KT-131-277

INTN
Roth

THE INTERNATIONAL LAW OF THE SEA

The law of the sea provides for the regulation, management and governance of the ocean spaces that cover over two-thirds of the Earth's surface. This book provides a contemporary explanation of the foundational principles of the law of the sea, a critical overview of the 1982 United Nations Convention on the Law of the Sea and an analysis of subsequent developments including the many bilateral, regional and global agreements that supplement the Convention.

The second edition of this acclaimed text takes as its focus the rules and institutions established by the Convention on the Law of the Sea and places the achievements of the Convention in both historical and contemporary context. All of the main areas of the law of the sea are addressed including the foundations and sources of the law, the nature and extent of the maritime zones, the delimitation of overlapping maritime boundaries, the place of archipelagic and other special states in the law of the sea, navigational rights and freedoms, military activities at sea, and marine resource and conservation issues such as fisheries, marine environmental protection and dispute settlement.

As the Convention is now well over a quarter of a century old, the book takes stock of contemporary oceans issues that are not adequately addressed by the Convention. Overarching challenges facing the law of the sea are considered, including how new maritime security initiatives can be reconciled with traditional navigational rights and freedoms, and the need for stronger legal and policy responses to protect the global ocean environment from climate change and ocean acidification.

The University of Law, Birmingham

B27392

The International Law of the Sea

Second Edition

Donald R Rothwell
and
Tim Stephens

·HART·
PUBLISHING

OXFORD AND PORTLAND, OREGON
2016

Published in the United Kingdom by Hart Publishing Ltd
16C Worcester Place, Oxford, OX1 2JW
Telephone: +44 (0)1865 517530
Fax: +44 (0)1865 510710
E-mail: mail@hartpub.co.uk
Website: http://www.hartpub.co.uk

Published in North America (US and Canada) by
Hart Publishing
c/o International Specialized Book Services
920 NE 58th Avenue, Suite 300
Portland, OR 97213-3786
USA
Tel: +1 503 287 3093 or toll-free: (1) 800 944 6190
Fax: +1 503 280 8832
E-mail: orders@isbs.com
Website: http://www.isbs.com

© Donald R Rothwell and Tim Stephens 2016

First edition published by Hart Publishing Ltd, 2010

Donald R Rothwell and Tim Stephens have asserted their right under the Copyright,
Designs and Patents Act 1988, to be identified as the authors of this work.

Hart Publishing is an imprint of Bloomsbury Publishing plc.

All rights reserved. No part of this publication may be reproduced, stored in a
retrieval system, or transmitted, in any form or by any means, without
the prior permission of Hart Publishing, or as expressly permitted by
law or under the terms agreed with the appropriate reprographic
rights organisation. Enquiries concerning reproduction which
may not be covered by the above should be addressed to
Hart Publishing Ltd at the address above.

British Library Cataloguing in Publication Data
Data Available

Library of Congress Cataloging-in-Publication Data

Names: Rothwell, Donald, 1959– author. | Stephens, Tim (Law teacher), author.

Title: The international law of the sea / Donald R. Rothwell and Tim Stephens.

Description: Second edition. | Oxford ; Portland, Oregon : Hart Publishing, 2016. | Includes
bibliographical references and index. | Description based on print version record and CIP data provided by
publisher; resource not viewed.

Identifiers: LCCN 2015042683 (print) | LCCN 2015042535 (ebook) | ISBN 9781782256854
(Epub) | ISBN 9781782256847 (pbk. : alk. paper)

Subjects: LCSH: Law of the sea. | Maritime law.

Classification: LCC KZA1145 (print) | LCC KZA1145 .R68 2016 (ebook) | DDC 341.4/5—dc23
LC record available at http://lccn.loc.gov/2015042683

ISBN: 978-1-78225-684-7

Typeset by Compuscript Ltd, Shannon
Printed and bound in Great Britain by
CPI Group (UK) Ltd, Croydon CR0 4YY

ACKNOWLEDGEMENTS

In preparing this second edition we continue to acknowledge the great debt to the many people who have inspired and assisted us through our voyages both in the law of the sea and in international law more generally. A number of scholars and mentors have been profoundly influential in our thinking and appreciation of the law of the sea, and we owe an immense intellectual debt to James Crawford, RD Lumb, DP O'Connell, Ivan Shearer and Gillian Triggs in that regard. Given our connections with the Law School of the University of Sydney we wish particularly to acknowledge its great tradition of international legal scholarship, and the encouragement we have received from colleagues over two decades to pursue our research interests in this field with particular thanks to Ben Boer, Christine Chinkin and Jeremy Webber.

In the course of writing both the first and second editions we were very grateful to have received comments and feedback from our students and a number of valued colleagues who read and commented on various drafts. We acknowledge our special thanks to Rachel Baird, Ben Boer, Chester Brown, Henry Burmester, J-P Fonteyne, Greg French, Sonia Gaal, Marcus Haward, Stuart Kaye, Natalie Klein, David Leary, Ted McDorman, Rob McLaughlin, Rosemary Rayfuse, Andrew Serdy, Ivan Shearer and Robin Warner. We are especially grateful to Alex G Oude Elferink, Karen N Scott and David VanderZwaag for their collaboration on a number of law of the sea projects over many years which have contributed to our current thinking on contemporary law of the sea issues. The constructive feedback that each of these distinguished scholars provided immeasurably improved the quality of this work, although we remain responsible for any errors and omissions.

The second edition was written over a number of months between 2014 and 2015, during which time we both enjoyed significant support from our home institutions. Donald acknowledges the support received from the ANU College of Law, Australian National University during this time and the wonderful collegiate environment fostered within the College by the Dean, Professor Stephen Bottomley, who was very supportive in terms of ensuring sufficient 'space' to complete this project. Tim acknowledges the support of his colleagues at the University of Sydney, in particular the international law cluster at the Sydney Centre for International Law, which provides a collegial and dynamic environment for research and teaching in international law.

Donald thanks the ANU College of Law College Research Committee for their assistance via a grant under the College Small Grant Scheme. Thanks are also extended to our researchers who were engaged with this edition: Zoe Winston-Gregson and Nishadee Perera in Canberra.

We also wish to acknowledge the staff at Hart Publishing for their support of this project. Particular thanks must be extended to Richard Hart, who provided guidance when we conceived the first edition, and Bill Asquith and Mel Hamill, who have guided the second edition to publication.

Finally, we wish to acknowledge our families who have had to endure a great deal during the writing of this second edition. We dedicate this work to them with our love and appreciation.

Donald R Rothwell
Tim Stephens

PREFACE TO THE SECOND EDITION

Since publication of the first edition of this book in 2010, the international law of the sea, consistent with its history as one of the most dynamic areas of international law, has continued to develop in response to new challenges facing the oceans. Historically, the development of the law of the sea was dominated by the state practice of the great powers and the views of publicists such as Grotius, but then gradually there emerged a distinctive and more expansive body of customary international law. The twentieth century proved to be the most significant to date for the law of the sea. Early efforts were made to codify the law, and then when these failed the International Law Commission was called upon to consider the issues, and the Commission's work was a major catalyst for the First United Nations Conference on the Law of the Sea and the eventual adoption of the four 1958 Geneva Conventions.

The middle of the twentieth century was a tumultuous time for international affairs coinciding with the Cold War, the development of the United Nations system, and decolonisation resulting in the emergence of many new states which sought to challenge the existing order, including the 'Eurocentric' focus of international law. These geopolitical currents exerted great force on the Third United Nations Conference on the Law of the Sea, and impacted upon the way in which the 1982 United Nations Convention on the Law of the Sea was negotiated and eventually settled.

Upon its conclusion and opening for signature at Montego Bay, Jamaica on 10 December 1982 the international law of the sea was irrevocably transformed. Not only did the Convention provide certainty to the law and settle ongoing arguments about matters such as the breadth of the territorial sea, it also took the law in new directions in its provisions dealing with the deep seabed, archipelagic states, marine environmental protection, marine scientific research and compulsory dispute settlement.

Importantly, the law of the sea now sought to achieve a balance between the respective rights and interests of coastal states and maritime states, and provided a clear framework for the way in which the various maritime zones now recognised under the law could be accessed, utilised and managed. In perhaps the most important 'mixed zone', the law recognised the exclusive economic zone as an area in which the legitimate sovereign rights and interests of a coastal state could be blended with the traditional freedoms of navigation enjoyed over what otherwise would have been high seas.

While providing certainty on many core questions, the 1982 Convention did not fix or freeze the law of the sea, but it has provided a stable and principled foundation for responses to contemporary challenges. Two important implementing agreements were adopted in the 1990s dealing with modifications to the Part XI deep seabed provisions of the Convention, and extending the Convention so as to deal more effectively and comprehensively with straddling and highly migratory fish stocks. State practice has continued to expand and develop the application and interpretation of parts of the Convention, especially those dealing with navigational rights and freedoms, archipelagos, marine environmental protection, and marine scientific research. There has also been a growth in the institutions associated with the law of the sea as was envisaged by the Convention. The International Tribunal for the Law of the Sea, the International Seabed Authority, and the Commission on the Limits of the Continental Shelf are all making significant contributions to the interpretation and operationalisation of the law. The United Nations continues to play its role hosting the annual meetings of the state parties, an informal consultative process, and through the United Nations Division on Ocean Affairs and the Law of the Sea (UNDOALOS) disseminates information and data on the law of the sea.

In keeping with its history, the law of the sea is therefore not standing still but is developing and expanding. State practice continues to 'thicken' in established areas such as maritime claims, resource management, marine pollution and maritime security, while in others it is only beginning to emerge fully developed, as is the case with claims to an outer continental shelf. In this regard, the expanding jurisprudence of the International Tribunal for the Law of the Sea is beginning to have an impact in areas as diverse as maritime boundary delimitation to the seizure of protest vessels and their crew within the exclusive economic zone. The international law of the sea is also being confronted with new challenges principally deriving from the effects of climate change, ocean acidification and other environmental impacts. As it becomes clear how climate change will transform the oceans, there is a need for rethinking how the community of states address coastal erosion, shifting baselines, disappearing low tide elevations and islands, and the effects of ocean warming upon marine living resources and the ocean environment. The commencement in 2015 of a negotiating process for a new agreement on high seas biodiversity is further recognition of the gaps in the 1982 Convention and the need to strengthen environmental mechanisms. Likewise, the 2014 judgment of the International Court of Justice in *Whaling in the Antarctic* serves as a reminder that, notwithstanding the breadth of the 1982 Convention, there remain parallel treaty regimes which are of significance for global oceans governance.

What these recent events teach us is that while the international law of the sea has secure foundations it cannot remain complacent in dealing with new challenges. The law will, therefore, as it has over many centuries, continue on its evolutionary path, presenting an ever-present challenge to balance a firm appreciation of the roots of the contemporary international law of the sea with a willingness to adapt the law to resolve modern dilemmas.

* * *

In writing this book we have been conscious of the voluminous literature on the international law of the sea. We have referred to the major historical and contemporary works in the discipline, but do not pretend to have done so in any exhaustive fashion. At the conclusion of each chapter we direct our readers to those works that we consider to be particularly useful and authoritative.

Treaties noted throughout the text are listed in the accompanying Table of Treaties where full references to those instruments can be found. In the case of those treaties and other international instruments which have been reproduced in AV Lowe and SAG Talmon, *The Legal Order of the Oceans: Basic Documents on the Law of the Sea:* (Oxford, Hart Publishing, 2009) (*Basic Documents*), we also include a reference in the footnotes to the relevant document in that excellent compendium. *Basic Documents* should be read as a companion to this volume.

Consistent with the tradition of the law of the sea, this book refers to nautical miles (nm), which is 1.15 statute miles or 1852 metres. Where alternate forms of measurement are used, those measurements are clearly identified. We acknowledge that M is an accepted abbreviation for a nautical mile but have preferred nm to avoid confusion with metres.

The law as stated in the text is current as at 1 July 2015.

Canberra and Sydney
31 August 2015

CONTENTS

LIST OF ABBREVIATIONS

ACCOBAMS	1996 Agreement on the Conservation of Cetaceans of the Baltic Sea, Mediterranean Sea and Contiguous Atlantic Area
AMIS	Australian Maritime Identification System
APEC	Asia-Pacific Economic Cooperation
ASCOBANS	1992 Agreement on the Conservation of Small Cetaceans of the Baltic and North Seas
ASEAN	Association of Southeast Asian Nations
ASLP	archipelagic sea lanes passage
BGR	Federal Institute for Geosciences and Natural Resources of Germany
CBD	1992 Convention on Biological Diversity
CCAMLR	1980 Convention on the Conservation of Antarctic Marine Living Resources
CCSBT	1993 Convention for the Conservation of Southern Bluefin Tuna
CFP	Common Fisheries Policy
CITES	1973 Convention on International Trade in Endangered Species of Wild Fauna and Flora
CLC	1992 Convention on Civil Liability for Oil Pollution Damage
CLCS	Commission on the Limits of the Continental Shelf
COLREG	1972 Convention on the International Regulations for Preventing Collisions at Sea
COLREGs	Collision Regulations
COMRA	China Ocean Mineral Resources Research and Development Association
CTI	APEC Leaders of the Coral Triangle Initiative
DDT	Dichlorodiphenyltrichloroethane
DOALOS	Division for Ocean Affairs and the Law of the Sea
DORD	Deep Ocean Resources Development Company
DPRK	Democratic People's Republic of Korea (North Korea)
ECJ	European Court of Justice
EEZ	Exclusive Economic Zone
EFZ	Exclusive Fishing Zone
EIA	Environmental Impact Assessment
EU	European Union
EUNAVFOR	European Union-led Naval Force
FAO	Food and Agriculture Organization
FFA	Forum Fisheries Agency
FON	Freedom of Navigation

FSA	1995 Agreement for the Implementation of the Provisions of the United Nations Convention on the Law of the Sea of 10 December 1982 Relating to the Conservation and Management of Straddling Fish Stocks and Highly Migratory Fish Stocks
GATT	1947 General Agreement on Tariffs and Trade
GESAMP	Joint Group of Experts on the Scientific Aspects of Marine Environmental Protection
GPA	1995 Global Programme of Action for the Protection of the Marine Environment from Land-Based Activities
GPASL	General Provisions on the Adoption, Designation and Substitution of Archipelagic Sea Lanes
HNS Convention	1996 Convention on Liability and Compensation for the Carriage of Hazardous and Noxious Substances by Sea
IAEA	International Atomic Energy Authority
IATTC	Inter-American Tropical Tuna Commission
IBC	International Bulk Chemical
ICAO	International Civil Aviation Organization
ICJ	International Court of Justice
ICP	United Nations Open-Ended Informal Consultative Process on Oceans and the Law of the Sea
ICRW	1946 International Convention for the Regulation of Whaling
IGC	International Code for the Construction and Equipment of Ships Carrying Liquefied Gases in Bulk
IHO	International Hydrographic Organization
ILC	International Law Commission
IMDG	International Maritime Dangerous Goods
IMO	International Maritime Organization
IOC	Intergovernmental Oceanographic Commission
IOM	Interoceanmetal Joint Organization
IOPCF	International Oil Pollution Compensation Fund
ISA	International Seabed Authority
ITLOS	International Tribunal for the Law of the Sea
IUCN	International Union for Conservation of Nature
IUU	illegal, unreported and unregulated
IWC	International Whaling Commission
LLGDS	landlocked and geographically disadvantaged states
LME	Large Marine Ecosystem
LOSC	1982 United Nations Convention on the Law of the Sea
MARPOL	1973 International Convention for the Prevention of Pollution from Ships, as Modified by the Protocol of 1978 Relating Thereto
MoU	Memoranda of Understanding
MSP	marine spatial planning
MSR	marine scientific research
1979 MSR	1979 International Convention on Maritime Search and Rescue
MSY	maximum sustainable yield
NAMMCO	1992 Agreement on Research, Conservation and Management of Marine Mammals in the North Atlantic
NATO	North Atlantic Treaty Organization
nm	nautical miles

OILPOL	1954 International Convention for the Prevention of Pollution of the Sea by Oil
OPPRC Convention	1990 Convention on Oil Pollution Preparedness, Response and Cooperation
OPRC-HNS Protocol	2000 Protocol on Preparedness, Response and Co-operation to Pollution Incidents by Hazardous and Noxious Substances
OSPAR Convention	1992 Convention for the Protection of the Marine Environment of the North-East Atlantic
PCA	Permanent Court of Arbitration
PCB	Polychlorinated biphenyls
PCIJ	Permanent Court of International Justice
pH	Potential for Hydrogen
POPs	persistent organic pollutants
PSI	Proliferation Security Initiative
PSSA	particularly sensitive sea area
ReCAAP	2004 Regional Cooperation Agreement on Combating Piracy and Armed Robbery against Ships in Asia
RFMO	regional fisheries management organisation
RMP	Revised Management Procedure
RMS	Revised Management Scheme
RSP	Regional Seas Programme
SDR	Special Drawing Rights
SEAFO	South-East Atlantic Fisheries Organisation
SOLAS	1974 International Convention for the Safety of Life at Sea
SPLOS	Meeting of States Parties to the United Nations Convention on the Law of the Sea
STCW Convention	1978 Convention on Standards of Training, Certification and Watchkeeping for Seafarers
SUA Convention	1988 Convention for the Suppression of Unlawful Acts against the Safety of Maritime Navigation
SUA Fixed Platforms Protocol	1988 Protocol for the Suppression of Unlawful Acts against the Safety of Fixed Platforms Located on the Continental Shelf
SWG	Small Working Group on the Future of the International Whaling Commission
TAAF	French Southern and Antarctic Territories
TFG	Transitional Federal Government
TSS	traffic separation schemes
UN	United Nations
UNCLOS	United Nations Conferences on the Law of the Sea
UNCLOS I	First United Nations Conference on the Law of the Sea
UNCLOS II	Second United Nations Conference on the Law of the Sea
UNCLOS III	Third United Nations Conference on the Law of the Sea
UNCTAD	United Nations Conference on Trade and Development
UNDOALOS	United Nations Division for Ocean Affairs and the Law of the Sea
UNEP	United Nations Environment Programme
UNESCO	United Nations Educational, Scientific and Cultural Organization
UNGA	United Nations General Assembly

UNICPOLOS	United Nations Open-ended Informal Consultation Process on Oceans and the Law of the Sea
UNTAET	United Nations Transitional Administration in East Timor
Virginia Commentaries	*United Nations Convention on the Law of the Sea 1982: A Commentary* (The Hague, Martinus Nijhoff, 1985–2002) vols 1–6
WCPFC	Western and Central Pacific Fisheries Commission
WMD	Weapons of Mass Destruction
WTO	World Trade Organization

LIST OF TABLES AND FIGURES

Tables:

Figures:

TABLE OF CASES

Abbreviations used in this table

ER *English Reports*
Ex D Law Reports, Exchequer Division
HCA High Court of Australia
ICLQ International and Comparative Law Quarterly
ILM *International Legal Materials*
ILR *International Law Reports*
Moore John Bassett Moore, *History and Digest of the International Arbitrations to Which the United States has Been a Party* (1898) vols I–VI
QB Law Reports, Queens Bench Division
RGDIP *Revue générale de droit international public*
RIAA United Nations Reports of International Arbitral Awards

TABLE OF TREATIES

Abbreviations used in this table

A Adopted
AJIL American Journal of International Law
ATNIF Australian Treaties Not In Force
ATS Australian Treaty Series
CTS Consolidated Treaty Series
EIF Entry into Force
EPL Environmental Policy and Law
IJMCL International Journal of Marine and Coastal Law
ILM International Legal Materials
IMO International Maritime Organization
LNTS League of Nations Treaty Series
LOSB Law of the Sea Bulletin
OJ Official Journal of the European Union
OS Open for Signature
TIAS Treaties and other International Acts Series (US)
UKTS United Kingdom Treaty Series
UNTS United Nations Treaty Series

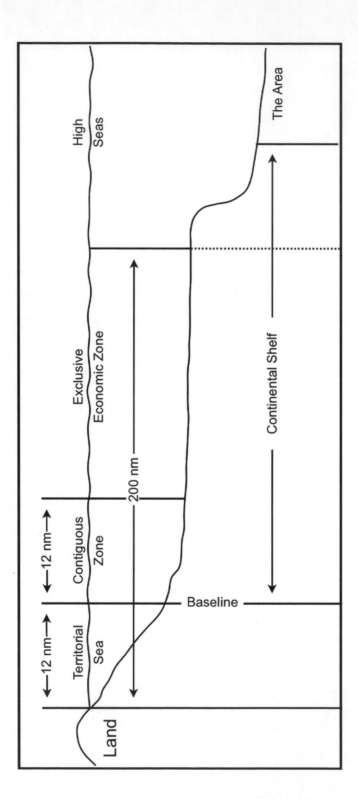

Maritime Zones

1

The History and Sources of the
International Law of the Sea

I. Introduction

The international law of the sea is one of the most important areas of contemporary international law, encompassing not only the 'constitution of the oceans', the 1982 United Nations Convention on the Law of the Sea (LOSC),[1] but an ever-growing body of additional treaties, frameworks and state practice for the governance and management of the world's oceans. Whilst the law of the sea had its initial origins in determining the status and control of ocean space, the contemporary law extends well beyond issues of coastal state sovereignty and jurisdiction, to address the interests of the international community in the deep seabed, high seas, fish stocks, the regulation of marine scientific research, military uses of the oceans, and marine environmental protection. In this regard, the law of the sea, like many other areas of international law, has become more detailed over time, expanding in scope and deepening in content. The result is that aspects of the law of the sea now interact with nearly every other mainstream area of international law and, given the critical importance of the oceans, the law of the sea will have implications for new areas of international law as they are developed.

The international law of the sea has developed across several quite distinctive phases, ranging from early theoretical debates between scholars over the status of the oceans, to the dominance of the freedom of the seas doctrine, to the gradual codification of the law throughout the twentieth century. Although the treaty law at the start of the twenty-first century is relatively well settled, the ongoing march of state practice means that the law remains in a state of evolution and new regulatory efforts are being made to address a wide array of contemporary challenges, ranging from ocean fertilisation to help mitigate climate change, to bioprospecting to discover pharmaceutical products, to a new treaty to protect high seas biodiversity, and to the regional management of strategic ocean spaces such as the South China Sea and the Arctic Ocean. Contemporary challenges to maritime security and oceans governance are also impacting upon the law of the sea, prompting not only a review of established law addressing matters such as piracy and flag state jurisdiction, but also how the myriad of issues posed by climate change for ocean space can be tackled at state, regional and global levels. Climate change poses considerable challenges as it introduces many variables into how the law is to be applied and interpreted. Whilst this is not a completely new dynamic, in that changing ocean and coastline conditions have always

---

[1] *Basic Documents* No 36.

had to be addressed by the law of the sea, rapid climate change has the potential to transform nearly all aspects of ocean activity and involves unpredictable consequences for many coastal states. How flexible the law of the sea is in responding to these challenges will be its greatest test.

What follows in this chapter is an outline of the historical developments in the international law of the sea from early periods until contemporary times. Particular attention will be given to the three United Nations Conferences on the Law of the Sea (UNCLOS) which were convened in the second half of the twentieth century and the issues which arose during those negotiations, and the distinctive sources of international law which comprise the international law of the sea. Consideration will also be given to some of the current challenges facing the law of the sea that are explored in more depth in later chapters of the book.

II. Historical Development of the International Law of the Sea

The history of the international law of the sea up until the mid-twentieth century was dominated by European practice. Europeans developed not only sophisticated maritime technology allowing exploration of the furthest reaches of the earth and providing a conduit to the development of maritime trading routes, but also through their naval technology they acquired the means to control and regulate activity on the oceans. Initially the oceans were seen as maritime highways allowing trade and commerce to flourish. However, it was soon realised that naval power gave a state the capacity to control and regulate access to the oceans and this could be used to defeat or control enemies. Accordingly, whilst Roman law provided that the sea was free and common to all,[2] by the Middle Ages many seas were subject to various forms of appropriation and control by powerful states.[3] Whether such claims were completely defendable is doubtful. Nevertheless, this did not deter some expansive claims being made. In a Papal Bull of Pope Alexander VI based upon discoveries made by Columbus and given effect in the 1494 Treaty of Tordesillas, a line drawn on a meridian of longitude through Brazil effectively allocated the known world into an area of Portuguese expansion to the east and Spanish expansion to the west, with consequential impacts upon the adjoining seas.[4] Such claims were ultimately unsustainable. As Fulton observed: 'It was those preposterous pretensions to the dominion of the immense waters of the globe that caused the great juridical controversies regarding *mare clausum* and *mare liberum*, from which modern international law took its rise.'[5]

---

[2] Jessup was prepared to assert that 'Roman Law did pass on to posterity the concept of the 'freedom of the seas' which concept exerted profound influence upon the development of international law': Philip C Jessup, *The Law of Territorial Waters and Maritime Jurisdiction* (New York, Jennings, 1927, 1970 rep) 4, n 3.

[3] Thomas Wemyss Fulton, *The Sovereignty of the Sea* (Edinburgh, Blackwood, 1911, 1976 rep) 3.

[4] DP O'Connell, *The International Law of the Sea*, vol 1 (Oxford, Clarendon Press, 1982) 2.

[5] Fulton, *The Sovereignty of the Sea* (n 3) 5.

A. The Grotian View of the Oceans

Into this realm of conflicting state practice entered the views of publicists who sought to bring a theoretical construct to the debate over the oceans, but also certainty to the debate over access to and ownership of the oceans. One of the earliest, and ultimately the most significant, contributions was made by the Dutch scholar Hugo Grotius with the publication in 1608 of his work *Mare Liberum*.[6] In Chapter V Grotius observes how under the law of nations the sea has at various times been referred to as the property of no one (*res nullius*), a common possession (*res communis*) and public property (*res publica*). However, it is clear that the oceans cannot be appropriated because 'that which cannot be occupied, or which has never been occupied, cannot be the property of any one, because all property has arisen from occupation'.[7] Likening the sea to the air, which Grotius observed was not susceptible to occupation and whose use was destined for all, he argued:

> For the same reasons the sea is common to all, because it is so limitless that it cannot become a possession of any one, and because it is adapted for the use of all, whether we consider it from the point of view of navigation or of fisheries.[8]

Whilst *Mare Liberum* was influenced by Dutch concerns at the time that the growing East India trade would be hampered by Portuguese maritime power, the Grotian notion of the freedom of the seas gained considerable momentum. Whether Grotius was drawing upon Roman law doctrine, or also received support from Asian state practice as it applied to the Indian Oceans and waters around Southeast Asia, remains debateable,[9] however his work did provoke a response from numerous other publicists of the age, including the Scottish lawyer William Welwood, Italian scholars such as Pacius, Mattherius, Francipani, Megenius and Zambono, and English authors such as Gerard Malynes, Alberico Gentilis and Lord Chief Justice Coke, who were drawn into what has often been termed the 'battle of the books'.[10] The most substantive response to Grotius came from the English scholar John Selden whose work *Mare Clausum* (*The Closed Sea*) was published in 1635 under the express command of King Charles. Selden sought to assert not only the sovereignty and dominion of the crown of England in British seas, but also to prove that there was long-standing state practice of dominion over the oceans.[11] Yet, as observed by Fulton: 'It was Selden's misfortune that the cause he championed was moribund, and opposed to the growing spirit of freedom throughout the world.'[12] Ultimately, the Grotian view of the oceans prevailed and freedom of the seas became the doctrine of the time.

---

[6] Hugo Grotius, *The Freedom of the Seas or the Right which Belongs to the Dutch to Take Part in the East Indian Trade* (New York, Oxford University Press, 1633 trans, 1916 rep).

[7] Ibid 27.

[8] Ibid 28.

[9] See comments by the Indian scholar RP Anand in *Origin and Development of the Law of the Sea* (The Hague, Martinus Nijhoff, 1983) 80.

[10] Ibid 102.

[11] Ibid 105.

[12] Fulton, *The Sovereignty of the Sea* (n 3) 370.

B. The Freedom of the Sea and Territorial Sea Claims

With the apparent resolution of this debate over the ownership of the seas, the legal regime of the oceans enjoyed a period of stability from the seventeenth to the nineteenth century. Yet the potential for the unrestrained use of naval capacity remained an issue, both in terms of the ability of naval powers to control certain waters and also to launch raids and bombardments against coastal towns and cities. This was the catalyst for rethinking whether a doctrine of absolute freedom of the seas, which effectively permitted vessels to sail close to foreign coastlines and allowed hostile navies to launch attacks with relative ease, was compatible with the ability of a state to defend itself against foreign forces. Gradually at first, coastal states began to claim a right to control the waters adjoining their coasts. Over time, these claims began to resemble those made over land and territory, such that by the later part of the nineteenth century a distinctive sea area akin in legal status to land territory— the territorial sea—began to emerge.

The territorial sea was an area over which the adjacent coastal state exercised jurisdiction and control, principally for the purposes of security, but also in relation to resources that may have been found close to the coast such as fisheries. These claims were often poorly defined and difficult to enforce unless the state also possessed some level of naval power. Nevertheless, such was the emerging influence of territorial sea claims that it was clear there was a need to accommodate this emerging state practice within the dominant paradigm of the law of the sea which remained the freedom of the seas.

C. 1930 Hague Conference

The formation of the League of Nations after World War I provided the impetus for new initiatives for the codification of international law, which in 1924 led to a decision of the Assembly of the League to request the appointment of a Committee of Experts whose task would be to formulate questions for consideration by League members on areas of law suitable for common agreement. In the following years this resulted in League members being consulted on their views on state practice with respect to the law of the sea, with particular emphasis given to the territorial sea and the treatment of foreign vessels.[13] This was not the only initiative at the time seeking possible codification of the law of the sea, with other bodies throughout the 1920s also addressing similar issues, including the Institut de Droit International, the International Law Association, the German and Japanese Societies of International Law, the American Institute of International Law and the Harvard Law School.[14]

Eventually, in 1930, the League of Nations convened the Hague Codification Conference, which was attended by 44 states. However, the meeting was unable to reach any agreement on the law of the sea and no treaty emerged. The principal point of contention was the regime of the territorial sea, especially its breadth and relationship with an adjacent

---

[13] Antonio Sanchez de Bustamante y Sirven, *The Territorial Sea* (New York, Oxford University Press, 1930) 63–78.

[14] O'Connell, *The International Law of the Sea*, vol 1 (n 4) 20–21.

contiguous zone.[15] Despite the failure of the 1930 Hague Conference, state practice continued to develop in the years which followed, most notably in the form of the 1936 Convention Regarding the Regime of Straits done at Montreux which regulated the freedom of transit and navigation through the Black Sea straits.[16] Whilst the onset of World War II put paid to any resumption of codification efforts, state practice remained active with various claims made by states to territorial sea type zones.

D. Truman Proclamation

The end of the war presented multiple opportunities for the development of the law of the sea, and in September 1945 the United States took an initiative that was to have a profound impact upon the law for many decades. In United States Presidential Proclamation No 2667,[17] commonly referred to as the 1945 Truman Proclamation, the United States sought by way of a unilateral declaration to exercise jurisdiction and control over the natural resources of the subsoil and sea bed of the contiguous continental shelf. This was the area of the seabed immediately adjacent to the coastline which extended out into the ocean as an undersea extension of the landmass. With the Truman Proclamation the United States argued that the 'the exercise of jurisdiction over the natural resources of the subsoil and sea bed of the continental shelf by the contiguous nation is reasonable and just' on the basis that 'the continental shelf may be regarded as an extension of the land-mass of the coastal nation and thus naturally appurtenant to it'.[18] Though undefined as to its outer limits, and not designed to impact upon the freedom of navigation, the Truman Proclamation was the first substantive claim by a coastal state to a distinctive offshore resources zone, which was completely separate from the territorial sea as it had been developed to that point. It paved the way for the similar resource-type claims by other coastal states which would become a dominant feature of state practice in the late 1940s, and into the 1950s and 1960s.[19]

Parallel to these developments was the emergence of a body of jurisprudence from international courts on law of the sea matters. There had been occasional law of the sea cases before the arbitral tribunals prior to the establishment of the Permanent Court of International Justice (PCIJ), and its successor the International Court of Justice (ICJ). However, it was the creation of these permanent international courts, with their capacity to develop an authoritative jurisprudence on law of the sea, that proved to have a significant impact upon the law of the sea. The ICJ's first decision, the 1949 *Corfu Channel* case,[20] allowed the Court an opportunity to consider the developing regime of the territorial sea, and in particular navigational rights and freedoms in international straits during peacetime. This was followed soon after by the 1951 *Fisheries* case,[21] which again raised issues of the territorial sea

---

[15] Anand, *Origin and Development of the Law of the Sea* (n 9) 140–41.

[16] *Basic Documents* No 3.

[17] United States Presidential Proclamation No 2667: Policy of the United States with Respect to the Natural Resources of the Subsoil and Sea Bed of the Continental Shelf, *Basic Documents* No 5.

[18] Ibid.

[19] For example, in 1947 Chile proclaimed a 200 nm zone over the adjacent continental shelf: Presidential Declaration Concerning Continental Shelf, 23 June 1947 (Chile), discussed in Ann L Hollick, 'The Origins of 200-Mile Offshore Zones' (1977) 71 *AJIL* 494, 495.

[20] *Corfu Channel (United Kingdom v Albania)* [1949] ICJ Rep 4.

[21] *Fisheries (United Kingdom v Norway)* [1951] ICJ Rep 116.

regime, and specifically the capacity of a coastal state to draw so-called 'straight baselines' around the outer edge of the coast from which the territorial sea was proclaimed. These developments, in both state practice and jurisprudence, were testament to the rapidly developing law of the sea in the immediate post-war era.

III. Work of the International Law Commission

With the creation of the International Law Commission (ILC) by the United Nations, a body charged with the codification and progressive development of international law, an opportunity was immediately presented to resume serious work on treaty-making in the law of the sea. Indeed, at its first session in 1949 the ILC agreed that the 'Regime of the High Seas' would be given priority. In 1950, the United Nations General Assembly (UNGA) recommended that the ILC also address territorial waters and this was formally added to the ILC's agenda in 1951. The result was that throughout the 1950s the ILC gave considerable attention to the law of the sea, with the members considering various theoretical and scientific aspects of the law, and also taking into account the views of governments. This work culminated in 1956 when the ILC reached agreement on draft articles with an accompanying commentary.[22] The work of the ILC had a profound impact upon the development of the international law of the sea in the twentieth century. Not only were a set of draft articles prepared, but the commentary provided a basis for future interpretation of key provisions. This work remains of major continuing significance. With the work of the ILC completed, the opportunity presented itself for a United Nations diplomatic conference on the law of the sea at Geneva. In anticipation of the 1958 Geneva conference, in 1957 the ILC's final draft articles were circulated by the UNGA to governments for their comment, with 25 responses received later that year.[23]

IV. The First United Nations Conference on the
Law of the Sea and the Geneva Conventions

The First United Nations Conference on the Law of the Sea (UNCLOS I), held in Geneva from 24 February to 27 April 1958, resulted in the conclusion of four, relatively short, conventions. These were the Convention on the Territorial Sea and Contiguous Zone,[24] the Convention on the Continental Shelf,[25] the Convention on the High Seas,[26] and the

---

[22] International Law Commission, 'Articles concerning the Law of the Sea with Commentaries' (1956) *Yearbook of the International Law Commission*, vol 2, 265–301.

[23] 'Comments by Governments on the Draft Articles Concerning the Law of the Sea Adopted by the International Law Commission at its Eighth Session' in United Nations Conference on the Law of the Sea, *Official Records*, vol 1 (Geneva, United Nations, 1958) 75.

[24] *Basic Documents* No 9.

[25] *Basic Documents* No 12.

[26] *Basic Documents* No 10.

Convention on Fishing and Conservation of the Living Resources of the High Seas.[27] In addition, an Optional Protocol of Signature concerning the Compulsory Settlement of Disputes arising out of the Law of the Sea Conventions[28] was also agreed, and there were nine resolutions addressing a range of miscellaneous matters such as nuclear tests, pollution of the high seas by radioactive materials, coastal fisheries and historic waters.[29] When the conference commenced it was anticipated that only one convention would be endorsed based upon the 73 ILC draft articles. However, as a consequence of conference procedures, and the referral of parts of the convention text to four committees, four complementary treaties emerged. A fifth committee was also formed to consider the question of free access to the sea for landlocked countries,[30] but no consensus was reached on the drafting of an additional convention and recommendations were made that the special interests of these states be reflected in the text of the agreed conventions.[31]

A total of 86 states attended the Geneva Conference, making it one of the largest postwar international law-making conferences. A number of important dynamics were apparent during the conference. The first was the East–West cold war rivalry which had particular impact upon important security aspects of the law of the sea, especially navigational matters and military uses of the oceans.[32] Another factor was the emergence of developing states as a significant grouping at international negotiations with the potential to outnumber the core western and allied states that up to that time had been dominant. Finally, there was also the grouping of landlocked states which, whilst small in number, were keen to ensure access rights to the ocean.

The Convention on the Territorial Sea and Contiguous Zone was predominantly a codification of existing customary international law, and for the first time provided significant content in treaty law to the regime of the territorial sea. Several aspects of the Convention were noteworthy. The most significant was the failure to indicate the breadth of the territorial sea. Article 6 only addresses the outer limit of the territorial sea by providing for a technical rule that the limit is a line 'every point of which is at a distance from the nearest point of the baseline equal to the breadth of the territorial sea' and remains silent as to what the breadth actually is. Ultimately the position taken by key western states such as Britain, France, West Germany and the United States that the customary territorial sea limits of three nautical miles (nm) should not be disturbed proved to be decisive, and a significant split existed between those states which supported the status quo and those promoting more expansive territorial sea claims.[33] The status of bays is addressed in Article 7 with both a geographical and technical definition provided, though no attempt was made to apply these provisions to historic bays which remained subject to customary international law.[34] The right of innocent passage, that being the passage of foreign-flagged ships through

[27] *Basic Documents* No 11.
[28] *Basic Documents* No 13.
[29] Arthur H Dean, 'The Geneva Conference on the Law of the Sea: What was Accomplished' (1958) 52 *AJIL* 607, 627.
[30] Those states surrounded by land which have no direct access to the ocean, eg Switzerland.
[31] United Nations Conference on the Law of the Sea, *Official Records*, vol 7 (Geneva, United Nations, 1958).
[32] James B Morell, *The Law of the Sea: The 1982 Treaty and Its Rejection by the United States* (Jefferson, NC, McFarland, 1992) 6.
[33] Dean, 'The Geneva Conference' (n 29) 610.
[34] O'Connell was particularly critical of these provisions, arguing they were 'so artificial as to be contrivances rather than rules of customary law': O'Connell, *The International Law of the Sea*, vol 1 (n 4) 23.

the territorial sea of the coastal state, and related matters dealing with passage through international straits were also addressed.[35] In doing so, the Convention addressed several issues considered by the ICJ in the *Corfu Channel* case. Finally, the Convention articulated for the first time in treaty law the regime of the contiguous zone, which in Article 24 is defined as a zone for the enforcement of customs, fiscal, immigration and sanitary laws and regulations that may not extend beyond 12 nm.

The Convention on the Continental Shelf, agreed just 13 years after the Truman Proclamation, reflected the rapidly developing state practice and customary international law in this area. Whilst the parameters of the developing continental shelf regime were outlined in the Convention, some important aspects remained unsettled. The outer limits of the continental shelf, addressed in Article 1, were not clearly defined, with an initial limit being the 200 metre isobath but beyond that 'to where the depth of the superjacent waters admits of the exploitation of the natural resources', thereby giving to developed states a potentially greater capacity than other states to exploit the continental shelf seabed because of their technological superiority. The rights over the shelf were clearly outlined and defined as being 'sovereign rights', in distinction to sovereignty simpliciter which applied only to the territorial sea.[36] However, the sovereign rights extended only to the natural resources of the shelf which included the mineral and other non-living resources of the seabed and subsoil and 'living organisms belonging to sedentary species'.[37] Given the potential for neighbouring state continental shelf claims to overlap, the Convention also provided in Article 6 for rules with respect to the delimitation of continental shelf boundaries.

The Convention on the High Seas had the strongest basis of all of the four conventions in customary international law, and this is reflected in the Convention's preamble, which stated an intention 'to codify the rules of international law relating to the high seas' and that the Convention's provisions were adopted 'as generally declaratory of established principles of international law'. To that end, the high seas was defined in Article 1 as being those parts of the sea not included within the territorial sea or the internal waters; thereby suggesting that the high seas were in parts conterminous with the contiguous zone and continental shelf. The key freedoms of the high seas were identified,[38] although their content was not fleshed out. Basic provisions were included regarding the flagging and nationality of ships,[39] whilst the customary rules relating to piracy[40] and hot pursuit[41] were codified.

The Convention on Fishing and Conservation of the Living Resources of the High Seas sought to place some constraints on high seas fishing freedoms with a view to achieving the 'conservation of the living resources of the high seas'.[42] State parties were obliged to engage in cooperation with other states to achieve this objective which in Article 2 was defined to mean attaining the 'optimum sustainable yield' of the living resources of the high seas so as to 'secure a maximum supply of food and other marine products'. Subsequent provisions in the Convention sought to operationalise this objective further.

---

[35] Convention on the Territorial Sea and Contiguous Zone, Section III Right of Innocent Passage, arts 14–23.
[36] Convention on the Continental Shelf, art 2(1).
[37] Ibid art 2(4).
[38] Convention on the High Seas, art 2.
[39] Ibid arts 5–10.
[40] Ibid arts 14–22.
[41] Ibid art 23.
[42] Convention on Fishing and Conservation of the Living Resources of the High Seas, art 1(2).

UNCLOS I was given the task of codifying the existing customary international law of the sea, and whilst this was possible in many instances, as the ILC's debates proved and the text of the conventions confirm, there are instances where progressive development of the law occurred.[43] Yet whilst UNCLOS I achieved a great deal, there remained significant gaps in the legal framework. As the chair of the United States delegation wrote soon after UNCLOS I: 'In nine weeks it is difficult to settle the accumulated problems of a generation.'[44] The acceptance of the conventions proved to be variable, and although they had all entered into force by 1966, at that time there were a range of factors at play which resulted in some provisions being overtaken by developing state practice.[45] The ICJ had occasion to consider the application of the Convention on the Continental Shelf in the 1969 *North Sea Continental Shelf* cases,[46] and in the 1973 *Fisheries Jurisdiction* case[47] reviewed aspects of the Convention on the High Seas.

In sum, therefore, the Geneva Conventions provided the foundation for the contemporary international law of the sea. They represented an important phase in the development of the law as it was transformed from a body of international law having an almost exclusive customary basis to one founded upon a multilateral treaty framework.

V. The Second United Nations Conference on the Law of the Sea

A Second United Nations Conference on the Law of the Sea (UNCLOS II) was convened in Geneva only two years after UNCLOS I. The UNGA called for the convening of the conference in December 1958, however, there was no intention of reopening the recently concluded Geneva Conventions but rather to focus on only two issues: the breadth of the territorial sea and fishery limits.[48] The conference, which lasted for six weeks, was spilt between two groups, those favouring a six nm territorial sea and those supporting a 12 nm territorial sea. The conference was dominated by concerns with respect to security, fisheries, and associated economic problems.[49] Ultimately, the principal proposal was a compromise put forward by the United States and Canada in which the limit of the territorial sea was proposed as being six nm beyond which a six nm fishing zone would exist. However, the so-called 'Six plus Six' proposal failed to achieve the necessary two thirds support by a single vote,[50] as a result of which UNCLOS II failed to reach agreement on any reforms or

---

[43] Philip C Jessup, 'The Geneva Conferences on the Law of the Sea: A Study in International Law-Making' (1958) 52 *AJIL* 730, 732.

[44] Dean, 'The Geneva Conference' (n 29) 628.

[45] O'Connell commented that 'the Geneva Conventions had barely come into force before their psychological basis became threatened by the political changes of the 1960s': O'Connell, *The International Law of the Sea*, vol 1 (n 4) 24.

[46] *North Sea Continental Shelf (Federal Republic of Germany v Denmark; Federal Republic of Germany v The Netherlands)* [1969] ICJ Rep 3.

[47] *Fisheries Jurisdiction (United Kingdom v Iceland)* (Merits) [1974] ICJ Rep 3.

[48] UNGA Resolution 1307 (XIII) (1958).

[49] DW Bowett, 'The Second United Nations Conference on the Law of the Sea' (1960) 9 *International and Comparative Law Quarterly* 415, 416–21.

[50] Whilst the Canadian/United States proposal received a vote of 54 in favour, 28 against, with 5 abstentions, this did not reach the necessary two-thirds majority required for adoption by the Conference in plenary: ibid 432.

modifications to the Geneva Conventions. The conference was therefore effectively a failure and made no contribution to the development of the law of the sea, although it did highlight the importance of seeking to gain agreement on key aspects of the law of the sea such as the limits of maritime zones when any future conference was convened.

VI. The Third United Nations Conference on the Law of the Sea

The failure of UNCLOS II did not halt the development of state practice in the 1960s and it became readily apparent that whatever consensus did exist with respect to key aspects of the Geneva Conventions was not going to prevent some states from asserting distinctive maritime claims. The period between UNCLOS II and UNCLOS III was characterised by a variety of new coastal state claims, the emergence of new groups of states seeking to play an active role in the development of the law of the sea, and proposals with respect to the regime of the deep seabed.

A. Claims to New Maritime Zones in the 1960s

With the collapse of UNCLOS II, the international law of the sea in the 1960s was an amalgam of the Geneva Conventions and rapidly developing customary international law which not only was filling the voids left in the conventions but which was also on the verge of creating new coastal state rights. Because the level of acceptance of the Geneva Conventions was not high, especially among newly independent developing states, there was not a great deal of allegiance to provisions which were seen as placing constraints on certain coastal state rights. This was particularly reflected in the rapidly developing state practice with respect to claims to fishing zones. Many of these claims were to 12 nm fishery zones or 'exclusive fishing zones' (EFZ), but there were also more extensive claims to offshore areas, including up to 50, 100, 200 and 400 nm. For the most part, European states asserted claims to 12 nm EFZs. Iceland (1958) was one of the first to do so, followed by Norway (1961). On the other hand, African, Asian and Latin American states sought to assert much more extensive EFZ claims. Latin American states including Ecuador (1966), Argentina (1966), Panama (1967), Uruguay (1969) and Brazil (1970) extended their claims to 200 nm, while African states such as Guinea (1964) claimed a 130 nm territorial sea in order to have greater security of access to offshore fish stocks.[51]

The claims to EFZs were not only made unilaterally by coastal states but were also recognised in bilateral and regional agreements. At the bilateral level, a number of agreements were reached that gave mutual recognition to a 12 nm fisheries zone. Examples included agreements between the United Kingdom and Norway (1960), Japan and South Korea (1965), Japan and New Zealand (1967), United States and Mexico (1967), and Spain and

---

[51] Anand, *Origin and Development of the Law of the Sea* (n 9) 199–200; O'Connell, *The International Law of the Sea*, vol 1 (n 4) 556–58.

Morocco (1969). The most significant regional initiative was the 1964 London Fisheries Convention concluded by 12 European states which provided for the mutual recognition of 12 nm fisheries zones.[52]

B. The Regime of the Deep Seabed

The other major development in the law of the sea during the 1960s resulted from the growing interest in the legal status of the deep seabed on the high seas. The Geneva Conventions had not sought to address the deep seabed, primarily because at that time there was no capacity to engage in deep seabed exploitation. Accordingly, other than in relation to scientific research and the laying of submarine cables and pipelines,[53] little attention was given to this issue. However, as improved technology opened the potential for not only exploration but also exploitation of the deep seabed, several key states and the international community more generally began to consider whether there was a need to develop a distinctive legal regime. Newly independent developing states, many of which relied upon the export of mineral resources for a substantial proportion of their national income, were particularly concerned that the free exploitation of the deep seabed would not only lead to industrial state dominance of this new resource frontier, but would also lead to a glut of minerals on commodity markets and falling resource prices.

Then, in a landmark moment for the law of the sea, the UNGA in 1967 was presented with a proposal by the Ambassador for Malta, Arvid Pardo, that the seabed and ocean floor be declared a part of the 'common heritage of mankind'.[54] Later that year the General Assembly agreed to the creation of an Ad Hoc Committee to Study the Peaceful Uses of the Sea-Bed and the Ocean Floor Beyond the Limits of National Jurisdiction (Sea-Bed Committee), and this effectively set in train a process for the development of a regime to govern the deep seabed. However, in order to maintain the status quo with respect to the deep seabed, the UNGA took the precautionary step in December 1969 of adopting a resolution which purported to place a moratorium on deep seabed resource activities beyond the limits of national jurisdiction, including any claims to the resources of that area.[55] These developments set in place a process whereby in 1970 the UNGA adopted Resolution 2749 (XXV) titled 'Declaration of Principles Governing the Sea-Bed and Ocean Floor, and the Subsoil Thereof, Beyond the Limits of National Jurisdiction',[56] which in addition to proclaiming the seabed and ocean floor as part of the common heritage of humankind, called upon the Sea-Bed Committee to act as a preparatory committee for a Third United Nations Conference on the Law of the Sea (UNCLOS III). The conference was eventually convened at the United Nations headquarters in New York from 3 to 15 December 1973.

---

[52] O'Connell, *The International Law of the Sea*, vol 1 (n 4) 543–44.

[53] Convention on the High Seas, art 2(3).

[54] Morell, *The Law of the Sea* (n 32) 18.

[55] UNGA Resolution 2574D (XXIV) (1969) 'Question of the Reservation Exclusively for Peaceful Purposes of the Sea-Bed and Ocean Floor, and the Subsoil Thereof, Underlying the High Seas Beyond the Limits of Present National Jurisdiction, and the Use of Their Resources in the Interests of Mankind' (Moratorium Resolution), *Basic Documents* No 16; the Resolution was adopted by a vote of 62 in favour, 28 against, with 28 abstentions.

[56] UNGA Resolution 2749 (XXV) (1970), *Basic Documents* No 17; the Resolution was adopted by a vote of 108 in favour, none against, with 14 abstentions.

C. UNCLOS III Conference Dynamics

UNCLOS III was a very different conference and negotiation from its predecessors. Unlike UNCLOS I there were no ILC draft articles upon which to base a convention text. Accordingly, the negotiation of the convention text had to take place within the Conference framework. The conference was conducted over a nine year period between 1973 and 1982, with 11 negotiating sessions spread across 585 days and held in three countries.[57] One consequence of the length of the negotiation was that state practice evolved significantly over the life of the conference.

UNCLOS III was far more representative than the earlier conferences. A much larger gathering of states attended the conference compared to both UNCLOS I and II, with the final numbers at the last substantive sessions in 1982 totalling 151. There were also many more observers in attendance.[58] A number of national liberation movements, specialised agencies and United Nations organisations, intergovernmental organisations and non-governmental organisations were also admitted as observers.[59] With such a large number of states present at the negotiations, there was also a very different political dynamic than at UNCLOS I or II. At the first session, five regional groups were recognised for the purpose of distributing seats in the various conference committees. These were the African group, the Asian group, the Latin American group, the Western European group and the Eastern European group.

As the conference developed, the 'Group of 77' emerged as a particularly significant negotiating bloc with the capacity to promote initiatives that specifically reflected developing country perspectives.[60] Throughout UNCLOS III the role of the Group of 77 was perhaps one of the most influential in its impact upon the key conference outcomes. Not only were the UNCLOS III negotiations occurring at a time when developing states were beginning to acquire greater political significance within United Nations forums, but there was also a sense that given the incomplete nature of the law there was a real opportunity for these states to shape a post-colonial legal regime and to reap significant economic and other benefits. Anand, reflecting upon the position taken by many of these states at the first substantive UNCLOS III negotiations at Caracas in 1974, noted

> the under-developed countries of the Third World were determined to play an active, indeed aggressive, role in the formulation of a new law in place of the old, time-worn, sparse rules, which had left unlimited freedom to a few maritime Powers to use the oceans according to their own sweet will.[61]

State practice in the law of the sea was in considerable flux in the period immediately prior to UNCLOS III, as reflected in the widely varying claims to different maritime zones

[57] Whilst the principal conferences venues were the United Nations Headquarters in New York and Geneva, the Second session (20 June–29 August 1974) was held in Caracas, Venezuela.

[58] Such as Papua New Guinea which originally attended as a territory of Australia but by the end of the conference was in attendance as an independent state.

[59] A complete list of attending states can be found in 'Final Act of the Third United Nations Conference on the Law of the Sea' at www.un.org/Depts/los/convention_agreements/texts/final_act_eng.pdf.

[60] By the conclusion of the conference this group encompassed over 100 states, and also included major powers such as China: Jeanette Greenfield, *China's Practice in the Law of the Sea* (Oxford, Clarendon Press, 1992) 194.

[61] Anand, *Origin and Development of the Law of the Sea* (n 9) 209.

and the equivocal decision of the ICJ in the *Fisheries Jurisdiction* case.[62] Nevertheless, by the time UNCLOS III convened in 1973 there was a developing momentum within the international community for recognition of an expanded offshore resources zone that encompassed elements of then existing fishing zone claims and also the continental shelf. This was consistent with the development of a 'New International Economic Order' within the international community. This found expression in a law of the sea context in the 1970 Montevideo Declaration on the Law of the Sea which called for the development of a new law of the sea recognising as a basic principle 'the right of the coastal states to avail themselves of the natural resources of the sea adjacent to their coasts'.[63] Latin American states further developed this principle with their endorsement of the concept of a 'patrimonial sea' that encompassed claims to a 200 nm zone over which sovereignty could be exercised with respect to the natural resources of the area.[64] These debates, which eventually formed the basis for the recognition of the Exclusive Economic Zone (EEZ), had a significant impact upon how coastal state claims to regulate offshore fishing activities were eventually perceived. With rapid agreement reached at UNCLOS III on the EEZ, many states in the 1970s unilaterally proclaimed expanded fisheries zones or an EEZ. These claims were reflected both in individual maritime claims, and also in bilateral and regional agreements. The effect of this state practice was that even prior to the conclusion in 1982 of UNCLOS III there was considerable acceptance of either a separate fisheries zone or the more complex EEZ.[65]

Notwithstanding the long agenda and the duration of the negotiations, for the most part debate at UNCLOS III was harmonious. Agreement was reached at an early stage on the breadth of the territorial sea as 12 nm, thereby immediately addressing one of the dominant sticking points at UNCLOS I and II. There was agreement that once the territorial sea was extended then greater attention needed to be given to the innocent passage navigation regime through the territorial sea and international straits, and so consideration was given to clarifying the navigational regime throughout the proposed convention. The rights of archipelagic states were also acknowledged as being in need of recognition, as were landlocked and geographically disadvantaged states. The debates of the 1950s and 1960s over an EFZ were subsumed into support for a more comprehensive offshore resources zone in the form of an EEZ, and it was seen as important to have a clear relationship between the EEZ and the continental shelf. There was also general consensus on the need to address the regime of the deep seabed, and the common heritage of humankind principles, which Pardo had promoted in 1967, received general endorsement.

Given the wide range of ocean governance challenges addressed at UNCLOS III, touching upon the interests of virtually all states, it was recognised throughout the negotiations that the outcome would have to be a 'package deal' if it were to be widely accepted. Hence,

---

[62] *Fisheries Jurisdiction (United Kingdom v Iceland)* (Merits) [1974] ICJ Rep 3.

[63] S Houston Lay, Robin Churchill and Myron Nordquist (eds), *New Directions in the Law of the Sea* vol 1 (Dobbs Ferry, NY, Oceana, 1973) 235.

[64] 'Text of the Declaration of Santo Domingo approved by the Meeting of Ministers on June 7, 1972' in *New Directions in the Law of the Sea*, vol 1, ibid 247.

[65] See *Delimitation of the Maritime Boundary in the Gulf of Maine Area (Canada/United States of America)* [1984] ICJ Rep 246, [94] where the Court observed that even through the LOSC was not yet in force, and that 'a number of States do not appear inclined to ratify it' the EEZ was 'adopted without any objections' and that the United States had proclaimed an EEZ in 1983.

a consensus position was reached on many issues which reflected that the interests of all states had been taken into account to ensure an appropriate balancing of those interests in the final draft convention. Accordingly, the interests of coastal states in attaining a 12 nm territorial sea were counter-balanced against the interests of maritime states which were guaranteed navigational freedoms. Likewise, archipelagic states such as Indonesia and the Philippines achieved recognition of their unique maritime status for the first time in return for maritime states being able to enjoy navigational freedoms through waters that previously would have been high seas or at least territorial sea.

D. The United States Position on Common Heritage and the Deep Seabed

The emerging consensus within the conference was challenged in 1981 following the election of the Reagan administration in the United States. The United States delegation to UNCLOS III began to express significant reservations about the deep seabed mining regime of the proposed convention, especially those aspects which gave effect to certain 'common heritage' principles such as technology transfer. Whilst the United States sought certain adjustments to the convention text, this proved impossible given the advanced state of the negotiations and the apparent about-turn by the United States delegation on the common heritage regime. However, the United States was able to force UNCLOS III to a vote on the convention text at the eleventh session in New York in April 1982, with 130 states in favour, 4 against and 17 abstentions. Israel, Turkey and Venezuela joined the United States in voting against the convention text,[66] however this did not prove to be an impediment to the eventual conclusion of the conference negotiations. UNCLOS III resumed its eleventh session in New York in September 1982, where the convention text was concluded, as was the Final Act. The Convention opened for signature at a further meeting at Montego Bay, Jamaica on 10 December 1982.[67] In a speech to the assembled states during the signing ceremony, then United Nations Secretary-General, Javier Pérez de Cuéllar, was able to proclaim with ample justification that 'international law is now irrevocably transformed, so far as the seas are concerned'.[68]

VII. The United Nations Convention on the Law of the Sea

The LOSC remains one of the most comprehensive international law-making instruments of its time. The Convention comprises 320 articles, and nine additional annexes and establishes a truly comprehensive regime for the law of the sea that both reaffirms well settled

---

[66] Morell, *The Law of the Sea* (n 32) 83.

[67] This has resulted in some instances of the LOSC being referred to as the 'Montego Bay Convention', reflecting its formal place of conclusion and also to distinguish it from the four 1958 Geneva Conventions.

[68] Javier Pérez de Cuéllar, 'International Law is Irrevocably Transformed' (10 December 1982) in *The Law of the Sea: Official Text of the United Nations Convention on the Law of the Sea with Annexes and Index* (New York, United Nations, 1983) xxix.

areas of the law but also expansively develops other areas of the law, and in some instances creates completely new international law.

A. Core Provisions

The LOSC contains 17 Parts or chapters. Part I comprises only Article 1 and mainly contains definitional provisions. The regime of the territorial sea and contiguous zone is found in Part II and whilst this mainly duplicates the 1958 Geneva Convention on the High Seas, there are some significant additions. The breadth of the territorial sea is not to exceed 12 nm from the territorial sea baselines,[69] with the adjacent contiguous zone not permitted to extend beyond 24 nm from the baselines.[70] More content is also given to the right of innocent passage, further defining the rights and interests of coastal states and maritime states. In recognition of the consequences of an expanded territorial sea for navigation through straits, Part III creates a new regime of transit passage through straits used for international navigation with variations on this right applicable in allied waters.[71] Related to these provisions dealing with 'coastal waters' is Part IV, which recognises 'Archipelagic States'.[72] These are states comprised of one or more geographical archipelagos and which meet certain technical criteria. Special provisions are created for these states and for navigation within their waters.[73]

The coastal state resource regimes of the Convention are found in Parts V and VI dealing with the EEZ and continental shelf. Both zones entitle coastal states to certain rights of resource sovereignty up to 200 nm in the case of the EEZ,[74] and in the case of the continental shelf a minimum zone of 200 nm is recognised, although in some instances it may be possible for a coastal state to proclaim an outer continental shelf which goes well beyond those limits.[75] The high seas regime is set out in Part VII, and largely reflects the key provisions of the 1958 Geneva Convention on the High Seas,[76] although it also recognises additional high seas freedoms, including the right to construct artificial islands and other installations and the right to conduct scientific research.[77]

Parts VIII to X deal with a variety of special circumstances. Part VIII comprises Article 121 and addresses the regime of islands, identifying the extent that islands are entitled to generate maritime zones. Part IX deals with enclosed or semi-enclosed seas, first providing a definition for such regions and then creating a framework for cooperation between the coastal states fronting such areas. The particular issues confronting landlocked and geographically disadvantaged states are addressed in Part X, rectifying the failure at UNCLOS I to include specific provisions to cater for this group of states.[78]

---

[69] LOSC, art 3. Discussed in more detail in ch 3.
[70] Ibid art 33. Discussed in more detail in ch 3.
[71] Discussed in more detail in ch 11.
[72] Discussed in more detail in ch 8.
[73] Discussed in more detail in ch 11.
[74] Discussed in more detail in ch 4.
[75] Discussed in more detail in ch 5.
[76] Discussed in more detail in ch 7.
[77] LOSC, art 87(1); discussed in more detail in ch 14.
[78] Discussed in more detail in ch 9.

Part XI deals with the regime of the deep seabed and is one of the lengthiest and most detailed parts of the Convention. The deep seabed, referred to for the purposes of the Convention as the 'Area', is the subject of a regime based on the principle of common heritage of humankind.[79] Under Part XI an institution known as the International Seabed Authority (ISA) has oversight of the operationalisation of the regime, while another body, the 'Enterprise', has the capacity to undertake exploration and exploitation of the deep seabed consistent with common heritage principles. A distinguishing feature of Part XI is that distinctive provisions are also included for the settlement of disputes.

Part XII deals with the protection and preservation of the marine environment and builds upon developing principles of international environmental law as applicable to oceans and seas. A series of general principles are outlined, in addition to mechanisms to facilitate global and regional cooperation to address marine environmental issues. Whilst there are no detailed provisions for the regulation of individual pollution sources, Part XII provides a framework for such rules to be adopted under other international legal frameworks and significantly enhances enforcement rights (in particular, the capacity for port state enforcement).[80]

Marine scientific research is addressed in Part XIII, thereby filling a gap which had emerged from the Geneva Conventions. Reference is made to the rights and responsibilities of all states in conducting marine scientific research in certain settings, and Part XIII seeks to achieve a balance between the interests of coastal states within their maritime zones and the broader interest of the international community in the freedom of scientific discovery. Related to this are provisions in Part XIV dealing with the development and transfer of marine technology.

Another central feature of the LOSC is found in Part XV dealing with the settlement of international disputes.[81] Unique to international law at the time, the Convention creates a regime of compulsory procedures for the settlement of disputes which builds upon the basic framework of peaceful dispute settlement found in Chapter VI of the Charter of the United Nations (UN Charter). Part XV seeks to utilise not only existing dispute settlement bodies such as the ICJ, but also establishes new mechanisms via a permanent International Tribunal for the Law of the Sea (ITLOS). Parts XVI and XVII round out the LOSC with general provisions addressing the importance of good faith in exercising convention rights,[82] and calling on the oceans to be used for peaceful purposes,[83] along with procedural provisions dealing with signature, ratification, and entry into force.

A significant procedural issue which needed to be dealt with in the LOSC was its relationship with the four 1958 Geneva Conventions, and with other instruments either of a regional or bilateral nature that may have application in a law of the sea context. Article 311(1) provides that the LOSC 'shall prevail, as between State Parties' over the Geneva Conventions. The effect of this is that for those states which had adopted both the Geneva Conventions and the LOSC, the LOSC prevails as a matter of treaty law between two states parties. But in the case of those states which had become Geneva parties, but not LOSC

---

[79] LOSC, art 136; discussed in more detail in ch 6.
[80] Ibid art 218; discussed in more detail in ch 15.
[81] Discussed in more detail in ch 18.
[82] LOSC, art 300.
[83] Ibid art 301.

parties, then the LOSC would not apply in the relations between a LOSC state party and a Geneva state party.[84] With respect to other pre-existing treaty agreements, they are to remain in place provided they are 'compatible' with the LOSC.[85] This was an important recognition of the need to maintain the status quo with respect to maritime boundary and fisheries treaties which pre-dated the LOSC. The Convention also includes nine additional Annexes. These deal with matters ranging from the identification of highly migratory fish stocks,[86] to more technical provisions which supplement the Part XV mechanisms for dispute settlement.

One of the important additions to the conceptual framework of the international law of the sea made by the LOSC is the manner in which the Convention distinguishes between coastal, flag and port states. Although coastal states are not defined in the Convention, they are simply states with a coastline entitled to a territorial sea and the associated sovereign rights and jurisdiction over other maritime zones. Flag states are those states which have set conditions for the grant of nationality to ships, giving them an entitlement under domestic law to fly the flag of that state. A flag state acquires certain duties under Article 94 of the LOSC to exercise jurisdiction over each ship flying its flag which extends not only to when that ship is within the flag state's own waters, but also when it is upon the high seas, or within the waters of other coastal states.[87] Port states have distinctive, but limited, enforcement jurisdiction with respect to vessels voluntarily within their ports. They exercise neither coastal or flag state jurisdiction because none of the laws of the port state enacted under their prescriptive jurisdiction have been infringed. Rather, they exercise enforcement jurisdiction at the request of another coastal or flag state where there is evidence to suggest that an infringement of coastal state or flag states laws have taken place.[88]

Whilst the LOSC was concluded at the resumed eleventh session in New York in September 1982, the Final Act was concluded and the Convention opened for signature on 10 December 1982. The LOSC remained open for signature for a further two years, during which time all states, and a range of other state entities were entitled to append their signature.[89] Ratification of the LOSC was open to all states which had signed,[90] whilst the Convention remained open for accession to all states even if they had not originally signed.[91] Entry into force of the LOSC required ratification or accession by 60 states. However, consistent with the 'package deal' notion of the Convention, Article 309 provided that no reservations or exceptions could be made unless expressly permitted. This provision was at the time contrary to the then trend in treaty law that large multilateral conventions could be subject to reservation, primarily in order to ensure the broadest possible participation. In recognition of this strict provision, the LOSC does, however, permit under

[84] This is an important matter of treaty law given that the LOSC has not been accepted by all Geneva state parties, of which the United States is perhaps the most prominent Geneva state party which still has yet to ratify or accede to the LOSC.
[85] LOSC, art 311(2).
[86] Ibid Annex I.
[87] Discussed in more detail in ch 7.
[88] Discussed in more detail in ch 15.
[89] LOSC, art 305; this included Namibia—at the time represented by the United Nations Council for Namibia; and self-governing associated states such as the Cook Islands.
[90] Ibid art 306.
[91] Ibid art 307.

Article 310 the making of declarations and statements, provided they do not in effect take the form of a reservation that may otherwise have been made.[92]

B. Entry into Force

The conclusion of UNCLOS III resulted in an initial burst of enthusiasm for the LOSC from states which had much to gain from its acceptance and entry into force. Fiji, for example, ratified the Convention on the day it was concluded on 10 December 1982, becoming the first state to do so. However, it soon became apparent that the concerns expressed by the United States over the provisions of Part XI were gaining support from other states. In the early 1980s the United States and some other western states enacted legislation permitting the issuing of licences for deep seabed mining,[93] and in order to reduce possible conflict over exploitation of deep seabed areas an agreement was reached in 1984 between many of these states to avoid overlapping licences.[94] Throughout the 1980s the status quo with respect to the Convention and the deep seabed remained in place. The LOSC had not entered into force, although the number of ratifications and accessions were growing, and the deep seabed legal regime was not being tested due to a lack of interest in exploration. However, in the early 1990s this position began to shift due to the realisation that the LOSC had attracted sufficient levels of support to bring it into force in the near future. Although this was a positive development for the law of the sea, the fact that a large number of western states still had not ratified the Convention meant there was the prospect that it would enter into force without large-scale support, and that its various institutions would struggle to command legitimacy without the full backing of the international community.

C. 1994 Implementing Agreement

Some form of breakthrough was required in this impasse and this occurred with the intervention of the United Nations Secretary-General, who was able to bring together key states and broker a resolution which effectively resulted in modifications and adjustments to Part XI of the LOSC prior to its entry into force. This occurred via a 1994 UNGA resolution[95] that formally agreed upon an Agreement Relating to the Implementation of Part XI of the United Nations Convention on the Law of the Sea of 10 December 1982 (1994 Implementing Agreement).[96] This Agreement sought to address many of the key concerns which had

---

[92] Ibid art 310 expressly notes on this point 'provided that such declarations or statements do not purport to exclude or modify the legal effect of the provisions of this Convention in their application to that State'. This was highlighted by the Australian objection to the Declaration lodged by the Philippines when it signed and subsequently ratified the LOSC; Australia's concern related to how the Philippines sought to interpret the archipelagic waters provisions of the LOSC: 'United Nations Convention on the Law of the Sea—Ratification, with Understanding by the Philippines—Objection by Australia' (1992) 12 *Australian Year Book of International Law* 383–85.

[93] See, eg, *Deep Seabed Hard Mineral Resources Act 1980* (US); *Deep Sea Mining (Temporary Provisions) Act 1981* (UK).

[94] 1984 Provisional Understanding Regarding Deep Seabed Matters between Belgium, France, the Federal Republic of Germany, Italy, Japan, the Netherlands, the United Kingdom, and the United States, *Basic Documents* No 38.

[95] UNGA Resolution 48/263 (1994).

[96] *Basic Documents* No 37.

been raised by the United States and others in the aftermath of UNCLOS III dealing with issues such as the institutional costs for state parties in giving effect to the Part XI arrangements, the operation of the Enterprise, decision-making procedures within the Assembly of the International Seabed Authority, the transfer of technology, and the production and economic assistance policies of the Authority.[97] Procedurally, the 1994 Implementing Agreement also needed to address its relationship with Part XI of the LOSC and it provided that the two were to be 'interpreted and applied together as a single instrument',[98] with the Agreement to prevail in the event of any inconsistency. Provision was also made in the Agreement for its adoption, which could occur through LOSC ratification or accession, or, in the case of those states which had already become parties to the LOSC at the time of the Agreement's adoption, by way of separate procedures indicating acceptance of the Agreement.[99]

The LOSC eventually entered into force on 16 November 1994, consistent with the provisions of Article 308, one year after the date of deposit of the sixtieth instrument of ratification or acceptance. By January 2015 a total of 167 states and the European Union had indicated their acceptance of the Convention. Allied with the LOSC is the 1994 Implementing Agreement, which entered into force on 28 July 1996 and has 147 parties. The most recent party to accede to the LOSC and the 1994 Implementing Agreement is the State of Palestine, which joined both conventions on 2 January 2015. Palestine joins three other parties to the LOSC and 1994 Implementing Agreement that are not members of the United Nations.[100] In respect of Palestine, it should be recalled that the Palestinian Liberation Organization was one of several national liberation movements invited to participate in the deliberations at UNCLOS III and which signed the Final Act of the conference.

Notwithstanding the high level of acceptance of the LOSC, there are several key states which remain outside of the Convention. In all there are 14 coastal states that are not parties to the LOSC.[101] Whilst United States opposition to the Convention has been reversed, as seen in the attitudes of recent Republican and Democrat administrations, the United States has not been able to ratify the Convention because of opposition within the United States Senate. Israel, Turkey and Venezuela have also not yet become parties to the Convention and have maintained their opposition to the Convention expressed at the conclusion of UNCLOS III.

D. 1995 Fish Stocks Agreement

To complete a missing plank in the LOSC framework of instruments, in 1995 an additional agreement was negotiated to supplement the provisions of the Convention relating to straddling and highly migratory fish stocks. Whilst the LOSC makes reference to these fish stocks, there was no comprehensive regime agreed upon to regulate these high

---

[97] See 1994 Implementing Agreement, Annex.
[98] Ibid art 2(1).
[99] Ibid arts 4, 5.
[100] Cook Islands, European Union and Niue.
[101] Cambodia, Colombia, El Salvador, Eritrea, Iran, Israel, Libya, North Korea, Peru, Syria, Turkey, United Arab Emirates, United States and Venezuela.

seas and related fisheries during UNCLOS III. This reflected an understanding during the conference that it would not be possible to resolve every law of the sea issue, and that some matters would need future resolution via additional agreements or protocols. To that end, Articles 63 and 64 of the LOSC provided only for very broad principles for the management of straddling stocks[102] and highly migratory fish stocks,[103] whilst several Part VII provisions dealing with high seas fish stocks also provided a framework for management of these fisheries.[104] Accordingly during the early 1990s, once again in contemplation of the pending entry into force of the LOSC but also in response to growing concerns about the management of these fisheries, the United Nations facilitated the negotiation and eventual conclusion of an Agreement for the Implementation of the Provisions of the United Nations Convention on the Law of the Sea of 10 December 1982 Relating to the Conservation and Management of Straddling Fish Stocks and Highly Migratory Fish Stocks (Fish Stocks Agreement).[105] The Agreement reflects some of the significant advances in marine living resource management since the 1970s, and also relevant developments in international environmental law. Its core objective is the 'long-term conservation and sustainable use of straddling fish stocks and highly migratory fish stocks',[106] and it seeks to achieve that objective through the application of the precautionary principle in the management of these stocks. Enhanced compliance and enforcement mechanisms are provided for, with the role of flag, port and coastal states all expanded. In an interesting point of distinction from the 1994 Implementing Agreement, the 1995 Fish Stocks Agreement is to be 'interpreted and applied in the context of and in a manner consistent' with the LOSC.[107] The Fish Stocks Agreement entered into force on 11 December 2001 and had 82 state parties as at 1 July 2015.

VIII. Institutional Frameworks

Another impact of the LOSC upon the international law of the sea was the creation of new institutions tasked with implementing various parts of the Convention, whilst also in a de facto manner creating a framework within which other associated institutional arrangements have developed. Three institutions created by the LOSC are of particular relevance. The ISA, headquartered in Jamaica, is at the core of the operation of Part XI dealing with the deep seabed. Although aspects of its operation were the subject of disagreement, their eventual resolution in the 1994 Implementing Agreement has meant that the ISA had an operational role soon after the LOSC entered into force. A key aspect of the ISA as it has developed has been its attention to the environmental impacts associated with deep

---

[102] These are fish stocks which 'occur within the exclusive economic zone of two or more coastal States', or 'occur both within the exclusive economic zone and in an area beyond and adjacent to the zone': LOSC, art 63.
[103] These stocks are identified in ibid Annex I.
[104] See ibid arts 118, 119.
[105] *Basic Documents* No 56; discussed in more detail in ch 13.
[106] Fish Stocks Agreement, art 2.
[107] Ibid art 4.

seabed mining activities, and the need for those impacts to be managed and limited as the Authority moves forward in the development of large-scale commercial seabed mining.[108]

ITLOS is the permanent international court for law of the sea dispute resolution created by the LOSC, and is the centrepiece of the Part XV mechanisms for the settlement of disputes contained within the Convention. Permanently located in Hamburg, the tribunal was established in 1996 and has developed a distinctive jurisprudence across several areas of the law of the sea, especially that relating to the prompt release of fishing vessels detained by coastal states[109] and the application of environmental principles to the law of the sea.[110]

The third LOSC institution is the Commission on the Limits of the Continental Shelf (CLCS), which is only briefly referred to in Article 76, but whose constitution, mandate and operation is further expanded upon in Annex II. The CLCS, which was founded in 1997 has been through three phases: organisational, primary and secondary.[111] These phases partly reflected the workload of the Commission, which has received 77 submissions of outer continental shelf data since 2001. The Commission's principal role is to make recommendations to coastal states on the outer limits of their continental shelves based on information provided to the Commission by coastal states. Unlike the ISA and ITLOS, no allowance was made for the CLCS to have a permanent seat, although in practice the Commission principally operates from United Nations headquarters in New York.

In addition to these permanent institutional arrangements, Article 319 of the LOSC also envisaged that, as appropriate, meetings of the state parties to the Convention could also be convened from time to time. This practice has been adopted and the Secretary-General of the United Nations, in the role as depositary of the Convention, convenes annual meetings of the State Parties to the United Nations Convention on the Law of the Sea (SPLOS) which are held in New York. Whilst the agenda of these meetings has varied, a principal point of focus is a review of the work of the ITLOS, the ISA and the CLCS. Consideration is also often given to the annual Report of the Secretary-General on the Law of the Sea, and budgetary matters associated with the operation of the Convention and its institutions.[112] As the mandate of the SPLOS is not clearly defined, there has been some capacity for it to respond to evolving issues confronting the LOSC and the law of the sea more generally. One particular issue has been the workload of the CLCS and its capacity to deal in a timely fashion with increasing submissions. This is highlighted by the fact that, as at 1 July 2015, the CLCS had adopted only 22 recommendations. Aligned with this process since 2000 there has been an annual United Nations Open-Ended Informal Consultative Process on Oceans and the Law of the Sea (ICP) which is designed to allow states parties to the LOSC to gather informally

---

[108] Michael Lodge, 'Current Legal Development: International Seabed Authority' (2009) 24 *International Journal of Marine and Coastal Law* 185, 186; discussed in more detail in ch 6.

[109] See the discussion in Donald R Rothwell and Tim Stephens, 'Illegal Southern Ocean Fishing and Prompt Release: Balancing Coastal and Flag State Rights and Interests' (2004) 53 *International and Comparative Law Quarterly* 171–87.

[110] Donald R Rothwell, 'The International Tribunal for the Law of the Sea and Marine Environmental Protection: Expanding the Horizons of International Oceans Governance' [2003] 17 *Ocean Yearbook* 26–55; discussed in more detail in ch 18.

[111] See the discussion in Donald R Rothwell 'Issues and Strategies for Outer Continental Shelf Claims' (2008) 23 *International Journal of Marine and Coastal Law* 185–211; discussed in more detail in ch 5.

[112] For general discussion see Alex G Oude Elferink, 'Reviewing the Implementation of the LOS Convention: The Role of the United Nations General Assembly and the Meeting of States Parties' in Alex G Oude Elferink and Donald R Rothwell (eds), *Oceans Management in the 21st Century: Institutional Frameworks and Responses* (Leiden/Boston, Martinus Nijhoff, 2004) 295–312.

to discuss key or emerging issues regarding the law of the sea that may be in need of further elaboration either within the LOSC or in related United Nations frameworks. In addition to these processes, the UNGA has also regularly reviewed the operation and implementation of the law of the sea and from time to time, when the occasion demands, the United Nations Security Council has adopted resolutions directly impacting upon the law of the sea in certain matters.[113] In addition to these United Nations organs, note also needs to be made of the role of other United Nations bodies, especially the International Maritime Organization (IMO), the Food and Agriculture Organization (FAO) and the United Nations Environment Programme (UNEP).[114]

IX. Sources of the International Law of the Sea

A. Customary International Law

The sources of the international law of the sea, as would be self-evident from the discussion above, are principally customary international law and treaties. However, consistent with Article 38(1) of the Statute of the International Court of Justice, all of the recognised sources of international law have a capacity to, and do in fact, contribute to the body of law. Whilst the law of the sea was clearly dominated by state practice and customary international law until the mid-twentieth century, the ongoing impact of customary international law cannot be ignored, especially with respect to those areas of conventional law which are not clearly articulated in the existing treaties or in areas where state practice may have extended the application of some of the treaty provisions. This phenomenon has been clearly recognised by the ICJ in its multiple decisions on law of the sea matters,[115] and is particularly evident in the law that has developed on maritime boundary delimitation. In the *North Sea Continental Shelf* case[116] the ICJ was called upon to determine the customary status of Article 6 of the Convention on the Continental Shelf as between Denmark, the Netherlands and the Federal Republic of Germany, and to establish continental shelf boundaries. The Court's judgment, which set out important general principles for determining customary international norms, also laid the foundation for subsequent judicial determinations by the ICJ and other international tribunals as to the methods and techniques for maritime boundary delimitation predominantly based upon state practice and customary international law. Notwithstanding the later development of the LOSC, these principles of maritime boundary delimitation as developed in custom, remain the relevant law in the field.

---

[113] See in particular United Nations Security Council Resolutions 1816 (2008), 1838 (2008), 1846 (2008) and 1851 (2008), *Basic Documents* Nos 86–89 dealing with piracy off the coast of Somalia and in the northwest Indian Ocean.

[114] Other international organisations with an interest in law of the sea matters include the International Atomic Energy Authority (IAEA), International Civil Aviation Organization (ICAO), International Hydrographic Organization (IHO), and the World Trade Organization (WTO).

[115] See *Delimitation of the Maritime Boundary in the Gulf of Maine Area (Canada/United States of America)* [1984] ICJ Rep 246, [79]–[96]; *Continental Shelf (Libyan Arab Jamahiriya/Malta)* [1985] ICJ Rep 13, [26]–[34].

[116] *North Sea Continental Shelf (Federal Republic of Germany v Denmark; Federal Republic of Germany v The Netherlands)* [1969] ICJ Rep 3.

B. Treaties and Conventions

With respect to treaty law, the contemporary international law of the sea since the conclusion of the four 1958 Geneva Conventions has been dominated by multilateral treaties, of which the LOSC is now clearly the central international instrument. An interesting feature of the LOSC has been its changing status. Soon after its conclusion in 1982, the President of UNCLOS III, Tommy TB Koh of Singapore, observed that the LOSC was not a codification Convention. He noted that:

> The argument that, except for Part XI, the Convention codifies customary law or reflects existing international practice is factually incorrect and legally insupportable. The regime of transit passage through straits used for international navigation and the regime of archipelagic sea lanes passage are two examples of many new concepts in the Convention.[117]

This analysis is certainly an accurate reflection of the 'mixed' status of the LOSC at the time in that in some instances it duplicated parts of the Geneva Conventions, in other instances it extended the Geneva Conventions, whilst in other areas it developed completely new law. Its impact upon the law of the sea was immediate, so that even though it took 12 years to enter into force, in some respects it was de facto operative as soon as it was concluded with some parts of the Convention, such as that dealing with the EEZ, being actively implemented prior to the Convention's formal conclusion. Now in the first decades of the twenty-first century, the LOSC represents a mature convention regime. The LOSC, however, has not stood still and in addition to the 1994 Implementing Agreement has been subject to extension by way of the 1995 Fish Stocks Agreement. Accordingly, when assessing the status of the LOSC and its impact as a source of law upon the law of the sea, not only must consideration be given to the core instrument but also those associated with it and the state practice which has developed around its implementation.[118]

A related aspect of the international law of the sea based on treaties which should not be ignored is the growing body of additional multilateral treaties at both a global and regional level which address an ever expanding range of matters which have a law of the sea dimension. Most prominent are the multilateral treaties that have been adopted under the auspices of the IMO relating to marine pollution,[119] and an expanding list of regional treaties dealing with fisheries management that are pivotal to the implementation of Parts V and VII.[120] In addition, there are numerous bilateral treaties that also give effect to various provisions of the contemporary international law of the sea, especially concerning maritime boundaries. When all of these additional multilateral and bilateral treaties are added to the core treaty framework found within the LOSC, not only is the body of international law comprising the law of the sea extensive, but its reach and depth are also apparent.

---

[117] Tommy TB Koh, 'A Constitution for the Oceans' in *The Law of the Sea: United Nations Convention on the Law of the Sea* (New York, St Martin's Press, 1983) xxxiv.

[118] To that end, domestic legislation, statutes, decrees and official acts by states giving effect to the provisions of the LOSC are also important sources of the law in the field, see, eg, Australian Maritime Safety Authority, Marine Notice 8/2006: Revised Pilotage Requirements for Torres Strait (2006), *Basic Documents* No 82.

[119] See, eg, 1973 International Convention for the Prevention of Pollution from Ships, as Modified by the Protocol of 1978 Relating Thereto (MARPOL 73/78), *Basic Documents* No 21.

[120] See, eg, 1993 Convention for the Conservation of Southern Bluefin Tuna, *Basic Documents* No 55.

C. Unilateral Declarations

An interesting aspect of the law of the sea is the role that unilateral declarations have played in its development. There are two distinctive types of unilateral declarations in a law of the sea context. The first are those declarations made by states that seek to extend the existing law and state practice in the field, of which the 1945 Truman Proclamation is a clear example. State practice with respect to the development of various maritime claims is replete with examples of unilateral declarations being made, often with little or no reference to the existing law. As is evident in the debate which took place as to the outer limit of the territorial sea, in some instances these declarations may or may not have influence on the development of the law. The impact of these unilateral declarations which seek to extend the development of the law of the sea have also been influential before the ICJ.[121] The second type of unilateral declaration is the assertion of a new maritime claim consistent with the existing law. Such claims, however, are contemplated under the law of the sea and reflect the assertion of a state's right to claim certain maritime areas consistent with the law.

D. Subsidiary Sources of Law

The law has also been considerably influenced by what technically may be considered 'subsidiary' sources of international law,[122] but which in a law of the sea context have been regarded as mainstream influences. There have been few other bodies of international law so substantially influenced by the views of publicists as the law of the sea and the ongoing influence of Grotius is evidence of this phenomenon. Likewise, the law of the sea has also been decisively shaped by decisions of international courts and tribunals. Since the ICJ's first decision in *Corfu Channel*,[123] there has been a steady caseload of law of the sea matters, especially with respect to maritime boundary delimitation. This is highlighted by the fact that in the period since 1969 and the decision in *North Sea Continental Shelf* the ICJ has delivered over a dozen judgments on maritime boundary delimitation matters. Other, ad hoc, tribunals have also contributed to the development of the law,[124] and with the establishment of ITLOS the capacity of international courts and tribunals to expand the law has been enhanced even further. In the process of some of these decisions, it should be noted that reference has been made to the importance of equity as a principle of law recognised under Article 38(1)(c) of the ICJ's Statute as also being influential for the development of the law.

E. Soft Law

Finally, as with many contemporary areas of international law, the law of the sea has also been influenced by 'soft law'[125] which over time has grown in significance and in some

---

[121] O'Connell, *The International Law of the Sea*, vol 1 (n 4) 31.
[122] Statute of the International Court of Justice, art 38(1)(d).
[123] *Corfu Channel case (United Kingdom v Albania)* [1949] ICJ Rep 4.
[124] See, eg, *Anglo-French Continental Shelf Arbitration* (1979) 18 ILM 397.
[125] That is law which is not yet completely formed by way of treaty or custom and accordingly is not binding upon states, but which may in time evolve into 'hard' law in the form of a binding treaty or custom.

instances has become hard law. This is evident from the UNGA resolutions of 1969 and 1970[126] concerning the deep seabed which became reflective of the common heritage of humankind principles embedded in Part XI of the LOSC, but can also be seen in the influence of the 1991 UNGA Resolution on Drift-Net Fishing[127] which though non-binding created the foundation for a moratorium on that practice. Other examples of soft law having an influence on the law of the sea include Agenda 21 adopted in 1992 with its Chapter 17 devoted to protection of the oceans;[128] the 1995 FAO Code of Conduct for Responsible Fisheries;[129] the 2001 FAO International Plan of Action to Prevent, Deter and Eliminate Illegal, Unreported and Unregulated Fishing;[130] and the 2009 IMO Code of Conduct Concerning the Repression of Piracy and Armed Robbery Against Ships in the Western Indian Ocean and the Gulf of Aden.[131] As is generally the case with soft law, its attractiveness lies with its capacity to develop such instruments on a relatively rapid basis without all of the formality associated with a treaty negotiation, and therefore to respond to newly emerging issues requiring action.

X. Challenges for the International Law of the Sea

A feature of the international law of the sea is that it has been in an ongoing state of development based on developing state practice, the views of publicists, or via new international treaties and instruments. As the law increasingly seeks to manage environmental impacts, there is better understanding of the dynamics of regulating the oceans from multiple integrated perspectives. When new geopolitical challenges are added to this mix, it becomes apparent that the law of the sea needs to be responsive to developments in order for it to remain relevant and effective in managing the oceans.

A. Climate Change and Ocean Acidification

Of all these contemporary challenges, during the twenty-first century the impact of climate change and the related phenomenon of ocean acidification will prove to be the most significant.[132] The impacts of climate change for the world's oceans include sea level rise, changes in sea surface temperature, coastal erosion, ocean acidification and increased frequency of extreme weather events. The impact upon the marine environment is significant, extending from the melting of the polar ice caps, resulting in the appearance of open water across the

---

[126] UNGA Resolution 2574 D (XXIV), *Basic Documents* No 16; UNGA Resolution 2749 (XXV), *Basic Documents* No 17.

[127] UNGA Resolution 46/215 (1991), *Basic Documents* No 47.

[128] Agenda 21, Chapter 17: Protection of the Oceans, All Kinds of Seas, Including Enclosed and Semi-Enclosed Seas, and Coastal Areas and the Protection, Rational Use and Development of Their Living Resources (1992), *Basic Documents* No 48.

[129] *Basic Documents* No 58.

[130] *Basic Documents* No 67.

[131] *Basic Documents* No 90.

[132] J-P Gattuso, 'Contrasting Futures for Ocean and Society from Different Anthropogenic CO_2 Emission Scenarios' (2015) 349 *Science* 45.

Arctic Ocean and significant icebergs in the Southern Ocean, to the redistribution of many fish stocks as their habitats change.[133]

Whilst many uncertainties surround the consequences of climate change for the world's oceans, several impacts can clearly be anticipated. Rising sea levels will create challenges for declared territorial sea baselines, including reliance upon certain low-tide elevations and reefs as basepoints.[134] The consequences for potential baseline modification arising from climate change are considerable with respect to navigation, as it may result in greater access rights by foreign vessels within coastal state waters. That baselines may need to be recalibrated as a result of sea level rise will also result in general uncertainty as to the outer limits of already claimed maritime zones. Such uncertainty would not be helpful for maritime confidence in general, as it could lead to increased tensions over already disputed areas such as the South China Sea. Navigational hazards may also increase, particularly as a result of the melting of sea ice with consequences for increased iceberg activity, but also as a result of more intense storm activity and shifts in prevailing winds and currents. Major changes in the habitats of some marine living resources are already being detected, with the consequence that jurisdictional regimes which have been devised to regulate certain fish stocks will need to be revisited. For instance, there will be a need to adjust existing fisheries treaties and negotiate new agreements to reflect the shifting ranges of some straddling stocks and highly migratory species.[135]

B. Marine Environmental Security

A flow on impact from climate change is that marine environmental security will become an even more pressing issue. One of the early examples of the significance attached to this issue was Australia and New Zealand's 1973 challenge to France's Pacific Ocean nuclear weapons testing programme in the *French Nuclear Test* cases[136] and the subsequent adoption of the 1985 Treaty of Raratonga,[137] which placed limitations on the testing and use of nuclear weapons within the South Pacific. In the coming decade it must therefore be anticipated that as climate change effects become more prevalent and concern for the environment becomes even stronger, that the political and public demand for protection of the marine environment will continue to grow. Likewise, contemporary marine environmental issues such as ocean fertilisation,[138] and the effects of ocean acidification highlight ongoing issues regarding threats to marine biodiversity. Access to and utilisation of genetic resources in the oceans has also been a matter under consideration since 2007, as have the legal issues

---

[133] See the discussion in T Stephens, 'Warming Waters and Souring Seas: Climate Change and Ocean Acidification' in DR Rothwell, AG Oude-Elferink, KN Scott and T Stephens (eds), *The Oxford Handbook of the Law of the Sea* (Oxford, Oxford University Press, 2015) 777.

[134] Ibid, 787–94.

[135] Stephens, 'Warming Waters and Souring Seas' (n 133).

[136] *Nuclear Tests (Australia v France)* [1974] ICJ Rep 253; *Nuclear Tests (New Zealand v France)* [1974] ICJ Rep 457.

[137] 1985 South Pacific Nuclear Free Zone Treaty.

[138] R Rayfuse, MG Lawrence and KM Gjerde, 'Ocean Fertilisation and Climate Change: The Need to Regulate Emerging High Seas Uses' (2008) 23 *International Journal of Marine and Coastal Law* 297–326.

arising from bioprospecting.[139] Linked to this is the introduction of invasive alien species into the world's oceans, a matter which the IMO has sought to control through its measures dealing with ballast water, but which will require further attention to protect fisheries and aquaculture.

C. Creeping Jurisdiction

A further challenge for the law of the sea is one that been a common thread throughout its history and goes to the heart of the Grotian vision for the oceans; that is the gradual encroachment by coastal states over their adjacent maritime domain. First with the territorial sea, then the continental shelf, and then during the 1960s and 1970s a raft of new claims to EFZs and EEZs, the law of the sea has witnessed an ever expanding assertion of coastal state rights over adjacent waters. Whilst the legitimacy of all of these maritime zones has now been confirmed by the LOSC, there remains an ongoing capacity for coastal states to assert unilateral claims over some of these zones with considerable impacts upon the rights and interests of many states. The effect of uncontained creeping jurisdiction or 'territorialisation' of the oceans would be profound, especially with respect to its potential impacts upon the freedoms of navigation, fishing, and marine scientific research.

There are two particular dynamics at play in this regard. The first is the ability of a coastal state to interpret the provisions of the LOSC unilaterally so as to gain as extensive a maritime claim as is possible. This can apply with respect to the drawing of baselines (both straight and archipelagic), the assertion of maritime zones from islands and rocks, and the proclamation of outer continental shelves. The second is the capacity of some coastal states to adopt a unilateral interpretation of the LOSC so as to assert more extensive claims to sovereign rights or jurisdiction than was originally envisaged by the Convention's framers. Though some caution must be exercised when considering unilateral claims in the context of the oceans, given the role that such actions played in the progressive development of the modern law of the sea, the active assertion of new sovereign rights and jurisdiction within existing maritime zones remains very contentious as has been highlighted by ongoing tensions in the South China Sea between various claimants as a result of excessive baselines claims and island disputes.[140]

XI. Review and Reform of the International Law of the Sea

Although the LOSC and its supporting network of treaties provide an extensive body of law, there remain gaps and uncertainties within the regime of the law of the sea, including

---

[139] See T Scovazzi, 'Bioprospecting on the Deep Seabed: A Legal Gap Requiring to be Filled' in F Francioni and T Scovazzi (eds), *Biotechnology and International Law* (Oxford, Hart Publishing, 2006) 81–97; S Adelle Bonney, 'Bioprospecting, Scientific Research and Deep Sea Resources in Areas Beyond National Jurisdiction: A Critical Legal Analysis' (2006) 10 *New Zealand Journal of Environmental Law* 41–91.

[140] Hayley Roberts, 'Responses to Sovereign Disputes in the South China Sea' (2015) 30 *International Journal of Marine and Coastal Law* 199.

the LOSC. With the adoption of the 1994 Implementing Agreement and the 1995 Fish Stocks Agreement it has been possible to fill some of those gaps and to extend the LOSC into new areas. However, technological developments and environmental challenges may in the future further test the capacity of the regime of the international law of the sea to cope and there has been speculation as to whether there may be a need for a Fourth United Nations Conference on the Law of the Sea. This question goes to the stability of the LOSC and whether the legal regime which has developed around it is capable of continuing to provide the basis for the contemporary international law of the sea. In other words, can the LOSC continue to act as a 'constitution of the oceans'?[141]

This question can be partly answered by how the current law of the sea is conceptualised. If the law of the sea is seen as a distinctive body of international law that seeks to regulate all of the activities in the world's oceans, from the territorial sea out to the high seas, then clearly the LOSC does perform that function. If, on the other hand, the legal regime of the oceans as reflected in the law of the sea is seen as requiring an integrated approach between the land, sea and air, then a newly conceived law of the sea may be more appropriate.[142] Indeed, the reality is that the law of the sea has proven itself capable of being subject to modification and expansion, not only through formal instruments such as the 1994 Implementing Agreement, but also via state practice, and the actions of international organisations which have built upon the law of the sea framework to regulate related activities ranging from land-based activities resulting in marine pollution to the shore-based actions of pirates that have ramifications for the safety of international shipping. This does not necessarily demonstrate a flexibility in the LOSC, but rather highlights the nature of the law of the sea regime more generally and its ability to be developed and broadened by both traditional and non-traditional sources.

The LOSC will, however, remain pivotal to the regime in the future and its broad base and detailed coverage of the 'core' of the law of the sea means that it will remain relevant and operative for some decades. Accordingly, the capacity of the LOSC to be adjusted and modified will be essential to its longevity. There are three main ways in which this can occur. The first is via the mechanism adopted for the 1994 Implementing Agreement; however this was clearly a response to a unique situation that is unlikely to arise again. The second is via the mechanism which created the 1995 Fish Stocks Agreement, which is effectively supplementary to the LOSC. There would be nothing to stop similar agreements being negotiated in the future, and indeed the United Nations General Assembly has set in motion the negotiating process for a new LOSC implementing agreement to protect biodiversity in areas beyond national jurisdiction.[143] The third mechanism would rely upon the formal amending procedures provided for in the LOSC, in which three types were provided for. Articles 312 and 313 deal with general amendments to the Convention other than those dealing with the deep seabed. Article 312 provides for a review conference mechanism, whilst Article 313 provides for a simplified mechanism which dispenses with the need for a conference. Amendments to the deep seabed regime are provided for in Article 314 which

---

[141] Koh, 'A Constitution for the Oceans' (n 117).
[142] See discussion in Philip Allott, '*Mare Nostrum*: A New International Law of the Sea' (1992) 86 *AJIL* 764.
[143] UN Doc A/69/L.65 (2015).

also provided for a simplified mechanism, however, that process now needs to be read alongside Section 4 of the Annex to the 1994 Implementing Agreement, which envisages that the Assembly of State Parties to the ISA may undertake a review of certain deep seabed measures.

XII. Further Reading

RP Anand, *Origin and Development of the Law of the Sea* (The Hague, Martinus Nijhoff, 1983)

David J Bederman, 'The Sea' in Bardo Fassbender and Anne Peters (eds), *The Oxford Handbook of the History of International Law* (Oxford, Oxford University Press, 2012) 359

ED Brown, *The International Law of the Sea*, vols 1–2 (Aldershot, Dartmouth, 1994)

RR Churchill and AV Lowe, *The Law of the Sea*, 3rd edn (Manchester, Manchester University Press, 1999)

James Crawford, *Brownlie's Principles of Public International Law*, 8th edn (Oxford, Oxford University Press, 2012)

James Harrison, *Making the Law of the Sea: A Study in the Development of International Law* (Cambridge, Cambridge University Press, 2011)

S Houston Lay, Robin Churchill and Myron Nordquist (eds), *New Directions in the Law of the Sea*, vols 1–10 (Dobbs Ferry, NY, Oceana, 1973+)

Vaughan Lowe and Stefan Talmon (eds), *The Legal Order of the Oceans: Basic Documents on Law of the Sea* (Oxford, Hart Publishing, 2009)

DP O'Connell, *The International Law of the Sea*, vols 1–2 (Oxford, Clarendon Press, 1982/1984)

Alex G Oude Elferink (ed), *Stability and Change in the Law of the Sea: The Role of the LOS Convention* (Leiden, Martinus Nijhoff, 2005)

T Treves, 'Historical Development of the Law of the Sea' in Donald R Rothwell, Alex G Oude-Elferink, Karen N Scott and Tim Stephens (eds), *The Oxford Handbook of the Law of the Sea* (Oxford, Oxford University Press, 2015)

2

Coastal Waters

I. Introduction

Much of the focus in the development of the international law of the sea has been upon the entitlements of coastal states to assert a variety of offshore maritime claims. However, it has always been recognised that coastal states enjoy certain rights over waters immediately adjacent to their land. These areas encompass various bodies of water closely linked to the land, including bays, bights, fjords, gulfs, sounds, river mouths, estuaries, and the waters adjacent to and within ports and harbours. These are waters over which states have traditionally exercised rights of sovereignty, jurisdiction and control, and in many instances have never been considered as a part of the high seas. In addition to being under sovereign control, these waters may also have been the subject of long-standing historical usage for internal navigation and for fishing, including for sedentary stocks found on shallow seabeds.

The legal status of coastal waters raises important jurisdictional issues and ultimately questions as to sovereignty and title, in contrast to waters well beyond the shoreline, which are considered part of the high seas. With the development of the regime of the territorial sea, how a coastal state delimited its coastal waters was of great significance because of the recognition of navigational freedoms within the territorial sea. The developing law of the sea therefore sought to maintain a distinction between the territorial sea and other 'traditional' or 'historic' waters over which the coastal state had always asserted control. Many examples of such waters could be found in the territory of the major European powers influential in the development of the law of the sea in the nineteenth century, especially in England, where in addition to the exercise of such sovereign rights there was also common law and developing statute law all affirming controls over adjacent waters. Perhaps not surprisingly given the way in which the law of the sea was developing at this time, many different terms were used to describe coastal waters, including 'territorial waters', 'jurisdictional sea', 'marginal sea' and 'littoral sea'.[1]

One of the major challenges for the law of the sea as the territorial sea began to be recognised in the nineteenth and early twentieth century was to distinguish the territorial sea and other coastal waters over which a state had traditionally asserted jurisdiction and control. During the latter part of the nineteenth century increasingly explicit claims were made by states over coastal waters, and by the twentieth century clear differentiations were

---

[1] Philip C Jessup, *The Law of Territorial Waters and Maritime Jurisdiction* (New York, GA Jennings, 1927) xxxvii.

emerging between adjacent coastal waters and the territorial sea beyond, in some cases facilitated through the use of artificial lines drawn across the sea from various geographical features. This practice eventually gained recognition when in 1951 the ICJ was called upon to determine the legitimacy of a baseline system used by Noway to delimit the outer points of the *skjærgaard* along the western limits of the Norwegian coast fronting the North Sea. In the *Anglo-Norwegian Fisheries* case,[2] the ICJ recognised for the first time the legitimacy of a coastal state relying upon 'straight baselines' as a means of delimiting the territorial sea. This judgment had considerable influence upon the work of the ILC when it considered these issues in the 1950s, and ultimately upon the drafting of the 1958 Convention on the Territorial Sea and Contiguous Zone,[3] which not only included provisions dealing with straight baselines, but also related provisions dealing with bays. The recognition in the law of the sea of baselines raised other issues with respect to the geographical features which could be relied upon when drawing these artificial lines. In addition to coastline configuration, other natural features including islands, islets, reefs, shoals, rocks and ice attracted legal significance and attention, whilst issues arose over the status of artificial features such as lighthouses, harbour works and installations. The drawing of baselines also provoked disputes, not only because baselines impacted upon fishing rights of other states, as seen in the *Anglo-Norwegian Fisheries* case, but also because they had security implications within large areas of sea in which high seas navigational freedoms have traditionally been enjoyed. In the case of Libya's 1973 declaration of the Gulf of Sidra as an historic bay, and accordingly as internal waters, some states lodged strong protests that in the case of the United States was accompanied by a show of force which resulted in open conflict with Libya.[4] The delimitation and status of coastal waters, against the backdrop of their sensitivity, were given due consideration at the United Nations Conferences on the Law of the Sea. The notion of the internal waters of a state also was recognised in the Convention on the Territorial Sea and Contiguous Zone and the basic framework for the entitlements over coastal waters and their delimitation was put in place. These measures were further developed by the LOSC[5] in 1982.

II. History

Early state practice in the delimitation of maritime claims from a baseline adopted the low-water mark as the point from which those claims could be asserted.[6] Such an approach gave to the coastal state a capacity to assert as broad a maritime claim as possible, and in cases of significant tidal variations the reliance upon the low-water mark was clearly beneficial to the coastal state. The 1839 Fishery Convention between Great Britain and

---

[2] *Fisheries (United Kingdom v Norway)* [1951] ICJ Rep 116.

[3] *Basic Documents* No 9.

[4] Francesco Francioni, 'The Status of the Gulf of Sirte in International Law' (1984) 11 *Syracuse Journal of International Law and Commerce* 311, 311. The Gulf of Sidra is also at times referred to as the Gulf of Sirte.

[5] *Basic Documents* No 36.

[6] DP O'Connell, *The International Law of the Sea*, vol 1 (Oxford, Clarendon Press, 1982) 171 referring to Roman Law at the basis for reliance upon the low-water mark.

France referred to the low-water mark, and by 1882 the North Sea Convention amongst European states also reflected this standard. However, whilst there was ready acceptance of the point from which claims could be asserted, early state practice reflected divergent views as to which geographical features could legitimately be the foundation for a claim. As Jessup observed in 1927, whilst there was general agreement that the low-water mark applied along the coast, the great difficulty which remained was determining what the coast actually was.[7] Varying practices applied in the case of coastlines fringed with rocks, shoals, reefs and islands making it difficult to state with any certainty the law at the time.

Whilst there was acceptance that islands generated a territorial sea,[8] there was debate as to the entitlement of a claim depending on the size of the island and its proximity to the coastline. In an 1812 Royal Ordinance of Norway, territorial waters were proclaimed from 'the outermost islands or islets which are not submersed by the sea',[9] which raised issues as to how the effect of tides should be measured upon features that may be submerged at high tide but visible and 'drying' at low tide. The 'portico doctrine' was developed by Lord Stowell in two early nineteenth century English decisions, *Twee Gebroeders*[10] and *The Anna*,[11] in which interconnected offshore features such as rocks, sandbanks and small islands were relied upon for the purposes of recognising coastal state claims.[12] These judgments provided the basis for official British legal opinions in nineteenth century disputes England had with Spain over waters adjacent to Cuba and with the United States regarding Bermuda, and the assertion of maritime jurisdiction in colonial Australia adjacent to the Great Barrier Reef.[13]

Another area of controversy related to the status of bays and gulfs and whether it was possible for a coastal state to claim all or only a part of the waters of such features as internal or 'national' waters. A separate approach towards bays, gulfs and other large indentations of the sea arose under the common law in England in which a branch or 'arm of the sea' was considered to be within *fauces terrae*, or the 'jaws of the land'.[14] The effect of such a characterisation was to treat the waters of the bay similarly to land and over which extensive rights and controls could be exercised.[15] The 1839 Fishery Convention accepted that in the case of bays which did not exceed ten miles in width a straight line could be drawn from headland to headland, and variations on this provision were adopted in subsequent treaties throughout a number of European states in the following years.[16] However, in addition to the emergence of these generic rules regarding bays, distinctive state practice also developed with respect to certain bays including Chesapeake and Delaware Bay (United States), Conception Bay, Newfoundland (England) and Hudson Bay (Canada), and also bays that

---

[7]   Jessup, *The Law of Territorial Waters* (n 1) 66.

[8]   *The Anna* (1805) 165 ER 809.

[9]   Jessup, *The Law of Territorial Waters* (n 1) 67.

[10]   (1800) 3 Admiralty Cases 162.

[11]   (1805) 165 ER 809.

[12]   O'Connell, *The International Law of the Sea* (n 6) 186.

[13]   Ibid 186–90.

[14]   WR Edeson, 'Australian Bays' (1968–1969) *Australian Year Book of International Law* 5.

[15]   C John Colombos, *The International Law of the Sea*, 6th edn (London, Longmans, 1967) 182 also refers to the so-called 'headland theory' permitting a line to be drawn across the headland entrances to a bay or gulf and the enclosure of those waters as part of the 'King's Chambers'; Thomas Wemyss Fulton, *The Sovereignty of the Sea* (Edinburgh, Blackwood, 1911) 118–20, 548.

[16]   Colombos, *The International Law of the Sea*, ibid 178–79.

were bounded by two or more states such as the Gulf of Fonseca (Nicaragua, Honduras and El Salvador),[17] and the Bay of Fundy (Canada/United States). Certain rules therefore became recognised for so-called 'historic bays' which were often of a large scale and of considerable historic importance, while lesser bays were subject to the developing rules of the law of the sea.

III. Baselines

The baseline is the legal expression of a state's coastal front, and serves three functions.[18] First, the baseline divides the land and internal waters of a coastal state from the territorial sea. Secondly, it is from the baseline that the outer limits of the territorial sea, the contiguous zone, the EEZ and the juridical (200 nm) continental shelf are measured. Thirdly, the baseline is relevant to the delimitation of the maritime boundary between two states with overlapping maritime zones.

Early in its development, the law of the sea accepted that the low-water mark was the normal baseline from which maritime claims, starting with the territorial sea, could be asserted. However, given the wide variety of coastline configurations, in the nineteenth and early part of the twentieth century state practice highlighted the need for baseline rules to address irregular coastlines and a variety of coastal formations such as fringing islands. As the law developed throughout the later part of the twentieth century considerable attention was given to setting rules dealing with straight baselines and the features and formations from which they can be drawn. These issues were highlighted at a pivotal moment in 1951, when the ICJ delivered its judgment in the *Anglo-Norwegian Fisheries* case at a time when the ILC was on the brink of commencing its detailed consideration of the regime of the territorial sea, and just seven years before UNCLOS I convened in Geneva.

A. The *Anglo-Norwegian Fisheries* Case

The 1951 *Anglo-Norwegian Fisheries* case arose out a claim by the United Kingdom that the straight baseline system developed by Norway, connecting the islands of the *skjærgaard* along the west coast including both large and small islands and in some instances reefs, rocks and islets only above water at low tide,[19] was not supported by international law. In addition to contesting the legitimacy of the Norwegian fisheries zone and territorial sea claim,[20] the United Kingdom argued that Norway was unable to draw baselines other than from the low-water mark on permanently dry land, and contested Norway's definition of a bay and historic waters.

---

[17] *El Salvador v Nicaragua* (1917) 11 *AJIL* 674.

[18] International Law Association, Committee on Baselines under the International Law of the Sea, Final Report (2012).

[19] *Fisheries (United Kingdom v Norway)* [1951] ICJ Rep 116, 127.

[20] Ibid 125; these two zones were conterminous and that was how they were viewed in the argument made to the Court.

The Court by majority found in favour of Norway's method for the delimitation of its fisheries zone and its reliance upon the baselines drawn around the *skjærgaard*.[21] Noting that the parties were in agreement as to the use of the low-water mark for the purpose of measuring the breadth of the territorial sea, the Court endorsed that method and observed that: 'This criterion is the most favourable to the coastal State and clearly shows the character of territorial waters as appurtenant to the land territory'.[22] The Court then turned to determining the relevant low-water mark in the case where the mainland was fringed by the *skjærgaard* and immediately noted the distinctive nature of the Norwegian coastline as being one in which the 'coast of the mainland does not constitute, as it does in practically all other countries, a clear dividing line between land and sea'.[23] Having reviewed the particular geographical nature of the coastline, the Court endorsed the use of baselines which could 'within reasonable limits' depart from the 'physical line of the coast'.[24] The United Kingdom submission that straight baselines could only be drawn across bays was rejected, and it was accepted that in addition to bays a straight baseline could also be drawn between islands, islets and rocks that make up the *skjærgaard* even if those waters do not fall within the conception of a bay.[25]

Nevertheless, the ICJ was not prepared to concede that the delimitation of these areas of the sea was merely a unilateral act of the coastal state which could be undertaken without any reference to international law, and certain basic considerations were identified which courts could apply in assessing the legitimacy of straight baselines. These included the close dependence of the territorial sea upon the land domain, that the baselines must not depart to any appreciable extent from the general direction of the coast, the close relationship between certain sea areas and the adjoining land formations, and the economic interests peculiar to the region which may be evidenced by long usage.[26] On this point, the Court concluded:

> The real question raised in the choice of base-lines is in effect whether certain sea areas lying within these lines are sufficiently closely linked to the land domain to be subject to the regime of internal waters. This idea, which is at the basis of the determination of the rules relating to bays, should be liberally applied in the case of a coast, the geographical configuration of which is as unusual as that of Norway.[27]

Ultimately the Court concluded that the method of straight baselines used by Norway was a result of the particular geography of the coastline, and that Norway's approach had been consolidated through long practice which had not been contested by other states as being contrary to international law.[28] The judgment generated considerable academic commentary, much of which was critical.[29] However, as observed by Colombos, whilst the decision

---

[21] Ibid 143; by respective majorities of 10:2, and 8:4; Judges McNair and Read wrote dissenting opinions.
[22] Ibid 128.
[23] Ibid 127.
[24] Ibid 129.
[25] Ibid 130.
[26] Ibid 133; on this last point Norway was able to point to various Royal decrees and other orders dating back to 1812 which reflected the use of a baseline system for some of the waters within the *skjærgaard*.
[27] Ibid 133.
[28] Ibid 139.
[29] Jens Evensen, 'The Anglo-Norwegian Fisheries Case and its Legal Consequences' (1952) 46 *AJIL* 609–30; Teruo Kobayashi, *The Anglo-Norwegian Fisheries Case of 1951 and the Changing Law of the Sea* (Gainesville, University of Florida, 1965) 49.

could be confined to the particular circumstances of the Norwegian coastline the judgment was 'confirmation that straight lines which follow the general direction of the coast and satisfy the criteria laid down for the enclosure of inland waters are not inconsistent with international law'.[30]

B. International Law Commission

When the ILC came to consider the question of baselines and associated issues it had the benefit of the decision of the ICJ in the *Anglo-Norwegian Fisheries* case, various examples of state practice, and also the commentaries and reports of learned associations and bodies which in the early part of the twentieth century had investigated the regime of the territorial sea and the related issues of baselines.[31] It also benefited from a 1953 report which had been prepared by a Committee of Experts on 'technical questions concerning the territorial sea'.[32] The experts were given a set of questions to address and their report supported the low-water mark as the baseline for the territorial sea, a ten mile closing line across juridical bays, and straight baselines of no longer than ten miles between headlands and islands.[33] This technical report proved to be influential for the ILC, and although the Commission was unable to reach agreement on the breadth of the territorial sea, there were agreed positions as to measuring the territorial sea from baselines and other coastal features. These were eventually reflected in four draft articles, which included provisions dealing with normal baselines, straight baselines, bays and ports.[34]

i. *International Law Commission Draft Articles*

Article 4 of the ILC's draft articles affirmed that the normal baseline is the low-water mark along the coast, as provided for in large-scale charts officially recognised by the coastal state. Whilst the ILC noted that this was the position affirmed by the ICJ in the *Anglo-Norwegian Fisheries* case, the term 'low-water mark' was potentially subject to different meanings and there was 'no uniform standard by which States in practice determine this line'.[35] However, notwithstanding the potential for variable practices,[36] the Commission was content not to provide more detailed provisions on this point. In the case of

---

[30] Colombos, *The International Law of the Sea* (n 15) 117.

[31] O'Connell, *The International Law of the Sea* (n 6) 192–93 describes the work of the early codification conferences in this area.

[32] 'Report of the Committee of Experts on Technical Questions Concerning the Territorial Sea' reproduced in *Virginia Commentaries*, vol 2, 59–63; the experts comprised Professor LEG Asplund (Norway), S Whittemore Boggs (United States), PRV Couillault (France), RH Kennedy (United Kingdom), and AS Pinke (the Netherlands).

[33] The distinction between 'closing' lines and 'straight baselines' reflected that a 'closing line' would close off the entrance to a bay and would be a single line, whilst a straight baseline would be multiple lines connecting various geographical features adjacent to the coast: JRV Prescott, 'Straight and Archipelagic Baselines' in Gerald Blake (ed), *Maritime Boundaries and Ocean Resources* (London, Croom Helm, 1987) 38, 39.

[34] International Law Commission, 'Articles Concerning the Law of the Sea with Commentaries' (1956) *Yearbook of the International Law Commission*, vol 2, 266–71.

[35] Ibid 267.

[36] O'Connell, *The International Law of the Sea* (n 6) 173–74 refers to eight different methods for determining low water for hydrographical purposes.

straight baselines, Article 5 of the ILC draft articles substantively reflected the judgment of the *Anglo-Norwegian Fisheries* case, making clear that the baseline may be independent of the low-water mark where 'circumstances necessitate a special regime because the coast is deeply indented or cut into or because there are islands in its immediate vicinity'.[37] This approach suggested that straight baselines could only be relied upon where the coastline had one of three characteristics: that it was 'deeply indented' as in the case of a gulf; 'cut into' as would be the case with a fjord; or where there were islands proximate to the coastline. Straight baselines were not to be drawn between drying rocks and drying shoals.[38] The ILC did not recommend limits on the length of the baselines, although an earlier draft had proposed a maximum length of ten miles, and that islands to or from which the baselines were drawn could be only five miles from the coast.[39] In the case of ports, draft Article 8 provided that the 'outermost permanent harbour works' that were an integral part of the harbour system could be regarded as forming part of the coast so that effectively straight baselines could be drawn across these points so as to delimit the territorial sea from internal waters. Jetties and other coastal protective works were assimilated to harbour works for this purpose.[40]

Article 7 of the ILC draft articles outlined the regime dealing with bays other than 'historic bays', which were excluded. Bays were defined for the purposes of Article 7 as being 'a well-marked indentation whose penetration is in such proportion to the width of its mouth as to certain landlocked waters and constitute more than a mere curvature of the coast'.[41] A semicircle method was proposed as a means for classifying the bay, by which the indentation had to be larger, or as large as, a semicircle drawn across the mouth of the bay. Waters within the bay were considered internal waters if the baseline did not exceed 15 miles. The length of lines 'closing' a bay had been the subject of comment in the *Anglo-Norwegian Fisheries* case, where it had been argued that a ten mile limit was reflective of international law. The Court, however, was unable to endorse that position, noting that there was variable state practice on point.[42] It was, therefore, not surprising that the ILC had similar difficulties in reaching agreement as to the appropriate length of bay 'closing lines' and whilst 15 miles was settled upon, earlier versions of the draft had a figure of 25 miles.[43]

Finally, note should be made of the work of the ILC with respect to the delimitation of the territorial sea at the mouth of a river, which in draft Article 13 provided that the territorial sea was to be 'measured from a line drawn *inter fauces terrarum* across the mouth of the river'.[44] This effectively conceded that river mouths could be subject to the drawing of straight baselines in a similar fashion to the rules developed for bays.

---

[37] ILC, 'Articles Concerning the Law of the Sea' (n 34) 267.
[38] Ibid 270–71, art 11 did, however, separately provide that drying rocks and drying shoals which fell within the territorial sea 'may be taken as points of departure for measuring the extension of the territorial sea'.
[39] Ibid 267.
[40] Ibid 269–70.
[41] Ibid 268, art 7(1).
[42] *Fisheries (United Kingdom v Norway)* [1951] ICJ Rep 116, 131.
[43] ILC, 'Articles Concerning the Law of the Sea' (n 34) 269.
[44] Ibid 271, art 13(1).

C. UNCLOS I

When UNCLOS I convened in Geneva in 1958 the delegates faced a vast task in concluding an agreed text reflecting the then existing international law of the sea, and in some instances developing the law beyond what was accepted as customary international law. The delegates at UNCLOS I were presented with three documents which contributed to a better understanding of some of the issues associated with territorial sea delimitation. The first, and most extensive, was a memorandum by the Secretariat of the United Nations titled 'Historic Bays'.[45] This comprehensive report addressed issues associated with the definition of bays, gulfs, historic bays and historic waters, assessed state practice and the decisions of international courts—including reviewing the relevant aspects of the *Anglo-Norwegian Fisheries* case and the opinions of authors and governments—and also provided an analysis of the so-called 'theory of historic bays'. Of particular note is that the report identified 50 bays within single states which were considered to be, or which had been claimed as, historic bays.[46] The second report, prepared by Commander RH Kennedy,[47] studied the status of bays and estuaries the coasts of which belonged to different states.[48] This study sought to fill in some of the gaps in the ILC's studies of bays and estuaries and equipped UNCLOS I with a fuller appreciation of those bays and estuaries claimed by two or more states. A total of 50 bays and estuaries were identified as falling into one of these two categories, although the report did not purport to be comprehensive.[49] In addition, a paper was prepared for UNCLOS I on the special question of the delimitation of the territorial waters of archipelagos,[50] which directly addressed the implications of the ICJ's judgment in the *Anglo-Norwegian Fisheries* case for drawing straight baselines around the outer islands that comprise mid-ocean archipelagos.[51]

Prior to the commencement of the conference, some delegations had also responded to a letter from the United Nations Secretary-General inviting them to comment on the ILC's draft articles.[52] A total of 21 states responded prior to the commencement of UNCLOS I with Canada, China, Denmark, Federal Republic of Germany, the Netherlands, Norway, Sweden and the United Kingdom commenting on Article 5 dealing with straight baselines, and China, Denmark, the Netherlands and Norway commenting on Article 7 on bays. The principal criticism of the straight baselines provisions were that they were too vague, and concerns were also expressed that the proposed 15 mile bay closing lines were too short.

---

[45] 'Historic Bays: Memorandum by the Secretariat of the United Nations' in *United Nations Conference on the Law of the Sea: Official Records,* vol 1, 1.

[46] Ibid 3–8; 16 of these bays were located within Australia.

[47] Kennedy worked with the Hydrographic Department of the British Admiralty, and had given 'technical explanations' to the ICJ in the *Anglo-Norwegian Fisheries* case.

[48] RH Kennedy, 'A Brief Geographical and Hydrographical Study of Bays and Estuaries the Coasts of which Belong to Different States' in *United Nations Conference on the Law of the Sea: Official Records,* vol 1, 198.

[49] Ibid 199.

[50] Jens Evensen, 'Certain Legal Aspects Concerning the Delimitation of the Territorial Waters of Archipelagos' in *United Nations Conference on the Law of the Sea: Official Records,* vol 1, 289.

[51] See the detailed discussion in ch 8.

[52] 'Comments by Governments on the Draft Articles Concerning the Law of the Sea Adopted by the International Law Commission as its Eighth Session' in *United Nations Conference on the Law of the Sea: Official Records,* vol 1, 75.

When UNCLOS I did convene, some of the discussion which focussed on delimitation of the territorial sea related to historic bays, and whether there was a need for more substantive study and analysis of that topic. However, ultimately the decision of the conference was in essence to adopt the ILC's draft article on that point. In addition, there was extensive debate over the question of bay closing lines, with many delegates suggesting alternative lengths to the original 15 miles proposed by the ILC. Eventually consensus was reached at the Conference on closing lines of 24 miles.[53]

D. Convention on the Territorial Sea and Contiguous Zone

Whilst the Convention on the Territorial Sea and Contiguous Zone did not ultimately contain any provisions on the breadth of the territorial sea, in Part I it outlined the regime of the territorial sea, and in Section II of Part I dealt with the limits of the territorial sea. Within these provisions, the Convention sought to incorporate the ILC's draft articles on the limits and measurement of the territorial sea, subject to modifications agreed during UNCLOS I. Nine articles dealt with different aspects of baselines and related coastal features that impact upon the territorial sea, and whilst it is clear that the ICJ's judgment in the *Anglo-Norwegian Fisheries* case was influential in the final convention text, the Convention also sought both to codify customary international law on point and to incorporate some aspects of progressive development of the law.

Although the outer limit of the territorial sea remained unresolved, Article 6 made clear that the territorial sea was to be determined from a baseline.[54] Article 3 of the Convention provides that the 'normal baseline' for measuring the breadth of the territorial sea is the low-water mark along the coast. No definition is provided as to what the low-water mark is, thereby permitting some latitude in state interpretation on this point. Nor does the Convention specify what constitutes the 'coast', which also allows for some variation in state practice subject to the other provisions in the Convention dealing with bays and other coastal features. The low-water mark was also to have been marked on large-scale charts and recognised as such by the coastal state. With respect to straight baselines, Article 4 builds upon the ILC draft and has six sub-paragraphs. The key points outlined in Article 4 are: straight baselines may be employed in cases where the coast is deeply indented or cut into or where there are a fringe of islands in the immediate vicinity of the coast;[55] the baselines must not depart to any appreciable extent from the general direction of the coast and the sea areas lying within the baselines must have a close linkage with the land domain;[56] the economic interests of a region could be taken into account, including evidence of long usage, in the drawing of straight baselines;[57] and the baselines should not be drawn so as to cut off from the high seas the territorial sea of another state.[58] One significant alteration

---

[53] Kobayashi, *The Anglo-Norwegian Fisheries Case* (n 29) 57.

[54] The baseline from which the breadth of the territorial sea was to be determined was also utilised for the purposes of measuring the breadth of the contiguous zone: Convention on the Territorial Sea and Contiguous Zone, art 24(2).

[55] Ibid art 4(1).

[56] Ibid art 4(2).

[57] Ibid art 4(4).

[58] Ibid art 4(5).

in the text from that proposed by the ILC was with respect to what had been termed drying rocks and drying shoals, and which in the Convention were described as low-tide elevations.[59] A low-tide elevation is defined in Article 11 as 'a naturally-formed area of land which is surrounded by and above water at low-tide but submerged at high-tide',[60] and if situated within the territorial sea may be used as a baseline for measuring the breadth of the territorial sea. However, Article 4 makes clear that such features may not be used for the purpose of drawing straight baselines 'unless lighthouses or similar installations which are permanently above sea level have been built on them'.[61]

In the case of bays, the Convention substantially reproduced the ILC draft article, excluding historic bays and bays which are within the territory of more than one state. A geographical and technical definition of a bay is given in Article 7(2), which extends to those features which are 'a well-marked indentation whose penetration is in such proportion to the width of its mouth as to contain landlocked waters' and more than a mere curvature of the coast. In addition, the semicircle method is employed to require that the area of the bay exceed that of a semicircle drawn across the mouth of the indentation. A closing line of no more 24 nm could be drawn across the entrance to the bay, and if the width of the bay exceeded that limit then a 24 nm straight baseline could be drawn within the area of the bay so as to enclose the maximum area of water.[62]

The Convention also made provision for permanent harbour works, with the outermost limits of such features that formed an integral part of a harbour system considered to be a part of the coast. As such, they could be utilised for the purposes of drawing a baseline.[63] In the case of rivers which flow directly into the sea the baseline was to be a straight line drawn across the mouth of the river.[64] Other related provisions included: where a straight baseline had the effect of enclosing waters which were previously considered territorial sea then the right of innocent passage remained within those waters,[65] and the definition in Article 10 of an island as being 'a naturally-formed area of land, surrounded by water, which is above water at high-tide'.

E. Post-UNCLOS I State Practice

In the wake of UNCLOS I and the adoption of the Convention on the Territorial Sea and Contiguous Zone, much of the attention with respect to state practice regarding baselines was directed at the actions of the Philippines and Indonesia which during this period were seeking to assert their status as archipelagos by drawing straight baselines that linked their

---

[59] 'Low-tide elevations' was a term introduced into the Conference by the United States: 'United States of America: Proposal' (UN Doc A/CONF.13/C.1/L.115) in *United Nations Conference on the Law of the Sea: Official Records*, vol 3, 243.

[60] Convention on the Territorial Sea and Contiguous Zone, art 11(1).

[61] Ibid art 4(3). The ICJ has observed that this provision is an indication that low-tide elevations cannot be equated with islands with respect to their being used as basepoints for the purpose of drawing straight baselines: *Maritime Delimitation and Territorial Questions between Qatar and Bahrain (Qatar v Bahrain)* (merits) [2001] ICJ Rep 40, [208].

[62] Convention on the Territorial Sea and Contiguous Zone, art 7(5).

[63] Ibid art 8.

[64] Ibid art 13.

[65] Ibid art 5.

outer islands.[66] During UNCLOS II in 1960, there was no substantive debate over the baseline provisions adopted in the Convention, even though a major focus of the conference was the breadth of the territorial sea. Despite efforts by Indonesia and the Philippines to win support at UNCLOS II for the straight baseline principle to be applied to archipelagos, there was no support for such an extension of the law at that time.[67] There was concern, however, as to how some states might seek to interpret some aspects of the baseline system, with McDougal and Burke observing in 1962 that:

> [O]ne way of limiting undesirable extensions of the *Ango-Norwegian Fisheries* judgment may be to demand a concrete demonstration of the coastal interest alleged to justify the claimed delimitation and to emphasize, as did the Court, the need for a realistic assessment of the coastal interest alleged to be at stake.[68]

In the aftermath of the ICJ's 1951 judgment, a number of states had sought to take advantage of that decision by declaring straight baselines around portions of their coast, including Albania, China, Cuba, Egypt, Ethiopia and Iceland.[69] Ireland was one of the first states to rely upon the Convention on the Territorial Sea and Contiguous Zone when it enacted its Maritime Jurisdiction Act 1959, specifying the low-water mark as the baseline other than where straight baselines had been drawn. A particular feature of Ireland's practice was the extensive system of straight baselines,[70] which was implemented via the Maritime Jurisdiction Act (Straight Baseline) Order 1959. This Order, which came into force in 1960,[71] proclaimed 44 straight baselines in the north, east and south of the country and had the effect of closing off several Irish bays, the Shannon river, and the mouth of Cork Harbour.[72] Notwithstanding doubts raised as to the legitimacy of the Irish baseline system, especially the use of isolated islands off the Irish west and south coasts,[73] these baselines were not adjusted. O'Connell estimated that in the period between UNCLOS I and the conclusion of UNCLOS III, a total of 50 states proclaimed straight baseline systems, and that whilst some of these claims were questionable as to their reliance upon offshore islands and whether they were truly 'fringes' of islands, there was little evidence of protest over this state practice.[74]

F. LOSC

When it came to UNCLOS III and the negotiation of the LOSC, the principal issues regarding the delimitation of the territorial sea and baselines related to the breadth of the territorial sea and the use of straight baselines in the case of archipelagos. Given the sensitivity

---

[66] RP Anand, *Origin and Development of the Law of the Sea* (The Hague, Martinus Nijhoff, 1983) 202.

[67] See the discussion of this issue in ch 8.

[68] Myres S McDougal and William T Burke, *The Public Order of the Oceans* (New Haven, New Haven Press, 1987, 1962 rep) 387.

[69] O'Connell, *The International Law of the Sea* (n 6) 211–12.

[70] *Fisheries (United Kingdom v Norway)* [1951] ICJ Rep 116, 169; Judge McNair in his Dissenting Opinion expressly referred to 'the heavily indented' west coast of Northern Ireland as bearing 'much resemblance to the Norwegian coast'.

[71] Clive R Symmons, *Ireland and the Law of the Sea* (Dublin, Round Hall Press, 1993) 27.

[72] Ibid 23.

[73] Ibid 29.

[74] O'Connell, *The International Law of the Sea* (n 6) 211–12.

associated with the delimitation of the territorial sea and the impact baselines had upon distinguishing internal waters from the territorial sea, there was a reluctance to modify the provisions of the Convention on the Territorial Sea and Contiguous Zone, other than where state practice had highlighted gaps. Accordingly, during the conference and in the resulting convention, minimal attention was given to the provisions dealing with the delimitation of the territorial sea and related coastal features. Nevertheless, one of the important outcomes of UNCLOS III was that the baselines from which the breadth of the territorial sea was measured acquired additional significance as also being the baseline from which the EEZ[75] and the continental shelf[76] were measured. This meant that the territorial sea baselines delimited five maritime zones: the boundary between internal waters and the territorial sea, the territorial sea, the contiguous zone, EEZ, and the continental shelf.

The provisions on the limits of the territorial sea are found in Part II of the LOSC dealing with the territorial sea and contiguous zone, Section 2 of which deals with the 'Limits of the Territorial Sea'. The 'normal baseline' is provided for in Article 5, which effectively duplicates Article 3 of the Convention on the Territorial Sea and Contiguous Zone and retains the low-water mark along the coast for that purpose. The special case of reefs is addressed in a new Article 6 which provides that in the case of atolls or islands with fringing reefs, the baseline is the seaward low-water line of the reef. This is a reflection of the fact that reefs have both a maritime and terrestrial dimension, and that in the absence of this rule reefs would otherwise be a part of the territorial sea with their accompanying navigational hazards. The use in Article 6 of the term 'fringing reefs' is significant given the Article 7 reference to 'fringe of islands' which suggests there should be a consistency in interpretation of the relationship of these features with the coastline.[77]

Straight baselines are addressed in Article 7, and these provisions also predominantly duplicate those of the Convention on the Territorial Sea and Contiguous Zone, other than for an allowance made for a delta or where the coastline is highly unstable due to natural conditions, in which case the points for a baseline may be selected from the 'furthest seaward extent of the low-water line'.[78] In an important concession to the unstable nature of the coastline, the baseline remains effective 'notwithstanding subsequent regression of the low-water line' until such time as it is adjusted by the coastal state. This provision has the potential to have increasing significance as coastlines become more unstable as a result of the effects of erosion caused by large tides and ocean storms arising from climate change. With respect to the drawing of straight baselines to low-tide elevations which have had lighthouses built upon them, the LOSC has extended that provision further to instances where 'the drawing of baselines to and from such elevations has received general international recognition'.[79]

---

[75] LOSC, art 57.

[76] LOSC, art 76.

[77] Peter B Beazley, 'Coral Reefs and the 1982 Convention on the Law of the Sea' in Gerald H Blake (ed), *Maritime Boundaries* (London, Routledge, 1994) 59, 71 who concludes that '[t]he term "fringing reefs" is ambiguous, and often there is no clear distinction between fringing and barrier reef. The baseline of an island with a true fringing reef is the low-water line of the reef under the provisions of Article 5. Fringing reef in Article 6 refers rather to reefs forming a fringe around an island.'

[78] LOSC, art 7(2).

[79] Ibid art 7(4); which sought to reflect an acknowledgement of Norwegian practice recognised in the *Anglo-Norwegian Fisheries* case: *Virginia Commentaries*, vol 2, 102–103.

Article 10 of the LOSC deals with bays, and effectively duplicates Article 7 of the Convention on the Territorial Sea and Contiguous Zone. Once again, historic bays are exempt from this straight baseline system, and the LOSC made no effort to further define historic bays, preferring to rely upon settled state practice. Articles dealing with ports,[80] roadsteads,[81] and low-tide elevations[82] duplicate provisions found in the Convention on the Territorial Sea and Contiguous Zone, other than Article 11 which makes clear that offshore installations and artificial islands shall not be considered as permanent harbour works for the purposes of a port or harbour system. Finally, in order to resolve any potential ambiguity, a new Article 14 appears in the LOSC making clear that a coastal state may rely upon a combination of the methods provided for in that section of the Convention in order to determine baselines.

IV. Key Issues in the Delimitation of Coastal Waters

The LOSC provisions concerning coastal waters and baselines are now well settled in international law, with almost 60 years of practice associated with many of the provisions as a result of the continuity between the Convention on the Territorial Sea and Contiguous Zone and the LOSC. It is therefore possible to review both the terms of the LOSC and implementation of the provisions dealing with the delimitation of the territorial sea against the backdrop of considerable state practice and commentary.

A. Low-Water

The term 'low-water line' in Article 5 is not defined and this allows for some variation in its interpretation. This is generally not contentious, except for some coastlines where there are significant tidal variations that may lead coastal states to adopt interpretations that place adjacent territorial sea within their internal waters. There is no single international standard for determining the low-water line, and accordingly individual states may adopt their own approach.[83] The United Nations has observed, in reliance upon a resolution of the International Hydrographic Organization, that the level to be relied upon as the low-water mark should be 'a plane so low that the tide will not frequently fall below it. In practice this will be close to the lowest tidal level.'[84]

By linking the normal baseline to the low-water line it is inevitable that baselines will be affected as sea levels rise due to human induced climate change. The Intergovernmental Panel on Climate Change, in its Fifth Assessment Report, projects that sea levels could rise

---

[80] LOSC, art 11.
[81] Ibid art 12.
[82] Ibid art 13.
[83] O'Connell, *The International Law of the Sea* (n 6) 177; Clive Schofield, 'Shifting Limits? Sea Level Rise and Options to Secure Maritime Jurisdictional Claims' (2009) 4 *Carbon and Climate Law Review* 405, 408.
[84] Office for Ocean Affairs and the Law of the Sea, United Nations, *The Law of the Sea: Baselines* (New York, United Nations, 1989) 2–3.

by between 0.26 and 0.55 m by 2100 if greenhouse gas emissions are aggressively curbed, and by between 0.52 and 0.98 m if emissions continue to rise.[85] Sea levels will continue to rise due to thermal expansion and the continued melting of glaciers and ice sheets for many centuries, and if there are high atmospheric concentrations of CO_2 then global average sea level rises of 4 m by 2300 are possible.[86]

Observed and projected sea level rise raises the issue of whether there is a need to recalibrate normal baselines where coastlines have been changed.[87] Whilst the LOSC does make allowance for situations where a coastline is highly unstable due to a delta or other natural features,[88] it is questionable whether the impacts of climate change were sufficiently appreciated at UNCLOS III for the LOSC to be capable of dealing with the significant rises in sea level that are now inevitable. Whilst there has been some attention given to the drawing of baselines along highly unstable coastlines, as is the case in Antarctica and parts of the Arctic where the coastline is ice fringed,[89] these issues have not to date been sufficiently mainstream so as to result in major shifts in state practice. The widely accepted view in both practice and among commentators is that under the LOSC baselines are ambulatory, and move as the land recedes.[90] The consequence of this is that the outer edge of coastal state maritime zones also move landwards (with the exception of the limits of the continental shelf beyond 200 nm, which are set by reference to the physical characteristics of the seafloor). As the sea rises this will have an impact upon not only the low-water mark from which the territorial sea baseline is measured, but also low-tide elevations which may be used as basepoints, which, if they are fully submerged, will result in coastal states losing their entitlement to rely upon those features as generating a territorial sea.

It must be anticipated that in coming years many coastal states will develop strategies designed to respond to the impact of sea level rise and climate change upon their baselines, and associated vulnerable basepoints such as low-tide elevations.[91] Coastal states may decide to declare unilaterally the continued applicability of their baselines and/or the outer limits of their maritime zones to preserve the extent of the maritime estate under coastal state sovereignty and jurisdiction.[92] In the absence of protest by other states, this may be effective to maintain the status quo. However, the difficulty remains that there is no support in the LOSC for this approach. While coastal states may also seek to protect their coastlines through physical reinforcement (which will be of dubious cost-effectiveness for most states

[85] IPCC, *Climate Change 2013: The Physical Science Basis. Contribution of Working Group I to the Fifth Assessment Report of the Intergovernmental Panel on Climate Change* (Cambridge, Cambridge University Press, 2013) 9.

[86] Ibid 26.

[87] Clive Schofield, 'Shifting Limits?' (n 83) 405; David Freestone and John Pethick, 'Sea Level Rise and Maritime Boundaries' in Gerald H Blake (ed), *Maritime Boundaries* (London, Routledge, 1994) 73; David D Caron, 'When Law Makes Climate Change Worse: Rethinking the Law of Baselines in Light of Rising Sea Level' (1990) 17 *Ecology Law Quarterly* 621.

[88] LOSC, art 7(2).

[89] Donald R Rothwell, 'Antarctic Baselines: Flexing the Law for Ice-Covered Coastlines' in Alex G Oude Elferink and Donald R Rothwell (eds), *The Law of the Sea and Polar Maritime Delimitation and Jurisdiction* (The Hague, Martinus Nijhoff, 2001) 49–68.

[90] Tim Stephens, 'Warming Waters and Souring Seas: Climate Change and Ocean Acidification' in DR Rothwell, AG Oude-Elferink, KN Scott and T Stephens (eds), *The Oxford Handbook of the Law of the Sea* (Oxford, Oxford University Press, 2015) 777.

[91] Schofield, 'Shifting Limits?' (n 83) 410–14.

[92] Ibid 406.

in the longer term), under the LOSC coastal states may not use a 'legal fiction' of a charted line that bears no resemblance to the receding low-water line.[93] Uncertainty in the placement of maritime boundaries and the breadth of zones is anathema to the certainty than the modern law of the sea seeks to engender. There is also unfairness inherent in low-lying states losing maritime entitlements while the international community gains a 'windfall' as the high seas expand.[94] For these reasons it is strongly desirable that the baseline rules are adjusted to address sea-level rise.

More serious still is the situation facing some low-lying small island states, where baselines may not only recede but where the entire territory of some states will be submerged or rendered uninhabitable because of salt water intrusion, or periodic inundation as a result of storm surges. This situation raises not only law of the sea issues concerning baselines but fundamental questions concerning the indicia of statehood upon which any assertions of maritime sovereignty and jurisdiction are premised.[95] The existence of territory and a permanent population are vital requirements for the acquisition of statehood, and the loss of these attributes, certainly if permanent, would appear to deprive an existing state of its status as such.[96]

B. Straight Baselines

The straight baselines allowed for under Article 7 of the LOSC are the centrepiece of the juridical system established in the Convention permitting the use of artificial lines to be drawn from the coast to adjoining geographical features so as to create a continuous front from which the territorial sea is delimited. The system is supported by extensive state practice, the decision of the ICJ in the *Anglo-Norwegian Fisheries* case, and the continuity given to this regime by the core provisions of the Convention on the Territorial Sea and Contiguous Zone and the LOSC.[97] The recognition accorded to straight baselines also provided the basis for the eventual recognition of claims to archipelagic status by countries such as Indonesia and the Philippines.

Straight baselines may be drawn in the following circumstances:

1. where the coastline is deeply indented and cut into;
2. where there is a fringe of islands in the immediate vicinity of the coast;
3. where there is a river which flows directly into the sea;
4. where there is a river delta making the coastline highly unstable;
5. where there are other natural conditions which make the coastline highly unstable;

---

[93] International Law Association (n 18) 30.

[94] See Caron, 'When Law Makes Climate Change Worse' (n 87).

[95] See, in particular, L Yamamoto and M Esteban, *Atoll States and International Law: Climate Change Displacement and Sovereignty* (Heidelberg, Springer, 2014); J McAdam (ed), *Climate Change and Displacement: Multidisciplinary Perspectives* (Oxford, Hart Publishing, 2010).

[96] E Crawford and R Rayfuse, 'Climate Change and Statehood' in R Rayfuse and S Scott (eds), *International Law in the Era of Climate Change* (Cheltenham, Edward Elgar, 2012) 243.

[97] See further International Law Association, Committee on Baselines under the International Law of the Sea, First Report (2014).

6.   to and from low-tide elevations with lighthouses or similar installations built upon them; and
7.   to and from low-tide elevations which have received general international recognition.

In addition, closing lines, which have been considered by the ICJ as equivalent to straight baselines,[98] may be drawn across bays in the case of:

1.   historic bays;
2.   juridical bays which have an entrance of less than 24 nm; and
3.   within juridical bays which have an entrance of more than 24 nm.

In recognition of the variable conditions that may exist along a coastline, the LOSC also makes clear that one or a combination of these provisions may be used to determine baselines.[99] However, the mere existence of these features does not give a coastal state a uni-lateral right to draw straight baselines, as there are additional criteria which must be taken into account, many of which were factors addressed by the ICJ in the *Anglo-Norwegian Fisheries* case. These include that the straight baselines do not depart from the general direction of the coast; that the areas of sea lying within the lines be sufficiently linked to the land; that the economic interests of the region—including evidence of long usage—be considered; and that the baselines do not cut off from the EEZ or high sea the territorial sea of another state.

   The straight baseline system has within it many subjective aspects which give to the coastal state considerable latitude in the interpretation of the LOSC provisions and this has meant that Article 7 has had expansionary effects in enclosing ocean space within inter-nal waters.[100] The subjective elements include assessing whether a coast is deeply indented or cut into, whether there is an offshore fringe of islands, whether the coastline is highly unstable, whether the baselines which have been drawn follow the 'general direction' of the coast, and whether the sea areas enclosed by the baselines are sufficiently linked to the land domain. Given the significance that can be attached to the length of baselines and how they can be used effectively to connect various parts of the mainland and islands, the LOSC remains silent on the permitted length of straight baselines other than those which are used within juridical bays and mid-ocean archipelagos.[101]

   The United Nations has commented that:

> The spirit of article 7, in respect of indented coasts and fringing islands, will be preserved if straight baselines are drawn when the normal baseline and closing lines of bays and rivers would produce a complex pattern of territorial seas and when those complexities can be eliminated by the use of straight baselines. It is not the purpose of straight baselines to increase the territorial sea unduly.[102]

This approach reflects the ICJ's jurisprudence in the *Anglo-Norwegian Fisheries* case. Once it was accepted that the islands, islets and low-tide elevations that made up the *skjærgaard*

---

[98]   *Land, Island and Maritime Frontier Dispute (El Salvador/Honduras; Nicaragua intervening)* [1992] ICJ Rep 351, [417].

[99]   LOSC, art 14.

[100]   S Kopela, *Dependent Archipelagos in the Law of the Sea* (Boston, MA, Martinus Nijhoff Publishers/Brill Academic, 2013) 74.

[101]   See the discussion which follows concerning bays; and ch 8 for the discussion regarding archipelagos.

[102]   Office for Ocean Affairs and the Law of the Sea, United Nations, *The Law of the Sea: Baselines*, 17, 20.

generated a territorial sea, and, because those features were so closely connected and inter-related that the territorial sea overlapped via a series of circles drawn around each of these features, then much of the relevant area became enclosed within the territorial sea. However, the real significance ultimately lies in the fact that the waters on the landward side of the baselines become part of the internal waters of the state, whilst those on the seaward side of the baselines would fall within the territorial sea.

The requirement that there be a 'fringe' of islands in the vicinity of the coast is one factor which suggests that straight baselines no longer than 24 nm in length may legitimately be used to connect offshore islands.[103] The LOSC also suggests that more than one island must be located offshore in order to utilise a straight baseline system; indeed, the term 'fringe of islands' is suggestive of a cluster, so a few isolated islands would not meet this criterion.[104] Comments made by the ICJ, the work of the ILC, and state practice would support this approach in instances where there is a tight cluster of islands which are closely connected with the mainland—as in the case of the Norwegian *skjærgaard*—or where there are a large number of islands which effectively 'screen' the coast such as in the case of an adjacent archipelago offshore the mainland.[105] In the *Qatar/Bahrain* case the ICJ, after observing that the method of straight baselines was to be 'applied restrictively', was not prepared to find that a number of islands along the coast of Bahrain constituted a fringe of islands, but rather that it was more appropriate to refer to a 'cluster of islands' or an 'island system'. Bahrain's claim to draw straight baselines was therefore denied.[106]

C. Low-Tide Elevations

The law of the sea has grappled with how to deal with low-tide elevations, and this is reflected in some of the debates which took place over these features within the ILC and at UNCLOS I.[107] The principal difficulty is their characterisation; which was highlighted in the *Qatar/Bahrain* case when the ICJ was presented with conflicting submissions as to whether certain features were either islands or low-tide elevations.[108] Often because they are disconnected from the coastline, they are not part of the geographical coast. Likewise, their size and the fact that they are washed at high tide excludes them from being considered islands.[109] The ICJ confirmed in *Territorial and Maritime Dispute*[110] what it had said in *Qatar/Bahrain*, namely that low-tide elevations, unlike islands, cannot be appropriated,

---

[103] Ibid 21.

[104] *Virginia Commentaries*, vol 2, 100.

[105] Ibid.

[106] *Maritime Delimitation and Territorial Questions between Qatar and Bahrain (Qatar v Bahrain)* (merits) [2001] ICJ Rep 40, [212]–[214].

[107] Geoffrey Marston, 'Low-Tide Elevations and Straight Baselines' (1972–1973) 46 *British Yearbook of International Law* 405–23.

[108] *Maritime Delimitation and Territorial Questions between Qatar and Bahrain (Qatar v Bahrain)* (merits) [2001] ICJ Rep 40, [191]–[195] where the Court was eventually satisfied that Qit'at Jaradah was an island as it fulfilled the criteria set out in LOSC, art 121. In this case the Court was also confronted with how to address competing sovereignty claims over these features; see [200]–[209].

[109] LOSC, art 121(1) defines an island as being 'a naturally formed area of land, surrounded by water, which is above water at high tide'.

[110] *Territorial and Maritime Dispute (Nicaragua v Colombia)* [2012] ICJ Rep 624.

although a coastal state will have sovereignty over low-tide elevations situated within its territorial sea as it has sovereignty over the territorial sea itself.[111] As Article 6 of the LOSC separately refers to reefs, there is a further distinction between those features and low-tide elevations. Article 13 makes clear that a low-tide elevation must meet three criteria: that it is a naturally formed area of land, that it is surrounded by and above water at low tide, and that it is submerged at high tide. Such a feature could therefore include a rock or rocks (of varying size), shoals, and sandbars.[112] That sandbars could be legitimately included in this category emphasises that the LOSC does not make any reference to the permanence of the feature, other than that it is submerged at high tide.

The LOSC establishes two scenarios where low tide elevations may be relevant for the determination of baselines. Under Article 13, a low-tide elevation within the territorial sea may itself generate a territorial sea baseline. However, a low-tide elevation beyond the territorial sea has no territorial sea of its own (Article 13(2)). Article 7(4) provides that low-tide elevations cannot be relied upon for the drawing of straight baselines unless lighthouses or other similar installations which are permanently above sea level have been built upon it,[113] or there has been general international recognition of the legitimacy of the use of the low-tide elevation for drawing baselines. Therefore, in a concession to the fact that some low-tide elevations may serve useful maritime purposes as being the location for navigational aids,[114] the LOSC allows an exception for low-tide elevations with artificial structures upon them. This has inevitably encouraged some states to build structures upon these features and, depending on the particular circumstances, this could prove to be very helpful to a state seeking to extend its territorial sea by drawing straight baselines between rocks and groups of fringing islands. Nevertheless, the limitation still remains that the use of low-tide elevations for the drawing of straight baselines must not depart to any appreciable extent from the general direction of the coastline. Moreover, the ICJ has cautioned against the use of the so-called 'leap-frogging' method which seeks to generate a territorial sea from a low-tide elevation outside the territorial sea, but situated less than 12 nm from another low-tide elevation within the territorial sea.[115]

Another dimension of low-tide elevations is that their physical status may be susceptible to change. This is especially the case with shoals and sandbars which may appear on one chart but not the other because of their shifting nature.[116] Sea-level rise also has the potential to have significant impact upon these features which may result in the need for their reclassification with consequent impact upon how straight baselines have been drawn.[117]

---

[111] Ibid [26].

[112] Office for Ocean Affairs and the Law of the Sea, United Nations, *The Law of the Sea: Baselines*, 14 states that a low-tide elevation is 'an intertidal feature and is only visible in calm seas at certain stages of the tide, but not at high tide'.

[113] The LOSC is silent as to the length of time a lighthouse or similar feature should have been in situ, suggesting that a coastal state is free to build such a structure after which it may become eligible for the drawing of a straight baseline: Marston, 'Low-Tide Elevations and Straight Baselines' (n 107) 423.

[114] Office for Ocean Affairs and the Law of the Sea, United Nations, *The Law of the Sea: Baselines*, 24 refers to where a low-tide elevation has a foghorn, beacon or radar reflector.

[115] *Maritime Delimitation and Territorial Questions between Qatar and Bahrain (Qatar v Bahrain)* (merits) [2001] ICJ Rep 40, [207].

[116] In ibid [190]–[195] where the ICJ considered the changing status of the Qit'at Jaradah and different claims reflected in various charts as to the stability of the feature.

[117] Clive Schofield, 'Shifting Limits?' (n 83) 409–10.

D. Juridical Bays

Any historical review of the law of the sea will immediately reveal the importance of bays to the development of the law, and the way in which coastal states first sought to regulate activities in their adjacent offshore waters. It should therefore be of no surprise that when the modern law of the sea came to develop specific rules regarding bays some difficulty was encountered in devising provisions which reflected the nature of the different bodies of waters which may comprise a bay, let alone being sensitive to the multitude of domestic laws which may have been applied to bays.

Article 10 of the LOSC explicitly and implicitly recognises five types of bays:

1. historic bays, which are not subject to the straight baseline system under Article 7 or generally dealt with under Article 10;
2. bays which have been enclosed within internal waters as a result of the drawing of straight baselines under Article 7;[118]
3. bays which are subject to claims by more than one state, which are not subject to the provisions of Article 10;
4. bays which meet the criteria for recognition as a juridical bay with natural entrance points of less than 24 nm;
5. bays which meet the criteria for recognition as a juridical bay with natural entrance points greater than 24 nm.

Accordingly, there may be some parts of a coast which have traditionally been referred to as a bay but which are not recognised as such under the Convention because they are a 'mere curvature of the coast'.[119] Such features would not, therefore, qualify as a juridical bay and straight baselines could not be drawn in their vicinity unless other factors were present.

The importance attached to the recognition of a juridical bay for the purpose of the LOSC is that a closing line may be drawn across the entrance to the bay, or within the bay, with the effect that the waters on the landward side of the line become internal waters and the coastal state is able to delimit the territorial sea from the baseline rather than the coastline of the bay, which depending on the size of the bay may be significant for the ultimate area of territorial sea the coastal state may be able to claim. The criteria for determining a juridical bay are a mix of subjective and objective factors. The bay must meet the geographical criteria of being a 'well-marked indentation' which is in such proportion to the width of its mouth that it contains landlocked waters. As noted above, a mere curvature of the coast is insufficient. In addition, the bay must also meet the objective 'semicircle test', such that the bay must be as large as or larger than a semicircle whose diameter is a line drawn across the mouth of the bay.[120] In the case where islands create different mouths of the bay, the semicircle test is to be applied by drawing a line along the sum total of the lengths of the lines across the different mouths.

---

[118] This would be the case where there are offshore fringing islands adjacent to the bay which have permitted the drawing of straight baselines between the mainland and those islands, effectively enclosing the bays within those offshore straight baselines.

[119] LOSC, art 10(2).

[120] Ibid.

If a bay meets the relevant criteria and is less than 24 nm across the entrance points, then a closing line may be drawn between the two low-water marks creating a baseline from which the territorial sea may be measured.[121] If the bay is greater than 24 nm in breadth, but otherwise meets the criteria as a juridical bay, then a 24 nm straight baseline may be drawn within the bay in such a manner so as to enclose the largest body of water. This allows the coastal state some flexibility to take advantage of geographical features which may exist within the bay. Waters on the landward side of these baselines become internal waters of the coastal state.

These definitions are not without difficulty. The first is determining the 'natural entrance points' to a bay. Where there are coastal features such as headlands marking the entrance to the bay that will not be an issue, but other bays may have more gradual curved entrance points. Another question relates to the measurement of the inner limits of the bay, especially when there may be a variety of coastal features within the bay such as broad river estuaries, deltas, or distinctive arms of the bay.[122] A further question arises in determining the natural entrance point of a bay in the case where a large island fronts the bay, effectively creating an entrance point between the island and the mainland. Such a situation arises in the case of Long Island Sound, off the coast of the state of New York in the United States, where Long Island fringes the coastline so that the effective entrance to the Sound is between Long Island and the mainland.

E. Historic Bays

State practice regarding historic bays has developed over many centuries as a result of municipal laws being applied by coastal states to significant bays which due either to their size or location were considered to be so economically, politically or strategically significant that they were equated to the land area of that state for the purposes of sovereignty and jurisdiction. The status of historic bays gained greater recognition during the nineteenth century, and during the twentieth century was directly referred to in early codifications of the law of the sea, and ultimately in the Convention on the Territorial Sea and Contiguous Zone and the LOSC. However, both conventions specifically excluded historic bays from the regime of juridical bays, leaving their regulation to customary international law. Historic bays must be distinguished from the broader concept of historic waters, which as the ICJ noted in the *Anglo-Norwegian Fisheries* case would extend to 'waters that are treated as internal waters but which would not have that character were it not for the existence of an historic title'.[123] Nevertheless, whilst there is a clear linkage between the two types of waters, the ICJ noted in its 1982 decision in *Continental Shelf (Tunisia v Libyan Arab Jamahiriya)*, by reference to the way the matter had been considered during UNCLOS III, that:

There are, however, references to 'historic bays', or 'historic titles' or historic reasons in a way amounting to a clear reservation to the rules set forth therein. It seems clear that the matter

---

[121] *Land, Island and Maritime Frontier Dispute (El Salvador/Honduras; Nicaragua intervening)* [1992] ICJ Rep 351, [417] in which the ICJ equated a 'closing line' with a 'baseline'.

[122] Office for Ocean Affairs and the Law of the Sea, United Nations, *The Law of the Sea: Baselines*, 24.

[123] *Fisheries (United Kingdom v Norway)* [1951] ICJ Rep 116, 130; Yehuda Z Blum, *Historic Titles in International Law* (The Hague, Martinus Nijhoff, 1965) 262. This broader concept of historic waters may extend to the waters that fall within archipelagos, straits, or estuaries, or areas akin to bays such as gulfs.

continues to be governed by general international law which does not provide for a *single* 'regime' for 'historic waters' or 'historic bays', but only for a particular regime for each of the concrete, recognized cases of 'historic waters' or 'historic bays'.[124]

This approach was endorsed by the Court in the 1992 *Case Concerning the Land, Island and Maritime Frontier Dispute*, where the Court also observed that the regime of an historic bay in the case the Gulf of Fonseca was *sui generis*,[125] suggesting that each historic bay may have its own distinctive legal regime.

Two principal issues are associated with historic bays. The first is whether an area qualifies as an historic bay. In the 1957 study undertaken by the United Nations in preparation for UNCLOS I the following were identified as historic bays: Sea of Azoz (Russia), Bay of Cancale (France), Bay of Chaleur (Canada), Chesapeake Bay (United States), Conception Bay (Canada), Delaware Bay (United States), Bay of El-Arab (Egypt), Hudson Bay (Canada), Miramichi Bay (Canada), Bays of Laholm and Skelderviken (Sweden), the Zuyder Zee (Netherlands), Gulf of Fonseca (Nicaragua, Honduras and El Salvador) and additional miscellaneous bays and fjords in Norway and Portugal.[126] An additional 37 other historic bays were also identified as having been claimed or regarded as such, including the River Plate estuary (Argentina), Spencer Gulf (Australia), Bristol Channel (United Kingdom) and Long Island Sound (United States).[127] Since that time the ICJ in the *Case Concerning the Land, Island and Maritime Frontier Dispute* has confirmed that the Gulf of Fonseca is an historic bay, describing it as a 'pluri-State bay' because of joint sovereignty exercised by El Salvador, Honduras and Nicaragua over the bay.[128] Panama has also declared an historic bay when upon its 1996 ratification of the LOSC, it took the unusual step of lodging a declaration in which it declared 'that it has exclusive sovereignty over the "historic Panamanian bay" of the Golfo de Panamá'.[129]

In 2003 the American Branch of the International Law Association proposed that the term 'historic bay', as used in the LOSC 'means a bay over which a coastal State has publicly claimed and exercised jurisdiction, and this jurisdiction has been accepted by other States. Historic bays need not meet requirements prescribed in the definition of 'bay' in the Convention, Article 10 (2).'[130] In 2012 the American scholars Roach and Smith, in reflecting United States Department of State views, identified 34 historic bays claimed by 19 states,[131] many of which have been subject to protest by the United States as not meeting the international legal standard.[132] Whilst some caution must be exercised in assessing the United States position on these historic bay protests, given the importance the United

---

[124] *Continental Shelf (Tunisia v Libyan Arab Jamahiriya)* [1982] ICJ Rep 18, 74.
[125] *Land, Island and Maritime Frontier Dispute (El Salvador/Honduras; Nicaragua intervening)* [1992] ICJ Rep 351, [384], [412].
[126] 'Historic Bays: Memorandum by the Secretariat of the United Nations', (n 45) 3–10.
[127] Ibid 8.
[128] *Land, Island and Maritime Frontier Dispute (El Salvador/Honduras; Nicaragua intervening)* [1992] ICJ Rep 351, [393].
[129] 'Declarations and Statements' at www.un.org/Depts/los/convention_agreements/convention_declarations. htm.
[130] George K Walker and John E Noyes, 'Definitions for the 1982 Law of the Sea Convention—Part II' (2003) 33 *California Western International Law Journal* 191, 265; in which the author of this report conceded that 'This definition appears to follow the United States position'.
[131] J Ashley Roach and Robert W Smith, *Excessive Maritime Claims*, 3rd edn (The Hague, Martinus Nijhoff, 2012) 36–38.
[132] Ibid 38–54.

States accords to ensuring its actions negate acquiescence by the international community in response to excessive maritime claims,[133] these studies do highlight not only variations in state practice but also how these claims have been received by the international community.

The second issue is the delimitation of an historic bay claim from that of the adjoining waters. The ICJ considered this issue in the *Case Concerning the Land, Island and Maritime Frontier Dispute* and noted that a 'normal geographical closing line' for the waters of the Gulf of Fonseca between the two natural entrance points into the gulf had been that which the three coastal states had recognised in their practice.[134] Therefore a closing line for an historic bay reflecting general principles of international law in its delimitation and which has been accepted by other states would have legitimacy. State practice in this regard is, however, variable, with some states applying a modified version of the straight baseline provisions in the LOSC to draw a closing line across the entrance to the bay, and in other instances closing lines have been drawn within the limits of the bay. Which approach is adopted may depend upon the extent of the claim which is being asserted; in the case of Libya's claim over the Gulf of Sidra a 300 nm closing line is drawn within the limits of the gulf,[135] whilst Italy has drawn a 63 nm closing line across the entrance to the Gulf of Taranto.[136] Notwithstanding the variable approaches used in these two instances, the United States lodged protests with both Libya and Italy over these claims.[137]

F. Contemporary State Practice

Because all coastal states wishing to assert maritime claims rely upon baselines, there is a considerable body of state practice relating to interpretation of the LOSC regarding the delimitation of the territorial sea and the associated limits of internal waters. State practice in this area is especially well developed as the LOSC confirmed all of the core provisions of the Convention on the Territorial Sea and Contiguous Zone regarding baselines. Some states nevertheless have lodged declarations under the LOSC dealing with baselines. Chile and Malta have asserted that their baselines are drawn in conformity with the Convention, while the Netherlands and United Kingdom have rejected these generic assertions.[138] There are 93 coastal states that have provided for straight baselines in their national legislation,[139] though not all may have actually proclaimed straight baselines at that time. Given the subjective criteria which can be applied in many of the relevant provisions, it is perhaps not surprising that some coastal states have sought to interpret the baseline provisions of the LOSC liberally.

---

[133] *Land, Island and Maritime Frontier Dispute (El Salvador/Honduras; Nicaragua intervening)* [1992] ICJ Rep 351, [394] where the importance of acquiescence was discussed.

[134] Ibid [410]; the line is 19.75 nm in width.

[135] Francioni, 'The Status of the Gulf of Sirte' (n 4) 312.

[136] Natalino Ronzitti, 'Is the Gulf of Taranto An Historic Bay?' (1984) 11 *Syracuse Journal of International Law and Commerce* 275, 275.

[137] Roach and Smith, *Excessive Maritime Claims* (n 131) 44–47.

[138] 'Declarations and Statements' at www.un.org/Depts/los/convention_agreements/convention_declarations. htm.

[139] 'Table of Claims to Maritime Jurisdiction' at www.un.org/depts/los/LEGISLATIONANDTREATIES/ PDFFILES/table_summary_of_claims.pdf.

In a 1987 study of state practice concerning straight baselines, Prescott identified five common breaches of Article 7 of the LOSC. These were as follows:

1.   the drawing of straight baselines along coasts which are smooth rather than deeply indented;
2.   the drawing of straight baselines to and from islands which do not constitute a fringe;
3.   the use of basepoints in the sea rather than from the low-water mark;
4.   the drawing by continental states of straight baselines around offshore archipelagos; and
5.   the drawing of straight baselines which are never published.[140]

To this list Roach and Smith have added instances where waters are not closely linked to the land domain, improper use of low-tide elevations, where a terminus is located on a maritime boundary at sea, where a terminus is located on the territory of another state, where a terminus is not located on mainland of the state relying upon the straight baseline, overlarge bays and gulfs, and estuary closing lines.[141]

Some examples of excessive straight baseline claims include Bangladesh's 1974 proclamation of a straight baseline measuring 221 nm which runs through a series of eight points located in the sea;[142] Egypt's 1990 claim to straight baselines along almost all of its coastline despite the fact that it is generally smooth and undulating and with few offshore fringing islands;[143] claims by Portugal in 1985 and Denmark in 1976 to a system of baselines around the Azores and Faroe Islands respectively notwithstanding that neither meet the criteria for archipelagic state status;[144] Burma's straight baseline system developed in 1977 which encloses waters not closely linked to the land domain and includes one baseline 222 nm in length,[145] which has been further amended in 2008 to include baselines around the Preparis and CoCo island groups on the basis they are an offshore archipelago;[146] and Mauritania's 1967 drawing of a 90 nm straight baseline across a juridical bay.[147] Canada's declaration of straight baselines around the islands which comprise its Arctic Archipelago has been particularly contentious not only because of the length of the baselines but also because of their impact upon the waters of the Northwest Passage, a navigation route through the Arctic Archipelago connecting the Beaufort Sea to the Davis Strait which then runs into the North Atlantic Ocean.[148]

The ICJ has also been called upon to comment on the legitimacy of some straight baseline claims in maritime delimitation cases. In the *Qatar/Bahrain* case, the Court observed generally with respect to the straight baseline system that they were an 'exception' and 'may only be applied if a number of conditions are met', suggesting that the system should be applied 'restrictively'.[149] In that case, Bahrain's attempt to declare straight baselines around

---

[140]   Prescott, 'Straight and Archipelagic Baselines' (n 33) 41–46.

[141]   Roach and Smith, *Excessive Maritime Claims* (n 131) 116–30.

[142]   Prescott, 'Straight and Archipelagic Baselines' (n 33) 45.

[143]   Giampiero Francalanci and Tullio Scovazzi, 'The Old and New Egyptian Legislation on Straight Baselines' in Gerald H Blake (ed), *Maritime Boundaries* (London, Routledge, 1994) 127, 132–35.

[144]   Roach and Smith, *Excessive Maritime Claims* (n 131) 108.

[145]   Ibid 116–17.

[146]   (2009) 69 *Law of the Sea Bulletin* 69–73.

[147]   Roach and Smith, *Excessive Maritime Claims* (n 131) 130.

[148]   Donald R Rothwell, *The Polar Regions and the Development of International Law* (Cambridge, Cambridge University Press, 1996) 273.

[149]   *Maritime Delimitation and Territorial Questions between Qatar and Bahrain (Qatar v Bahrain)* (merits) [2001] ICJ Rep 40, [212].

its adjacent islands was rejected as it had not declared itself as an archipelagic state, and the offshore islands were not considered to constitute a fringe.[150]

It is clear that there is a great diversity of state practice with respect to baselines. As base-line declarations are made unilaterally, they are only subject to protest from those states directly affected by such claims or those which are vigilant in monitoring excessive baseline claims such as the United States. International courts will only consider the legitimacy of baselines once cases have been brought before them, and excepting the *Anglo-Norwegian Fisheries* case, these issues have only arisen in recent decades in maritime boundary delimi-tation cases. Whether the straight baseline provisions of the LOSC have become a part of customary international law is questionable.[151] Given the scope for subjective interpreta-tion of the straight baseline rules in particular, and the fact that in contrast to the closing line limits for bays there is no defined limit on the length of straight baselines, it is doubtful whether these provisions are of a fundamentally norm creating character.[152] Nevertheless, whilst the straight baseline provisions may not reflect customary international law the ICJ has declared the Article 10 LOSC provisions on bays to 'express general customary law',[153] and states parties to the LOSC are bound to adhere to them in good faith. Through the process of claim, protest and counter-claim state practice on the law of baselines will it seems remain contentious for some time to come.

V. Internal Waters

With the recognition in the international law of the sea throughout the twentieth century of the legitimacy of straight baselines, it accordingly became possible to distinguish more clearly those bodies of water properly classified as 'internal waters' from the adjacent ter-ritorial sea. This process gained momentum following the *Anglo-Norwegian Fisheries* case recognising the status of Norwegian waters on the landward side of the claimed baselines as being part of the 'regime of internal waters'.[154] It was inevitable then that some reference would be given to these waters as the law of the sea began its codification process through the work of the ILC and subsequently at UNCLOS I.

A. Views of the ILC

Sensitive to the fact that these waters had traditionally not been the subject of international concern and had overwhelmingly been regulated only by municipal legal systems, the ILC

---

[150] Ibid [213]–[214].

[151] Robin Churchill, 'The Impact of State Practice on the Jurisdictional Framework Contained in the LOS Convention' in Alex G Oude Elferink (ed), *Stability and Change in the Law of the Sea: The Role of the LOS Convention* (Leiden, Martinus Nijhoff, 2005) 91, 106; International Law Association (n 97) [60].

[152] *North Sea Continental Shelf (Federal Republic of Germany v Denmark; Federal Republic of Germany v The Netherlands)* [1969] ICJ Rep 3.

[153] *Land, Island and Maritime Frontier Dispute (El Salvador/Honduras; Nicaragua intervening)* [1992] ICJ Rep 351, [383].

[154] *Fisheries (United Kingdom v Norway)* [1951] ICJ Rep 116, 133.

was careful in its considerations not to suggest the development of a distinctive regime for this area. Accordingly, internal waters were addressed in a rather low key fashion, even extending to the inclusion of the definition of internal waters within the 'High Seas' part of the ILC's draft articles and commentary. Draft Article 26(2) simply provided that 'Waters within the baseline of the territorial sea are considered 'internal waters' and in the accompanying Commentary the ILC observed that the state exercises its sovereignty over this area in the same way as it does over the land 'subject to the provisions of international law limiting the rights of the State'.[155] The ILC did make clear that large stretches of water entirely surrounded by dry land known as 'lakes' or 'seas' were not bodies of water to which the regime of high seas, and by implication that of the developing law of the sea, was applicable. Draft Article 5 also made clear that waters which fell on the landward side of a straight baseline would be subject to the 'régime of internal waters'. No comment was made as to the extent of that regime, other than in the proposal found in draft Article 5(3) that when straight baselines had the effect of enclosing as internal waters, areas which were previously considered to be territorial sea, then a right of innocent passage would be recognised within those waters.

B. Convention on the Territorial Sea and Contiguous Zone

In the Convention on the Territorial Sea and Contiguous Zone the provisions proposed by the ILC dealing with internal waters were consolidated in Article 5 of the Convention. This article made clear that waters on the landward side of the baseline of the territorial sea formed part of the internal waters of the state,[156] and that where the establishment of straight baselines had the effect of enclosing as internal waters areas previously considered to be a part of the territorial sea, then a right of innocent passage existed within those waters.[157] However, whilst not in any way attempting to define the regime of internal waters, the Convention did provide some further indications as to the extent of the regime, so that Article 1(1) refers to the sovereignty of a state extending beyond the land territory and internal waters to encompass the territorial sea. This reference by implication acknowledges coastal state sovereignty over internal waters, which in Article 4(2) is referred to as a 'régime of internal waters' in the context of waters enclosed within baselines as being sufficiently linked to the land domain. The Convention therefore primarily concerned itself with the delimitation of the territorial sea in instances where the territorial sea and internal waters abutted, and whilst acknowledging the sovereignty of the coastal state over internal waters, did make that right subject to innocent passage by foreign ships in instances where straight baselines enclosed waters previously considered territorial sea.

C. LOSC

When the issue of internal waters was considered at UNCLOS III, one of the immediate issues which confronted the conference were the claims made by Indonesia and the

---

[155] ILC, 'Articles Concerning the Law of the Sea' (n 34) 277.
[156] Convention on the Territorial Sea and Contiguous Zone, art 5(1).
[157] Ibid art 5(2).

Philippines that all of the waters which fell within the limits of the straight baselines they had proclaimed around the outer limits of their archipelagos were internal waters. Whilst Indonesia had made a concession that the right of innocent passage existed within these waters,[158] these declarations creating vast areas as internal waters had no precedent in international law. Ultimately, this potentially divisive issue for the regime of internal waters was dealt with at UNCLOS III by recognition accorded to 'archipelagic waters' within the archipelagic baselines proclaimed by recognised archipelagic states, including Indonesia and the Philippines. This compromise did, however, require a minor adjustment to the regime of internal waters recognised in the Convention on the Territorial Sea and the Contiguous Zone and the LOSC provides in Article 8(1) that except as provided for in Part IV of the Convention dealing with archipelagic states, waters on the landward side of the baseline of the territorial sea form part of the internal waters of the state. Nevertheless, the Part IV Archipelagic State regime also recognised that within archipelagic waters an archipelagic state may be able to draw closing lines for the delimitation of internal waters in accordance with Articles 9, 10 and 11 of the LOSC. Therefore, an archipelagic state may have internal waters within the islands which make up the outer limits of the archipelago and directly face the territorial sea, and also have internal waters within islands encompassed by archipelagic baselines. One consequence of these circumstances is that in some instances ships would transit from internal waters to territorial sea, and in other instances from internal waters to archipelagic waters. Another minor adjustment to the regime of internal waters appears in Article 8(2), which was extended so as to permit a right of innocent passage though all waters previously not considered as internal waters, thereby extending the operation of the exception originally found in the Convention on the Territorial Sea and Contiguous Zone to include the contiguous zone and EEZ. In all other respects, the LOSC duplicates the relevant provisions of that convention with respect to internal waters, with Article 2 noting that the sovereignty of the coastal state extends beyond its internal waters to the territorial sea, and Article 7(3) referring to the need for a close linkage between the land domain and waters within baselines that are subject to the regime of internal waters. Importantly, with the exception of a right of innocent passage being enjoyed within internal waters previously considered territorial sea until straight baselines had been drawn, or when the right of innocent passage by foreign ships is being exercised through the territorial sea to access internal waters,[159] the LOSC does not in any way seek to interfere with the regime of internal waters.

D. State Practice

The development of the contemporary international law of the sea since World War II assisted with the delimitation of internal waters from those maritime zones which fall on the seaward side of the baselines, which in most cases will be the territorial sea and in the case of internal waters situated within archipelagic baselines, archipelagic waters. The regime of internal waters is therefore all of those waters which fall on the landward side

---

[158] See the discussion in ch 8.
[159] LOSC, art 18(1).

of the baselines, wherever they may be located. This will include the waters found within coastal areas enclosed by straight baselines such as bays, bights, gulfs, sounds, ports and harbours, and also between offshore fringing islands and the mainland. The status of these waters as internal under contemporary international law is closely linked to the similar status accorded some of these waters under the *fauces terrae* principle in English common law and its equivalent in European civil law.[160] Internal waters would also include river mouths, estuaries, canals and the waters within inland lakes, dams and seas. However, for the purposes of the law of the sea only those waters which are directly accessible to the ocean become subject to the operation of aspects of the law of the sea. Accordingly, whilst non-navigable rivers, inland lakes and seas are part of a state's internal waters, these are not bodies of water with which the law of the sea is concerned. The Saint Lawrence Seaway which provides access for ocean-going vessels from the Atlantic Ocean to the Great Lakes is an example of internal waters comprising a river, lakes and interconnecting canal systems which while regulated by Canada and the United States, is subject to very minimal law of the sea provisions. Likewise, access to the Panama and Suez Canals is covered by specific international convention not subject to the law of the sea, though recognition is given to the freedom of navigation.[161] The Black Sea, on the other hand, whilst only accessible to the Atlantic Ocean via the Turkish Straits and Mediterranean Sea, is considered subject to the law of the sea.[162]

i. Territorial Sovereign Rights and Internal Waters

As internal waters fall within the sovereign territory of a coastal state,[163] the state has recognised sovereignty over those waters fully encompassing prescriptive and enforcement jurisdiction, subject only to the limitations imposed under international law. The regime of internal waters is interpreted by some states so as to reflect bilateral treaty arrangements where neighbouring states share certain waters,[164] or on constitutional documents which affirm certain rights over these waters.[165] The most prominent exception to the regime of internal waters contemplated by the LOSC is the ongoing right of innocent passage within internal waters that were previously not considered as such, and a number of states reflect this provision in their national legislation.[166] Another relevant exception is foreign state immunity, which accords visiting foreign warships immunity from the laws of the coastal

---

[160] O'Connell, *The International Law of the Sea* (n 6) 385.

[161] As these canals are not considered to be part of the territorial sea, they are not subject to the limitation of LOSC, art 26 prohibiting the imposition of charges by virtue of passage through the territorial sea.

[162] See *Maritime Delimitation in the Black Sea (Romania v Ukraine)* [2009] ICJ Rep 61.

[163] *Military and Paramilitary Activities in and Against Nicaragua (Nicaragua v United States)* (merits) [1986] ICJ Rep 14, [213] ('*Nicaragua*').

[164] 'Chile—Statement Made upon Signature (10 December 1982) and Confirmed upon Ratification (25 August 1997)' in 'Declarations and Statements' at www.un.org/Depts/los/convention_agreements/convention_declarations.htm, making reference to its 1984 Treaty of Peace and Friendship with Argentina regarding navigation through internal waters.

[165] 'Philippines—Understanding Made upon Signature (10 December 1982) and Confirmed upon Ratification (8 May 1984) in 'Declarations and Statements' at www.un.org/Depts/los/convention_agreements/convention_declarations.htm.

[166] For example, *Maritime Jurisdiction Act 1959* (Ireland), s 5: Symmons, *Ireland and the Law of the Sea*, (n 71) 32.

state.[167] Nonetheless, the coastal state still retains the capacity to close access to its ports and other internal waters to vessels which it considers constitute an undue risk or hazard, such as nuclear-armed vessels.[168]

ii. Port Access

The LOSC is silent as to whether foreign ships have a right of access to a port. However, there is both treaty law and case law in support of the general principle that a state does not have an unlimited power to prohibit access to its ports.[169] The 1923 Convention and Statute on the International Regime of Maritime Ports[170] provides for a general recognition of equality of treatment between the state parties with respect to reciprocal rights of port access.[171] This principle was later recognised in the 1958 *Saudi-Arabia v Aramco* arbitration, where the arbitrator observed that:

> According to a great principle of public international law, the ports of every State must be open to foreign merchant vessels and can only be closed when the vital interests of the State so require.[172]

In the 1986 *Nicaragua* case, the ICJ also referred to certain rights linked to the freedom of communications and maritime commerce conferring a 'right of free access enjoyed by foreign ships' to ports.[173] Nevertheless, there are examples where states have on a non-discriminatory basis barred port access to certain types of vessels. Australia prohibits access by foreign whaling vessels, unless a special permit has been sought or if force majeure conditions apply,[174] whilst New Zealand bars port access to any ship that is partly or wholly nuclear powered.[175] There are also examples of instances during times of tension between states, short of armed conflict, that port access may be denied to certain flagged vessels.[176] The status of vessels in distress has become contentious in recent years as a result of some states barring port access to vessels carrying asylum seekers, including some who have been rescued at sea. In 2001 Australia barred the Norwegian flagged *Tampa* access to the port

---

[167] *The ARA Libertad Case (Argentina v Ghana)*, Provisional Measures, Order of 15 December 2012, [95] ('in accordance with general international law, a warship enjoys immunity, including in internal waters', but *cf* Separate Opinion of Judges Wolfrum and Cot at [45]: 'prima facie [Art. 32] is meant to be applicable in the territorial sea only'); US Supreme Court, *The Schooner Exchange v M'Faddon*, (1812) 11 US 116 (in which the United States Supreme Court held that a French warship in port in the United States was immune from proceedings in local courts).

[168] This has been an issue for a number of countries, including Ireland—Symmons, *Ireland and the Law of the Sea*, 33–34; and New Zealand—*New Zealand Nuclear Free Zone, Disarmament and Arms Control Act 1987* (NZ); Joanna Mossop, 'Maritime Security in New Zealand' in Natalie Klein, Joanna Mossop and Donald R Rothwell (eds), *Maritime Security* (London, Routledge, 2009) 54, 61–62.

[169] O'Connell, *The International Law of the Sea* (n 6) 848; Colombos, *The International Law of the Sea* (n 15) 176–77.

[170] *Basic Documents* No 1.

[171] Convention and Statute on the International Regime of Maritime Ports, art 2; art 1 defines a 'maritime port' as being 'All ports which are normally frequented by sea-going vessels and used for foreign trade shall be deemed to be maritime ports within the meaning of the present Statute'.

[172] *Saudi-Arabia v Arabian American Oil Company (ARAMCO)* (1963) 27 ILR 117.

[173] *Nicaragua* [1986] ICJ Rep 14, [214].

[174] *Environmental Protection and Biodiversity Conservation Act 1999* (Australia), s 236.

[175] *New Zealand Nuclear Free Zone, Disarmament, and Arms Control Act 1987* (NZ), s 11.

[176] The United States in 1985 declared a total trade embargo against Nicaragua with the effect that all Nicaraguan vessels were barred from United States ports: *Nicaragua* [1986] ICJ Rep 14, [125].

of Christmas Island after that vessel had conducted a successful search and rescue of 433 asylum seekers in the north-eastern Indian Ocean.[177] In 2002, Norway was successful in having agreement reached at the IMO for adjustment of the relevant provisions in the 1974 International Convention for the Safety of Life at Sea (SOLAS) permitting vessels having conducted search and rescue operations at sea to disembark persons rescued at sea at the nearest available port.

iii. Jurisdiction over Foreign Ships in Port

Excepting sovereign immune vessels, all foreign vessels within internal waters or a port are subject to the criminal and civil laws and regulations of a coastal state, subject to the coastal state's discretion as to whether jurisdiction will be exercised in all instances.[178] In cases of minor criminal matters concerning the internal discipline of a ship, the coastal state may not seek to apply its criminal laws. However, if a criminal offence affects the interests of the coastal state, then the coastal state will most probably seek to prosecute.[179] Greater difficulty exists with respect to those vessels which have entered internal waters or a port under conditions of *force majeure* or distress. State practice has traditionally granted such vessels a limited immunity from prosecution,[180] however, there is emerging evidence that providing lives are not at risk some states will bar access to vessels that pose a substantial marine pollution risk even though that vessel may technically be in distress.

One particular limitation which applies to foreign ships passing from the territorial sea into internal waters, such as a port,[181] is relevant coastal state laws dealing with the design, construction, manning and equipment of foreign ships. If the coastal state adopts such standards then they must conform to generally accepted international rules or standards,[182] which would include IMO instruments such as SOLAS.[183] Importantly, the LOSC does not demand that a coastal state apply identical pollution prevention laws and regulations within both the territorial sea and internal waters, leading to the potential for more stringent provisions being applied to ships within internal waters. This is contemplated in LOSC, Art 211(3) which requires states that establish 'particular requirements for the prevention, reduction and control of pollution of the marine environment as a condition for the entry of foreign vessels into their ports or internal waters' to give appropriate publicity to this requirement and also advise the IMO. In recent years some coastal states have adopted stringent pollution prevention measures in the wake of major maritime incidents, including the United States following the 1989 *Exxon Valdez* incident,[184] and Spain following the

---

[177]   Donald R Rothwell, 'The Law of the Sea and the MV Tampa Incident: Reconciling Maritime Principles with Coastal State Sovereignty' (2002) 13 *Public Law Review* 118–27.

[178]   Jessup, *The Law of Territorial Waters* (n 1) 144–45.

[179]   Ibid 169, observing that: 'The theory that foreign merchant vessels are completely subject to the jurisdiction of the littoral state has found its most consistent application in England and has come to be known as the English rule'.

[180]   Erik Jaap Molenaar, *Coastal State Jurisdiction over Vessel-Source Pollution* (The Hague, Kluwer Law International, 1998) 187.

[181]   LOSC, art 18(1) considers this to be an act of innocent passage.

[182]   Ibid art 21(2).

[183]   *Basic Documents* No 22.

[184]   Michael J Uda, 'The Oil Pollution Act of 1990: Is there a Bright Future beyond Valdez?' (1991) 10 *Virginia Environmental Law Journal* 403–33.

2002 *Prestige* incident. Spain, for example, announced that from 2003 single-hull tankers flying any flag and carrying heavy fuel oil, coal tar or heavy crude oil would be prohibited from entering Spanish ports, terminals or anchorage areas.[185] Related to these provisions is the extent of coastal state[186] and port state[187] jurisdiction with respect to vessels voluntarily within a port being subject to inspection and possible prosecution for breach of marine pollution laws and regulations.[188]

VI. Further Reading

Philip C Jessup, *The Law of Territorial Waters and Maritime Jurisdiction* (New York, GA Jennings, 1927)

DP O'Connell, *The International Law of the Sea*, vol 1 (Oxford, Clarendon Press, 1982)

Coalter Lathrop, 'Baselines' in Donald R Rothwell, Oude G Oude Elferink, Karen N Scott and Tim Stephens (eds), *The Oxford Handbook of the Law of the Sea* (Oxford, Oxford University Press, 2015) 69

Victor Prescott and Clive Schofield, *Maritime Political Boundaries of the World*, 2nd edn (Leiden, Martinus Nijhoff, 2004)

Michael W Reisman and Gayl S Westerman, *Straight Baselines in Maritime Boundary Delimitation* (New York, St Martin's Press, 1992)

J Ashley Roach and Robert W Smith, *Excessive Maritime Claims*, 3rd edn (Leiden, Martinus Nijhoff, 2012)

Gayl S Westerman, *The Juridical Bay* (New York, Oxford University Press, 1987)

---

[185] Eric R Jaworski, 'Developments in Vessel-based Pollution: Prestige Oil Catastrophe Threatens West European Coastline, Spurs Europe to Take Action against Aging and Unsafe Tankers' (Fall 2002) *Colorado Journal of International Environmental Law and Policy* 101–109.

[186] LOSC, art 220.

[187] Ibid art 218.

[188] Molenaar, *Coastal State Jurisdiction over Vessel-Source Pollution* (n 180) 186–90.

3

Territorial Sea and Contiguous Zone

I. Introduction

The history of the international law of the sea is dominated by the contest between the freedom of the sea (*mare liberum*) and the doctrine of the closed sea (*mare clausum*). From the time of Grotius and Selden until the later part of the twentieth century this contest continued and it was not until the regime of the territorial sea became relatively settled as a result of the codifications of the law through the various Law of the Sea Conferences that a degree of certainty began to prevail. There was only then a clear acceptance that coastal states were entitled to claim a narrow adjacent maritime zone as the territorial sea. This fundamental shift in the law laid the foundation for subsequent acceptance and codification in the various conventions of the additional maritime zones which comprise the modern international law of the sea, of which the EEZ and the continental shelf are the most significant.

The development of the territorial sea regime is not only a cornerstone in the development of the law, but it is also the cornerstone maritime zone in the modern law of the sea, as it not only encompasses the greatest extent of coastal state sovereignty and jurisdiction but is also the area of greatest maritime activity because of its proximity to the coast. The territorial sea therefore secures all of the key interests of the coastal state in one relatively narrow maritime area. It extends to sovereignty over the waters, seabed and airspace, and complete jurisdiction over all activities which occur within the area subject only to those limitations recognised by international law. All of the resources of the territorial sea are within the reach of the adjoining coastal state, including not only the living and non–living resources that may be available for commercial exploitation, but also the waters and seabed which may be used for a range of development activities, including the building of airports, artificial islands, bridges and port facilities.

The territorial sea is also an area of considerable security sensitivity for coastal states. Whilst the right of innocent passage is recognised for foreign flagged vessels within the territorial sea, this still has the potential to become a flashpoint in some instances, especially in matters concerning foreign warships and for those states with a heightened sense of security that place constraints on access to the territorial sea. These contemporary tensions reflect the historical view that the territorial sea was seen as a security zone for the coastal state, giving it protection from hostile forces seeking to plunder coastal towns and cities.

Related to this security dimension of the territorial sea has been the contemporary development of the contiguous zone, the maritime zone adjacent to the territorial sea which confers distinctive jurisdictional capacities upon the coastal state. The contiguous zone has only been recognised through developments in modern customary international law, and more recently through the codifications of the law of the sea, but has become of increasing importance as coastal states seek to extend their jurisdictional reach to address specialised concerns such as customs and immigration laws and regulations.

II. Territorial Sea in Customary International Law

The standard history of the law of the sea is presented as a victory of the Grotian view of *mare liberum* over *mare clausum* in the seventeenth century, with *mare clausum* only regaining support during the twentieth century. The reality is that while the freedom of the seas prevailed and was the dominant theory and approach towards the oceans, it was not the unanimous view of both publicists and in state practice. Grotius himself was prepared to concede in his book *De Jure Belli ac Pacis* published in 1625 that sovereignty over the sea could be 'acquired in the same way as sovereignty elsewhere, that is … through the instrumentality of persons and of territory'.[1] Another Dutch scholar and jurist, Bynkershoek, proclaimed in his 1703 work *Dominion of the Sea*, that the 'power of the land properly ends where the force of arms ends'[2] promoting the view that a state was able to exert control over adjacent seas on the basis of either land or sea-based forces.

Whilst these and other publicists pondered the extent, if any, of some form of coastal state control over adjacent coastal waters, there was also emerging state practice in the seventeenth and eighteenth centuries. The predominant concern of coastal states at the time was their capacity to control the security of their coastal waters and adjoining seas, including the waters of bays, gulfs, fjords, estuaries, ports and harbours as well as the seas adjoining the outer coasts. This concern over coastal security was crucial for European states as naval technology continued to develop during this time resulting in larger and more capable warships which through their use of cannon had the potential to devastate coastal towns and cities. An additional factor, which more gradually rose to prominence, was the concern of the coastal state over the protection of coastal fish stocks traditionally fished by local fishermen but which were coming under threat from foreign fishers. This was initially a matter of concern principally within Europe. However, following the Industrial Revolution which saw the development of enhanced ship building and fishing technologies, this became a truly global concern as the phenomenon of 'distant water fishing' emerged and foreign fishing vessels and whalers plundered fish and whale stocks where they were most easily located close to shorelines.

Examples of some state practice from this era include a 1565 decree by King Philip II of Spain proclaiming that '[n]o one can come to our coasts, harbours, roadsteads, or rivers or within sight of our land',[3] whilst a 1774 Treaty between France and Spain sought to prohibit ships carrying smuggled goods from entering an area within two leagues of the

---

[1] Hugo Grotius, *De Jure Belli Ac Pacis* (The Hague, Martinus Nijhoff, 1625, 1948 trans) book 2, ch III; see also RP Anand, *Origin and Development of the Law of the Sea* (The Hague, Martinus Nijhoff, 1983) 138.

[2] Cornelius van Bynkershoek, *De Dominio Maris Dissertatio* (New York, Oceana, 1744, 1923 trans, 1964 rep) 44.

[3] Royal Decree of Philip II, King of Spain (October 1565), reprinted in Henry G Crocker (ed), *The Extent of the Marginal Sea* (Washington, Government Printing Office, 1919, 1974 rep) 622 (this work was reprinted as *The Inquiry Handbooks*, vol 10 (Wilmington, Del, Scholarly Resources, 1974)).

land, including ports and the mouths of rivers.[4] Denmark has some particular examples of state practice as they relate to fisheries, with a 1599 ordinance declaring that English vessels found to be hovering or fishing within two Norwegian leagues of the coast were subject to capture.[5] With respect to whaling in Danish waters, which at the time included Iceland and the Faroe islands, these activities were prohibited or regulated via a series of seventeenth century declarations and licenses at a distance of four, six and ten Norwegian leagues from the coast.[6] For Great Britain, greater emphasis was placed on coastal security and this was reflected in a series of seventeenth-century peace treaties with Tripoli and Algiers principally concerning protection of the British garrison at Tangier on the northwest African coast which prohibited 'cruising near or in sight of any of His Majesty's raids, havens, or ports, towns and places, nor in any way disturb the peace of the same.'[7]

Notwithstanding the development of this state practice, the type of claims made to these adjacent waters, in addition to the breadth of the claims varied considerably, and were dictated by several variables, including the extent of peaceful relations between the interested states, the value of the marine resources within these adjacent waters, and the capacity of a coastal state to enforce these claims. Nevertheless by the nineteenth century, state practice had developed to such a degree that it was now becoming increasingly common for European states to assert some level of jurisdiction, control and even sovereignty over their adjoining coastal waters.[8] As a result of the enactment of laws and regulations governing activities in these waters, which were applicable to both nationals and non-nationals, courts were also beginning to consider the extent of coastal state regulation. This not only applied to developing maritime law regulating trade and commerce, but also to criminal and other civil matters occurring onboard ships and also to activities within the seabed.[9]

While the regime of the territorial sea was initially developing, there remained enormous variations in the breadth of the maritime zone and this was reflected both in state practice and the views of publicists. One approach which did find favour was the so-called 'cannon-shot rule',[10] whereby foreign vessels were not to approach the shore at any lesser distance than that which could be covered by a cannon-shot, thereby providing some level of security to the coastal state from potential attacks by foreign warships. As Fulton explained, '[i]t was the rule, in England at least, that "the sea should salute the land," and the range of guns determined the limit within which the salute ought to be rendered. Beyond

---

[4] Treaty between France and Spain (27 December 1774) art 8, reprinted in Crocker (ed), *The Extent of the Marginal Sea*, ibid 521. One nautical league is equal to 3 nm or 5.556 km.

[5] Ordinance—Denmark (10 May 1598), reprinted in Crocker (ed), *The Extent of the Marginal Sea*, ibid 513; an accompanying note to this extract discusses the range of a 'Norwegian league' as being between 6 and 8 km.

[6] Declaration of Christian IV to Charles I (13 December 1631); Licence granted to Iceland Whaling Company (16 April 1636); Manifesto regarding the management of the trade and fishing along Iceland and the Færø group (13 May 1682); reprinted in Crocker (ed), *The Extent of the Marginal Sea*, ibid 514.

[7] Treaty of Peace and Commerce with Algiers (5 April 1686), art VIII, reprinted in Crocker (ed), *The Extent of the Marginal Sea*, ibid 534.

[8] John Rawson Elder, *The Royal Fishery Companies of the Seventeenth Century* (Glasgow, Maclehose, 1912) 4, discussing the practices in England of Kings Edward III, Henry V, Henry VI and Henry VII making proclamations asserting the rights of British fishers to the exclusion of Dutch fishers.

[9] Geoffrey Marston, *The Marginal Seabed* (Oxford, Clarendon Press, 1981) 1–159, discussing United Kingdom practice regarding the seabed between 1829 and 1883.

[10] Bynkershoek, *De Dominio Maris Dissertatio*, 44; discussed in Wyndham L Walker, 'Territorial Waters: The Cannon Shot Rule' (1945) 22 *British Yearbook of International Law* 210.

the reach of cannon no salute was expected; within it usage, international courtesy, or the law, required it.'[11]

With divergent state practice it was difficult to pinpoint with any certainty the clear development of customary international law with respect to the territorial sea. This was also reflected in the various theoretical approaches that developed in the nineteenth century seeking to provide a firm legal foundation for coastal state claims over these adjacent waters whilst at the same time also not undermining the principles of *mare liberum* which remained dominant. O'Connell identified three theories which had developed at the time: the property theory of the territorial sea—encompassing the notion that the territorial sea was part of the property of the coastal state; the police theory based on the notion that the territorial sea was an area from which all foreigners could be excluded; and the competence theory—which asserted that the coastal state had competence to assert either sovereignty, jurisdiction or control over the waters.[12] All of this uncertainty in the law suggested that the time was quickly approaching for clarification by way of codification.

III. Codification of the Territorial Sea

A. The Views of the International Associations

The codification of the law of the sea commenced with the work of a number of international associations which began studying a variety of law of the sea questions towards the end of the nineteenth century and in the early part of the twentieth century. Whilst none of these bodies formally concluded a treaty or convention on the territorial sea, their studies did prove influential for the work of the ILC in the 1950s.

None of the international associations denied the existence of a territorial sea; however, there were considerable variations in the approaches taken as to the breadth of the territorial sea and the extent of coastal state rights within those waters. The Institute of International Law resolved in 1888 to study the territorial sea and in a 1892 report proposed that a coastal state would have absolute sovereignty within the territorial sea other than for a right of innocent passage. The use of the term 'sovereignty' to describe coastal state rights over the area was at the time distinctive, and a clear divergence from the 'property theory' of the territorial sea.[13] In its 1894 session, the Institute adopted six nm from the low-water mark as the breadth of the territorial sea.[14] In the 1920s the German Society of International Law, American Institute of International Law, Japanese Association of International Law, and the Harvard Law School draft articles all endorsed the territorial sea as a maritime zone over which coastal states had sovereignty.[15] The International Law Association at its 1924 Conference proposed a 'right of jurisdiction' over the territorial sea, but in 1926 adjusted this to 'territorial jurisdiction'.[16]

---

[11] Thomas Wemyss Fulton, *The Sovereignty of the Sea* (Edinburgh, Blackwood, 1911, 1976 rep) 557.
[12] DP O'Connell, *The International Law of the Sea*, vol 1 (Oxford, Clarendon Press, 1982) 60–67.
[13] Ibid 67–68.
[14] C John Colombos, *The International Law of the Sea*, 6th edn (London, Longmans, 1967) 102.
[15] O'Connell, *The International Law of the Sea*, vol 1 (n 12) 75.
[16] Ibid.

The most significant early attempt at codification occurred during the 1930 Hague Codification Conference convened under the auspices of the League of Nations. The Conference gave the most detailed consideration to the territorial sea regime that had existed until that time with the Rapporteur of the Preparatory Commission, Schücking, proposing that the coastal state had 'dominion' over the territorial sea 'within fixed limits'.[17] The Hague Conference ultimately endorsed the view that a coastal state had sovereignty over the territorial sea, but was unable to reach agreement as to the breadth of that zone, with proposals ranging from three, four, to six nm.[18] Whilst no treaty was agreed upon, the draft on the 'Legal Status of the Territorial Sea' embodied in the Final Act of the conference provided a template for the ILC when it came to consider the issue 20 years later.

B. International Law Commission

Prior to the ILC commencing its consideration of the law of the sea, the ICJ had delivered two judgments relevant to the developing territorial sea regime. In the *Corfu Channel* case,[19] the ICJ accepted the legitimacy of Albania's claim to 'territorial waters' within the Corfu Channel, observing that the United Kingdom's minesweeping operations in the strait had been 'a violation of Albanian sovereignty'.[20] In the *Fisheries* case,[21] where the Court was considering the legitimacy of Norway's baselines which had been drawn along its coast so as to delimit its internal waters, the ICJ directly referred to the territorial sea and the use of the low-water mark and straight baselines as a legitimate means of measuring its breadth.[22] Whilst neither case discussed in detail the regime of the territorial sea, including its breadth, by implication the ICJ was clearly indicating an acceptance of the territorial sea for the purposes of customary international law.

When the ILC did commence its review of the law of the sea regime, it was confronted by well-developed customary international law concerning the high seas, developing customary international law with respect to the continental shelf, and vast amounts of state practice with respect to the territorial sea which at that time had little consistency.[23] The ILC was therefore in a position not only to codify the territorial sea regime, but also to make proposals that would clarify the law and ultimately advance the progressive development of the regime.[24] A total of 25 draft articles concerning the territorial sea were proposed by the ILC in its 1956 'Articles concerning the Law of the Sea with commentaries'.[25] Whilst a number

---

[17] Ibid 76.

[18] Jesse S Reeves, 'The Codification of the Law of Territorial Waters' (1930) 24 *AJIL* 486; Colombos, *The International Law of the Sea* (n 14) 104–105.

[19] *Corfu Channel (United Kingdom v Albania)* [1949] ICJ Rep 4.

[20] Ibid 35.

[21] *Fisheries (United Kingdom v Norway)* [1951] ICJ Rep 116.

[22] Ibid 128.

[23] This was highlighted by a dispute between Sweden and the Soviet Union in 1948 over a purported 12 nm Soviet Union territorial sea claim in the Baltic Sea; in the midst of this dispute in 1952 two unarmed Swedish reconnaissance planes were shot down over the Baltic resulting in the loss of life: Gene Glenn, 'The Swedish-Soviet Territorial Sea Controversy in the Baltic' (1956) 50 *AJIL* 942.

[24] For an analysis of some of the ILC debates see Burdick H Brittin, 'Article 3, Regime of the Territorial Sea' (1956) 50 *AJIL* 934.

[25] International Law Commission, 'Articles Concerning the Law of the Sea with Commentaries' (1956) *Yearbook of the International Law Commission*, vol 2, 265–301.

of these provisions dealt with delimitation of the territorial sea, including the baselines of the territorial sea, and innocent passage within the territorial sea, draft Articles 1, 2, 3, and 6 proposed the core components of the territorial sea regime. This included that the sovereignty of the coastal state extended to the sea adjacent to the coast which was described as the territorial sea,[26] that coastal state sovereignty extended to the air space, seabed and subsoil of the territorial sea,[27] and that the outer limit of the territorial sea was a line measured from the baseline.[28] However, most importantly the ILC in draft Article 3 did not propose a fixed breadth for the territorial sea, other than to observe that 'international law does not permit an extension of the territorial sea beyond twelve miles'.[29] This reflected the divergent positions within the Commission, and in its accompanying Commentary to the draft articles the ILC noted that 'the Commission came out clearly against claims to extend the territorial sea to a breadth which, in its view, jeopardises the principle that has governed maritime law since Grotius, namely the freedom of the seas. On the other hand, the Commission did not succeed in fixing the limit between three and twelve miles'.[30]

C. UNCLOS I

In preparation for UNCLOS I, states attending the conference were invited to comment on the ILC's draft articles, with 14 states making specific comments on the territorial sea regime.[31] These pre-conference observations reflected the variations in state practice which the ILC had identified, with some states supporting a narrow band for the territorial sea on the grounds that this had less impact upon navigation rights, while others advocated a broader territorial sea, as this provided potentially greater access to offshore fisheries. The connection between offshore fish stocks and the territorial sea was at the time becoming increasingly important, especially following the development of the continental shelf regime in the wake of the 1945 Truman Proclamation,[32] and the detailed consideration given to the issue by the ILC. Developing states were increasingly frustrated that coastal state fishery resource rights were not receiving the same detailed attention as resource rights to non-living resources in the continental shelf, and one response to this was to argue in support for a broader territorial sea thereby enhancing rights over fish stocks in that area.[33] Chile, for example, commented that the ILC's work on the breadth of the territorial sea reflected primarily a 'juridical interpretation' when there were other political and

---

[26] Ibid 265, art 1.

[27] Ibid 266, art 2.

[28] Ibid 268, art 6.

[29] Ibid 265, art 3.

[30] Ibid 266.

[31] 'Comments by Governments on the Draft Articles Concerning the Law of the Sea Adopted by the International Law Commission at its Eighth Session', *United Nations Conference on the Law of the Sea: Official Records*, vol 1 (Geneva, United Nations, 1958) 75–113 these being Canada, Chile, China, Cuba, Denmark, Ethiopia, India, Italy, the Netherlands, Norway, Peru, Poland, Sweden and the United Kingdom.

[32] *Basic Documents* No 5.

[33] 'Comments by Governments on the Draft Articles Concerning the Law of the Sea Adopted by the International Law Commission at its Eighth Session', *United Nations Conference on the Law of the Sea: Official Records*, vol 1 (Geneva, United Nations, 1958) 86 where Iceland commented: 'The most important problem as far as the Icelandic Government is concerned is the question of coastal jurisdiction over fisheries'.

economic factors which should also be taken into account.[34] Ethiopia observed that whilst it had proclaimed a 12 nm territorial sea, it recognised how divisive this issue was becoming and that it preferred to 'see this question left aside, if that were possible, rather than have the convention embody a statement which would be unacceptable to any large group of States'.[35]

This is precisely the position which UNCLOS I ultimately took, in that while agreement was reached on the development of the 1958 Convention on the Territorial Sea and Contiguous Zone,[36] which contained within it the core provisions of the territorial sea regime as recommended by the ILC, the breadth of the territorial sea remained undefined. The effect of this compromise was that there was ongoing uncertainty in the law of the sea with respect to the most pivotal of all maritime zones. The incapacity to reach a clear consensus on the issue was the catalyst for the remarkable reassembling of the states at UNCLOS II in 1960.

D. Convention on the Territorial Sea and Contiguous Zone

The Convention on the Territorial Sea and Contiguous Zone was adopted in Geneva on 29 April 1958 and entered into force on 10 September 1964. It was the first treaty of its type to define the foundations of the territorial sea regime, and also recognised for the first time a contiguous zone. The Convention substantially replicated the ILC draft articles which had been proposed in 1956 and contained three parts dealing respectively with the territorial sea, contiguous zone, and procedural articles relating to entry into force and revision. The territorial sea provisions are the main body of the Convention and comprise 23 articles, of which 13 relate to the limits of the territorial sea and general aspects of the regime and the remainder address innocent passage. Other than those provisions dealing with the delimitation of the territorial sea from baselines, the core provisions are those found in Articles 1, 2 and 6.

Article 1 of the Convention affirmed that the 'sovereignty of the state' extends to the territorial sea and that this was an area beyond the land territory and internal waters which encompassed 'a belt of sea adjacent to the coast'. This simple statement made clear that the territorial sea was an area over which a coastal state exercised sovereignty, and whilst Article 1 did not expressly refer to a 'coastal state', as the territorial sea was immediately adjacent to the coast of a state, this was the implication. Importantly, however, it was made clear that coastal state sovereignty was not absolute as it was 'exercised subject to the provisions of these articles and to other rules of international law'[37] a formulation broad enough to include relevant provisions found in the three other 1958 Geneva Conventions, customary international law, and any existing bilateral and regional treaties dealing with territorial sea matters.[38]

---

[34] Ibid 98.

[35] Ibid 112.

[36] *Basic Documents* No 9.

[37] Convention on the Territorial Sea and Contiguous Zone, art 1(2).

[38] Prior to adoption of the 1958 Convention, the territorial sea was often referred to in treaties and conventions as 'territorial waters': 1924 Convention between the United States of America and United Kingdom Respecting the Regulation of Liquor Traffic, *Basic Documents* No 2, art 1—indicating that three marine miles was the limit of

The sovereignty of the coastal state with respect to the territorial sea was expanded upon in Article 2, which provided that sovereignty extended to the air space over the territorial sea, as well as the bed and subsoil. This provision, which reflected the ILC draft articles, was in turn taken from the articles proposed by the 1930 Hague Codification Conference, and was subject to minimal ILC comment.[39] This is significant for two reasons. The first is that up until this point in time the principal focus upon the territorial sea regime had been with respect to its regulation of maritime affairs. However, as aerial navigation developed in the late nineteenth century and early twentieth century, issues began to arise with respect to the regulation of air navigation above the territorial sea. Once it had been established that states had sovereignty with respect to the air space over their sovereign territories,[40] and that the territorial sea was an area over which the coastal state had sovereignty, it followed that this sovereignty also extended to the air space above the territorial sea. As observed by Pépin, who prepared a report for UNCLOS I on those provisions in the ILC draft articles dealing with the law of the air, this provision was 'fully consistent with existing air law'.[41] It was also significant that Article 2 made clear that the sovereignty of the coastal state extended to the seabed and subsoil of the territorial sea. Likewise with air space, this had not been a traditional area of concern for the territorial sea regime. However, with the development of the continental shelf regime, as reflected in the 1958 Convention on the Continental Shelf,[42] there was a need to make clear that coastal state sovereignty extended over the seafloor in the territorial sea. Given the emerging interest at this time in the development of offshore oil and gas resources, this represented a timely clarification on the ambit of a coastal state's territorial sea sovereignty.

Notwithstanding these important provisions as to the extent of the regime, the breadth of the territorial sea remained unresolved and accordingly the Convention was silent on the matter other than in Article 6, which provided that '[t]he outer limit of the territorial sea is the line every point of which is at a distance from the nearest point of the baseline equal to the breadth of the territorial sea'. This was only a technical provision, which allowed for a mechanism by which the territorial sea was to be delimited from the baseline but without addressing what the actual defined breadth was to be. Accordingly, the Convention left it to state practice to determine the outer limit of the territorial sea which at that time could have varied from anywhere between three to 12 nm. Significantly, the Convention provided in Article 24 for a 12 nm outer limit of the contiguous zone, which by implication suggested that the territorial sea should not seek to extend beyond this limit.

Undoubtedly the fact that the Convention left unresolved the breadth of the territorial sea was a very significant gap not only in the Convention but also in the developing regime of the territorial sea, though the Convention needed to be read alongside existing

---

territorial waters; 1942 Treaty between Great Britain and Northern Ireland and Venezuela Relating to the Submarine Areas of the Gulf of Paria, *Basic Documents* No 4, art 1; 1951 Treaty of Peace with Japan, arts 1, 3.

[39] International Law Commission, 'Articles Concerning the Law of the Sea with Commentaries' (1956) *Yearbook of the International Law Commission*, vol 2, 265.

[40] 1919 Paris Convention relating to the Regulation of Aerial Navigation, art 1; 1944 Chicago Convention on International Civil Aviation, art 1.

[41] 'The Law of the Air and the Draft Articles Concerning the Law of the Sea Adopted by the International Law Commission at its Eighth Session', *United Nations Conference on the Law of the Sea: Official Records*, vol 1 (Geneva, United Nations, 1958) 64, 65.

[42] *Basic Documents* No 12.

customary international law. Bowett characterised the two major challenges arising from this issue as being the reconciliation of security interests and economic interests.[43] Western powers were particularly concerned about the impact of an expanded territorial sea upon navigational rights and freedoms, and given the Convention had only briefly addressed the sensitive issue of international straits in Article 16(4), it was deficient in leaving unresolved a core security issue, the importance of which was obvious during the Cold War.[44] With respect to economic issues, because recognition of a coastal state fisheries zone was not on the UNCLOS I agenda, many states economically dependent on fisheries which favoured such a zone were inclined instead to support an extended territorial sea.[45] Given the ongoing debates over these issues it was not surprising that efforts were made to reach a resolution in 1960.

E. UNCLOS II

UNCLOS II met in Geneva from 17 March to 26 April 1960 and was attended by 88 states. There were only two substantive items on its agenda. The first was the 'Consideration of the questions of the breadth of the territorial sea and fishery limits in accordance with Resolution 1307 (XIII) adopted by the General Assembly on 10 December 1958', and the second was the adoption of conventions or other instruments related to that process.[46] Numerous proposals were presented to the conference as to the limit of the territorial sea, and a co-related fishing zone. As to the breadth of the territorial sea, the conference appeared evenly divided between support for a three nm and 12 nm limit. After nearly five weeks of discussion on this key point, Canada and the United States on 22 April 1960 introduced a proposal which would have entitled a state to fix the breadth of the territorial sea up to a maximum of six nm, and to also establish a fishing zone 'in the high seas contiguous to the territorial sea' extending to a maximum of 12 nm.[47] This so-called 'six plus six' proposal would therefore have permitted an outer limit of the territorial sea of six nm, reflecting the middle ground in the debate between those states favouring a three nm and 12 nm territorial sea, whilst also permitting a new and distinctive fishing zone adjacent to the territorial sea, thereby seeking to meet the demands of those states who were dependent upon the fishery resources in those waters. However, the joint North American proposal failed to achieve the necessary two thirds support by a single vote,[48] and accordingly the conference concluded without any agreement on the breadth of the territorial sea, nor an adjacent fishing zone.

---

[43]   DW Bowett, *The Law of the Sea* (Manchester, Manchester University Press, 1967) 7–12.

[44]   Ibid 9.

[45]   Ibid 10.

[46]   Final Act of the Second United Nations Conference on the Law of the Sea (26 April 1960), UN Doc A/CONF.19/L.15, reprinted in Second United Nations Conference on the Law of the Sea, *Summary Records of Plenary Meetings and of Meetings of the Committee of the Whole* (Geneva, United Nations, 1960) 175.

[47]   'Canada and United States of America: Proposal' (22 April 1960), UN Doc A/CONF.19/L.11 reprinted in Second United Nations Conference on the Law of the Sea, *Summary Records of Plenary Meetings*, 173.

[48]   Whilst the Canadian/United States proposal received a vote of 54 in favour, 28 against, with 5 abstentions, this did not reach the necessary two thirds majority required for adoption by the Conference in plenary: DW Bowett, 'The Second United Nations Conference on the Law of the Sea' (1960) 9 *International and Comparative Law Quarterly* 415, 432.

F. State Practice

Given the circumstances surrounding UNCLOS I and UNCLOS II, it is of no surprise that in 1960 there was considerable variation in state practice as to the breadth of the territorial sea. A study prepared by the United Nations for UNCLOS I, which was updated in 1960 for UNCLOS II, showed that of the states with clear territorial sea limits, 22 had declared a three nm territorial sea, three a four nm, one a five nm, 10 a six nm, one a nine nm, one a 10 nm, and 13 a 12 nm territorial sea. In addition, Chile at the time claimed a 50 km zone, and El Salvandor a 200 nm zone.[49] Those states supporting a three nm limit were principally European and maritime states, and included Australia, Canada, China, Denmark, France, Ireland, Japan, the Netherlands, Poland, South Africa, the United Kingdom and the United States. States supporting a 12 nm limit were principally newly independent and developing states, and included Bulgaria, Ecuador, Ethiopia, Indonesia, Iran, Libya, Panama, Romania, Saudi Arabia, Soviet Union, United Arab Republic and Venezuela. Nordic states were principally in support of a four nm limit, whilst both developed and developing states from the east and west supported a six nm limit. Whilst most states therefore at this time claimed at least a three nm territorial sea, a limit set at this distance did not reflect the majority position, and accordingly even when allowance is made for inclusion of those states supporting a four, five and six nm territorial sea, it becomes apparent how difficult it was to secure the necessary two-thirds support for the 'six plus six' proposal at UNCLOS II.

In light of the ongoing uncertainty as to the breadth of the territorial sea and support at UNCLOS II for at least a six nm limit, following the conclusion of the conference a number of states began to revisit the breadth of their territorial sea claims. In 1964 the United States Department of State reported that the number of states claiming a three nm territorial sea was 19, with a further 19 states claiming a 12 nm territorial sea, and six others making variable claims in excess of that distance.[50] As Bowett observed at the time 'it seems tolerably clear that the breadth of the territorial sea is, on the basis of state practice, gradually widening'.[51] However, during the 1960s the phenomenon of the 'exclusive fishing zone' began to emerge partly in response to the frustration felt by some states at the failure of UNCLOS II to reach agreement on the fishery zone issue, but also as a means to assert newly found independence and economic resource security. Whilst the legitimacy of these fishery claims were highly contested, the disassociation of the territorial sea from a number of these claims meant that some states were no longer seeking to assert excessive territorial seas.

The trend, however, in more expansive territorial sea claims and the move away from the three nm limit continued throughout the 1960s and until UNCLOS III. In a survey in October 1972, Brown put the number of three nm claimant states at 27, and those claiming 12 nm at 50.[52] This demonstrated conclusively that newly emerging states, which would

---

[49] 'Synoptical table concerning the breadth and juridical status of the territorial sea and adjacent zones' (8 February 1960), UN Doc A/CONF.19/4, reprinted in *Second United Nations Conference on the Law of the Sea, Summary Records of Plenary Meetings*, 157.

[50] 'Jurisdiction Claimed Over Territorial Waters and Fishing' (1964) 3 *International Legal Materials* 469.

[51] Bowett, *The Law of the Sea* (n 43) 13.

[52] ED Brown, 'Maritime Zones: A Survey of Claims' in Robin Churchill, KR Simmonds and Jane Welch (eds), *New Directions in the Law of the Sea*, vol 3 (London, British Institute of International and Comparative Law, 1973) 157, 161.

eventually form themselves into the 'Group of 77' at UNCLOS III, were overwhelmingly supporting a 12 nm territorial sea limit. Another factor which needed to be taken into account was the position of the United States, which was outlined in a statement by President Nixon in May 1970, that supported a new oceans treaty and which made clear that '[t]his treaty would establish a twelve-mile limit for territorial seas and provide for free transit through international straits'.[53]

Although there was general consistency in state practice regarding the extent of coastal state sovereignty over the territorial sea,[54] there were variations as to the methods used to delimit the territorial sea based on the low-water mark and baselines,[55] and also as to the extent of navigational rights and freedoms, especially as they applied to warships,[56] and also the methods utilised to delimit the territorial sea based on the low-water mark and baselines.[57] There were also several variations in nomenclature used by states in describing their territorial seas. Yugoslavia, for example, combined its claim over internal waters and the territorial sea to proclaim its sovereignty over what it referred to as 'marginal seas', of which the territorial sea breadth was 10 nm.[58] Given the considerable fluidity which existed at the time not only with respect to the breadth of territorial sea claims, but also the jurisdictional rights claimed within them, and related claims to fishing and economic zones, it was particularly challenging to assess state practice during this period with any level of certainty.[59]

IV. UNCLOS III and the LOSC

When UNCLOS III was convened a pivotal issue for initial determination was the outer limit of the territorial sea, as how the conference settled this issue would have a major impact upon a range of other related issues especially international straits. Prior to the conference commencing in 1972 and 1973 the Sea-Bed Committee of the United Nations considered submissions supporting the right of states to proclaim a territorial sea of up to 12 nm. Whilst there were variable proposals offered during the second UNCLOS III session in 1974, it was clear that the majority of states favoured a 12 nm territorial sea and this was in turn reflected in the 1975 Informal Single Negotiation Text for the putative convention.[60] Another factor helping to establish consensus on this matter was the support within UNCLOS III for some form of 'economic' or fishing zone to address the concerns

---

[53] 'Announcement by President Nixon on United States oceans policy, Saturday, 23 May 1970' (1970) 9 *International Legal Materials* 807, 809.

[54] 'France: Law Extending Territorial Waters to 12 Miles' reprinted in S Houston Lay, Robin Churchill and Myron Nordquist (eds), *New Directions in the Law of the Sea*, vol 1 (Dobbs Ferry, NY, Oceana Publications, 1973) 24.

[55] This was especially the case with the archipelagos of Indonesia and the Philippines; see discussion in ch 8.

[56] 'Regulations of 5 August 1960 for the Defence of the State Frontier of the Union of Soviet Socialist Republics' reprinted in Houston Lay, Churchill and Nordquist (eds), *New Directions in the Law of the Sea* (n 54) vol 1, 29.

[57] 'Republic Act No 3046 of 17 June 1961. An Act to Define the Baselines of the Territorial Sea of the Philippines' reprinted in ibid vol 1, 27.

[58] Art 1 of 'Law of 22 May on Yugoslavia's Marginal Seas, Contiguous Zone and Continental Shelf' reprinted in ibid vol 1, 35.

[59] Brown, 'Maritime Zones: A Survey of Claims' (n 52) 165.

[60] *Virginia Commentaries*, vol 2, 79–80.

expressed by many states during the 1960s that a narrow territorial sea did not meet their needs with respect to fish stocks. In particular, these developments met the concerns of Latin American states which had been particularly proactive in seeking to assert very broad territorial sea claims for precisely that reason.

Once the 12 nm breadth of the territorial sea had been settled, it became possible to make constructive progress on the important and related issue of the regime of international straits, which it was now estimated would play a much greater role in the law of the sea given the potential enclosure of many straits less than 24 nm in breadth. Whilst some adjustments were also made to the LOSC with respect to the territorial sea baseline provisions, and rights of innocent passage, the key functional aspects of the territorial sea regime as established in the Convention on the Territorial Sea and Contiguous Zone remained in place.

Part II of the LOSC deals with the territorial sea and contiguous zone, with the Section 1 General Provisions laying the key foundational aspects of the regime. Article 2 effectively combines Articles 1 and 2 of the Convention on the Territorial Sea and Contiguous Zone, reflecting the necessary updating required following the recognition given in the LOSC to archipelagic states. The legal status of the territorial sea is therefore described as an area which extends beyond the land territory, internal waters, and in the case of an archipelagic state its archipelagic waters, to encompass an 'adjacent belt of sea' known as the territorial sea. The sovereignty which exists over this area extends to the air space, bed and the subsoil. Whilst the extent of coastal state sovereignty in the territorial sea is not clearly articulated, it is possible to discern its extent from a review of customary international law, state practice, and other relevant provisions of the Convention. It is clear that the coastal state has sovereignty over all the resources which are found within the territorial sea, and unlike allowances which are made in the EEZ or continental shelf regime for access rights by third states or even the equitable sharing of resources, nothing equivalent prevails within the territorial sea except in the case of arrangements that may predate the LOSC or have a historic basis.[61] The coastal state is also recognised as having an 'exclusive right' of sovereignty with respect to marine scientific research within the territorial sea.[62]

However, as was the case with the Convention on the Territorial Sea and Contiguous Zone, under LOSC the sovereignty of the coastal state is exercised in the territorial sea subject to the LOSC and other rules of international law.[63] This makes clear that other relevant treaties dealing with the territorial sea have ongoing application,[64] as do other treaties and customary international law which applies within the territorial sea.[65]

---

[61] See, eg, 1974 Memorandum of Understanding between the Government of Australia and the Government of the Republic of Indonesia regarding the operations of Indonesian Traditional Fishermen in Areas of the Australian Exclusive Fishing Zone and Continental Shelf.

[62] LOSC, art 245.

[63] Ibid art 2(3).

[64] Such as relevant provisions of the 1974 International Convention for the Safety of Life at Sea, *Basic Documents* No 22, Annex, ch V, reg 12 dealing with vessel traffic services within the territorial sea.

[65] International human rights law obligations which extend to the 'territory' of a state include the territorial sea, see generally Guy Goodwin-Gill and Jane McAdam, *The Refugee in International Law* 3rd edn (Oxford, Oxford University Press, 2007) 254–55; while in some instances treaties make clear that territory includes land and the territorial sea/waters: 1969 Agreement between the Government of Australia and the Government of Nauru Relating to Air Services, art 1(b).

In Article 3 the LOSC addresses the breadth of the territorial sea and confirms that every state has the right to establish a territorial sea 'up to a limit not exceeding 12 nautical miles' which is to be measured from the baselines as provided for in the LOSC. Archipelagic states,[66] islands and rocks all generate a territorial sea.[67] Low-tide elevations situated beyond the limits of the territorial sea[68] and offshore structures, installations and artificial islands do not generate a territorial sea.[69] Once a coastal state has determined the limits of the territorial sea generated from its various coastal and maritime features, then Article 16 requires that these limits be shown on charts, to which due publicity is given, and the geographical coordinates and relevant charts are lodged with the United Nations.

These key provisions prompt several observations. The first is that consistent with the juridical history of the regime of the territorial sea, the LOSC refers to the 'sovereignty' of the coastal state over that area, in distinction to several other maritime zones in the LOSC where the terms 'sovereign rights'[70] and 'jurisdiction'[71] are used. In this respect there is some similarity in the LOSC between the recognition of coastal state sovereignty over the territorial sea and archipelagic state sovereignty over archipelagic waters.[72] Sovereignty suggests the possession of plenary rights to control activities within the area, and also to use and enjoy the resources found within the area. However, consistent with the history of the regime, territorial sea sovereignty is not in fact absolute, and is not equivalent to that which a state possesses in respect of its land domain or even its internal waters.

The sovereignty of the coastal state needs to be read carefully alongside the other relevant provisions of the LOSC, and more generally other relevant provisions of international law especially those found in IMO conventions dealing with shipping and the rights of the coastal state to regulate matters concerning ship-sourced marine pollution within the territorial sea. The provisions found in Section 3 of Part II of the LOSC have particular application. Articles 17 to 26 deal with the navigational regime of innocent passage for foreign flagged ships within the territorial sea, and provides for the right of passage subject to certain constraints. These provisions also provide further guidance as to the extent of coastal state sovereignty over the territorial sea, indicating that it extends to the enactment of laws and regulations dealing with living resources within the area, including fisheries, the protection of the environment, the movement of shipping, marine scientific research, the laying of cables and pipelines, and customs, immigration, fiscal and sanitary matters.[73] The seabed rights of the coastal state also clearly permit the development of that area for living and non-living resources, the construction of shipping facilities, and related infrastructure.[74]

---

[66] LOSC, art 48.

[67] LOSC, art 121. On the distinction between rocks and low-tide elevations see discussion in *Sovereignty over Pedra Branca/Pulau Batu, Middle Rocks and South Ledge (Malaysia/Singapore)*, Judgment of 23 May 2008 [2008] ICJ Rep 12, [288]–[299].

[68] LOSC, art 13(2).

[69] LOSC, arts 11, 60(8).

[70] LOSC, arts 56(1)(a), 77(1).

[71] Ibid art 56(1)(b). As the ICJ noted in *Territorial and Maritime Dispute (Nicaragua v Colombia)* [2012] ICJ Rep 624, [177], 'In accordance with long-established principles of customary international law, a coastal State possesses sovereignty over the sea bed and water column in its territorial sea ... By contrast, coastal States enjoy specific rights, rather than sovereignty, with respect to the continental shelf and exclusive economic zone.'

[72] LOSC, art 49(1).

[73] Ibid art 21.

[74] This would also extend to the construction of artificial islands. Consideration has been given in the Netherlands to the construction of an airport within an area of the territorial sea: Erik Jaap Molenaar, 'Airports at Sea: International Legal Implications' (1999) 14 *International Journal of Marine and Coastal Law* 371.

The LOSC also includes provisions addressing the potential coastal state enforcement of both criminal and civil laws against not only foreign ships within that area but also foreign nationals. Article 27 provides that coastal state criminal jurisdiction should not be exercised on board a foreign ship so as to effect an arrest of a person on board a ship engaged in innocent passage unless certain conditions are met. The most important of these is that the crime is one which extends to the coastal state, disturbs the peace of the country or good order of the territorial sea, is a drug related matter, or arises from the master of the ship requesting assistance. These conditions make clear that the criminal offence must pass a severity threshold before the coastal state would become involved. A common assault would not do so, whilst serious criminal offences such as sexual assault or murder would clearly be of concern to the coastal state, even if none of its nationals were involved and would be regarded as a disturbance of the 'good order' of the territorial sea.[75]

With respect to civil jurisdiction aboard foreign ships, the coastal state has an even more limited capacity when that ship is engaged in innocent passage through the territorial sea. Jurisdiction cannot be exercised unless it relates to liabilities arising from a visit to the coastal state's internal waters, or assumed in the course of its voyage through the territorial sea. Civil liability arising from a marine pollution incident aboard a foreign ship within the territorial sea would fall into this category.[76] Articles 29 to 32 address issues arising with respect to jurisdiction over warships and other government ships operated for non-commercial purposes. These provisions require coastal state respect for immunities enjoyed by these vessels,[77] but in recognition of the potential marine environmental damage that may arise from a major maritime incident involving such vessels, Article 31 reaffirms flag state responsibility for any loss or damage to the coastal state.

V. Contemporary Territorial Sea in State Practice

A. Breadth of the Territorial Sea

It might have been assumed that given the consensus reached at UNCLOS III regarding the breadth of the territorial sea, the debates of the twentieth century would have been conclusively settled. However, while state practice reveals that there is very substantial support for the 12 nm territorial sea, it is not unanimous. Some states remained sufficiently conscious of potential challenges to the 12 nm limit and the elements of the territorial sea regime that they addressed these issues in declarations made upon their signature or ratification of the LOSC. Belgium, for example, stated in its 1984 Declaration that 'The limitation of the breadth of the territorial sea, as established by Article 3 of the Convention, confirms and codifies a widely observed customary practice which it is incumbent on every State

---

[75] LOSC, art 27(1)(b).
[76] See LOSC, art 220(2), giving to the coastal state the capacity to institute proceedings against vessels that have violated its pollution laws and regulations while within the territorial sea.
[77] Ibid art 32. See further *ARA Libertad (Argentina v Ghana)* (2014) 156 ILR 186.

to respect, as it is the only one admitted by international law'.[78] Belgium further indicated that it would not recognise any territorial sea claims beyond 12 nm. Germany in its 1994 Declaration emphasised that the provisions concerning the territorial sea 'represent in general a set of rules reconciling the legitimate desire of coastal states to protect their sovereignty and that of the international community to exercise the right of passage'.[79] This was a common theme in the declarations of a number of states concerned to ensure an appropriate balance between coastal state rights over the territorial sea and the freedoms of navigation. A small group of other states, including Egypt and Oman[80] took the opportunity via their LOSC Declarations to indicate adjustments to their territorial sea limits in conformity with the Convention, whilst Uruguay and Vietnam in their Declarations reaffirmed that the LOSC provisions were consistent with their own national sovereignty and laws concerning the territorial sea.[81]

Roach and Smith asserted in 2012 that 'the State practice of territorial sea claims has become, by large measure, stable and in line with the customary international law' reflected in the LOSC.[82] At that time 143 of 152 states, or 94 per cent of states, asserted a territorial sea of 12 nm or less, with only seven states asserting claims in excess of that limit.[83] Either as a result of protest, especially from countries such as the United States, or through a desire to ensure compliance in good faith with the LOSC, Roach and Smith tracked the rolling back of excessive territorial sea claims by 26 states, which included such diverse states as Albania (15 nm), Argentina (200 nm), Congo (200 nm), Gabon (100 nm), Germany (16 nm), Haiti (100 nm), Nicaragua (200 nm) and the Maldives and Tonga, whose claims partly reflected so-called rectangle baseline claims made around the limits of their archipelagos.[84] States asserting claims in excess of 12 nm were Togo (30 nm), and Benin, Ecuador, El Salvador, Peru and Somalia (200 nm).[85] The Philippines territorial sea remains determined by a set of coordinate points which reflect the outer limits of the Philippines archipelagic claim.[86]

These figures clearly indicate a very high level of acceptance and adherence to the current 12 nm limit of the territorial sea; however, a number of observations may still be made. The first is that the LOSC does not require coastal states to establish a 12 nm territorial sea. Article 2 is clear that coastal states do not need to claim a territorial sea, in that it is inherent to coastal states, and Article 3 is also clear that the territorial sea is not to exceed 12 nm. While a territorial sea is therefore recognised under general international law and the LOSC as being part of a coastal state's sovereign territorial entitlement, the outer limit

---

[78] Belgium (5 December 1984), 'Declarations and Statements' at www.un.org/Depts/los/convention_agreements/convention_declarations.htm.

[79] Germany (14 October 1994), 'Declarations and Statements' at www.un.org/Depts/los/convention_agreements/convention_declarations.htm.

[80] Egypt (26 August 1983); Oman (1 July 1983), 'Declarations and Statements' at www.un.org/Depts/los/convention_agreements/convention_declarations.htm.

[81] Uruguay (10 December 1982); Vietnam (25 July 1994), 'Declarations and Statements' at www.un.org/Depts/los/convention_agreements/convention_declarations.htm.

[82] J Ashley Roach and Robert W Smith, *Excessive Maritime Claims*, 3rd edn (The Hague, Martinus Nijhoff, 2012) 136.

[83] Ibid.

[84] Ibid 139–43.

[85] Ibid 148.

[86] See discussion of this claim in ch 8.

of that claim needs to be identified not only for the purposes of the LOSC,[87] but also for the purposes of municipal law enforcement with respect to activities taking place within the waters offshore the coastal state. Accordingly claims of a territorial sea of less than 12 nm made by states such as Jordan (three nm) and Greece (six nm) are in conformity with the Convention. Likewise for Turkey, which though not a party to the LOSC has established a six nm territorial sea in the Aegean Sea, but claims a 12 nm territorial sea in the Black Sea. A number of states also have variable territorial sea limits which in some instances arise from boundary delimitations with opposite states resulting in boundary limitations being imposed upon territorial sea limits. Some states have established a three nm territorial sea in some selected areas so as to reduce tension with respect to those waters, particularly in the case of straits. Japan, for example, applies a three nm limit to the Soya Strait, Tsugaru Strait and to the eastern and western channels of the Tsushima and Osumi Straits,[88] whilst the United Kingdom claims a three nm territorial sea from many of its overseas territories such as Gibraltar and Pitcairn.[89] In other cases, territorial sea limits may be fixed by treaty provisions, as is the case for certain islands in the Torres Strait between Australia and Papua New Guinea which only generate a three nm territorial sea whilst other islands in the same group are recognised as having a 12 nm territorial sea.[90]

Those states with a territorial sea in excess of 12 nm have long asserted such claims, and they have regularly been subject to protest by a number of states, including the United States.[91] These excessive claims certainly are not reflective of either the LOSC or customary international law and the legitimacy associated with such claims is further compromised by the difficulties in effectively policing claims to a territorial sea of up to 200 nm which would be essential if the claim were to be maintained according to the traditional notion of effective control, which was the basis for the development of the territorial sea regime.

B. Sovereignty and Jurisdiction

The extent of coastal state sovereignty and jurisdiction over the territorial sea is vast and even taking into account the limitations imposed by the LOSC in relation to innocent passage, relatively unfettered with respect to core areas of state interest. The coastal state is therefore able to engage in a range of development activities within the territorial sea which include the building of artificial islands, bridges, ports and roadsteads, and the installation of navigational aids such as lighthouses.[92] Land reclamation associated with these activities is also permissible, so as to allow for the extension of airports into the territorial

---

[87] LOSC, art 16.

[88] 'Table of Claims to Maritime Jurisdiction (as at 31 March 2007)' (2007) 63 *Law of the Sea Bulletin* 87.

[89] Ibid 92.

[90] Treaty between Australia and the Independent State of Papua New Guinea concerning Sovereignty and Maritime Boundaries in the area between the two Countries, including the area known as Torres Strait, and Related Matters.

[91] Roach and Smith, *Excessive Maritime Claims* (n 82) 144–48.

[92] These features will not necessarily result in adjustment of the normal baseline or straight baseline from which the breadth of the territorial sea is measured; for example, while LOSC, art 11 provides that the outermost permanent harbour works that form an integral part of the harbour system are regarded as forming part of the coast, offshore installations and artificial islands are not similarly classified.

sea outwards from the coast, subject to not unduly impairing the rights and interests of neighbouring states.[93] Nevertheless, there remain some areas of coastal state practice within the territorial sea which have generated some level of disagreement.[94]

Since the terrorist attacks on the United States in 2001, there has been a marked assertion by many coastal states of security jurisdiction in the territorial sea. This is particularly relevant with respect to the interdiction rights of coastal states within their territorial sea over both ships and aircraft approaching their coasts. In some instances, coastal states have sought to expand notification requirements over sea and airspace not only beyond the territorial sea and contiguous zone, but also into the EEZ and in some cases the high seas.[95] There has likewise been a more vigorous approach taken towards policing and law enforcement within the territorial sea as a result of the rise of transnational crime resulting in an upsurge of drug and people smuggling. To that end, some coastal states have taken a more proactive approach towards search and inspection of vessels approaching the coast. This has become particularly contentious in the case of the interdiction of vessels suspected of carrying refugees and asylum seekers. These vessels are often interdicted within the contiguous zone and EEZ with the objective of preventing them from reaching the territorial sea because once they do so obligations of the coastal state under international refugee and human rights law become applicable in ways they are not beyond the territorial sea.[96] Likewise, some states have sought to close access to their territorial sea by vessels carrying migrants or refugees.[97] Prominent examples include Australia's 'Operation Sovereign Borders', in effect from 2013, in which boats suspected of carrying migrants and refugees have been towed back into the EEZ and high seas.[98] In 2015, the United Nations Secretary-General sought to intervene after Indonesia, Malaysia and Thailand were reported to have 'pushed back' from their territorial sea boats carrying migrants and refugees which had sailed across the Andaman Sea.[99]

There has also been an increased concern for marine environmental security of which the territorial sea is one of the most sensitive areas for a coastal state given its proximity to the coastline and population centres and the potential for maritime incidents to have

---

[93] See discussion in *Land Reclamation by Singapore in and Around the Straits of Johore (Malaysia v Singapore)* (provisional measures) 8 October 2003 www.itlos.org.

[94] A number of these matters relate to baseline claims and controls placed upon navigation, which are discussed in chs 2, 10 and 11; with respect to an overview of the Chinese state practice on these matters see Hyun-Soo Kim, 'The 1992 Chinese Territorial Sea Law in Light of the UN Convention' (1994) 43 *International and Comparative Law Quarterly* 894.

[95] N Klein, 'Legal Limitations on Ensuring Australia's Maritime Security' (2006) 7 *Melbourne Journal of International Law* 306, discussing the Australian Maritime Identification System.

[96] This practice has been especially contentious with respect to interdiction practices adopted by the United States in the Caribbean, and some European states in the Mediterranean; see Stephen H Legomsky, 'The USA and Caribbean Interdiction Program' (2006) 18 *International Journal of Refugee Law* 677; Thomas Gammeltoft-Hansen, 'The Refugee, the Sovereign, and the Sea: EU Interdiction Policies in the Mediterranean' (2008) *Danish Institute for International Studies Working Paper* 6.

[97] Donald R Rothwell, 'The Law of the Sea and the MV Tampa Incident: Reconciling Maritime Principles with Coastal State Sovereignty' (2002) 13 *Public Law Review* 118–27, discussing Australia's actions in 2001 towards the Norwegian-flagged MV *Tampa* which had rescued persons at sea who were seeking asylum in Australia.

[98] Joyce Chia, Jane McAdam and Kate Purcell, 'Asylum in Australia: "Operation Sovereign Borders" and International Law' (2014) 32 *Australian Year Book of International Law* 33.

[99] Ban Ki-moon, 'Statement: Statement Attributable to the Spokesman for the Secretary-General on the Situation in the Andaman Seas and the Straits of Malacca' United Nations Secretary-General (17 May 2015) at www.un,org/sg/statements/index.asp?nid=8635.

an impact not only upon the living resources within the area, but the overall health of the marine environment. Prima facie a coastal state is able to implement rigorous marine environmental protection provisions which apply within its territorial sea consistent with its sovereignty over the area. This would extend to the declaration of marine protected areas, reserves and parks, the closure of commercial and recreational fishing areas, the imposition of moratoria upon seabed mining activities, and special protection for areas such as reefs and sites with underwater cultural significance such as indigenous sites and historic wrecks, and ships routeing and reporting measures.

A coastal state will have little difficulty in applying and enforcing these provisions against its own nationals, including its own flagged vessels, and also its own military forces. However, challenges arise in uniformly applying similar provisions to foreign flagged vessels because of the innocent passage provisions of the LOSC. Nevertheless, Article 21 makes clear that the coastal state has considerable capacity to regulate many of these activities even when foreign ships are engaged in innocent passage, though in some instances there is a need for conformity with the generally accepted international rules or standards which are found in the principal international conventions. The most relevant of these is the 1973/1978 International Convention for the Prevention of Pollution from Ships (MARPOL 73/78),[100] which establishes the international regime for the regulation of ship-sourced marine pollution. Whilst MARPOL has been the subject of ongoing modification to reflect enhanced environmental standards and safeguards, there nevertheless remain some issues as to whether coastal states may impose stricter requirements, consistent with Article 21 of the LOSC.[101] In this regard, while the LOSC respects the capacity of the coastal state to exercise its sovereignty in the territorial sea with respect to marine pollution, the innocent passage of foreign vessels must not be hampered.[102]

Coastal states also possess absolute rights to regulate all resource activity within the territorial sea. This recognises the capacity of the coastal state to enjoy its sovereign rights over all of the resources which are found within the area—which extends to both the living and non-living resources. Occasionally the capacity to fully enjoy these rights may be impacted upon by the territorial sea of an adjoining state and it may be appropriate in those instances for joint development areas to be agreed upon in recognition of the shared resources.[103] In the case of non-living resources, the coastal states may seek to regulate the exploration, exploitation and development of those resources in whatever manner that it sees fit. It may grant exclusive access to its own nationals or it may license foreign miners to undertake that task in which case there are no constraints upon the royalties that may be levied by the coastal state. The only factor which a coastal state would need to take into account would be the potential for such mining activities to result in transboundary pollution thereby incurring state responsibility as a result of the activities having occurred within its territory. Likewise, in the case of living resources the coastal state is also able to completely regulate the conservation and exploitation of those resources entirely as it sees fit, consistent with its own environmental and resource policies. In doing so it may

[100] *Basic Documents* No 21.
[101] Erik Jaap Molenaar, *Coastal State Jurisdiction over Vessel-Source Marine Pollution* (The Hague, Kluwer Law International, 1998) 201; also relevant is LOSC, art 211(4). See further ch 15.
[102] LOSC, art 211(4).
[103] *Grisbådarna (Norway and Sweden)* (1909) 11 RIAA 147.

issue licences and permits to its own nationals to conduct such an activity, either on a commercial or recreational basis, or it may seek to provide access rights to foreign nationals by way of bilateral or regional arrangements. Unlike the EEZ regime, the coastal state has no obligations towards third states in relation to fishing access. An exception may apply in the case of historic waters, which would also include those waters within an historic bay, where they may exist long-standing rights of foreign state access to fish stocks which remain notwithstanding the waters in question being either territorial sea or internal waters.

Finally, as the coastal state is recognised as having sovereignty with respect to marine scientific research (MSR) within the territorial sea, there is no obligation to grant third states access to the territorial sea to conduct MSR. Of course, this does not prevent a coastal state from expressly permitting other states to conduct MSR either independently, or in cooperation with the coastal state. Indeed the facilitation of MSR would be entirely consistent with the general principles found within the LOSC promoting MSR and international cooperation to that end.[104]

C. Innocent and Transit Passage

One of the most long-standing areas of contention with respect to the territorial sea regime has been the right of foreign vessels to enter the territorial sea and navigate within it.[105] The modern international law of the sea reflects these rights in two ways. The first is the right of innocent passage which generally applies to foreign vessels within the territorial sea. The second is the right of transit passage which applies within the territorial sea of an international strait which is subject to overlapping territorial sea from the adjoining coasts. These rights of passage are long-standing, and have undergone significant refinement in the LOSC. Notwithstanding the development of the law, there remains variable state practice with respect to these territorial sea navigation rights which are partly reflected in Declarations made accompanying signature or ratification of the LOSC. For present purposes it can be observed that a number of states seek to place significant constraints upon the ability of certain vessels to enjoy innocent passage consistent with the LOSC. For example, Bangladesh, Egypt and Malaysia do not permit nuclear-powered ships or those carrying nuclear or other inherently dangerous or noxious substances from entering their territorial sea without prior authorisation.[106] China, Iran and Oman, likewise impose a prior notification requirement upon warships seeking to pass through the territorial sea.[107] This position remains contested, and is not only evident in contrary positions reflected in Declarations made by other states,[108] but also through protest and assertions of navigational freedoms within the territorial sea.[109]

---

[104] LOSC, arts 239, 242.

[105] See detailed consideration of these issues in chs 10 and 11.

[106] Bangladesh (27 July 2001); Egypt (26 August 1983), Malaysia (14 October 1996), 'Declarations and Statements' at www.un.org/Depts/los/convention_agreements/convention_declarations.htm.

[107] China (7 June 1996); Iran (10 December 1982); Oman (1 July 1983), 'Declarations and Statements' at www.un.org/Depts/los/convention_agreements/convention_declarations.htm; discussed in more detail in ch 12.

[108] Germany (14 October 1994); Netherlands (28 June 1996), ibid, stating that: 'None of the provisions of the Convention, which in so far [as they] reflect existing international law, can be regarded as entitling the coastal State to make the innocent passage of any specific category of foreign ships dependent on prior consent or notification'.

[109] Roach and Smith, *Excessive Maritime Claims* (n 82) 226–66, outlining the United States position and its response with respect to these claims.

However, there is a strong sense that the counter-balancing of a 12 nm territorial sea with rights of innocent and transit passage was an essential part of the 'package deal' of the LOSC which reflected in this particular instance the differing views of coastal and maritime states. As Germany highlighted in its Declaration to the LOSC, '[a] prerequisite for the recognition of the coastal state's right to extend the territorial sea is the regime of transit passage through straits used for international navigation' and accordingly there is an expectation from those states which made concessions on these issues during UNCLOS III that commitments reflected in the LOSC will be honoured. Notwithstanding the navigational rights granted to foreign shipping within a coastal state's territorial sea, the coastal state nevertheless retains significant rights so as the maintain its sovereignty and national security. It has a capacity to apply and enforce its laws against foreign merchant shipping, and has a limited right to temporarily suspend innocent passage.[110] Given the various positions on this issue and their sensitivity, navigation rights within the territorial sea will remain a law of the sea flashpoint for some time to come.

One exceptional right which exists under customary international law and the LOSC for ships to enter the territorial sea on a temporary basis is to provide assistance to vessels in distress or persons in jeopardy at sea. The right of 'assistance entry' is founded upon fundamental practices of the sea to provide humanitarian assistance to persons in distress and can generally be found in the Article 98 duty to render assistance to ships and persons at sea, and also in the 1974 International Convention for the Safety of Life at Sea.[111] Article 18(2) of the LOSC likewise recognises an exception to passage through the territorial sea when assistance is being rendered to persons, ships or aircraft in distress. This practice is also reflected in the doctrine of some navies which recognise the right of assistance entry into the territorial sea of a foreign coastal state.[112]

VI. Contiguous Zone

In addition to the territorial sea, state practice had throughout the early part of the twentieth century begun to recognise some level of coastal state jurisdiction in offshore areas for the purposes of enforcing a specific collection of laws and regulations relating to matters such as customs laws which, among other things, were designed to prevent the smuggling of unlawful goods and contraband through coastal waters. Some foundation for this practice can be found in the British Hovering Acts which were adopted in the eighteenth century and applied 'beyond the range of canon' so as to prohibit foreign ships from 'hovering' or anchoring at sea so as to provide a base for illegal activities ashore.[113] The United States was also a strong proponent of this type of jurisdiction being exercised within the high seas, having enacted laws as early as 1799 providing for a right to interdict ships bound for

---

[110] LOSC, art 25 (3).

[111] *Basic Documents* No 22.

[112] AR Thomas and James C Duncan (eds), 'Annotated Supplement to The Commanders Handbook on the Law of Naval Operations' (1999) 73 *International Legal Studies* 120, outlining United States practice.

[113] O'Connell, *The International Law of the Sea*, vol 1 (n 12) 90.

a United States port in order to inspect the manifest.[114] In 1891 the Supreme Court of the United States observed with respect to state jurisdiction only extending to the edge of the territorial sea that 'all governments, for the purpose of self-protection in time of war or for the prevention of frauds on its revenue, exercise an authority beyond this limit',[115] and the extent of United States extra-territorial jurisdiction with respect to liquor smuggling so as to deal with 'rum runners' gained particular notoriety during the 'Prohibition era' between 1919 and 1933.[116] At the 1930 Hague Conference this influenced debate upon a 'contiguous zone' which in turn was considered by the ILC.

A. ILC

Consistent with the manner in which the ILC conducted its analysis of the law of the sea regime, the contiguous zone was seen as part of the regime of the high seas. This is because the contiguous zone partly overlaps the high seas, and also raises issues of hot pursuit on to the high seas for the infringement of relevant laws within the contiguous zone. The ILC at an early stage of its deliberations considered a contiguous zone, and recommended the recognition of such a zone in ILC draft Article 66. The ILC made clear that the zone would be within the high seas and 'contiguous' to the territorial sea but would not extend beyond 12 nm from the baselines of the territorial sea. Within the zone draft Article 66 acknowledged the capacity of the coastal state to 'prevent infringement' of customs, fiscal or sanitary laws and regulations within the territorial sea, and to 'punish infringement' of these laws and regulations when they had taken place within the territory of the coastal state or its territorial sea.[117]

The ILC's commentary on the contiguous zone is illuminating in that it makes clear that despite designating the area as a new and distinctive jurisdictional 'zone', it is described as a 'belt of the high seas' in which the legal status of the waters is essentially unchanged.[118] As such, the zone is not one in which a coastal state exercises sovereignty but rather only has 'rights', and this in the view of the ILC was reflective of state practice at the time. Notwithstanding the views of some coastal states, the Commission did not support the contiguous zone as being one which conferred special security rights in the coastal state, or as a zone in which special fishing rights were conferred.[119] There appeared to be little debate within the ILC that on the basis of state practice the contiguous zone could not exceed 12 nm.

B. UNCLOS I and the Geneva Convention

Despite the fractious debates at UNCLOS I regarding the breadth of the territorial sea and whether recognition should be granted to a distinctive fishing zone, the contiguous zone as

---

[114] Philip C Jessup, *The Law of Territorial Waters and Maritime Jurisdiction* (New York, Jennings, 1927, 1970 rep) 80.
[115] *Manchester v Massachusetts* (1891) 139 US 240, 258.
[116] Jessup, *The Law of Territorial Waters and Maritime Jurisdiction* (n 114) 211–38.
[117] International Law Commission, 'Articles Concerning the Law of the Sea with Commentaries', art 66.
[118] Ibid 294.
[119] Ibid 294–95.

recommended by the ILC remained unchallenged. It was ultimately recognised as a distinctive maritime zone within the 1958 Convention on Territorial Sea and Contiguous Zone, with the title of the new convention reflecting the recognition now being granted to this maritime zone. Article 24 of the Convention was therefore the first time the contiguous zone had been codified in contemporary international law. The fact that it was not located in the Convention on the High Seas[120] highlighted the view that its principal operational focus as a zone supplemented the territorial sea regime, both with respect to law enforcement and in protecting the rights and interests of the coastal state.

The zone was affirmed as one which could not extend more then 12 nm from the territorial sea baseline,[121] which given the ongoing debates as to the breadth of the territorial sea is remarkable, as in some instances it meant a coastal state would have had no distinctive entitlement to a contiguous zone if it also claimed a 12 nm territorial sea. The zone was also affirmed as being within the high seas and contiguous to the territorial sea, and no reference is made to any form of sovereignty being exercised over this area other than the limited jurisdictional control provided for. The power to prevent and punish infringement of a narrow band of laws remained in Article 24. However, UNCLOS I elected to expand the scope of the provision beyond customs, fiscal and sanitary laws to also include immigration matters.[122] Finally, Article 24 also addressed the issue of the delimitation of contiguous zones between opposite and adjacent states.[123]

C. UNCLOS III and the LOSC

The status of the contiguous zone was not up for debate at UNCLOS II, and the failure to resolve the outer limit of the territorial sea and ongoing issues regarding the status of a distinctive fishing zone resulted in minimal attention being given to the contiguous zone during the 1960s. The resolution of these outstanding issues at UNCLOS III meant that it was possible to retain the contiguous zone in the LOSC, though there was some debate during the early stages of UNCLOS III as to whether the expanded breadth of the territorial sea and the proposed EEZ would render the need for a contiguous zone superfluous.[124] During the second session of the conference in 1974, by which time it was becoming clear that the outer limit of the territorial sea would be 12 nm, the view firmed that the distinctive nature of the contiguous zone, which gave to the coastal state an additional form of jurisdiction that was quite separate from that being envisaged for the EEZ, was one that should be retained. Accordingly, the conference agreed to recognise the contiguous zone in the LOSC,

---

[120] *Basic Documents* No 10.

[121] Convention on the Territorial Sea and Contiguous Zone, art 24(2).

[122] The inclusion of immigration within the category of contiguous zone laws and regulations had been considered but ultimately rejected by the ILC: International Law Commission, 'Articles Concerning the Law of the Sea with Commentaries', 295.

[123] Convention on the Territorial Sea and Contiguous Zone, art 24(3).

[124] *Virginia Commentaries*, vol 2, 269.

essentially duplicating Article 24 of the Convention on the Territorial Sea and Contiguous Zone as Article 33 of the LOSC, with an expansion of its breadth to 24 nm.[125]

Article 33 of the LOSC differs in three ways to its previous incarnation as Article 24 of the Geneva Convention. First, the zone is described as being contiguous to the territorial sea. This reflects the fact that under the LOSC both the EEZ and the continental shelf regime are also adjacent to the outer limit of the territorial sea and accordingly the previous connection that existed between the contiguous zone and the high seas no longer remain. Secondly, there is no direct reference made to the delimitation of overlapping contiguous zone claims. This is in recognition of the fact that any coastal state maritime claims beyond 12 nm would not only possibly encompass a contiguous zone, but also most certainly an EEZ/continental shelf and as such the contiguous zone would be delimited as part of a 'multi-zone' single maritime boundary between the states.[126] Thirdly, Article 303(2) creates a legal fiction whereby coastal state laws applicable to customs, fiscal, immigration and sanitary matters are also extended to the removal of archaeological and historical objects found on the seabed within the contiguous zone.[127]

D. State Practice

In 2011, a total of 90 states claimed a contiguous zone, of which 83 (92 per cent) claimed a 24 nm zone. Those states which claimed a contiguous zone less than the permitted limit were Finland (14 nm), Venezuela (15 nm), Bangladesh, Gambia, Saudi Arabia and Sudan (18 nm). Lithuania had a claim based on coordinates of points, while the Democratic People's Republic of Korea (DPRK) claimed a 50 nm military zone.[128] Compared to all of the other maritime zones which coastal states are entitled to assert under the LOSC, the contiguous zone is the least popular and this is highlighted when it is considered that 152 coastal states claim a territorial sea but that only 59 per cent of those same states also assert a contiguous zone. There may be multiple reasons why some states have not opted to proclaim a contiguous zone, though since the 1990s there has been an upward trend in contiguous zone claims. In 1996 Roach and Smith identified 66 states claiming a contiguous zone,[129] and this trend, reflecting a 36 per cent increase in claims over 15 years to 2011, may be directly related to the increased concerns regarding maritime security in the wake of the 11 September 2001 terrorist attacks upon the United States.

---

[125] See generally regarding this history, and the development of the concept of the contiguous zone: AV Lowe, 'The Development of the Concept of the Contiguous Zone' (1981) 52 *British Yearbook of International Law* 109.

[126] There is minimal state practice in the delimitation of contiguous zone maritime boundaries; David Colson, 'The Legal Regime of Maritime Boundary Arrangements' in Jonathan I Charney and Lewis M Alexander (eds), *International Maritime Boundaries*, vol 1 (Dordrecht, Martinus Nijhoff, 1993) 41, 42.

[127] See discussion in Mariano J Aznar, 'The Contiguous Zone as an Archaeological Maritime Zone' (2014) 29 *International Journal of Marine and Coastal Law* 1.

[128] See United Nations Division of Ocean Affairs and Law of the Sea, 'Table of claims to maritime jurisdiction (as at 15 July 2011)' at www.un.org/Depts/los/convention_agreements/convention_declarations.htm.

[129] Roach and Smith, *Excessive Maritime Claims* (n 82) 151.

Contiguous zone jurisdiction is specifically related to outward and inward bound movement of ships. With respect to inward bound ships, the coastal state has within its contiguous zone the capacity to 'prevent infringement' of customs, fiscal, immigration and sanitary laws and regulations. Importantly, the contiguous zone does not confer upon the coastal state the extended operation of its laws and regulations in these fields and accordingly the entry into the contiguous zone of a vessel engaged in people smuggling for example could not be subject to coastal state law enforcement operations, but could result in the interdiction of the vessel and its removal from the contiguous zone.[130] This is reflective of state practice in this area with some coastal states using their navy to interdict these vessels and tow them out beyond the contiguous zone into the EEZ. Detaining a vessel within the contiguous zone that had entered the zone from the adjoining EEZ and which was not subject to arrest or investigation presents another fact scenario, which on its face would be beyond coastal state jurisdiction. In that regard, when a coastal state goes about seeking to 'prevent infringement' it needs to take into account the freedom of navigation which vessels enjoy within the contiguous zone, as it overlaps with the EEZ in which high seas freedoms of navigational apply.[131]

In the case of outbound ships, the contiguous zone confers upon the coastal state the capacity to 'punish infringement' of laws and regulations relating to customs, fiscal, immigration and sanitary matters which occurred within its territory or the territorial sea. This gives to the coastal state additional enforcement capacity with respect to these matters that circumvent some of the constraints that operate when exercising the right of hot pursuit in equivalent law enforcement operations. Therefore, ships seeking to flee from the jurisdiction of the coastal state following an infringement of those laws do not enjoy any form of effective immunity by virtue of the fact that they have reached the territorial sea limit.

While the contiguous zone does provide to the coastal state enhanced enforcement capacity, it is not a general security zone. The Unites States has been very proactive in protesting what is considers to be excessive claims made by coastal states with respect to any security dimension associated with the territorial sea that go beyond what is permissible under Article 33.[132] China's 1992 Law on the Territorial Sea and Contiguous Zone, for example, sought to confer jurisdiction within the contiguous zone to prevent or punish with respect to security laws and regulations.[133]

---

[130] In 2015 the High Court of Australia observed with respect to the capacity of the coastal state within the contiguous zone: 'It may be accepted that exercising the control necessary to prevent infringement of laws of the kind described in Art 33 of UNCLOS would include a coastal state stopping in its contiguous zone an inward-bound vessel reasonably suspected of being involved in an intended contravention of one of those laws. Because there must be a power to stop the vessel, it may be accepted that there is a power to detain the vessel (at least for the purposes of investigating whether there is a threat of a relevant contravention). But whether, for the purposes of international law, Art 33 permits the coastal state to take persons on the vessel into its custody or to take command of the vessel or tow it out of the contiguous zone remains controversial': *CPCF v Minister for Immigration and Border Protection* [2015] HCA 1, [79] per Hayne and Bell JJ.

[131] LOSC, art 58(1).

[132] Roach and Smith, *Excessive Maritime Claims* (n 82) 154–57, referring to United States protests with respect to aspects of the contiguous zone claims made by Bangladesh, Burma, China, Pakistan, Sri Lanka, Sudan, Syria, Venezuela, Vietnam and Yemen.

[133] Kim, 'The 1992 Chinese Territorial Sea Law' (n 94) 903.

VII. Further Reading

Philip C Jessup, *The Law of Territorial Waters and Maritime Jurisdiction* (New York, Jennings, 1927)

AV Lowe, 'The Development of the Concept of the Contiguous Zone' (1981) 52 *British Yearbook of International Law* 109

John E Noyes, 'The Territorial Sea and Contiguous Zone' in Donald R Rothwell, Alex G Oude Elferink, Karen N Scott and Tim Stephens (eds), *The Oxford Handbook of the Law of the Sea* (Oxford, Oxford University Press, 2015) 91

DP O'Connell, *The International Law of the Sea*, vol 1 (Oxford, Clarendon Press, 1982)

J Ashley Roach and Robert W Smith, *Excessive Maritime Claims*, 3rd edn (The Hague, Martinus Nijhoff, 2012)

4

The Exclusive Economic Zone

I. Introduction

The EEZ established by the LOSC is a comparatively recent innovation in the law of the sea, which confers upon coastal states sovereign rights for the purpose of exploring and exploiting, conserving and managing, the living and non-living resources of the water column, seabed and subsoil to a distance of 200 nm. A major impetus in the development of this zone was the ambition of southern states for a new international economic order in which they would obtain a fair share of coastal marine resources, including both living and non-living resources. Another justification for the EEZ was the expectation that it would address the tragedy of the oceanic commons resulting from the unregulated exploitation of marine living resources. As the majority of the world's fisheries are found within 200 nm of coastlines, it was hoped that the enclosure of large swathes of the high seas within EEZs would lead to more effective resource management by assigning resource rights to the states which were best placed to regulate them and which valued them most.[1] The continuing poor state of wild ocean fisheries globally, three quarters of which are fished at, or beyond, sustainable limits,[2] attests to the fact that the high expectations of the EEZ as a mechanism for sustainable fisheries management have not yet been attained.[3] Also unrealised have been the economic aspirations of many coastal states that have been unable to develop endogenous fishing industries to exploit their new resources. Instead many continue to rely on limited economic returns from access fees received from distant water fishing fleets, and have found it difficult to manage their EEZs effectively.[4]

The customary international law status of the EEZ was recognised by the ICJ in 1984,[5] and in 1985 the ICJ concluded in *Continental Shelf (Libyan Arab Jamahiriya/Malta)* that

---

[1] For an analysis of the economic logic of the EEZ regime see Eric A Posner and Alan O Sykes, 'Economic Foundations of the Law of the Sea', John M Olin Law and Economics Working Paper No 504, December 2009, ssrn.com/abstract=1524274.

[2] Food and Agriculture Organization, *The State of World Fisheries and Aquaculture* (Rome, FAO, 2006) 36.

[3] Richard Barnes, 'The Convention on the Law of the Sea: An Effective Framework for Domestic Fisheries Conservation' in David Freestone, Richard Barnes and David M Ong (eds), *The Law of the Sea: Progress and Prospects* (Oxford, Oxford University Press, 2006) 233. See also ch 13.

[4] Tim Stephens, 'Fishing-Led Development in the South Pacific: Charting a Pacific Way to a Sustainable Future' (2008) 39 *Ocean Development and International Law* 257.

[5] *Delimitation of the Maritime Boundary in the Gulf of Maine (Canada/United States of America)* [1984] ICJ Rep 246, [94].

'the institution of the EEZ with its rule on entitlement by reason of distance is shown by the practice of states to have become part of customary law'.[6] That the ICJ was prepared to confer this status upon the EEZ within three years of the LOSC being concluded reflects the rapid acceptance of the EEZ concept through state practice at that time. While to some extent problematic in its implementation, the EEZ concept and regime established by the LOSC nonetheless represents a revolutionary development in the law of the sea, bringing around one-third of ocean space within coastal state jurisdiction. Not only does the EEZ effect an extension of coastal state resource rights seawards, it also establishes a new capacity for coastal states to protect and preserve the marine environment from pollution and other environmental threats out to 200 nm. In recent years there has also been a discernible trend to give the EEZ a security emphasis, with several states purporting to restrict navigational freedoms in their EEZs on account of national security concerns such as terrorism, weapons proliferation, piracy and people trafficking.[7] This illustrates the ongoing tension that surrounds the EEZ regime in which coastal states and other states enjoy a range of shared rights and duties, not all of which are defined clearly by the LOSC. In this respect, Shearer has remarked that, in addition to high seas fisheries and marine environmental protection, the main 'unfinished business' of the LOSC is settling the juridical character of the EEZ as a distinctive maritime zone that is *sui generis* and *sui juris*.[8]

II. The Concept of the EEZ

The EEZ concept first acquired clear legal definition in Part V of the LOSC, although it had been foreshadowed by developments in state practice before UNCLOS III was convened in 1973. The most important pre-UNCLOS III development was the assertion of EFZs. Several states had long-standing claims to EFZs, such as Iceland which had asserted an EFZ in 1948, and subsequently extended its claim in 1952 (from 3 to 4 nm), 1958 (to 12 nm) and 1971 (to 50 nm). Parallel with assertions of fisheries jurisdiction, other states also claimed jurisdiction over economic resources on appurtenant continental shelves, such as the United States through the 1945 Truman Proclamation.[9] In the *Fisheries Jurisdiction* case,[10] in which Germany and the United Kingdom contested Iceland's EFZ claims, the ICJ confirmed that an EFZ up to 12 nm from the baselines could be claimed consistently with customary international law as a *tertium genus* distinct from both the territorial sea and the high seas. Although many aspects of the decision in this case were soon overshadowed by rapidly developing state practice, the Court's encapsulation of the nature of an adjacent

---

[6] *Continental Shelf (Libyan Arab Jamahiriya/Malta)* [1985] ICJ Rep 13, [34].

[7] Jon M Van Dyke, 'The Disappearing Right to Navigational Freedom in the Exclusive Economic Zone' (2005) 29 *Marine Policy* 107, 121. See further ch 10.

[8] Ivan Shearer, 'Oceans Management Challenges for the Law of the Sea in the First Decade of the 21st Century' in Alex G Oude Elferink and Donald R Rothwell (eds), *Oceans Management in the 21st Century: Institutional Frameworks and Responses* (Leiden, Martinus Nijhoff, 2004) 10.

[9] Proclamation 2667, 'Policy of the United States With Respect to the Natural Resources of the Subsoil and Seabed of the Continental Shelf', 28 September 1945, *Basic Documents* No 5.

[10] *Fisheries Jurisdiction (United Kingdom v Iceland)* (merits) [1974] ICJ Rep 3; *(Germany v Iceland)* (merits) [1974] ICJ Rep 175.

EFZ remains an authoritative description of the essence of the EEZ as a novel maritime zone.

Developments in the emergence of the EEZ concept were brought to a head in state practice before the convening of UNCLOS III in 1974, with developing states rallying around a proposal by Kenya to the United Nations Seabed Committee for the EEZ to be a zone relating to all of the natural resources of adjacent seas, including the seabed and water column.[11] The proposal met with approval from major maritime states as it was conceived primarily as a jurisdictional zone, rather than one of absolute sovereignty, and therefore would not interfere with traditional high seas freedoms, except as regards access to living and non-living resources. This undermined claims by some Central and South American nations such as El Salvador, and African nations such as Benin, for a 200 nm territorial sea in which full coastal state sovereignty appeared to be asserted.[12] Moreover, the EEZ directly benefited several major maritime states such as Canada, Japan, Russia and the United States which were among the top ten states in terms of the area of ocean space that they could acquire as EEZ.[13] Throughout the 1970s and 1980s a range of states claimed EEZs or EFZs up to 200 nm, so that the concept of a 200 nm EEZ was generally recognised as part of customary international law well before the LOSC entered into force in 1994.[14]

The 200 nm outer-limit of the EEZ was accepted from the start of negotiations in UNCLOS III for the practical reason that it represented the most extensive claims then in existence, and not for geological, geographical, economic or ecological reasons. However, although this distance was settled upon mostly because of political expediency, it has in fact tended to coincide with the distribution of living and non-living resources. The vast majority of commercially exploitable fish stocks and submarine hydrocarbon resources are found within 200 nm of most coasts. Adjacent to some coastlines the resources are found further seawards, and during UNCLOS III early proposals by west European states sought a limit to the zone set by reference to geographical characteristics and fisheries resources.[15] However, this was rejected in favour of a clear demarcation line set up to a maximum claimable distance, for many of the same reasons that the definition of the continental shelf by reference to exploitability was discarded in negotiations in UNCLOS III on Part VI of the LOSC.

The LOSC sets out the regime for the EEZ in Part V. As with many aspects of the LOSC that draw upon one or more of the 1958 Geneva Conventions, the drafters of Part V were able to refer to the 1958 Geneva Convention on the Continental Shelf[16] in relation to some aspects of the EEZ. In other respects there was no guidance, as the EEZ represented an important innovation, especially as regards jurisdiction over environmental matters, and hence many features of the EEZ regime had to be fashioned anew.

The EEZ combines characteristics of the territorial sea and the high seas, but cannot be assimilated to either. It is a *sui generis* zone with its own distinctive regime. Unlike the territorial sea it is not an area in which coastal states have a plenary and *ipso jure* entitlement

---

[11] Lawrence Juda, *International Law and Ocean Management: The Evolution of Ocean Governance* (London, Routledge, 1996) 195.

[12] Ibid 215.

[13] Lewis M Alexander and Robert D Hodgson, 'The Impact of the 200-Mile Economic Zone on the Law of the Sea' (1974–1975) 12 *San Diego Law Review* 569, 574–575.

[14] Over 60 states had claimed 200 EEZs or EFZs prior to 1982.

[15] *Virginia Commentaries*, vol 2, 549.

[16] *Basic Documents* No 12.

to sovereignty, and in contrast to the high seas it is not a zone in which other states have unfettered freedoms. It is an amalgam, or 'multifunctional' zone, in which coastal states enjoy sovereign rights in relation to economic resources, and also jurisdiction not only in relation to these rights but also for certain other matters, including environmental protection.[17]

For most of the history of the law of the sea this intermediate ocean space between the *mare liberum* and the *mare clausum* would have been inconceivable;[18] however, the EEZ successfully melds aspects of both sovereign rights (ownership or *dominium*) and jurisdiction (competence or *imperium*) in what Article 55 of the LOSC describes as a 'specific legal regime'. It is one that has proved remarkably durable and free from major controversy, although in recent times the EEZ regime has been subject to the phenomenon of 'creeping jurisdiction',[19] whereby a number of coastal states have sought gradually to extend the scope of their jurisdiction in the EEZ beyond matters of a resource or environmental character.

III. Breadth of the EEZ and its Relationship with Other Maritime Zones

The EEZ is established by the LOSC as a claimable maritime zone, which sets it apart from the continental shelf which vests inherently in coastal states. This is made clear in Article 57, which indicates that states may claim an EEZ up to 200 nm from the baselines from which the breadth of the territorial sea is measured. If a state does claim an EEZ of 200 nm this means that the zone is constituted by a band of waters, seabed and subsoil that is effectively 188 nm in breadth (taking into account the 12 nm territorial sea).[20]

Most states, including non-parties to the LOSC, have claimed an EEZ to the 200 nm limit, and many have passed legislation applicable in these waters to give effect to Part V.[21] As of 15 July 2011, 132 of the 152 coastal states in the international community had made EEZ claims.[22] None of these claims exceeded 200 nm, whether made by parties or non-parties to the LOSC.[23] States are free to claim an EEZ of lesser breadth than 200 nm if they wish, and also to assert less than the full complement of rights afforded by the EEZ regime. The United Kingdom did not proclaim an EEZ until 2014, preferring to keep in place a 200 nm EFZ for most of the British Isles on the grounds that an EFZ accorded sufficient protection

---

[17] Barbara Kwiatkowska, *The 200 Mile Exclusive Economic Zone in the New Law of the Sea* (Dordrecht, Martinus Nijhoff, 1989) 4.

[18] DP O'Connell, *The International Law of the Sea*, vol 1 (Oxford, Clarendon Press, 1982) 15.

[19] On the concept of 'creeping jurisdiction' see Erik Franckx, 'The 200-mile Limit: Between Creeping Jurisdiction and Creeping Common Heritage?' (2007) 39 *George Washington International Law Review* 467, 476.

[20] Note also that if a coastal state claims a contiguous zone of 12 nm beyond the limits of the territorial sea, as permitted by Article 33, then the second 12 nm of the EEZ will overlap with the contiguous zone.

[21] For a summary of the state practice in relation to EEZ claims see *Basic Documents* App 3.

[22] United Nations Division of Ocean Affairs and Law of the Sea, 'Table of Claims to Maritime Jurisdiction (as at 15 July 2011)' at www.un.org/Depts/los/convention_agreements/convention_declarations.htm. States that have not claimed an EEZ include Albania, Ecuador, El Salvador, Greece, Iraq, Jordon, Kuwait, Peru and Sudan.

[23] Robin Churchill, 'The Impact of State Practice on the Jurisdictional Framework Contained in the LOS Convention' in Alex G Oude Elferink (ed), *Stability and Change in the Law of the Sea: The Role of the LOS Convention* (Leiden, Martinus Nijhoff, 2005) 91, 126.

of its water column resource rights and that its access to, and management of, non-living seabed resources was adequately guaranteed by the continental shelf regime applicable in Part VI of the LOSC.[24]

It may also be noted in relation to the seaward limits of the EEZ that the 200 nm maximum will not be able to be reached in certain places where the distance between opposite coastal states is less than 400 nm. In such circumstances, and also for adjacent states which both maintain EEZ claims, a maritime boundary will need to be delimited in accordance with the procedure and principles set out in Article 74 of the LOSC.[25] The potential for overlapping EEZs in enclosed or semi-enclosed seas such as the Mediterranean Sea[26] and Adriatic Sea[27] has given rise to significant disputes at a political level as to how best to manage the waters of these ocean spaces pending delimitation of a boundary. In these areas, and other places where potential EEZ areas overlap, disputes have been avoided or provisionally put to one side through coastal states partially implementing the EEZ regime, or entering into agreements for the joint management of living and non-living resources.[28]

A claim to an EEZ may be projected from the baselines from which the breadth of the territorial sea is measured. This therefore encompasses claims from normal and straight baselines, and bay closing lines, drawn along coastlines consistent with Part II of the LOSC. The regime for archipelagic states established in Part IV of the LOSC also allows for an EEZ to be claimed from archipelagic baselines drawn in conformity with Article 47, which has allowed many archipelagic states, such as a number of Pacific microstates, to acquire economic sovereignty over areas of ocean space vastly greater in area than their land masses. For instance Tuvalu, with a land area of a mere 26 square kilometres, has an EEZ of 900,000 square kilometres.

The only exceptions to the capacity of coastal states to claim an EEZ from their territory relates to artificial islands, installations and structures (LOSC, Article 60(8)), and 'rocks which cannot sustain human habitation or economic life of their own' (Article 121(3)). Such 'rocks', when not forming part of an archipelago, are deprived of the capacity to generate either an EEZ or a continental shelf, on the grounds that economic zones should not apply or inhere to territory that itself lacks any capacity for economic productivity. In practice, however, states have maintained, largely without protest, EEZ claims around remote and uninhabited islands and asserted the full range of sovereign and jurisdictional rights under the LOSC. Examples in this regard include the sub-Antarctic island territories of Australia (Heard and McDonald Islands, and Macquarie Island) and France (Kerguelen Island).[29]

---

[24] Only six states maintain EFZs: Algeria, Denmark (for Greenland and the Faroe Islands), Gambia, Malta, Papua New Guinea and Spain (in the Mediterranean Sea); United Nations Division of Ocean Affairs and Law of the Sea, 'Table of Claims' (n 22). See Shalva Kvinikhidze, 'Contemporary Exclusive Fishery Zones or Why Some States Still Claim an EFZ' (2008) 23 *International Journal of Marine and Coastal Law* 271.

[25] See ch 16.

[26] Angela Del Vecchio Capotosti, '*In Maiore Stat Minus:* A Note on the EEZ and the Zones of Ecological Protection in the Mediterranean Sea' (2008) 39 *Ocean Development and International Law* 287.

[27] Davor Vidas, 'The UN Convention on the Law of the Sea, the European Sea and the Rule of Law: What is Going on in the Adriatic Sea?' (2009) 24 *International Journal of Marine and Coastal Law* 1.

[28] In relation to the East China Sea for instance see the 1997 Japan-China Fisheries Agreement. See Mark J Valencia and Yoshihisa Amae, 'Regime Building in the East China Sea' (2003) 34 *Ocean Development and International Law* 189.

[29] In relation to the EEZs of several of these islands Australia and France have carried out enforcement action against IUU fishing vessels which has given rise to several cases in ITLOS, in the course of which no serious doubt has been cast on the legitimacy of these EEZ. The exception has been a lone dissentient, Judge Vukas, who has

A different situation has been encountered in relation to much smaller islets that are truly 'rocks', such as Rockall in the North Atlantic that is less than 0.1 hectare, and around which the United Kingdom relinquished an EEZ claim in 1997 on acceding to the LOSC.

Article 121(3) of the LOSC is somewhat of an anomalous provision as it applies only to 'rocks', and not to more substantial territory that may be as incapable of sustaining human habitation or economic life as a remote islet. Antarctica presents an obvious example in this respect, although the effects of global warming may change this in the longer term, particularly for the Antarctic Peninsula, the northernmost part of the Antarctic mainland, which is one of the fastest warming places on earth.[30] In any event Antarctica is a special case by virtue of the 1959 Antarctic Treaty, Article IV of which provides that 'no new claim, or enlargement of an existing claim, to territorial sovereignty in Antarctica shall be asserted'. This formulation is designed to put on hold any contest over sovereignty in Antarctica, and thereby allow states to cooperate in the protection of the continent and its surrounding seas up to 60 degrees south latitude. As the EEZ concept was not accepted until after the Antarctic Treaty entered into force in 1961, proclamations of Antarctic EEZ areas by three of the seven claimants to territory in Antarctica (Argentina, Australia and Chile) could be said to amount to an impermissible enlargement of an existing claim or assertion of a new claim.[31] In practice, however, these three states, and other parties to the Antarctic Treaty, have not exercised jurisdictional rights in these EEZs to their full extent, and have instead cooperated in the management of the marine living resources of the Southern Ocean collectively on the basis of the 1980 Convention on the Conservation of Antarctic Marine Living Resources.

IV. Coastal State Rights and Obligations in the EEZ

In Part V the LOSC draws a distinction between the rights enjoyed by, and duties incumbent on, two categories of state: coastal states and other states. It deals fairly extensively with each, in specifying the content of their relevant rights and duties in the EEZ. However, it does not do so exhaustively, and Article 59 addresses the possibility that certain rights and jurisdiction will be asserted that are not specifically attributed by the LOSC to coastal states or other states. Article 59 directs that if a conflict arises between the interests of a coastal state and another state in relation to unregulated matters in the EEZ then the dispute should be resolved 'on the basis of equity and in light of all relevant circumstances', including the 'importance of the interests involved to the parties' and to 'the international community as a whole'.

---

argued that these islands fall within the exception in Article 121(3), LOS Convention: *Monte Confurco (Seychelles v France)* (prompt release) (2000) 125 ILR 203, 254, *Volga (Russian Federation v Australia)* (prompt release) (2003) 42 ILM 159, 179–80.

[30] J Bockheim et al, 'Climate Warming and Permafrost Dynamics in the Antarctic Peninsula Region' (2013) 100 *Global and Planetary Change* 215.

[31] Donald R Rothwell, *The Polar Regions and the Development of International Law* (Cambridge, Cambridge University Press, 1996) 280–81.

This is an open-ended formulation,[32] which can only be given meaning by concrete practice through agreement between states, or through guidance by arbitration or judicial determination pursuant to Part XV, in the event that a disagreement arises and is not settled by the parties. The words of Article 59 suggest that in the case of unattributed rights neither coastal nor other states are presumed to have priority. However, given the nature of the EEZ as a coastal state economic zone, Article 59 could conceivably be interpreted so that unattributed economic rights would usually fall to coastal states, while unattributed rights of a non-economic nature will fall to other states.[33] As some coastal states seek to expand their jurisdictional reach in the EEZ, Article 59 may prove to be increasingly significant in balancing the rights and interests of coastal and other states within the EEZ.

In relation to the rights attributed to coastal states, the key provision in Part V is Article 56 which accords to coastal states (1) sovereign rights for the purpose of exploring, exploiting, conserving and managing natural resources of the seabed, subsoil, and water column, (2) jurisdiction in relation to artificial structures, marine scientific research and environmental preservation and protection. The enjoyment of these sovereign and jurisdictional rights is obviously contingent on a coastal state claiming an EEZ (or EFZ in relation to fisheries rights alone), and these rights are exercisable only in relation to that claim.

A. Sovereign Rights

The sovereign rights of coastal states in the EEZ apply both to living and non-living resources.

i. Living Resources

Under Article 56 coastal states are accorded sovereign rights for the purpose of exploring, exploiting, conserving and managing the living resources of the water column, seabed and subsoil in the EEZ. The main significance of this is that the coastal state is thereby given exclusive sovereign rights over fisheries and extensive jurisdiction to regulate fishing in the EEZ.[34] The coastal state is given sole discretion in setting allowable catches for fisheries,[35] taking into account the best scientific evidence,[36] and the responsibility to conserve and manage fisheries so that they are not endangered by over-exploitation[37] while at the same time aiming towards their optimum utilisation.[38] Part V contains additional provisions in relation to specific types of fisheries (anadromous and catadromous species, marine mammals, straddling and highly migratory stocks), and specifically leaves sedentary species, that is those organisms constantly in contact with the seabed or subsoil, to be regulated under

---

[32] It is the only provision in the Convention to make specific reference to 'equity', as opposed to the more general term 'equitable' which is used in several contexts, including in relation to maritime boundary delimitation where the objective is to secure an 'equitable solution': arts 74(1), 83(1).

[33] *Virginia Commentaries*, vol 2, 569.

[34] See LOSC, art 62(4). See further ch 13.

[35] LOSC, art 61(1).

[36] Ibid art 61(2).

[37] Ibid art 61(3).

[38] Ibid art 62(1).

the continental shelf regime in Part VI.[39] In principle a coastal state is required to give access to other states to its EEZ living resources if it has insufficient capacity to harvest the allowable catch it has set,[40] with particular regard to landlocked, geographically disadvantaged and least developed states.[41] In practice, however, this right of access to the surplus accorded to foreign states is unenforceable because coastal state decisions determining the allowable catch, the extent of harvesting capacity, and the allocation of surpluses, fall within one of the few exceptions to the compulsory dispute settlement system set out in Part XV.[42]

Coastal states therefore have very close to plenary rights and jurisdiction in EEZ fisheries, an outcome that was sought by many newly independent states at UNCLOS III. They also have the capacity to regulate a wide array of activities connected with fishing consistent with Article 62. In the 2014 case of the *Virginia G*, ITLOS dealt with a dispute relating to bunkering activities of Panamanian flagged vessels in support of foreign vessels in the Guinea-Bissau EEZ.[43] At issue was whether Guinea-Bissau as the coastal state with sovereign rights over natural resources in the EEZ could regulate bunkering,[44] or whether bunkering was more properly characterised as an activity associated with the freedom of navigation. The tribunal held that Article 56 needed to be read together with the provisions on living resources in Articles 61 to 68,[45] and that there was a clear connection between bunkering and fishing activities as bunkering at sea allowed fishing activities to be continued without interruption.[46] On this point, the tribunal concluded that:

> the regulation by a coastal State of bunkering of foreign vessels in its exclusive economic zone is among those measures which the coastal State may take in its exclusive economic zone to conserve and manage its living resources under article 56 of the Convention read together with article 62, paragraph 4, of the Convention. This view is also confirmed by State practice which has developed after the adoption of the Convention.[47]

ii. Non-Living Resources

In relation to non-living resources found in the seabed and subsoil, the EEZ regime overlaps in its entirety with the continental shelf.[48] Under both the EEZ and continental shelf regimes coastal states enjoy essentially unrestricted rights of exploration and exploitation for non-living seabed resources such as hydrocarbons and minerals, without any obligation

---

[39] Ibid art 68.

[40] Ibid art 62(2).

[41] Ibid arts 69, 70.

[42] Ibid art 297(3).

[43] *M/V Virginia G (Panama/Guinea-Bissau)* (2014) 53 ILM 1164.

[44] Panama defined 'bunkering' as a 'term used in the shipping industry to describe the selling of fuel from specialised vessels, such as oil tankers, which supply fuel (such as light fuel, gas oil and marine diesel) to other vessels whilst at sea'; Guinea-Bissau accepted this description: ibid [162].

[45] Ibid [209].

[46] Ibid [215].

[47] Ibid [217]. In *M/V Saiga (No 1) (Saint Vincent and the Grenadines v Guinea)* (prompt release) (1997) 110 ILR 736, the first case before ITLOS, which related to the arrest of a bunkering vessel, ITLOS considered arguments that art 62(4) should extend to cover such ancillary activities, but did not come to a clear conclusion, stating at [63] that bunkering could 'arguably be classified' as a matter within coastal state EEZ jurisdiction. See also *M/V Saiga (No 2) (Saint Vincent and the Grenadines v Guinea)* (admissibility and merits) (1999) 120 ILR 143, [137]–[138].

[48] See ch 5.

of conservation or judicious use.[49] These non-living resource rights are exclusive in the fullest sense, and import no requirement for coastal states to share access, let alone any benefits from their exploitation. At UNCLOS III the Group of 77 called for a system of equitable distribution of these resources, arguing that coastal states should remit a percentage of economic returns from non-living resource exploitation in their EEZs to landlocked and geographically disadvantaged states. This proposal was not accepted.[50]

Another non-living economic resource in the EEZ receiving specific mention in Article 56(1)(a) is 'energy from the water, currents and winds'. Article 56 was drafted broadly, in the expectation that it would need to be able to embrace future scientific and technological developments, and this has proven to be the case as states develop renewable sources of energy in order to abate greenhouse gas emissions from fossil-fuel based energy sources. Parties to the LOSC may rely upon this provision for the granting of licenses in their EEZs for renewable energy facilities such as offshore tidal power generators, wave barrages and wind farms.[51] However, this is not an unlimited sovereign right, in that Article 56(2) makes clear that coastal states must have due regard to other states and act in a manner compatible with the Convention. In particular, coastal states will not be able to derogate from the freedom and safety of navigation, nor cause damage to the marine environment contrary to the obligations under Part XII of the LOSC, or more stringent regional regimes.

The EEZ and continental shelf regimes give sovereign rights to coastal states only over natural resources, and therefore do not extend to cover shipwrecks and other potentially significant cultural artefacts. The LOSC does not deal with shipwrecks in Part V, but instead provides in Article 303(2) that coastal states may exercise jurisdiction over archaeological and historical objects found within their contiguous zone. As such, any claim to title in, or jurisdiction over, underwater cultural heritage in the EEZ beyond the contiguous zone would need to be assessed by reference to Article 59, discussed above, which provides for an assessment of unattributed rights in the EEZ. The outcome of this process is uncertain,[52] and so to avoid doubt, and to ensure the adequate protection of shipwrecks wherever found, in 1993 the United Nations Educational, Scientific and Cultural Organization (UNESCO) initiated negotiations on what was to become the 2001 UNESCO Convention on the Protection of Underwater Cultural Heritage,[53] which entered into force in 2009. Article 10 of the UNESCO Convention addresses the protection of underwater cultural heritage in the EEZ and on the continental shelf, and has the effect of making coastal states 'Co-Ordinating States' for the purposes of protecting underwater cultural heritage 'on behalf of the States Parties as a whole and not in [their] own interest' (Article 10(6)).[54] Moreover the coastal state will, in certain circumstances, be empowered not only to lead

[49] See David M Ong, 'Towards an International Law for the Conservation of Offshore Hydrocarbon Resources within the Continental Shelf?' in David Freestone, Richard Barnes and David M Ong (eds), *The Law of the Sea: Progress and Prospects* (Oxford, Oxford University Press, 2006) 93.

[50] *Virginia Commentaries*, vol 1, 533.

[51] Karen N Scott, 'Tilting at Offshore Windmills: Regulating Wind Farm Development within the Renewable Energy Zone' (2005) 18 *Journal of Environmental Law* 89, 95–96.

[52] Although several states including Malaysia and Portugal have claimed jurisdiction over archaeological items in the EEZ: Churchill, 'The Impact of State Practice' (n 23) 133.

[53] *Basic Documents* No 65.

[54] See Tullio Scovazzi, 'The Law of the Sea Convention and Underwater Cultural Heritage' (2012) 27 *International Journal of Marine and Coastal Law* 753.

the coordination of cooperative measures to protect underwater cultural heritage, but will be able to take immediate action to prevent the looting of a shipwreck found on its EEZ to ensure its effective *in situ* conservation for the international community as a whole.

B. Jurisdictional Rights

Article 56 makes reference to three specific categories of coastal state jurisdiction in the EEZ, namely jurisdiction with regard to (1) the establishment and use of artificial islands, installations and structures, (2) marine scientific research, and (3) the protection and preservation of the marine environment. Also referred to are 'other rights and duties' provided for in the LOSC, which includes those jurisdictional and enforcement rights in relation to customs, fiscal, immigration and sanitary matters provided under the Contiguous Zone regime that overlaps with the first 12 nm of the EEZ. It is clear from the Article 56 formulation that coastal states are not accorded general or residual jurisdictional rights in the EEZ.[55]

i. Artificial Islands, Installations and Structures

Under Article 60, coastal states have the exclusive jurisdiction to construct, and to authorise and regulate the construction and operation of, artificial islands and installations and structures for economic purposes in the EEZ. In relation to artificial islands, installations and structures coastal states also have exclusive jurisdiction in relation to customs, fiscal, health, safety and immigration laws and regulations.[56]

These rights overlap to a substantial extent with the rights of coastal states in relation to such infrastructure built in and upon the continental shelf, as provided in Article 80 (which applies Article 60 *mutatis mutandis*), and it is therefore unsurprising that the text of Article 60 draws substantially on Article 5 of the 1958 Geneva Convention on the Continental Shelf which addressed the issue of artificial structures. However, whereas Article 80 of the LOSC deals only with those facilities used to explore and exploit continental shelf resources, Article 60 is far broader and allows facilities to be constructed to take advantage of all economic resources in and on the seabed, and in and above the water column. It is upon this provision that coastal states must rely in order to construct renewable power generation facilities in the EEZ, or to place other installations such as fish aggregation devices (buoys, attached to the seabed, designed to attract pelagic fish species such as tuna).

It is significant that Article 60(1)(b) of the LOSC extends coastal state jurisdiction only over installations and structures having an economic purpose.[57] Proposals at UNCLOS III to make all installations, including military installations constructed by other states, subject

---

[55] This was the position taken in the declarations of Germany, Italy, the Netherlands and the United Kingdom on ratifying the LOSC. This view is also endorsed in *The Arctic Sunrise (Netherlands v Russian Federation)* (provisional measures) (2014) 53 ILM 607; Joint Separate Opinion of Judge Wolfrum and Judge Kelly [13].

[56] LOSC, art 60(2).

[57] This interpretation was reinforced by Germany in its Declaration: see United Nations Division for Ocean Affairs and the Law of the Sea (UNDOALOS), 'United Nations Convention on the Law of the Sea: Declarations Made upon Signature, Ratification, Accession or Succession or Anytime Thereafter' at www.un.org/Depts/los/convention_agreement/convention_declarations.htm.

to Article 60 were rejected.[58] However, under Article 60(1)(a) jurisdiction over artificial islands is not circumscribed by reference to economic purposes in the same way as for installations and structures under Article 60(1)(b), which suggests that coastal states may regulate very substantial infrastructure in the EEZ regardless for what purpose it was placed there. However, 'artificial islands', 'installations', and 'structures' are all undefined in the LOSC, which renders a distinction between artificial islands and other artificial facilities difficult to determine. Nonetheless, what is certain is that even very sizeable artificial islands, such as those constructed in the Persian Gulf offshore Dubai for residential housing and tourism purposes, would not have the status of islands for the purpose of the LOSC, and as such may not possess maritime zones of their own, nor affect maritime boundary delimitation.[59] Similar considerations apply to artificial islands constructed in the South China Sea, although in some instances those islands have been constructed upon reefs and rocks that would fall within the territorial sea.

As with coastal state rights in the EEZ generally,[60] in relation to artificial structures coastal states must have due regard to the rights of other states utilising the EEZ, particularly in relation to the freedom of navigation and overflight enjoyed in the EEZ under Article 58(1). To this end, due notice must be given of the construction of such structures, mechanisms must be in place to give warning of their presence, and abandoned or disused facilities are to be removed.[61] Other steps may also be taken to ensure the safety of navigation, such as through the establishment of reasonable safety zones (out to a maximum distance of 500 metres), taking into account applicable international standards as determined by the IMO.[62] Artificial structures and any surrounding safety zones may not be established in circumstances where they would cause inference with 'the use of recognized sea lanes essential to international navigation'.[63] While the LOSC is silent as to whether overflight constraints may be imposed around these features, reasonable limitations on overflight would be permissible if directed to securing the safety of the features. Likewise, other than the due regard provisions, there are no limitations imposed upon the coastal state as to the size of these features.

In the 2013 case of the *Arctic Sunrise*, a ship operated by Greenpeace and registered in the Netherlands was boarded by Russian authorities in the EEZ of the Russian Federation after Greenpeace crew members had sought to board the drilling platform *Prirlomnaya*. Following the arrest of both the ship and its crew the Netherlands commenced proceedings against the Russian Federation under the LOSC before an Annex VII arbitral tribunal, while also seeking provisional measures from ITLOS for the release of the *Arctic Sunrise* and its crew.[64] ITLOS granted the Netherlands provisional measures, and in doing so acknowledged the differing views of the Netherlands and the Russian Federation over the rights and obligations of a coastal state and a flag state within the EEZ.[65] In a Dissenting Opinion, Judge Golitsyn observed with respect to Article 60 that under the LOSC a coastal state

---

[58] *Virginia Commentaries*, vol 1, 584.
[59] See LOSC, art 60(8).
[60] See ibid art 56(2).
[61] Ibid art 60(3).
[62] Ibid art 60(4), (5), (6).
[63] Ibid art 60(7).
[64] *The Arctic Sunrise (Netherlands v Russian Federation)* (2014) 53 ILM 607.
[65] Ibid [68].

'has the authority to take appropriate measures to ensure compliance with its regulations governing activities within safety zones, in other words to take the necessary enforcement measures'.[66] However, Judges Wolfrum and Kelly observed in their Separate Opinion that while the Russian Federation enjoyed 'enforcement functions in respect of the protection of the platform within the safety zone' it had no such right in the EEZ.[67] This suggests a need to ensure a balancing between the rights and interests of the coastal state over a safety zone within an EEZ established with respect to an artificial installation and the more general rights and interests of flag and other states that exist immediately beyond that zone within the much larger EEZ.

ii. Marine Scientific Research

The regulation by the LOSC of marine scientific research is extensive, and is addressed in Part XIII.[68] The EEZ regime makes reference in Article 56(1)(b)(ii) to the exclusive jurisdiction of coastal states with regard to marine scientific research, and this right must be read in light of Article 246 in Part XIII. Consistent with this provision, other states and international organisations may only carry out marine scientific research within the EEZ with the consent of the relevant coastal state.[69] This consent should be granted in 'normal circumstances', which are intended to be understood broadly given that Article 246(3) provides that they will include situations where a coastal state and a researching state do not maintain diplomatic relations. However, coastal states may in their discretion withhold consent to marine research in the EEZ in certain circumstances, such as where the research is directly concerned with the search for living or non-living resources, and/or involves the construction, operation or use of artificial islands, installations and structures.[70] This regime for the regulation of marine scientific research in the EEZ is generally intended to be permissive in respect of all research except that which has the exclusive or predominant purpose of resource exploration. However, some states, most notably the People's Republic of China, have interpreted Article 56(1)(b)(ii) and Part XIII broadly, arguing that intelligence gathering, and even hydrographic surveys conducted for the purpose of aiding navigational safety, cannot be undertaken in the EEZ without coastal state consent.[71]

iii. Marine Environmental Protection

One of the most important reforms brought about by the EEZ regime is the extension of coastal state jurisdiction over not only the living and non-living resources of the zone, but also more generally to encompass 'the protection and preservation of the marine environment' consistent with the 'relevant provisions' of the LOSC.[72] As a result, the EEZ confers on coastal states extensive rights and powers to protect all living and non-living

---

[66] Ibid, Dissenting Opinion of Judge Golitsyn [25]; see also Joint Separate Opinion of Judge Wolfrum and Judge Kelly [12] making similar observations.

[67] Ibid, Joint Separate Opinion of Judge Wolfrum and Judge Kelly [14]. The Annex VII arbitral tribunal heard argument on the merits of this case in 2015.

[68] See ch 14.

[69] LOSC, art 246(2).

[70] Ibid art 246(5)(a), (c).

[71] See J Ashley Roach and Robert W Smith, *Excessive Maritime Claims*, 3rd edn (The Hague, Martinus Nijhoff, 2012) 383–85, discussing US responses to the Republic of Korea (2001) and China (2007).

[72] Ibid art 56(1)(b)(iii).

components of the marine environment found within 200 nm in an integrated manner. In relation to marine pollution in the EEZ, Part XII deals with three main heads of prescriptive and enforcement jurisdiction: pollution from seabed activities and in relation to artificial structures;[73] pollution by dumping[74] which cannot be carried out in the EEZ without express consent by the coastal state; and incidental pollution from vessels.[75] In relation to installations and dumping, coastal states have a wide margin of appreciation, and may adopt measures more stringent than international rules and standards. In respect of operational vessel-source pollution their powers are more limited, in that laws adopted for the EEZ must be in conformity with generally accepted international rules and standards such as those set under the auspices of the IMO.

V. Rights and Duties of Other States in the EEZ

Given the expansion of the sovereign rights and jurisdiction of coastal states in the EEZ achieved by the LOSC there was an awareness of the need to protect the interests of other states, particularly the major naval powers and states with large merchant and fishing fleets. Whereas the EFZs claimed by many states prior to the emergence of the EEZ concept at UNCLOS III interfered only with the high seas freedom to fish and to conduct fisheries research, the EEZ regime apportioned to coastal states far broader powers that needed to be tightly circumscribed.

Article 58 is the key provision in Part V that seeks to safeguard the interests of the major maritime states. First, in relation to rights, Article 58(1) provides that in the EEZ all states, whether coastal or landlocked, enjoy the freedoms identified in Article 87 of navigation and overflight, the laying of submarine cables and pipelines, and 'other internationally lawful uses of the sea related to these freedoms'. Further, Article 58(2) states that several provisions of the LOSC (Articles 88 to 115) relating to the high seas apply in the EEZ to the extent that they are compatible with Part V. These provisions go to issues such as the nationality of ships,[76] the duties of flag states,[77] the immunity of warships,[78] and the suppression of piracy.[79] Secondly, in respect to the duties of states other than coastal states, Article 58(3) stipulates that due regard must be had to the rights and duties of the coastal state, and there must be compliance with the laws and regulations adopted by the coastal state in conformity with the LOSC.

A. Navigation and Overflight

Article 58(1) imports into the EEZ regime the high seas freedoms of navigation and overflight referred to in Article 87. This means that in the EEZ the navigation and overflight

---

[73] Ibid art 208.
[74] Ibid art 210(5).
[75] Ibid art 211(5), (6).
[76] Ibid art 91.
[77] Ibid art 94.
[78] Ibid art 95.
[79] Ibid arts 100–107.

rights accorded to states other than coastal states are akin to those rights as enjoyed on the high seas, and attempts by some states parties to the LOSC to limit these rights in the EEZ by defining them as rights of innocent passage are inconsistent with Part V.[80] The United States has been vigilant in protesting against interpretations of the LOSC that would inter- fere with EEZ freedoms of navigation, as have a number of European states.[81]

Nonetheless, it is clear that the rights of navigation and overflight in the EEZ are not as extensive as those exercisable on the high seas given the regulatory powers accorded to coastal states by Part V.[82] To that end, in *Virginia G*, ITLOS made it clear that Article 58 was to be read together with Article 56.[83] Accordingly, coastal states can regulate bunker- ing of foreign vessels engaged in fishing in their EEZ.[84] Coastal states may also stop and search any fishing vessel to ensure compliance with its fisheries laws adopted in conform- ity with the Convention,[85] on the proviso that arrested vessels and their crews are to be released promptly on the posting of a reasonable bond.[86] Coastal states may also lawfully pass pollution control legislation consistent with applicable international standards, and take enforcement action in respect of egregious breaches.[87] It is also possible for coastal state regulation of EEZ fisheries to impose some fetters on the freedom of navigation by merchant vessels through sensitive marine environments essential for the health of fisheries such as coral reefs, although no provision in Part V is explicit on this point. A clearer exam- ple of the potential for coastal state jurisdiction to limit navigational rights in the EEZ is in relation to artificial islands, installations and structures which will inevitably have some impact on navigation, although Article 60(7) seeks to limit this by prohibiting the estab- lishment of such facilities within recognised sea lanes essential to international navigation.

i. Environmental Security

Part V permits the freedom of navigation to be curtailed in regulating marine pollution. However, since the conclusion of the LOSC there has been some creeping of jurisdiction with several states relying on the environmental jurisdiction they possess in the EEZ to object to the passage by foreign vessels carrying ultra-hazardous cargoes, particularly nuclear materials in transit to power plants, reprocessing facilities or to repositories for dis- posal. Some states assert that the risk of environmental harm is so great that they are entitled not only to be notified of planned voyages of vessels carrying such cargoes (a right of 'prior notification'), but may even deny passage through their EEZs (a right of 'prior informed consent'). For example, Ecuador lodged a declaration upon accession to the LOSC in 2012 providing that within its 'maritime spaces', which included the EEZ, 'prior notification and authorization shall be required for the transit through its maritime spaces of ships powered

---

[80] Such as Portugal: Act No 33/77 of 28 May 1977 Regarding the Juridical Status of the Portuguese Territorial Sea and the Exclusive Economic Zone.

[81] Roach and Smith, *Excessive Maritime Claims* (n 71) 379–401.

[82] Navigational rights within the EEZ were the subject of consideration in *The Arctic Sunrise (Netherlands v Russian Federation)* (2014) 53 ILM 607.

[83] *M/V Virginia G (Panama/Guinea-Bissau)* (2014) 53 ILM 1164 [222].

[84] This can extend to the payment of a fee for authorisation of bunkering. Ibid [223].

[85] LOSC, art 73(1).

[86] Ibid art 73(2).

[87] Ibid art 220(5).

by nuclear energy or transporting radioactive, toxic, hazardous or harmful substances'.[88] Ecuador's declaration provoked responses from Belgium, the European Union, Finland, Ireland, the Netherlands, Spain, Sweden and the United Kingdom.

Voyages carrying nuclear materials between Europe and Japan since the 1990s have provoked significant controversy, with states including Argentina, Chile, Antigua and Barbuda, Colombia, the Dominican Republic, New Zealand, South Africa and Mauritius claiming a right to exclude these vessels from their territorial seas *and* also their EEZs.[89] The capacity of coastal states unilaterally to regulate the transport of oil within their EEZs consistent with the LOSC has also been a point of contention. Following the break up of the oil tanker *Prestige* off the coast of Spain in November 2002, which resulted in substantial damage along the French, Portuguese and Spanish coastlines, these three states established new controls requiring oil tankers to give advance notice before travelling through their EEZs, and allowing for spot inspections in their EEZs of single-hull tankers more than 15 years old, and summary expulsion from these waters if found on inspection to be unseaworthy.[90] As these measures were, at the time, stricter than the international standards set under the auspices of the IMO they were not consistent with the requirements of Article 211 of the LOSC.[91]

The difficulty for those states seeking notice of shipments of certain dangerous substances, or which reserve the right to exclude particular vessels carrying these materials, is that Part V contains no provision that allows coastal states to regulate the transport of goods per se. Accordingly, foreign vessels carrying hazardous materials appear entitled to navigate freely in the EEZ. It is relevant here that Article 23 clearly permits such voyages within the territorial sea, subject to special obligations to 'carry documents and observe special precautionary measures established for such ships by international agreements'.[92] Despite the silence of Part V on the subject, it would be curious if the same rights afforded in the territorial sea were not also applicable in the EEZ. Alternatively, it may be argued that Part V should be read as far as possible consistently with Part XII which allows (and indeed requires) coastal states to protect the marine environment within their EEZs. Several states have also argued that rules and principles of international environmental law have application in this context, as seen in New Zealand's invocation of the precautionary principle to contest the legality of shipments of nuclear cargoes by Japanese vessels through New Zealand's EEZ.[93]

ii. Military Security

Since the conclusion of the LOSC there has been a growing body of practice indicating the willingness of coastal states to interfere with navigational rights and freedoms on grounds

---

[88] See UNDOALOS, 'United Nations Convention on the Law of the Sea' (n 57).

[89] Stuart Kaye, 'Freedom of Navigation in a Post 9/11 World: Security and Creeping Jurisdiction' in David Freestone, Richard Barnes and David M Ong (eds), *The Law of the Sea: Progress and Prospects* (Oxford, Oxford University Press, 2006) 347, 362; Jon M Van Dyke, 'The Legal Regime Governing Sea Transport of Ultrahazardous Radioactive Materials' (2002) 33 *Ocean Development and International Law* 77.

[90] Van Dyke, 'The Disappearing Right to Navigational Freedom' (n 7) 109–10.

[91] See further ch 15.

[92] See Churchill, 'The Impact of State Practice' (n 23) 115.

[93] Van Dyke, 'The Disappearing Right to Navigational Freedom' (n 7) 111.

of maritime security, particularly since the September 2001 terrorist attacks in the United States. One of the more dramatic illustrations of this practice took place in March 2001, when a United States Navy EP-3 reconnaissance aircraft collided with a Chinese F-8 fighter aircraft that had intercepted the EP-3 in China's EEZ, around 70 nm south-east of China's Hainan Island. The Chinese pilot died when his aircraft crashed into the sea; however, the EP-3 managed to make a distress landing at a Chinese military base on Hainan. The Chinese government detained the aircraft and its crew, and contended that the United States had abused the rights of overflight in the EEZ and failed to have 'due regard to the rights and duties' of China as the coastal state, as required by Article 58(3) of the LOSC. China specifically asserted a right to interfere with EEZ overflight by foreign aircraft posing a threat to the natural security of China.[94] This incident raised the issue as to the effect of Article 58, which applies high seas navigational and overflight rights in the EEZ. Does Article 58 protect such rights on the EEZ to the same extent as Article 87 does in relation to the high seas?

The EEZ regime does not expressly authorise foreign states to carry out surveillance or other military activities such as military exercises or weapons testing, but neither does it prohibit such uses of the EEZ. Some states have nonetheless maintained that weapons testing cannot lawfully be carried out in the EEZ.[95] However, it is significant that the freedoms set out in Article 87 are referred to as main examples of high seas freedoms, rather than the only such freedoms. Moreover, these freedoms are to be exercised subject to conditions set not only by the LOSC but also 'other rules of international law'. The only express condition set down in Articles 58(3) and 87(2) is the vague stipulation that foreign states must have 'due regard' to the rights and duties of coastal states and other states. And the reference in Article 87 to 'other rules of international law' would seem to suggest that general international law can be turned to in determining the legitimate uses to which the high seas and the EEZ may be put. As such there would be a clear prohibition on the carrying out of activities in the EEZ that constituted a threat or use of force contrary to the UN Charter.[96]

On the other side of the coin is the issue whether coastal states may assert any kind of security jurisdiction in the EEZ. Many states have done so, prohibiting not only military exercises, manoeuvres and weapons testing, but also seeking to restrict navigation and overflight in the EEZ more generally in the interests of national security such as to prevent the proliferation of weapons of mass destruction (WMD). Other states have sought to impose lesser restrictions. An example is the Australian Maritime Identification System announced in 2004, under which Australian authorities seek information from vessels making for Australian ports when entering a 'Maritime Identification Zone' 1000 nm from an Australian coastline, and all vessels, except day recreational vessels, entering the Australian EEZ.[97] The stated purpose of the system is to enhance the quality of maritime surveillance and protect the resource and national security interests of Australia. Information sought

---

[94] Eric Donnelly, 'The United States–China EP-3 Incident: Legality and *Realpolitik*' (2004) 9 *Journal of Conflict and Security Law* 25, 30.

[95] See, eg, the declarations on ratifying the LOSC by Cape Verde (in 1987), Brazil (in 1988), India (in 1995), Malaysia (in 1996), Pakistan (in 1997) and Bangladesh (in 2001). For the countervailing view see the declaration on accession by the United Kingdom (in 1997).

[96] See the more detailed discussion in ch 12.

[97] Natalie Klein, 'Legal Implications of Australia's Maritime Identification System' (2006) 55 *International and Comparative Law Quarterly* 337.

from vessels entering the EEZ for the purposes of fisheries protection is likely to be regarded as consistent with Part V given the broad powers given to coastal states over marine living resources in the EEZ. However, as the information is sought from all vessels, and not only fishing vessels, this raises the question of whether the system interferes with the rights of other states in the EEZ, contrary to Article 58. The mere request for information is unlikely to amount to such an infringement; however, an attempt to prevent passage by a ship that has refused to provide such information would be, unless the vessel concerned is reasonably suspected to be intending to violate valid coastal state laws relating to marine resources, or pollution. One argument that has been made in favour of the legality of the monitoring of all vessels in the EEZ is that it may be an assertion of an unattributed right consistent with Article 59 if directed to suppressing activities such as terrorism, which could legitimately be regarded as an issue of importance to the international community as a whole.[98]

B. Submarine Cables and Pipelines

In addition to navigation and overflight rights, Article 58(1) also refers to the rights of other states to lay submarine cables and pipelines in the EEZs of coastal states. These rights are elaborated in several provisions of Part VII concerning the exercise of such rights on the high seas, to which Article 58(2) cross-refers. As a result, flag states must take responsibility to ensure that their vessels and nationals do not wilfully, or through culpable negligence, break or injure a cable or pipeline.[99] The laying of a submarine cable or pipeline within the EEZ also necessarily brings into application the continental shelf regime as such infrastructure is laid on the seafloor. There is in Article 76(3) a pertinent restriction on the freedom in Article 58(1) to lay cables and pipelines, in that the course that this infrastructure may follow is made subject to the consent of the coastal state.

VI. Further Reading

Gemma Andreone, 'The Exclusive Economic Zone' in Donald R Rothwell, Alex G Oude Elferink, Karen N Scott and Tim Stephens (eds), *The Oxford Handbook of the Law of the Sea* (Oxford, Oxford University Press, 2015) 134

Robert C Beckman and Clive H Schofield, 'Defining EEZ Claims from Islands: A Potential South China Sea Change' (2014) 29 *International Journal of Marine and Coastal Law* 193

Robin Churchill, 'The Impact of State Practice on the Jurisdictional Framework Contained in the LOS Convention' in Alex G Oude Elferink (ed), *Stability and Change in the Law of the Sea: The Role of the LOS Convention* (Leiden, Martinus Nijhoff, 2005) 91

Barbara Kwiatkowska, *The 200 Mile Exclusive Economic Zone in the New Law of the Sea* (Dordrecht, Martinus Nijhoff, 1989)

Francisco Orrego Vicuña, *The Exclusive Economic Zone Regime and Legal Nature under International Law* (Cambridge, Cambridge University Press, 1989)

---

[98] Ibid 359–60.
[99] LOSC, arts 112–15.

5

The Continental Shelf

I. Introduction

The continental shelf is the relatively shallow area of the seafloor adjacent to the coast where what is known as the continental margin slopes down gradually from the landmass into the sea until it begins to drop more sharply towards the deep ocean floor.[1] The contemporary law of the sea vests in coastal states not only sovereign rights in the continental shelf in the scientific sense, but rather in the entire physical continental margin, that is the submerged prolongation of the land territory. The continental shelf doctrine is therefore more accurately described as the continental margin doctrine, but because of its historical use 'continental shelf' has become the accepted term in international law.[2]

The continental margin is comprised of three main physical components: the seabed and subsoil of the *continental shelf*, the *continental slope*, and the *continental rise* (see Figure 5.1, below).[3] Seawards from the scientific continental shelf there is the slope that falls steeply (usually at a gradient more than 1.5 degrees), sometimes to a third section of the margin, the rise, where there is an accretion of sediments and the gradient is less steep (around 0.5 degrees). Beyond the rise lies the abyssal plain or deep ocean floor which for the purposes of the law of the sea is that part of the seabed known as the 'Area'.

By the early part of the twentieth century it was apparent that the continental shelves of many coastal states held significant potential as a source of non-living resources, principally oil and gas, and·also for several valuable seafloor fisheries such as pearl oysters. Developments in marine technology by the mid twentieth century allowed the cost-effective exploitation of these resources, and in the absence of a legal regime to regulate access, a number of coastal states sought to protect their interests by making unilateral claims to a continental shelf. The most influential was the proclamation by United States President Harry S Truman, that claimed for the United States exclusive rights in the resources of the adjacent seabed out to a depth of 100 fathoms (around 200 metres), while disavowing any interference with high seas freedoms in the water column above.[4] The Truman Proclamation was followed by similar declarations by other states, and the continental shelf doctrine was soon recognised

---

[1] See Philip A Symonds et al, 'Characteristics of Continental Margins' in Peter J Cook and Chris M Carleton (eds), *Continental Shelf Limits: The Scientific and Legal Interface* (Oxford, Oxford University Press, 2000) 25.

[2] DP O'Connell, *The International Law of the Sea*, vol 1 (Oxford, Clarendon Press, 1982) 491.

[3] Ibid 443–45.

[4] Proclamation 2667, 'Policy of the United States With Respect to the Natural Resources of the Subsoil and Seabed of the Continental Shelf', 28 September 1945, *Basic Documents* No 5. See AL Hollick, 'US Oceans Policy: The Truman Proclamation' (1976–77) 17 *Virginia Journal of International Law* 23.

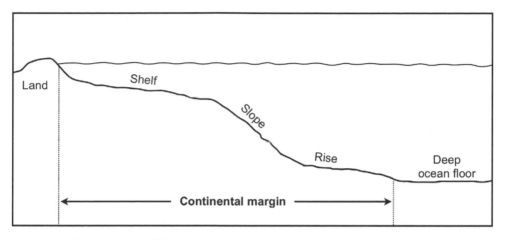

Figure 5.1: The Continental Margin

in bilateral treaties, the 1958 Geneva Convention on the Continental Shelf, in customary international law, by decisions of the ICJ, and ultimately in the LOSC.

The LOSC has adopted a more expansive definition of the continental shelf than either the Truman Proclamation or that found in the Geneva regime, giving to coastal states an entitlement to a continental shelf of 200 nm regardless of seafloor configuration, and a continental shelf reaching out to the limits of the continental margin where the outer edge extended beyond 200 nm. The juridical 200 nm continental shelf endorsed by the LOSC resolved many of the problems that bedevilled the Geneva regime, in so far as the outer limits of the continental shelf are concerned. Nonetheless state practice in relation to the continental shelf is now in a particularly dynamic phase, not seen since the 1940s, because of the process the LOSC establishes for verifying outer continental shelf limits that can in some places extend beyond 200 nm. To establish an outer[5] continental shelf beyond the 200 nm continental shelf, coastal states that are parties to the LOSC must submit data to the CLCS, a technical body established by the LOSC that considers the information and makes recommendations as to the extent of a coastal state's seafloor estate. As of 1 January 2015 there had been 77 full or partial submissions of data to the CLCS,[6] and although the Commission had only been able to consider less than half of these, it is clear that over time

---

[5] In the literature the terms 'extended continental shelf' and 'outer continental shelf' have been used interchangeably. However, although these assist in distinguishing the area of continental shelf within 200 nm and areas of shelf that may lie beyond, the arbitral tribunal in *Barbados v Trinidad and Tobago* (2006) 45 ILM 798 pointed out (at [213]) that 'there is in law only a single "continental shelf" rather than an inner continental shelf and a separate extended or outer continental shelf'.

[6] There have also been extensive submissions of preliminary information indicative of the outer limit of the continental shelf, pursuant to a decision of the Meeting of States Parties to the LOSC regarding the workload of the CLCS, and the ability of states, especially developing states, to meet the requirement for states to submit data under LOSC, annex II, art 4. Under the decision, preliminary information is taken to satisfy the submission requirements: UN Doc SPLOS/183, [1(a)].

it will approve the enclosure of a very substantial area of seafloor beyond 200 nm. One hundred and seventeen of the 152 coastal states in the international community have made continental shelf claims.[7]

II. The Truman Proclamation

Following the Second World War there was significant commercial interest in the mineral resources of the continental shelf, which were then open to exploitation by all states under the prevailing freedom of the seas doctrine. The seabed, including both the deep ocean floor and the continental margins of states, was not clearly characterised as either a *res communis*, available to all states, or a *res nullius*, subject to national claim by occupation or prescription.[8] The issue had received relatively little international legal attention until this time for the simple reason that exploitation of this area was difficult or impossible under existing technologies, which only allowed oil and gas rigs to operate close to shore within the territorial sea. Hence the objects of extended maritime claims had been fisheries rather than the seabed per se.[9] A Committee of Experts convened under the auspices of the League of Nations made reference to the fact that the 'bottom of the sea is marked by a sort of great step, almost always abrupt, which divides it into two quite distinct regions', but did not seek to set out any clear legal limits to the continental shelf.[10]

The Truman Proclamation on 28 September 1945, which asserted a claim to the natural resources of the subsoil and seabed of the continental shelf adjacent to the United States (but not the superjacent waters),[11] was the first initiative by any state both to assert a claim to that area of the seabed, and to clarify the associated legal rights and entitlements. The Truman Proclamation took note of the 'world-wide need for new sources of petroleum and other minerals' and recognised that 'jurisdiction over these resources is required in the interest of their conservation and prudent utilisation'. The Proclamation's preamble further asserted several practical and geographical bases for the United States claim, one which was described as 'reasonable and just', namely that the effectiveness of any measures to utilise or conserve continental shelf resources would depend on coastal state cooperation, that the continental shelf can be regarded as the natural extension of the land mass, that seabed mineral resources often form a seaward extension of resources found on the land, and that 'self-protection' compels the coastal state to keep a 'close watch' on activities close to shore.

---

[7] United Nations Division of Ocean Affairs and Law of the Sea, 'Table of Claims to Maritime Jurisdiction (as at 15 July 2011)' at www.un.org/Depts/los/convention_agreements/convention_declarations.htm. States that have not claimed a continental shelf but had claimed an EEZ include Belize, Democratic People's Republic of Korea, Congo, Egypt, Grenada, Honduras, Kiribati, Lebanon, Liberia, Libya, Maldives, Marshall Islands, Nauru, Niue, Romania, St Vincent and the Grenadines, Samoa, Singapore, Thailand, Turkey, and Tuvalu.

[8] Although the early attitude of some states such as Great Britain was that the Truman Proclamation could be supported by the theory of occupation: O'Connell, *The International Law of the Sea* (n 2) vol 1, 456–57.

[9] David J Attard, *The Exclusive Economic Zone in International Law* (Oxford, Clarendon Press, 1987) 129–31.

[10] 'League of Nations Committee of Experts for the Progressive Codification of International Law: Questionnaire No 2: Territorial Waters' (1926) 20 *AJIL Supplement* 62, 126.

[11] *Basic Documents* No 5.

The operative part of the Truman Proclamation stated that:

[T]he Government of the United States regards the natural resources of the subsoil and sea bed of the continental shelf beneath the high seas but contiguous to the coasts of the United States as appertaining to the United States, subject to its jurisdiction and control. … The character as high seas of the waters above the continental shelf and the right to their free and unimpeded navigation are in no way thus affected.

The Truman Proclamation set out in definitive terms the nature of the continental shelf as a natural and contiguous appurtenance of the land, in which the natural resources would be within the sole jurisdiction and control of the coastal state and where the water column and airspace above would remain free for the use of other states. It differed, therefore, from the earlier proclamation by Argentina in 1944, that made an ambit claim to a 200 nm territorial sea and all the resources found within it.

There were few protests to the Truman Proclamation and indeed other states quickly followed, and in some cases surpassed, the United States lead.[12] Kuwait and Saudi Arabia asserted claims to the subsoil and seabed of parts of the Persian Gulf,[13] while Mexico and some states in South America claimed not only rights in the resources of the continental shelf, but sovereignty in full over the seabed, water column and airspace (in the case of Mexico and Chile, following the Argentine approach). Moreover the claims were often not limited to the extent of the continental shelf in a geomorphological or geographical sense, but rather extended to a fixed distance of 200 nm (in the case of Chile, Costa Rica, El Salvador and Honduras; these claims were the Latin American forerunners to the EEZ). Although the United States protested those claims that exceeded its own, there is little doubt that the unilateral approach taken in the Truman Proclamation had been the catalyst for a welter of independent rather than cooperative state practice.

Writing in 1950 Sir Hersch Lauterpacht stated that the continental shelf doctrine had become 'instant customary international law' because of the claims and the general acquiescence to them as seen by the absence of protest.[14] However, despite the clarity of the Truman Proclamation itself, the body of state practice it provoked was not uniform. This led Lord Asquith, while sitting as arbitrator in a dispute relating to the granting of a concession to mineral oil resources in the 'sea waters' of Abu Dhabi, to conclude that not only had the doctrine of the continental shelf not been in existence in 1939, at the time of the concession contract, but by 1951 was not yet 'admitted to the canon of international law'.[15] However, Asquith accepted that it was highly desirable for there to exist an *ipso jure* entitlement to a continental shelf, as free access would promote a 'perilous scramble' by states seeking to assert and perfect title to an area that was otherwise *res nullius*.[16] Nonetheless he concluded that:

there are in this field so many ragged ends and unfilled blanks, so much that is merely tentative and exploratory, that in no form can the doctrine claim as yet to have assumed hitherto the hard lineaments or the definitive status of an established rule of international law.[17]

---

[12]   Richard Young, 'Recent Developments with Respect to the Continental Shelf' (1948) 42 *AJIL* 849, 851.
[13]   Richard Young, 'Saudi Arabian Offshore Legislation' (1949) 43 *AJIL* 530.
[14]   Hersch Lauterpacht, 'Sovereignty over Submarine Areas' (1950) 27 *British Yearbook of International Law* 376, 431.
[15]   *Petroleum Development (Trucial Coast) Ltd and the Sheikh of Abu Dhabi* (1952) 1 *International and Comparative Law Quarterly* 247, 253.
[16]   Ibid 257.
[17]   Ibid 256.

The only caveat entertained by Asquith was that in certain very rare circumstances coastal states might hold a customary right to harvest sedentary, seabed fisheries such as sponges, coral, oysters, pearls and chank (sea snails, such as those which produce conch shells). Indeed, well before 1945 a number of states had asserted jurisdiction over adjacent sedentary fisheries on their continental shelves, beginning with pearl fisheries legislation in the British colony of Ceylon in 1811, and similar claims made later by other states, including Panama, Venezuela, and France in the Bay of Granville.[18]

III. UNCLOS I and the Geneva Convention

A. Work of the International Law Commission

The ILC began work on the continental shelf and other law of the sea topics in 1951 in preparation for UNCLOS I in Geneva. The basic concept of the continental shelf did not prove to be particularly difficult for the ILC to address in its Draft Articles Concerning the Law of the Sea which it adopted in 1956, and which formed the basis for the four Geneva Conventions, including the 1958 Convention on the Continental Shelf.[19] By contrast, settling the seawards limit of the shelf was controversial, and not satisfactorily resolved by the ILC, or by states themselves at UNCLOS I.

From the outset the ILC accepted that coastal states should be entitled to exercise control and jurisdiction over the continental shelf, with the qualification that this was only for the purpose of exploiting seabed resources, and not as an incident of any generalised sovereignty in the seabed. Once it was acknowledged that the continental shelf could not be *res communis* in the same way as the high seas because, as Lumb put it, 'no country would be prepared to stand idle while the drilling rigs of other countries were set up to appropriate … the mineral wealth … beneath its adjacent continental shelf',[20] it followed that there would have to be coastal state control of the shelf.

At a relatively early stage the ILC was confronted with the argument that continental shelf resources should not as a matter of principle be arrogated to coastal states, but rather should be vested in the international community generally, and exploited under the oversight of an international agency. The ILC considered however, that 'such internationalization would meet with insurmountable practical difficulties, and would not ensure the effective exploitation of natural resources necessary to meet the needs of mankind'.[21] This was a precursor to the debate that was to follow many years later at UNCLOS III in relation to the deep seabed, which did result in the internationalisation of the seafloor beyond the continental margin.

When it came to the status of the water column above the continental shelf, the ILC considered that it should remain open to all nations for the purposes of navigation and

---

[18] Suzette V Suarez, *The Outer Limits of the Continental Shelf: Legal Aspects of their Establishment* (Berlin, Springer, 2008) 21–22; O'Connell, *The International Law of the Sea* (n 2) vol 1, 451ff.
[19] *Basic Documents* No 12.
[20] RD Lumb, 'The Continental Shelf' (1967–68) 6 *Melbourne University Law Review* 357, 357.
[21] [1956] *Yearbook of the International Law Commission*, vol 1, 296.

fishing. Unlike the EEZ regime, which began to emerge in the 1970s, the continental shelf was therefore conceived as still being part of the high seas rather than an entirely distinctive maritime zone. Indeed the ILC considered the freedom of the seas over the shelf to be the 'paramount principle',[22] and proposed articles to ensure that the exploration of the continental shelf and the exploitation of its natural resources would not result in any unjustified interference with high seas freedoms.

An immediate issue confronting the ILC beyond the nature of the continental shelf was what limit it should extend to. The inner limit of the continental shelf was, and had always been, clear: it commenced where the territorial sea ended. In the ILC's 1951 first set of draft articles on the topic, the outer limit of the continental shelf was defined by reference to 'where the depth of the superjacent waters admits of the exploitation of the natural resources of the seabed and subsoil'. In subsequent deliberations the ILC rejected this elastic criterion of exploitability, because it 'might give rise to disputes and uncertainty',[23] in favour of a fixed limit where the sea reached a depth of 200 metres. This was in line with a recommendation from the International Committee on the Nomenclature of Ocean Bottom Features, which had noted in 1952 that the edge of the continental margin was normally found around the 200 metre isobath.[24] However, this depth limit proved politically unfeasible as state practice had begun to recognise exploitability, as was the case at the Inter-American Specialized Conference on 'Conservation of Natural Resources: Continental Shelf and Oceanic Waters' held at Ciudad Trujillo in the Dominican Republic in 1956.

In the result, the ILC therefore adopted an amalgam provision combining both a fixed depth criterion and a fluid exploitability limit, which was subsequently repeated in essentially the same terms in Article 1 of the Convention on the Continental Shelf. There the term 'continental shelf' was defined to mean:

> the seabed and subsoil of the submarine areas adjacent to the coast but outside the area of the territorial sea, to a depth of 200 metres or, beyond that limit, to where the depth of the superjacent waters admits of the exploitation of the natural resources of the said areas.[25]

Some ILC members considered that the addition of the exploitability criterion 'unjustifiably and dangerously impaired the stability of the limit'.[26] As Johnston has noted, the formula did indeed combine two quite different elements, and gave rise to a considerable degree of uncertainty in legal interpretation.[27] On one view the exploitability criterion was the only relevant limit, and was entirely ambulatory (the 'broad shelf' interpretation), while on another view there could be some reasonable limits to the continental shelf implied by the term 'adjacent' that suggested a requirement for propinquity between the shelf and the coastal state (the 'narrow shelf' view).[28]

---

[22] Ibid 298.

[23] Ibid 296.

[24] O'Connell, *The International Law of the Sea* (n 2) vol 1, 489. This was inaccurate, as it is often only the first of a series of escarpments.

[25] See further B H Oxman 'The Preparation of Article 1 of the Convention on the Continental Shelf' (1972) 3 *Journal of Maritime Law and Commerce* 245; B H Oxman 'The Preparation of Article 1 of the Convention on the Continental Shelf' (1972) 3 *Journal of Maritime Law and Commerce* 445; BH Oxman, 'The Preparation of Article 1 of the Convention on the Continental Shelf' (1972) 3 *Journal of Maritime Law and Commerce* 683.

[26] [1956] *Yearbook of the International Law Commission*, vol 1, 296–97.

[27] Douglas M Johnston, *The Theory and History of Ocean Boundary Making* (Kingston and Montreal, McGill-Queens University Press, 1988) 87.

[28] Ibid 88. For a defence of the formula see DW Bowett, *The Law of the Sea* (Manchester, Manchester University Press, 1967) 34.

The ILC and the Geneva regime's definition divorced the legal and scientific meanings of the continental shelf, not least because the exploitability criterion allowed control to be extended beyond the physical limits of the shelf. Indeed the difference between the law and the science was so great that there was some acknowledgment that it would have been better to have adopted a more neutral concept such as 'submarine area'. However, the term 'continental shelf' had such widespread usage that this was not practical, and it continues to be used today.

When it came to determining the rights and duties of coastal states in continental shelf areas, the ILC sought to make clear that these did not amount to sovereignty such that freedoms of the seas and the airspace above might be threatened. Hence 'sovereignty' gave way to 'sovereign rights', with the latter including not only exclusive rights of exploration and exploitation of resources, but also jurisdiction to prevent and enforce violations of the law. In terms of the resources within the continental shelf the early draft articles embraced only 'mineral resources'. However, this was later extended to include 'natural resources' so as also to incorporate sedentary fisheries, that is those which are permanently attached to the seabed, but not bottom-fish which only occasionally rest on the seabed, such as when reproducing. One seabed item which the ILC clearly considered not to be included in 'natural resources' was sea wrecks and any treasure that they may contain such as bullion.[29]

There was some controversy on the issue of sedentary fisheries because their inclusion in the continental shelf regime removed them from the high seas freedom to fish, and had impacts in many places such as northern Australia where there was extensive Japanese involvement in pearl fisheries. Moreover there was, and remains, a degree of artificiality in the distinction between sedentary and free-swimming species.[30] While sessile species may be said to be part of the continental shelf (such as mussels, corals and the like), other species also considered sedentary are only present on or in the continental shelf for part of their life cycle (such as oysters, crabs and lobsters).

In relation to maritime boundary delimitation, the ILC set out a formulation that was subsequently at issue in the *North Sea Continental Shelf* cases.[31] Namely that the apportionment of a shared continental shelf should be resolved by agreement in the first instance, but in the absence of agreement and unless another line is justified by special circumstances, by adopting the median or equidistance line. In this the ILC adopted the same formulation it deployed for the delimitation of overlapping territorial seas.

One particularly unique feature of the draft articles in relation to the continental shelf was a provision for the ICJ to have compulsory jurisdiction over disputes concerning the continental shelf. The Commission explained that this was justified because the articles on the continental shelf were a novel compromise between high seas freedoms and coastal state resource sovereignty which incorporated a high degree of discretion as to the lawfulness of activities permitted within the zone (such as the requirement that there be no 'unjustifiable' interference by the coastal state with navigation or fishing). So that the new regime did not 'endanger the higher principle of the freedom of the seas' it was 'essential that States which

---

[29] For discussion of the issues surrounding wrecks ('lagan') and the 2001 UNESCO Convention on the Protection of Underwater Cultural Heritage, *Basic Documents* No 65, see ch 4.

[30] Bowett, *The Law of the Sea* (n 28) 35–36.

[31] *North Sea Continental Shelf (Federal Republic of Germany v Denmark; Federal Republic of Germany v The Netherlands)* [1969] ICJ Rep 3 ('*North Sea Continental Shelf*').

disagree concerning the exploration and exploitation of the continental shelf should be required to submit any dispute arising on this subject to an impartial authority'.[32]

B. The Convention on the Continental Shelf

The 1958 Convention on the Continental Shelf adopted at UNCLOS I largely followed the articles adopted by the ILC in 1956. Although the idea of the continental shelf itself attracted general support and consensus at UNCLOS, there was significant debate at the conference in relation to the combined distance and exploitability definition of the limits of the continental shelf as proposed by the ILC. The conference ultimately adopted the ILC's definition with no major changes, in Article 1. The Convention then went on to elaborate on the nature of the continental shelf and the rights of coastal and other states. The rights of the coastal state extended to the exploration for and exploitation of the living and non-living resources of the continental shelf.[33] The living resources include only sedentary species, that is organisms which at a harvestable stage are either immobile or unable to move except in constant physical contact with the ocean floor.[34] Coastal state seabed resource rights were exclusive,[35] and not dependent on occupation by the coastal state, nor on any express proclamation.[36] This was an important statement of the nature of the continental shelf as belonging inherently to coastal states *ipso facto*, *ipso jure* and *ab initio* in much the same way as the territorial sea. O'Connell has noted that from the inherent nature of the continental shelf followed the retroactivity of continental shelf doctrine, the effect of which was to 'annul any priority of claim in time or nature over the rights of the coastal State, so that, for example, the doctrines of historic rights or acquisitive prescription would not be available'.[37]

The coastal state is entitled under the Geneva regime to take reasonable measures to explore and exploit the continental shelf, so long as this does not impede the laying or maintenance of submarine cable or pipes by other states,[38] nor constitute an unjustifiable interference with navigation, fishing or conservation, nor result in any interference with pure oceanographic or other scientific research.[39] Subject to these limitations, coastal states are entitled to establish installations and other devices necessary to the exploration and exploitation of continental shelf natural resources, and to establish safety zones no greater than 500 metres around such infrastructure.[40] Given that the continental shelf was a new resource zone in which the coastal state had exclusive sovereign rights, it was important to ensure that the regime was not undermined by research conducted by other states focussed on continental shelf resources. Hence coastal state consent was to be obtained in

[32] [1956] *Yearbook of the International Law Commission*, vol 1, 301.
[33] 1958 Convention on the Continental Shelf, art 2(1).
[34] Ibid art 2(4).
[35] Ibid art 2(2).
[36] Ibid art 2(3).
[37] O'Connell, *The International Law of the Sea* (n 2) vol 1, 482.
[38] 1958 Convention on the Continental Shelf, art 4.
[39] Ibid art 5(1).
[40] Ibid art 5(2), (3).

respect of any research concerning the continental shelf and undertaken there, whereas the coastal state should not normally withhold its consent for purely scientific research into the physical or biological characteristics of the shelf.[41]

Finally, the Convention on the Continental Shelf specifically provided that it had no application to tunnelling under the seafloor from *terra firma*.[42] The ILC in its commentary stated that regardless of the depth of the superjacent waters, there was no limit to the exploitation of the subsoil of the high seas by the use of tunnels, cuttings or wells.[43] The subsoil is thereby effectively susceptible to claim by occupation out to an indeterminate distance from the land and depth under the sea surface, so long as there is no interference with the water column.[44]

There was no provision included in the Convention on the Continental Shelf to give the ICJ compulsory jurisdiction as recommended by the ILC, indicating that these provisions were no more likely to excite disputation than those found in the three other Geneva conventions. The Convention on the Continental Shelf had attracted 56 parties by the time the LOSC was concluded, and virtually all of these states went on to join the LOSC to take advantage of the latter's more expansive definition of the continental shelf. The most notable exception is the United States, which ratified the Convention in 1961, and there are only a handful of others: Cambodia, Colombia, Israel, and Venezuela. For these states the Geneva Convention is the prevailing treaty law; however, the core of the LOSC definition of the continental shelf, in Article 76(1), (2) and (3), has almost certainly now become part of customary international law through a combination of the number of state parties to the LOSC and state practice endorsing 200 nm continental shelf claims.

C. *North Sea Continental Shelf* Cases

The customary status of the continental shelf regime may have been doubted in the early 1950s, but following UNCLOS I and the adoption of the Convention on the Continental Shelf it quickly became assured.[45] Nevertheless, in a 1968 study on the status of the regime, Slouka concluded that at the time of its conclusion Article 1 of the Convention could not be said to have been a codification of customary international law.[46] It was pointed out that:

> the definition by the criterion of exploitability of the extent of the exclusive shelf rights was then a reciprocally established and recognized policy between but a few of the participants, while the Convention articles determining the functional limits of exclusive coastal rights on the shelf, i.e., the definition of the exclusively controlled resources and the method of their exploitation, represented merely one among several existing international systems, some of them more and others less restrictive.[47]

---

[41] Ibid art 5(8).
[42] Ibid art 7.
[43] [1956] *Yearbook of the International Law Commission*, vol 1, 297.
[44] CJ Colombos, *International Law of the Sea*, 6th edn (London, Longmans, 1967) 407.
[45] See generally Zdenek J Slouka, *International Custom and the Continental Shelf: A Study in the Dynamics of Customary Rules of International Law* (The Hague, Martinus Nijhoff, 1968).
[46] Ibid 169.
[47] Ibid.

This view was reinforced in 1969 by a resolution of the UNGA which stated that the Convention on the Continental Shelf:

> does not define with sufficient precision the limits of the area over which a coastal State exercises sovereign rights for the purpose of exploration and exploitation of the natural resources, and that customary international law on the subject is inconclusive.[48]

However, in the *North Sea Continental Shelf* cases in the same year the Court found that Articles 1 to 3 did indeed represent customary international law.[49] The ICJ had been requested by Germany, Denmark and the Netherlands to articulate those principles and rules of international law applicable to the delimitation of areas of the continental shelf in the North Sea beyond those where there had been partial agreement by the parties.

The central conclusion of the Court was that Article 6(2) of the Convention on the Continental Shelf relating to the delimitation of the continental shelf did not codify, nor subsequently give rise to, an identical norm of customary international law. The ICJ found that this provision was not of a 'fundamentally norm creating character' that could be regarded 'as forming the basis of a general rule of law',[50] and that the state practice and *opinio juris* was far from being extensive or uniform. By contrast, the Court did find that Articles 1 to 3 of the Convention on the Continental Shelf represented customary international law. It was not made clear precisely when this crystallisation occurred; however, the Court noted that Articles 1 to 3 were, at the Geneva Conference, 'regarded as reflecting, or as crystallizing, received or at least emergent rules of customary international law'.[51] Critical to the Court's reasoning was the fact that Articles 1 to 3 (concerning the nature of the continental shelf) could not be subject to reservation unlike Article 6 (concerning delimitation) which could.[52]

In the *North Sea Continental Shelf* cases the Court took the concept of continental shelf further than Article 1 of the Convention on the Continental Shelf, adopting the *ipso jure* doctrine and repeatedly emphasising the notion of 'natural prolongation':

> the rights of the coastal State in respect of the area of continental shelf that constitutes a natural prolongation of its land territory into and under the sea exist *ipso facto* and *ab initio*, by virtue of its sovereignty over the land, and as an extension of it in an exercise of sovereign rights for the purpose of exploring the seabed and exploiting its natural resources. In short, there is here an inherent right.[53]

The concept of natural prolongation was described as the most fundamental of all the rules of law relating to the continental shelf, and relevant both to the issue of the entitlement of a coastal State and delimitation of the seabed boundary between adjacent coastal states.[54]

---

[48] UNGA Resolution 2574 A(XXIV) (1969).

[49] *North Sea Continental Shelf* [1969] ICJ Rep 3.

[50] Ibid [72].

[51] Ibid [63].

[52] See the 1958 Convention on the Continental Shelf, art 12.

[53] *North Sea Continental Shelf* [1969] ICJ Rep 3, [19].

[54] See O'Connell, *The International Law of the Sea* (n 2) vol 1, 495. See also D N Hutchinson, 'The Concept of Natural Prolongation in the Jurisprudence Concerning Delimitation of Continental Shelf Areas' (1984) 55 *British Yearbook of International Law* 133.

IV. UNCLOS III

By the commencement of UNCLOS III, the main elements of the continental shelf doctrine had entered into customary international law.[55] However, a number of issues remained to be addressed by the new convention that was being negotiated.

At UNCLOS III it was apparent that the march of marine technology had rendered the depth and exploitability based definition of the outer limit of the continental shelf in the Geneva regime deeply problematic. Moreover in 1970 the UNGA adopted a pivotal declaration of principles in relation to the deep seabed calling for the establishment of a regime including appropriate institutional machinery for the exploration and exploitation of the area for the benefit of all humankind.[56] This emphasised further the critical need to establish the limits of national jurisdiction over submarine areas because it would be the residual area that would become the common heritage of humankind.

A new formula for the outer limits therefore needed to be found which balanced a range of values including equity, precision, stability, and uniformity.[57] One approach favoured by some delegations was an outer limit that matched the EEZ—namely 200 nm—regardless of the natural configuration of the appurtenant seafloor. This was based on the physical fact that most states do not have a continental margin beyond 200 nm. However, this approach was not acceptable for those, relatively few, states known as the 'margineers' with continental margins extending in places substantially beyond 200 nm, to areas that in some cases included concessions already granted for oil and gas exploitation. The 'margineers group' therefore initially supported the exploitability criterion in Article 1 of the Convention on the Continental Shelf, and the 'creeping boundary' theory that it encapsulated.[58] They argued that it would be fundamentally unfair to overlook the legal position of those coastal states that had established sovereign rights to the edge of the continental margin for many years through state practice, bilateral agreements, domestic legislation and the issue of permits.[59]

Continental shelf issues were considered by the Second Committee at UNCLOS III, which had general responsibility for resolving issues concerning the limits of the maritime zones. An acceptable compromise on the limits of the continental shelf took nine years, across 10 of the 11 negotiating sessions at UNCLOS III, to reach. At the second session of UNCLOS III, the first in which substantive debates were held, states were divided over fundamental issues as to whether there should be a continental shelf doctrine at all in view of the new EEZ regime; how the continental shelf could coexist with the EEZ; whether the limit of the continental shelf should be 200 nm or beyond; and how a limit seawards of 200 nm would relate to the deep seabed regime.

As regards the outer limits of the continental shelf, at an early stage of UNCLOS III the exploitability criterion of the Convention on the Continental Shelf was rejected and most of the discussion around the continental shelf issue was what should replace it. A range

---

[55] O'Connell, *The International Law of the Sea* (n 2) vol 1, 475–76.
[56] 'Declaration of Principles Governing the Sea Bed', UNGA Resolution 2749 (XXV) (1970).
[57] Johnston, *The Theory and History of Ocean Boundary Making* (n 27) 86–87.
[58] O'Connell, *The International Law of the Sea* (n 2) vol 1, 493–94.
[59] *Virginia Commentaries*, vol 2, 846.

of proposals were made, beginning with six competing formulae presented at the second session, that sought to include both geological and geomorphological criteria to bring scientific clarity and certainty to the question. The importance of a scientific and technical assessment of the limits was recognised by many delegations, as was the ultimate need for an international commission to apply agreed methodology to data submitted by coastal states in determining the outer limits of the continental shelf.

Basic agreement on the nature of the continental shelf was reached at the third session which incorporated the language of 'natural prolongation' used by the ICJ in the *North Sea Continental Shelf* cases. Part II of the Single Negotiating Text included an article that was eventually to appear without modification as Article 76(1) of the LOSC:

> The continental shelf of a coastal state comprises the sea-bed and subsoil of the submarine areas that extend beyond its territorial sea throughout the natural prolongation of its land territory to the outer edge of the continental margin, or to a distance of 200 nautical miles from the baselines from which the breadth of the territorial sea is measured where the outer edge of the continental margin does not extend up to that distance.

Negotiations continued, however, on how a regime for a continental shelf beyond 200 nm would interact with the international seabed regime. While several states continued to insist that the continental shelf should not be recognised beyond 200 nm because this would interfere with the deep seabed, states with wide continental margins proposed an accommodation whereby there would be an equitable sharing of revenues from any exploitation of the outer continental shelf. This ultimately proved acceptable, including to landlocked and geographically disadvantaged states that were advocating for the greatest area possible to be recognised as part of the deep seabed common heritage regime.

There remained the question of precisely how to delineate the outer continental shelf given the range of different geographical and geological conditions where margins extended beyond 200 nm. At the seventh session in 1978, Ireland proposed two alternative methods to delineate the outer limits in a formulation which was to be the basis for Article 76(4) of LOSC. The Irish proposal sought to give states a choice between two approaches in an effort to bring most of the continental rise where hydrocarbon resources are found within coastal state jurisdiction.[60] The continental margin could be determined by a line delineated by reference to the outermost fixed points at each of which the thickness of sedimentary rocks is at least one per cent of the shortest distance from such point to the foot of the continental slope (this is known as the Irish formula). Alternatively, the continental shelf could be delineated by reference to fixed points not more than 60 nm from the foot of the continental slope.[61] Further negotiations at the ninth session resulted in additional proposals from the Soviet Union to place a maximum seawards limit on the continental shelf of 350 nm from the territorial sea baselines or not in excess of 100 nm from the 2,500 metre isobath, that is a line connecting the depth of 2,500 metres.

By the conclusion of the ninth session in 1980 the fundamentals of the continental shelf provisions of the LOSC had been agreed. This was very much in the spirit of the negotiations

---

[60] Robert W Smith and George Taft, 'Legal Aspects of the Continental Shelf' in Peter J Cook and Chris M Carleton (eds), *Continental Shelf Limits: The Scientific and Legal Interface* (Oxford, Oxford University Press, 2000) 17, 19.

[61] This is the 'Hedberg formula', named after the United States geologist Hollis D Hedberg, who originated it.

as a whole towards a consensus-based, package deal convention in which compromise had to be reached, and differing interests were accommodated.

V. LOSC

The LOSC addresses the continental shelf in 10 provisions in Part VI. Article 76(1) defines the continental shelf in terms which the ICJ found to represent customary international law in *Territorial and Maritime Dispute*.[62] However, the Court did not rule on the customary status of the other paragraphs of Article 76, including those relating to the outer continental shelf, noting that it was unnecessary to do so in the circumstances of the case.[63]

The basic elements of the Geneva regime are adopted in the LOSC with the important exception of the outer limits of the continental shelf beyond 200 nm. The continental shelf is reaffirmed as a resource zone that does not need to be claimed (unlike the EEZ). As the CLCS has been assessing data associated with outer continental shelf submissions, there has been a tendency for the language of 'claim' to creep in, but strictly speaking such submissions constitute not a claim as such, but rather the establishment of the legal limits of the continental shelf by reference to physical characteristics of the seabed.[64]

Under the LOSC, coastal states are entitled to a juridical continental shelf comprising the seabed and subsoil of the submarine area out to a distance of 200 nm irrespective of whether the continental margin extends this far. The only limitation that applies to the land features that generate a continental shelf is with respect to rocks 'which cannot sustain human habitation or an economic life of their own'. Under Article 121 these features generate neither a continental shelf nor an EEZ. The result is that small island states generate the same entitlements to a continental shelf as a continental state. For states with narrow continental margins the 200 nm continental shelf therefore clearly differentiates the legal shelf from the physical continental shelf.[65] In addition, coastal states with margins beyond 200 nm also have sovereign rights and jurisdiction over the area beyond, out to certain limits. The juridical definition of the continental margin and the methods and procedure for determining its outer extent are found in Article 76, one of the lengthiest and most complex single articles in the Convention. This is because it seeks to include predominantly scientific criteria while also brokering a compromise between states in a legal text. Article 76 must also be read in conjunction with a Statement of Understanding included as Annex II to the Final Act of UNCLOS III to address the specific situation pertaining to the Bay of Bengal because the thickness of the sediments in that bay results in the generation of a very large continental margin most of which would be lost by the strict application of Article 76(5). This statement was included at the urging of Sri Lanka.[66]

---

[62] *Territorial and Maritime Dispute (Nicaragua v Colombia)* [2012] ICJ Rep 624, [118].

[63] Ibid.

[64] See LOSC, art 76(8), which refers to the 'limits of the shelf established' by the coastal state.

[65] Attard, *The Exclusive Economic Zone in International Law* (n 9) 133.

[66] See Suarez, *The Outer Limits of the Continental Shelf* (n 18) 61; George Taft and Bilal Haq, 'Deep Sea Fan Issues' in Peter J Cook and Chris M Carleton (eds), *Continental Shelf Limits: The Scientific and Legal Interface* (Oxford, Oxford University Press, 2000) 308.

The key provision in respect of the outer continental shelf is Article 76(4), which gives states two options. First, states may delineate a line by reference to the outermost fixed points at each of which the thickness of the sedimentary rocks is at least one per cent of the shortest distance from the point to the foot of the continental slope.[67] To support the location of a point 100 nm from the foot of the continental slope, the sedimentary rock on the continental rise must therefore be at least 1 nm thick. Alternatively, coastal states can apply a combined geomorphological and geographical criterion, delineating a line by reference to fixed points not more than 60 nm from the foot of the continental slope.[68] In either case it will be critical to determine the foot of the continental slope, which is defined by Article 76(4)(b) as the point of maximum change in the gradient at its base, in the absence of evidence to the contrary. States need not adopt one or other approach for their entire continental margin—they are free to apply either formula to the various sectors that make up their continental margin to achieve the outcome most advantageous to them. In terms of the actual drawing of the delineation line for the outer limits of the continental shelf beyond 200 nm, states are to draw straight lines not exceeding 60 nm in length connecting fixed points that are defined by geographical coordinates.[69]

Important constraints are set by Article 76(5), which provides that the outer limit of the continental shelf set by either approach shall not exceed 350 nm from the territorial sea baselines or 100 nm from the 2500 metre isobath (which in some cases will exceed 350 nm). Notwithstanding Article 76(5), Article 76(6) provides that on submarine ridges the outer limit of the continental shelf shall not exceed 350 nm. On submarine ridges, which are elongated elevations of the seafloor that constitute a natural prolongation of the land territory but which are not components of the continental margin, recourse therefore cannot be had to a line that runs 100 nm from the 2,500 metre isobath.[70] However, Article 76(6) makes clear that this limitation does not apply to 'submarine elevations that are natural components of the continental margin, such as its plateaux, rises, caps, banks and spurs'. Oceanic ridges are regarded as neither part of the continental margin, nor part of the natural prolongation of the land territory, but rather are part of the deep ocean floor.[71] Whether or not a satisfactory distinction may be drawn between submarine ridges, submarine elevations that are natural components of the continental margin, and oceanic ridges has given rise to considerable discussion, and will need to be resolved on a case-by-case basis by the CLCS as it considers submissions by coastal states.[72] One area where the issue has particular prominence is in the Arctic Ocean where if the submarine ridges are considered submarine elevations most of the seabed could fall within national jurisdiction.[73]

---

[67] LOSC, art 76(4)(a)(i).
[68] Ibid art 76(4)(a)(ii).
[69] Ibid art 76(7).
[70] *Virginia Commentaries*, vol 2, 880.
[71] LOSC, art 76(3).
[72] 'Scientific and Technical Guidelines of the Commission on the Limits of the Continental Shelf', UN Doc CLCS/11 (1999), 52–55.
[73] R Macnab, 'The Outer Limits of the Continental Shelf in the Arctic Ocean' in MH Nordquist, JN Moore and TH Heidar (eds), *Legal and Scientific Aspects of Continental Shelf Limits* (Leiden, Martinus Nijhoff, 2004) 301.

A. Commission on the Limits of the Continental Shelf

One of the major innovations of the LOSC in relation to the continental shelf is the establishment of a standing institution—the CLCS. Once it was accepted that coastal states could have a continental shelf extending beyond a fixed distance of 200 nm, attention had to turn to how to ensure that the delineation of the outer limits would adhere to the agreed formula. In the discussions in the Sea Bed Committee that was the precursor to UNCLOS III, China proposed that the maximum limits should be determined by states through direct consultation.[74] However, at UNCLOS III it became apparent that this would not provide the necessary certainty on an issue of such importance as the limits of a maritime zone with major resource implications. Accordingly proposals were put for the creation of an international body to consider continental shelf data. The United States at the third session contended that there should be a Continental Shelf Boundary Commission to review coastal state delineations and that the adoption of a seaward boundary on the basis of this review would be final and binding.[75]

What finally emerged from UNCLOS III was the CLCS, the mandate of which is set out in Article 76(8) of the LOSC. This provides that information on the limits of the continental shelf beyond 200 nm from the territorial sea baselines 'shall be submitted' by the coastal state to the Commission established under Annex II of LOSC.[76] The Commission 'shall make recommendations to coastal States' on the establishment of the outer limits of their continental shelf, and '[t]he limits of the shelf established by a coastal State on the basis of these recommendations shall be final and binding'. Annex II of LOSC provides additional details on the composition, function, role and procedures of the CLCS. There are also Rules of Procedure that have been adopted by the CLCS.[77] To provide direction to coastal states on the scientific and technical evidence admissible before the CLCS, and to clarify scientific, technical and legal terms in the LOSC, the CLCS adopted Scientific and Technical Guidelines in 1999.[78] These very detailed and extensive guidelines (which run to over 80 pages) are of great importance given that a number of terms in the LOSC are open to a number of equally valid interpretations and there is a need for consistency in the way states and the CLCS approach outer continental shelf issues.

The two functions of the CLCS are first to consider data that is submitted by coastal states and make recommendations, and second to provide scientific and technical advice to coastal states when requested to do so.[79] The CLCS consists of 21 members who are experts in the fields of geology, geophysics or hydrography elected by state parties to the LOSC having regard to considerations of equitable geographical representation,[80] and they serve in an individual and not representative capacity, although this is somewhat undermined by the way in which members' costs are met by governments. The CLCS is therefore an

---

[74] *Virginia Commentaries*, vol 2, 843.

[75] Ibid 849.

[76] Submissions made to the CLCS are available at www.un.org/Depts/los/clcs_new/commission_submissions. htm.

[77] 'Rules of Procedure of the Commission on the Limits of the Continental Shelf', UN Doc CLCS/40/Rev.1 (2008). These are the revised version of the rules first adopted in 1997.

[78] 'Scientific and Technical Guidelines of the Commission on the Limits of the Continental Shelf', UN Doc CLCS/11 (1999).

[79] LOSC, annex II, art 3.

[80] Ibid annex II, art 2.

independent scientific and technical body, rather than a political or legal institution. The mode of its functioning, which is via subcommissions that assess submissions and make recommendations to be considered, and approved or amended by the CLCS, is set out in the CLCS Rules of Procedure.[81]

Over the course of its operation to date it is possible to characterise the CLCS's work as falling within three phases: organisational, primary and secondary.[82] In the organisational stage from 1997 until 2001, the CLCS was concerned mainly to address procedural issues, such as the formulation of its Rules of Procedure. In the primary stage, which began in 2001 when the CLCS received its first submission, from the Russian Federation, the Commission's procedures were tested, and working methods were adopted. This primary phase extended until 2004, during which time the CLCS received an additional two submissions, from Brazil and Australia, and delivered its first set of recommendations in relation to Russia. Hence in the first stage the CLCS had received three very substantial submissions from two states with among the largest outer continental shelf areas that will ever come before the CLCS. The secondary phase commenced in 2005 and continues to this day, and is marked by the CLCS establishing more streamlined processes for addressing submissions. This has been a practical necessity given the very substantial workload of the CLCS, and the delays between receipt of submissions and the making of recommendations. In the case of the Russian submission this was only a seven month period, but by contrast in the case of the Australian submission it was 41 months. Although this partly reflected the size and complexity of the Australian submissions, others have taken two to three years to be reviewed by the relevant CLCS subcommission and for final recommendations to be made by the CLCS.

Coastal states that are parties to LOSC are required by Annex II of the LOSC to submit particulars of any outer continental shelf beyond 200 nm with supporting scientific and technical data as soon as possible, but in any case within 10 years of the entry into force of the LOSC for those states.[83] Given the substantial number of ratifications of the LOSC by the time it entered into force on 16 November 1994, a large number of submissions needed to be completed by 16 November 2004. It soon became clear that this deadline would not be realistic for many states given the considerable volume of data that they needed to collect to substantiate the establishment of an outer continental shelf. Accordingly, in 2001 a meeting of State Parties to the Convention resolved that for those states for which the LOSC entered into force prior to 13 May 1999 the ten-year period would begin to run from that date.[84] Hence for most states the deadline became 13 May 2009, and this explains the many submissions received in the first half of 2009. However, this new timeframe has also proven too demanding for some coastal states, particularly developing and least developed states. Accordingly there was a further decision of the States Parties to LOSC in 2008

---

[81] 'Rules of Procedure of the Commission on the Limits of the Continental Shelf', UN Doc CLCS/40/Rev.1 (2008).

[82] Donald R Rothwell, 'Issues and Strategies for Outer Continental Shelf Claims' (2008) 23 *International Journal of Marine and Coastal Law* 185, 193.

[83] LOSC, annex II, art 4. It has been argued that while not being required to, non-parties to the LOSC may also utilise the CLCS in establishing the outer limits of their continental shelf in view of the general acceptance that Article 76 is part of customary international law: Ted L McDorman, 'The Entry Into Force of the 1982 LOS Convention and the Article 76 Outer Continental Shelf Regime' (1995) 10 *International Journal of Marine and Coastal Law* 165, 179ff.

[84] UN Doc SPLOS/72 (2001).

that the ten-year time period referred to in Article 4 of Annex II to UNCLOS may be satisfied by submitting 'preliminary information', including an intended date for making a submission.[85] In any event it may be questioned whether the procedural requirement to meet the original or extended deadline affects a coastal state's substantive and inherent right to a continental shelf as accorded by Article 77(3) of LOSC which provides that 'the rights of the coastal state … do not depend on occupation, effective or notional, or on any express proclamation'.[86] There is certainly no penalty stipulated for failing to meet the deadline.

The work of the CLCS began relatively slowly but has steadily increased. By the end of 2007 it had received nine submissions, and made recommendations in relation to three of these. However, the workload has since grown dramatically, and for the period 2015–2017 the Commission agreed to meet for a total of 21 weeks each year.[87] By the beginning of 2015 the CLCS had received 77 full or partial submissions, yet made recommendations only in relation to 22 of these (see Table 5.1, below). It had also received 46 submissions of preliminary information, mostly from developing states, indicative of the outer limits of the continental shelf beyond 200 nm. Nine subcommissions were also active in 2015, meaning that only 31 of the 77 submissions to the CLCS (or 40 per cent) had been actively considered or resolved at that time. In view of the substantial workload that remains for the CLCS, it will be some time before most coastal states will be in a position to establish the outer limits of their continental shelf on the basis of CLCS recommendations.

One significant aspect of the developing practice of the CLCS process has been the making of a variety of different submissions short of complete submissions of data to address matters such as the capacity of coastal states to meet the May 2009 deadline, the existence of overlapping continental shelves, and unresolved land or maritime disputes. The CLCS Rules of Procedure address the situation where the outer continental shelves of coastal states overlap. Hence Annex I, Rule 3 of the Rules of Procedure provides that '[a] submission may be made by a coastal State for a portion of its continental shelf in order not to prejudice questions relating to the delimitation of boundaries'. In addition, Annex I Rule 5 of the Rules of Procedure stipulate that '[i]n cases where a land or maritime dispute exists, the Commission shall not consider and qualify a submission by any of the States concerned in the dispute'. However, 'the Commission may consider one or more submissions in the areas under dispute with prior consent given by all States that are parties to such a dispute'.

The partial submission strategy adopted by some coastal states have seen submissions based on staggered partial submissions,[88] uncontested partial submissions with future identified submissions reserved,[89] and uncontested partial submissions with future unidentified submissions reserved.[90] Another strategy has been to make a complete submission, but to request the CLCS for the time being not to consider aspects of the submission that are contested. This is the case with Australia's 2004 submission as it applies to the Australian

---

[85] UN Doc SPLOS/183 (2008).

[86] Suarez, *The Outer Limits of the Continental Shelf* (n 18) 183. See also Ted L McDorman, 'The Role of the Commission on the Limits of the Continental Shelf: A Technical Body in a Political World' (2002) 17 *International Journal of Marine and Coastal Law* 301, 305–306.

[87] 'Progress of work in the Commission on the Limits of the Continental Shelf: Statement by the Chair' UN Doc CLCS/88 (2015) [13].

[88] See, eg, the 2005 partial submission by Ireland in relation to the Porcupine Abyssal Plain.

[89] See, eg, the 2006 submission by New Zealand.

[90] See, eg, the 2007 partial submission by Mexico.

Antarctic Territory.[91] Recognising the sensitivity that the inclusion of Antarctic data raises for the international community and under the 1959 Antarctic Treaty, Australia asked that the CLCS not take any action for the time being in relation to the Antarctic data. Despite this the Australian submission generated a significant response by other states, with six parties to the Antarctic Treaty lodging objections with the CLCS.[92] The United States response was typical of these in stating that it 'does not recognize any State's claim to territory in Antarctica', or to 'the seabed and subsoil of the submarine areas beyond and adjacent to the continent of Antarctica'.[93]

A contentious issue for the CLCS has been submissions that have sought to rely upon maritime features more properly described as rocks than islands, and accordingly not entitled to generate claims to a continental shelf under Article 121(3). Japan's 2008 submission to the CLCS sought to rely upon Okinotorishima, a marine feature claimed by Japan in the western Pacific. Notes were submitted by both China and South Korea in response to the Japanese CLCS submission asserting that Okinotorishima was a rock and not an island,[94] and the matter was discussed at the 19th (2009) and 21st (2011) Meeting of State Parties to the LOSC.[95] At the time the Chairman of the CLCS indicated that the Commission acknowledged it had no role in interpreting Article 121.[96] China subsequently indicated that, with respect to the CLCS, 'As a body consisting of experts in the fields of geology, geophysics and hydrography, the Commission should avoid the situation in which its work influences the interpretation and application of relevant provisions of the Convention, including Article 121'.[97] In 2012 the CLCS finalised its recommendations to Japan and in doing so declined to take action on the submission relating to the Southern Kyushu-Palau Ridge Region until such time as the status of Okinotorishima was resolved.[98]

The CLCS is not an adjudicative body such as the ICJ and its recommendations are only that—recommendatory, and not legally binding.[99] If a coastal state bases the proclamation of its continental shelf outer limits on CLCS recommendations then these become 'final and binding'[100] for the coastal state. There is some debate as to whether they would also

[91] Compare this with the 2009 full submission by Argentina which included the 'Argentina Antarctic Sector' and which was accompanied by a request not to consider the Antarctic data. See Alan D Hemmings and Tim Stephens, 'Reconciling Regional and Global Dispensations: The Implications of Subantarctic Extended Continental Shelf Penetration of the Antarctic Treaty Area' (2008) 6 *New Zealand Year Book of International Law* 273, 276.

[92] Germany, India, Japan, the Netherlands, the Russian Federation and the United States. These are available at www.un.org/Depts/los/clcs_new/submissions_files/submission_aus.htm.

[93] United States, 'Note to the United Nations Secretary-General' (2004) at www.un.org/depts/los/clcs_new/submissions_files/aus04/clcs_03_2004_los_usatext.pdf.

[94] Communication of China (6 February 2009) at www.un.org/Depts/los/clcs_new/submissions_files/jpn08/chn_6feb09_e.pdf; Communication of Republic of Korea (27 February 2009) at www.un.org/Depts/los/clcs_new/submissions_files/jpn08/kor_27feb09_e.pdf.

[95] 'Report of the Nineteenth Meeting of States Parties' UN Doc SPLOS/203 (2009) [70]–[78]; 'Report of the Twenty-first Meeting of States Parties' UN Doc SPLOS/231 (2011) [87].

[96] 'Statement by the Chairmain of the Commission on the Limits of the Continental Shelf on the Progress of the Work in the Commission' UN Doc CLCS/62 (2009) [59].

[97] Communication of China (3 August 2011) at www.un.org/Depts/los/clcs_new/submissions_files/jpn08/chn_3aug11_e.pdf.

[98] 'Progress of Work in the Commission on the Limits of the Continental Shelf: Statement by the Chairperson' UN Doc CLCS/74 (2012) [19].

[99] McDorman, 'The Role of the Commission' (n 86) 313–17.

[100] LOSC, art 76(8).

be binding for the international community as a whole.[101] However, in practical terms the litmus test will be the presence or absence of state protest. Article 76(9) requires coastal states to deposit with the United Nations Secretary-General charts and relevant information 'permanently describing' the outer limits of the continental shelf, and the Secretary-General must give due publicity to these. Hence following a reasonable period after the recommendations are acted upon and charts drawn and deposited, if there is no objection from other states then there will be little doubt that the limits are indeed final and binding *erga omnes*.[102] In accordance with Article 76(9) and based on the recommendations of the CLCS, by 2015 Australia, Ireland, Mexico and the Philippines (Benham Rise) had deposited coordinates of the outer limits of their continental shelf beyond 200 nm with the Secretary-General.

Table 5.1: Submissions to the CLCS (as at 3 June 2015)

	Submission	Date of submission	Recommendations
1.	Russian Federation (including revisions)	20 December 2001	27 June 2002/ 11 March 2014 (revised)
2.	Brazil	17 May 2004	4 April 2007
3.	Australia	15 November 2004	9 April 2008
4.	Ireland—Porcupine Abyssal Plain	25 May 2005	5 April 2007
5.	New Zealand	19 April 2006	22 August 2008
6.	Joint submission by France, Ireland, Spain and the United Kingdom of Great Britain and Northern Ireland—in the area of the Celtic Sea and the Bay of Biscay	19 May 2006	24 March 2009
7.	Norway—in the North East Atlantic and the Arctic	27 November 2006	27 March 2009
8.	France—in respect of the areas of French Guiana and New Caledonia	22 May 2007	2 September 2009
9.	Mexico—in respect of the western polygon in the Gulf of Mexico	13 December 2007	31 March 2009
10.	Barbados (including revisions)	8 May 2008	15 April 2010/13 April 2012 (revised)
11.	United Kingdom of Great Britain and Northern Ireland—Ascension Island	9 May 2008	15 April 2010
12.	Indonesia—North West of Sumatra Island	16 June 2008	28 March 2011
13.	Japan	12 November 2008	19 April 2012

(continued)

---

[101] Judge Nelson of the ITLOS has argued, *extra curia*, that they would be: LDM Nelson, 'The Settlement of Disputes Arising From Conflicting Outer Continental Shelf Claims' (2009) 24 *International Journal of Marine and Coastal Law* 409, 418–19. But see McDorman, 'The Role of the Commission' (n 86) 315–16.

[102] McDorman, 'The Role of the Commission', ibid 317.

Table 5.1: *(Continued)*

	Submission	Date of submission	Recommendations
14.	Joint submission by the Republic of Mauritius and the Republic of Seychelles—in the region of the Mascarene Plateau	1 December 2008	30 March 2011
15.	Suriname	5 December 2008	30 March 2011
16.	Myanmar	16 December 2008	
17.	France—areas of the French Antilles and the Kerguelen Islands	5 February 2009	19 April 2012
18.	Yemen—in respect of south east of Socotra Island	20 March 2009	
19.	United Kingdom of Great Britain and Northern Ireland—in respect of Hatton Rockall Area	31 March 2009	
20.	Ireland—in respect of Hatton-Rockall Area	31 March 2009	
21.	Uruguay	7 April 2009	
22.	Philippines—in the Benham Rise region	8 April 2009	12 April 2012
23.	The Cook Islands—concerning the Manihiki Plateau	16 April 2009	
24.	Fiji	20 April 2009	
25.	Argentina	21 April 2009	
26.	Ghana	28 April 2009	5 September 2014
27.	Iceland—in the Ægir Basin area and in the western and southern parts of Reykjanes Ridge	29 April 2009	
28.	Denmark in the area north of the Faroe Islands	29 April 2009	11 March 2014
29.	Pakistan	30 April 2009	13 March 2015
30.	Norway—in respect of Bouvetøya and Dronning Maud Land	4 May 2009	
31.	South Africain respect of the mainland of the territory of the Republic of South Africa	5 May 2009	
32.	Joint submission by the Federated States of Micronesia, Papua New Guinea and Solomon Islands concerning the Ontong Java Plateau	5 May 2009	
33.	Joint submission by Malaysia and Viet Nam—in the southern part of the South China Sea	6 May 2009	

(continued)

Table 5.1: *(Continued)*

	Submission	Date of submission	Recommendations
34.	Joint submission by France and South Africa—in the area of the Crozet Archipelago and the Prince Edward Islands	6 May 2009	
35.	Kenya	6 May 2009	
36.	Mauritius—in the region of Rodrigues Island	6 May 2009	
37.	Viet Nam—in North Area (VNM-N)	7 May 2009	
38.	Nigeria	7 May 2009	
39.	Seychelles—concerning the Northern Plateau Region	7 May 2009	
40.	France—in respect of La Réunion Island and Saint-Paul and Amsterdam Islands	8 May 2009	
41.	Palau	8 May 2009	
42.	Côte d'Ivoire	8 May 2009	
43.	Sri Lanka	8 May 2009	
44.	Portugal	11 May 2009	
45.	United Kingdom of Great Britain and Northern Ireland—in respect of the Falkland Islands, and of South Georgia and the South Sandwich Islands	11 May 2009	
46.	Tonga	11 May 2009	
47.	Spain—in respect of the area of Galicia	11 May 2009	
48.	India	11 May 2009	
49.	Trinidad and Tobago	12 May 2009	
50.	Namibia	12 May 2009	
51.	Cuba	1 June 2009	
52.	Mozambique	7 July 2010	
53.	Maldives	26 July 2010	
54.	Denmark—Faroe-Rockall Plateau Region	2 December 2010	
55.	Bangladesh	25 February 2011	
56.	Madagascar	29 April 2011	
57.	Guyana	6 September 2011	
58.	Mexico—eastern polygon in the Gulf of Mexico	19 December 2011	
59.	United Republic of Tanzania	18 January 2012	
60.	Gabon	10 April 2012	

(continued)

Table 5.1: *(Continued)*

	Submission	Date of submission	Recommendations
61.	Denmark—Southern Continental Shelf of Greenland	14 June 2012	
62.	Tuvalu, France and New Zealand (Tokelau)—Robbie Ridge	7 December 2012	
63.	China—East China Sea	14 December 2012	
64.	Kırıbatı	24 December 2012	
65.	Republic of Korea	26 December 2012	
66.	Nicaragua—southwestern Caribbean Sea	24 June 2013	
67.	Federated States of Micronesia—Eauripik Rise	30 August 2013	
68.	Denmark—North-Eastern Continental Shelf of Greenland	26 November 2013	
69.	Angola	6 December 2013	
70.	Canada—Atlantic Ocean	6 December 2013	
71.	Bahamas	6 February 2014	
72.	France—Saint-Pierre-et Miquelon	16 April 2014	
73.	Tonga—western Lau-Colville Ridge	23 April 2014	
74.	Somalia	21 July 2014	
75.	Cabo Verde, The Gambia, Guinea, Guinea-Bissau, Mauritania, Senegal and Sierra Leone—Atlantic Ocean	25 September 2014	
76.	Denmark—Northern Continental Shelf of Greenland	15 December 2014	
77.	Spain—Canary Islands	17 December 2014	

Source: www.un.org/Depts/los/clcs_new/commission_submissions.htm

B. Rights and Duties of Coastal and Other States

The rights and duties of coastal states in the continental shelf are not substantially modified by the LOSC from the Geneva regime. The coastal state exercises over the continental shelf sovereign rights for the purpose of exploring and exploiting its natural resources.[103] These rights are exclusive in that coastal states can decide whether or not to explore or exploit their continental shelves and whether or not to grant access to other states.[104] Additionally, the coastal state has the exclusive right to authorise and regulate drilling on the continental

---

[103] LOSC, art 77(1).
[104] Ibid art 77(2).

shelf for all purposes.[105] In a 2015 ITLOS ruling on a request for provisional measures brought by Côte D'Ivoire against Ghana regarding oil exploration and exploitation in a disputed area of continental shelf, a Special Chamber of Tribunal observed:

> the rights of the coastal State over its continental shelf include all rights necessary for and connected with the exploration and exploitation of the natural resources of the continental shelf and that the exclusive right to access to information about the resources of the continental shelf is plausibly among those rights.[106]

Based on concerns that Ghana's planned exploration and exploitation activities may cause 'irreparable prejudice to the sovereign and exclusive rights' of Côte D'Ivoire and the risk of such prejudice was imminent,[107] ITLOS granted provisional measures in favour of Côte D'Ivoire.[108]

The resources that fall within the sovereign rights of coastal states include all natural resources, both living and non-living.[109] However, in relation to living resources it includes only sedentary species, that is those which at their harvestable stage are either immobile on or under the seabed, or are unable to move except in constant physical contact with the seabed or the subsoil.[110] Coastal states have the exclusive right to construct and authorise the construction of artificial islands, installations and structures for economic purposes, with the EEZ equivalent provisions being extended to the continental shelf.[111] One consequence of this coastal state right is that when the continental shelf extends beyond 200 nm, safety zones established in association with an artificial island, installation or structure would have a consequential impact upon the capacity of shipping to exercise the freedom of navigation upon what would otherwise be high seas.

Where a coastal state has a continental shelf that extends beyond 200 nm, its rights in this outer continental shelf are not as extensive as those within 200 nm. The rights over living resources are the same as those pertaining within 200 nm, but this is not the case for non-living resources. While coastal states still have exclusive sovereign rights over non-living resources, Article 82 requires the coastal states to make payments or contributions in kind to the ISA. Such payments or contributions are to be made annually after the first five years of production from a site on the outer continental shelf. For the sixth year the rate is to be one per cent of the value or volume of production, rising by one per cent for each year until the twelfth year, and remaining at seven per cent thereafter.[112] An exception applies to developing states that are net importers of a mineral resource produced from its continental shelf—these states are not required to make payments or contributions to

---

[105]   Ibid art 81.
[106]   *Dispute Concerning Delimitation of the Maritime Boundary between Ghana and Côte D'Ivoire in the Atlantic Coast (Ghana/Côte D'Ivoire)* (provisional measures) 25 April 2015 www.itlos.org [94].
[107]   Ibid [96].
[108]   Ibid [108]. The dispute between Ghana and Côte D'Ivoire with respect to the maritime boundary between the two states is being separately determined by a Special Chamber of ITLOS following the commencement of proceedings in December 2014.
[109]   Ibid art 77(4).
[110]   Ibid.
[111]   Ibid arts 60, 80.
[112]   Ibid art 82(2).

the ISA.[113] The payments or contributions are to be distributed by the ISA 'on the basis of equitable sharing criteria', having regard to 'the interests and needs of developing states', especially 'the least developed and the land-locked among them'.[114]

As for other states, Article 78 seeks to safeguard their interests. The sovereign rights and jurisdiction of the coastal state in the continental shelf do not affect the legal status of the water column above the seabed, or indeed the airspace.[115] In addition, the exercise by the coastal state of its continental shelf rights are not to infringe or result in an unjustifiable interference with navigation and the other freedoms of states as provided for in LOSC.[116] Unlike the Geneva regime where reference is made to the high seas freedom of fishing, this was not possible in the context of Article 78(2) of LOSC because of the new EEZ regime, that displaces this freedom up to 200 nm.

An additional safeguard for the interests of other states is found in Article 79 which provides that all states are entitled to lay submarine cables and pipelines on the continental shelf.[117] Coastal states may not impede the laying or maintenance of such cables or pipelines except when taking reasonable measures for exploring the continental shelf, exploiting its resources, or regulating pollution from pipelines.[118] Submarine cables may be laid following any route, but the course of pipelines is subject to the consent of the coastal state.[119] When laying submarine cables or pipelines, states must have due regard to existing infrastructure of this character already in place, and not prejudice the possibility of repairing existing cables or pipelines.[120]

C. Relationship with the EEZ Regime

There are substantial overlaps between the continental shelf and EEZ regimes. Up to 200 nm both regimes give to coastal states essentially the same rights to exploit the non-living resources found in and on the seabed and subsoil. However, there are some important differences between the two regimes. First, the continental shelf need not be proclaimed, and vests inherently in coastal states, whereas the EEZ must be asserted. Secondly, the two regimes differ in the way they regulate the exploitation of living resources. The EEZ regime seeks to promote the conservation and management of fisheries in the EEZ, whereas the continental shelf regime makes no mention of this objective in relation to sedentary fisheries. As sedentary fisheries are expressly excluded from the EEZ regime by Article 68 this means that coastal states may exploit them to extinction should they wish. Indeed, under the continental shelf regime there is no duty on coastal states to conserve any resources within the continental margin, whether living or non-living. This is consistent with the theory of the continental shelf as a natural prolongation of land territory, in respect of which there is no general duty to conserve resources. Whether it is appropriate in an era

[113] Ibid art 82(3).
[114] Ibid art 82(4).
[115] Ibid art 78(1).
[116] Ibid art 78(2).
[117] Ibid art 79(1).
[118] Ibid art 79(2).
[119] Ibid art 79(3).
[120] Ibid art 79(5).

of growing resource scarcity is another question entirely.[121] Moreover, the corollary of an exclusive right to explore and exploit would appear to be a right to conserve sedentary species on the outer continental shelf, which would permit coastal states to adopt policies of sustainable development, or outright preservation through the designation of a marine protected area.[122] It is in the outer continental shelf where the distinction between sedentary and non-sedentary species remains relevant (unlike the 200 nm continental shelf, which overlaps with the EEZ).

VI. Further Reading

Peter J Cook and Chris M Carleton (eds), *Continental Shelf Limits: The Scientific and Legal Interface* (Oxford, Oxford University Press, 2000)

Hersch Lauterpacht, 'Sovereignty over Submarine Areas' (1950) 27 *British Yearbook of International Law* 376

Ted L McDorman, 'The Continental Shelf' in Donald R Rothwell, Alex G Oude Elferink, Karen N Scott and Tim Stephens (eds), *The Oxford Handbook of the Law of the Sea* (Oxford, Oxford University Press, 2015) 181

MH Nordquist, JN Moore and TH Heidar (eds), *Legal and Scientific Aspects of Continental Shelf Limits* (Leiden, Martinus Nijhoff, 2004)

Zdenek L Slouka, *International Custom and the Continental Shelf* (The Hague, Martinus Nijhoff, 1968)

Suzette V Suarez, *The Outer Limits of the Continental Shelf: Legal Aspects of their Establishment* (Berlin, Springer, 2008)

---

[121] See David M Ong, 'Towards an International Law for the Conservation of Offshore Hydrocarbon Resources within the Continental Shelf?' in David Freestone, Richard Barnes and David M Ong (eds), *The Law of the Sea: Progress and Prospects* (Oxford, Oxford University Press, 2006) 93.

[122] Joanna Mossop, 'Protecting Marine Biodiversity on the Continental Shelf Beyond 200 Nautical Miles' (2007) 38 *Ocean Development and International Law* 283, 289.

6

The Deep Seabed

I. Introduction

One of the most important and contentious areas in the law of the sea relates to the regulation of the deep seabed, the submarine area of the seafloor beyond the continental shelf where a wealth of mineral resources can be found. Until the 1960s the deep seabed was regarded as part of the high seas, subject to high seas freedoms, and therefore amenable to exploitation by all states. This position had gone largely unchallenged as there was no real prospect that deep seabed resources could feasibly be exploited. However, with developments in mining technologies, rising mineral prices and the emergence of new developing states in the 1960s keen to secure a fairer international economic order, there came a major shift in international opinion. This led fairly rapidly to the seabed being designated as the 'common heritage of mankind' and, on the basis of this principle, to the detailed regime in Part XI of the LOSC to regulate deep seabed mining activities.

The main components of the common heritage of humankind doctrine in the context of the deep seabed are: the non-appropriation of seabed areas and seabed resources by states or private entities; a system of international management of deep seabed mining through the ISA, which was established by the LOSC; the sharing of benefits from deep seabed mining for the common good of humanity; and the peaceful use of deep seabed areas.[1] There have been suggestions that the common heritage of humankind principle could be extended to the conservation and sustainable use of biodiversity beyond national jurisdiction. However, in the law of the sea as it currently stands the principle has only direct relevance and application to the mineral resources of the deep seabed.

The debates prior and during UNCLOS III over the legal status of the deep seabed were foreshadowed to some extent in the ILC in the 1950s as it formulated draft articles on the law of the sea that formed the basis for the four Geneva Conventions agreed at UNCLOS I.[2] However, it was only with the decolonisation process that reached its peak in the 1960s that sustained pressure began to build for deep seabed resources to be declared the common heritage of humankind and subject to a regime for equitable exploitation. Even with the shift in legal doctrine that this dynamic had brought about by the 1970s, many issues surrounding the actual implementation of the common heritage regime remained abstract.

---

[1] See generally Christopher C Joyner, 'Legal Implications of the Concept of the Common Heritage of Mankind' (1986) 35 *International and Comparative Law Quarterly* 190, 191–95.

[2] At UNCLOS I several delegations proposed that the continental shelf be exploited for the benefit of all humanity: *Virginia Commentaries*, vol 6, 8–9.

These issues were subsequently addressed at UNCLOS III and in Part XI of the LOSC, but the regime was controversial and led to the United States declining to sign the LOSC because of the particular balance it struck between the interests of industrialised states and developing states in relation to seabed resources and their management.

Twelve years after the LOSC was concluded, and on the eve of the Convention entering into force, its complex seabed mining provisions were modified by a supplementary agreement, the 1994 Agreement Relating to the Implementation of Part XI (1994 Agreement).[3] The 1994 Agreement satisfied many of the concerns that western states harboured in relation to the common heritage regime, thereby enabling most of these states (with the notable exception of the United States) to ratify the LOSC secure in the knowledge that their mining interests would be protected. However, only relatively recently has deep seabed mining started to become both technically and economically feasible, and it is only in this context that the applicable provisions of the LOSC and the 1994 Agreement have begun to have real impact for the law of the sea and states have enacted domestic legal frameworks to enable deep seabed mining to take place consistently with the LOSC.[4]

The ISA, which was established by Part XI of the LOSC, is now actively discharging several of the primary functions for which it was created.[5] Headquartered in Kingston, Jamaica, the ISA has drafted and adopted regulations towards the conclusion of a complete 'mining code' that deal not only with issues such as contractual arrangements with miners, but also the protection of unique and vulnerable seafloor habitats during exploration and exploitation of the deep seabed. Full-scale commercial mining still appears some distance away. However, since 2010 there has been a significant increase in seabed exploration. The ISA has entered into 22 contracts for exploration for polymetallic nodules and polymetallic sulphides covering around 900,000 square kilometres of the seafloor. Fourteen of these contracts are to explore for polymetallic nodules in the Pacific Ocean (the Clarion-Clipperton Fracture Zone) and the central Indian Ocean, five are to explore for polymetallic sulphides in the South West Indian Ridge, Central Indian Ridge and the Mid-Atlantic Ridge, and three are to explore for cobalt-rich crusts in the Western Pacific Ocean. The protection of the deep seabed environment has been a major focus for the ISA, and the environmental protection provisions of the deep seabed regime were considered in detail by the Seabed Disputes Chamber of ITLOS in *Responsibilities and Obligations of States Sponsoring Persons and Entities with Respect to Activities in the Area (Seabed Mining Advisory Opinion)*.[6]

II. The Deep Seabed: Environment and Resources

The deep seabed, or the 'Area', is defined by Article 1(1) of the LOSC to mean 'the seabed and ocean floor and subsoil thereof, beyond the limits of national jurisdiction'. These limits of national jurisdiction are either 200 nm from the territorial sea baselines, or

---

[3] *Basic Documents* No 37.

[4] See, eg, Deep Sea Mining Act 2014 (UK).

[5] For an overview see Michael Wood, 'International Seabed Authority: The First Four Years' (1999) 3 *Max Planck Yearbook of United Nations Law* 173; Michael Wood, 'The International Seabed Authority: Fifth to Twelfth Sessions (1999–2006)' (2007) 11 *Max Planck Yearbook of United Nations Law* 47.

[6] (2011) 50 ILM 458.

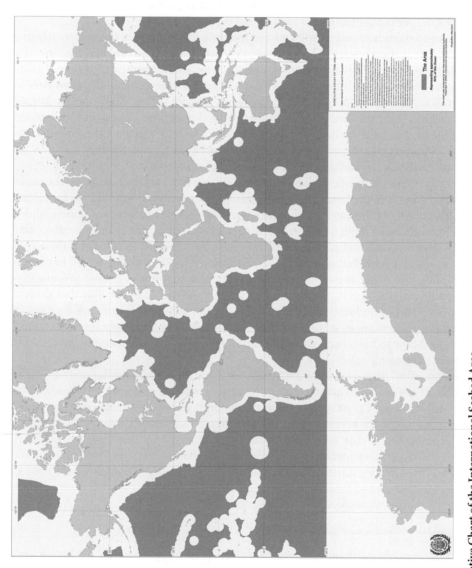

Figure 6.1: Indicative Chart of the International Seabed Area

Source: International Seabed Authority, www.isa.org.jm/files/documents/EN/Areamap.pdf

further beyond this distance out to the limits of the outer continental shelf established by states in conformity with Article 76 of the LOSC. Because of the procedure under Article 76, which requires data for extended continental shelves to be submitted to the Commission on the Limits of the Continental Shelf, with the limits to be established by coastal states on the basis of the Commission's recommendations, it will be some time before the extent of the Area can be determined conclusively. In approximate terms, however, the Area constitutes a remarkable 50 per cent of the earth's surface (see Figure 6.1, above).[7]

The Area contains a variety of mineral and hydrocarbon resources, but it is metals that have attracted the most interest. The first resource to be identified on the abyssal plains were polymetallic nodules, which were found during the 1872–77 scientific expedition of HMS *Challenger*.[8] These are small ball-like rock concretions, between 0.5 and 25 centimetres in diameter, scattered on the deep seabed at depths of about 4,000 to 6,000 metres. Among other materials, these nodules contain manganese, nickel, copper, cobalt, aluminium and iron. While polymetallic nodules are distributed widely, only three areas have attracted attention by industrial prospectors: the north central Pacific Ocean, the Peru Basin in the south-east Pacific Ocean and the middle of the north Indian Ocean.

The composition of specific nodules and their aggregation and abundance on the ocean floor varies substantially. Hence while they are found in many locations, it is speculated that there may only be three to ten sites where there are sizeable quantities of 'good nodules' containing sufficiently high concentrations of nickel, copper, manganese and cobalt.[9] Various systems for mining nodules have been designed and tested since the 1970s, not only by developed states but also by India, a prominent G-77 member, which has established a pilot processing plant.[10] The mining technique that appears most promising is the 'hydraulic mining system', which involves a self-propelled collector unit that dredges the seafloor, crushes nodules, and then pumps the ore to the surface as a slurry via an umbilical hose. There are as yet no commercial scale nodule mining operations, and there remain significant technical and economic hurdles to be overcome before it can compete with terrestrial mining.

There are also major environmental concerns surrounding nodule mining.[11] The disruption of the seafloor that it necessarily involves, and the generation of waste-water plumes, will affect a range of species found on the deep seabed. It will also destroy species on the surface and in the crevices of the nodules themselves (indeed, one theory as to how nodules concretised is that their precipitation was catalysed by these microorganisms). Surveys of nodules have identified a rich variety of characteristic and endemic abyssal fauna, and there is a legitimate apprehension that nodule mining, which would need to occur over a large area to be economically viable, would result in the extinction of many unique and undiscovered species.[12]

---

[7] Michael Lodge, 'Collaborative Marine Scientific Research on the International Seabed' (2008) *The Journal of Ocean Technology* 30, 30.

[8] See ISA, *Polymetallic Nodules* at www.isa.org.jm/files/documents/EN/Brochures/ENG7.pdf; Hjalmar Thiel, 'Use and Protection of the Deep Sea—An Introduction' (2001) 38 *Deep Sea Research II* 3427.

[9] ISA, *Polymetallic Nodules*, ibid 3.

[10] NK Mittal and PK Sen, 'India's First Medium-Scale Demonstration Plant for Treating Poly-Metallic Nodules' (2003) 16 *Minerals Engineering* 865.

[11] Lahrs Suhr, 'Environmental Protection in Deep Seabed Mining: International Law and New Zealand's Approach' (2008) 12 *New Zealand Journal of Environmental Law* 97, 108 ff.

[12] See, eg, Julie Veillette et al, 'Ferromanganese Nodule Fauna in the Tropical North Pacific Ocean: Species Richness, Faunal Cover and Spatial Distribution' (2007) 54 *Deep-Sea Research I* 1912.

A second potential source of resources on the deep seabed are cobalt-rich ferromanganese crusts, that are found on and around volcanic seamounts, the tens of thousands of undersea mountains throughout the world's oceans. The resources of relatively few seamounts have been sampled; however, large deposits of cobalt crusts have been identified in several sites in the Pacific Ocean.[13] As with nodules, these crusts have formed through a process of precipitation of minerals from the seawater. They are up to 25 cm in thickness, and may cover as much as 1.7 per cent of the total ocean floor.[14] They are often in more accessible locations than nodules, as they are found in depths anywhere from 400 to 4,000 metres. Cobalt-rich crusts are a potentially important source not only of cobalt but also manganese and nickel. However, although many crusts can be found at relatively shallow depths they are not as readily recoverable as nodules because of the attachment to substrate rock which makes it difficult for operators to mine the minerals without also taking excessive amounts of the substrate.

Seamounts are also more biologically variegated than the abyssal plains where nodules are found and support many species of bottom-dwelling and demersal marine life. The upwelling of water at these sites means that there are large quantities of nutrients available to support complex ecological communities, including pelagic fish and seabirds.[15] The physical environmental impacts of crust mining is likely to be similar to nodule mining, although these will be confined to smaller areas. Nonetheless, as with the organisms of the abyssal plain, the species found on seamounts indicate a high degree of endemism, and therefore there is a high likelihood of extinction of some species during mining operations.

The third focus for industrial miners are deposits of polymetallic sulphides found near hydrothermal vents, up to 4,000 metres in depth.[16] Hydrothermal vents were discovered in the late 1970s, and occur at the boundaries of tectonic plates where seawater seeps into the ocean crust, later to emerge superheated, and rich in minerals. These minerals precipitate out of solution quickly when the mineralised water comes into contact with the water column, which is near freezing point, and generate chimney-like formations (known as white or black 'smokers', according to the colour of the plume of mineral-rich water they discharge). This results in the accumulation of many thousands, and in some cases millions, of tonnes of sulphides containing high concentrations of the base metals lead, zinc and copper, and also precious metals gold and silver. Sulphide mining at hydrothermal vents appears more economically viable than either nodule or cobalt crust mining because of the accessibility of some vents that are relatively close to shore, are found in relatively shallow waters and contain very high mineral grades.[17] The world's first massive sulphide recovery operation is planned in the territorial sea of Papua New Guinea.[18] As this project is to be in territorial waters, it does not fall within the purview of the LOSC deep seabed regime. However, its success or otherwise will be a harbinger for potential exploration and exploitation of massive sulphides within the Area.

The environment of hydrothermal vents is highly unique and productive, and supports many species that were previously completely unknown to the scientific community. These

[13] See ISA, *Cobalt-Rich Crusts* at www.isa.org.jm/files/documents/EN/Brochures/ENG9.pdf, 1.
[14] Ibid 2.
[15] Suhr, 'Environmental Protection in Deep Seabed Mining' (n 11) 109.
[16] ISA, *Polymetallic Sulphides* at www.isa.org.jm/files/documents/EN/Brochures/ENG8.pdf.
[17] Porter Hoagland et al, 'Deep-sea Mining of Seafloor Massive Sulfides' (2010) 34 *Marine Policy* 728, 729.
[18] For a schematic diagram of the mining plan for this deposit see Hoagland et al, 'Deep-sea Mining' ibid 730.

include organisms that produce energy from chemosynthesis (chemical reactions with hydrogen sulphide) rather than photosynthesis. Much remains unknown about the biota near vents, which like other seafloor habitats also appears to be highly endemic. Given the highly unusual nature of hydrothermal vent ecological communities they are a focus of significant MSR effort, including bioprospecting for organisms of value to the pharmaceutical industry. By way of example, a species of bacteria found on a deep sea vent (*Thermococcus litoralis*) is used for DNA replication in laboratories because of its capacity to endure the repeated heating and cooling that DNA testing involves.

With no mining operations currently being undertaken at hydrothermal vents, MSR currently poses the most serious threat to biodiversity at vent sites. However, as the ISA does not have general oversight over such activities (unless carried out directly under its own auspices), calls have been made for marine researchers to adopt a voluntary code of conduct.[19] More generally it has been recommended that a precautionary approach should be taken and that marine protected areas should be established around selected vent sites, with MSR and mining to take place only under tightly controlled conditions.[20]

III. Early Debates: Sedentary Fisheries and the Deep Seabed

Well before advances in MSR revealed mineral resources of economic value on the deep seabed, there was a significant amount of state practice in relation to another seafloor resource—sedentary fisheries. From the early nineteenth century a range of claims were made in relation to pearl, mollusc and other sessile fisheries on the seabed beyond the territorial sea. There was considerable debate as to the international legal significance of this practice.[21] Did it amount to the acquisition of seabed areas that were *res nullius*, that is, belonging to no state until effectively occupied? Did long-standing arrangements for harvesting sedentary species give rise to historic rights in certain seabed areas, in derogation of the freedom of fishing? Alternatively, should seafloor fishing be regarded as an exercise of the freedom to fish in a *res communis* area that was open to all states and not subject to appropriation, so that all that was acquired was the resource itself, and not the area from which it was harvested?

Some of these issues were canvassed in argument in the *Bering Fur Seals* case[22] in the late nineteenth century. That arbitration concerned the legality of enforcement action taken by the United States against Canadian (and therefore British-flagged) vessels that were hunting Alaskan fur seals on the high seas. The United States argued on several grounds that it had jurisdiction beyond the territorial sea over the seals, including on the basis that the

---

[19] Lyle Glowka, 'Putting Marine Scientific Research on a Sustainable Footing at Hydrothermal Vents' (2003) 27 *Marine Policy* 303.

[20] Jochen Halfar and Rodney M Fujita, 'Precautionary Management of Deep-Sea Mining' (2002) 26 *Marine Policy* 103, 105. See also Andrew J Davies et al, 'Preserving Deep-Sea Natural Heritage: Emerging Issues in Offshore Conservation and Management' (2007) 138 *Biological Conservation* 299, 304–306.

[21] DP O'Connell, *The International Law of the Sea*, vol 1 (Oxford, Clarendon Press, 1982) 450–57. See also [1956] *Yearbook of the International Law Commission*, vol 1, 293.

[22] *Bering Sea Fur Seals (Great Britain v United States)* (1898) 1 Moore 755.

substantial connection of the species with Alaska meant that they could be compared with immobile seafloor fisheries. The British government argued in response that there was no similarity between pelagic and seafloor fisheries. Nonetheless it was accepted that a state may 'claim portions of the soil under the sea' and that pearl fisheries and other sedentary fisheries may therefore be claimed in the same way that 'mines within the territory may be worked out under the sea below the low-water mark'.[23] The arbitral tribunal did not need to rule on this issue, and it rejected the United States' claim by applying the freedom of the seas doctrine. However, it is significant that both Britain and the United States took a view that was consistent with the idea that the seabed was *res nullius*, and therefore able to be acquired by occupation.[24]

The idea that certain organisms should be regarded as fixtures in the soil of the seabed, because of their attachment to it, was therefore closely connected with the view that the seabed beyond national jurisdiction could be subject to state sovereignty.[25] This view had some currency, if not widespread support, well into the twentieth century,[26] with the British government responding favourably to the Truman Proclamation in 1945,[27] which claimed for the United States sovereign rights in the continental shelf, on the grounds that it could be justified by the occupation theory.[28] However, the *res nullius* doctrine when applied to the seabed always had a high degree of unreality, in that conventional theories of occupation could not be reconciled with the reality that the deep seafloor could not be effectively claimed or controlled by states. As O'Connell put it, more would be required than mere 'paper claims to sovereignty', and there would have to be 'physical presence sufficiently permanent to guarantee the exclusion of others'.[29] Intermittent harvesting of living and non-living resources would not be sufficient, and there would need to be some kind of lasting presence such as mining infrastructure located on, or attached to, the seafloor.[30] This, however, could not be squared with the way in which it was thought that seabed mining would actually have to take place at great depths by suction and scooping, rather than by permanent installations.[31]

IV. The Moratorium Resolution and Principles Resolution

The Truman Proclamation, and other similar assertions of coastal state entitlement to the continental shelf, dramatically raised the profile of the legal issues surrounding the deep seabed. Beyond establishing clear limits to the continental shelf, it was also critical to determine the status of the deep seabed. Despite isolated statements to the contrary, the general view was that the deep seabed had the same status as the high seas. This was certainly

---

[23] Quoted in O'Connell, *The International Law of the Sea* (n 21) vol 1, 454.
[24] Ibid 454.
[25] Ibid 456.
[26] See Cecil JB Hurst, 'Whose Is the Bed of the Sea—Sedentary Fisheries Outside the Three-Mile Limit' (1923–24) 4 *British Year Book of International Law* 34.
[27] *Basic Documents* No 5.
[28] O'Connell, *The International Law of the Sea* (n 21) vol 1, 456.
[29] Ibid 457.
[30] Ibid 457–58.
[31] Ibid 458.

implicit in the work of the ILC in the 1950s, which suggested that except in relation to certain historic seafloor fisheries the seabed was part of the high seas.[32] This view prevailed at UNCLOS I where the ILC's draft articles were considered and transformed into four separate conventions.[33]

The assumption that the seabed was open to all states to exploit meant that as technologies improved it would be likely that industrialised states would monopolise seabed resources. It was therefore anticipated that there would soon be a scramble for minerals in this new frontier, to the great detriment of the newly independent states that would be effectively locked out of deep seabed mining. Moreover many of these new developing states were heavily dependent on export earnings from terrestrial mining of the many minerals that would be exploited on the seafloor, and their economies would be seriously affected if global commodity prices fell or collapsed as seafloor minerals were brought to market.

With these concerns in mind, in 1967 in the UNGA the Maltese Ambassador to the United Nations, Dr Arvid Pardo, called for the deep seabed and its resources to be designated as the 'common heritage of mankind'.[34] Under the Maltese proposal neither states, nor any other legal entity, including mining companies, would be able to acquire rights in the seabed or its mineral resources. Pardo not only advocated for an equitable seabed regime, he also expressed particular concern at the risk of militarisation of the deep seabed. Much as the Truman Proclamation in 1945 had reflected the views of many states in relation to continental shelf resources, Pardo's proposal to internationalise the deep seabed captured the zeitgeist of the late 1960s and quickly gained support.[35] Developing states regarded the common heritage of humankind concept as an integral part of the New International Economic Order that would bring some level of equity to the world economy,[36] and several UNGA resolutions were subsequently adopted to give effect to the Maltese initiative.[37] The UNGA also established the Committee to Study the Peaceful Uses of the Seabed and the Ocean Floor Beyond the Limits of National Jurisdiction, with the mandate to examine legal rules for the deep seabed that would foster international cooperation in the exploitation of seabed resources for the benefit of all humanity.[38] The work of the Seabed Committee proved to be an important catalyst for UNCLOS III, as it was soon realised that agreement on deep seabed mining could only realistically be achieved by simultaneously resolving a complete package of law of the sea questions, including addressing the interaction of the deep seabed regime with the continental shelf regime.[39]

Before UNCLOS III was convened, the UNGA adopted a series of resolutions on the topic of the deep seabed, of which two were particularly important. The first of these was a 1969 resolution on the 'Question of the Reservation Exclusively for Peaceful Purposes of the Sea-Bed and the Ocean Floor, and the Subsoil Thereof, Underlying the High Seas Beyond

---

[32] [1956] *Yearbook of the International Law Commission*, vol 1, 293.

[33] AV Lowe, 'The International Seabed: A Legacy of Mistrust' (1981) 5 *Marine Policy* 205, 205.

[34] UN Doc A/C.1/PV 1515 and A/C.1/PV 1516 (1967).

[35] ED Brown, 'Neither Necessary Nor Prudent at this Stage' (1993) 17 *Marine Policy* 81, 82.

[36] Robert L Friedheim, *Negotiating the New Ocean Regime* (Columbia, South Carolina, University of South Carolina, 1993) 221; Roderick C Ogley, 'The Law of the Sea Draft Convention and the New International Economic Order' (1981) 5 *Marine Policy* 240.

[37] The first of which was UNGA Resolution 2340 (XXII) (1967) which recognised 'the common interest of mankind in the sea-bed and ocean floor, which constitute the major portion of the area of this planet'.

[38] UNGA Resolution 2467 A (XXIII) (1968), [2].

[39] O'Connell, *The International Law of the Sea* (n 21) vol 1, 461.

the Limits of Present National Jurisdiction, and the Use of Their Resources in the Interests of Mankind'.[40] This resolution, known as the Moratorium Resolution, attracted 62 votes in favour, 28 against, and 28 abstentions. It affirmed that the exploitation of the resources of the seabed and ocean floor beyond the limits of national jurisdiction should be carried out for the benefit of mankind as a whole, and taking into account the special needs and interests of developing states. In order to achieve this outcome the resolution observed that it was essential for an international regime and accompanying international machinery to be established. The resolution concluded by declaring, in its final paragraph, that pending the establishment of such a regime:

(a)   States and persons, physical or juridical, are bound to refrain from all activities of exploitation of the resources of the area of the sea-bed and ocean floor, and the subsoil thereof, beyond the limits of national jurisdiction;

(b)   No claim to any part of that area or its resources shall be recognized.

The legal effect of the resolution was heavily contested. Many of those states that had voted in its favour argued that the resolution established new, or recognised existing, customary norms on the point. However, given that the resolution was supported by only 62 of a total of 118 United Nations members, it could not be argued that it instantly created new law. The major powers certainly took the view that the resolution was recommendatory only, while at the same time, and somewhat paradoxically, taking steps to restrain deep seabed mining.[41] This practice suggested that they accepted the common heritage doctrine in general terms, while having concerns about how it would be given effect. In this regard it needs to be noted that the primary concern of the industrialised states was to ensure investment certainty and to minimise the chance of confrontation on the high seas, and it was becoming increasingly clear this would be more readily achieved by an internationalised regime, than by a free-for-all under an open-access regime.[42]

The Moratorium Resolution was followed in 1970 by another, more detailed, General Assembly resolution: the 'Declaration of Principles Governing the Sea-Bed and the Ocean Floor, and the Subsoil Thereof, Beyond the Limits of National Jurisdiction'.[43] In an indication of the rapid coalescing of consensus on the issue, the Declaration of Principles attracted 108 votes in favour, none against, and only 14 abstentions. The Declaration of Principles expanded on the common heritage of humankind concept that had been articulated by Ambassador Pardo.

The Declaration of Principles expressly proclaimed that the seabed and ocean floor, and the subsoil thereof, beyond national jurisdiction (which it referred to as 'the Area') and its resources were the 'common heritage of mankind'. The Area was not to be subject to appropriation by states or non-state entities, nor could states claim or exercise sovereignty or sovereign rights over any part of it. No state or person could assert rights in the Area or to its resources in a way that was incompatible with the international regime to be established. All activities of exploration and exploitation were to be governed by the regime. The Area was to be used exclusively for peaceful purposes. And, above all, its exploration and exploitation was to be carried out 'for the benefit of mankind as a whole, irrespective of

---

[40]   UNGA Resolution 2574 D (XXIV) (1969), *Basic Documents* No 16.
[41]   O'Connell, *The International Law of the Sea* (n 21) vol 1, 461.
[42]   Ibid 462–63.
[43]   UNGA Resolution 2749 (XXV) (1970), *Basic Documents* No 17.

the geographical location of States, whether landlocked or coastal, and taking into account particular consideration the interests and needs of the developing countries'. States were to promote international cooperation in scientific research in the Area, and take appropriate measures to prevent pollution and contamination of the marine environment.

Although setting out broad and important principles, the Declaration of Principles left a range of issues to be resolved in a treaty establishing the regime foreshadowed in the resolution. Both the Moratorium Resolution and the Declaration of Principles were adhered to by industrialised states in practice, as deep seabed mining remained uncommercial. They were also heeded in word by the dominant industrialised state, the United States, which tabled a draft treaty with the Seabed Committee in 1970 that ruled out national jurisdiction beyond the continental margin, and would have established an International Seabed Resources Authority with authority to license miners and collect royalties.[44] However, until such a regime was established, the United States and other industrialised states took the view that although the deep seabed could not be subject to occupation[45] it could in principle be mined in the exercise of high seas freedoms.[46] Even if this position was contrary to the Moratorium and Principles Resolutions, industrialised states did not accept that these declarations had established customary rules, still less peremptory norms from which no derogation is permitted.

V. UNCLOS III

The need to resolve the deep seabed question was a major reason behind the convening of UNCLOS III. However, it was also the issue that gave rise to some of the most deep-seated divisions at the conference, which continued to be unresolved to some extent for more than a decade after the LOSC was concluded. What follows is only a brief account of these developments, which are now primarily of historical interest because of the successful conclusion of the 1994 Agreement which modified the deep seabed provisions of the LOSC to the satisfaction of most states.

The original form that Part XI took in the LOSC was one in which the ISA possessed extensive capacity to regulate seabed mining to give effect to the common heritage of humankind principle.[47] Provisions of a general character are found at the outset of Part XI in Articles 133 to 135, which serve among other things to define the resources embraced by the regime, and the scope of the deep seabed. They are followed by provisions which articulate principles governing the Area, including the 'common heritage of mankind',[48] a term that is not defined, but the meaning of which is made clear in successive provisions

---

[44] O'Connell, *The International Law of the Sea* (n 21) vol 1, 462.

[45] Hence the United States rejected a claim in 1974 by a United States corporation, Deepsea Ventures Inc, for exclusive mining rights in an area in the Clarion-Clipperton Zone. See Edward Guntrip, 'The Common Heritage of Mankind: An Adequate Regime for Managing the Deep Seabed?' (2003) 4 *Melbourne Journal of International Law* 376, 388–89.

[46] For a defence of this position see Theodore G Kronmiller, *The Lawfulness of Deep Seabed Mining* (Dobbs Ferry, New York, Oceana, 1980) vol 1.

[47] For a comprehensive commentary on the original Part XI provisions and the changes effected by the 1994 Agreement, see *Virginia Commentaries*, vol 6.

[48] LOSC, art 136.

addressing a variety of matters, including the legal status of the Area;[49] the requirement that activities in the Area be carried out for the benefit of humankind;[50] the use of the Area exclusively for peaceful purposes;[51] the transfer of mining technologies from developed countries to the Enterprise and to developing states;[52] and the effective participation of developing states in Area activities.[53] These principles are in turn followed by more complex provisions addressing development of Area resources, which include complicated formulae relating to the rate of production of seabed minerals to protect existing developing country producers.[54] In Article 153 provision is made for a parallel system of exploration and exploitation whereby the Enterprise could engage in mining alongside other miners, in sites 'banked' by successful mining applicants specifically for the purpose of the ISA. There are then extensive provisions setting out the functions and powers of the ISA.[55]

Much of the controversy at UNCLOS III in relation to the deep seabed turned on the nature and powers of the ISA.[56] Developing states argued for an authority that would have far reaching powers to regulate deep seabed mining and to engage in mining itself, whereas the industrialised countries (in which the major mining companies were based) sought a more skeletal institution that would operate essentially as a registry for concessions.[57] Underlying industrial state concerns about the ISA was the fear that it would act against their interests because developing states would have a substantial numerical advantage in the institution's governing bodies.

Failure to reach universal agreement on these and other issues lead to the somewhat unsatisfactory conclusion of UNCLOS III in 1982. The LOSC was adopted not by consensus as had been hoped and expected, but rather by vote which meant that some level of dissent would be openly expressed. In the event only four states, including the United States, voted against the LOSC, but a further 17 abstained, including the United Kingdom, Belgium, the Federal Republic of Germany, Italy, the Netherlands, the Soviet Union and the Eastern bloc states. Therefore, with few exceptions, those states involved or interested in deep seabed mining did not vote in support of the LOSC.

This outcome might seem surprising given the concurrence of views that had been attained on deep seabed issues in 1980, following eight years of negotiations in UNCLOS III. However, the reasons behind the 1982 vote lie in the disarray into which negotiations were thrown by the United States. Just before the tenth session of UNCLOS III began in 1981, the United States delegation announced that there was to be a wholesale policy review of the negotiating text by the new Reagan administration, which identified a range of concerns with Part XI, including the preferential treatment for the Enterprise; the mandatory transfer of technology; production limitations to benefit land-based producers; no guaranteed United States representation on the ISA Council; the potential for a Review Conference to adopt amendments binding on the United States without its assent; revenue

---

[49] Ibid art 137.
[50] Ibid art 140.
[51] Ibid art 141.
[52] Ibid art 144.
[53] Ibid art 148.
[54] Ibid art 151.
[55] Ibid pt XI, s 4.
[56] Lowe, 'The International Seabed: A Legacy of Mistrust' (n 33) 205.
[57] Ibid.

sharing obligations attaching to contractors; and the absence of protection for preparatory investors.[58] This effectively placed negotiations on seabed matters in limbo. Then, prior to the eleventh session in 1982, the United States indicated that it would return to negotiations subject to its concerns being addressed. The United States formulated detailed proposed amendments that were debated by the conference, but initially resisted by the G-77 states.

Despite significant concessions subsequently granted by the G-77 group, the regime remained unsatisfactory for the United States and other major industrialised states because it was thought that it would discourage seabed mining, and would not allow industrialised states an appropriate role in the decision-making of the ISA. This was despite the fact that the adoption of UNCLOS III was accompanied by a Final Act that included two resolutions which accommodated the position of the United States and other industrialised states that had not yet endorsed the LOSC.

Resolution I of UNCLOS III established a Preparatory Commission which, as its name suggests, was tasked with making preparations for the establishment and operation of the ISA, including by agreeing on the organisation's rules of procedure. The Preparatory Commission was also charged with giving effect to Resolution II of UNCLOS III, which made provision for the protection of pioneer enterprises which had already made substantial investments in seabed mining. The Preparatory Commission continued its work until being dissolved in 1994 on the entry into force of the LOSC, and the formal establishment of the ISA.

Under Resolution II, 'pioneer investors' were given preferential treatment, and could immediately carry out 'pioneer activities' that included not only prospecting, but also activities normally considered to be exploratory, such as the recovery of polymetallic nodules to aid in the design, fabrication and testing of nodule mining equipment.[59] There were three categories of pioneer investors: four states or their enterprises (France, Japan, India and the Soviet Union), four multinational consortiums, and pioneers from developing states. To be registered as a pioneer investor, an applicant needed to establish that before 1 January 1983 it had expended at least US$30 million on pioneer activities. Pioneer investors were required to pay a substantial registration fee (of US$250,000), along with an annual fee of US$1 million per annum when the pioneer area was allocated. Pioneer investors could be required to undertake exploration on behalf of the Enterprise, the mining arm of the ISA, on an essentially at-cost basis. In terms of the pioneer area, pioneer investors were to be allocated only one such area, to be no greater in area than 150,000 square kilometres. Pioneers also had to nominate a second area to be allocated to the ISA, which could be exploited by the Enterprise or by developing states.

Although the pioneer scheme sought to give immediate and interim protection to investors, it was in important respects contingent on the LOSC entering into force. Only preliminary 'pioneer activity' could be conducted until the pioneer had submitted a plan of work to the ISA and had it approved. This had to take place within three years of the entry into force of the LOSC. Furthermore, commercial mining required the granting of a production authorisation by the ISA on application by a pioneer, and this could only occur once the LOSC entered into force.

[58] *Virginia Commentaries*, vol 6, 48–49.
[59] Brown, 'Neither Necessary nor Prudent at this Stage' (n 35) 85.

A. Reciprocating States Regime

Resolution II was not the last word on the deep seabed mining issue before the 1994 Agreement was adopted and the LOSC entered into force. A number of understandings and agreements were concluded after 1982 that adapted and amended the operation of Resolution II, including the 1984 Provisional Understanding Regarding Deep Seabed Matters[60] between eight industrialised states (Belgium, France, the Federal Republic of Germany, Italy, Japan, the Netherlands, the United Kingdom and the United States). This agreement addressed potential conflicts arising from overlapping areas of interest to pioneer investors, by seeking to ensure that two or more parties would not grant permission to carry out seabed mining in the same area.

The parties to the agreement considered it necessary to harmonise the development of the seabed through legislation that had been introduced in the United States and the Federal Republic of Germany in 1980, in France and the United Kingdom in 1981, in the Soviet Union and Japan in 1982, and in Italy in 1985.[61] Most of these statutes followed a similar template. They provided reciprocal recognition of licences granted for exploration or exploitation of seabed resources by other states, and prohibited exploration or exploitation unless there was such a licence. The laws and regulations were said by these states to be wholly interim in nature, and without prejudice to Part XI of the LOSC, and in no way an assertion of sovereignty or sovereign rights in the resources of the deep seabed.[62] Indeed, most of the statutes included provisions for amendment or repeal on entry into force of the LOSC for the states concerned. One interesting feature of the legislation was the levying of an amount of 3.75 per cent of the value of recovered minerals to be deposited into a central fund for general distribution, a mechanism that was essentially the same as that provided for in Part XI of the LOSC, although it was less than half the levy that would be imposed under Part XI. Although this gave effect to the common heritage idea, other aspects of the legislation of the reciprocating states clearly did not. For instance, there was no arrangement made for site banking, so that the Enterprise would not be given access to mining areas as valuable as those which had been exploited by miners. And there were no production controls to maintain mineral prices, and thereby safeguard the existing export incomes of developing states with large mining sectors.[63]

VI. The LOSC and 1994 Agreement

The reciprocating states regime was criticised by the G-77 and by Eastern European states as being against the letter and spirit of the LOSC. However, it was considered necessary by industrialised states because of the inevitable delay surrounding the entry into force of the

---

[60] *Basic Documents* No 38.
[61] For discussion of the United States and German legislation see David D Caron, 'Deep Seabed Mining: A Comparative Study of US and West German Municipal Legislation' (1981) 5 *Marine Policy* 4.
[62] Brown, 'Neither Necessary Nor Prudent at this Stage' (n 35) 93.
[63] Ibid 94.

LOSC.[64] However, while substantial, the hiatus was not as lengthy as was initially expected, and certainly not so long as to witness any change to deep seabed mining conditions, which remained commercially unfavourable.

Article 308 of the LOSC provided that it was to enter into force twelve months after the date of deposit of the sixtieth instrument of ratification or accession. On 16 November 1993 Guyana deposited the sixtieth instrument of ratification, meaning that the LOSC would enter into force in November 1994. After several years of impasse over the interim arrangements made by some states prior to the LOSC regime becoming operational, the prospect that the Convention would soon enter in force proved to be a powerful impetus for final agreement to be reached on a workable compromise on Part XI. Most of the ratifications had been by developing states, and it appeared that the LOSC would come into effect with very limited participation by developed countries, an unattractive outcome not only because wide ratification of the regime was needed to be make it a truly effective treaty, but also because there were significant costs involved in maintaining the LOSC institutions, including the ISA, ITLOS and the CLCS. From 1990 onwards two successive Secretaries-General of the United Nations, Perez de Cuéller and Boutrous Ghali, facilitated consultations among the permanent representatives in New York with a view to resolving problem areas for industrialised states in Part XI in eight issue areas: the costs to parties, the Enterprise, decision-making in the ISA, the review conference that was to occur 15 years after commercial production commenced, provisions for technology transfer, production policy, the compensation fund and the financial terms of contracts.[65]

In late 1993 an informal group of representatives from both developing and developed states was formed which developed a draft UNGA resolution together with a draft agreement on the implementation of Part XI of the LOSC.[66] This document became known as the 'Boat Paper' because of a simple image of a mining vessel placed on its cover by the Australian representative on the informal group, Dr Greg French. Over the ensuing months the Boat Paper was heavily discussed and revised and formed the basis of the 1994 Agreement. The 1994 Agreement was adopted by the UNGA under the terms of its resolution 48/263 in July 1994. One hundred and twenty-one states voted in favour of the resolution, there were no votes against, and seven abstentions (only one of which, Russia, was an industrialised state). The United States had occupied a pivotal position throughout these negotiations because it was clear that without its participation other industrialised states would not join the new regime. Consensus on significant changes to Part XI via the 1994 Agreement resulted in the United States changing its position and indicating that it would become a party to the LOSC.[67] However, despite support from successive presidents, ratification of the LOSC by the United States has not been possible because of opposition in the United States Senate.[68]

---

[64] A delay for which, of course, they were in large part responsible.
[65] DH Anderson, 'Efforts to Ensure Universal Participation in the UN Convention on the Law of the Sea' (1993) 42 *International and Comparative Law Quarterly* 654.
[66] DH Anderson, 'Further Efforts to Ensure Universal Participation in the UN Convention on the Law of the Sea' (1994) 43 *International and Comparative Law Quarterly* 886, 887.
[67] Lawrence Juda, *International Law and Ocean Use Management: The Evolution of Ocean Governance* (London, Routledge, 1996) 258.
[68] Scott G Borgerson, *The National Interest and the Law of the Sea* (New York, Council on Foreign Relations, 2009) 12–13.

A. The Main Revisions in the 1994 Agreement

As a result of the lengthy and complex negotiations during and after UNCLOS III, the contemporary regime for the deep seabed is found in several places, rather than in a single, omnibus text. Of primary importance is the LOSC, with its Part XI, Annex III that includes the Basic Conditions for Prospecting, Exploration and Exploitation, and Annex IV that sets out the statute of the Enterprise. Many of the provisions found in the LOSC were then modified substantially by the 1994 Agreement. The LOSC and the 1994 Agreement are to be interpreted and applied as a single instrument, and where there is any inconsistency between the two treaties it is the provisions of the 1994 Agreement that prevail.[69]

The 1994 Agreement was a novel approach in the law of treaties, and sought to modify the LOSC without infringing the prohibition on reservations to the LOSC in Article 309.[70] Ruling out reservations to the LOSC was considered essential at UNCLOS III in order to produce a comprehensive multilateral convention that would address the full gamut of ocean governance issues. Allowing reservations could make the regime complex and unworkable by parties opting out of any number of provisions. The 1994 Agreement gets around the prohibition on reservations, and the consensus-based amendment process,[71] by providing in Article 4(1) that after the adoption by the UNGA of the 1994 Agreement, any state joining the LOSC shall also be consenting to be bound by the 1994 Agreement. Furthermore, in Article 4(2) it provides that no state or entity may establish its consent to be bound by the 1994 Agreement unless it has previously established, or establishes at the same time, its consent to be bound by the LOSC.[72]

The revised deep seabed mining system is not as visionary as Pardo's original conception of the common heritage regime,[73] but it does retain several of its core features. The modified LOSC deep seabed regime applies to the entirety of the Area, that is, the 'seabed and ocean floor and subsoil thereof beyond the limits of national jurisdiction'.[74] The Area and its resources are defined as the common heritage of humankind, and may not be subject to claims to sovereignty or sovereign rights.[75] The regime does not affect the legal status of superjacent waters, or the airspace above those waters.[76] Seabed resources in the Area are not subject to alienation; however, title may be obtained in the minerals recovered pursuant to the scheme.[77] States and non-state entities may only claim, acquire or exercise rights with respect to minerals recovered in accordance with the LOSC and the 1994 Agreement.[78]

The regime also has some application to the continental shelves of coastal states that extend beyond 200 nm, without affecting the legal status of these waters as being within the national jurisdiction of coastal states. Under Article 82 of the LOSC, coastal states are

---

[69]   1994 Agreement, art 2(1).

[70]   Reservations are also not permitted to the 1994 Agreement: 1994 Agreement, art 2(2).

[71]   LOSC, art 314.

[72]   For discussion see ED Brown, 'The 1994 Agreement on the Implementation of Part XI of the UN Convention on the Law of the Sea: Breakthrough to Universality?' (1995) 19 *Marine Policy* 5, 6–7.

[73]   A Carlsson, 'The US and UNCLOS III—The Death of the Common Heritage of Humankind Concept?' (1997) *Maritime Studies* 27.

[74]   LOSC, art 1(1).

[75]   Ibid arts 136, 137.

[76]   Ibid art 135.

[77]   Ibid art 137(2).

[78]   Ibid art 137(3).

to make payments or contributions in kind in respect of the exploitation of the non-living resources in the extended continental shelf.[79] Payments and contributions are to be made annually after the first five years of production at a site, so that in the sixth year the rate shall be one per cent of the value or volume of production, increasing by one per cent for each following year until the twelfth year, and remaining at seven per cent thereafter.[80] While mining in outer continental shelf areas does not itself come within the competence of the ISA, the body is charged with distributing payments or contributions to state parties to the LOSC on the basis of equitable sharing criteria, and taking into account the interests and needs of developing states, particularly the least developed and landlocked among them.[81]

The LOSC in its original guise included complex provisions to limit the extent of minerals production in the Area.[82] The 1994 Agreement dispensed with these production limitations as part of a general effort to make the regime more market-orientated in line with the demands of the major industrialised states. Development of the resources of the Area is therefore to take place in accordance with sound commercial principles.[83] The 1994 Agreement also made substantial modifications to the way in which the ISA was to operate so as to make it more responsive, cost-effective and commercially orientated.[84] The Enterprise was placed on equal footing with private contractors, rather than giving it an advantage.[85] In addition, the technology transfer provisions of the LOSC were watered down. They had provided for compulsory transfer of technology from a contractor to the Enterprise or to developing country miners if the latter were unable to obtain the technology on the open market, or through participation in a joint venture.[86] Instead there is now simply a general duty for states sponsoring contractors to facilitate the acquisition of deep seabed mining technology where the Enterprise or the developing state is unable to obtain technology on the open market.[87]

VII. The International Seabed Authority and the Seabed Mining System

A. The ISA

Critical to reaching agreement on Part XI and the Agreement was the clear delineation of the responsibilities and powers of the ISA. The creation of the ISA was made necessary by the designation of the area as the common heritage of humankind, as there would need to be a central institution that could protect investors developing deep seabed resources by

[79] Ibid art 82(1). For a comprehensive analysis see International Law Association, Committee on the Outer Continental Shelf, *Report on Article 82 of the 1982 UN Convention on the Law of the Sea* (2008).
[80] LOSC, art 82(2).
[81] Ibid art 82(4).
[82] Ibid art 151.
[83] 1994 Agreement, Annex, s 6(1)(a).
[84] Ibid s 1(2).
[85] Ibid s 2(4).
[86] LOSC, annex III, art 5.
[87] 1994 Agreement, annex, s 5.

granting them exclusive access to nominated sites. According to Article 157(1) of the LOSC, it is the ISA through which states parties shall 'organize and control activities in the Area, particularly with a view to administering the resources of the Area'. The powers and functions of the ISA are those that are expressly conferred upon it by the LOSC as modified by the 1994 Agreement, and such incidental powers as are implicit in and necessary for their exercise.[88]

The ISA does not have plenary powers over the deep seabed; instead, its competence relates solely to seabed mineral resources, that is, all solid, liquid or gaseous mineral resources in or beneath the seabed, including polymetallic nodules.[89] Hence activities that have an impact on the seabed, but which are unconnected with mineral resources, are unregulated by the ISA, whether they be deep sea trawling, the laying of pipelines and submarine cables, military activities, or the conduct of MSR. The ISA therefore does not have any general environmental jurisdiction over the deep seabed.[90]

Article 145 of the LOSC indicates that the ISA is to adopt rules, regulations and procedures for effectively protecting the marine environment from damage from prospecting, exploring, and mining resources on the deep seabed. But these are to be directed to mitigating the environmental impact of mineral resource activities, not any and all activities on the deep seabed that would include practices such as bioprospecting and pure MSR. The same is true of cultural heritage as represented by archaeological and historical objects on the deep seabed. Article 149 provides that such objects are to be preserved or disposed of for the benefit of humankind as a whole, having particular regard to those states with a direct interest, such as the country of origin. However, the ISA itself has no authority to supervise this protection; its only role is to pass on notifications from prospectors of discovery of such objects to the UNESCO Secretary-General.

The 1992 Convention on Biological Diversity (CBD) applies alongside LOSC to the genetic resources of the deep seabed and has some relevance to its conservation. The obligations of the Convention pertaining to sustainable utilisation, the preservation of species diversity, the facilitation of access, and fair and equitable sharing of benefits from their exploitation all apply. However, the specific provisions of the LOSC must take precedence over the CBD which is a more general convention, and does not deal specifically with the flora and fauna of the deep seabed. For this reason it is desirable that an implementing agreement under the LOSC be concluded to address the need to protect marine biodiversity in areas beyond national jurisdiction.[91]

The membership of the ISA embraces all parties to the LOSC, which are *ipso facto* members of the organisation. As of 1 July 2015 there were 167 parties to the LOSC, including the European Union, but 20 fewer parties to the Agreement. This disparity is significant in that a small number of states which ratified the LOSC before the conclusion of the Agreement, but which have not since ratified the Agreement, could potentially insist on their rights under Part XI in its original form. In practice this is highly unlikely to occur given that the ISA is functioning on the basis of the modified regime, in accordance with the wishes of a substantial majority of states.

---

[88] LOSC, art 157(2).

[89] Ibid art 133.

[90] Wood, 'The International Seabed Authority: Fifth to Twelfth Sessions' (n 5) 59.

[91] Louise de La Fayette, 'A New Regime for the Conservation and Sustainable Use of Marine Biodiversity and Genetic Resources beyond the Limits of National Jurisdiction' (2009) 24 *International Journal of Marine and Coastal Law* 221–80.

The ISA has a tripartite constitutional structure as set out in the LOSC. The principal organs of the ISA are the Assembly, the Council and the Secretariat. Also established is the Enterprise, which is the organ through which the ISA engages in seabed mining directly. In addition there are two subsidiary bodies: the Legal and Technical Commission and the Finance Committee. The Legal and Technical Commission deals with scientific and other technical issues, and provides assistance to the Council and the Assembly. Its 15 members are experts in fields of geology, oceanography, economics and law, and are elected in their personal and not representative capacity.

Decision-making as a general rule in the organs of the ISA is to be by consensus, and it is only if all efforts to reach consensus have failed that decisions may be taken by vote.[92] In practice all decisions on matters of substance have been by consensus.[93]

i. The Assembly

The Assembly is the plenary body of the ISA and its supreme decision-making organ.[94] It has the power to establish general policies in conformity with the LOSC.[95] One of its most important roles is to consider and adopt regulations, rules and procedures relating to prospecting, exploration and exploitation in the Area.[96] It is also able to consider and approve the rules, regulations and procedures for the equitable sharing of financial and other economic benefits derived from activities in the Area and the payments and contributions made by Article 82, with particular attention being given to the interests and needs of developing states.[97] The powers of the Assembly were significantly limited by the 1994 Agreement to give industrialised states a greater say in the decision-making process of the ISA. As a result, in respect of matters also falling within the competence of the Council the decisions of the Assembly must be based on the recommendations of the Council.[98]

ii. The Council

The Council comprises 36 members, and is the executive arm of the ISA with the general responsibility for supervising and coordinating the implementation of the deep seabed mining regime.[99] The Council's powers and functions are set out in Article 162 of the LOSC, including the approval of plans of work for exploration or exploitation following review by the Legal and Technical Commission.[100] The Council is elected by the Assembly, and must include members from several different groups of states.[101] Four members must be from parties which, during the last five years, have been major consumers or importers of minerals, four must be from the parties that have made the largest investments in seabed mining either directly or through their nationals, four must be from parties that are major

---

[92] 1994 Agreement, Annex, s 3(2)–(3).
[93] Satya Nandan, 'Administering the Mineral Resources of the Deep Seabed' in David Freestone, Richard Barnes and David M Ong (eds), *The Law of the Sea: Progress and Prospects* (Oxford, Oxford University Press, 2006) 83.
[94] LOSC, art 160.
[95] Ibid art 160(1).
[96] Ibid art 160(2)(f)(ii).
[97] Ibid art 160(2)(f)(i).
[98] 1994 Agreement, Annex, s 3(4).
[99] LOSC, art 162(2)(a).
[100] Ibid art 162(2)(j).
[101] 1994 Agreement, Annex, s 3(15).

net exporters of minerals, six must be from developing states that represent special interests such as those large populations and landlocked or geographically disadvantaged states, and 18 must be elected according to the principle of ensuring an equitable geographical distribution of seats in the Council as a whole. These requirements which establish four 'chambers' representing specific interest groups, coupled with the decision-making system effectively give industrialised states, most prominently the United States should it accede to the LOSC, a potential blocking or veto role in the Council that they did not have in the original Part XI regime. Decisions are to be reached by consensus where possible, but where efforts towards this objective have been exhausted decisions on most questions of substance are to be taken by a two-thirds majority of members present and voting, provided that such decisions are not opposed by a majority in any one of the chambers.[102]

In relation to applications to explore or exploit mineral resources in the Area, there is a streamlined process under the 1994 Agreement that is designed to promote the development of the mining industry. The Legal and Technical Commission first considers applications, and if they meet the criteria (which are discussed below) recommends to the Council that they be approved by simple majority. The applications must then automatically be approved by the Council, unless by a two-thirds majority of members present and voting, including a majority of members present and voting in each of the special interest chambers, decides to disapprove a plan of work.[103]

B. The Seabed Disputes Chamber and the *Seabed Mining Advisory Opinion*

The Seabed Disputes Chamber is established by Part XI of the LOSC and has compulsory jurisdiction over disputes between states parties concerning activities in the Area.[104] Significantly, the Chamber, whose 11 members are selected by ITLOS, also has competence to render Advisory Opinions on legal questions arising within the scope of the activities of the Assembly or Council of the ISA.[105] The Chamber is, therefore, charged with providing authoritative decisions on the interpretation and application of the provisions of the LOSC and the 1994 Agreement relating to mining in the Area.

In 2011 the Chamber rendered its first and so far only decision in the *Seabed Mining Advisory Opinion*, an Opinion that carries major significance for the operation of the seabed mining regime and the law of the sea more generally.[106] The Opinion was sought by the ISA following a request by Nauru and Tonga for clarification of their potential liabilities for sponsoring deep seabed mining activities. Nauru and Tonga are two small island developing states that have been actively pursuing deep seabed mining, and have sponsored multinational mining companies in seeking contracts with the ISA for prospecting and exploration for polymetallic nodules in areas reserved under the deep seabed regime for exploitation by developing states.[107] In 2010 Nauru and Tonga requested that their applications for

---

[102] Ibid s 3(5).

[103] Ibid s 3(11)(a).

[104] LOSC, art 187.

[105] Ibid art 190.

[106] *Seabed Mining Advisory Opinion* (2011) 50 ILM 458. See generally Duncan French, 'From the Depths: Rich Pickings of Principles of Sustainable Development and General International Law on the Ocean Floor—the Seabed Disputes Chamber's 2011 Advisory Opinion' (2011) 26 *International Journal of Marine and Coastal Law* 525.

[107] See ISA, *Seabed Authority And Nauru Ocean Resources Inc Sign Contract For Exploration* (22 July 2011) at www.isa.org.jm/en/node/666.

approval for a plan of work in a reserved area be placed on hold pending a request through the ISA of an Advisory Opinion from the Seabed Disputes Chamber concerning the nature and extent of liabilities that sponsoring states incur in respect of deep seabed mining. The ISA put three specific questions to the Seabed Disputes Chamber:

1. What are the legal responsibilities and obligations of states parties to the LOSC with respect to the sponsorship of activities in the Area in accordance with the LOSC, in particular Part XI, and the 1994 Agreement? What is the extent of liability for any failure by a sponsored entity to comply with the requirements of the regime?
2. What is the extent of liability of a state party for any failure to comply with the provisions of the LOSC, in particular Part XI, and the 1994 Agreement, by an entity it has sponsored under Article 153(2)(b) of the LOSC?
3. What are the necessary and appropriate measures that a sponsoring state must take in order to fulfil its responsibility under the LOSC, in particular Article 139 and Annex III, and the 1994 Agreement?

In response to the first question, the Chamber clarified the meaning of 'activities' in the Area. It concluded that the term as used in the LOSC meant the recovery of minerals from the seabed and their lifting to the surface but did not include other associated activities, such as processing of mineral ores on land or the transportation of minerals to land.[108] The Chamber also considered the content of the responsibilities and obligations of sponsoring states under the relevant provisions of the LOSC, principally Articles 139(1) and 153(4), and Article 4(4) of Annex III. The Chamber noted that the 'responsibility to ensure' that activities carried out in conformity with the LOSC is not an obligation of result, but rather one to deploy adequate means, to exercise best possible efforts and to do the utmost in order to obtain this result.[109] The Chamber also found that, in addition to the general due diligence obligation to ensure that mining activities conform with the LOSC, there were several direct obligations owed by sponsoring states. These included obligations: to assist the ISA in controlling activities in the Area; to apply a precautionary approach (the Chamber said not only was the approach integral to the mining regulations developed by the ISA, but also that there was a 'trend towards making this approach part of customary international law'); to apply best environmental practices; to assist in an emergency to protect the environment; to ensure recourse to compensation in respect of pollution damage; and to conduct an environmental impact assessment. Significantly, the Chamber advised that the obligations on sponsoring states apply equally to developed and developing states, unless specifically provided otherwise in the applicable provisions. Equality of treatment was said by the Chamber to be of utmost importance to avoid the phenomenon of 'sponsoring states of convenience', which might become a problem akin to 'flag states of convenience': 'The spread of sponsoring States "of convenience" would jeopardize uniform application of the highest standards of protection of the marine environment, the safe development of activities in the Area and protection of the common heritage of mankind.'[110]

---

[108] *Seabed Mining Advisory Opinion* (2011) 50 ILM 458 [84].
[109] Ibid [110].
[110] Ibid [159].

In relation to the second question, concerning the liability of a party for any failure by a sponsored entity to comply with the seabed regime, under Article 139(2) of the LOSC a party is liable for damage caused by its failure to meet its responsibilities under the regime, but is not liable for damage caused by the failure of a sponsored entity if it has taken all necessary and appropriate measures to secure effective compliance. The Chamber observed, therefore, that the liability of sponsoring states derives from their own failure to fulfil their obligations, and the mere failure of a contractor to comply with its obligations does not give rise to the liability of the sponsoring state if it has discharged its due diligence obligation to take 'all necessary and appropriate measures to secure effective compliance'.[111] This means that there is no strict liability on the part of sponsoring states. It also means that there are two potentially significant gaps in liability. The first is a situation where a sponsoring state has discharged its due diligence obligation but a contractor nonetheless causes damage that results from its own breach of its obligations and is unable to provide redress for the damage. The second is a situation where both the sponsoring state and the contractor fully discharge their obligations but damage nonetheless occurs. In order to address these gaps in liability, the Chamber suggested that the ISA consider the establishment of a trust fund to compensate for damage not covered by the liability regime.[112] Further, the Chamber noted that the regime of responsibility and liability is not static and that Article 304 of the LOSC allows for the development of further rules and regulations for the liability regime for deep seabed mining.

The Chamber had addressed most of the issues raised by the third question, which concerned the necessary and appropriate measures that a sponsoring state must take in fulfilling its duties under the LOSC in its response to the first two questions. The Chamber observed that the liability of sponsoring states is determined having regard to a due diligence obligation to take all necessary and appropriate measures to secure effective compliance. This obligation requires the sponsoring state to adopt laws and regulations, and to take administrative measures, to ensure that the sponsored contractor complies with its obligations under the LOSC. This may include the establishment of enforcement mechanisms for active supervision of the activities of the contractor. Contractual obligations between the sponsoring state and the sponsored contractor were not considered a sufficient substitute for the adoption of laws, regulations and administrative measures. The content of the measures was left to the states to determine, but measures must be 'reasonably appropriate' to ensure compliance and must be no less effective than the rules of international law.[113] The rules, regulations and procedures concerning environmental protected adopted by the ISA (Annex III, Article 21(3)) provide a minimum standard; however, it is open for a state to impose more demanding standards.

i. Recent Activities of the ISA and the Mining Code

As noted at the opening of this chapter, the ISA has entered into contracts for exploration for marine mineral resources with 22 contractors. In addition, four pending contracts are expected to be finalised in 2015. This surge in interest in deep seabed resources has meant a

---

[111] LOSC, art 139(2).
[112] *Seabed Mining Advisory Opinion* (2011) 50 ILM 458 [205].
[113] Ibid [228].

corresponding increase in the activity of the ISA, which includes not only mining applications, but also continuing work on a comprehensive Mining Code to govern prospecting, exploration and exploitation for nodules, sulphides and ferromanganese crusts in the Area. The Mining Code comprises the Regulations adopted by the ISA, which, together with the LOSC and the 1994 Agreement, provides the legal framework within which mining activities in the Area must take place.[114] The Mining Code brings the various relevant provisions of the LOSC and the 1994 Agreement together with the ISA regulations so that a prospective contractor need only have reference to the Mining Code to identify the process that applies. As a former Secretary-General of the ISA has remarked: 'This makes the mining system, which otherwise appears to be complex, more coherent and simple and more readily understood.'[115] Another aspect of the Mining Code that is designed to lower the transaction costs of seabed mining is the two page standard form contract, which means that the ISA will not need to negotiate terms with individual contractors, and a set of standard clauses. Hence the basic terms and conditions will be the same for all contractors, with the differences in the exploration area and programme of activities reflected in schedules to the contract.

As it stands, the Mining Code comprises three sets of regulations (the Regulations on Prospecting and Exploration for Nodules, the Regulations on Prospecting and Exploration for Sulphides and the Regulations on Prospecting and Exploration for Crusts) and several Recommendations (including the Recommendations to Guide Contractors on Assessing Environmental Impacts of Exploring Minerals). Work is continuing on the remainder of the Mining Code, with the next step being the adoption of Exploitation Regulations for the three types of seabed minerals. The Mining Code has a strong environmental focus, consistent with Article 145 of the LOSC, which requires parties to take necessary measures in respect of seabed mining activities in order to provide effective protection of the marine environment. The ISA is acutely aware that all forms of seabed mining involve significant disturbance to the seabed and the bathypelagic layer of water near to the seafloor, and mining activities and the plumes, light and noise that they involve will damage deep seabed species and their habitats. To ameliorate this, the Mining Code includes some of the strictest environmental protections found in any international instrument, as can be seen in the provisions of the Nodule Regulations.

The Nodule Regulations deal with notifications of intended prospecting and approval for plans of work. Prospecting is not to be undertaken if there is substantial evidence of risk of serious harm to the marine environment,[116] with 'marine environment' defined expansively as:

> the physical, chemical, geological and biological components, conditions and factors which interact and determine the productivity, state, condition and quality of the marine ecosystem, the waters of the seas and oceans and the airspace above those waters, as well as the seabed and ocean floor and subsoil thereof.[117]

---

[114] LOSC, art 153.
[115] Nandan, 'Administering the Mineral Resources of the Deep Seabed' (n 93) 88–89.
[116] Nodules Regulations, reg 2(2).
[117] Ibid reg 1(3)(c).

Part V of the Nodules Regulations includes several environmental safeguards. The ISA is to keep under periodic review its rules, regulations and procedures to ensure the protection of the marine environment from harmful effects that may arise from activities in the Area.[118] States are to apply a 'precautionary approach' as reflected in Principle 15 of the Rio Declaration.[119] Contractors must take measures to prevent, reduce and control pollution to the marine environment as far as reasonably possible using the best available technology.[120] Contracts entered into with contractors must include the requirement that contractors obtain baseline environmental data and establish environmental baselines against which to assess the environmental impact of its activities.[121] The Legal and Technical Commission has issued recommendations to assist contractors implement this aspect of the regulations.[122] The Secretary-General is empowered, pending any action by the Council, to issue emergency orders when made aware of serious environmental harm or the likelihood of such harm.[123]

In addition to the development of the Mining Code, the substantive programme of work of the ISA has been focused on the supervisory functions of the Authority over exploration contracts, monitoring trends and developments relating to seabed mining activities, including world metal market conditions, the promotion and encouragement of MSR in the Area, information-gathering and the establishment of databases of scientific and technical information relating to the deep ocean environment, and ongoing assessment of data relating to prospecting and exploration for nodules in the Clarion-Clipperton Zone.[124]

One particularly interesting development in the ISA in relation to the protection of the Area environment is the ongoing work to consider a proposal to establish a network of ecologically related areas in the Clarion-Clipperton Zone, described as 'areas of particular environmental interest', where there would be no exploration or other mining activity. A basis for the designation of such areas is found in Article 162(2)(x) of the LOSC, which provides that the Council shall 'disapprove areas for exploitation by contractors of the Enterprise in cases where substantial evidence indicates the risk of serious harm to the marine environment'. The Legal and Technical Commission appointed an informal working group which has considered the findings of a collaborative project known as the Kaplan Project from 2002 until 2007 that assessed levels of biodiversity in abyssal nodule provinces in the Pacific Ocean so as to evaluate better the threats to biodiversity from nodule mining. Three key faunal groups were examined (polychaete worms, nematode worms and protozoan foraminifera) which together constitute more than 50 per cent of faunal abundance and species richness in abyssal sediments. The results of the project indicated that there were very high levels of species diversity for all three groups, and that the total number of species from these three groups alone in one site in the Clarion-Clipperton Zone could be far greater than 1,000 species. The researchers concluded that appropriate measures need to be taken in order to protect biodiversity. The informal working group proposed the

---

[118] Ibid reg 31(1).
[119] Ibid reg 31(2).
[120] Ibid reg 31(3).
[121] Ibid reg 31(4).
[122] Doc No ISA/7/LTC/1/Rev.1 (2002).
[123] Nodules Regulations, reg 32.
[124] Report of the ISA Secretary-General, 20th Session, Informal Advance Text (2014), 2.

establishment of nine sanctuary zones, with a total area of 1,440,000 square kilometres, which would result in around 25 per cent of the total Clarion-Clipperton Zone management area being placed under protection. Following this work, in 2011 the ISA adopted an Environmental Management Plan for the Clarion-Clipperton Zone, which identified nine areas of particular environmental interest within biogeographic subregions.[125] As Kaye has noted, the powers of the ISA to protect seafloor habitats are extensive, and if the ISA takes the lead to preserve habitats around hydrothermal vents and other significant features, this may place pressure upon coastal and flag states and regional fisheries organisations to seriously consider what protective measures they might also be willing to agree to in order to protect high seas biodiversity more effectively.[126]

C. Utilising the Deep Seabed Mining Regime

The deep seabed mining regime deals with the three stages of mining: prospecting, exploration and exploitation. The three terms were not defined in the LOSC or the 1994 Agreement, but have now been given meaning by the Mining Code. Although these regulations apply only in respect of prospecting and exploration, and not exploitation, they do set out a clear road map for most of the steps of the ISA process that will be generalised across the Mining Code as it is added to over time with additional regulations.

Under the Nodules Regulations, prospecting means 'the search for deposits of polymetallic nodules in the Area ... without any exclusive rights'.[127] Exploration means 'searching for deposits of polymetallic nodules in the Area with exclusive rights', and includes 'studies of the technical, economic, commercial and other appropriate factors that must be taken into account in exploitation'.[128] Exploitation means 'the recovery for commercial purposes of polymetallic nodules in the area and the extraction of minerals therefrom'.[129]

Prospecting may be freely undertaken by any party to the LOSC and the 1994 Agreement, with relatively few limitations. The prospector must notify the ISA of its intention to engage in prospecting, and give a written undertaking that it will comply with the LOSC.[130] Prospecting may not be undertaken if there is substantial evidence of risk of serious environmental harm, within an area covered by an approved plan of work for exploration, in a reserved area, or in an area which the Council has disapproved for exploitation for environmental reasons.[131] Prospecting does not confer on prospectors any rights in relation to the resources, although prospectors may recover a reasonable amount of minerals for testing purposes.[132] Prospecting may continue until such time that a plan of work for exploration is approved with regard to the area,[133] and it may be conducted simultaneously by more

---

[125] ISA/17/LTC/7 (2011).
[126] Stuart Kaye, 'Implementing High Seas Biodiversity Conservation: Global Geopolitical Considerations' (2004) 28 *Marine Policy* 221, 225.
[127] Nodules Regulations, reg 1(3)(e).
[128] Ibid reg 1(3)(b).
[129] Ibid reg 1(3)(a).
[130] LOSC, annex III, art 2(1)(b); Nodules Regulations, reg 3.
[131] Nodules Regulations, reg 2(3).
[132] LOSC, annex III, art 2(2).
[133] Nodules Regulations, reg 2(5).

than one prospector in the same area or areas.[134] Notification of prospecting is to take the form set out in Annex 1 of the Nodule Regulations.[135] The ISA Secretary-General must review and act on the notification within 45 days of its receipt.[136]

When it comes to exploration, the Enterprise, states parties, state enterprises, or natural or juridical persons possessing the nationality of states parties (or effectively controlled by them) or any combination of these may apply to the ISA for approval of plans of work for exploration.[137] Applications from a state enterprise or non-state entities must be accompanied by a certificate of sponsorship by the state of which the enterprise or entity is a national, or by the state by whose nationals it is effectively controlled.[138] Applicants must meet additional qualification conditions. The applicant must be financially and technically capable of carrying out the proposed plan of work, and be able to fulfil its financial obligations to the ISA.[139] All applicants, including the Enterprise, must as part of the application process provide a written undertaking to the ISA that they will accept as enforceable, and comply with, the provisions of the LOSC and the rules, regulations and procedures of the ISA and the terms of the contracts with the ISA.[140]

One of the key elements of the regime for exploration and exploitation is the so-called 'parallel' system set out in Article 153 of the LOSC. Under this system miners must identify a site that can be banked or reserved for exploration in the future, by the Enterprise itself (alone, or in partnership with developing states, or the contractor itself). The idea behind this system is to ensure that there will be no monopolisation of the seabed, and also to ensure that there will be sufficient resources available for later contractors, especially those from developing states.[141] Hence under Regulation 15 of the Nodule Regulations, applications for approval for a plan of work for exploration must cover a total area, which need not be a single area, sufficiently large and of sufficient commercial value to permit two mining operations.[142] In this regard applications must contain sufficient data and information to allow the Council, on the recommendation of the Legal and Technical Commission, to designate a reserved area based on the estimated commercial value of the two parts.[143] If satisfactory, the Council may designate a reserved area, which becomes operative as soon as the plan of work for exploration of the non-reserved area is approved and the contract is signed.[144] Developing states, or natural or juridical persons sponsored by them, or the Enterprise may submit a plan of work for exploration of a reserved area.[145] If there is no such application within 15 years from the date on which the area was reserved, then the contractor may apply for a plan of work for that area, provided it offers in good faith to include the Enterprise as a joint-venture partner.[146]

---

[134] Ibid reg 2(6).
[135] Ibid reg 3(2).
[136] Ibid reg 4(2).
[137] LOSC, annex III, arts 3 and 4; Nodules Regulations, reg 9.
[138] LOSC, annex III, art 4; Nodules Regulations, reg 11.
[139] LOSC, annex III, art 4; Nodules Regulations, reg 12.
[140] Nodules Regulations, reg 14.
[141] Nandan, 'Administering the Mineral Resources of the Deep Seabed' (n 93) 86.
[142] See also LOSC, annex III, art 8.
[143] Nodules Regulations, reg 16(1).
[144] Ibid reg 16(2).
[145] Ibid reg 17.
[146] Ibid reg 17(3).

The fee for an application for exploration is US$500,000, which must be paid at the time the application is submitted.[147] The level of the fee is to be reviewed from time to time by the Council.[148] And when exploration begins there will be an additional, annual fee payable. In terms of processing applications, the Legal and Technical Commission is to consider applications in the order in which they are received.[149] There are only limited bases upon which an application may be refused, such as where the application relates to an area included in a plan of work already approved by the Council.[150] Another basis upon which an application will be refused is if the state applicant, or the state sponsor, (i) already has plans of work for exploration or exploitation in non-reserved areas that, together with either part of the area covered by the application, exceed in size 30 per cent of a circular area of 400,000 square kilometres around the centre of either area, or (ii) already has plans of work for exploration or exploitation in non-reserved areas that taken together constitute two per cent of the Area which is not reserved or disapproved for exploitation for environmental reasons.[151]

After a plan of work has been approved by the Council it is to be prepared in the form of a contract between the ISA and the Applicant. If it relates to exploration for polymetallic nodules, then it is to take the form of Annex 3 of the Nodules Regulations, and incorporate the standard clauses set out in Annex 4.[152] A contractor has exclusive rights to explore or exploit the area covered by a plan of work (unlike prospecting which confers no such exclusivity).[153] The total area allocated to a contractor under a contract is not to exceed 150,000 square kilometres.[154] And where the area allocated is greater than 75,000 square kilometres, then the contractor is to relinquish a proportion of the area over time, which will revert back to become a part of the Area.[155] A plan of work for exploration is to be approved for a period of 15 years, after which time the contractor must renounce its rights in the area, apply for a five-year extension for exploration, or apply for a plan of work for exploitation.[156]

During the period of a contract the ISA is to monitor performance by the contractor with the terms of the contract. The contractor is to permit the ISA to send its inspectors on board vessels and installations used by the Contractor.[157] The Council may suspend or terminate the contract if, despite written warnings by the Authority, the Contractor has violated the fundamental terms of this contract, Part XI of the LOSC, the 1994 Agreement and the rules, regulations and procedures of ISA.[158]

---

[147]   Ibid reg 19(1).
[148]   Ibid reg 19(2).
[149]   Ibid reg 21(2).
[150]   Ibid reg 21(6)(a).
[151]   Ibid reg 21(6)(d).
[152]   Ibid reg 23(1).
[153]   Ibid reg 24(1).
[154]   Ibid reg 25.
[155]   Ibid reg 25.
[156]   Ibid reg 26.
[157]   Standard Clauses for Exploration Contract at www.isa.org.jm/files/documents/EN/Regs/Code-Annex4.pdf, s 14.
[158]   Ibid s 21.

VIII. Further Reading

RP Anand, *Legal Regime of The Sea-Bed and The Developing Countries* (New Delhi, Thomson Press, 1976)

Yves Fouquet and Denis Lacroix (eds), *Deep Marine Mineral Resources* (Dordrecht, Springer, 2014)

Duncan French, 'From the Depths: Rich Pickings of Principles of Sustainable Development and General International Law on the Ocean Floor—the Seabed Disputes Chamber's 2011 Advisory Opinion' (2011) 26 *International Journal of Marine and Coastal Law* 525

James Harrison, *Making the Law of the Sea: A Study in the Development of International Law* (Cambridge, Cambridge University Press, 2011) chapter 5

Lawrence Juda, *International Law and Ocean Management: The Evolution of Ocean Governance* (London, Routledge, 1996) chapters 6, 7, 8

David Leary, *International Law and the Genetic Resources of the Deep Seabed* (The Hague, Martinus Nijhoff, 2007)

Michael W Lodge, 'The Deep Seabed' in Donald R Rothwell, Alex G Oude Elferink, Karen N Scott and Tim Stephens (eds), *The Oxford Handbook of the Law of the Sea* (Oxford, Oxford University Press, 2015) 226

Satya Nandan, 'Administering the Mineral Resources of the Deep Seabed' in David Freestone, Richard Barnes and David M Ong (eds), *The Law of the Sea: Progress and Prospects* (Oxford, Oxford University Press, 2006)

Satya N Nandan, Michael W Lodge and Shabtai Rosenne (eds), *United Nations Convention on the Law of the Sea 1982: A Commentary*, vol VI (The Hague, Martinus Nijhoff, 2002)

7

High Seas

I. Introduction

The high seas have a central place in the history of the international law of the sea. When a distinctive body of international law for the sea began to emerge in the seventeenth century, the high seas dominated state practice and developing customary international law and it retained that central position until the middle of the twentieth century. Whilst the territorial sea gradually gained recognition as an additional maritime zone, its relatively narrow breadth meant that the importance of the high seas remained undiminished. Only since 1945, with the onset of new maritime zones in the form of the continental shelf, fisheries zones and the EEZ, has the importance of the high seas to the law of the sea been eroded. Nevertheless, the high seas remain the largest of the maritime zones and retain many of the fundamental characteristics associated with the Grotian vision of the freedom of the oceans. Marine areas beyond national jurisdiction account for around 60 per cent of the ocean surface, and 90 per cent of the ocean volume.

The centrality of the high seas to the international law of the sea derives in large part from their historic importance. In Roman times the seas and oceans were considered free for all to access and sail upon with the only constraints arising from controls exercised by certain naval powers. Political communities in those times did not seek to assert any permanent control equivalent to sovereign rights over the oceans, with the only exception made in the case of inland or coastal waters such as bays, gulfs, estuaries and river mouths.[1] All of the known seas and oceans were therefore high seas and the freedoms associated with those waters meant that they were open to all for navigation and fishing.

The reason why, historically, the law of the sea placed such weight in the debates between publicists such as Grotius and Selden[2] was that the high seas and the freedoms associated with it were so embedded in the consciousness that any suggested variations represented a radical change to the established legal order. While the Grotian vision for the freedom of the high seas prevailed, since the nineteenth century the law of the sea has witnessed a steady but gradual erosion of the geographical extent of the high seas. During that time the high seas have also become more regulated, not only as a result of the development of a convention-based regime found especially in the LOSC, but also as a result of the narrowing

---

[1] See the discussion in ch 2.
[2] See the discussion of the debate in ch 1.

of the breadth of the high seas and an increase in global concerns over oceans management in areas beyond national jurisdiction.

A. The High Seas as a Managed Common Area

As an area beyond national appropriation and not subject to state sovereignty, the high seas have been subject to a significant transformation in the extent of their legal regulation through specialist treaties dealing with biodiversity,[3] high seas fisheries,[4] managed stocks such as whales,[5] navigational safety[6] and maritime security.[7] The result has been that the high seas have now become a managed common area rather than one where traditional high seas freedoms may be fully exercised. Whilst these developments have placed constraints on some traditional high seas freedoms, the high seas face major ongoing challenges. Some have arisen as a result of global overfishing combined with the recognition of coastal state rights to an EEZ, thereby pushing fishing fleets further from the coast into the more distant and less regulated high seas. The effect has been to concentrate high seas fishing activities into some oceans, resulting in very considerable pressure on some high seas fish stocks.[8] Another key challenge has been to address other environmental pressures faced by the world's oceans as a whole, or the high seas in particular. The impact of vessel-sourced pollution, land-based marine pollution and ocean acidification are creating significant challenges for the international community in maintaining the health of the high seas marine environment.[9] This has spawned a debate over whether marine protected areas may be designated over the high seas and how such areas may be effectively managed.[10] When combined, these developments are creating issues with respect to oceans governance of the high seas which whilst challenging some traditional notions of the freedom of the high seas are also highlighting the need for the international community to assume greater responsibility for global ocean health.[11]

---

[3] 1992 Convention on Biological Diversity.

[4] 1995 Agreement for the Implementation of the Provisions of the United Nations Convention on the Law of the Sea of 10 December 1982 Relating to the Conservation and Management of Straddling Fish Stocks and Highly Migratory Fish Stocks, *Basic Documents* No 56.

[5] 1946 International Convention for the Regulation of Whaling, *Basic Documents* No 7.

[6] 1974 International Convention for the Safety of Life at Sea, *Basic Documents* No 22.

[7] 2005 Convention for the Suppression of Unlawful Acts against the Safety of Maritime Navigation, *Basic Documents* No 79.

[8] This issue is discussed in more detail in chs 13 and 16.

[9] Rosemary Rayfuse, Mark G Lawrence and Kristina M Gjerde, 'Ocean fertilisation and climate change: the need to regulate emerging high seas uses' (2008) 23 *International Journal of Marine and Coastal Law* 297; these issues are discussed in more detail in ch 15.

[10] Robin Warner, *Protecting the Oceans Beyond National Jurisdiction* (Leiden, Martinus Nijhoff, 2009) 207–34; Tullio Scovazzi, 'Marine Protected Areas on the High Seas: Some Legal and Policy Considerations' (2004) 19 *International Journal of Marine and Coastal Law* 1.

[11] See David Freestone et al, 'Workshop in high seas governance for the 21st century' (2008) 23 *International Journal of Marine and Coastal Law* 359; Rosemary Rayfuse and Robin Warner, 'Securing a Sustainable Future for the Oceans Beyond National Jurisdiction: The Legal Basis for an Integrated Cross-Sectoral Regime for High Seas Governance for the 21st Century' (2008) 23 *International Journal of Marine and Coastal Law* 399; and discussion of oceans governance in ch 19.

II. Historical Development of the High Seas

A. Pre-Grotian Freedoms of the High Seas

The early development of the high seas regime needs to be understood alongside the development of international law at a time when the modern nation state did not exist, and international law-making through customary international law and conclusion of treaties was at a very rudimentary stage. Nevertheless, there is evidence of significant practices having developed with key maritime states holding a pivotal role during ancient times. Two regions stand out with respect to their maritime practices. The first are the predominantly European states adjoining the Mediterranean Sea, the North Sea and the Baltic. There is evidence of significant trade within the Mediterranean by 1500 BCE with the Phoenicians having several trading colonies around the coast. By 200 BCE the Aegean island of Rhodes had become especially significant due to its strategic location in the Mediterranean between Egypt, Cyprus and the Greek cities.[12] Rhodes developed its own laws and practices regulating commercial aspects of maritime trade and Rhodian sea law 'gave rise to several maritime codes and assumed a binding character freely recognised by the seafaring states of the Mediterranean'.[13] From time to time, however, some Mediterranean and European states did seek to assert control over their adjacent seas, including the Greeks and Romans in ancient times, certain Italian republics in the Middle Ages, and Denmark and Sweden over parts of the Baltic.[14]

The second region of importance was Asia, where there is evidence of developing sea trade by the third century BCE between parts of India and Arabia. The Roman conquest of Egypt in 30 BCE eventually opened the way for trade between Rome and India. Trade routes were also developed between India and China, though they were dependent upon favourable winds and avoiding pirates.[15] Whilst there may have been minor variations in state practices in Europe and Asia up until the Middle Ages, all of these very early developments in maritime trade and commerce depended upon a recognition of the freedom of the seas.

B. Grotian Vision of the High Seas

Notwithstanding the prevailing influence of the freedom of the seas in both doctrine and maritime practice by the time *Mare Liberum* was published in 1608,[16] sufficient variations in state practice were beginning to emerge such that there was a real prospect that the freedom of the seas could be threatened by accepting the legitimacy of some state claims over the seas. The Scandinavian claims to maritime dominion in parts of the North Sea,

---

[12] RP Anand, *Origin and Development of the Law of the Sea* (The Hague, Martinus Nijhoff, 1983) 10–11.
[13] Ibid 11.
[14] Thomas Wemyss Fulton, *The Sovereignty of the Sea* (Edinburgh, Blackwood, 1911, 1976 rep) 3–4.
[15] Anand, *Origin and Development of the Law of the Sea* (n 12) 12–20.
[16] Hugo Grotius, *The Freedom of the Seas or the Right which Belongs to the Dutch to Take Part in the East Indian Trade* (New York, Oxford University Press, 1916 rep).

Baltic Sea and into parts of the North Atlantic, became more extensive during the Middle Ages.[17] However, it was the 1494 Treaty of Tordesillas founded upon a Papal Bull of Pope Alexander VI which, via a line drawn on a meridian of longitude through Brazil divided the world including the oceans into a Portuguese sphere of influence to the east and a Spanish sphere of influence to the west, had the most significant impact upon thinking regarding the freedom of the seas.

This was the setting in which *Mare Liberum* was published and whilst it seems clear that its publication was politically motivated by the desire of the Dutch to maintain their freedom of access to the seas, its impact upon the legal and doctrinal discourse on what became the regime of the high seas was formidable. Seeking to build upon principles of *res nullius*, *res communis*, and *res publica*, Grotius asserted that the oceans could not be appropriated because they could not be occupied. As the oceans were therefore not susceptible to occupation, and accordingly not capable of ownership by any one state, the oceans like the air were available for all to use freely.[18] This Grotian vision for the oceans was subject to sustained critique from many other European scholars, and whilst John Selden's *Mare Clausum* (The Closed Sea) is the most famous response to Grotius, many other works were published which contributed to the debate over the status of the high seas.[19] Whilst Grotius did eventually modify his views to such an extent that with the 1625 publication of *De Jure Belli ac Pacis*[20] it was conceded the high seas had to be distinguished from inland seas, straits and bays, the core of the freedom of the high seas doctrine had become well accepted and reflected in state practice in the seventeenth century.

C. The High Seas in Customary International Law

Although the freedom of the high seas was accepted from the seventeenth century onwards the content of the legal regime in customary international law remained imprecise. As a result, several important debates arose. The most significant of these was the extent of the high seas and whether they comprised all the world's oceans and seas such as to prevent any claim to a portion of the seas, or whether it was possible to accommodate claims to a narrow coastal strip of waters in the form of a territorial sea. Despite the variations in state practice, especially with respect to breadth, international law clearly recognised the existence of the territorial sea as a legitimate maritime zone by the turn of the twentieth century.[21] While it took the conclusion of the LOSC in 1982 for definitive agreement to be reached on the breadth of the territorial sea, it had long been conceded that an area of high seas immediately adjacent to the coast was subject to appropriation. Likewise, the gradual acceptance throughout the twentieth century in customary international law of other maritime zones, such as fisheries zones and the EEZ, also impacted upon the extent

---

[17] Fulton asserts that these claims were 'probably indeed the most important in history': Fulton, *The Sovereignty of the Sea* (n 14) 4.

[18] Grotius, *The Freedom of the Seas* (n 16) 27.

[19] Frans De Pauw, *Grotius and the Law of the Sea* (Brussels, Institut de Sociologie, Université de Bruxelles, 1965) 13.

[20] Hugo Grotius, *De Jure Belli ac Pacis* (J Barents and AJS Douma (eds)) (The Hague, Martinus Nijhoff, 1948) 41–42, ch III, [VIII], 19–20.

[21] See discussion in ch 3.

of the high seas. However, once it was accepted that coastal states had certain sovereign rights and jurisdiction over these zones, it was accepted that certain high seas freedoms that may have previously been exercised in those areas of the ocean were now diminished and in some cases lost.[22]

More significantly perhaps, was the debate which emerged as to the extent of the rights and freedoms that could be exercised over the high seas. Whilst it was accepted that the high seas were an area that was not subject to appropriation, extending principally to the control of the water surface, but also the water column and by implication to the adjacent seabed, there was little clear articulation in state practice as to precisely what the freedoms of the high seas entailed other than navigation and fishing. However, even the freedom of navigation was subject in the eighteenth and nineteenth centuries to the realities of maritime power enjoyed by the leading states. This period was one where British maritime and naval power was particularly predominant, and Britain claimed for itself the right to stop and inspect neutral vessels on the high seas and remove and destroy contraband goods.[23] While these practices were closely aligned with the then laws of naval warfare, which permitted the blockade of ports, and the seizure of vessels flying the flags of a belligerent power, their effect was to place de facto limitations upon the freedoms of high seas navigation. The principle of the freedom of the seas was also influential in the gradual abolition of tolls that had been demanded by some states for passage through certain waters.[24]

The freedom of the seas also encouraged states to take action against piracy, which was seen as being disruptive to international maritime communication and commerce. In addition to state practice criminalising pirate acts, and conferring upon all states certain capacities to arrest and prosecute pirates, some navies took direct action against pirate fleets.[25] Similar action was eventually taken against vessels engaged in the slave trade. With the Industrial Revolution and significant growth in commerce throughout Europe, the capacity of European powers to engage in global trade became a possibility with markets developing in the Americas, Asia and Australia and New Zealand. During this period the 'freedom of the seas became a necessity'[26] and many of the principles of the modern high seas regime became well established in customary international law.

i. Jurisdiction Over Vessels on the High Seas

Closely associated with the principle of the freedom of the high seas is a principle of international law that states may not generally exercise authority or jurisdiction beyond their territory. The principle of territoriality is fundamental to international law, and has particular application on the high seas where no state possesses territorial jurisdiction. The high seas are not, however, a jurisdictional vacuum, and it has long been recognised that states may exercise extraterritorial jurisdiction over their own nationals whilst on the high seas, including ships that are flying the state's flag. As Colombos observed, this jurisdiction rests

---

[22] See, eg, *Fisheries Jurisdiction (United Kingdom v Iceland)* (merits) [1974] ICJ Rep 175, [72].

[23] Anand, *Origin and Development of the Law of the Sea* (n 12) 115.

[24] C John Colombos, *The International Law of the Sea*, 6th edn (London, Longmans, 1967) 55.

[25] Ibid 57 referring to an incident in 1816 when the British navy accompanied by Dutch naval vessels engaged and destroyed Algerian pirates.

[26] Anand, *Origin and Development of the Law of the Sea* (n 12) 130.

on the grounds that the vessels 'are property in a place where no local jurisdiction exists'[27] and accordingly it is the jurisdiction of the flag state which fills this void when a vessel is on the high seas. However, flag state jurisdiction on the high seas is not exclusive and over time it has also come to be recognised that certain limited forms of universal jurisdiction may be exercised by a non-flag state over vessels on the high seas, especially with respect to piracy and slavery.[28]

These high seas jurisdictional principles were tested before the PCIJ in its 1927 decision in the *Lotus* case.[29] This case arose out of a 1926 high seas collision between the French registered *Lotus* and the Turkish registered *Boz-Kourt*, which resulted in the latter vessel sinking with the loss of eight Turkish nationals. After rescuing ten of the shipwrecked crew of the *Boz-Kourt*, the *Lotus* arrived in Constantinople (Istanbul), whereupon its Master was arrested, prosecuted and convicted on criminal charges of manslaughter. France protested this conduct, and the matter went to the PCIJ for its determination.

In relation to enforcement jurisdiction the Court observed that:

> [J]urisdiction is certainly territorial; it cannot be exercised by a state outside its territory except by virtue of a permissive rule derived from international custom or from a convention. It does not, however, follow that international law prohibits a state from exercising jurisdiction in its own territory, in respect of any case which relates to acts which have taken place abroad, and in which it cannot rely on some permissive rule of international law.[30]

In rejecting the notion that international law recognises the exclusive jurisdiction of the flag state on the high seas, the Court observed that there was nothing in international law which forbade 'Turkey to take into consideration the fact that the offence produced its effects on the Turkish vessel and consequently in a place assimilated to Turkish territory in which the application of Turkish criminal law cannot be challenged, even in regard to offences committed there by foreigners'.[31] Finding that the 'effects' of the offence had occurred on the Turkish vessel, there was nothing in international law which prohibited Turkey from prosecuting the French master of the *Lotus*.[32] The decision was at the time subject to extensive criticism,[33] and attempts were made to circumvent the judgment through various international initiatives prior to UNCLOS I.[34] Attempts to explain the decision on the basis of a ship being equivalent to 'floating territory' on the high seas have been discredited[35] and, as the ICJ has observed, the judgment has been 'significantly overtaken'[36] by developments in both general international law and the law of the sea.[37]

---

[27] Colombos, *The International Law of the Sea* (n 24) 55.
[28] Robert CF Reuland, 'Interference with Non-national Ships on the High Seas: Peacetime Exceptions to the Exclusivity Rule of Flag-state Jurisdiction' (1989) 22 *Vanderbilt Journal of Transnational Law* 1161.
[29] *Lotus (France v Turkey)* [1927] PCIJ Rep ser A no 10.
[30] Ibid 18–19.
[31] Ibid 23.
[32] Ibid 23.
[33] See, eg, JL Brierly, 'The 'Lotus' Case' (1928) 44 *Law Quarterly Review* 154.
[34] Colombos, *The International Law of the Sea* (n 24) 306.
[35] DP O'Connell, *The International Law of the Sea*, vol 2 (Oxford, Clarendon Press, 1982) 800.
[36] *Arrest Warrant of 11 April 2000 (Democratic Republic of Congo v Belgium)* [2002] ICJ Rep 3, [51] (Joint Separate Opinion of Judges Higgins, Kooijmans and Buergenthal).
[37] See in particular LOSC, art 97.

III. Codification of the High Seas Regime

A. Pre-Geneva Codifications

The turn of the twentieth century saw the commencement of several processes which ultimately led to the ILC in the 1950s being asked to consider the law of the sea, which in turn resulted in UNCLOS I and the adoption of the 1958 Geneva Convention on the High Seas. The high seas regime was therefore the subject of significant and ongoing discussion amongst various international law bodies during the early part of the century. Unlike debates over the regime of the territorial sea, the high seas was not as contentious, and in most instances proposals were made for the codification of what was existing customary international law. Of significance in the efforts to codify the high seas regime was the fact that several multilateral treaties had already been adopted which dealt with a number of high seas issues. For example, following the sinking of the *Titanic* in 1912,[38] significant efforts were made to improve international cooperation for safety of life at sea and this resulted in a series of conventions which placed obligations upon states to come of the aid of shipwrecked persons on the high seas.[39] Likewise, the 1884 Convention for the Protection of Submarine Cables, without referring directly to the high seas, dealt with 'all legally established submarine cables' which were 'outside territorial waters',[40] thereby implicitly recognising the capacity of states to lay submarine cables on the seabed beneath the high seas. The international law on piracy, which was well established in customary international law by the early twentieth century without having been codified in a convention, had also been the subject of the 1932 Harvard Draft Convention on Piracy.[41]

Throughout the early part of the twentieth century there was also increasing attention being given to marine living resource management, not only in state practice and through the decisions of international arbitrations, but also via a growing body of multilateral treaties which all had implications for the high seas regime. The 1931 International Convention for the Regulation of Whaling sought to regulate aspects of high seas whaling, and was later replaced by the 1946 Convention. Aspects of what at the time were high seas fisheries were also being subject to initial regulation, through initiatives such as the 1946 Convention for the Regulation of Meshes of Fishing Nets and Size Limits of Fish and the 1949 North West Atlantic Fisheries Convention. Accordingly, by the time the ILC came to consider the regime of the high seas in the 1950s, it had a considerable body of customary and conventional international law to draw from.

---

[38] The *Titanic* collided during its maiden voyage with an iceberg in the northern Atlantic Ocean in April 1912 with the loss of 1503 passengers and crew. It was the largest and most advanced ocean cruise liner of its time; see generally Lawrence Beesley, *The Loss of the S.S. Titanic: By One of the Survivors* (New York, Houghton Mifflin Company, 1912).

[39] 1929 International Convention for the Safety of Life at Sea; 1948 International Convention for the Safety of Life at Sea.

[40] 1884 Convention for the Protection of Submarine Cables, art 1.

[41] The Committee of Experts for the Progressive Codification of International Law, 'Part VII—Piracy' (1932) 26 *AJIL (Supplement)* 739.

B. Work of the ILC

The ILC's work on the law of the sea reflected in the 'Articles concerning the Law of the Sea with Commentaries'[42] ultimately devoted the majority of its draft to the high seas. Part II of the draft text encompassed a total of 40 articles dealing with provisions for a general regime of the high seas, navigation, fishing, and submarine cables and pipelines. This not only reflected the breadth of the high seas regime, but also the amount of customary international law on the subject which the ILC felt able to codify. Draft Article 27 identified the freedom of the high seas as encompassing the freedom of navigation, freedom of fishing, freedom to lay submarine cables and pipelines, and the freedom to fly over the high seas. The accompanying ILC Commentary observed that '[t]he principle generally accepted in international law that the high seas are open to all nations governs the whole regulation of the subject. No State may subject any part of the high seas to its sovereignty; hence no State may exercise jurisdiction over any such stretch of water.'[43] The list of high seas freedoms was not considered by the ILC to be exhaustive, and in its accompanying commentary the ILC made express reference to the freedom of overflight of the high seas as following 'directly from the principle of the freedom of the sea' while also observing that it had refrained from making any express reference to nuclear weapon tests on the high seas.[44]

With respect to the remaining high seas draft articles, the ILC observed:

> Any freedom that is to be exercised in the interests of all entitled to enjoy it, must be regulated. Hence, the law of the high seas contains certain rules, most of them already recognized in positive international law, which are designed, not to limit or restrict the freedom of the high seas, but to safeguard its exercise in the interests of the entire international community.[45]

The accompanying draft articles then proceeded to address issues such as the right of navigation, nationality and status of ships, immunities of certain ships, navigational safety, including the duty to render assistance, slavery, piracy, the rights of visit and hot pursuit, high seas pollution, fishing, and submarine cables and pipelines.[46]

C. UNCLOS I

UNCLOS I adopted the core recommendations of the ILC with respect to the high seas, with one significant exception. Whereas the ILC had included high seas fisheries conservation within the high seas draft articles, UNCLOS I elected to have this matter separately considered by the Third Committee, whilst the Second Committee considered the general regime of the high seas. The result was the eventual adoption of two conventions addressing

---

[42] International Law Commission, 'Articles Concerning the Law of the Sea with Commentaries' (1956) *Yearbook of the International Law Commission*, vol 2, 265–301.

[43] Ibid 278.

[44] Ibid, where the Commentary refers to its general observation that 'States are bound to refrain from any acts which might adversely affect the use of the high seas by nationals of other States'.

[45] Ibid.

[46] An interesting insight into the ILC's work is that its proposal for the contiguous zone was also contained within these high seas provisions, on the grounds that this zone was 'a belt of the high seas contiguous' to the territorial sea: ibid 294.

high seas issues; the Convention on the High Seas,[47] and the Convention on Fishing and Conservation of the Living Resources of the High Seas.[48] The Convention on the High Seas reflected the main provisions found in the ILC's draft and encompassed a total of 29 substantive articles and a number of procedural and technical articles. One contentious issue which arose during the conference deliberations related to the testing of nuclear weapons on the high seas.[49] Czechoslovakia, Poland, Yugoslavia and the Soviet Union jointly proposed a new article for adoption which would have provided that states were to refrain from the testing of nuclear weapons on the high seas.[50] However, via a procedural mechanism this proposal was never put to the vote.[51] With this exception, the Convention on the High Seas did not prove to be particularly contentious at UNCLOS I.[52] The acceptance of the Convention as being essentially reflective of customary international law was highlighted by it entering into force only four years after UNCLOS I and two years prior to the Convention on the Territorial Sea[53] and Contiguous Zone and the Convention on the Continental Shelf.[54]

As to the Convention on Fishing and Conservation of the Living Resources of the High Seas, that UNCLOS I sought to address this as a distinctive issue and ultimately conclude a separate convention, highlights the significance attached to fisheries issues at the conference. It was the last of the four Geneva Conventions to enter into force and ultimately never received the same levels of support as the others. This is also reflected in the issues which arose for consideration at UNCLOS II, and ultimately became part of the debate over a distinctive fishing zone and EEZ at UNCLOS III.[55]

D. UNCLOS III

When UNCLOS III convened high seas issues were not ones that were anticipated to dominate the discussions. As the 1958 Convention on the High Seas had principally sought to codify existing customary international law, and implementation of the Convention had not proven to be particularly contentious, the major task for the conference was to absorb the high seas provisions into a more general convention on the law of the sea. Whilst there were ongoing concerns as to the management of high seas fish stocks, this issue was directly related to how UNCLOS III dealt with proposals for a distinctive fisheries zone. What was

---

[47]   *Basic Documents* No 10.

[48]   *Basic Documents* No 11.

[49]   Following the conclusion of World War Two, the United States commenced a nuclear testing programme in parts of the Pacific Ocean and during 1946–62 a total of 109 nuclear weapons were detonated in an area known as the 'Pacific Proving Grounds' which were principally Enewetak and Bikini Atolls on the Republic of the Marshall Islands, resulting in increased sensitivity as to nuclear-weapons testing on the high seas: see generally David D Caron and Harry N Scheiber (eds), *The Oceans in the Nuclear Age: Legacies and Risks* (Leiden, Martinus Nijhoff, 2010).

[50]   UN Doc A/CONF.13/C.2/L/30 (21 March 1958).

[51]   O'Connell, *The International Law of the Sea*, vol 2 (n 35) 811–12.

[52]   This was reflected in a post-UNCLOS I assessment of the conference by the Head of the United States delegation, in which of the four conventions concluded, the Convention on the High Seas received the briefest of mentions: Arthur H Dean 'The Geneva Conference on the Law of the Sea: What was accomplished' (1958) 52 *AJIL* 607.

[53]   *Basic Documents* No 9.

[54]   *Basic Documents* No 12.

[55]   For more detailed analysis see ch 4.

clear at the opening of the conference, however, was that the regime of the high seas, which at that time under conventional law commenced at the outer edge of the territorial sea, would inevitably be impacted upon by claims for a fisheries zone and also claims for a new regime to deal with the deep seabed beneath the high seas. This raised several uncertainties as to the operation of the traditional freedoms of the high seas, and the interaction of the high seas regime with other maritime zones.

By 1976, Hamilton Shirley Amerasinghe, the President of UNCLOS III, acknowledged the challenges the conference faced in dealing with the interaction of the high seas with the juridical nature of the then still developing EEZ:

> [T]he special character of this new legal concept calls for a clear distinction to be drawn between the rights of the coastal state and the rights of the international community in the zone. A satisfactory solution must ensure that the sovereign rights and jurisdiction accorded to the coastal state are compatible with well-established and long-recognized rights of communication and navigation which are indispensable to the maintenance of international relations, commercial and otherwise.[56]

Ultimately these issues could only be addressed by carefully ensuring the retention of traditional high seas freedoms, subject to concessions granted to coastal states with respect to their specific interests in the EEZ. Accordingly, whilst coastal states are granted certain sovereign rights and jurisdiction with respect to the EEZ,[57] those rights are not to interfere with high seas freedoms which may apply within those waters. Therefore, high seas freedoms of navigation may continue to be exercised within the EEZ provided they are not incompatible with coastal state rights, which extend to controlling marine pollution. On the other hand, the freedom of high seas fishing cannot be exercised within the EEZ as this would directly impair a coastal states' sovereign right over the marine living resources of the area.

With the exception of this need to ensure appropriate interaction between the high seas regime and the other maritime zones created under the LOSC, the Convention retains the core high seas regime provisions of the 1958 Convention on the High Seas subject to minor modification and updating. With respect to high seas fisheries, the LOSC did not outline a detailed regime, nor did it seek to duplicate the provisions of the 1958 Convention on Fishing and Conservation of the Living Resources of the High Seas. There was, however, allowance made for enhanced future cooperation in dealing with the living resources of the high seas,[58] and this provided one of the grounds for the eventual adoption of the 1995 Fish Stocks Agreement.[59]

IV. The LOSC and the High Seas

The LOSC in Part VII deals with the high seas and immediately in Article 86 seeks to situate Part VII alongside other relevant parts of the Convention, especially those dealing with

---

[56] *Third United Nations Conference on the Law of the Sea: Official Records*, vol 6 (New York, United Nations, 1976) 122, 123.

[57] LOSC, art 56.

[58] Ibid art 118.

[59] 1995 Agreement for the Implementation of the Provisions of the United Nations Convention on the Law of the Sea of 10 December 1982 Relating to the Conservation and Management of Straddling Fish Stocks and Highly Migratory Fish Stocks, *Basic Documents* No 56.

related maritime zones. Article 86 makes clear that the high seas extend to 'all parts of the sea' that are not included within the EEZ, territorial sea, the internal waters of a coastal state or the archipelagic waters of an archipelagic state. The effect of this is that where a coastal state has claimed an EEZ of 200 nm, the high seas commence from that limit. Beyond 200 nm the high seas will be the water surface and column above any extended continental shelf established by states beyond 200 nm or above the Area.[60]

Whilst the true high seas therefore commence beyond the limits of the EEZ, the LOSC provides for interaction between the high seas and EEZ regimes with Article 86 making clear that it 'does not entail any abridgement of the freedoms enjoyed by all States in the exclusive economic zone in accordance with article 58'. Article 58 in turn makes clear that certain of the high seas freedoms are also to be enjoyed within the EEZ. The LOSC in Article 89 also provides that no state may seek to subject any part of the high seas to its sovereignty and this is consistent with the customary international law on this matter, although it is important to distinguish between the limitations on the capacity to assert sovereignty and the ability of states to exercise certain forms of jurisdiction over the high seas.

A. Freedom of the High Seas

Article 87 of the LOSC identifies the freedom of the high seas, making clear that the high seas are open to all states whether coastal or landlocked. Six high seas freedoms are listed in Article 87(1), two more than were listed in the 1958 Convention on the High Seas with the additions being to carry out scientific research, and to construct artificial islands and other installations. The list is not exhaustive and is prefaced by the words *inter alia*. This is of significance with respect to the capacity of states to engage in other activities consistent with the freedom, such as to conduct military exercises and weapons testing on the high seas.[61] The freedoms of the high seas are not, however, absolute and are to be exercised consistent with the LOSC and other relevant rules of international law,[62] and with due regard to the interests of other states and rights under the LOSC with respect to the Area.[63] This suggests that from time to time there will need to be taken into account the rights and interests of all users of the high seas in exercising certain freedoms.

i. Freedom of Navigation

Given its historical importance to the high seas regime, the listing of the freedom of navigation as the first freedom of the high seas is iconic. This term reflects considerable state practice and customary international law and is confirmed by the absence of any further elaboration in the convention text. Whilst the freedom of navigation on the high seas needs to be read alongside the exercise of that right in the territorial sea, including international

---

[60] Ibid art 1.

[61] O'Connell, *The International Law of the Sea*, vol 2 (n 35) 809–13.

[62] An example of which is the 1972 Convention on the International Regulation for Preventing Collisions at Sea (COLREG), *Basic Documents* No 20, as amended, Rule 1 of which makes clear that 'These Rules shall apply to all vessels upon the high seas'.

[63] LOSC, art 87(3).

traits, and archipelagic waters, the major distinction is that upon the high seas ships do not pass through the waters of any state and accordingly their navigational freedoms are not subject to any limitations. Consistent with the LOSC, however, the mere presence of a ship on the high seas does not guarantee that its navigation will not be subject to interference. In addition to the recognised but limited right of visit upon certain vessels on the high seas,[64] particular acts are prohibited such as piracy and illicit traffic in narcotic drugs.

ii. Freedom of Overflight

In distinction to the 1958 Convention on the High Seas, the LOSC refers to the freedom of 'overflight' on the high seas as opposed to the previous formulation of 'freedom to fly over'.[65] The freedom of overflight applies to commercial, government or military aircraft and does not seek to distinguish between types of aircraft, and therefore would apply to spacecraft upon take off or re-entry into the earth's atmosphere when overflying the oceans. The law of the sea only seeks to identify the right to use airspace above the high seas, and does not regulate how that airspace is used other than in the exceptional case of aircraft which are engaged in piracy.[66] Navigational safety for aircraft engaged in overflight of the high seas is dealt with under separate international aviation law conventions.[67]

iii. Freedom to Lay Submarine Cables and Pipelines

The freedom to lay submarine cables and pipelines is listed as a high seas freedom with Article 112 making clear that such installations may be laid 'on the bed of the high seas beyond the continental shelf'. This is consistent with state practice which developed in the late nineteenth century and was also reflected in the 1958 Convention on the High Seas. However, this freedom within the high seas is only operational if carefully calibrated with the relevant provisions found in Part VI dealing with the continental shelf and the laying of cables and pipelines over that area. Article 79 sets out the conditions for the installation of cables and pipelines over the continental shelf and gives to all states a right to do so subject to certain conditions that may be established by the coastal state. Whilst the delineation of the course of cables and pipelines within the continental shelf is subject to the consent of the coastal state,[68] no such limitation exists in the high seas. Nevertheless, any state wishing to lay cables and pipelines through the high seas would need to take into account the interests of other users, and also the potential marine environmental impact of this activity. Articles 113 to 115 provide additional measures associated with the breaking of, or injury to, a submarine cable or pipeline, requiring coastal states to adopt relevant laws and regulations.

---

[64] Ibid art 110; this right has also been supplemented by the provisions of the 2005 Convention for the Suppression of Unlawful Acts against the Safety of Maritime Navigation, *Basic Documents* No 79; see the discussion in Natalie Klein 'The Right of Visit and the 2005 Protocol on the Suppression of Unlawful Acts Against the Safety of Maritime Navigation' (2007) 35 *Denver Journal of International Law and Policy* 287.

[65] Overflight is also referred to in Part IV dealing with archipelagic states, though in that context it is referred to as 'rights of ... overflight'; LOSC, art 53(3).

[66] LOSC, art 101 extends the act of piracy to acts of private aircraft; which are further defined in art 103.

[67] 1944 Convention on International Civil Aviation ('Chicago Convention').

[68] LOSC, art 79(3).

iv. *Freedom to Construct Artificial Islands and Other Installations*

As an addition to the 1958 Convention on the High Seas, Article 87(1)(d) refers to the right to construct 'artificial islands and other installations permitted under international law'. The freedom is, however, subject to other relevant provisions found in Part VI. There are two instances where artificial installations and islands may be constructed in the high seas. The first is where such structures are built in support of operations on the continental shelf beyond 200 nm in a zone where the high seas are conterminous with the outer continental shelf. In this case, the provisions of Article 80 and Part VI of the LOSC will control.[69] However, in a curious example highlighting the interconnections between certain parts of the LOSC, Article 80 makes Article 60 in Part V applicable *mutatis mutandis*, with the effect that certain EEZ provisions of the Convention are also applicable in the high seas. The principal limitations which exist with respect to these structures are: that due notice is given as to their construction; appropriate safety zones are established around them; there is no interference with sea lanes essential to international navigation; and abandoned or disused structures are removed.[70]

The second instance is where these structures are built within the high seas proper and there is no conterminous continental shelf. This area of the high seas would be conterminous with the deep seabed of the Area for the purposes of Part XI. Article 147(2) contains equivalent provisions to Article 60 where installations have been built in support of activities in the Area. In keeping with the status of the high seas as an area where coastal state sovereignty may not be exercised, the construction of artificial islands or installations on the high seas does not acquire for the relevant state any form of sovereignty over that area such as a capacity to generate maritime claims nor does it impact upon the delimitation of maritime boundaries.[71] States may also elect to construct artificial islands for the purposes of marine scientific research, in which case provisions found in Part XIII of the LOSC would also be applicable. An interesting issue arises in the case of co-called 'ice islands' which may be formed from icebergs which have broken away from ice shelves. Whilst these are natural features and so do not fall within the scope of Article 87(1)(d), issues will arise as to the ability of a state to appropriate the ice island, albeit on a temporary basis, and its ability to exercise jurisdiction over the persons engaging in activities on the island.[72]

v. *Freedom of Fishing*

The freedom of fishing, alongside the freedom of navigation, is one of the cardinal freedoms of the high seas and it continues to be recognised in Article 87 of the LOSC.[73] However, whilst in the 1958 Convention on the High Seas the freedom to fish was recognised without qualification, in the LOSC there is direct reference to 'conditions' which are imposed on

---

[69] Salah E Honein, *The International Law Relating to Offshore Installations and Artificial Islands* (London, Lloyd's of London Press, 1991) 17–22.

[70] LOSC, art 60.

[71] See, eg, ibid art 147(2), (3).

[72] In one instance, the United States courts were prepared to exercise jurisdiction in a case involving the murder of an American scientist stationed on an ice island in the Arctic Ocean; see *US v Escamilla* (1972) 467 F 2d 341; and discussion in Donat Pharand, 'State Jurisdiction over Ice Island T-3: The Escamilla Case' (1971) 24 *Arctic* 83.

[73] The discussion under this heading should be read in the light of the more detailed consideration of marine resource management in ch 13.

the freedom to fish found in Part VII, Section II which encompasses Articles 116 to 120. Importantly, Article 116 makes clear that whilst all states have the right for their nationals to engage in fishing on the high seas, this activity must be undertaken subject to their treaty obligations, certain rights and duties of coastal states as identified in Part V of the LOSC, and other relevant provisions of section II.

The freedom of high seas fishing is therefore subject to three broad constraints. First, with respect to other treaty obligations this could extend to other bilateral, regional or global multilateral treaties states are parties to which place constraints upon high seas fishing activities. A prominent example is the 1980 Convention on the Conservation of Antarctic Marine Living Resources which extends to large portions of the Southern Ocean,[74] including claimed EEZs and high seas, and which through conservation measures adopted under the Convention place significant restrictions upon fishing activities.[75] Secondly, high seas fishing needs to take into account the particular interests of coastal states with respect to straddling stocks, highly migratory species, marine mammals, anadromous stocks and catadromous species. With respect to straddling and highly migratory fish stocks, the special issues confronting those stocks have been further addressed in the Fish Stocks Agreement. Finally, high sea fishing also needs to take into account the other provisions found in Section II of Part VII which encompasses Articles 117 to 120 and particularly includes certain measures for the conservation and management of living resources of the high seas.

vi. Freedom of Scientific Research

The freedom of scientific research was a high seas freedom which the ILC acknowledged in its commentary to the draft articles but did not expressly refer to.[76] Given the extensive consideration given to scientific research in Part XIII of the LOSC, which itself makes clear the existence of certain rights to conduct research in areas within the high seas,[77] it is appropriate that part of the LOSC provides more detail on this high seas freedom. A further constraint with respect to high seas scientific research relates to those areas of outer continental shelf extending beyond the 200 nm limit and which are within the high seas in which case relevant provisions in Part VI are also applicable.[78]

B. Shipping

Part VII of the LOSC also contains a collection of provisions which address the status of ships and obligations upon ships whilst on the high seas. While located within Part VII of the Convention, the reality is that their application is much broader since they reflect the general international law on the topic and effectively apply wherever ships may be, although there are some particular duties upon flag states when their ships are on the high seas.

---

[74] 1980 Convention on the Conservation of Antarctic Marine Living Resources, art I.
[75] Ibid art IX.
[76] Marine scientific research is discussed in further detail in ch 14.
[77] LOSC, art 256 referring to the right to conduct marine scientific research in the Area; and Article 257 referring to the right to conduct marine scientific research in the area beyond the limits of the EEZ.
[78] Ibid art 81 particularly regulates all drilling that may take place on the continental shelf and extends to 'all purposes'.

An additional observation is that these provisions do not purport to be all encompassing or substitute for relevant maritime and shipping law, some of which itself has been subject to codification in instruments adopted under the auspices of the IMO. Nevertheless, these provisions complement the specific international maritime law on point.

i. Nationality of Ships

The nationality of ships is provided for in Article 91 which recognises the capacity of every state to fix the conditions for the grant of nationality thereby giving the ship the right to fly its flag.[79] The only condition imposed under Article 91 is that there must exist 'a genuine link between the State and the ship'. This requirement is reflective of the general principles of international law regarding nationality which were referred to by the ICJ in the *Nottebohm* case[80] and were restated in the 1986 United Nations Convention on Conditions for Registration of Ships.[81] One of the enormous challenges which exists in this area is characterising a genuine link between a state of registration and a ship, and ensuring that broadly uniform standards are adopted between states. This was recognised by the ILC, in the commentary to the equivalent provision in its draft articles when it observed that:

> Each State lays down the conditions on which ships may fly its flag. Obviously the state enjoys complete liberty in the case of ships owned by it or ships which are the property of a nationalized company. With regard to other ships, the state must accept certain restrictions.[82]

The ILC then went on to refer to the need for a 'minimum national element'.[83] One issue which has arisen in this field is the operation of so-called 'Open Registries' in which some states have very liberal domestic laws allowing for the registration of ships that have minimal connection with the state resulting in some ships flying what are often referred to as 'flags of convenience'.[84] States which operate these registries often have a reputation for taking little interest in the affairs of the ship and do not apply standards to ensure the safety of the ship and its crew. Such flags of convenience are undesirable and create significant legal challenges with respect to maritime regulation and enforcement,[85] but they do not contravene the requirement for the existence of a genuine link. In the *M/V Saiga (No 2)* case ITLOS had occasion in 1999 to review the relevant provisions of the LOSC and the ILC's commentaries on its draft articles. The tribunal observed that, for the purpose of the Convention:

> [T]he need for a genuine link between a ship and its flag State is to secure more effective implementation of the duties of the flag State, and not to establish criteria by reference to which the validity of the registration of ships in a flag State may be challenged by other States.[86]

---

[79] LOSC, art 93 also contemplates the possibility that ships may fly the flag of an international organisation, such as the UN.

[80] *Nottebohm (Liechtenstein v Guatemala)* (second phase) [1955] ICJ Rep 4.

[81] 1986 United Nations Convention on Conditions for Registration of Ships, art 1.

[82] International Law Commission, 'Articles Concerning the Law of the Sea with Commentaries' (n 42) 279.

[83] Ibid 280.

[84] H Edwin Anderson, 'The Nationality of Ships and Flags of Convenience: Economics, Politics and Alternatives' (1996) 21 *Tulane Maritime Law Journal* 139; cf LOSC, art 92(2) which refers to ships using the flags of two or more states for 'convenience'.

[85] This has particularly been the case with respect to enforcement of fisheries laws, regulations and measures: Jessica K Ferrell, 'Controlling Flags of Convenience: One Measure to Stop Overfishing of Collapsing Fish Stocks' (2005) 25 *Environmental Law* 323.

[86] *M/V Saiga (No 2) (Saint Vincent and the Grenadines v Guinea)* (admissibility and merits) (1999) 120 ILR 143, [83].

In that instance, the tribunal concluded that there was no legal basis for Guinea to refuse to recognise the right of the *Saiga* to fly the flag of Saint Vincent and the Grenadines on the basis that there was no genuine link.[87] This was reaffirmed by the tribunal in *M/V Virginia G*, and the tribunal went further in spelling out flag state duties that flow from the nationality of vessels:

> In the view of the Tribunal, once a ship is registered, the flag State is required, under article 94 of the Convention, to exercise effective jurisdiction and control over that ship in order to ensure that it operates in accordance with generally accepted international regulations, procedures and practices. This is the meaning of 'genuine link'.[88]

Closely related to Article 91 is Article 92 which deals with the status of ships. It affirms that ships are under the exclusive jurisdiction of the flag state whilst on the high seas. The only exception to this rule would arise if a vessel has been detained or arrested on the high seas for engaging in an act such as piracy, in which case it clearly falls under the jurisdiction of the arresting state. Ships are also not permitted to change their flag during a voyage or whilst in port other than following a change of registry or transfer of ownership.

ii. Duties of the Flag State

The duties of the flag state are outlined in Article 94 which is a significant expansion of the equivalent provision found in the 1958 Convention on the High Seas.[89] In doing so, Article 94 details both the extent and capacity of flag state jurisdiction, but also the particular responsibilities which arise for flag states.[90] A flag state is required to 'effectively exercise its jurisdiction and control in administrative, technical and social matters' over ships flying its flag and this extends to maintaining a register of all shipping flying its flag, and also assuming jurisdiction under its national law for both the ship and its crew in relation to administrative, technical and social matters. This creates a requirement that the flag state apply particular shipping and maritime laws to its flagged ships, and also relevant criminal and civil laws to the crew. Flag states are also to take certain measures with respect to ensuring the safety of life at sea of its flagged ships extending to the seaworthiness of the ship;[91] the manning of the ship including labour conditions; and the use of signals for the prevention of collisions. These measures are required to conform to generally accepted international regulations, the great majority of which are found in relevant IMO conventions.[92] These duties of the flag state have also been supplemented by the 1986 United Nations Convention on Conditions for Registration of Ships; however, that convention remains moribund and it is doubtful whether it will enter into force.[93]

---

[87] Ibid [86].
[88] *M/V Virginia G (Panama/Guinea-Bissau)* (2014) 53 ILM 1164, [113].
[89] 1958 Convention on the High Seas, art 10.
[90] Co-related provisions with respect to the extent of flag state jurisdiction can be found in LOSC, art 217.
[91] See also ibid art 219.
[92] These would include COLREG, *Basic Documents* No 20; and SOLAS, *Basic Documents* No 22.
[93] As of July 2015 the Convention had 15 parties, but requires 40 states with a combined tonnage of not less then 25 per cent of the world tonnage to become contracting parties; see discussion in Moira L McConnell, '"Business as Usual": An Evaluation of the 1986 United Nations Convention on Conditions for Registration of Ships' (1987) 18 *Journal of Maritime Law and Commerce* 435.

iii. Immunities

The immunities of warships and government ships used for non-commercial purposes are recognised in Articles 95 and 96. In both instances the LOSC provides that such ships have 'complete immunity from the jurisdiction of any State' other than the flag state. A supplementary provision can be found in Article 236 which reaffirms sovereign immunity for warships and other government vessels on non-commercial service with respect to certain provisions dealing with the protection and preservation of the marine environment.[94] These provisions reflect existing customary international law with respect to sovereign immunity of states which itself is founded upon extensive jurisprudence by domestic courts and relevant municipal legislation.[95]

iv. Collisions

Closely related to the issue of immunities, is the extent of flag state jurisdiction over ships that have been involved in a collision. Article 97 deals with penal jurisdiction following a collision or any other incident of navigation,[96] and provides that the institution of any proceedings against the master or any other person following such an incident must be by the flag state or the state of nationality of the person involved. A related procedural provision is that only the flag state can issue a request for arrest or detention of a ship following such an incident.[97] This provision, which had a predecessor equivalent in Article 11 of the Convention on the High Seas, was originally recommended by the ILC in direct response to the decision in the *Lotus* case. Observing that the PCIJ's judgment was 'strongly criticized and caused serious disquiet in international maritime circles' the Commission justified its support for the provision on the grounds that it was seeking to protect 'ships and their crews from the risk of penal proceedings before foreign courts in the event of collision on the high seas, since such proceedings may constitute an intolerable interference with international navigation'.[98] The consequence is that the state which has suffered an injury, either through the loss of a ship or its nationals, is effectively barred from instituting criminal proceedings against those who may have been responsible. One available option in this instance is for the aggrieved state to seek to request that the flag state properly exercise its jurisdiction following such an incident, including the conduct of an inquiry.[99] This provision, however, does not have any impact upon civil proceedings which may arise from such an incident.

v. Assistance to Persons at Sea

The duty to render assistance to ships and persons in distress on the high seas is articulated in Article 98 of the LOSC, which replicates an equivalent provision in the 1958 Convention

---

[94] However, LOSC, art 236 goes on to provide that 'each State, shall ensure, by the adoption of appropriate measures not impairing operations or operational capabilities of such vessels … that such vessels … act in a manner consistent, so far as is reasonable and practicable, with this Convention'.

[95] See, eg, *The Schooner Exchange v M'Faddon* (1812) 11 US 116; *Trendtex Trading v Central Bank of Nigeria* [1977] 1 QB 529; *ARA Libertad (Argentina v Ghana)*, Provisional Measures, Order of 15 December 2012.

[96] This is sufficiently broad to extend to an incident involving damage to a submarine cable or pipeline.

[97] LOSC, art 97(3).

[98] International Law Commission, 'Articles Concerning the Law of the Sea with Commentaries' (n 42) 281.

[99] LOSC, arts 94(6), 94(7).

on the High Seas, and also builds upon similar obligations found in SOLAS,[100] the 1979 International Convention on Maritime Search and Rescue (1979 MSR),[101] and the 1989 International Convention on Salvage.[102] If the Master can give assistance without 'serious danger, to the ship, the crew or the passengers', then assistance is to be provided to persons found at sea, persons in distress are to be rescued, and assistance is to be rendered following a collision.[103] In support of these obligations, there is also a requirement that every coastal state is to promote adequate mechanisms for maritime search and rescue. The requirement in Article 98 to rescue 'any person' makes clear that there should be no distinction exercised in the rescue of persons at sea. This is important given some variable practice which has arisen with respect to the rescue of asylum seekers. In 1985 the IMO and Executive Committee of the High Commissioner for Refugees sought to remind all states of their obligations in this regard.[104] In 2004 the IMO issued 'Guidelines on the Treatment of Persons Rescued at Sea' in order to clarify further the obligations under the LOSC, SOLAS and the 1979 MSR[105] to render assistance to persons following controversies when some states had refused to receive persons who had been rescued at sea.[106]

C. Prohibitions

i. Piracy

There is a long and eventful history of piracy in international law. As contemporary international trade routes developed, slow moving and undefended merchant ships were an easy target for pirates set on looting and plunder. Gradually throughout the nineteenth century a legal regime developed in response to the threat of piracy and customary international law evolved which rendered piracy the first universal crime over which all states assumed the right to arrest and prosecute offenders. These developments in custom found their way into the modern law of the sea first via the 1958 Convention on the High Seas, and then the LOSC. An important aspect of the response to piracy is inter-state cooperation, and this is reinforced in Article 100 of the LOSC.

Article 101 defines ship-based piracy as consisting of acts of violence or detention, or an act of depredation, committed for private ends by the crew of a private ship directed against another ship on the high seas or outside the jurisdiction of any state. Piracy also extends to the operation of a pirate ship which is a ship used by persons for the purposes of committing pirate acts. This general definition of piracy is consistent with the common expression that a pirate is *hostis humani generis*—an enemy of all humankind. However, by limiting the definition to acts committed for 'private ends' any actions taken for political motives such as terrorist attacks are excluded. A crucial element of this definition is that piracy is

---

[100] SOLAS, Annex, ch 5, reg 33.
[101] 1979 MSR, Annex, ch 2, [2.1].
[102] International Convention on Salvage, art 10.
[103] LOSC, art 98(1).
[104] *Virginia Commentaries*, vol 3, 175.
[105] IMO Resolution MSC 167 (78) (20 May 2004), *Basic Documents* No 75.
[106] See Donald R Rothwell 'The Law of the Sea and the MV Tampa Incident: Reconciling Maritime Principles with Coastal State Sovereignty' (2002) 13 *Public Law Review* 118–27.

an act which occurs on the high seas, and accordingly an equivalent act of violence which took place within the territorial sea would not be piracy for the purposes of international law. The definition of pirate ship or aircraft in Article 103 extends to one that is 'intended by the persons in dominant control' to be used for an act of piracy. The importance of the characterisation of a vessel as a pirate ship is highlighted by Article 105 which gives to any state on the high seas the capacity to seize a pirate ship and to arrest the persons on board and their assets. Additional consequential provisions are found in the LOSC dealing with piracy by a government ship or warship whose crew has mutinied,[107] and liability arising from the seizure of a pirate ship without adequate grounds.[108]

Notwithstanding the LOSC provisions on piracy reflecting international law, laws dealing with piracy can also be found in municipal law which may sometimes differ in important respects. Different approaches can be found in the elements of the offence, the types of offensive acts, and the locus of the offence,[109] with the effect that under municipal law acts of piracy may be committed within the territorial sea. However, in those instances, it will be the laws of the coastal state that will apply to any enforcement operations and unless exceptional arrangements have been put in place other states would have no jurisdiction over pirates within the territorial seas of a coastal state.[110] Exceptional arrangements have been put in place since 2008 in relation to Somalia and these are discussed below.

Since adoption of the LOSC, the international law in the area of vessel security has been significantly expanded by the 1988 Convention for the Suppression of Unlawful Acts against the Safety of Maritime Navigation (SUA Convention)[111] in response to the highjacking of the Italian cruise ship, *Achille Lauro*, in the Mediterranean, which resulted in the death of a passenger. Whilst the SUA Convention makes it an offence if a person 'seizes or exercises control over a ship by threat or use of force thereof or any other form of intimidation',[112] enforcement relies upon the traditional jurisdictional bases of nationality and territoriality. A 2005 Protocol has substantially expanded the scope of the Convention to include acts of maritime terrorism, including what may be termed 'political piracy'. However, the focus of the adjustments has not been acts of 'common' piracy or robbery at sea, and there remain important jurisdictional loopholes in the enforcement of criminal charges when non-nationals or non-state vessels are involved.

There have been some significant developments in state practice with respect to piracy since the 1990s. In response to an upsurge in pirate activity the International Maritime Bureau in 1992 established a Piracy Reporting Centre which has been steadily tracking pirate activity around the world.[113] During the 1990s much of the focus had been upon Southeast Asian waters, especially in the Straits of Malacca and within the Indonesian Archipelago.[114] However, from 2007 there was an unprecedented increase in piracy at sea,

---

[107] LOSC, art 102.
[108] Ibid art 106.
[109] O'Connell, *The International Law of the Sea*, vol 2 (n 35) 979.
[110] Ibid 979–83.
[111] Subsequently modified by a 2005 Protocol, *Basic Documents* No 79.
[112] SUA Convention, art 3.
[113] IMB Piracy Reporting Centre at icc-ccs.org/piracy-reporting-centre.
[114] Graham Gerard Ong (ed), *Piracy, Maritime Terrorism and Securing the Malacca Straits* (Singapore, Institute of Southeast Asian Studies, 2006); Robert C Beckman, 'Issues of Public International Law Relating to Piracy and Armed Robbery Against Ships in the Malacca and Singapore Straits' (1999) 3 *Singapore Journal of International and Comparative Law* 512.

resulting in significant international efforts to suppress pirate attacks. In 2008 an increase in the number of these attacks was evident off the east African coast, principally in the Gulf of Aden but also in the Indian Ocean offshore Kenya and Somalia. Global attention was focussed on these events in November 2008 with the seizure of the crude carrier *Sirius Star* some 450 nm southeast of Mombassa, Kenya. There were also reports of pirate attacks against cruise ships in the Indian Ocean. In 2009 there were a total of 406 reports of piracy and sea robbery, of which 217 were Somali sourced attacks involving 47 highjacked ships and 867 crew being held hostage.[115] In more recent years the number of piratical incidents has fallen significantly, with a total of 245 actual and attempted attacks globally in 2014; and there are now fewer attacks in the Gulf of Aden than in several other regions, such as Bangladesh, Indonesia and Nigeria.[116]

The scale of the pirate attacks in the Indian Ocean in 2008 and 2009 combined to create contemporary challenges for international shipping not previously encountered during peacetime since the 1956 closure of the Suez Canal. It called into account the international legal regime dealing with piracy and drew comparisons with international terrorism. In response, the United Nations Security Council proactively intervened in 2008 to adopt unprecedented resolutions conferring upon maritime powers the capacity to enter Somali waters to conduct anti-piracy operations and to facilitate the prosecution of suspected pirates.[117] In reliance upon this mandate, the EU launched operation 'Atlanta' to combat piracy off the coast of Somalia while the North Atlantic Treaty Organization (NATO) has also taken the lead in providing naval support. Other states which offered support included China, India, Iran, Malaysia and Russia. A further significant step was taken with the adoption of Security Council Resolution 1851 on 16 December 2008 which further authorised 'shiprider' agreements to facilitate more effective law enforcement capability, whilst also authorising capacity on the part of the international community to operate not only within Somali waters but also within the territory of Somalia so as to suppress acts of piracy and robbery at sea.[118] The effect of these agreements is that law enforcement officials of the relevant state parties are given reciprocal jurisdiction to undertake enforcement operations against suspect flagged vessels beyond the territorial sea thus facilitating enforcement operations against pirates by circumventing some of the limitations created by the international law against piracy.[119]

ii. Slavery

The abolition of slavery in international law had its foundations in developments in the United States and Europe during the nineteenth century which eventually resulted in

---

[115] IMB Piracy Reporting Centre, '2009 Worldwide Piracy Figures Surpass 400' (14 January 2010) at icc-ccs.org/piracy-reporting-centre.

[116] IMB Piracy Reporting Centre, *Piracy and Armed Robbery Against Ships: Report for 2014* (2015) 5.

[117] UN Security Council Resolution 1816 (2008), *Basic Documents* No 86; UN Security Council Resolution 1838 (2008), *Basic Documents* No 87; UN Security Council Resolution 1846 (2008), *Basic Documents* No 88; UN Security Council Resolution 1851 (2008), *Basic Documents* No 89.

[118] See detailed analysis in Douglas Guilfoyle, *Shipping Interdiction and the Law of the Sea* (Cambridge, Cambridge University Press, 2009) 61–74.

[119] See an example of a 'ship-rider' agreement in 2009 Code of Conduct Concerning the Repression of Piracy and Armed Robbery Against Ships in the Western Indian Ocean and the Gulf of Aden, *Basic Documents* No 90; and discussion in Guilfoyle, *Shipping Interdiction and the Law of the Sea*, ibid 72–73.

twentieth-century initiatives to prohibit slavery and adopt measures to stop the slave trade. As there was a history of transportation of slaves by sea, any international law prohibiting slavery needed to take measures to regulate the slave trade on the high seas. The 1926 International Convention to Suppress the Slave Trade and Slavery[120] was the first of a series of international initiatives to prohibit slavery, and these efforts were also reflected in Article 13 of the 1958 Convention on the High Seas. The LOSC in Article 99 essentially repeats the earlier provision requiring states to take effective measures to prevent and punish the transportation of slaves in ships flying its flag. Slaves taking refuge on board any ship, are *ipso facto* to be considered free. Enforcement of this provision is supported expressly by the right of visit on the high seas,[121] and more generally by the right of hot pursuit.[122] Whilst combating the slave trade may principally be seen as a matter of historical concern, in recent decades the trafficking of persons has become a recognised transnational crime with certain elements associated with the slave trade. However, responses to human trafficking have been distinctive from those developed for the slave trade, even though both share a maritime enforcement dimension.[123]

iii. Drug Trafficking

Reflective of the growth in international concern over the illicit traffic in narcotic drugs and psychotropic substances, Article 108 of the LOSC seeks to address this issue first by requiring states to cooperate in the suppression of high seas trafficking of such substances, and secondly by requesting the aid of other states in undertaking suppression activities against its own flagged ships. At the time of its conclusion, these obligations sought to complement existing international law dealing with drug trafficking as found in the 1961 Single Convention on Narcotic Drugs and the 1971 Convention on Psychotropic Substances. These measures have since been extended by the 1988 United Nations Convention against Illicit Traffic in Narcotic Drugs and Psychotropic Substances. In this respect, it is noteworthy that the latter convention in Article 17 directly addresses 'Illicit traffic by sea' and requires states to 'co-operate to the fullest extent possible to suppress illicit traffic by sea, in conformity with the international law of the sea'. To that end, provision is made for a right to board and search vessels of other state parties which are suspected of involvement in drug trafficking. However, as the LOSC is silent as to a right of high seas boarding, a state would need to point to its acceptance of the 1988 Convention if it undertook such measures on the high seas. Global initiatives in this area have in some instances been supplemented by regional arrangements such as the 2003 San José Agreement which applies within the Caribbean area.[124]

---

[120] See also the later 1956 Supplementary Convention on the Abolition of Slavery, the Slave Trade, and Institutions and Practices similar to Slavery; and 1957 ILO Convention (No 105) Concerning the Abolition of Forced Labour.

[121] LOSC, art 110(1).

[122] Ibid art 111.

[123] Guilfoyle, *Shipping Interdiction and the Law of the Sea* (n 118) 75–77; see also 2000 United Nations Convention against Transnational Organized Crime.

[124] 2003 Agreement Concerning Co-Operation in Suppressing Illicit Maritime and Air Trafficking in Narcotic Drugs and Psychotropic Substances in the Caribbean Area, *Basic Documents* No 72.

iv. Unauthorised Broadcasting

Unauthorised broadcasting on the high seas (often termed 'pirate' radio or television) was not an issue considered at UNCLOS I but by the time of UNCLOS III there was sufficient concern to include it on the main conference agenda. Several initiatives to address unauthorised high seas broadcasting predate the LOSC, including a 1965 European Agreement[125] and a Radio Regulation adopted by the International Telecommunications Union;[126] however, the state practice was variable.[127] Article 109 of the LOSC provides that states are to cooperate to suppress unauthorised broadcasting on the high seas, and provides a jurisdictional basis for a variety of states with particular interests to prosecute persons responsible. Included are the flag state of the ship engaged in the act, the state of registry of the installation, the state of which a person is a national, and the state in which transmissions can be received or which is suffering interference.[128] 'Unauthorised Broadcasting' is defined to extend to 'transmission of sound radio or television broadcasts from a ship or installation on the high seas intended for the reception by the general public contrary to international regulations'.[129] The transmission of distress calls are excluded from this definition. In the Internet age these provisions relating to unauthorised broadcasting which place the activity alongside piracy and the slave trade appear curiously anachronistic, and they no longer appear to have any significant relevance.

D. Enforcement

Part VII of the LOSC has a number of distinctive and significant enforcement provisions which build upon state practice reflected in customary international law and also the 1958 Convention on the High Seas.[130] Article 110 confers upon warships, and other duly authorised ships in government service,[131] including aircraft, a high seas 'right of visit' against certain ships. An important aspect of Article 110 is that it proceeds upon the basis that consistent with the freedom of high seas navigation, ships on the high seas are not to be interfered with, unless there is a 'reasonable ground' for suspecting that the ship is engaged in certain types of activity. If such grounds do exist, then warships or their equivalent have a right of visit which extends to boarding and inspection of the vessel. The right can only be exercised in a case where there are suspicions that the ship is engaged in piracy, the slave trade or unauthorised broadcasting, is without nationality, or though flying a foreign flag is really the same nationality as the warship.[132] The right does not apply to ships which enjoy immunity, which includes foreign warships and certain government vessels.[133] The right of

---

[125] 1965 European Agreement for the Prevention of Broadcasts Transmitted from Stations Outside National Territories.

[126] *Virginia Commentaries*, vol 3, 236.

[127] Guilfoyle, *Shipping Interdiction and the Law of the Sea* (n 118) 170–75; HF van Panhuys and Menno J van Emde Boas, 'Legal Aspects of Pirate Broadcasting: A Dutch Approach' (1966) 60 *AJIL* 303.

[128] LOSC, art 109(3).

[129] Ibid art 109(2).

[130] The provisions dealing with high seas enforcement will be addressed in more detail in ch 18.

[131] This would extend to clearly identifiable Coast Guard, Fisheries and Customs vessels.

[132] LOSC, art 110(1).

[133] Ibid arts 95, 96.

visit can also extend to an inspection of the ship if that is necessary to remove or confirm suspicion. This right would certainly be applicable in the case of pirate ships where it may be necessary to undertake a full inspection in order to verify the status of the ship, the crew and its activities. If a right of visit is exercised against a ship and the 'suspicions prove to be unfounded' the LOSC makes clear that the delayed ship 'shall be compensated' for any losses or damage.[134] As a complement to the right of visit, Article 109(4) also permits the arrest on the high seas of any person or ship engaged in unauthorised broadcasting by a state which has jurisdiction conferred upon it.

Whilst the right of visit permits a form of enforcement action to be taken against ships engaged in certain types of activities on the high seas, the right of hot pursuit allows a state to undertake enforcement operations against ships commencing within the territorial sea, contiguous zone, EEZ or the continental shelf, but which continues onto the high seas. O'Connell observed of hot pursuit that: 'The right of a State to pursue foreign ships on the high seas which have offended its law within its national jurisdiction was well-established in the nineteenth century, although the derivation of the right is obscure'.[135] There is considerable evidence of the doctrine in state practice, in the early efforts at codification of the law of the sea and also in the work of the ILC. The right of hot pursuit was recognised in Article 23 of the 1958 Convention on the High Seas, and other than modifications made to account for the existence of additional maritime zones which arose from the LOSC, that right has been retained with all its key features in Article 111 of the LOSC.

Hot pursuit may only be commenced once authorities in the coastal state believe that a ship has violated the laws and regulations of that state. The pursuit may commence within internal waters, archipelagic waters, the territorial sea or the contiguous zone, and in certain instances also within the EEZ and the continental shelf. A key element is that the pursuit must be continuous and not be interrupted and that an order to stop has been properly given to the ship subject to the pursuit. The right of hot pursuit may only be exercised by warships, military aircraft, or other ships or aircraft clearly marked as being on governmental service. This would extend to maritime police forces. The pursuit must cease as soon as to the delinquent ship has entered the territorial sea of another state,[136] in recognition of the cardinal principle that states may not exercise enforcement jurisdiction in the territory of other states. However, states may agree to allow other states to conduct hot pursuit through their territorial waters.[137] Ships that have been stopped or arrested outside of the territorial sea, including on the high seas, in instances where the circumstances did not justify the exercise of the right of hot pursuit, shall be compensated for any loss or damage.[138] In 2001 and 2003 two very lengthy hot pursuits were undertaken by Australia from the Southern

---

[134] Ibid art 110(3). The ILC in commenting on this requirement observed that 'The State to which the warship belongs must compensate the merchant ships for any delay caused … This severe penalty seems justified in order to prevent the right of visit being abused': International Law Commission, 'Articles Concerning the Law of the Sea with Commentaries' (n 42) 281.

[135] O'Connell, *The International Law of the Sea*, vol 2 (n 35) 1076.

[136] LOSC, art 111(3).

[137] See, eg, 2003 Treaty between the Government of Australia and the Government of the French Republic on Cooperation in the Maritime Areas Adjacent to the French Southern and Antarctic Territories (TAAF), Heard Island and the McDonald Islands, art 3.

[138] LOSC, art 111(8).

Ocean into the south Atlantic and the Indian Oceans, and these were concluded only with the cooperative assistance of other states.[139]

E. Conservation and Management of High Seas Living Resources and Biodiversity

Given the existence of the 1958 Convention on Fishing and Conservation of the Living Resources of the High Seas, one of the challenges faced by the LOSC was to define the extent to which those marine living resource conservation and management mechanisms should be transferred into the high seas regime, or whether they were more appropriately addressed within the EEZ.[140] Ultimately, UNCLOS III chose to do neither, and whilst Part V of the LOSC contains extensive provisions dealing with the conservation and management of the marine living resources of that area they needed to be balanced against coastal state resource sovereignty and jurisdiction. What was left for the high seas were five articles in Section II of Part VII dealing with conservation and management of living resources which effectively qualify the Article 87 freedom to fish on the high seas. The effect of these provisions is that whilst the high seas freedom to fish has been retained, there is no longer a right to engage in unlimited high seas fishing without any consideration of the conservation and management impacts upon high seas fisheries. This is made clear by Articles 118 and 119 of the LOSC and also by additional instruments regulating high seas marine living resources that have been adopted since the mid 1990s of which the Fish Stocks Agreement is the most prominent. Other relevant initiatives which have application include the 1995 FAO Code of Conduct for Responsible Fisheries,[141] and the 2001 FAO International Plan of Action to Prevent, Deter and Eliminate Illegal, Unreported and Unregulated Fishing.[142]

i. Conservation and Sustainable Use of Marine Biodiversity Beyond National Jurisdiction

The most significant recent development in relation to marine living resources and other elements of marine biodiversity on the high seas is the ongoing initiative to develop a new implementing agreement under the LOSC.[143] At the 2012 United Nations Conference on Sustainable Development, leaders committed 'to address, on an urgent basis ... before the end of the sixty-ninth session of the General Assembly, the issue of the conservation and sustainable use of marine biological diversity beyond areas of national jurisdiction, including by taking a decision on the development of an international instrument under the [LOSC]'.[144] This commitment recognises that while the range and intensity of threats to the

---

[139] See Erik Jaap Molenaar, 'Multilateral Hot Pursuit and Illegal Fishing in the Southern Ocean: The Pursuits of the Viarsa I and South Tomi' (2004) 19 *International Journal of Marine and Coastal Law* 19.

[140] This topic is considered in more detail in ch 13.

[141] *Basic Documents* No 58.

[142] *Basic Documents* No 67.

[143] See Robin M Warner, 'Conserving Marine Biodiversity in Areas Beyond National Jurisdiction' in Donald R Rothwell, Alex G Oude Elferink, Karen N Scott and Tim Stephens (eds), *The Oxford Handbook of the Law of the Sea* (Oxford, Oxford University Press, 2015) 752.

[144] UN Doc A/CONF.216/L.1 (2012), [162].

marine environment and its biodiversity are increasing, there is currently no comprehensive global regime for conserving the marine ecosystems of the high seas. Instead, there is a patchwork of regional agreements (mostly on fisheries), and specific sectoral regimes addressing some threats to marine biodiversity (eg, controls on marine pollution).

The origins of this initiative lie in the work of the United Nations Open-ended Informal Consultative Process on Oceans and the Law of the Sea (UNICPOLOS), which has addressed a wide variety of oceans issues since 1999. In 2004, the United Nations General Assembly accepted and acted on a recommendation by UNICPOLOS that it establish an 'Ad-Hoc Open-ended Informal Working Group' to study issues related to the conservation and sustainable use of marine biological diversity beyond areas of national jurisdiction (BBNJ Working Group). The BBNJ Working Group has met regularly since that time, and consensus has emerged on the need for the high seas to be more effectively managed by reference to the precautionary principle, ecosystem based approaches and environmental impact assessment.[145] In 2015 the BBNJ Working Group recommended to the General Assembly that it '[d]ecide to develop an international legally-binding instrument under the [LOSC] on the conservation of areas beyond national jurisdiction' and that prior to holding an intergovernmental conference the General Assembly establish a preparatory committee to make substantive recommendations on the elements of a draft text of such an agreement.[146] In June 2015 the General Assembly adopted a resolution in which it decided 'to develop an international legally-binding instrument under the [LOSC] on the conservation and sustainable use of marine biological diversity of areas beyond national jurisdiction' and to this end to establish a preparatory committee to meet in 2016 and 2017 prior to the holding of an intergovernmental conference thereafter.[147]

F. Relationship with Other Maritime Zones

A pivotal aspect of the contemporary high seas regime as it had existed in customary international law and conventional law under the 1958 Convention on the High Seas, is the accommodation which needed to be made between the high seas and the EEZ. Unlike the situation which had existed after UNCLOS I and the adoption of the Geneva Conventions, there was a need to dovetail aspects of the new EEZ regime with traditional freedoms of the high seas and associated aspects of that regime such as piracy and hot pursuit. Unless these accommodations could be made, UNCLOS III would have failed and the LOSC most certainly would not have won global support. This was self-evident in the case of the freedom of navigation where there was never any credible suggestion that coastal state rights over an EEZ would give to those states the capacity to interfere with traditional navigational freedoms that prior to the recognition of the EEZ were being enjoyed over high seas areas. It was, therefore, essential that the high seas freedom of navigation apply from the edge of the EEZ, which was the outer limit of the territorial sea, subject only to the legitimate EEZ rights and interests of the coastal state over that area.

---

[145] Warner, 'Conserving Marine Biodiversity' (n 143) 765.
[146] Outcome of the Ad Hoc Open-ended Informal Working Group to study issues relating to the conservation and sustainable use of marine biological diversity beyond national jurisdiction, 20–23 January 2015 at www.un.org/depts/los/biodiversityworkinggroup/documents/ahwg-9_report.pdf.
[147] UNGA RES 69/269, UN Doc A/69/L/65 (2015).

The linkage between the high seas and the EEZ is made clear in Article 86, making reference to the 'freedoms enjoyed by all States' within that area in accordance with Article 58 of the LOSC. Article 58 in Part V of the LOSC in turn makes clear that the Article 87 high seas freedoms of navigation and overflight, laying of submarine cables and pipelines, and other 'internationally lawful uses of the sea' related to those freedoms are enjoyed by all states. Three of the six identified high seas freedoms found in Article 87 are therefore made clearly applicable within the EEZ. The other three high seas freedoms—fishing, construction of artificial islands and installations, and scientific research—because they are subject to distinctive EEZ and related limitations cannot be considered as 'freedoms'. Additionally, Articles 88 to 115 of the high seas regime also apply within the EEZ to the extent they are not incompatible with that part. Accordingly, all of the high seas provisions dealing with ships and their status, prohibitions, and enforcement also have application within the EEZ subject to any express reservations.[148] The exercise of these high seas freedoms and rights within the EEZ is only constrained by an obligation to have 'due regard' to the rights and interests of the coastal state within that area, including compliance with relevant laws and regulations of the coastal state which are not incompatible with Part V of the LOSC. Whilst in some instances the obligation upon foreign ships to comply with coastal state marine pollution provisions within the EEZ are clearly compatible with the coastal states interests in that zone,[149] whether the coastal state can seek to obtain information about navigational movements by foreign ships within the EEZ without infringing the high seas freedom of navigation is more problematic.[150]

V. Further Reading

David D Caron and Harry N Scheiber (eds), *Bringing New Law to Ocean Waters* (Leiden, Martinus Nijhoff, 2004)

K Gjerde and C Breide (eds), *Towards a Strategy for High Seas Marine Protected Areas* (Gland, Switzerland, IUCN, 2003)

Douglas Guilfoyle, 'The High Seas' in Donald R Rothwell, Alex G Oude Elferink, Karen N Scott and Tim Stephens (eds), *The Oxford Handbook of the Law of the Sea* (Oxford, Oxford University Press, 2015) 203

Myres S McDougal and William T Burke, *The Public Order of the Oceans* (New Haven, CT, New Haven Press, 1987)

Graham Gerard Ong (ed), *Piracy, Maritime Terrorism and Securing the Malacca Straits* (Singapore, Institute of Southeast Asian Studies, 2006)

Robin Warner, *Protecting the Oceans Beyond National Jurisdiction* (Leiden, Martinus Nijhoff, 2009)

---

[148] An example can be found in LOSC, art 111, which makes express reference to the EEZ in the right of hot pursuit.

[149] See further discussion in ch 15.

[150] See, eg, 'Strengthening Australia's Offshore Maritime Security' (February 2005), *Basic Documents* No 77; and discussion in Natalie Klein, 'Legal Implications of Australia's Maritime Identification System' (2006) 55 *International and Comparative Law Quarterly* 337–68.

8

Archipelagic States

I. Archipelagos and International Law

One of the challenges which the law of the sea has faced is dealing with islands. It is a feature of the world's oceans and seas that islands are scattered throughout them, in some areas in clusters and in other places as isolated geographical features. The marine life that is often associated with islands can also make them important biological marine regions, and this has had particular significance with respect to the development of fisheries in adjacent island waters which become sources of food for island populations. During the eighteenth and nineteenth centuries, when maritime claims were motivated by security concerns, little thought was given to whether differential entitlements to maritime zones should exist depending on the size of the land mass and its associated outer-lying features. For example, Great Britain was an island state and leading maritime power, which placed value on the development of maritime claims, but given its associated outlying islands was also concerned with its national security over those lands. Whilst Australia was clearly an island, it was also a continent, and given the size of its continental land mass no case for special circumstances could be made out with respect to its adjacent maritime domain. Japan, on the other hand, was an island state composed of a number of larger islands and smaller outer lying islands with a strong maritime culture, and its capacity to assert maritime claims was never questioned. Therefore, as the law of the sea developed throughout the twentieth century and as more states emerged into the international system, greater consideration was given to whether island states had distinctive needs for the purposes of both international law and the law of the sea.

By the mid twentieth century when the modern law of the sea was truly emerging, three particular issues regarding islands were beginning to have prominence. The first was the impact islands could have upon maritime boundary delimitation between opposite and adjacent states, especially if they were located adjacent to a maritime boundary, thereby justifying the adjustment of the boundary to take account of their presence. This ultimately became a matter for so-called 'special circumstances' and has factored in the jurisprudence of the ICJ.[1] The second issue surrounded coastal archipelagos created by offshore islands, or offshore archipelagos that fringe or hug the coastlines of a number of states. If these coastal islands were each entitled to a territorial sea in the same manner as the adjacent mainland, then it was possible to argue that they should be factored into the drawing of baselines.

---

[1] See the discussion in ch 16.

This issue was addressed by the ICJ in the *Anglo-Norwegian Fisheries* case,[2] and its recognition of the legitimacy of Norway's claim to draw baselines around the outer edge of the Norwegian *skjærgaard* paved the way for developments in the law concerning baselines, and ultimately gave coastal states significant options to extend their maritime claims and to secure their internal waters.[3] The third issue was the dynamic created by so-called mid-ocean archipelagos, that is those clusters of islands and associated waters which themselves comprise a state, and from which a series of maritime claims could be made.[4] Whilst the developing law of the sea never denied these multi-island states their entitlements, it was conceded that they did raise some distinctive legal issues, especially as a result of territorial sea claims between the various islands often overlapping and having implications not only for resource sovereignty within those waters, but also jurisdiction, and the freedom of navigational entitlements of foreign vessels in waters between the islands.

In the period immediately following the end of World War II the status of island states began to take on greater significance, as a result of decolonisation and the rapid emergence of new states especially in Southeast Asia, the Pacific, and the Caribbean. Indonesia and the Philippines had particular prominence in this regard. Gradually emerging from independence achieved from the Netherlands in 1945, Indonesia was a mid-ocean archipelago comprising 17,508 islands, of which only approximately 6,000 were inhabited, and with a total coastline of 54,716 km.[5] Some of the larger islands were at that time also shared with neighbouring countries, including Portugal (East Timor), Australia (Papua New Guinea) and Great Britain (east Malaysian states of Sabah and Sarawak). Notwithstanding some of these internal boundaries with other states, Indonesia was a state principally comprised of an archipelago. The Philippines was in a similar situation. Emerging from World War II as an independent state in 1946, the Philippines archipelago comprised 7,107 islands spread throughout the South China Sea, Philippines Sea, Sulu Sea and Celebes Sea, giving the new country a total coastline of 36,289 km. The claims of these two countries to recognition as archipelagic states had a profound influence on the development of the law of sea in the latter part of the twentieth century, fundamentally changing the way in which international law recognised mid-ocean archipelagos.

As is evident from the above discussion, archipelagos take varying forms. There are coastal archipelagos which are comprised of multiple islands which effectively form an outer edge of the coastline, such as the Norwegian *skjaergaard*. In other cases, a coastal archipelago may result in the effective extension of the coastline via a series of islands, cays and reefs, of which the Florida Keys are an example. More common is where a cluster of

---

[2] *Fisheries (United Kingdom v Norway)* [1951] ICJ Rep 116.

[3] Noway has approximately 50,000 islands which fringe its coastline, which themselves have a coastline of 58,133 km; this is to be contrasted with the main Norwegian coastline which is 2,650 km in length: 'Norway', *The World Factbook*, Central Intelligence Agency (CIA), Washington, at https://www.cia.gov/library/publications/the-world-factbook/.

[4] '*Outlying (mid-ocean) archipelagos* are groups of islands situated out in the ocean at such a distance from the coasts of firm land as to be considered as an independent whole rather than forming part of or outer coastline of the mainland': Jens Evensen, 'Certain Legal Aspects Concerning the Delimitation of the Territorial Waters of Archipelagos' in *United Nations Conference on the Law of the Sea: Official Records*, vol 1 (Geneva, United Nations, 1958) 289, 290.

[5] 'Indonesia', *The World Factbook* (n 3).

islands of varying sizes and shapes fringe a coastline.[6] In some instances, such as the islands which comprise the Canadian Arctic Archipelago, the land mass of these islands may be extensive and clearly represent an extension of the continental land mass. In other cases, the islands are much smaller and may be remnants of coastal headlands.

Mid-ocean archipelagos are distinctive in that they are separated from continental land masses. Most of the islands within the Caribbean Sea whilst proximate to the American continent, would fall into this category. Many comprise large islands with scattered outlying islands, of which Cuba is a prominent example. Japan is also an archipelago with one of its distinctive features being the size of the four main islands. The Pacific Ocean also features many archipelagos. The Hawaiian Islands are a classic example of a tightly clustered group of related islands, whilst in other instances the islands may be more scattered as is the case with Vanuatu, French Polynesia, the Marshall Islands and the Federated States of Micronesia.[7]

II. Early Codifications

Whilst the status of the territorial sea attracted the attention of the major international law bodies in the late nineteenth century, little consideration was given to the issue of either coastal or mid-ocean archipelagos. This was despite the fact that by this time law officers in both Great Britain and the United States had considered the status of offshore fringing islands in the context of maritime claims.[8]

The first serious review of the issue by the community of international legal experts took place in the 1920s, when the Institut de Droit international, International Law Association and the American Institute of International Law all separately considered the impact of islands upon territorial sea claims.[9] The American Institute suggested that in the case of an archipelago, the islands 'shall be considered as forming a unit' with the territorial sea measured from the 'islands farthest from the center of the archipelago'.[10] At the 1930 Hague Codification Conference there was support amongst the experts for the American Institute of International Law's views that archipelagos could be considered as a single unit, but this was met with a mixed response from certain governments and no concluded position was reached on this question.[11]

---

[6] *Maritime Delimitation and Territorial Questions between Qatar and Bahrain (Qatar v Bahrain)* (merits) [2001] ICJ Rep 40, [214] where the ICJ refers to a 'cluster of islands' or an 'island system' in the context of offshore fringing islands.

[7] Mohamed Munavvar, *Ocean States: Archipelagic Regimes in the Law of the Sea* (Dordrecht, Martinus Nijhoff, 1995) 14–23; HP Rajan, 'The Legal Regime of Archipelagos' (1986) 29 *German Yearbook of International Law* 137, 139.

[8] DP O'Connell, 'Mid-Ocean Archipelagos in International Law' (1971) 45 *British Yearbook of International Law* 1, 2–3.

[9] Evensen, 'Certain Legal Aspects' (n 4) 290–91.

[10] (1926) 20 *American Journal of International Law Special Supplement* 318, 319; being art 7 of a set of draft articles on the 'National Domain'; a similar view was promoted by Jessup: Philip C Jessup, *The Law of Territorial Waters and Maritime Jurisdiction* (New York, GA Jennings, 1927) 457.

[11] CF Amerasinghe, 'The Problem of Archipelagoes in the International Law of the Sea' (1974) 23 *International and Comparative Law Quarterly* 539, 541; Evensen, 'Certain Legal Aspects' (n 4) 292.

When the International Law Commission considered this issue the first report of the Special Rapporteur, Professor François, proposed that in the case of 'a group of islands (archipelagos) and islands situated along the coast' a limit of 10 miles would apply to baselines connecting those islands, with the effect that the 'waters included within the group shall constitute inland waters'.[12] By his third report, François had adopted a less ambitious, but at the time a nonetheless novel approach, towards islands making up an archipelago. He proposed that:

> The term 'groups of islands', in the juridical sense shall be determined to mean three or more islands enclosing a portion of the sea when joined by straight lines not exceeding five miles in length, except that one such line may extend to a maximum of ten miles.[13]

Ultimately the ILC as a whole did not endorse these proposals and its 1956 *Articles concerning the Law of the Sea with commentaries*[14] made no direct reference to archipelagos. All that remained of some elements of the François drafts was reference in Article 10 to islands having their own territorial sea and an acknowledgment in the accompanying commentary of the difficulties associated with reaching agreement on the issues raised by archipelagos.[15] The only draft article which had significance for the future recognition of archipelagic claims was Article 5 dealing with 'Straight Baselines' which the ILC's commentary acknowledged could be relied upon to draw baselines to 'islands situated in the immediate vicinity of the coast'.[16]

III. UNCLOS I

Despite the ILC's ultimate position with respect to archipelagos, it seemed inevitable that UNCLOS I would need to give some consideration to the issues arising in both the case of coastal and mid-ocean archipelagos. The *Anglo-Norwegian Fisheries* case had certainly set an important precedent in the case of coastal archipelagos, while the initial archipelagic claims by Indonesia and the Philippines clearly indicated to the major maritime powers that the status of archipelagos in international law was a rapidly emerging issue. Expectations as to the intentions of UNCLOS I with respect to archipelagos were further raised by the preparation of a paper in 1957 by the Norwegian lawyer, Jens Evensen, on 'Certain legal aspects concerning the delimitation of the Territorial Waters of Archipelagos' which was included in the Preparatory Documents for the conference.[17] Evensen's paper reviewed

---

[12] 'Regime of the Territorial Sea', Doc A/CN.4/53, reprinted in (1952) *Yearbook of the International Law Commission*, vol 2, 31; see also Evensen, 'Certain Legal Aspects', ibid 292.

[13] 'Regime of the Territorial Sea', Doc A/CN.4/77, reprinted in (1954) *Yearbook of the International Law Commission*, vol 2, 1; and see Evensen, 'Certain Legal Aspects' ibid 293.

[14] (1956) *Yearbook of the International Law Commission*, vol 2, 265.

[15] (1956) *Yearbook of the International Law Commission*, vol 2, 270 observing that: 'It recognizes the importance of this question and hopes that if an international conference subsequently studies the proposed rules it will give attention to it.'

[16] (1956) *Yearbook of the International Law Commission*, vol 2, 268; though in the case of Article 10 'Bays' the Commentary observed at 270 that 'article 5 may be applicable to groups of islands lying off the coast'.

[17] Evensen, 'Certain Legal Aspects' (n 4) 289.

relevant state practice with respect to coastal archipelagos,[18] and mid-ocean archipelagos,[19] and assessed the significance of the *Anglo-Norwegian Fisheries* case. Summing up this review of state practice and the developments in the law, Evensen asserted that 'no hard and fast rules exist as to the delimitation of the territorial waters of archipelagos',[20] but nonetheless made recommendations for future consideration at the conference. With respect to mid-ocean archipelagos, Evensen concluded they should be considered:

> as a whole for the delimitation of territorial waters by drawing straight baselines from the outer-most points of the archipelago—that is from the outermost points of the constituent islands, islets and rocks—and by drawing the seaward limit of the belt of marginal seas at a distance of X nautical miles outside and parallel to such baselines. Thus the archipelago viewed as a unit has a continu-ous area of territorial water. Whether or not an outlying archipelago should be treated in such a manner, will, to a large extent, depend on the geographical features of the archipelago.[21]

Evensen concluded his paper with some observations as to the relevant criteria that would be taken into account in drawing baselines enclosing a mid-ocean archipelago, noting that they should not depart from the general direction of the coast of the archipelago and should not be 'exorbitantly long' so as to enclose 'vast areas' of the sea from navigation and fishing. Observations were also made as to the need to ensure the water and surrounding land were 'closely linked'.[22]

Notwithstanding Evensen's paper, which may have appeared to have been an impetus for UNCLOS I to deal with archipelagos, the Conference avoided any sustained discussion of the issue. Ultimately, the 1958 Convention on the Territorial Sea and Contiguous Zone[23] contained no provisions of particular application to archipelagos, other than generic articles dealing with straight baselines,[24] and Article 10 which sought to define an island and con-firm the method for determining its territorial sea. The Philippines did make a bold pro-posal to confirm the status of archipelagos, including that the waters on the landward side of baselines would be considered internal waters;[25] however, the United States firmly indicated its opposition, noting that the consequence of this proposal being accepted would be that 'areas of the high seas formerly used by ships of all countries would be unilaterally claimed as territorial waters or possibly even internal waters'.[26] Attempts were made to revive the debate within the First Committee, with Denmark and Iceland urging further considera-tion of the issue in the context of Article 10 of the Convention; however, Sir Gerald Fitz-maurice (for the United Kingdom) put forward the view that given the complexity of the issues, especially with respect to 'oceanic archipelagos', it was preferable to have the matter

---

[18] Referring to the practices adopted with respect to Norway, Iceland, Denmark, Sweden, Finland, Yogoslavia [sic], Saudi Arabia, Egypt, Cuba, the United Kingdom, Australia, and USA: Evensen, 'Certain Legal Aspects' ibid 295–97.

[19] Referring to the practices adopted with respect to the Faeroes, Svalbard, Iceland, Bermudas, Galapagos, Philippines, Fiji, Cook Island and the Hawaiian Islands: Evensen, 'Certain Legal Aspects' ibid 297–99.

[20] Evensen, 'Certain Legal Aspects', ibid 301.

[21] Ibid 302; the reference to X nautical miles was intentional so as to remain neutral on that issue.

[22] Ibid.

[23] *Basic Documents* No 9.

[24] Convention on the Territorial Sea and Contiguous Zone, art 4.

[25] 'Philippines: Proposal', UN Doc A/CONF/13/C.1/L.98, reprinted in *United Nations Conference on the Law of the Sea: Official Records*, vol 3 (Geneva, United Nations, 1958) 239; see also the 'Yugoslavia: Proposal', 227.

[26] *United Nations Conference on the Law of the Sea: Official Records*, vol 3 (Geneva, United Nations, 1958) 25.

deferred for further study, and this ultimately was the position adopted at the Conference.[27] Notwithstanding that UNCLOS II followed soon after UNCLOS I, and that there was a further attempt by the Philippines to introduce substantive debate on the question of archipelagos, no detailed consideration was given to the matter at UNCLOS II.[28]

IV. The Indonesian and Philippines Claims

As the two leading advocates for international legal recognition of the special status of archipelagic states, it is instructive to review the legislative history of the archipelagic claims asserted by Indonesia and the Philippines. Both had considerable influence not only in the development of state practice, but also in how the law was eventually shaped through the negotiations of UNCLOS III and in the final outcomes of Part IV of the LOSC.

A. Indonesia

Indonesia has long advocated that its status as a geographical archipelago should be given international recognition in the law of the sea. In support of this claim Indonesian governments have consistently argued, both domestically and internationally since Indonesia gained independence in 1945, that the Indonesian islands and waters between them constituted a singular, unified nation.[29] This was reflected in the concept of *wawasan nusantara* which aims for the unification of the land, waters and the people of Indonesia.[30] This concept encapsulates the attitude adopted by Indonesians towards their country, one in which they regard:

> all of their islands, and the waters around them and interconnecting those islands as one entity. The term fatherland in Indonesian is *tanah air* which means 'land and water'. The nationhood of Indonesia is built on the concept of unity between the Indonesian islands and the inter-connecting waters. Those seas are regarded as a unifying, not a separating, element.[31]

Wawasan nusantara was first officially expressed by Indonesia in the 1957 Djuanda Declaration which affirmed the concept of the Indonesian archipelago as an entity, encompassing the islands and waters.[32] It stated that:

> all waters around, between and connecting, the islands or parts of islands belonging to the Indonesian archipelago irrespective of their width or dimension are natural appurtenances of its

---

[27] Ibid 162–63.

[28] O'Connell, 'Mid-Ocean Archipelagos in International Law' (n 8) 21–22.

[29] These assertions became more developed in the light of the International Court of Justice decisions in the *Fisheries (United Kingdom v Norway)* [1951] ICJ Rep 116; John G Butcher, 'Becoming an Archipelagic State: The Juanda Declaration of 1957 and the "Struggle" to Gain International Recognition of the Archipelagic Principle' in Robert Cribb and Michelle Ford (eds), *Indonesia beyond the Water's Edge* (Singapore, Institute of Southeast Asian Studies, 2009) 28, 34–35.

[30] *Wawasan* means outlook; *nusantara* refers to people.

[31] N Wisnomoerti, 'Indonesia and the Law of the Sea' in C-H Park and JK Park (eds), *The Law of the Sea: Problems from the East Asian Perspective* (Honolulu, Law of the Sea Institute, 1987) 392.

[32] Butcher, 'Becoming an Archipelagic State' (n 29) 38–40.

land territory and therefore an integral part of the inland or national waters subject to the absolute
sovereignty of Indonesia. The peaceful passage of foreign vessels through these waters is guaranteed
as long and insofar as it is not contrary to the sovereignty of the Indonesian state or harmful to her
security.

The delimitation of the territorial sea, with a width of 12 nautical miles, shall be measured from
straight base lines connecting the outermost points of the islands of the Republic of Indonesia.[33]

Despite diplomatic protests from Australia, France, Japan, the Netherlands, New Zealand,
the United Kingdom and the United States,[34] the Declaration was implemented internally
in 1960. Act No 4 of 18 February 1960 indicated that 'Indonesian waters consist of the territorial sea and the internal waters of Indonesia'[35] and that Indonesian internal waters were
those laying within the baselines. The baselines were to be 'straight lines connecting the
outermost points of the low water mark of the outermost islands or part of such islands
comprising Indonesian territory'.[36] Whilst this claim had little basis in the then law of the
sea following UNCLOS I, Article 1(3) of Government Regulation No 4 did permit innocent
passage by foreign vessels through these 'internal' waters, suggesting that Indonesia was
seeking to develop a form of internal waters/territorial sea hybrid within its archipelago.
However, in a clarification of the regulations also issued at the same time, Indonesia sought
to distinguish innocent passage through the territorial sea and innocent passage within
'interior waters' which noted that this latter form of innocent passage 'constitutes a certain
facility granted intentionally by Indonesia, while innocent passage in territorial waters constitutes a right of the foreign ships which is recognized by international law'.[37] Indonesia's
position with respect to internal waters encompassing those waters on the landward side of
the baselines drawn around the edge of the Indonesian archipelago was further reinforced
by a Reservation which accompanied its ratification of the 1958 Convention on the High
Seas,[38] which restated the Indonesian concept of internal waters.[39]

    As O'Connell observed, Indonesia's indication that innocent passage was 'a "facility"
rather than a right had an ominous implication, and seemed to indicate that Indonesia
would resist passage through the enclosed seas when it was deemed necessary for national
security to do so'.[40] Nevertheless, whilst innocent passage was subsequently regulated by
government ordinance in 1962 with the enactment of a Government Regulation concerning

[33] MM Whiteman, *Digest of International Law*, vol 4 (Washington, United States Department of State, 1965)
284; cf alternative translations of the Indonesian text: JJG Syatauw, *Some Newly Established Asian States and the
Development of International Law* (The Hague, Martinus Nijhoff, 1961) 173–74.
    [34] Whiteman, *Digest of International Law*, ibid vol 4, 284–85; DP O'Connell, *The International Law of the Sea*,
vol 1 (Oxford, Clarendon Press, 1982) 249.
    [35] Act No 4 (18 February 1960) (Indonesia), art 1(1); reprinted in Syatauw, *Some Newly Established Asian States*
(n 33) 176.
    [36] Ibid art 1(2). Indonesia has conceded that the Declaration was 'prepared in some haste' in order to achieve
recognition of archipelagic waters prior to UNCLOS II: *Sovereignty over Pulau Ligitan and Pulau Sipadan
(Indonesia/Malaysia)* [2002] ICJ Rep 625, [130].
    [37] Article-by-Article Clarification, annexed to Government Regulation No 4, 1960, in lieu of an Act concern-
ing Indonesian Waters; O'Connell, 'Mid-Ocean Archipelagos in International Law' (n 8) 40; Syatauw, *Some Newly
Established Asian States* (n 33) 180–82 uses the terms 'inland', 'interior' and 'national' waters interchangeably with
'internal waters'.
    [38] *Basic Documents* No 10.
    [39] O'Connell, 'Mid-Ocean Archipelagos in International Law' (n 8) 40.
    [40] Ibid 41.

'Innocent Passage by Foreign Water Vehicles within Indonesian Waters', Article 1 of that regulation affirmed that innocent passage of foreign vessels was guaranteed within Indonesian waters while the remainder of the regulation substantially implemented the innocent passage regime of the Convention on the Territorial Sea and Contiguous Zone.[41] A significant point of distinction from the innocent passage regime of the Convention was that in Article 4(1) of the 1962 Regulation Indonesia sought to retain a right to 'place a temporary ban on innocent passage in certain parts of Indonesia's waters'. However, it appears that Indonesia never sought at that time to rely upon this provision to actually close its waters to innocent passage.[42]

The Djuanda Declaration marked a historic step in Indonesia's national development and was pivotal in laying the foundation for its claim to be recognised as an archipelagic state. Legally it set an important precedent, and although the major maritime powers clearly indicated their objections between 1957 and 1962, there was a gradual acceptance of the Indonesian claim, even extending to informal notification of the passage of warships through Indonesian waters.[43] The Indonesian claim also needed to be seen in the context of Indonesian national politics at the time, when concerns over internal security were especially sensitive and when the West also had its own concerns over whether Indonesia would fall to the communists.[44] The West had an incentive to see the development of a strong Indonesia robust enough to resist communism and this was reflected in the recognition of not only Indonesian territorial claims but also maritime claims to the waters within the archipelago.

B. The Philippines

The position of the Philippines with respect to its recognition as an archipelagic state differs from Indonesia in two major respects. The first is geographical in that the Philippines is a more tightly congested group of islands than Indonesia, and accordingly is often referred to as an 'island studded sea' rather than a group of interconnected islands.[45] The second is historic, and is based on a series of treaties and related instruments drawn up by colonial powers in the late nineteenth and early twentieth centuries which the Philippines asserts make clear that recognition was granted to rights over the waters that connect the islands of the archipelago. These claims commence with the 1898 Treaty of Paris,[46] where Article III provided that 'Spain cedes to the United States the archipelago known as the Philippines Islands' and the islands which fall within certain coordinates. The subsequent 1900 Treaty between Spain and the United States for the Cession of Outlying Islands of the Philippines sought to clarify which islands were ceded by Spain to the United States; however, no direct reference is made to the waters that lay between the islands as also having been transferred.

---

[41] Donald R Rothwell, 'The Indonesian Straits Incident: Transit or Archipelagic Sea Lanes Passage?' (1990) 14 *Marine Policy* 491, 496–97.

[42] M Kusumaatmadja, 'The Concept of the Indonesian Archipelago' (1982) 10 *Indonesian Quarterly* 12, 15.

[43] Butcher, 'Becoming an Archipelagic State' (n 29) 43.

[44] Andrew TH Tan, *Security Perspectives of the Malay Archipelago* (Cheltenham, Edward Elgar, 2004) 201–203.

[45] Munavvar, *Ocean States* (n 7) 21.

[46] 1898 Treaty of Peace between Spain and the United States (Treaty of Paris).

A later 1930 colonial treaty between the United Kingdom and the United States is also relied upon by the Philippines to support its claims to the waters within defined coordinates,[47] however, the treaty clarified the southern extent of the Philippines and the northern extent of the British Malay territory of Borneo and it is doubtful whether there was an intention to confer sovereignty over the waters.[48]

The first international indication of the extent of the Philippines claim to the waters between the islands of the archipelago came in 1955 and this was reinforced in 1956 during communications with the United Nations in response to the ILC's draft articles on the law of the sea.[49] In commenting on the definition of the high seas, a *note verbale* lodged by the Philippines stated that:

> All waters around, between and connecting different islands belonging to the Philippine Archipelago, irrespective of their width or dimension, are necessary appurtenances of its land territory, forming an integral part of the national or inland waters, subject to the exclusive sovereignty of the Philippines.

The *note verbale* further provided that all of the 'natural deposits or occurrences of petroleum or natural gas in public and/or private lands' within the archipelago and 'seaward from the shores of the Philippines which are not within the territories of other countries' belong to the Philippines 'subject to the right of innocent passage of ships of friendly foreign States over those waters'.

While the Philippines made these assertions in the 1950s, it did not at that time enact laws seeking to give effect to such a claim. This did not occur until 1961, with the adoption of the Republic Act No 3046.[50] In seeking to define for the first time the baselines that comprised the outer limits of the Philippines claim, Republic Act No 3046 reaffirmed aspects of the 1955 and 1956 *notes verbales*, including the historical basis for the claim, and asserted that:

> Whereas, all the waters within the limits set forth in the above-mentioned treaties have always been regarded as part of the territory of the Philippine Islands;

> Whereas, all the waters around, between and connecting the various islands of the Philippine archipelago, irrespective of their width or dimension, have always been considered as necessary appurtenances of the land territory, forming part of the inland or internal waters of the Philippines.[51]

Whilst the Republic Act No 3046 proceeded to identify the baselines from which the Philippine claim was being asserted, of particular concern to maritime powers was the failure to state unambiguously the position regarding innocent passage through these waters, and as the Philippines denied recognition of a customary international law right of innocent passage by warships, this issue was of particular sensitivity. Australia, the United

---

[47]   1930 Convention regarding the Boundary between the Philippine Archipelago and the State of North Borneo.

[48]   O'Connell, 'Mid-Ocean Archipelagos in International Law' (n 8) 26–27; Munavvar, *Ocean States* (n 7) 62–63. These treaties and agreements are also reviewed by the International Court of Justice in *Sovereignty over Pulau Ligitan and Pulau Sipadan (Indonesia/Malaysia)* [2002] ICJ Rep 625.

[49]   'Note Verbale Dated 20 January 1956 from the Permanent Mission of the Philippines to the United Nations' (1956) *Yearbook of the International Law Commission*, vol 2, 69–70.

[50]   'An Act to Define the Baselines of the Territorial Sea of the Philippines', reprinted in S Houston Law, Robin Churchill and Myron Nordquist (eds), *New Directions in the Law of the Sea*, vol 1 (Dobbs Ferry, NY, Oceana Publications, 1973) 27.

[51]   Ibid.

Kingdom and the United States all raised their concerns over the new Philippines law; however, the United States was on firmer ground in insisting on the navigational rights of its warships due to pre-existing bilateral arrangements.[52] Uncertainty remained over this issue for much of the 1960s and a number of minor incidents occurred involving British and Australian naval vessels.[53] Further reinforcement of the Philippines position regarding its claim over the waters within the archipelago was made in the 1973 Philippines Constitution, in which Article 1 asserted that 'The waters around, between and connecting the islands of the archipelago, irrespective of their breadth and dimensions, form part of the internal waters of the Philippines.'[54]

Of the two major archipelagic states, the Philippines took a more robust position during the negotiations at UNCLOS I and II on the issue of archipelagos and the need for recognition in the law of the sea of archipelagic baselines. Whilst these initiatives ultimately failed, the Philippines did not retreat from its assertion of archipelagic status during the 1950s and 1960s. Commenting in 1971, O'Connell argued that the Philippines claim 'is mainly aimed at security, and to this extent it is directed in the first instance at the unauthorised passage of warships. The emotional background is such that it is politically difficult to retreat from the contention that the enclosed waters are, like any other internal waters...'.[55]

V. UNCLOS III

By the time of UNCLOS III, nearly 15 years had passed during which both Indonesia and the Philippines had firmly asserted a form of archipelagic claim. Though the broad extent of the claims had not been widely recognised,[56] they had provoked debate amongst the international community and interest from other states which believed they could make similar claims. With the United Nations General Assembly beginning to promote the idea of a Third Conference on the Law of the Sea, and the establishment of the Seabed Committee to consider issues associated with the development of a new regime for that area, Fiji and Mauritius joined Indonesia and the Philippines to form a small bloc of states supporting wider recognition of the interests of states comprising mid-ocean archipelagos. Within the Group of 77, these views generated considerable additional support, and accordingly there was a great deal of momentum behind UNCLOS III addressing the issue of archipelagos by the time the conference convened.[57]

Given that there had been so little progress on issues associated with archipelagos at either UNCLOS I or II, much remained to be accomplished if there was to be the development

---

[52] J Ashley Roach and Robert W Smith, *Excessive Maritime Claims*, 3rd edn (Leiden, Martinus Nijhoff, 2012) 211–13.

[53] O'Connell, 'Mid-Ocean Archipelagos in International Law' (n 8) 33–36.

[54] Munavvar, *Ocean States* (n 7) 64.

[55] O'Connell, 'Mid-Ocean Archipelagos in International Law' (n 8) 37.

[56] ED Brown, 'Maritime Zones: A Survey of Claims' in Robin Churchill, KR Simmonds and Jane Welch (eds), *New Directions on the Law of the Sea*, vol 3 (London, British Institute of International and Comparative Law, 1973) 157, 160. 'There is increasing evidence of sympathy for the arguments skilfully deployed by Indonesian and Philippino spokesmen.'

[57] RP Anand, *Origin and Development of the Law of the Sea* (The Hague, Martinus Nijhoff, 1983) 202–203.

of any new provisions at UNCLOS III. Fortunately, however, there remained the legacy of the *Anglo-Norwegian Fisheries* case with respect to baselines, the very preliminary work of the ILC and other expert groups considering the status of archipelagos, and the state practice founded on the actions of Indonesia and the Philippines. Whilst this provided a foundation for development of a regime dealing with archipelagos at UNCLOS III, two of the principal issues were whether any distinctive status should be accorded to states comprising one or more archipelagos, which in turn raised important definitional issues with respect to which states may enjoy those entitlements, and the pivotal question of navigation rights through any waters, previously high seas, that may become enclosed through the drawing of baselines connecting up the islands of the archipelago and enclosing them within the territorial waters of the state. However, these issues could not be seen in isolation and were closely connected to other pivotal issues requiring resolution during UNCLOS III, including the breadth of the territorial sea and the navigational regime through international straits.

With a decision having been made to include the topic of 'Archipelagos' on the agenda of UNCLOS III, during sessions of the Seabed Committee in 1973, Fiji, Indonesia, Mauritius and the Philippines sought to advance debate by introducing proposals which outlined the principles for an archipelagic regime, including for a limited right of innocent passage through sea lanes within an archipelago.[58] These formed the basis for formal proposals eventually put to UNCLOS III in 1974.[59] An initial threshold issue which arose related to the eligibility of an archipelago to make certain claims. This was highlighted not only because of the great geographical variety among archipelagos, but also because of concerns that the definition could be expanded to cover a multitude of cases. The fact that the Bahamas, Papua New Guinea and Tonga also expressed their interest in having their claims recognised, and that the Bahamas put forward separate proposals for the recognition of its particular status as an archipelago, fuelled fears that the debate regarding archipelagos could become unwieldy and divisive. Nevertheless, the major maritime powers were prepared to recognise these archipelagic claims, in return for unimpeded navigational rights, and accordingly much of the debate at UNCLOS III was focussed on seeking to accommodate these positions.[60]

The pivotal UNCLOS III definitional issue was whether the new convention should only apply to mid-ocean archipelagos, or continental archipelagos, or both. Whilst the debate and development of state practice had predominantly been driven by the interests of mid-ocean archipelagos such as Indonesia and the Philippines, at UNCLOS III a group of states with continental archipelagos put forward proposals for draft articles in which they sought the extension of some of the principles under consideration to groups of outer lying islands offshore continental land masses.[61] An important breakthrough in the negotiations occurred in 1975 when the Bahamas introduced a document titled '18 Principles

---

[58] Ibid 203.

[59] 'Fiji, Indonesia, Mauritius, and Philippines: Draft Articles relating to Archipelagic States', Doc A/CONF.62/C.2/L.49, *Third United Nations Conference on the Law of the Sea, Official Records*, vol 3 (New York, United Nations, 1975) 226.

[60] Described as 'The Archipelago Package': Charlotte Ku, 'The Archipelagic States Concept and Regional Stability in Southeast Asia' (1991) 23 *Case Western Reserve Journal of International Law* 463, 471–74.

[61] This group included states such as Canada, Chile, Iceland, India, Mexico, New Zealand and Norway: *Virginia Commentaries*, vol 2, 402.

for Inclusion in Archipelagic Articles'[62] which had the effect of crystallising the debate with respect to those states possibly entitled to archipelagic status, and sought to give clarity to the issues associated with the drawing of baselines. By 1976, it was clear that agreement had been reached within UNCLOS III that the archipelagic regime would focus on mid-ocean archipelagos, and not those archipelagos associated with a continental state. However, this did not prevent those states still seeking to rely upon the baseline provisions of the convention from proclaiming extensive internal waters.[63] By the time of the final UNCLOS III session in 1982, a number of states during concluding debates sought to declare their status as archipelagic states, including the Bahamas, Cape Verde, Fiji, Indonesia, Netherlands Antilles, Papua New Guinea, the Philippines and the Solomon Islands.[64]

VI. The LOSC and Archipelagic States

Reflective of the eventual significance that came to be associated with the question of archipelagos during UNCLOS III, the LOSC devoted Part IV of the Convention to Archipelagic states. Part IV contains key definitional provisions concerning the classification of archipelagic states for the purposes of the Convention, the drawing of archipelagic baselines, and the rights and entitlements of archipelagic states. There are also detailed provisions dealing with the navigational regime which applies within archipelagos.[65] A co-related provision, which is of significance in the reading of Part IV, is Article 121 dealing with the regime of islands. Not only does that article identify the extent of the maritime claims that may be generated from islands, but it clarifies that for the purposes of the law of the sea an island is 'a naturally formed area of land, surrounded by water, which is above water at high tide'.[66] In *Territorial and Maritime Dispute*[67] the ICJ found that 'the legal régime of islands set out in … Article 121 forms an indivisible régime, all of which … has the status of customary international law'.

A. Archipelagic States

The fact that Part IV of the LOSC is headed 'Archipelagic States' is both symbolic and of great significance for the law of the sea and international law generally. Throughout contemporary international law the international system has increasingly accorded to states ever greater privileges and entitlements, and during the post 1945 United Nations era this has been heightened by the 'state centric' system which has been perpetuated under the UN Charter. The criteria for statehood are set down in international law,[68] and recognition as

---

[62] Ibid 405.
[63] Anand, *Origin and Development of the Law of the Sea* (n 57) 214.
[64] Office for Ocean Affairs and the Law of the Sea, United Nations, *The Law of the Sea: Archipelagic States* (New York, United Nations, 1990) 108–13.
[65] See ch 11 for detailed discussion of archipelagic navigation.
[66] LOSC, art 121(1).
[67] *Territorial and Maritime Dispute (Nicaragua v Colombia)* [2012] ICJ Rep 624, [139].
[68] 1933 Montevideo Convention on the Rights and Duties of States, art 1.

a state guarantees participation in the international system. One of these privileges is the capacity of 'coastal states' to proclaim a range of maritime zones,[69] whilst 'all states' enjoy the right of innocent passage.[70] States such as those which are landlocked or geographically disadvantaged also enjoy certain *sui generis* rights under the LOSC,[71] but they do not have as comprehensive a regime given over to them under the Convention.[72] Yet this is what is found in Part IV in the case of 'Archipelagic States' and to a degree is the culmination of the political campaigns of certain archipelagic states—especially Indonesia and the Philippines—for the recognition of their special status.[73]

To understand the definition in the LOSC of an 'Archipelagic State', it is first important to comprehend the juridical definition accorded to the term archipelago.[74] This definition, while focussing on the geographical features of an island group, also incorporates additional dimensions. Article 46(b) provides that an archipelago:

> means a group of islands, including parts of islands, interconnecting waters and other natural features which are so closely interrelated that such islands, waters and other natural features form an intrinsic geographical, economic and political entity, or which have historically been regarded as such.

This definition clearly reflects some of the essential elements that emerged in the campaign during the 1950s and 1960s for recognition of archipelagic status, with its focus not only upon the land but also the waters of the archipelago, and the notion that the two are 'closely interrelated'. Recognition is also given to other natural features that may make up the archipelago, such as cays, islets, reefs and sand banks. The stipulation that the archipelago must in total comprise an 'intrinsic ... entity' based on geographical, economic or political characteristics suggests the need for a high level of interaction between the islands of the archipelago, which may have existed historically even in the absence of these other factors and is a recognition that many states claiming archipelagic status have only emerged since 1945.[75] Importantly, the definition recognises that not all parts of an island must be a part of the archipelago. This blends a political dimension with a geographical one, and accommodates islands such as Borneo which is shared between Indonesia, Malaysia and Brunei, and the island of New Guinea which is shared between the two archipelagic states of Indonesia and Papua New Guinea.

An 'archipelagic state' is in turn defined as one that is 'constituted wholly by one or more archipelagos and may include other islands'.[76] This definition immediately excludes those groups of states that have offshore continental archipelagos, such as Canada with its adjacent northern islands in the Arctic,[77] and the United States with the Hawaiian Islands group.[78]

---

[69] LOSC, arts 2, 33, 55, 76.

[70] Ibid art 17; discussed in more detail in ch 10.

[71] Ibid arts 69, 70.

[72] See the discussion in ch 9.

[73] Ku, 'The Archipelagic States Concept' (n 60) 477.

[74] LL Herman, 'The Modern Concept of the Off-Lying Archipelago in International Law' (1985) 23 *Canadian Yearbook of International Law* 172, 179–85.

[75] Both Indonesia and the Philippines have consistently placed emphasis on their historic archipelagic claims.

[76] LOSC, art 46(a).

[77] Though Canada has sought to proclaim straight baselines around these islands: J Bruce McKinnon, 'Arctic Baselines: A Litore Usque ad Litus' (1987) 66 *Canadian Bar Review* 790.

[78] Nancy Barron, 'Archipelagos and Archipelagic States under UNCLOS III: No Special Treatment for Hawaii' (1981) 4 *Hastings International and Comparative Law Review* 509.

Likewise, France is unable to claim archipelagic status notwithstanding that several of its overseas territories would otherwise be considered to be archipelagos.[79] Importantly, an archipelagic state may be comprised of one or more archipelagos, and states may still be able to claim archipelagic status based on several archipelagos, or a central archipelago and a number of distant outlying islands.[80] As the situation of Indonesia and Papua New Guinea highlights, it is also possible for two archipelagic states to share a common island which is the case with New Guinea, and rely upon that part of the island over which they exercise sovereignty for the purpose of drawing baselines consistent with the LOSC. To that end, and setting aside the question of continental archipelagos, it is clear that the LOSC definition seeks to provide flexibility as to the groups of island states that may be entitled to claim archipelagic status.

B. Archipelagic Baselines

Article 46 provides the basis for recognition as an archipelagic state; however, the capacity to enjoy all of the rights and privileges of an archipelagic state ultimately rests with the ability of the state to proclaim archipelagic baselines consistent with the provisions of Article 47.[81] The ICJ in *Qatar v Bahrain* made it clear that Part IV straight archipelagic baselines can only be relied upon by a state which has declared itself to be an archipelagic state.[82] In response to Bahrain's assertion that it was a de facto archipelagic state, Judge ad hoc Torres Bernárdez observed that there is 'no such thing in conventional or general international law as a "secret archipelagic State" appearing in or disappearing from general international judicial proceedings or international relations in general'.[83] Therefore, even if a state meets all the generic criteria of Article 46, if the state is unable to comply with the specific requirements of the archipelagic baseline regime, its ability to proclaim itself as an archipelagic state will be compromised. This would not, however, impact upon the ability of that state to draw straight baselines consistent with Article 7.

The archipelagic baselines provisions in Article 47 are founded upon the general straight baselines provisions in the LOSC that have developed over time in the law of the sea, including the practice that developed following the *Anglo-Norwegian Fisheries* case and the 1958 Convention on the Territorial Sea and Contiguous Zone. They also reflect some of the specific state practice found in the Indonesian and Philippines baseline claims. While there is no direct link between Articles 7 and 47, they share common principles with respect to the drawing of straight baselines.

---

[79] For example, French Polynesia and New Caledonia.

[80] Office for Ocean Affairs and the Law of the Sea, United Nations, *The Law of the Sea: Baselines*, 37.

[81] This is reflected in the wording of LOSC, art 47(1) which notes that the 'archipelagic State may draw straight archipelagic baselines'.

[82] *Maritime Delimitation and Territorial Questions between Qatar and Bahrain (Qatar v Bahrain)* (merits) [2001] ICJ Rep 40, [214]; suggesting at [213] strict application of the baseline criteria; in this instance Bahrain had not declared itself an archipelagic state and was therefore unable to avail itself of the provisions of Part IV.

[83] Ibid Dissenting Opinion of Judge ad hoc Torres Bernárdez, 280 [56].

The core elements of the archipelagic baseline provisions in Article 47 must satisfy five criteria.[84] The baselines are to:

1. connect the outermost points of the outermost islands and drying reefs of the archipelago[85] and include the main islands;[86]
2. result in a ratio of the area of water to land of between 1 to 1 and 9 to 1;[87]
3. with one exception be no longer than 100 nm in length;[88]
4. with only 3 per cent of the total number of baselines being 101 to 125 nm in length;[89] and
5. not depart to any appreciable extent from the general configuration of the archipelago.[90]

These requirements, whilst technical in nature,[91] sit comfortably alongside the definitions of an archipelagic state and archipelago found in Article 46 and provide objective criteria that conform with the geography of the major archipelagic states engaged in the UNCLOS III negotiations.[92] They make clear that the archipelagic baselines are to enclose the main islands and extend to the outermost points of the archipelago, thereby thwarting any attempts to enclose small separate clusters of islands that may be distant from a larger island or groups of large islands.[93] In addition, the water to land ratio requirement ensures that the archipelagic state is one in which there is a focus upon the ocean spaces which connect the islands, rather than a state which is dominated by very large islands. The effect of this provision is to exclude states such as Australia and New Zealand, which, though states comprised of islands, would not meet the minimum 1 to 1 area of water to area of land ratio given the size of the land mass compared to waters that may be enclosed within legitimate baselines. Likewise, island states which comprise one large island, such as Cuba, Iceland, Ireland and Madagascar, are excluded.[94]

[84] JRV Prescott, 'Straight and Archipelagic Baselines' in Gerald Blake (ed), *Maritime Boundaries and Ocean Resources* (London, Croom Helm, 1987) 38, 46 observed that: 'Three of the five tests are incapable of consistent objective interpretation.'

[85] Cf LOSC, art 6 where the term 'fringing reefs' is used; *Virginia Commentaries*, vol 2, 430.

[86] Office for Ocean Affairs and the Law of the Sea, United Nations, *The Law of the Sea: Baselines* (New York, United Nations, 1989) 35, [82] comments: 'The expression "main islands" could be interpreted in a variety of ways. For different countries the main islands might mean the largest islands, the most populous islands, the most economically productive islands, or the islands which are pre-eminent in an historical or cultural sense.'

[87] LOSC, art 47(7) clarifies what 'land' can be included for the purpose of computing the water to land ratio, and is drawn from the '18 Principles for Inclusion in Archipelagic Waters' paper introduced by the Bahamas during UNCLOS III; *Virginia Commentaries*, vol 2, 405, 432.

[88] LOSC, art 47(2).

[89] Ibid art 47(2).

[90] Ibid art 47(3).

[91] Herman, 'The Modern Concept' (n 74) 185–87.

[92] *Virginia Commentaries*, vol 2, 429.

[93] Kiribati expressed its concern about this provision in its LOSC Declaration where it stated: 'Part IV calculations for archipelagic waters do not allow a baseline to be drawn around all the islands of each of the three Groups of islands that make up the Republic of Kiribati. These Group of islands are spread over an expanse of over three million square kilometres of ocean, and the existing formula…will divide Kiribati's three island groups into three distinct exclusive zone waters and international waters': 'Declarations and Statements' at www.un.org/Depts/los/convention_agreements/convention_declarations.htm.

[94] Prescott, 'Straight and Archipelagic Baselines' (n 84) 47, listed 15 archipelagic states prevented from drawing archipelagic baselines because they could not enclose an area of water equal to the area of land: Australia, Cuba, Haiti, Iceland, Ireland, Japan, Madagascar, Malta, New Zealand, Singapore, Sri Lanka, Taiwan, Trinidad and Tobago, and the United Kingdom and Western Samoa; though this does not bar those states from drawing straight baselines consistent with LOSC, art 7: Robin R Churchill, 'The Impact of State Practice on the Jurisdictional

In recognition of the geographical size of some archipelagos, and the distance that may exist between some of the islands, Article 47(2) provides archipelagic baselines shall not exceed 100 nm,[95] except that up to 3 per cent of the total number of baselines which enclose the archipelago may extend up to a maximum length of 125 nm. Whilst these provisions appear strict, there is nothing to prevent a state claiming archipelagic status from segmenting baselines so that by the drawing of multiple archipelagic baselines there be less then 3 per cent between 101 and 125 nm.[96] The baselines are also not to depart to 'any appreciable extent' from the general configuration of the archipelago.[97] These provisions are supplemented by limitations on the drawing of baselines to certain low-tide elevations,[98] and the cutting off of high seas or EEZ access from the territorial sea of another state.[99] Archipelagic baselines are to be shown on charts and due publicity is to be given to them, including the deposit of charts and relevant geographical coordinates with the United Nations.[100]

Baselines once declared are not fixed and may be subject to subsequent adjustment. Indonesia was faced with the need to adjust its archipelagic baselines following the independence of East Timor/Timor-Leste in 2002, which had the effect of limiting Indonesia's ability to continue previously drawn archipelagic baselines which extended to and from that territory, and also following the 2002 decision of the ICJ in the *Sovereignty over Pulau Ligitan and Pulau Sipadan* case between Indonesia and Malaysia which clarified sovereignty over certain disputed islands.[101]

C. The Legal Status of Archipelagic Waters

Once archipelagic baselines have been drawn, an archipelagic state enjoys two distinctive rights. The first, consistent with its ongoing status as a coastal state albeit one which is recognised as an archipelagic state for the purposes of the LOSC, is the entitlement to use the archipelagic baselines for delimiting adjacent maritime zones. This is a significant entitlement, and gives to some archipelagic states which have drawn long archipelagic baselines, an ability to assert claims to a territorial sea, contiguous zone, EEZ and continental shelf over areas of the ocean that previously would have been considered high seas.[102]

Framework contained in the LOS Convention' in Alex G Oude Elferink (ed), *Stability and Change in the Law of the Sea: The Role of the LOS Convention* (Leiden, Martinus Nijhoff, 2005) 91, 121.

[95] There does not appear to have been any firm grounding in prior state practice for the identification of 100 nm as the length of archipelagic baselines: Munavvar, *Ocean States* (n 7) 131–32.

[96] Office for Ocean Affairs and the Law of the Sea, United Nations, *The Law of the Sea: Baselines*, 35 noting that: 'Since there is no restriction on the number of segments a country can draw, and since the more segments used the closer the system is likely to be to the general configuration of the archipelago, it will usually be possible to adjust the number of segments to secure the necessary number of very long baselines.'

[97] LOSC, art 47(3).

[98] Ibid art 47(4).

[99] Ibid art 47(5).

[100] Ibid arts 47(8), (9).

[101] *Sovereignty over Pulau Ligitan and Pulau Sipadan (Indonesia/Malaysia)* [2002] ICJ Rep 625.

[102] Whilst an island generates all of the maritime claims that a continental landmass does, with the exception of those islands which 'cannot sustain human habitation or economic life of their own' which are not entitled to an EEZ or continental shelf (LOSC, art 121), the effect of drawing archipelagic baselines of up to 125 nm between certain islands is that as maritime claims are generated from those baselines larger areas of ocean are potentially subject to claim.

The second distinctive right, which is *sui generis* to the LOSC, is that waters that fall within archipelagic baselines are considered to be 'archipelagic waters' over which the archipelagic state is able to exercise its sovereignty extending not only to the waters but also to the air space above and the seabed below.[103] This sovereignty is exercised irrespective of the depth of the waters or their distance from the coast, making it clear that archipelagic waters are very different in conception from the other maritime spaces regulated in the LOSC. Sovereignty over archipelagic waters is exercised subject to Part IV of the LOSC, which includes making allowance for the right of foreign ships not only to exercise a right of innocent passage generally within those waters, but also to exercise a right of archipelagic sea lanes passage within archipelagic sea lanes or routes normally used for international navigation where no sea lanes have been designated, though this right is not one which in other respects affects the status of archipelagic waters.[104] However, the capacity of the archipelagic state to enforce its laws and regulations against vessels engaged in those different navigational rights, and the related prescriptive and enforcement jurisdiction of the archipelagic state, does raise some issues with respect to the adoption of jurisdictional regimes designed to apply within the territorial sea.[105] Consistent with its sovereignty over the air space, the archipelagic state also exercises complete sovereignty with respect to overflight of both the archipelagic land mass and archipelagic waters. Archipelagic sea lanes passage, however, does permit a right of overflight along sea lanes by aircraft.[106]

In addition, the LOSC expressly recognises that an archipelagic state may draw closing lines for the purpose of delimiting internal waters within archipelagic waters,[107] and this may be considered desirable especially for the purposes of regulating access to and from port and harbour facilities that exist within the archipelago.[108] That internal waters may exist within archipelagic waters raises for direct consideration the distinction that exists between these bodies of water. It is clear from the early Indonesian and Philippine claims that the waters within baselines were equated by both states with their internal waters, even though rights of innocent passage were recognised. When it came to the negotiation of the LOSC, and the recognition in Part IV of 'archipelagic waters' it was therefore important to make clear the extent of not only archipelagic state sovereignty and jurisdiction over archipelagic waters, but to also distinguish the new regime from previous practice.

Therefore, whilst the sovereignty of a state over internal waters and archipelagic waters is closely aligned, there are some important distinctions. The most significant is the prima facie right of navigation that exists through archipelagic waters, extending to innocent

---

[103] LOSC, art 49(1)(2).

[104] LOSC, art 49(4), 52; see discussion in ch 11 on navigational rights within archipelagic waters.

[105] Erik Jaap Molenaar, *Coastal State Jurisdiction over Vessel-Source Pollution* (The Hague, Kluwer Law International, 1998) 342–45; a clear example would be differential interests in the case of vessels carrying hazardous cargoes principally because of the much longer period of time that it could be anticipated such vessels would be within archipelagic waters, compared to vessels within the territorial sea, either for the purposes of a port visit or whilst undertaking some form of transit through the archipelago.

[106] LOSC, art 53.

[107] LOSC, art 50 which makes clear that the baselines may be drawn in accordance with LOSC, arts 9–11, thereby excluding LOSC, art 7 straight baselines; cf LOSC, art 8(1) which makes clear that the general provisions regarding internal waters being on the landward side of the baseline do not apply in the context of Part IV.

[108] Given the size and scale of the Indonesian and Philippine archipelagic claims, and some of the industrial and other port developments that are taking place within their archipelagic waters, this provision has particular application.

passage and archipelagic sea lanes passage. There is no equivalent right of navigation through internal waters. Not only does the recognition of these navigational rights permit the passage of foreign vessels through archipelagic waters, it also places certain limitations on the laws and regulations which can be applied to foreign ships within archipelagic waters. This is to be contrasted with the plenary powers that a coastal state has over its internal waters. The other distinction between the two regimes is that the archipelagic state is also bound to recognise 'existing rights and all other legitimate interests' adjacent neighbouring states may have 'traditionally exercised' in what are now archipelagic waters,[109] including pre-existing fishing agreements and 'traditional fishing rights',[110] and previously laid submarine cables which pass through what have become archipelagic waters.[111] These provisions collectively seek to address issues that arise when archipelagic waters of one state are located between two parts of a neighbouring country, which could have occurred in the case of Indonesian archipelagic waters potentially blocking access to East Malaysia from the Malaysian mainland.[112]

D. Archipelagic State Practice

By the time of the conclusion of the LOSC, as well as Indonesia and the Philippines, a number of additional states had taken steps towards achieving archipelagic status, either by way of enacting new laws providing a framework for archipelagic claims including the recognition of archipelagic waters, or by actually having declared baselines and proclaimed archipelagic waters.[113] These states included Cape Verde,[114] Fiji,[115] Papua New Guinea,[116] Sao Tome and Principe,[117] and Vanuatu.[118] Soon after the conclusion of the LOSC, Prescott observed that '[t]he requirement for the islands and the waters to be closely interrelated is a matter for subjective judgement and there are 35 archipelagic states which could be considered to meet the definition of Article 46', of which only 17 had the capacity to proclaim legitimate archipelagic baselines.[119]

---

[109] LOSC, art 47(6). This provision sought to reflect concerns Malaysia had raised over Indonesia's archipelagic claim: *Virginia Commentaries*, vol 2, 431.

[110] LOSC, art 51(1); this later term is not defined: Rajan, 'The Legal Regime of Archipelagos' (n 7) 149–50.

[111] LOSC, art 51(2) extends the rights with respect to submarine cables to their maintenance and replacement subject to notification.

[112] Office for Ocean Affairs and the Law of the Sea, United Nations, *The Law of the Sea: Baselines*, 36.

[113] For a review of that practice see Barbara Kwiatkowska, 'The Archipelagic Regime in Practice—Making or Breaking International Law?' (1991) 6 *International Journal of Estuarine and Coastal Law* 1.

[114] Decree Law No 126/77 (31 December 1977) (Cape Verde), reprinted in Myron Nordquist, S Houston Lay and Kenneth R Simmonds (eds), *New Directions in the Law of the Sea*, vol 7 (London, Oceana Publications, 1980) 363 declaring 'straight baselines' (art 2) and archipelagic waters (art 3).

[115] Marine Spaces Act 1977 (20 October 1977) (Fiji), reprinted in *New Directions in the Law of the Sea* vol 7, 391 declaring archipelagic waters to be subsequently proclaimed by further declaration of baselines (s 4).

[116] National Seas Act 1977 (7 February 1977) (Papua New Guinea), reprinted in *New Directions in the Law of the Sea*, vol 7, 485 describing archipelagic waters (s 7), and an 'Interim Delimitation of Archipelagic Waters' (s 9).

[117] Decree-Law No 14/78 (16 June 1978) (Sao Tome and Principe), reprinted in *New Directions in the Law of the Sea*, vol 7, 5 declaring 'straight lines' (art 2) and archipelagic waters (art 3).

[118] Maritime Zones Act No 23 of 1981 (6 October 1982) (Vanuatu), reprinted in *The Law of the Sea: Current Developments and State Practice* (United Nations, New York, 1987) 124 declaring archipelagic waters (s 4) and archipelagic baselines (sch).

[119] Prescott, 'Straight and Archipelagic Baselines' (n 84) 46–47; cf Kwiatkowska, 'The Archipelagic Regime in Practice' (n 113) 3 referring to the potential claim of 24 archipelagic states.

i. *Proclaimed Archipelagic States*

Since the conclusion of the LOSC and its entry into force, a total of 22 states have sought to proclaim themselves as archipelagic states (see Table 8.1, below). However, two of these states, Kiribati and the Marshall Islands, have not drawn archipelagic baselines as at 2015.

Table 8.1: Archipelagic States[120]

No	State	Legislation/Proclamation	Date
1	Antigua and Barbuda	Maritime Areas Act 1982 (CAP 260)	1 September 1982
2	The Bahamas	The Archipelagic Waters and Maritime Jurisdiction 1993; modified by The Archipelagic Waters and Maritime Jurisdiction (Archipelagic Baselines) Order 2008	4 January 1996; 8 December 2008
3	Cape Verde	Decree Law No 60/IV 92	21 December 1982
4	Comoros	Law No 82-005; Presidential Decree No 10-092	6 May 1982; 13 August 2010
5	Dominican Republic	Act 66-07	22 May 2007
6	Fiji	Marine Spaces (Archipelagic Baselines and EEZ) Order, Legal Notice No 117 of 1981	1 December 1981
7	Grenada	Grenada Territorial Sea and Maritime Boundaries Act 1989; Statutory Rules and Orders No 31 of 1992	25 April 1989; 16 November 1992
8	Indonesia	List of geographical coordinates of points of archipelagic baselines, Government Regulation No 38 of 2002 (as amended by Government Regulation No 37 of 2008)	19 May 2008
9	Jamaica	The Maritime Areas Act, 1996; baselines promulgated by the Exclusive Economic Zone (Baselines) Regulation, 1992	12 October 1992
10	Kiribati	Maritime Zones (Declaration) Act 1983 (straight archipelagic baselines not drawn)	16 May 1983
11	Maldives	Maritime Zones Act No 6/96	27 June 1996
12	Marshall Islands	Maritime Zones Declaration Act 1984 (straight archipelagic baselines not drawn)	13 September 1984
13	Mauritius	Maritime Zones Act 2005; Maritime Zones (Baselines and Delineating Lines) Regulations 2005	5 August 2005
14	Papua New Guinea	Offshore Seas Declaration 1978 (declaration of the baselines by method of coordinates of base points for purposes of the location of archipelagic baselines)	25 July 2002

(continued)

---

[120]   Based on data from Roach and Smith, *Excessive Maritime Claims* (n 52) 206–08 as updated.

Table 8.1: (*Continued*)

No	State	Legislation/Proclamation	Date
15	Philippines	Republic Act No 9522, 2009	10 March 2009
16	Saint Vincent and the Grenadines	Maritime Areas Act 1983 (straight archipelagic baselines not drawn)	19 May 1993
17	Sao Tome and Principe	Law No 1/98	31 March 1998
18	Seychelles	Maritime Zones Act 1999; Maritime Zones (Baselines) Order, 2008	6 November 2008
19	Solomon Islands	Legal Notice No 41 of 1979: Declaration of Archipelagic Baselines (The Delimitation of Marine Waters Act (No 32 of 1978))	31 August 1979
20	Trinidad and Tobago	Archipelagic Waters and Exclusive Economic Zone Act	11 November 1986
21	Tuvalu	Tuvalu Maritime Areas Act 2012; Declaration of Archipelagic Baselines 2012	4 May 2012; 22 November 2012
22	Vanuatu	Maritime Zones Act No 6 of 2010; Maritime Zones Act [CAP 138] Amendments of the Schedule, Order No 81 of 2009	18 June 2010; 29 July 2009

Given the significance associated with their claims, and the size of their archipelagos, the declaration and adjustment of archipelagic baselines by Indonesia and the Philippines is closely observed. In 2009 Indonesia deposited with the United Nations a revised set of geographical coordinates of points consistent with Article 47(9) of the LOSC. These coordinates are based on Government Regulation No 38 (2002) as amended by Government Regulation No 27 (2008).[121] A total of 183 baselines are identified in the Indonesian coordinates, which include a mix of normal and archipelagic baselines. The baselines range in length from as little as 0.51 nm to 122.75 nm.

In 2009 the Philippines also deposited with the United Nations a set of geographical coordinates of points, which for the first time proclaimed archipelagic baselines consistent with the LOSC.[122] These baselines were based upon Republic Act No 9522, which had in turn amended earlier Philippine legislation.[123] The Philippines identified a total of 101 basepoints and baselines which range in length from 0.08 nm to 122.83 nm. Republic Act No 9522 also reaffirms in section 3 that the Philippines 'has dominion, sovereignty and jurisdiction over all portions of the national territory as defined in the Constitution'. A separate declaration is also made in Republic Act No 9522 with respect to the islands that form the Kalayaan Island Group and Scarborough Shoal, which are determined as a 'Regime of Islands' for the purposes of Article 121 of the LOSC.[124] The Philippines baselines

---

[121] MZN67.2009 (Maritime Zones Notification) United Nations (25 March 2009).

[122] Mary Ann Palma, 'The Philippines as an Archipelagic and Maritime Nation: Interests, Challenges and Perspectives' (2009) *RSIS Working Paper* No 182, 4–5. Under the previous baselines, for example, a baseline across Moro Gulf was 140.05 nm in length.

[123] MZN 69.2009 (Maritime Zones Notification) United Nations (21 April 2009).

[124] Republic Act No 9522 (2009) (Philippines) s 3.

and provisions of Republic Act No 9522 have been protested by China with respect to their contested sovereignty over Huangyan Island, and the islands of the reefs of the Nansha Islands (which the Philippines refer to as the Kalayaan Island Group),[125] which are reflective of ongoing sovereignty tensions over islands within the South China Sea.

In addition to Indonesia and the Philippines, other archipelagic states are seeking to take advantage of various aspects of the archipelagic regime. Antigua and Barbuda, Fiji, Grenada, Mauritius, Saint Vincent and the Grenadines, and Tuvalu have sought to delimit internal waters within their archipelagic waters consistent with Article 50.[126] Tuvalu has also sought to mix its use of archipelagic baselines in the case of some atolls that are within the archipelago, in accordance with Article 6 in the case of isolated atolls.[127] Variations in state practice are, however, evident. Papua New Guinea's declared archipelagic baselines commence at a point approximately 40 nm off the northern coast in the Bismark Sea and terminate on Suau Island in the Coral Sea off the southern New Guinea coast.[128] Whilst these baselines effectively enclose New Guinea, they do not connect with the New Guinea coast at either their commencement or terminus points. In the case of the lengths of straight archipelagic baselines, one of the potentially more sensitive issues in state practice implementing Part IV, recent studies suggest that the great majority of archipelagic states are interpreting Article 47(2) consistently,[129] with the Maldives and Papua New Guinea the only exceptions.[130]

Some maritime states have been sensitive to the manner in which certain archipelagic baselines have been proclaimed and have challenged their consistency with Article 47 of the LOSC. The United States has been particularly vigilant in monitoring claims by archipelagic states,[131] including instances where continental states which do not meet the Article 46 definition of an archipelagic state have sought to enclose clusters of offshore islands in a manner similar to an archipelagic claim.[132] In 1980, the United States protested Cape Verde's claim to be an archipelagic state on the basis that the water to land ratio arising from that state's archipelagic baselines was 12.54 to 1, with the result that the baselines were modified to conform with the LOSC.[133] In 2007 following the declaration by the Dominican Republic that it was an archipelagic state,[134] the United Kingdom and the United States issued a joint demarche indicating they did not accept the Dominican Republic's claim and

---

[125] Communication from the Government of China received by the Secretary-General of the United Nations, CML/12/2009 (13 April 2009); which in turn promoted a response from Vietnam with respect to China's assertions of sovereignty: Communication from the Government of Vietnam received by the Secretary-General of the United Nations, No 86/HC-2009 (8 May 2009); at www.un.org/Depts/los/LEGISLATIONANDTREATIES/STATEFILES/PHL.htm.

[126] Kevin Baumert and Brian Melchior, 'The Practice of Archipelagic States: A Study of Studies' (2015) 46 *Ocean Development and International Law* 60, 71.

[127] Department of State (United States), *Limits in the Seas: No 139 Tuvalu's Maritime Claims and Boundaries* (Washington, Department of State, 2014) 3, 7, 18.

[128] Baumert and Melchior, 'The Practice of Archipelagic States' (n 126) 63–64.

[129] Ibid 65; see also Committee on Baselines under the International Law of the Sea (International Law Association), *Baselines under the International Law of the Sea* (Washington, 2014) [76]–[87] at www.ila-hq.org/en/committees/index.cfm/cid/1028.

[130] Baumert and Melchior, 'The Practice of Archipelagic States' (n 126) 65.

[131] See generally Baumert and Melchior, 'The Practice of Archipelagic States' (n 126), assessing recent United States studies of archipelagic state practice.

[132] Roach and Smith, *Excessive Maritime Claims* (n 52) 208, referring to United States protests following claims by Canada, Denmark, Ecuador, Portugal, Spain and the United Kingdom.

[133] Roach and Smith, *Excessive Maritime Claims*, ibid 209.

[134] Law No 66-07 of 22 May 2007 (Dominican Republic); see Sophia Kopela, '2007 Archipelagic Legislation of the Dominican Republic: An Assessment' (2009) 24 *International Journal of Marine and Coastal Law* 501.

challenging the reliance by the Dominican Republic upon certain low-tide elevations as basepoints for archipelagic baselines. The United Kingdom and United States asserted that these features were not above water at high tide and did not meet the particular requirements of Article 47.[135] In 2012, Timor-Leste sought to raise its concerns with respect to aspects of Indonesia's straight archipelagic baseline system as they directly impacted upon its interests as a neighbouring state, particularly highlighting that Indonesia had not taken into account the provisions of Article 47(5) with respect to the Timor-Leste enclave of Oecussi and access to the EEZ and high seas.[136]

ii. Archipelagic State Rights Over Archipelagic Waters

In addition to these controversies, there has also been tension over the manner in which some archipelagic states have sought to interpret their rights with respect to archipelagic waters. The Philippines declaration upon signature of the LOSC, and confirmed on ratification, with respect to its interpretation of archipelagic status in a manner consistent with the Constitution of the Philippines, and previous treaties ceding sovereign rights over the islands that comprise the Philippines, has been particularly contentious.[137] The Philippine's Declaration provided:

> 7. The concept of archipelagic waters is similar to the concept of internal waters under the Constitution of the Philippines and removes straits connecting these waters with the economic zone or the high seas from the rights of foreign vessels to transit passage for international navigation.

A number of states responded to aspects of the Philippine's Declaration, including Australia, Bulgaria, the Ukraine and the Soviet Union. The United States protested the Declaration in January 1986:

> The Government of the United States wishes to observe that, as generally understood in international law, including that reflected in the 1982 Law of the Sea Convention, the concept of internal waters differs significantly from the concept of archipelagic waters. Archipelagic waters are only those enclosed by properly drawn archipelagic baselines and are subject to the regimes of innocent passage and archipelagic sea lanes passage.[138]

Given some of the controversies which have been associated with the regime of archipelagic states, and the limited number of states capable of claiming the status of an archipelagic state under Part IV of the LOSC, there remains limited state practice in this particular area of the law of the sea. Nevertheless, the level of acceptance of the regime of archipelagic states, which has now de facto and de jure been operative since the 1950s, suggests that this area of the law of the sea is accepted as part of customary international law.[139]

---

[135] 'Text of a Joint Demarche Undertaken by the United Kingdom of Great Britain and Northern Ireland and the United States of America in relation to the Law of the Dominican Republic Number 66-07 of 22 May 2007, Done on 18 October 2007' (2008) 66 *Law of the Sea Bulletin* 98–99, which also asserts that as the turning points relied upon 'do not qualify as turning points under article 47, paragraph 1, of the Convention, and that the Dominican Republic does not meet the other requirements of article 47 to be an archipelagic state'.

[136] Timor-Leste, Diplomatic Note NV/MIS/85/2012 (6 February 2012) at www.un.org/Depts/los/LEGISLATIONANDTREATIES/PDFFILES/DEPOSIT/communicationsredeposit/mzn67_2009_tls.pdf.

[137] 'Declarations and Statements' at www.un.org/Depts/los/convention_agreements/convention_declarations.htm.

[138] Roach and Smith, *Excessive Maritime Claims* (n 52) 214.

[139] This view is certainly borne out by the practice of the United States in terms of it recognition of the claims of individual archipelagic states: Roach and Smith, *Excessive Maritime Claims*, ibid 204.

VII. Further Reading

Robert Cribb and Michelle Ford (eds), *Indonesia beyond the Water's Edge: Managing an Archipelagic State* (Singapore, Institute of Southeast Asian Studies, 2009)

Tara Davenport, 'The Archipelagic Regime' in Donald R Rothwell, Alex G Oude Elferink, Karen N Scott and Tim Stephens (eds), *The Oxford Handbook of the Law of the Sea* (Oxford, Oxford University Press, 2015) 134–58

Sophia Kopela, *Dependent Archipelagos in the Law of the Sea* (Leiden, Martinus Nijhoff, 2013)

Mohamed Munavvar, *Ocean States: Archipelagic Regimes in the Law of the Sea* (Dordrecht, Martinus Nijhoff, 1995)

DP O'Connell, 'Mid-Ocean Archipelagos in International Law' (1971) 45 *British Yearbook of International Law* 1

Office for Ocean Affairs and the Law of the Sea, United Nations, *The Law of the Sea. Archipelagic States: Legislative History of Part IV of the United Nations Convention on the Law of the Sea* (New York, United Nations, 1990)

9

Landlocked and Geographically Disadvantaged States

I. Introduction

One of the enduring concerns of the law of the sea has been to promote freedom of communication throughout the world's oceans, especially so as to facilitate international trade and commerce. This freedom is not one that landlocked states are able to enjoy without allowance being made for transit to and from the sea across the territory of adjoining coastal states. Geographically disadvantaged states, that is those states that possess a coastline, but one that is short, or configured in such a way as to restrict the extent of adjacent maritime zones, are also unable to take full advantage of ocean space.

At UNCLOS III the specific interests of landlocked and geographically disadvantaged states (LLGDS) received serious and detailed consideration and this resulted in the incorporation within LOSC of Part X, which is devoted to addressing these issues. This achievement was possible because LLGDS formed a negotiating bloc and advanced their collective interests in all three of the committees that undertook the work of UNCLOS III. The Group of LLGDS numbered 55 states, over a third of the participating states, and therefore wielded considerable influence because under the UNCLOS III Rules of Procedure such a 'blocking third' could veto proposed rules.[1]

The Group of LLGDS at UNCLOS III was remarkable in bringing together a diversity of developed and developing states (such as Switzerland and Nepal) which had limited or no access to the sea but otherwise shared little in common. The group was united in seeking recognition of existing rights of access to the sea and navigation upon it, together with new resource rights within the EEZ, the continental shelf and the deep seabed maritime zones being recognised by the LOSC.[2] However, their requests met with limited success and, beyond certain specific rights, LLGDS enjoy few hard and fast guarantees under the LOSC, especially as regards access to living and non-living resources. While the LOSC does to some extent correct for the natural inequality resulting from the geographical position of some states in relation to the sea, it does not systematically address the economic disadvantage faced by these states and LLGDS continue to be over-represented in the United Nations Development Programme's (UNDP's) list of least developed countries.[3] In 2014, the United Nations Secretary-General observed that the 32 'landlocked developing countries, with a

---

[1] *Rules of Procedure of UNCLOS III*, UN Doc A/CONF.62/30/Rev.3 (1975), rr 37, 39.
[2] Gerhard Hafner, 'The "Land-Locked" Viewpoint' (1981) 5 *Marine Policy* 281, 281.
[3] UNCTAD, *The Least Developed Countries Report 2014*, UN Doc UNCTAD/LDC/2014 (2014).

total population of about 450 million, face special challenges that are associated with their lack of direct territorial access to the sea and remoteness and isolation from international markets'.[4]

Table 9.1: Landlocked States and the LOSC

Landlocked States Parties to the LOSC	Landlocked States Not Parties to the LOSC
Armenia	Afghanistan
Austria	Andorra
Belarus	Azerbaijan
Bolivia	Bhutan
Botswana	Burundi
Burkina Faso	Central African Republic
Chad	Ethiopia
Czech Republic	Holy See (Vatican City)
Hungary	Kazakhstan
Laos	Kosovo
Lesotho	Kyrgyzstan
Luxembourg	Liechtenstein
Macedonia	Rwanda
Malawi	San Marino
Mali	South Sudan
Moldova	Tajikistan
Mongolia	Turkmenistan
Nepal	Uzbekistan
Niger	
Paraguay	
Serbia	
Slovakia	
Swaziland	
Switzerland	
Uganda	
Zambia	
Zimbabwe	

[4] UN General Assembly, *Ten-year Review of the Implementation of the Almaty Programme of Action: Addressing the Special Needs of Landlocked Developing Countries with a New Global Framework for Transit Transport Coopera-tion for Landlocked and Transit Developing Countries: Report of the Secretary-General*, UN Doc A/69/170 (2014) [1].

The LOSC defines a landlocked state as one that has no sea coast.[5] As of 1 January 2015 there were 45 such states, and over half of these states have ratified or acceded to the LOSC (see Table 9.1, above), five having done so since 2010. The African and European continents have the largest numbers of landlocked states, with 16 and 15 such states, respectively. There are 12 landlocked states in Asia, and two in South America (see Table 9.2, below). The total of 45 landlocked states out of around 200 states in the international community is a substantially larger group than at the time of UNCLOS III, when the landlocked states numbered 30.[6] However, at UNCLOS III the landlocked states were also joined and supported by a further group of coastal states that were considered to be 'geographically disadvantaged'. This was, and remains, a somewhat amorphous category, that embraces developed and developing coastal states that face various kinds of disadvantage in terms of their coastal and maritime areas.[7] These can include a short coastline, and therefore a limited capacity to generate maritime zones (as is the case for Iraq and the Democratic Republic of Congo, both of which are almost landlocked), so-called zone-locked states because of their coastline configuration (as was the case for the Federal Republic of Germany),[8] a narrow or resource-poor continental margin (as is the case for Finland), or an EEZ that contains unproductive fisheries (as is the case for Jamaica). The majority of the geographically disadvantaged states are in Africa, where for many of these states there is a combination both of long-standing economic disadvantage, and also highly restricted access to

Table 9.2: Landlocked States by Region

Africa
Botswana, Burkina Faso, Burundi, Central African Republic, Chad, Ethiopia, Lesotho, Malawi, Mali, Niger, Rwanda, South Sudan, Swaziland, Uganda, Zambia and Zimbabwe.
Asia
Afghanistan, Armenia, Azerbaijan, Bhutan, Kazakhstan, Kyrgyzstan, Laos, Mongolia, Nepal, Tajikistan, Turkmenistan and Uzbekistan.
Europe
Andorra, Austria, Belarus, Czech Republic, Holy See (Vatican City), Hungary, Kosovo, Liechtenstein, Luxembourg, Macedonia, Moldova, San Marino, Serbia, Slovakia and Switzerland.
South America
Bolivia[9] and Paraguay.

[5] LOSC, art 124(1).

[6] Lewis M Alexander, 'The "Disadvantaged" States and the Law of the Sea' (1981) 5 *Marine Policy* 185.

[7] At UNCLOS III the geographically disadvantaged states in the LLGDS were: Algeria, Bahrain, Belgium, Bulgaria, Ethiopia, Finland, Gambia, the German Democratic Republic, the Federal Republic of Germany, Greece, Iraq, Jamaica, Jordan, Kuwait, the Netherlands, Poland, Qatar, Romania, Singapore, Sudan, Sweden, Syria, Turkey, the United Arab Emirates, the United Republic of Cameroon and Zaire: SC Vasciannie, *Land-Locked and Geographically Disadvantaged States in the International Law of the Sea* (Oxford, Clarendon Press, 1990) 8.

[8] See *North Sea Continental Shelf (Federal Republic of Germany v Denmark; Federal Republic of Germany v The Netherlands)* [1969] ICJ Rep 3.

[9] Bolivia regards itself as unjustly deprived of a sea coast, and has an ongoing territorial dispute in this respect with Peru. Hence, it adopted a somewhat equivocal position at UNCLOS III regarding its inclusion in the LLGDS Group. See also the declaration of Bolivia of 1984 upon signing the LOSC: www.un.org/Depts/los/convention_agreements/convention_declarations.htm.

ocean resources. The flexibility of the 'geographical disadvantage' term is highlighted by the inclusion of the island state of Singapore which, while being surrounded by sea, is nonetheless disadvantaged because of its proximity to much larger states, one of which, Indonesia, is an archipelagic state. As a result Singapore is only able to claim a small, 100 square nm EEZ.[10] It may also be noted that the issue of geographical disadvantage in a broad sense is relevant not only to questions surrounding access to the sea, but also to maritime boundary delimitation (in which coastal configuration can be a key factor),[11] and the drawing of territorial sea and archipelagic baselines to ensure that these do not cut off the territorial sea of another state from the high seas, or an EEZ.[12]

The status of the Caspian Sea, and whether is it a sea that generates a 'sea coast' for the purposes of Article 124(1)(a), is of significance with respect to the status of those landlocked states which border the Caspian and the general application of the LOSC. The Caspian Sea, which at 143,200 square miles is the world's largest inland body of water, is bordered by five states: Azerbaijan, Iran, Kazakhstan, the Russian Federation and Turkmenistan. Only Iran and the Russian Federation are considered coastal states for the purposes of the LOSC (as they border other, recognised, seas), with the other Caspian Sea littoral states considered landlocked. Nevertheless, the size of the Caspian Sea, and the interests of its littoral states, has generated debates over its legal status and there have been ongoing negotiations between the five states with respect to their rights and entitlements.[13]

Traditionally, the special interests of landlocked states when it comes to the law of the sea have been twofold. The first is securing rights of transit across the territory of neighbouring states so as to obtain access to the sea. The second is obtaining the right to grant nationality to vessels, which are then permitted to navigate freely and gain access to the ports of a coastal state adjoining the landlocked state. At UNCLOS III landlocked states sought affirmation of these interests and, with the geographically disadvantaged states, also sought new rights of access to the resources of the EEZ, the continental shelf and the deep seabed.

II. Landlocked States and Access to the Sea

A. Early Developments

The LOSC gave recognition to the interests of LLGDS in Part X and several provisions found elsewhere in the Convention. However, this was not the first occasion in international law in which efforts had been made to address the interests of landlocked states in relation to maritime matters. As early as the eleventh century, a number of landlocked territories in Europe were able to secure rights under bilateral treaties to gain access to the sea across neighbouring territories, principally via international rivers. However, more

---

[10] Raymond SK Lim, 'EEZ Legislation of ASEAN States' (1991) 40 *International and Comparative Law Quarterly* 170, 171.

[11] See further ch 16.

[12] LOSC, arts 7(6), 47(5).

[13] Barbara Janusz-Pawletta, *The Legal Status of the Caspian Sea: Current Challenges and Prospects for Future Development* (Heidelberg, Springer, 2015).

extensive and important practice occurred in the twentieth century, beginning in earnest under the auspices of the League of Nations in the aftermath of World War I. While some writers at this time contended that landlocked states enjoyed a right of transit on the basis of natural law principles,[14] as a logical consequence of the freedom of the seas,[15] or as an international servitude of necessity,[16] in practice it was through bilateral and plurilateral treaties that access was sought and granted.[17] Early examples of such treaties included an 1816 agreement between Sardinia, the Swiss Confederation and the Canton of Geneva that facilitated the transit of goods.[18]

The 1919 Versailles Treaty included provisions which established a regime for transit for landlocked states on certain international rivers in Europe.[19] In the *River Oder* case the Permanent Court of International Justice affirmed that this regime effected the 'complete internationalization' of the River Oder, a position that benefited landlocked Czechoslovakia.[20] Also of importance was the 1919 Covenant of the League of Nations, which in Article 23(e) required members to 'make provision to secure and maintain freedom of communications and of transit and equitable treatment of the commerce of all Members'. In an early acknowledgment of geographical disadvantage, the article went on to encourage members in making such provision to bear in mind 'the special necessities of the regions devastated during the war'.

Much of the state practice relevant to access rights for landlocked states is concerned with the general facilitation of free movement of persons and goods from one territory to another, regardless of their particular geographical circumstances.[21] An example of this is the 1921 Convention and Statute on Freedom of Transit, agreed at a conference convened by the League of Nations in Barcelona in 1921. Article 2 of the Convention provided that states are to ensure that there is free and non-discriminatory transit across the territory of contracting states. However, the regime was limited in that it applied only to transit using international rivers and railways, rather than all forms of overland transport, including aviation, which was to become increasingly important as a mode of access for landlocked states in the twentieth century. Moreover, it was not a treaty specifically aimed at addressing issues of access for landlocked states but was rather a more general system for promoting international communication.

Another general transit regime is found in the 1947 General Agreement on Tariffs and Trade (GATT), which was subsequently reproduced in the 1994 General Agreement on Tariffs and Trade, the first and most important of the 'covered agreements' of the World Trade Organization. Article V of GATT provides that 'there shall be freedom

---

[14] See, eg, Charles De Visscher, *Le Droit International des Communications* (Ghent and Paris, Université de Gand, 1924) 6ff.

[15] See, eg, Georges Scelle, *Manuel de Droit International Public* (Paris, Domat-Montchrétien, 1941) pt I, 389.

[16] Ibid. An international servitude is a right under which part of a state's territory is placed under the permanent use of another state.

[17] DW Bowett, *The Law of the Sea* (Manchester, Manchester University Press, 1967) 50.

[18] For discussion of this and other early treaties see Secretariat of the United Nations, *Question of Free Access to the Sea of Land-Locked Countries, UNCLOS I Preparatory Document No 23*, UN Doc A/CONF.13/29 and Add 1 (1958), 312ff.

[19] 1919 Versailles Treaty, pt XII, s II.

[20] *Territorial Jurisdiction of the International Commission of the River Oder (Czechoslovakia, Denmark, France, Germany, Great Britain, Sweden/Poland)* [1929] PCIJ ser A no 23.

[21] Vasciannie, *Land-Locked and Geographically Disadvantaged States* (n 7) 183.

of transit through the territory of each contracting Party, via the routes most convenient for international transit'. The GATT provision, therefore, takes a similar approach to the Barcelona regime, but deals with all methods of transit across territory, including by road and air. However, it is limited in so far as it applies only to the transit of goods, and not to the free movement of persons.

B. UNCLOS I

The first specific treatment of transit rights for landlocked states to the sea in a multilateral treaty is found in the 1958 Convention on the High Seas.[22] The key provision in this respect is Article 3, the text of which was not drafted by the International Law Commission, as was most of the Geneva regime,[23] but was instead based on a draft prepared by Switzerland and inserted with the support of the other landlocked states at UNCLOS I.[24] In its comments on the ILC's draft articles, Nepal observed that the right of free access to the sea had been granted to landlocked countries in practice by common courtesy or convention, and that it was now time to codify this practice in legal form.[25]

The negotiating position taken by Switzerland and the other landlocked states at UNCLOS I was based upon a set of principles they had agreed prior to the conference. The most significant of these was the first principle, which stated that: 'The right of each land-locked State of free access to the sea derives from the fundamental principle of freedom of the High Seas.'[26] The 1958 Convention on the High Seas did not give effect to this principle in any strict sense. Article 3(1) provides that states having 'no sea-coast' should have 'free access to the sea' in order to enjoy 'the freedom of the seas on equal terms with coastal states'. Coastal states adjoining landlocked states are to accord, 'by common agreement', the landlocked states 'on the basis of reciprocity, free transit through their territory'.[27] In terms of access to, and use of, seaports, coastal states are also to afford treatment to the ships of landlocked states equal to that enjoyed by their own ships and the ships of other states.[28]

As landlocked states such as Czechoslovakia pointed out at the time, this provision fell short of a guarantee of transit, because the granting of 'free access to the sea' was made contingent on 'common agreement' between the states concerned.[29] Bowett noted that the 1958 Convention on the High Seas therefore endorsed the moral claim of landlocked states, but did not give them an enforceable legal right to access, a right that could only be made manifest via a 'specific, negotiated agreement'.[30]

---

[22]   *Basic Documents* No 10.

[23]   The 1956 ILC Articles on the Law of the Sea and accompanying commentaries make no mention of land-locked states: [1956] *Yearbook of the International Law Commission*, vol 2.

[24]   Koshor Uprety, *The Transit Regime for Landlocked States* (Washington DC, World Bank, 2006) 65.

[25]   United Nations Conference on the Law of the Sea, *Official Records, Volume I: Preparatory Documents*, UN Doc A/CONF.13/37 (1958) 92–93.

[26]   Bowett, *The Law of the Sea* (n 17) 51.

[27]   1958 Convention on the High Seas, art 3(1)(a).

[28]   Ibid art 3(1)(b).

[29]   Vasciannie, *Land-Locked and Geographically Disadvantaged States* (n 7) 186.

[30]   Bowett, *The Law of the Sea* (n 17) 51–52. See also JD Viall, 'The Transit of Persons to and from Lesotho' (1968) 1 *Comparative and International Law Journal of Southern Africa* 1–12; 188–208; 363–89.

C. Post-UNCLOS I Developments

Following UNCLOS I, landlocked states shifted strategy in their efforts to obtain greater recognition of their disadvantaged position. Rather than seeking access rights under the law of the sea, they instead sought to obtain benefits from emergent regimes that were advancing a global trade liberalisation agenda. This approach was evident in the negotiations at, and outcome of, the inaugural United Nations Conference on Trade and Development (UNCTAD) held in Geneva in 1964. By the time this conference was convened, the number of landlocked states had grown substantially as a result of the decolonisation process. These states were successful in advocating a specific new convention on access issues for landlocked states: the 1965 New York Convention on the Transit Trade of Land-Locked States.

The 1965 New York Convention is to a significant extent modelled on the Barcelona regime, and Article V of the GATT. However, it is notable in that it included for the first time recognition that landlocked states enjoy a legal 'right' of free transit.[31] Article 2 provided that freedom of transit is to be granted to 'traffic in transit and means of transport' on 'routes in use mutually acceptable for transit'.[32] No discrimination is to be exercised on the basis of 'the place of origin, departure, entry, exit or destination or on any circumstances relating to the ownership of the goods or the ownership, place of registration or flag of vessels, land vehicles or other means of transport used'.[33] The Convention applies not only to river and rail traffic, but to all means of transport, including 'seagoing and river vessels and road vehicles'.[34] In addition, traffic in transit is not to be subject to customs duties or taxes, although fees for service for supervising and administering transit may be imposed.[35] One of the strengths of the regime is its enforceability, in that Article 16 provides for the compulsory arbitration of disputes with respect to the interpretation or application of the Convention that cannot be settled by negotiation, or other peaceful means, within nine months. The 1965 New York Convention was the baseline for negotiations at UNCLOS III on the question of rights of transit for landlocked states.[36]

Although it was an important development, the relatively small number of ratifications of the 1965 New York Convention,[37] and in particular the failure of major transit states such as France and Pakistan to join the regime, makes it difficult to sustain an argument that the regime codified an existing, or generated a new, customary right of free access for landlocked states to the sea.[38] It was certainly not accepted at the time of its conclusion that the Convention reflected customary law on the point.[39] The position has not changed substantially with the conclusion and widespread ratification of the LOSC, Part X of which includes similar provisions as the 1965 New York Convention that fall short of clearly guaranteeing a right of access.

---

[31] 1965 New York Convention, Preamble, Principle I.
[32] Ibid art 2(1).
[33] Ibid.
[34] Ibid art 1(d)(i).
[35] Ibid art 3.
[36] See LC Caflisch, 'Land-Locked States and their Access to and From the Sea' (1978) 49 *British Year Book of International Law* 85.
[37] As at 1 January 2015 there are 43 parties to the Convention.
[38] Vasciannie, *Land-Locked and Geographically Disadvantaged States* (n 7) 208.
[39] Ibid, 206–207.

There is little other evidence to support the conclusion that landlocked states have a customary law right of access to the sea. Indeed the preponderance of practice suggests the opposite. A case in point is the *Right of Passage* case[40] decided on the merits by the ICJ in 1960. The case concerned a right of transit asserted by Portugal to apply to persons, officials and goods moving between its enclaved territories in India and the coast. The Court found that there was such a right of passage supported by a local, or regional, custom because of long-standing and consistent practice between the states that was accepted by them as law. In essence, the Court gave effect to an arrangement that was akin to a bilateral treaty providing access, rather than affirming a general right of access at customary international law.[41]

D. The LOSC

The LOSC devotes Part X, containing nine articles, to the access and certain other rights of landlocked states, and the concomitant obligations of transit states in the law of the sea. That a whole part of the LOSC's 17 parts is dedicated to LLGDS is indicative of the significance of these issues at UNCLOS III and the influential role that LLGDS played at the conference. In practical terms, however, the provisions of Part X have not attracted a great deal of attention by LLGDS or coastal states, and have not been the basis for any disputes brought under the Part XV dispute settlement system. This underscores the continuing importance of bilateral arrangements of both a formal and informal character in effectively accommodating the special interests of LLGDS.

'Transit state' is defined in Article 124(1)(b) of the LOSC as a state 'with or without a sea-coast' that is 'situated between a land-locked State and the sea, through whose territory traffic in transit passes'. 'Traffic in transit' means all persons and materials, including goods and baggage and means of transport, when the passage is only a portion of a complete journey that begins or terminates in the territory of a landlocked state.[42] The means of transport covered by Part X are railways, sea vessels, lake and river craft, and road vehicles, and, where local conditions require, porters and pack animals.[43] Hence the LOSC does not apply to air transport, and the rights of landlocked states to transit by air navigation depend on bilateral and multilateral agreements reached under the framework of the 1944 Convention on International Civil Aviation, such as the 2005 Paraguay–United States Open Skies Agreement, the 2007/2010 Air Transport Agreement between the United States and the European Union, and the 2010 United States–Laos Air Transport Agreement. In addition, the rights of access for landlocked states provided for in Part X do not extend to geographically disadvantaged states which, though under some level of disadvantage in terms of maritime zones and resources, nonetheless all have at least some coastline, and therefore access to the sea.

During the negotiations at UNCLOS III there was considerable discussion as to whether the convention being drafted should recognise a right of access to the sea for landlocked states as a general principle of international law. While landlocked states took the view that

[40] *Right of Passage over Indian Territory (Portugal v India)* [1960] ICJ Rep 6.
[41] Vasciannie, *Land-Locked and Geographically Disadvantaged States* (n 7) 214–15.
[42] LOSC, art 124(1)(c).
[43] Ibid art 124(1)(d).

there was such a right at customary law which should be acknowledged in the text, the transit states were divided on the question. Some states in the Eastern bloc, including the Soviet Union, supported such recognition, while others such as Iran and Pakistan maintained that the right was in fact only a privilege, and had to be based on bilateral agreements between transit and landlocked states.[44] Several transit states continue to maintain such a view, as evidenced by declarations on signing, ratifying or acceding to the LOSC which observe that the freedom of transit depends upon agreement between the transit state and the landlocked state concerned, and that in the absence of such an agreement, transit may be exercised only according to the national law of the transit state.[45]

The ultimate outcome in the LOSC is a somewhat ambiguous combination of an apparently enforceable right of transit, but one that depends upon bilateral, sub-regional or regional arrangements to be given effect. Article 125 is the central provision on point, balancing a concern with providing freedom of access for landlocked states, with the concern for maintaining territorial sovereignty for transit states. Article 125(1) provides that landlocked states 'shall have the right of access to and from the sea for the purpose of exercising the rights provided for in this Convention including those relating to the freedom of the high seas and the common heritage of mankind'. To this end this provision continues that 'land-locked States shall enjoy freedom of transit through the territory of transit States by all means of transport'. This formulation uses mandatory language in relation to access and transit rights, and is therefore more strongly in favour of landlocked states than Article 3 of the 1958 Convention on the High Seas.

The freedom of transit under Article 125 exists independently of any bilateral or other arrangement between landlocked and transit states, although such agreements will be necessary for the freedom to be given effect in practice.[46] Hence the right of access is tempered by Article 125(2) which provides that the 'terms and modalities for exercising freedom of transit shall be agreed between the land-locked States and transit States concerned through bilateral, subregional or regional agreements'. Additionally, Article 125(3) is directed at the interests of transit states, and provides that 'in the exercise of their full sovereignty over their territory' transit states 'have the right to take all measures necessary to ensure that the rights and facilities … for land-locked States shall in no way infringe their legitimate interests'. However, Article 132 does seek to safeguard any arrangements between transit and landlocked states that were more favourable than those provided for in LOSC, and does not preclude the grant of such facilities in the future.

The effect of Article 125 is that landlocked states do not have a self-executing right to access. Instead, transit states are under an obligation to engage in good faith negotiations to facilitate access for landlocked states. Hence while the right of access for landlocked states itself is not directly enforceable, landlocked states may none the less insist on their rights being considered by transit states. An outright refusal by a transit state to grant access or to engage in negotiations with a landlocked state would be an unreasonable assertion of

---

[44] Vasciannie, *Land-Locked and Geographically Disadvantaged States* (n 7) 46.

[45] See, eg, the declarations of Germany on accession in 1994 and Pakistan on ratification in 1997. Germany's declaration provoked a response by the Czech Republic in its declaration on ratification in 1996 that the German declaration 'cannot be interpreted with regard to the Czech Republic in contradiction with the provisions of Part X of the Convention': www.un.org/Depts/los/convention_agreements/convention_declarations.htm.

[46] *Virginia Commentaries*, vol 3, 418.

territorial sovereignty, and would constitute an abuse of rights, contrary to Article 300 of LOSC.[47] On this basis it could be litigated under the dispute settlement provisions in Part XV of the Convention, which provides no capacity for states to opt out of the compulsory dispute settlement system in relation to this type of dispute.

Part X continues in relation to access, providing that the exercise of the right of access to and from the sea is excluded from the application of the most favoured nation clause.[48] This means that rights enjoyed by landlocked states by operation of the LOSC and any special arrangements with transit states, do not apply to third states by operation of any most favoured nation clause that the third state has with a transit state.[49] Traffic in transit is not to be subject to any customs duties, taxes or other charge except fees for services rendered in connection with the traffic.[50] In addition, the means of transport in transit and other facilities provided for and used by landlocked states is not to be subject to taxes any greater than those levied for the use of means of transport of the transit state.[51] To promote convenience for traffic in transit, free zones or other customs facilities may be provided at the ports of entry and exit in transit states by agreement with the landlocked states.[52] Article 129 includes provision for transit and landlocked states to cooperate in the construction or improvement of facilities to give effect to the freedom of transit, by providing for means of transport in transit states that otherwise do not exist, or constructing port installations and equipment. Transit states are to take appropriate measures so as to avoid delays or other difficulties of a technical nature for traffic in transit.[53] And if such difficulties do arise, then the authorities of landlocked and transit states are to cooperate to eliminate them.[54]

While five landlocked states became parties to the LOSC in the period 2010–15, as Table 9.1 highlights, many landlocked states are yet to adhere to the LOSC, or take advantage of its provisions by seeking to negotiate access arrangements with neighbouring transit states, most of which are parties to the LOSC because they are coastal states. The slow take up of the LOSC by landlocked states has historically been an issue in Africa. As a response, in respect of African states that are members of the Commonwealth,[55] in 2005 the Commonwealth Secretariat sought to promote adoption of the LOSC by highlighting developmental benefits that may accrue from full use of the LOSC provisions to enter into negotiations with transit states and enact enabling legislation thereby establishing effective access corridors to the sea.[56] Three landlocked African members of the Commonwealth, Lesotho (2007), Malawi (2010) and Swaziland (2012), have since adhered to the LOSC.

---

[47] LOSC, art 300 provides that 'States Parties shall fulfil in good faith the obligations assumed under this Convention and shall exercise the rights, jurisdiction and freedoms recognized in this Convention in a manner which would not constitute and abuse of rights'.

[48] Ibid art 126.

[49] *Virginia Commentaries*, vol 3, 424.

[50] LOSC, art 127(1).

[51] Ibid art 127(2).

[52] Ibid art 128. See, eg, 1921 United Kingdom-Belgium Convention to Facilitate Belgian Traffic Through the Territories of East Africa.

[53] LOSC, art 130(1).

[54] Ibid art 130(2).

[55] The African members of the Commonwealth are Botswana, Lesotho, Malawi, Swaziland, Uganda and Zambia; Zimbabwe is not currently a member of the Commonwealth, having been suspended in 2002.

[56] See Cheryl Thompson-Barrow, 'A Corridor for Land-Locked States' (2006) 32 *Commonwealth Law Bulletin* 67, 71. See also 'Communiqué: 2005 Meeting of Commonwealth Law Ministers and Senior Officials' (2006) 32 *Commonwealth Law Bulletin* 73, 76.

In 2013 Bolivia instituted proceedings against Chile in the ICJ, asserting that Chile had failed in its obligation to Bolivia to negotiate access to the Pacific Ocean.[57] Although both states are parties to the LOSC, Bolivia chose not to invoke the LOSC in its application but instead to focus its legal grounds for the claim under general international law and commitments that Chile had made to negotiate access to the sea for Bolivia. In 2015 the ICJ heard preliminary objections raised by Chile in the matter.

United Nations bodies have continued to review the particular circumstances of landlocked states, and the challenges of their geographical location upon their ability to engage in transit and related aspects of trade. The 2003 Almaty Programme of Action, borne out of the 2000 Millennium Declaration and subsequent meetings of least developed countries, sought to facilitate infrastructure development and maintenance in this area with respect to rail and road transport, ports and inland waterways. With respect to ports, it was recognised that 'Landlocked and transit developing countries should seek cooperative arrangements to improve port facilities and services for transit goods, including the modernization of existing terminals, the establishment of new ones and the simplification of procedures where appropriate'.[58]

The United Nations General Assembly endorsed a ten-year review of the Almaty Programme of Action, which was undertaken in 2014 in conjunction with the Second United Nations Conference on Landlocked Developing Countries.[59] This resulted in the adoption of the Vienna Programme of Action for Landlocked Developing Countries for the Decade 2014–2024.[60] The Vienna Programme of Action is based on 'renewed and strengthened partnerships between landlocked developing countries and the transit countries and their development partners'.[61] Priority 1 addresses 'Fundamental Transit Policy Issues' and emphasises the importance for landlocked developing countries 'to have access to and from the sea, in accordance with applicable international law, in order to fully integrate into the global trading system'.[62]

III. Landlocked States and Rights of Navigation

The LOSC affirmed and strengthened the rights of access by landlocked states to the sea. For landlocked states, such access rights could be justified in large part because of the navigational rights of landlocked states which have attracted long-standing acceptance, and which received recognition in Part X. The argument is that if the freedom of the seas is a right accorded to all states of whatever geographical position, then rights of access must necessarily follow, otherwise the freedom of the seas would be deprived of meaning.

---

[57] *Obligation to Negotiate Access to the Pacific Ocean (Bolivia v Chile)*, Application Instituting Proceedings of 24 April 2013.

[58] UN Office of the High Representative for the Least Developed Countires, Landlocked Developing Countries and Small Island Developing States, *Almaty Programme of Action*, UN Doc A/CONF.2002/3 (2003) [23(a)].

[59] UNGA Resolution 68/270 (2014).

[60] Second United Nations Conference on Landlocked Developing Countries, *Vienna Programme of Action for Landlocked Developing Countries for the Decade 2014–2024*, UN Doc A/CONF.225/L.1 (2014).

[61] Ibid [16].

[62] Ibid [23].

For most of the history of the law of the sea, the nationality of ships depended upon the port of registration. As landlocked states possess no seaports, it was originally thought that landlocked states could not have their flag flown by vessels. However, the situation changed in the early twentieth century in the aftermath of World War I. Switzerland pressed at the Paris Peace Conference for recognition of the right of landlocked states to grant nationality to vessels, and to be accorded full rights of navigation upon the sea.[63] Without such rights, Switzerland argued, it would not be able to establish a commercial fleet in its own right. The Swiss request was agreed to in the 1919 Treaty of Versailles, which in Article 273 provided that recognition shall be accorded to the certificates and documents issued to their vessels by governments, whether or not they possessed a coastline. Vessels of landlocked states were to be registered in a specified place in their territory, which was to serve as the port of registry for such vessels.

At UNCLOS I the navigational rights of landlocked states were recognised more systematically. The 1958 Convention on the Territorial Sea and the Contiguous Zone[64] in Article 14(1) stipulated that all states, whether coastal or not, enjoyed the right of innocent passage through the territorial sea. The 1958 Convention on the High Seas declared in Article 2 that the high seas are open to all nations, and that coastal and non-coastal states enjoyed the established freedoms of the seas, including the freedoms of navigation and fishing. Under Article 4, every state, whether coastal or not, has the right to sail ships under its flag on the high seas.

These rights were affirmed in the LOSC. Article 17 provides that the ships of all states, whether coastal or landlocked, enjoy the right of innocent passage through the territorial sea. The same is true for the other navigational rights, including the right of transit passage through straits used for international navigation,[65] the right of innocent passage through archipelagic waters,[66] the right of archipelagic sea lanes passage,[67] and freedom of navigation on the high seas.[68] Article 90 affirms that every state, whether coastal or landlocked, has the right to sail ships flying its flag on the high seas. Although referring only to navigation on the high seas, it is clear by reference to the other provisions already cited that landlocked states may grant nationality to ships that then enjoy the other navigational rights and freedoms. There is no specific provision made for the modality by which nationality is to be granted to ships by landlocked states, and so the general conditions would apply as set out in Article 91. Many landlocked states have taken advantage of this provision, and three of these (Bolivia, Moldova and Mongolia) provide foreign shipowners with flags of convenience.

The final provision of the LOSC of relevance to navigational issues for landlocked states is Article 131, which is found in Part X. That article states that ships flying the flag of landlocked states enjoy treatment equal to that accorded to other foreign ships in maritime ports. This does not provide a right of access to ports which, as with internal waters, remain under the complete control and sovereignty of coastal states. Rather it is a provision of

---

[63] SP Menefee, '"The Oar of Odysseus": Landlocked and Geographically Disadvantaged States in Historical Perspective' (1992–93) 23 *California Western International Law Journal* 1, 34–35.
[64] *Basic Documents* No 9.
[65] LOSC, art 37.
[66] Ibid art 52.
[67] Ibid art 53.
[68] Ibid art 87.

non-discrimination, such that coastal states must not treat the vessels of landlocked states less favourably than the vessels of other states.[69]

IV. Landlocked and Geographically Disadvantaged States and Marine Resources

Historically, the gaining of access to the sea to secure access to trade and to facilitate the transit of persons, has been far more important for landlocked states than obtaining access to marine living and non-living resources. However, when coastal states began to assert sovereign rights and jurisdiction over new and broader maritime areas after World War II this served further to highlight the natural disadvantages experienced by the landlocked states when it came to the oceans.[70] The LOSC seeks to remedy this disadvantage, to give effect to the aspiration of a 'just and equitable international economic order' by taking into account the 'special interests and needs of developing countries, whether coastal or land-locked'.[71]

Part X deals only with issues of transit and access. Resource issues are addressed separately in other parts of the LOSC and include not only landlocked but also geographically disadvantaged states. These deal with the access to the living resources of the EEZ, the resources of the high seas, the mineral resources of the deep seabed (the Area), and the right to engage in marine scientific research and to have preferential access to the transfer of marine technology. There are no rights accorded to LLGDS to the mineral resources of the EEZ, or the resources of the continental shelf.[72] Coastal states successfully opposed requests by LLGDS for access to these resources, maintaining that it would be incompatible with the juridical nature of the continental shelf as a natural prolongation of land territory, in which coastal states had inherent sovereign rights.[73] For similar, indeed stronger, reasons, landlocked states have no access to the resources, living or non-living, of the territorial seas of coastal states.

However, one important concession was obtained from coastal states by the LLGDS in respect of the outer continental shelf, that is areas beyond 200 nm, if a coastal state's continental margin extends that far. Article 82 of the LOSC provides a formula for coastal states to make contributions to the ISA in respect of the exploitation of the non-living resources of this area,[74] and for the ISA to distribute contributions 'taking into account the interests and needs of developing States, particularly the least developed and the land-locked among them'. As exploitation of the Area under ISA regulatory oversight becomes ever more likely in the coming decade, Article 82 will take on greater significance for developing states, especially as the 2014 UNCTAD assessment found that 15 of the world's 48 least developed states were landlocked.[75]

---

[69] *Virginia Commentaries*, vol 3, 453.
[70] Ibid 371.
[71] LOSC, preamble, 5th recital.
[72] Ibid art 82(4).
[73] Vasciannie, *Land-Locked and Geographically Disadvantaged States* (n 7) 88–93.
[74] LOSC, arts 82(1)–(2).
[75] UNCTAD, *The Least Developed Countries Report 2014* (n 3); those states were Afghanistan, Bhutan, Burkina Faso, Burundi, Central African Republic, Chad, Ethiopia, Lesotho, Malawi, Mali, Nepal, Niger, Rwanda, South Sudan and Uganda.

A. Living Resources of the EEZ

Landlocked states consistently opposed the EEZ at UNCLOS III. However, when it became apparent that the EEZ regime would be adopted, the LLGDS pressed for compensation in the form of access to the resources of the EEZ.[76] In 1981 Nepal and several other land-locked states went so far as to propose a Common Heritage Fund to be funded out of a levy on profits obtained by coastal states in exploiting EEZ resources.[77] Other proposals from LLGDS included the establishment of regional EEZs in which neighbouring states, including coastal, geographically disadvantaged, and landlocked would have an equal right to fish.[78] However, a far more limited regime was adopted by the conclusion of UNCLOS III.

In the 200 nm EEZ coastal states have exclusive sovereign rights and jurisdiction for the purposes of exploring and exploiting, conserving and managing the living and non-living natural resources found in the seabed and water column. Under Part V of the LOSC which sets out the EEZ regime, special provision is made for access by LLGDS to the living resources of the EEZ of coastal states in the same subregion or region. This does not grant a defined share of the marine living resources of the EEZ, but instead seeks to guarantee access by the fishing industries of the LLGDS themselves to harvest marine resources under certain circumstances. Geographically disadvantaged states are defined in this context to mean both those coastal states, including states bordering enclosed or semi-enclosed seas, whose geographical situation makes them dependent on the exploitation of the living resources of the EEZ of other states in the subregion or region for adequate supplies of fish, and coastal states that can claim no EEZs of their own.[79]

Under Article 62(2) coastal states are to determine their capacity to harvest the living resources of the EEZ, and where they do not have the capacity to harvest the entire allowable catch of a fishery, are to give other states access to the surplus. In so doing they are to have particular regard to LLGDS, especially the developing states among them. LLGDS are given the right by Articles 69(1) and 70(1) respectively to participate on an equitable basis in the exploitation of an appropriate fraction of the surplus of the living resources of the EEZ of coastal states of the same region or subregion, taking into account relevant economic and geographical circumstances. The use of the terms 'equitable' and 'appropriate' rather than any kind of objective criteria suggests that considerable discretion lies with coastal states in determining the extent of access that LLGDS will have.[80] This conclusion is reinforced by the fact that the coastal state decisions on what access, if any, is to be given to LLGDS is not subject to challenge via the LOSC dispute settlement system in Part XV.[81] Hence, as Oxman has observed, what is granted to LLGDS 'amounts to little more than an

---

[76] Ibrahim J Wani, 'An Evaluation of the Convention on the Law of the Sea from the Perspective of the Land-locked States' (1981–82) 22 *Virginia Journal of International Law* 627, 647.

[77] DJ Attard, *The Exclusive Economic Zone in International Law* (Oxford, Clarendon Press, 1987) 192.

[78] Vasciannie, *Land-Locked and Geographically Disadvantaged States* (n 7) 65; Robert L Friedheim, *Negotiating the New Ocean Regime* (Columbia, South Carolina, University of South Carolina Press, 1993) 162.

[79] LOSC, art 70(2).

[80] Deborah Cass, 'The Quiet Revolution: The Development of the Exclusive Economic Zone and Implications for Foreign Fishing Access in the Pacific' (1987–88) 16 *Melbourne University Law Review* 83, 93.

[81] LOSC, art 297(3)(a).

apparent priority over third states with regard to agreed access to an undetermined part of a surplus of changing size calculated by the coastal state'.[82]

The modalities for such participation are to be given effect by bilateral, subregional or regional agreements taking into account, among other things, the need to avoid damaging the fishing communities and fishing industries of the coastal state, the extent to which the LLGDS are participating under existing agreements in the exploitation of living resources of the EEZs of other coastal states, the extent to which other LLGDS are participating in the exploitation of the living resources of the EEZ of the coastal state, and the nutritional needs of the respective states.[83] Developed LLGDS are entitled to participate in the exploitation of living resources only in the EEZs of developed coastal states of the same region or sub-region.[84] The upshot of these provisions is similar to the transit provisions which couple a right with a requirement for further negotiations. Hence LLGDS have a legitimate claim to be able to exploit the surplus, but the modalities for so doing must be elaborated on the basis of regional, subregional or bilateral agreement in a way that is satisfactory to the coastal state.[85] If instead of a surplus the coastal state is fully exploiting the entire allowable catch in its EEZ, then it is to cooperate with other states in establishing equitable arrangements to allow for the participation of developing LLGDS in the same region or subregion in the exploitation of the living resources taking into account the factors identified above in relation to access to the surplus.[86] While the rights accorded under Articles 69 and 70 are limited, they are designed to assist developing LLGDS, which are placed in a position of priority over other states in terms of access to surplus EEZ fisheries, and which retain access even where there is no surplus.[87] In practice, however, there are few instances where such access has been sought or granted, and few states have made reference to access for LLGDS in their fisheries or generic EEZ legislation. The 1991 Regional Convention on Fisheries Cooperation Among African States Bordering the Atlantic Ocean is an example of the type of regional agreement envisaged by the LOSC. Article 16 reaffirms the 'solidarity' of the parties with landlocked African states and geographically disadvantaged states of the region, and commits to 'active cooperation with them'. However, notwithstanding the Convention being open to states within the region, no landlocked African states have elected to join the Convention.

The Part V regime includes several safeguards in relation to access for LLGDS to EEZ fisheries. Article 71 provides that Articles 69 and 70 do not apply to coastal states whose economy is overwhelmingly dependent on the exploitation of the living resources of the EEZ. In addition, the rights that exist are exclusively for the benefit of the relevant LLGDS— the rights are not to be directly or indirectly transferred to third states or their nationals through any arrangement such as leases, licences or joint ventures.[88]

---

[82] Bernard H Oxman, 'Human Rights and the United Nations Convention on the Law of the Sea' (1998) 36 *Columbia Journal of Transnational Law* 399, 413.

[83] LOSC, arts 69(2), 70(3).

[84] Ibid arts 69(4), 70(5).

[85] WT Burke, 'The Law of the Sea Convention Provisions on Conditions on Access to Fisheries Subject to National Jurisdiction' (1984) 63 *Oregon Law Review* 73, 100.

[86] LOSC, arts 69(3), 70(4).

[87] Attard, *The Exclusive Economic Zone in International Law* (n 77) 201.

[88] LOSC, art 72(1).

B. Living Resources of the High Seas

In guaranteeing the rights of LLGDS to the freedom of the high seas, Article 87 of the LOSC specifically safeguards the freedom of fishing, subject to the general conditions applicable to all states in relation to the conservation and management of high seas living resources. In essence, therefore, LLGDS have the same high seas freedoms as any other state, a guarantee that was included prior to the LOSC in Article 2 of the 1958 Convention on the High Seas.

C. Mineral Resources of the Area

Part XI of the LOSC declares that the international seabed, and the resources found within it, constitute the common heritage of humankind.[89] Activities in the Area are to be carried out for the benefit of humankind as a whole 'irrespective of the geographical location of States, whether coastal or land-locked'.[90] In addition, effective participation by developing states in the Area is to be promoted, having regard 'in particular to the special need of the land-locked and geographically disadvantaged among them to overcome obstacles arising from their disadvantaged location'.[91]

While emphasising that LLGDS are not to be placed in an unfavourable position, Part XI of the LOSC, and the 1994 Agreement[92] which amended its operation, do not grant any specific or preferential resource rights, despite the difficulties most are likely to face in exploring and exploiting the resources of the Area. Hence LLGDS do not have any priority in terms of the distribution of the financial and other economic benefits derived from resource exploitation in the area. Instead, Part XI is geared towards developing states generally, for which particular consideration must be given.[93] Hence the only safeguards of practical importance are essentially procedural in nature. For instance elections to the Council, the 36 member executive body of ISA, are to ensure that 'land-locked and geographically disadvantaged States are represented to a degree which is reasonably proportionate to their representation in the Assembly'.[94] And more specifically there is to be a 'chamber' within the Council of six members representing developing states with special interests such as having the status of a LLGDS.[95]

D. Marine Scientific Research and Transfer of Marine Technology

All states have the right to conduct marine scientific research subject to the relevant provisions of the LOSC.[96] When it comes to marine scientific research on the high seas LLGDS are in the same position as any other state, as provided for in Article 87(1)(f). There is, however,

---

[89] Ibid art 136. See ch 6.
[90] Ibid art 140(1).
[91] Ibid art 148.
[92] 1994 Agreement Relating to the Implementation of Part XI, *Basic Documents* No 37.
[93] LOSC, art 160(2)(f)(i).
[94] Ibid art 161(2)(a).
[95] 1994 Agreement, annex, s 3(15)(d).
[96] LOSC, art 238.

special provision made for LLGDS when marine scientific research is being undertaken in the EEZ of a neighbouring coastal state. In such a case, the state or international organisation conducting the proposed research is to give notice to the neighbouring LLGDS of the proposed research project.[97] If consent is given by the coastal state to the research, then information about the project is to be provided to the neighbouring LLGDS,[98] and they shall be given the opportunity to participate in the project,[99] and given access to an assessment of the data, samples and research results.[100]

Related to the issue of marine scientific research is that of marine technology. Under Article 266(2) states are to cooperate in actively promoting the development and transfer of marine science and marine technology on fair and reasonable terms and conditions. States are to pay particular regard to developing the marine scientific and technological capacity of those states that need and request assistance 'particularly developing States, including land-locked and geographically disadvantaged States' in relation to maritime matters including exploiting marine resources, and marine scientific research.[101] The aim of this capacity building is 'accelerating the social and economic development of the developing States'.[102]

V. Further Reading

J Symonides, 'Geographically Disadvantaged States in the 1982 Convention on the Law of the Sea' (1988) 208 *Recueil des Cours* 283

Helmut Tuerk, 'Landlocked and Geographically Disadvantaged States' in Donald R Rothwell, Alex G Oude Elferink, Karen N Scott and Tim Stephens (eds), *The Oxford Handbook of the Law of the Sea* (Oxford, Oxford University Press, 2015) 325

Koshor Uprety, *The Transit Regime for Landlocked States* (Washington DC, World Bank, 2006)

SC Vasciannie, *Land-Locked and Geographically Disadvantaged States in the International Law of the Sea* (Oxford, Clarendon Press, 1990)

---

[97] Ibid art 254(1).
[98] Ibid art 254(2).
[99] Ibid art 254(3).
[100] Ibid arts 254(4), 249(1)(d).
[101] Ibid art 266(2).
[102] Ibid art 266(3).

10

Navigational Rights and Freedoms

I. Freedom of the Seas and Navigational Rights and Freedoms

A. Traditional Interests

The international law of the sea was principally founded on the freedom of the seas, a doctrine that has been critical to the recognition of navigational rights and freedoms in the law of the sea and which has continuing relevance in the twenty-first century. The predominant basis for the recognition of the freedom of the seas has been, and remains, the freedom of trade and commerce across the oceans. There is abundant evidence of trade across the oceans throughout recorded history, with some historians asserting evidence of trade between India and Babylon as early as 3000 BC.[1] This trade continued to build throughout the centuries, particularly in the Mediterranean where the Aegean island of Rhodes became an important crossroads for maritime traffic, which in turn resulted in the first maritime codes that became the foundation for contemporary maritime law. As observed by Anand, Rhodes 'believed in the practice of the freedom of the seas'[2] and this proved to be influential in subsequent practice and doctrine.

These practices, however, were not clearly reflected in any law at the time and accordingly during the later part of the Middle Ages, when the first maritime claims began to be asserted, the foundation for the pivotal debate on the future of the law of the sea was laid. The Grotian view of the freedom of the sea was reflected in his 1608 work, *De Mare Liberum*.[3] Notwithstanding the counter-arguments put forward by Selden[4] and other publicists such as Welwood,[5] the freedom of the seas prevailed and continued to have dominance over the law of the sea into the twentieth century. With the seas open for all to enjoy, the freedom to navigate across the world's oceans and seas permitted trade and commerce

---

[1] RP Anand, *Origin and Development of the Law of the Sea* (The Hague, Martinus Nijhoff, 1983) 10; cf Wolfgang Graf Vitzthum, 'From the Rhodian Sea Law to UNCLOS III' (2003) 17 *Ocean Yearbook* 56, 57.

[2] Anand, *Origin and Development*, ibid 11.

[3] Hugo Grotius, *The Freedom of the Seas or the Right which Belongs to the Dutch to Take Part in the East Indian Trade* (New York, Oxford University Press, 1916 rep).

[4] John Selden, *Mare Clausum: The Right and Dominion of the Sea* (London, Andrew Kembe and Edward Thomas, 1663).

[5] William Welwood, *An Abridgment of all Sea Lawes* (Amsterdam, Theatrum Orbis Terrarum, 1972 rep).

to flourish during an era in which European colonial powers developed a significant maritime capability often backed by formidable naval power. When this was combined with some of the technological breakthroughs which occurred during the Industrial Revolution in the nineteenth century, the oceans became the main highway for international trade and commerce between the continents and were vital for opening up new markets, especially in the Americas.

Any limits upon navigational rights and freedoms were therefore strongly resisted because of the constraints they placed upon imperial objectives and their possible commercial ramifications. However, the push for recognition of a territorial sea gained sufficient momentum that towards the end of the nineteenth and certainly by the early part of the twentieth century it was becoming more acceptable for coastal states to assert some form of narrow claim to a territorial sea. It was always recognised, however, that any right to claim a territorial sea needed to be countered by the continuing recognition of the freedom of navigation. The reconciliation between the views of coastal states seeking to claim a territorial sea, and the views of maritime states, which wished to ensure the maintenance of navigational freedoms became one of the pivotal relationships within the then emerging law of the sea which to this day is integral to the operation of the international law of the sea.

B. Contemporary Interests

A feature then of the modern law of the sea as it has evolved through the 1958 Geneva Conventions, the LOSC and state practice into the twenty-first century, has been a capacity to balance the rights and interests of coastal states with those of maritime states. Initially, when the territorial sea was developed the interests of coastal states were conceived in terms of national security and the limited assertion of state sovereignty over a narrow band of adjacent waters. However, those interests have now expanded to include concerns over the marine environment; the sustainable use of marine living resources; threats posed by non-state actors such as terrorist groups; and the management of ocean space extending from the territorial sea out through adjacent maritime zones to the edge of the continental shelf. Accordingly, whilst the LOSC sought to ensure a careful balance between the interests of coastal states and maritime states in the innocent passage regime through the territorial sea, as the concerns of coastal states over the security of the territorial sea expand, so too does the potential for increased interference with innocent passage.[6] Concerns which have arisen in the past for some coastal states over innocent passage by foreign warships[7] have in recent decades been extended to include vessels that are deemed to constitute an unacceptable environmental risk.[8] Such issues, however, do not end at the limits of the territorial sea, and

---

[6] See the discussion in Sam Bateman, Donald R Rothwell and David VanderZwaag, 'Navigational Rights and Freedoms in the New Millennium: Dealing with 20th Century Controversies and 21st Century Challenges' in Donald R Rothwell and Sam Batemen (eds), *Navigational Rights and Freedoms and the New Law of the Sea* (The Hague, Martinus Nijhoff, 2000) 314, 317–18.

[7] See Zou Keyuan, 'Innocent Passage for Warships: The Chinese Doctrine and Practice' (1998) 29 *Ocean Development and International Law* 195–223.

[8] Jon M Van Dyke, 'Sea Shipment of Japanese Plutonium under International Law' (1993) 24 *Ocean Development and International Law* 399–430.

one of the contemporary challenges of the current law is ensuring that there are reasonable limits to coastal state regulation of an expanding array of activities within the adjoining EEZ. Whilst some of these initiatives, including the creation of maritime identification zones, may be considered benign or consistent with coastal states rights created under a loose amalgam of United Nations Security Council resolutions and new conventional law dealing with maritime security, the impact of these measures upon the traditional freedom of the seas beyond the limits of the territorial sea needs to be carefully considered.[9]

The ICJ summed up the process of balancing these various rights and interests in the *Nicaragua* case in 1986, just four years after the conclusion of the LOSC. The Court observed that:

> Since freedom of navigation is guaranteed, first in the exclusive economic zones which may exist beyond territorial waters (Art 58 of the Convention), and secondly, beyond territorial waters and on the high seas (Art 87), it follows that any State which enjoys a right of access to ports for its ships also enjoys all of the freedom necessary for maritime navigation.[10]

This statement encapsulates some of the key principles upon which this body of the international law of the sea is based and which continues to have an impact.

The discussion below will track the development within the modern international law of the sea of navigational rights and freedoms with particular focus upon the territorial sea, EEZ and high seas. The particular issues arising in regard to navigational rights and freedoms within international straits and archipelagic waters are discussed elsewhere.[11]

II. Customary International Law Prior to UNCLOS I

A. Early State Practice

Whilst the freedom of the seas ensured the ongoing right of navigation on the high seas, it is not possible to identify clearly the historical development of a right of passage through the territorial sea. Unlike the assertion of a right to the territorial sea made by the claim of a coastal state, the assertion of a right of passage had to be made by a foreign vessel for it to have significance in terms of the development of state practice. In this respect, the status of the vessel was significant: merchant ships would have been more likely to be granted a right of passage, whereas warships were treated with great caution and often completely barred. Principles of reciprocity were also significant, especially if trade was to flourish. A further

---

[9] See, eg, the Australian Maritime Identification System (AMIS), in which vessels up to 1,000 nm or 48 hours steaming from the Australian coastline would be subject to a request for advanced arrival information, which would increase when the vessel was 500 nm or 24 hours steaming from the coast, until such time as the vessel actually entered the Australian EEZ; Commonwealth of Australia, Department of Transport and Regional Services, *Strengthening Australia's Offshore Maritime Security* (Industry Briefing Paper, February 2005); and discussion in Natalie Klein, 'Legal Implications of Australia's Maritime Identification System' (2006) 55 *International and Comparative Law Quarterly* 337, 338–39.

[10] *Military and Paramilitary Activities in and Against Nicaragua (Nicaragua v United States)* (merits) [1986] ICJ Rep 14, [214].

[11] See ch 11.

point of distinction existed in the case of vessels seeking to pass through the territorial sea en route to a port, or seeking passage through the waters of a strait enclosed within territorial sea limits.

O'Connell claims that a right of passage was an element in the law of the Roman Empire,[12] but it is clear that the publicists took variable views prior to the nineteenth century.[13] The modern law of innocent passage through the territorial sea eventually began to take shape throughout the nineteenth century, partly driven by changes in technology which allowed steamships to navigate by the most direct routes and therefore through the territorial sea.[14] It is possible during this time to find references to rights of passage not only in state practice,[15] but also in the decisions of municipal courts. Two English decisions of the time are of particular importance.[16] In 1801 in *The Twee Gebroeders*, Lord Stowell asserted that 'the act of inoffensively passing over such parts of water, without any violence committed there, is not considered as any violation of territory belonging to a neutral state—permission is not usually required'.[17] Later, in *R v Keyn* in 1876, the English courts reaffirmed the right of passage by foreign vessels within English territorial waters.[18]

With the efforts in the early part of the twentieth century to codify the emerging law of the sea, there appeared for the first time a much clearer articulation of the status of the right of passage through the territorial sea.[19] Jessup, writing in 1927, firmly asserted that: 'As a general principle, the right of innocent passage requires no supporting argument or citation of authority; it is firmly established in international law';[20] though he did concede that there existed divergent opinion on the rights of passage of warships and the extent of the authority coastal states could exercise over passing vessels. In 1930, de Bustamante Sirven, writing immediately prior to the Hague Codification conference, observed that whilst there was general agreement in state practice as to the existence of a right of passage through the territorial sea, the title accorded that passage and the content of the right varied. It was noted that various expert bodies of international law and scholars had referred to a right of 'inoffensive passage', 'free passage', 'innocuous passage', and 'innocent passage'.[21]

---

[12] DP O'Connell, *The International Law of the Sea*, vol 1 (Oxford, Clarendon Press, 1982) 260.

[13] Francis Ngantcha, *The Right of Innocent Passage and the Evolution of the International Law of the Sea* (London, Pinter, 1990) 38.

[14] O'Connell, *The International Law of the Sea* (n 12) vol 1, 260.

[15] See John Bassett Moore, *A Digest of International Law*, vol 1 (Washington, Government Printing Office, 1906) 720–21 recording an 1886 Opinion of the US Secretary of State, Mr Bayard, that in reference to a US claim to territorial waters the US did not 'deny the free right of vessels of other nations to pass, on peaceful errands, through this zone, provided they do not by loitering produce uneasiness on the shore or raise a suspicion of smuggling'.

[16] As noted by Ngantcha, 'as a major maritime nation, and, as such, a torch-bearer for rules governing the seas, British conduct may best reflect 'customary' practice in this issue': Ngantcha, *The Right of Innocent Passage* (n 13) 39.

[17] *Twee Gebroeders* 165 ER 485, 491.

[18] *R v Keyn* (1876) 2 Ex D 63, a case which provoked exhaustive and ongoing commentary because of issues which arose as to the extraterritorial application of certain English laws; see O'Connell, *The International Law of the Sea* (n 12) vol 1, 263–65.

[19] See 1921 Barcelona Convention and Statute on Freedom of Transit, art 2 of which provided: 'In order to ensure the application of the provisions of this Article, Contracting States will allow transit in accordance with the customary conditions and reserves across their territorial waters'; and 1936 Convention Regarding the Status of Straits (Montreux Convention), *Basic Documents* No 3, art 1 which in referring to navigation through the Straits of the Dardanelles (commonly referred to as the Black Sea straits) noted the 'principle of freedom of transit and navigation by sea in the Straits'.

[20] Philip C Jessup, *The Law of Territorial Waters and Maritime Jurisdiction* (New York, Jennings, 1927) 120.

[21] Antonio de Bustamante Sirven, *The Territorial Sea* (New York, Oxford University Press, 1930) 113–15.

These divergent views were perpetuated at the Hague Conference,[22] where there was disagreement not only with respect to the title associated with territorial sea passage but also the content of the right.

B. The *Corfu Channel* Case

In light of this variable state practice, the 1949 *Corfu Channel* case between the United Kingdom and Albania in the ICJ[23] presented an opportunity for the Court to consider significant law of the sea issues with respect to navigation and the right of innocent passage. The Corfu Channel is a strait within the Albanian territorial sea and in October 1946 two British warships sustained damage from mines that had been laid in the waters of the channel, resulting in death and injury to British personnel. No notification had been given of the presence of the mines and the potential danger they posed to navigation through the waters of the strait. In response to this incident in November 1946 the British Royal Navy undertook a minesweeping operation in the Albanian waters of the Corfu Channel in order to clear any remaining mines, an operation conducted against the wishes of the Albanian government. In determining the claims and counter-claims of Britain and Albania the ICJ therefore had a number of matters to consider, including important principles of international law relating to state responsibility for the damage to the British warships. Of particular significance, however, was the regime of innocent passage, how warships could exercise the right of innocent passage,[24] and the status of the Corfu Channel.

Whilst the United Kingdom and Albania took differing positions with respect to the rights of warships to enjoy innocent passage,[25] the ICJ was firm in its finding, concluding that:

> It is, in the opinion of the Court, generally recognized and in accordance with international custom that States in time of peace have a right to send their warships through straits used for international navigation between two parts of the high seas without the previous authorization of a coastal State, provided that the passage is *innocent*.[26]

This conclusion is significant in that it was the first time that an international court had clearly articulated the existence of a right of innocent passage, although the ICJ did make clear that its finding was limited to a strait, and given that the matter involved warships, some caution needs to be exercised in stating a rule of general application with respect to innocent passage more generally within the territorial sea.[27]

The ICJ was, however, more explicit when it came to assessing what constituted innocent passage, and here its observations have more general application in reflecting the then position under customary international law. Albania had contended that the October 1946

---

[22] O'Connell, *The International Law of the Sea* (n 12) vol 1, 266–67.

[23] *Corfu Channel (United Kingdom v Albania)* [1949] ICJ Rep 4.

[24] The innocent passage of warships had been a matter of great sensitivity in the first half of the twentieth century and there was extensive and variable state practice during World War I and II and between the wars: O'Connell, *The International Law of the Sea* (n 12) vol 1, 274–83.

[25] Prior to the events in October and November 1946, two British cruisers had been fired upon by an Albanian battery in May 1946 during which time Britain had stated that 'innocent passage through straits is a right recognized by international law': *Corfu Channel (United Kingdom v Albania)* [1949] ICJ Rep 4, 27.

[26] Ibid 28 (emphasis in original).

[27] See O'Connell, *The International Law of the Sea* (n 12) vol 1, 286–87.

passage was not innocent because of the manner in which the British ships were manoeuvring, the positioning of their guns, and that the crews were at action stations, and it was not contested by the United Kingdom that the purpose of the passage in addition to navigation through the waters of the strait was to also test Albania's attitude.[28] On this point the ICJ observed that the United Kingdom was 'not bound to abstain from exercising its right of passage, which the Albanian Government had illegally denied',[29] and that the manner in which the passage was conducted was consistent with the principles of innocent passage.[30] As to the later minesweeping operation, the United Kingdom did not seek to justify this action as an exercise of the right of innocent passage and the Court accepted that position, ultimately finding Albanian sovereignty had been violated as a result of the minesweeping operation.[31] This decision, coming on the cusp of the International Law Commission's consideration of the law of the sea during the course of the 1950s, had ongoing significance.

III. UNCLOS I and the Geneva Conventions

A. The Work of the International Law Commission

The International Law Commission, tasked with codifying and progressively developing the international law of the sea, first began a serious assessment of the regime of navigation, including through the territorial sea and straits, when it convened in 1952 to consider the first report of Special Rapporteur, Mr JPA François. This work was strongly influenced by the deliberations at the 1930 Hague Conference and the *Corfu Channel* case, with particular care being taken to ensure that the recommendations being put forward were consistent with that judgment.[32] Heavily relying upon draft articles agreed to at the Hague Conference, the work of the Commission progressed satisfactorily between 1953 and 1955, with ready agreement on the existence of a right of innocent passage, the need to account for the situation in straits, and also the distinctive issues raised by warships. At the eighth ILC session in 1956, an effort was made to take into account the views of states which had commented upon draft articles. Some particular issues raised by Turkey with respect to conformity of the draft articles with the 1936 Montreux Convention Regarding the Regime of Straits were considered, as was the need to distinguish the application of the articles in times of peace from war time. However, few substantive changes were made to the draft articles.[33]

The 1956 ILC Articles Concerning the Law of the Sea with Commentaries[34] were adopted at the conclusion of the eighth session of the Commission, and formed the basis

---

[28]   *Corfu Channel (United Kingdom v Albania)* [1949] ICJ Rep 4, 30.

[29]   Ibid.

[30]   The ICJ gave some weight in its judgment to the actual positioning of the guns on the warship, noting that they were in the 'normal position': ibid 31.

[31]   Ibid 36.

[32]   See comments at the 6th Session in 1954, by Mr Lauterpacht (later Sir Hersch Lauterpacht): (1954) *Yearbook of the International Law Commission*, vol 1, 112, [62].

[33]   See (1956) *Yearbook of the International Law Commission*, vol 1, 199–216.

[34]   International Law Commission 'Articles Concerning the Law of the Sea with Commentaries' (1956) *Yearbook of the International Law Commission*, vol 2, 265–301.

for the negotiations which took place at Geneva during UNCLOS I. The provisions dealing with innocent passage were found in Section III, which in turn were divided into four sub-sections dealing with General Rules, Merchant Ships, Government Ships other then Merchant Ships, and Warships. The ILC made clear that these provisions only applied during times of peace and that they did not affect rights and obligations under the UN Charter.[35] Article 15 stated the core proposition that the ships of all states enjoyed a right of innocent passage which included the act of passing through the territorial sea, or of proceeding to or from internal waters. It included the act of stopping or anchoring, if incidental to navigation or arising from *force majeure* or distress. Passage was to be considered innocent 'so long as a ship does not use the territorial sea for committing any acts prejudicial to the security of the coastal state'. The ILC Commentary on this point referred to 'hovering ships', that is foreign ships lingering in the territorial sea for the express purpose of defeating import and export controls, as an example of an activity that could not be regarded as innocent. Coastal states had duties not to hamper innocent passage and to give due publicity to dangers to navigation,[36] whilst the coastal state could also take 'necessary steps' within the territorial sea to protect itself against acts prejudicial to its security.[37] Foreign ships engaging in innocent passage were required to comply with laws and regulations enacted by the coastal state, in particular those dealing with transport and navigation.[38] With respect to the particular provisions applicable to certain types of ships, it was made clear that no charges could be levied against foreign ships only because of their passage through the territorial sea, although an exception was made for charges levied for specific services.[39] Government ships operated for commercial purposes enjoyed all of these rights,[40] but government ships operated for non-commercial purposes did not enjoy the exemption from charges.[41] Finally, the passage of warships through the territorial sea could be made subject to prior authorisation; although there was a presumption in favour of the granting of a right of innocent passage.[42] In a related provision, submarines were required to navigate on the surface whilst exercising innocent passage.[43]

With respect to the freedom of navigation on the high seas, a matter that had been the subject of little debate during the ILC's deliberations, the ILC Articles made clear that the freedom of the high seas encompassed the freedom of navigation.[44] This was supplemented by a right of navigation by all states to sail ships under their flag on the high seas.[45]

[35] Ibid 272.
[36] Ibid art 16; this is an issue that arose during the ICJ's deliberations in the *Corfu Channel* case with respect to Albania's obligations to warn of the dangers posed by the mines in the channel: *Corfu Channel (United Kingdom v Albania)* [1949] ICJ Rep 4, 22.
[37] International Law Commission 'Articles Concerning the Law of the Sea with Commentaries' (n 34) art 17.
[38] Ibid art 18; the ILC Commentary at 274 referred to five examples of laws and regulations that may be applicable in this instance, including the safety of traffic, protection of the waters of the coastal state from pollution, and the conservation of living resources.
[39] Ibid art 19.
[40] Ibid art 22.
[41] Ibid art 23.
[42] Ibid art 24.
[43] Ibid art 15(5).
[44] Ibid art 27.
[45] Ibid art 28.

B. UNCLOS I

The ILC Articles were subject to extensive discussion at UNCLOS I. The First Committee considered Articles 15 to 25, which eventually formed the basis for the provisions dealing with navigation embodied within the Convention on the Territorial Sea and Contiguous Zone.[46] Amendments and adjustments to the text were suggested by 26 states during the course of deliberations, prior to a final text being presented to the Plenary of the Conference for adoption. Bowett argued that part of the conflict which existed at UNCLOS I was between states seeking a narrow territorial sea and those seeking fishery resource rights within a broader territorial sea, and that at times navigation within the territorial sea, which was a different and distinctive right, became confused within the broader debate over the breadth or existence of maritime zones.[47]

The Convention on the Territorial Sea and Contiguous Zone addressed the issue of navigation through the territorial sea in Section III, Articles 14 to 23 and follows the same structure as the ILC had recommended in terms of first addressing the rules applicable to all ships, then merchant ships, government ships other than warships, and finally warships. All of the principal provisions found in the Draft Articles were retained, subject to some minor adjustments and additions. In Article 14(4) of the Convention, the right of passage was deemed to be innocent 'so long as it is not prejudicial to the peace, good order and security of the coastal State', which differed from the ILC draft which focussed upon the ship using the territorial sea for the purposes of committing acts prejudicial to coastal state security. Specific reference was made to fishing vessels in a newly inserted Article 14(5), providing that their passage would not be innocent if they failed to observe laws preventing fishing in the territorial sea. The right of the coastal state to suspend innocent passage temporarily was retained in the Convention, although now limited in Article 16(3) by a requirement that there be no discrimination against foreign ships. The most significant adjustment which was made at Geneva, however, related to the rights of passage of warships. Removed from the text was the ILC's Draft Article 24, whilst Draft Article 25 was retained in modified form as Article 23 of the Convention resulting in a presumption that warships enjoyed a right of passage which could be curtailed by a request from the coastal state to leave the territorial sea if there was a failure to comply with coastal state regulations concerning passage.[48] Nevertheless, this was an important modification to the text as the result was that the Convention did not contemplate prior authorisation or notification in the case of passage by warships. On this point then, the Convention sought to uphold what for maritime states was a crucial navigational right. Likewise, UNCLOS I did not consider it necessary to develop a more extensive regime for international straits than what was eventually provided for in Article 16(4), in which the Convention made it clear that there was to be no suspension of innocent passage by foreign ships through straits. This reflected not only the ICJ's judgment in *Corfu Channel*, but also the fact that at that time very few international straits were the subject of overlapping territorial sea claims. Because of the narrow width of most territorial sea claims there often existed a high seas corridor within many international straits through which shipping could pass.

---

[46] *Basic Documents* No 9.
[47] DW Bowett, *The Law of the Sea* (Manchester, Manchester University Press, 1967) 6–7.
[48] See discussion in O'Connell, *The International Law of the Sea* (n 12) vol 1, 288–92.

With respect to high seas navigation, the relevant ILC Draft Articles were taken up within the Convention on the High Seas,[49] which in Article 2 made clear that the freedom of the high seas comprised, among other rights, the freedom of navigation. Importantly, some constraint was placed upon what could have been interpreted as an absolute freedom, by Article 2 making clear that the freedoms were to be exercised 'with reasonable regard to the interests of other States in their exercise of the freedom of the high seas'.

IV. UNCLOS III and the LOSC

The major issues before UNCLOS III impacting upon navigational rights and freedoms mainly related to the extension of existing maritime zones and the assertion of new maritime claims. The status of the territorial sea and the confirmation of its outer limit as being 12 nm was a matter of particular sensitivity as it would mean that vessels that previously would have enjoyed high seas freedoms of navigation if sailing within a corridor of between six to 12 nm would now fall within an innocent passage regime of the territorial sea that could from time to time be suspended. Accordingly, consistent with the balancing approach adopted during the LOSC negotiations, any extension of the territorial sea required a countervailing clarification of the precise rights enjoyed by foreign vessels whilst engaged in innocent passage and a more detailed statement of the rights of the coastal state in regulating that shipping. Likewise, any extension of the territorial sea would have a very significant impact upon the regime of straits and result in many straits now falling completely within the limits of a territorial sea and removing high seas corridors that may previously have existed within those waters.[50]

For maritime powers such as the United States, this resulted in an insistence on the development of a new regime specially applying to straits that would replace the innocent passage provisions that had originally applied under the Convention on the Territorial Sea and Contiguous Zone.[51] Proposals promoted by countries such as Indonesia and the Philippines for the recognition of their status as archipelagic states, which resulted in Part IV of the LOSC, also created significant issues for the ongoing recognition of navigational rights and freedoms through waters that in most instances had previously been high seas, and this too required accommodation within the LOSC. Whilst the principle of the freedom of the high seas was not contested at UNCLOS III, the emergence and acceptance of the EEZ as extending beyond the territorial sea to an outer limit of 200 nm had important implications for surface and submarine navigation within waters that were previously high seas. This also required accommodation within the LOSC, though there was never any doubt that core elements of high seas navigational rights would need to be retained within the new EEZ if that regime was to win acceptance at the conference.

Another element of the negotiations was the ongoing impact of the decision at UNCLOS I to remove ILC Draft Article 24 regulating innocent passage by warships, and the push from some states to insert into the new convention text a capacity to bar foreign warship access

---

[49] *Basic Documents* No 10.
[50] Anand, *Origin and Development* (n 1) 206–07.
[51] See discussion in ch 11.

to the territorial sea.[52] In the context of the UNCLOS III negotiations, this was a matter that also actively engaged the NATO and Warsaw Pact blocs, and more generally raised issues as to how the LOSC should address military activities during peacetime.[53] Ultimately UNCLOS III was able to reach a conclusion on all of these matters and what is remarkable is how influential the work of the ILC and the text and regime created by the Convention on the Territorial Sea and Contiguous Zone were upon the innocent passage regime in Part II of the LOSC, and how the Grotian vision of the freedom of the sea continued to prevail with respect to high seas freedom of navigation in both Parts V and VII, dealing with the EEZ and high seas respectively. However, as with much of the contemporary international law of the sea, the LOSC represented a balancing of various rights and interests in addressing navigational rights and freedoms, especially within the territorial sea. The implementation of the Convention and state practice surrounding it has therefore been pivotal in respecting that balancing process.[54]

V. Territorial Sea

Following a similar structure to the Convention on the Territorial Sea and Contiguous Zone, the innocent passage provisions of the LOSC are embedded within Part II of the Convention dealing with the territorial sea, of which Section 3 concerns 'Innocent Passage in the Territorial Sea'. There is likewise a breakdown of these provisions into three subsections addressing the rules applicable to all ships, rules applicable to merchant ships and government ships operated for commercial purposes, and rules applicable to warships and government ships operated for non-commercial purposes.

A. Coastal State Rights in the Territorial Sea

A contemporary assessment of the navigation regime within the territorial sea requires a sound appreciation of the rights and interests that the coastal state has within that area. It is important therefore to recall that LOSC, Article 2 makes clear that the sovereignty of the coastal state extends 'beyond its land territory and internal waters' to the territorial sea and that sovereignty includes both the air space above as well as the bed and subsoil beneath the water column. The sovereignty of the coastal state therefore is as complete as that which pertains in and over the land and internal waters, contingent only in the qualification that it is 'subject to this Convention and to other rules of international law'.[55] Therefore, just as state sovereignty over land may be constrained by the recognition of diplomatic immunity or air services agreements permitting overflight by aircraft on commercial air routes, so can sovereignty over the territorial sea be subject to similar constraints. The most significant of

---

[52] A matter which China strongly promoted, see Jeanette Greenfield, *China's Practice in the Law of the Sea* (Oxford, Clarendon Press, 1992) 199.

[53] See discussion in O'Connell, *The International Law of the Sea*, vol 1 (n 12) 292–93.

[54] Cf ibid 270–271.

[55] LOSC, art 2(3).

these limitations is clearly with respect to the navigational rights of foreign ships within the waters of the territorial sea, but other limitations also exist.[56]

Whilst the innocent passage regime of the LOSC therefore represents a concession on the part of the coastal state towards foreign ships which, in practical terms, results in a diminution of state sovereignty, it may be noted that the right is reciprocal so that coastal states acquire navigational rights in the territorial seas of other states. Finally, the focus of the innocent passage regime vis-à-vis the coastal state is entirely directed towards foreign flagged ships exercising the right of innocent passage. The coastal state, consistent with its sovereignty, is entitled to regulate its own flagged shipping within the waters of the territorial sea, extending to the exercise of both criminal and civil jurisdiction; however, with respect to navigational safety within the territorial sea often uniform laws and regulations will be applied as between domestic and foreign flagged vessels.[57] This is especially significant for small intra-coastal, cross strait and inter-island craft which may operate for commercial purposes, in addition to small in-shore fishing vessels used by both recreational and commercial fishers.

B. The Right of Innocent Passage

The key provisions in the LOSC dealing with the right of innocent passage, and how it is to be exercised, are found in Part II, Section 3, subsection A (with the rules applicable to all ships contained within Articles 17 to 20). Consistent with the historical development of the law of the sea, the right of innocent passage through the territorial sea in Article 17 applies only to the ships of states, whether coastal or landlocked. It does not apply to aircraft, and here a distinction needs to be made with international straits and archipelagic sea lanes where there is recognition of a right of overflight by aircraft.[58] The right of innocent passage is subject to the Convention, which suggests that the right is subject to limitations not only in Part II, Section 3, but also elsewhere in the LOSC.[59] Innocent passage, as a right recognised under both treaty and customary international law, does not depend upon coastal state recognition in domestic law. Nevertheless, some coastal states have addressed the right of innocent passage in their municipal law so as to make clearer the rights of foreign vessels within the territorial sea, and the coastal state's obligations towards those vessels.[60]

---

[56] In many instances, the right of overflight by foreign aircraft on scheduled commercial services will also involve a right of overflight of the territorial sea either on approach to an airport adjacent to the coast or to airports which are further inland. This is a matter which will have been determined under agreed bilateral air services agreements between the relevant states.

[57] This is reflected in the 1972 Convention on the International Regulations for Preventing Collisions at Sea (COLREG), *Basic Documents* No 20, under COLREG pt A, r 1 which makes clear that 'These Rules shall apply to all vessels upon the high seas and in all waters connected therewith navigable by seagoing vessels'. The Regulations then go on to distinguish between the capacity of the coastal state to make special rules for internal waters such as roadsteads and harbours.

[58] See LOSC, art 38 'Right of transit passage' and art 53 'Right of archipelagic sea lanes passage', which provide for a right of transit and overflight by aircraft within the territorial sea of a strait or an archipelagic sea lane within an archipelagic state.

[59] See, eg, LOSC, art 45 'Innocent Passage' within straits used for international navigation, and art 52 'Right of innocent passage' as applicable within Archipelagic States.

[60] J Ashley Roach and Robert W Smith, *United States Responses to Excessive Maritime Claims*, 2nd edn (The Hague, Martinus Nijhoff, 1996) 230–31 identified 34 states which expressly recognised innocent passage under their municipal law.

The physical act of navigation by way of passage through the territorial sea is defined in Article 18, with three types of passage provided for:

1. traversing the territorial sea without entering internal waters or calling at a roadstead or port facility outside of internal waters, in which case the ship is effectively traversing the territorial sea and using it as a maritime highway;
2. proceeding to or from internal waters or after having called at a roadstead or port facility outside internal waters, in which case the ship will have called at either a port or other facility within the coastal state in order to offload or load cargo, disembark or embark passengers, or required bunkering or related shipping services;[61] and
3. stopping or anchoring within the territorial sea when rendered necessary by force majeure or distress to the ship, or to other persons, ships or aircraft in danger of distress,[62] or when incidental to ordinary navigation, which would include the taking onboard of a pilot to assist with navigation within the territorial sea or in order to enter a port.

With the exception of the third type of passage, the activity is to be continuous and expeditious, and accordingly ships undertaking innocent passage should do so with due speed taking into account their capacity and navigational conditions. Therefore, consistent with the history of innocent passage, hovering by a foreign ship is not legitimate passage. Likewise, a foreign-flagged cruise ship which sails within the territorial sea between the coast and adjacent islands to provide its passengers with scenic views would not be engaged in passage.[63] However, the same cruise ship sailing by the most expeditious route through the territorial sea between two ports in the same coastal state would be engaged in passage. Submarines within the territorial sea are required to navigate on the surface and show their flag.[64]

The act of innocent passage is fully expanded upon in Article 19, which builds on the Article 18 definition of passage. Article 19(1) retains the core language of the Convention on the Territorial Sea and Contiguous Zone and states that:

> Passage is innocent so long as it is not prejudicial to the peace, good order or security of the coastal State. Such passage shall take place in conformity with this Convention and other rules of international law.

The right of innocent passage is therefore conditional upon the foreign ship refraining from acts which pose a threat to the adjacent coastal state, adherence to other relevant provisions in the LOSC, and other relevant international laws. Masters of vessels exercising innocent passage therefore need to be conscious of how their actions may be interpreted by the coastal state, whilst also being mindful of any other obligations they have under the Convention and international law more generally.[65] Here an obvious difficulty with the

---

[61] Which the ICJ has described as being part of a 'customary right of innocent passage in territorial waters for the purposes of entering or leaving internal waters': *Military and Paramilitary Activities in and Against Nicaragua (Nicaragua v United States)* (merits) [1986] ICJ Rep 14, [214].

[62] This is consistent with a general duty to render assistance to persons in danger at sea, LOSC, art 98.

[63] Scenic cruising by regularly scheduled cruise ships within the territorial sea of a coastal state is permissible if granted in advance by the coastal state; common examples would be cruises undertaken in the Mediterranean Sea and along the coast of Alaska.

[64] LOSC, art 20.

[65] Relevant rules of the LOSC would include adherence to navigational safety provisions allowing for the coastal State to declare sea lanes, LOSC, art 22; while more general rules of international law would include the COLREG;

definition of innocent passage in Article 19(1) is that it is capable of subjective assessment by the coastal state, possibly resulting in the denial of innocent passage for acts that would otherwise be considered benign and posing no threat to the coastal state. To address this issue, Article 19(2), in distinction to the Convention on the Territorial Sea and Contiguous Zone, provides a non-exhaustive but nonetheless detailed list of actions that would be deemed to be considered prejudicial to the peace, good order and security of the coastal state if engaged in by a foreign ship.[66] This list effectively identifies categories of accepted 'non-innocent' passage.[67] The list includes:

— any threat or use of force against the coastal state, or in violation of international law principles embodied in the UN Charter;[68]
— weapons exercises;
— acts aimed at collecting information to the prejudice of the defence or security of the coastal state;
— acts of propaganda that affect the defence or security of the coastal state;
— the launching, landing or taking on board of any aircraft or military device;
— the loading or unloading of any commodity, currency or person contrary to relevant laws and regulations of the coastal state;
— wilful and serious pollution contrary to the LOSC;[69]
— fishing activities;
— research and survey activities; or
— any act aimed at interfering with communications or other facilities or installations of the coastal state.

In addition, 'any other activity not having a direct bearing on passage'[70] is included as a matter considered prejudicial to the interests of the coastal state. Reference to an 'activity' suggests a positive act by the vessel whilst in passage, rather than an omission.[71] The phrasing here is troubling and potentially open to abuse by a coastal state which deems that an activity of a foreign vessel whilst in passage is not directly related to passage; however, there is little state practice to suggest that this provision has in fact been misused.

Whilst the Article 19(2) list is clearly helpful, some difficulty arises in assessing what test is to be applied in determining whether the actions of a ship are contrary to its provisions.[72] This is especially relevant given the sensitivity associated with the right of innocent passage for some coastal states, and the potential for over-generous interpretations of the

and 1973/78 International Convention for the Prevention of Pollution from Ships, as modified by the Protocol of 1978 Relating Thereto (MARPOL 73/78), *Basic Documents* No 21.

[66] Cf USA–USSR Joint Statement on the Uniform Interpretation of Rules of International Law Governing Innocent Passage, *Basic Documents* No 42, [3] asserting that 'Article 19 of the Convention on 1982 sets out in paragraph 2 an exhaustive list of activities that would render passage not innocent'.

[67] The 1930 Hague Conference draft used the term passage that is 'not innocent': *Virginia Commentaries*, vol 2, 166.

[68] This is effectively a restatement of UN Charter, art 2(4); see also LOSC, art 301; cf *Corfu Channel (United Kingdom v Albania)* [1949] ICJ Rep 4, 30–31 where the ICJ accepted that though the British warships were at action stations whilst passing through the strait this was consistent with innocent passage.

[69] Which needs to be read with LOSC, art 1 and pt XII.

[70] LOSC, art 19(2)(l).

[71] K Hakapää and EJ Molenaar, 'Innocent passage—Past and Present' (1999) 23 *Marine Policy* 131, 132.

[72] William K Agyebeng, 'Theory in Search of Practice: The Right of Innocent Passage in the Territorial Sea' (2006) 39 *Cornell International Law Journal* 371, 382.

Article 19(2) list resulting in questionable limitations being placed upon the freedom of territorial sea navigation. It is possible to envisage a number of scenarios where subjective interpretations by a coastal state could result in denial of innocent passage contrary to the intention of the Convention.[73] In order to address any potential disagreements that may have arisen over the interpretation of Article 19(2), the United States and former Soviet Union in 1989 issued a Joint Statement on the Uniform Interpretation of Rules of International Law Governing Innocent Passage which provided as follows:

> A coastal State which questions whether the particular passage of a ship through its territorial sea is innocent shall inform the ship of the reason why it questions the innocence of the passage, and provide the ship an opportunity to clarify its intentions or correct its conduct in a reasonably short period of time.[74]

Such an approach essentially gives the foreign vessel the benefit of the doubt and, reflecting international comity and the very particular nature of the right of innocent passage within the territory of another state, affords the foreign vessel the opportunity to rectify any potentially delinquent behaviour.[75]

C. Coastal State Rights and Duties Regarding Innocent Passage

i. Prevention of Passage

The LOSC outlines the rights and duties of a coastal state with respect to innocent passage in Articles 24 and 25, building upon equivalent provisions in the Convention on the Territorial Sea and Contiguous Zone.[76] Closely aligned with the Article 19 criteria for determining that a ship was not engaged in innocent passage, Article 25 permits coastal states to take 'the necessary steps' to prevent passage which is not innocent. In the case of ships proceeding to internal waters or a territorial sea port facility, the coastal state is also entitled to take similar measures to prevent a breach of any relevant conditions of admission to those waters or facilities. Article 25 is broadly drafted and gives to the coastal state considerable scope for a variety of responses depending on the circumstances. This could include an exchange of communications requesting a delinquent ship to refrain from certain acts, a request that the ship leave the territorial sea immediately, the positioning of vessels to prevent the ship from continuing its passage, the intervention of state authorities such as a Coast Guard or Maritime Police in order to board the vessel to direct it away from the territorial sea, or subject to threat posed to the coastal state by the delinquent ship the use of armed force.[77] The LOSC is intentionally silent on this issue as ultimately it goes to the question of state

---

[73] For example, art 19(2)(d) prohibits an act of propaganda. However, difficulty would arise in objectively interpreting such an act in the context of passage through the territorial sea; see Donald R Rothwell, 'Coastal State Sovereignty and Innocent Passage: The Voyage of the *Lusitania Expresso*' (1992) 16 *Marine Policy* 427.

[74] USA–USSR Joint Statement on the Uniform Interpretation of Rules of International Law Governing Innocent Passage (n 66) para 4.

[75] See discussion in Vaughan Lowe, 'Uniform Interpretation of the Rules of International Law Governing Innocent Passage' (1991) 6 *International Journal of Estuarine and Coastal Law* 73.

[76] Convention on the Territorial Sea and Contiguous Zone, arts 15, 16.

[77] See for a description of the practice of 'bumping off' delinquent vessels within the territorial sea, JC Hilt Jr, 'Oceans Law and Superpower Relations: The Bumping of the Yorktown and Caron in the Black Sea' (1989) 29 *Virginia Journal of International Law* 713–43.

sovereignty and how a state may choose to protect itself from what may be perceived, or actually is, a threat to the interests of the coastal state. Nevertheless, a permissible response would ultimately depend upon the circumstances and as the International Tribunal for the Law of the Sea observed in *The M/V Saiga (No 2)* case would be subject to general principles of international law such as necessity and proportionality.[78]

A related right of protection for the coastal state, is the capacity to suspend innocent passage temporarily in specific areas of the territorial sea where this is essential for the protection of its security.[79] Such a right of temporary suspension, which expressly extends to allow weapons exercises, may only take effect after having been duly published, thereby preventing ad hoc suspensions of passage.[80] Some states specifically allow for suspension of innocent passage within their national legislation.[81] This right of the coastal state would extend to the capacity to suspend innocent passage in cases of internal unrest requiring police or military operations to quell that unrest.[82] It is also sufficiently broad to deal with military exercises which may be conducted by the coastal state either on its own or in conjunction with military allies requiring the closure of the territorial sea on a temporary basis. What constitutes a 'temporary' closure is undefined in the LOSC, and how that term is interpreted may depend upon the circumstances, including whether the events justifying the closure were anticipated, as would be the case with military exercises; have arisen with little notice; or require an ongoing response.[83] In 1986 the United States had occasion to protest the actions of Sri Lanka which purported to require all vessels, with certain exceptions, to obtain permission prior to entering the territorial sea. Whilst the United States acknowledged the ongoing efforts of Sri Lanka to interdict armed anti-government groups it was asserted that its actions were not consistent with the LOSC. Sri Lanka responded by noting its right to 'the protection of Sri Lanka's security, in the light of the prevailing security situation' which was a temporary measure and not permanent.[84]

ii. Regulation of Passage

An additional right of the coastal state, consistent with its sovereignty over the territorial sea and capacity to adopt and enforce laws and regulations against its own flagged vessels, is

[78] In *M/V Saiga (No 2) (Saint Vincent and the Grenadines v Guinea)* (1999) 120 ILR 143, [155], where ITLOS observed as follows: 'Although the Convention does not contain express provisions on the use of force in the arrest of ships, international law, which is applicable by virtue of article 293 of the Convention, requires that the use of force must be avoided as far as possible and, where force is unavoidable, it must not go beyond what is reasonable and necessary in the circumstances'; see generally IA Shearer, 'Problems of Jurisdiction and Law Enforcement Against Delinquent Vessels' (1986) 35 *International and Comparative Law Quarterly* 320.
[79] LOSC, art 25(3).
[80] See United Nations Division for Ocean Affairs and the Law of the Sea, 'Suspension of Innocent Passage' at www.un.org/Depts/los/convention_agreements/innocent_passages_suspension.htm listing notifications of suspensions of innocent passage within the territorial sea received by the United Nations Secretary General.
[81] Maritime Zone Act 2005 (Mauritius), art 10(4); Law No 28(8) 2003 (Syria), art 13.
[82] Cf exclusion zones which have been declared on security grounds; in May 1990 Papua New Guinea declared a 50 nm exclusion zone around the island of Bougainville, in response to a secession movement on that island, Australia protested this claim and the exclusion zone was revoked: (1992) 13 *Australian Year Book of International Law* 297.
[83] In the case of where internal civil disturbance is taking place, it may be possible to justify suspension of innocent passage for a considerable period of time in order to ensure the safety of foreign vessels within those waters.
[84] J Ashley Roach and Robert W Smith, *Excessive Maritime Claims*, 3rd edn (The Hague, Martinus Nijhoff, 2012) 226–27.

the capacity under Article 21 to adopt laws and regulations relating to innocent passage by foreign flagged vessels. Such laws can extend to a wide array of activities related to passage, including navigational safety and the regulation of maritime traffic, conservation of living resources, preservation of the marine environment including the prevention of pollution, marine scientific research and surveying, and customs, fiscal, immigration and sanitary matters.[85] Foreign ships exercising a right of innocent passage are expected to comply with these coastal state laws.[86] In this respect there are clear correlations between activities considered non-innocent under Article 19 and activities subject to legitimate regulation under Article 21. Two of the most relevant for many vessels are those relating to pollution prevention and those addressing fishing. In addition to an act of wilful and serious pollution constituting non-innocent passage, the coastal state is also able to regulate other forms of pollution within the territorial sea for which foreign vessels may be responsible. Any such laws, however, must be consistent with both the LOSC and other relevant provisions of international law.[87] Likewise, in addition to prohibiting foreign fishing within the territorial sea, the coastal state may legislate to prevent the infringement of fisheries laws and regulations, which may, for example, extend to the stowing of fishing gear while foreign fishing vessels undertake innocent passage.[88]

Closely related to, but distinctive from, the laws and regulations applicable to innocent passage, is the capacity of the coastal state to apply its criminal law to persons aboard ships engaged in innocent passage.[89] Such criminal laws are only applicable when the consequences of the crime extend to the coastal state or disturb the peace and good order of the coastal state; if assistance has been requested by the master of the ship; or if the matter relates to drug trafficking. More limited provisions apply to the application of civil jurisdiction against ships enjoying innocent passage.[90]

iii. Obligation not to Hamper Innocent Passage

The duties of the coastal state with respect to ships undertaking innocent passage are expressed as being not to 'hamper' passage through the territorial sea.[91] This is consistent with the intention of the LOSC to permit the free flow of international maritime traffic through the territorial sea, providing that passage is innocent. Prima facie, therefore, ships exercising the right of innocent passage are not to be denied the right of passage, and whilst undertaking passage are not to be subject to interference. One area of contention has been whether a coastal state may legitimately require that all ships take on board a pilot while navigating through the territorial sea. In the absence of international recognition by a body such as the IMO that the waters of the territorial sea were either particularly hazardous

---

[85] No equivalent list appeared in the Convention on the Territorial Sea and Contiguous Zone, cf (1956) *Yearbook of the International Law Commission*, vol 2, 274.

[86] LOSC, art 21(4).

[87] Erik Jaap Molenaar, *Coastal State Jurisdiction over Vessel-Source Pollution* (The Hague, Kluwer Law International, 1998) 199–240.

[88] Alex Oude Elferink, 'Rules of Navigation of Ships through the Territorial Sea and the Internal Waters of Estonia' (1993) 8 *International Journal of Marine and Coastal Law* 422, 424 referring to Estonian practice.

[89] LOSC, art 27.

[90] Ibid art 28.

[91] Ibid art 24(1).

or particularly sensitive thereby requiring the services of a pilot to ensure safe passage,[92] compulsory pilotage enforced by way of coastal state laws and regulations would be considered to hamper innocent passage.[93]

In order to distinguish between the legitimate application of certain coastal state laws and regulations with the obligation not to hamper passage, laws which have the practical effect of denying or impairing the right of innocent passage, or which discriminate against ships from certain states or which are carrying certain cargoes, are not permissible.[94] A related duty of the coastal state is to publicise dangers to navigation within its territorial sea, of which it has knowledge. No charges may be levied against ships engaged in innocent passage, other than for services rendered to the ship.[95]

iv. Sea Lanes and Traffic Separation Schemes

Related to the interests of the coastal state in ensuring safe navigation within its territorial sea, and its capacity to enact certain laws and regulations, the LOSC confers significant rights upon a coastal state with respect to the designation and regulation of sea lanes within the territorial sea. Article 22(1) permits the coastal state to require foreign ships exercising innocent passage to use designated or prescribed sea lanes or traffic separation schemes (TSS) in order to ensure the safety of navigation. The coastal state does not have a unilateral right to designate sea lanes or a TSS, and shall take into account the 'recommendations' of the accepted competent international organisation, which is recognised as being the IMO. Other factors the coastal state shall take into account, include those channels which have customarily been used for international navigation, the special characteristics of ships and channels, and the density of traffic.[96] Nuclear-powered ships or those which are carrying nuclear or other inherently dangerous or noxious substances may be required to confine their passage to such sea lanes in order to ensure the safety of navigation.[97] There is no requirement that the coastal state designate sea lanes in order to facilitate the safety of navigation, and in their absence the right of innocent passage is still capable of being enjoyed.[98] Generally applicable international rules concerning the safety of navigation at sea found within the COLREG would still be applicable, and all foreign ships within the territorial sea would be expected to comply with those provisions preventing collisions at sea.[99]

---

[92] Michael White, 'Navigational Rights in Sensitive Marine Environments: The Great Barrier Reef' in Donald R Rothwell and Sam Bateman (eds), *Navigational Rights and Freedoms and the New Law of the Sea* (The Hague, Martinus Nijhoff, 2000) 230 discussing compulsory pilotage within the waters of the Great Barrier Reef.

[93] Roach and Smith, *Excessive Maritime Claims* (n 84) 231, referring to United States responses to the practice of Finland and Italy.

[94] Likewise, LOSC, art 21(2) makes clear that laws and regulations of the coastal state relating to design, construction, manning or equipment of foreign ships are only applicable if they reflect generally accepted international rules and standards. See also LOSC, art 227 regarding non-discrimination against foreign vessels in Part XII.

[95] LOSC, art 26. However, this would permit the levying of charges for pilotage services in those parts of the territorial sea where this would be necessary to ensure safe navigation.

[96] Ibid art 22(3).

[97] Ibid art 22(2).

[98] See, eg, USA–USSR Joint Statement on the Uniform Interpretation of Rules of International Law Governing Innocent Passage (n 66) [5].

[99] LOSC, art 21(4).

D. The Rights of Foreign Flagged Vessels

Other than the broad right of innocent passage in Article 17, the LOSC does not provide much detail as to the precise rights of foreign flagged vessels whilst engaged in innocent passage. The broad statement as to what constitutes innocent passage in Article 19 is clearly capable of wide interpretation, and although assisted by the listing of non-innocent acts outlined in Article 19(2), still gives to the coastal state a firm basis upon which to revoke passage if it so determines.[100] The duty of the coastal state not to hamper passage outlined in Article 24 gives foreign vessels some confidence in their capacity to enjoy innocent passage, but the LOSC is silent as to what a foreign vessel can do if its innocent passage rights have been denied or improperly terminated. The gap which exists in the LOSC is an indication of an evidentiary question as to whether a vessel is undertaking non-innocent passage, and in particular whether an objective or subjective standard is applicable. When this issue arose in the *Corfu Channel* case, the ICJ focussed more on the manner in which the passage of the British warships was being conducted than the actual motive of the passage.[101]

E. Warships

Notwithstanding the variable approaches taken towards innocent passage for warships by the ILC and at UNCLOS I and III, the LOSC retains a right of innocent passage for warships in their capacity as 'ships of all States' under Article 17.[102] Nevertheless, Subsection C of Part II, Section 3 contains four articles which specifically apply to some aspects of innocent passage through the territorial sea by warships and other government ships operated for non-commercial purposes.[103] A warship is defined under Article 29 as being a ship belonging to the armed forces of a state, with distinguishing external marks, under the command of a commissioned officer and manned by a crew under regular armed forces discipline.[104] Article 30 then addresses how a coastal state may respond to a warship which is not complying with relevant laws and regulations applicable to innocent passage; potentially one of the most sensitive issues which can arise in the innocent passage regime. A graduated response from the coastal state is envisaged: first requesting compliance with the relevant laws, and secondly requiring the warship to immediately leave the territorial sea if the request is disregarded. Whilst the LOSC is silent as to how full compliance with a request to leave the territorial sea could be achieved, as noted above there are a range of options open to the coastal state consistent with the Convention and international law. Further guidance on

---

[100] Ngantcha emphasises that the coastal State's subjective appraisal of passage as non-innocent should be limited by the objective requirement that any violation which is alleged to have occurred took place while the vessel was in passage; Ngantcha, *The Right of Innocent Passage* (n 13) 51.

[101] *Corfu Channel (United Kingdom v Albania)* [1949] ICJ Rep 4, 30 stating that 'It remains, therefore, to consider whether the manner in which the passage was carried out was consistent with the principle of innocent passage'.

[102] The navigational rights of warships are addressed in more detail in ch 12.

[103] These other ships would include government research and survey vessels, and vessels operated by heads of state.

[104] This definition is broadly consistent with that which applies under international humanitarian law; see Louise Doswald-Beck (ed), *San Remo Manual on International Law Applicable to Armed Conflicts at Sea* (Cambridge, Cambridge University Press, 1995) 9, r 13(g).

state practice in this area is provided by the 1989 United States and Soviet Union Uniform Interpretation of Rules which makes clear that:

> If a warship engages in conduct which violates such law or regulations or renders its passage not innocent and does not take corrective action upon request, the coastal State may require it to leave the territorial sea ... In such case the warship shall do so immediately.[105]

Articles 31 and 32 address questions relating to international responsibility arising from any loss or damage to the coastal state as a result of non-compliance by a warship or other government non-commercial vessel, and the immunities those vessels enjoy under general international law. Therefore, whilst a foreign warship could not be prosecuted for an oil spill within the territorial sea, state responsibility would rest with the flag state for any damage which resulted to the coastal state.

Some states maintain the position that foreign warships are only entitled to enter the territorial sea and undertake innocent passage with permission.[106] This cannot be reconciled with the LOSC. Nevertheless, whilst warships enjoy a right of innocent passage under the LOSC, it is clear from the categories of non-innocent passage listed in Article 19(2) that specific attention is given to some particular issues that may arise from the presence of warships within the territorial sea. In addition to prohibiting their use of force, warships are also prohibited from engaging in weapons exercises, the collection of intelligence aimed at prejudicing the security of the coastal state, and the launching, landing or taking on board of any aircraft or military device. Accordingly, aircraft carriers or warships with helicopter support may not operate those craft whilst undertaking innocent passage.

F. Nuclear Vessels and Vessels Carrying Hazardous Substances

The LOSC directly addresses the issue of nuclear-powered ships and ships carrying nuclear or other 'inherently dangerous or noxious substances' in Article 23. Innocent passage by these vessels is permitted, provided they carry documentation and 'observe special precautionary measures' that may have been adopted by relevant international agreements.[107] Hence it would seem clear that provided these conditions, which in essence require such vessels to comply with recognised international standards, are met, then such vessels enjoy a right of innocent passage.[108] As some warships, including submarines, are both

---

[105] USA–USSR Joint Statement on the Uniform Interpretation of Rules of International Law Governing Innocent Passage (n 66) [7].

[106] See, eg, LOSC Declaration by China (1996) stating that: 'The People's Republic of China reaffirms the provisions of the United Nations Convention on the Law of the Sea concerning innocent passage through the territorial sea shall not prejudice the right of a coastal state to request, in accordance with its laws and regulations, a foreign State to obtain advance approval from or give prior notification to the coastal State of the passage of its warships through the territorial sea of the coastal State'. Note other LOSC Declarations made by Bangladesh (2001), Croatia (1995), Egypt (1983), Iran (1982), Malta (1993), Montenegro (2006), Oman (1983); cf Germany (1994), the Netherlands (1996): United Nations Division for Ocean Affairs and the Law of the Sea (UNDOALOS), 'United Nations Convention on the Law of the Sea: Declarations made upon signature, ratification, accession or succession or anytime thereafter', at www.un.org/Depts/los/convention_agreement/convention_declarations.htm.

[107] This would include SOLAS (Ch VII), MARPOL (Annex II), the International Maritime Dangerous Goods (IMDG) Code, the International Bulk Chemical (IBC) Code, and the International Code for the Construction and Equipment of Ships Carrying Liquefied Gases in Bulk (IGC).

[108] cf LOSC Declarations by Egypt (1983), and Oman (1983) indicating they require prior authorisation of such vessels, see also Malta (1993): UNDOALOS, United Nations Convention on the Law of the Sea: Declarations.

nuclear- powered and nuclear-armed, this provision has particular relevance to the free-dom of navigation of navies. Nevertheless, some states have adopted measures requiring prior authorisation of innocent passage by nuclear-powered ships,[109] and the United States has protested such actions.[110]

Notwithstanding this apparently clear provision in the LOSC, the capacity of coastal states to impair the freedom of navigation of vessels carrying inherently dangerous cargoes has been a matter of debate since the 1990s and some states still insist on such measures.[111] In 1992 the Japanese registered *Akatsuki Maru* was engaged to carry reprocessed pluto-nium from Europe to Japan via the Cape of Good Hope, the Indian Ocean and the Pacific Ocean. Several states in the Asia Pacific denied access by the vessel to their territorial seas due to their concerns over the potential for environmental devastation if this vessel was involved in a maritime incident.[112] Indonesia, Malaysia and Singapore also opposed the passage of the vessel through the Straits of Malacca, thereby effectively closing access to the territorial sea.[113] Despite these protests and closure of some navigation routes, the voyage of the *Akatsuki Maru* was completed, only for similar issues to arise in 1999 when the *Pacific Pintail* and the *Pacific Teal* undertook similar voyages from France to Japan.[114]

G. Vessels in Distress

One dimension of the LOSC that is unclear, and that has implications for the regime of innocent passage, is the status of vessels in distress. This is relevant in a number of con-texts, including the capacity of such vessels to enter internal waters and seek refuge dur-ing inclement weather. In the context of the territorial sea, a vessel in distress may not be one which is able to continue its passage, however allowance is made for this scenario in Article 18(2) and vessels are permitted to stop or anchor as a result of *force majeure* or distress. The issue which arises in this context is who has the capacity to classify whether a ship is truly in distress? In certain circumstances a ship will clearly be in distress such as fol-lowing a maritime incident when damage is visible, or when it is floundering in heavy seas. The case where passengers and crew are in distress is more difficult, and objective determi-nations from ashore will be nearly impossible to make. Accepted practice in these cases is therefore that it is for the Master of the ship to assert a situation of *force majeure* or distress, either directly or through the shipowner or an agent.[115] However, given the immunities applicable to a ship in distress,[116] the Master's declaration of distress should not be irrebut-table and a coastal state should have a right to question dubious claims.

---

[109] Oude Elferink, 'Rules of Navigation of Ships' (n 88) 423 referring to Estonian practice.

[110] Roach and Smith, *Excessive Maritime Claims* (n 84) 254–58.

[111] Maritime Zone Act 2005 (Mauritius), s 10(3); Law No 66-07 2007 (Dominican Republic), art 12.

[112] Van Dyke, 'Sea Shipment of Japanese Plutonium' (n 8) 407–08, indicating that Argentina, Chile, Indonesia and the Philippines asked the vessel to not enter their territorial sea.

[113] Ibid 411.

[114] Duncan EJ Currie and Jon M Van Dyke, 'The Shipment of Ultrahazardous Nuclear Materials in Interna-tional Law' (1999) 8 *RECIEL* 113–24.

[115] Jean-Pierre L Fonteyne, 'All Adrift in a Sea of Illegitimacy: An International Law Perspective on the Tampa Affair' (2001) 12 *Public Law Review* 249, 250.

[116] A ship which enters a port or internal waters under conditions of *force majeure* or distress is not subject to the application of local laws, the British–United States Claims Commission having noted that: 'The reason for this rule is obvious. It would be a manifest injustice to punish foreigners for a breach of certain laws, uninten-tionally committed by them, and by reason of circumstances over which they had no control'; see *The Enterprise*

VI. High Seas

The modern articulation of the freedom of the seas is to be found in Part VII of the LOSC dealing with the high seas. While prima facie these provisions apply to those parts of the sea not included within the territorial sea, the EEZ or the archipelagic waters of an archipelagic state,[117] there is also the capacity for a number of the high seas freedoms to apply within the EEZ to the extent that they are not incompatible with the rights and duties that exist therein.[118] Article 87 sets out the contemporary framework for the freedom of the seas as originally developed by Grotius, and in addition to the freedom of navigation, also extends to the freedom of overflight, the laying of submarine cables and pipelines, construction of artificial islands and installations, fishing, and marine scientific research. Freedom in this context needs to be qualified by an appreciation that several of these activities are subject to extensive regulation in other parts of the LOSC, and in the case of high seas fishing, by other related international instruments. The freedom of navigation is not, however, so qualified other than that it is exercised subject to conditions found in the LOSC and other rules of international law.

The freedom of high seas navigation is open to all states: both coastal and landlocked.[119] This reflects the ongoing position within the law of the sea that the high seas is *res communis* and open for all states to use and enjoy. With respect to landlocked states, Article 87 is consistent with the rights granted to those states in Part X, and especially Article 125 which makes clear that such states 'have the right of access to and from the sea for the purpose of exercising … the freedom of the high seas'. A key term in this context is 'navigation'; which is inexorably linked with the notion of the freedom of the seas. Whilst navigation is not defined in Part II of the LOSC, its context when referred to with respect to innocent passage clearly suggests some act of physical movement through the water, whether on the surface or beneath.[120] Article 90 refers to a 'Right of navigation' but avoids any precise definition as to what the act of navigation is, instead relying upon 'sail' as being a broad enough maritime term to encompass all means of vessel propulsion at sea.[121]

The freedom of high seas navigation is only lightly regulated under the LOSC. Ships are expected to fly a flag reflecting a grant of nationality by a flag state[122] and are subject to the jurisdiction of the flag state whilst on the high seas[123] which may result in the ships being bound to conform with a number of relevant international conventions such as those dealing with SOLAS, collisions (COLREG), and marine pollution (MARPOL). Certain ships enjoy immunity on the high seas, including warships[124] and state vessels on government

---

in JB Moore, *History and Digest of the International Arbitrations in which the United States has been a Party*, vol 4 (Washington, DC, Government Printing Office, 1898) 4349, 4363.

[117] LOSC, art 86.
[118] Ibid arts 58(2), 86.
[119] Ibid art 87(1).
[120] Ibid art 20 stating that 'submarines and other underwater vehicles are required to navigate on the surface'.
[121] The term 'sail' is also referred to in the context of ibid art 92(1) 'Ships shall sail under the flag of one State'; cf the French language version of the LOSC which in art 90 uses the term 'naviguer'.
[122] Ibid arts 91, 92.
[123] Ibid art 94.
[124] Ibid art 95.

non-commercial service.[125] In order to avoid some of the controversy that arose from the *Lotus* case where the PCIJ recognised certain rights by a non-flag state following a high seas collision,[126] Article 97 outlines procedures for penal jurisdiction arising from collisions or other navigational incidents on the high seas.[127] Other than the enforcement-related provisions of the LOSC dealing with the right of visit and hot pursuit,[128] the only other limitations which exist under the LOSC upon the freedom of high seas navigation are those which relate to the transportation of slaves,[129] piracy,[130] drug trafficking[131] and unauthorised high seas broadcasting.[132]

The freedom of high seas navigation has in recent decades come under increasing strain as growing international and regional security concerns have led the international community to take more proactive measures to regulate acts at sea beyond national jurisdiction, but which have the potential to pose a threat to international peace and security. There have been two particular dimensions to these developments. The first has been the increasing role of the United Nations Security Council and resolutions adopted by the Council to have some impact upon high seas freedoms of navigation. This has arisen in the context of Chapter VII resolutions responding to threats to international peace and security of which the proliferation of nuclear materials has been a particular concern. For instance, the Security Council has adopted measures directed towards placing constraints on North Korea's nuclear programme which has also provided a limited capacity to stop and inspect vessels on the high seas suspected of carrying prohibited nuclear materials.[133] Likewise, United Nations Security Council Resolution 1540 (2004) outlined a range of general measures states should take to combat the proliferation of nuclear, chemical and biological weapons. States are called upon to not provide support to non-state actors dealing with these WMD, and to develop appropriate domestic measures to that end. The resolution called upon states to cooperate on non-proliferation issues 'in accordance with their national legal authorities and legislation and consistent with international law, to take cooperative action to prevent illicit trafficking in nuclear, chemical and biological weapons, their means of delivery and related materials'.[134] Security Council Resolution 1540 provides a potential basis for cooperation amongst Members States to stop WMD proliferation at sea, and in reliance upon these measures states have adopted a more proactive stance with respect to high seas interdiction via the United States-led 'Proliferation Security Initiative'.[135]

The second basis for interference with high seas freedoms of navigation can be found in treaty law. The SUA Convention was adopted in response to the terrorist attack upon the Italian cruise ship the *Achille Lauro* in the Mediterranean Sea which resulted in the murder

---

[125] Ibid art 96.
[126] *Lotus (France v Turkey)* [1927] PCIJ Rep ser A no 10; discussed in more detail in ch 7.
[127] See also Convention on the High Seas, art 11.
[128] For detailed discussion see ch 17.
[129] LOSC, art 99.
[130] Ibid arts 100–07.
[131] Ibid art 108.
[132] Ibid art 109.
[133] UN Security Council Resolution 1874 (2009), [12] which: 'Calls upon all Members States to inspect vessels, with the consent of the flag States, on the high seas'.
[134] UN Security Council Resolution 1540 (2004), [10].
[135] See discussion in Craig Allen, *Maritime Counterproliferation Operations and the Rule of Law* (Westport, Conn, Praeger, 2007) 50–52; discussed in more detail in ch 12.

of a passenger.[136] The Convention created a series of offences related to terrorist acts at sea and conferred upon state parties certain rights to interdict vessels on the high seas with flag state consent. These rights have been further expanded in the 2005 SUA Convention,[137] which was modified to take into account further maritime security concerns raised by the New York and Washington terrorist attacks in 2001. Under the 2005 SUA Convention non-flag states have expanded capacities to interdict on the high seas foreign vessels with the consent of the flag state where there are reasonable suspicions that the vessel is improperly transporting WMD or related materials.

These developments over the past decade highlight that even on the high seas the freedoms of navigation are coming under ever increasing controls. They reinforce observations O'Connell made in 1984 that:

> The concept of the freedom of the seas is neither absolute or static: it embodies the balance of jurisdictional functions among States which at any time best serve the community of nations, and its content is subject to constant modification as that community adjusts itself to the solution of new problems.[138]

VII. Exclusive Economic Zone

Whilst the EEZ was developed as a distinctive regime to sit between the territorial sea and high seas with a predominant focus upon coastal state sovereign rights over living and non-living natural resources, there was an immediate appreciation during the UNCLOS III negotiations of the need to make significant allowances for navigational freedoms. If not, then the recognition of this new and very highly significant maritime zone would have been impossible. Accordingly, Part V of the LOSC makes clear that all states, both coastal and landlocked, enjoy similar freedoms within the EEZ as those outlined in Article 87, which includes the freedom of navigation.[139] However, unlike the manner in which navigational freedoms may be capable of exercise on the high seas, within the EEZ another dynamic exists and Article 58(3) notes that in the exercise of their rights 'States shall have due regard to the rights and duties of the coastal state and shall comply with the laws and regulations adopted by the coastal state in accordance with the provisions of this Convention and other rules of international law'. While not strictly necessary, some states have enacted municipal laws which recognise the freedom of navigation of foreign flagged vessels within their EEZ.[140]

In many respects any balancing of the rights and interests of the coastal state within its EEZ and those of other states seeking to navigate within those waters should not be the cause of conflict. The freedom of navigation for foreign vessels does not prima facie include

---

[136] Malvina Halberstam, 'Terrorism on the High Seas: The Achille Lauro, Piracy and the IMO Convention on Maritime Safety' (1988) 82 *AJIL* 269.

[137] *Basic Documents* No 79.

[138] O'Connell, *The International Law of the Sea* (n 12) vol 2 (1984), 797.

[139] LOSC, art 58(1).

[140] China's Law on the Exclusive Economic Zone and the Continental Shelf is an example: Zou Keyuan, 'Navigation of Foreign Vessels within China's Jurisdictional Waters' (2002) 29 *Marine Policy and Management* 351, 364.

a freedom to fish such that there would be a clear incompatibility with coastal state laws and regulations dealing with fishing activities. Likewise, marine scientific research is a separate activity and can be regulated by a coastal state consistent with the LOSC without interference with navigation. If the coastal state were to construct artificial islands and installations, then navigational freedoms would be subject to minor constraints, but of no greater inconvenience than similar structures in the territorial sea. Therefore, in principle, the Part V EEZ rights of a coastal state should not have significant impact upon the freedoms of navigation being exercised by other states. Nevertheless, some coastal states concerned about the transhipment of hazardous cargoes have sought to impose prior notification requirements upon vessels seeking to transit their EEZ. The controversy raised by the voyages of the *Akatsuki Maru* and *Pacific Pintail* also saw some states prohibit the transit of those vessels through their EEZs.[141]

Three freedom of navigation aspects have attracted controversy within the EEZ. The first is the right of transit of fishing vessels across the EEZ. Such vessels enjoys the same rights to freedom of navigation as other vessels, including warships and other merchant ships, however, there has been some sensitivity associated with the navigation of fishing vessels within the EEZ because of the fear that such vessels may use the opportunity to illegally engage in fishing activities.[142] A fishing vessel with its gear stowed and operating in a manner that does not attract suspicion that it is intending engage in fishing, should be permitted to transit the EEZ without interference. However, this would not prevent the coastal state undertaking visual surveillance of the fishing vessel, or requiring it to comply with maritime identification procedures while it is within the EEZ.

The second is the freedom of navigation of military vessels and their ability to undertake certain activities within the EEZ. Whilst the navigation of warships within the EEZ has not been the subject of equivalent concerns to those raised over their passage within the territorial sea, concerns have been expressed over foreign naval vessels undertaking certain military activities within the EEZ. Several Declarations made by states on signing or becoming parties to the LOSC reflect this position.[143] For example, Cape Verde in 1987 indicated that:

> In the exclusive economic zone, the enjoyment of the freedoms of international communication, in conformity with its definition and other relevant provisions of the Convention, excludes any non-peaceful use without the consent of the coastal State, such as exercises with weapons or other activities which may affect the interests of the said state.[144]

These interpretations raise issues as to whether weapons exercises are part of recognised navigational freedoms, or whether they are a distinctive aspect of the customary freedoms of the high seas, in which case the ability to conduct weapons exercises by naval warships would then depend upon an interpretation of Article 58. Some distinctions do, however,

---

[141] Molenaar, *Coastal State Jurisdiction over Vessel-Source Pollution* (n 87) 379–80. See the Netherlands (1996) making clear in its LOSC Declaration that: 'Nothing restricts the freedom of navigation of nuclear-powered ships or ships carrying nuclear or hazardous waste in the [EEZ], provided such navigation is in accordance with the applicable rules of international law': UNDOALOS, United Nations Convention on the Law of the Sea: Declarations.

[142] Roach and Smith, *Excessive Maritime Claims* (n 84) 395–97, referring to United States protests against the actions of Costa Rica requiring prior notification of EEZ transit.

[143] See Brazil (1988), Ecuador (2012), Malaysia (1996), Uruguay (1982); cf Italy (1984): UNDOALOS, United Nations Convention on the Law of the Sea: Declarations.

[144] Ibid.

need to be made between the act of engaging in weapons exercises, and the normal mode of operations of warships which for aircraft carriers would extend to the take-off and landing of aircraft, and underwater navigation in the case of submarines. Such actions would, in those instances, be entirely consistent with normal modes of navigation for such vessels.[145]

The third contentious matter is the freedom of navigation within the EEZ of vessels protesting certain actions of the coastal state. Such a scenario arose in the 2013 case of the *Arctic Sunrise*, a vessel operated by Greenpeace that was flagged to the Netherlands. Greenpeace was at the time engaging in protest activities in the Russian Arctic, seeking to highlight concerns over offshore oil and gas development in the EEZ. Greenpeace crew members from the *Arctic Sunrise* sought to board an oil platform in the Russian EEZ, which prompted the Russian authorities to launch a security operation that resulted in the arrest of the *Arctic Sunrise* and the detention of the crew. The Netherlands responded by commencing proceedings before an Annex VII arbitral tribunal and seeking provisional measures before ITLOS.[146] Before both ITLOS and the Annex VII arbitral tribunal, the Netherlands asserted that Russia's actions were inconsistent with the Article 58(1) freedom of navigation within the EEZ.[147] While Russia did not appear before either ITLOS or the Annex VII arbitral tribunal, in a *note verbale* to the Netherlands Foreign Ministry it was made clear that Russia was of the view that it had a legal basis under Articles 56 and 60 of the LOSC for its actions.

VIII. Further Reading

Zou Keyuan, *The Law of the Sea in East Asia: Issues and Prospects* (London, Routledge, 2005)

Francis Ngantcha, *The Right of Innocent Passage and the Evolution of the International Law of the Sea* (London, Pinter, 1990)

Alex G Oude Elferink (ed), *Stability and Change in the Law of the Sea: The Role of the LOS Convention* (Leiden, Martinus Nijhoff, 2005)

Donald R Rothwell and Sam Bateman (eds), *Navigational Rights and Freedoms and the New Law of the Sea* (The Hague, Martinus Nijhoff, 2000)

Yoshifumi Tanaka, 'Navigational Rights and Freedoms' in Donald R Rothwell, Alex G Oude Elferink, Karen N Scott and Tim Stephens (eds), *The Oxford Handbook of the Law of the Sea* (Oxford, Oxford University Press, 2015)

United Nations, *The Law of the Sea: Navigation on the High Seas* (New York, United Nations, 1989)

Jon M Van Dyke et al (eds), *International Navigation: Rocks and Shoals Ahead?* (Honolulu, Law of the Sea Institute, 1988)

---

[145] Military operations within the EEZ as a distinctive issue is addressed in more detail in ch 12.

[146] *The Arctic Sunrise Case (Netherlands v Russia)* (2014) 53 ILM 607.

[147] Ibid [33].

11

International Straits and Archipelagic Navigation

I. Recognising Rights of Navigation Through Straits

As the international law of the sea has developed throughout the centuries and there has been a growing acceptance of the legitimacy of a range of maritime zones, there has been a need to provide certainty with respect to the freedom of navigation. The initial focus was to assure freedom of navigation in the territorial sea, and this saw the gradual recognition of innocent passage which guaranteed rights of navigation by foreign-flagged vessels. The innocent passage regime developed alongside the ever expanding claims by coastal states to a broader territorial sea, and as long as expansive claims to a territorial sea were kept under check significant disruption to maritime traffic through straits used by international navigation was minimised. However, as the territorial sea regime became more accepted as a part of customary international law, and then was recognised in the 1958 Geneva Convention on the Territorial Sea and Contiguous Zone,[1] it was evident that the particular issues that arise with respect to navigation through straits would have to be addressed.

The need for a distinctive law of the sea regime dealing with straits arose because of the significance of international straits, or 'international maritime highways', to commerce. International maritime trade had historically developed using the shortest navigable route between ports and this naturally involved the use of straits connecting one high seas area with another as a means of safe and expeditious passage. In Europe, the Strait of Gibraltar, Dover Strait, the Danish Straits and the Turkish Straits all acquired considerable strategic, political and commercial significance because of the volume of maritime traffic supplying international trade that passed through those waters.[2] Beyond Europe, other straits had similar strategic, political and commercial importance, including the Straits of Malacca and Singapore, Sunda Strait, Taiwan (Formosa) Strait, Torres Strait, Bass Strait, Behring Strait, Juan da Fuca Strait, Florida Strait and the Straits of Magellan.[3] The risk posed to the international community if passage through the straits was prevented or impaired by the adjacent coastal state, resulted in the early development of some specific regimes which directly addressed navigational rights through certain straits. Various political arrangements, declarations and treaties were agreed upon in the nineteenth and early part of the twentieth

---

[1] *Basic Documents* No 9.
[2] Erik Brüel, *International Straits*, vol 2 (London, Sweet & Maxwell, 1947).
[3] Ibid vol 1, 44–45.

centuries with respect to the Danish Straits,[4] Strait of Gibraltar[5] and Turkish Straits,[6] which sought to recognise certain navigational rights on the part of user states.[7] In light of these developments, various initiatives were undertaken by professional associations to identify the relevant law that applied in straits and attempts to codify that law in writing. Projects undertaken by the Institut de Droit International, International Law Association, and the Hague Codification Conference between 1894 and 1930 all advanced the thinking on straits without coming to a conclusive view.[8] Whilst these developments were taking place there was also in the late nineteenth and early twentieth centuries a movement for the building of various inter-oceanic canals which resulted in the construction of the Suez, Panama and Kiel Canals. However, it has always been understood that the legal regimes of the canals were separate and distinct from that of the international law of the sea,[9] and accordingly the developments in the law with respect to straits never sought to address international canals.

A. The *Corfu Channel* Case

In his landmark study of international straits in 1947, Brüel conceded the right of merchant ships to pass through international straits and suggested very limited rights on the part of the coastal state to close a strait to shipping. Similar rights were conceded to warships in time of peace.[10] Recognition of a distinctive customary international law with respect to straits came with the 1949 decision of the International Court of Justice in the *Corfu Channel* case.[11] On the question of the navigational rights of the British warships through the Corfu Channel, the ICJ made clear that in a time of peace states had 'a right to send their warships through straits used for international navigation between two parts of the high seas' provided that the passage was innocent.[12] The Court went on to note that unless otherwise prescribed by a convention, a coastal state could not prohibit innocent passage through a strait in peacetime.[13]

Whilst the decision made clear then that a right of innocent passage existed in straits, until that point in time there had been no legal determination of whether a distinctive navigational regime applied in straits. In this respect, the ICJ's decision in *Corfu Channel* gave, for the first time, an authoritative legal definition as to which straits may be subject to such a regime. The Court asked the question as to whether the volume of traffic passing through

---

[4] 1857 Treaty for the Redemption of the Sound Dues; 1857 Special Convention between Belgium and Denmark relative to the Extinction of the Sound Dues.

[5] Declaration between Great Britain and Spain for the Abolition of the Practice of Firing on Merchant Vessels from British and Spanish Forts in the Straits of Gibraltar (adopted 2 March 1865); Declaration between France and Great Britain respecting Egypt and Morocco (adopted 8 April 1904).

[6] 1936 Montreaux Convention Regarding the Regime of the Straits, *Basic Documents* No 3.

[7] Myres S McDougal and William T Burke, *The Public Order of the Oceans* (New Haven, Connecticut, New Haven Press, 1962, 1987 rep) 196–201.

[8] DP O'Connell, *The International Law of the Sea*, vol 1 (Oxford, Clarendon Press, 1982) 301–306.

[9] See C John Colombos, *The International Law of the Sea*, 6th edn (London, Longmans, 1967) 200–16, 221.

[10] Brüel, *International Straits* (n 2) vol 1, 230.

[11] *Corfu Channel (United Kingdom v Albania)* [1949] ICJ Rep 4.

[12] Ibid 28.

[13] Ibid.

the strait or the importance of the strait for international navigation was significant, and responded:

> [I]n the opinion of the Court the decisive criteria is rather its geographical situation as connecting two parts of the high seas and the fact of its being used for international navigation.[14]

The Court observed that it was not 'decisive' that the strait was not a necessary route between two parts of the high seas, but only an alternative route of passage between the Aegean and Adriatic Seas. However, it noted that the Corfu Channel had nevertheless 'been a useful route for international maritime traffic'.[15] Following consideration of the volume of international maritime traffic passing through the Corfu Channel, and noting that the North Corfu Channel was the frontier between Greece and Albania, the Court concluded:

> [T]he North Corfu Channel should be considered as belonging to the class of international highways through which passage cannot be prohibited by a coastal State in time of peace.[16]

The ICJ's judgment therefore provided considerable clarity to the then developing customary international law with respect to the innocent passage rights of warships through straits, and the types of straits through which innocent passage could be enjoyed, of which both geographical and functional criteria were emphasised. Commenting on the Court's conception of a strait, McDougal and Burke observed in 1962 that this:

> emphasizes the pronounced preference for free maritime communication by rejecting frequency of use as a criterion for the applicability of the right of innocent passage—no such qualification as 'substantial use' or 'customarily used' were incorporated in the definition.[17]

Nevertheless, it remained essential that some level of usage of a strait for international navigation had to be proven.

B. The ILC and UNCLOS I

The ILC's consideration of the territorial sea regime during the 1950s was influenced by the decision in *Corfu Channel*. However, it devoted little attention to the development of a comprehensive regime for international straits and all that was eventually recommended in the ILC Draft Articles was a single provision providing for no suspension of innocent passage through straits 'normally used for international navigation between two parts of the high seas';[18] the insertion of the word 'normally' was believed by the ILC to be in conformity with the ICJ's decision.[19]

When UNCLOS I convened in 1958 it had the benefit of a geographical and hydrographical study commissioned by the United Nations of 33 straits constituting routes

---

[14] Ibid.
[15] Ibid.
[16] Ibid 29.
[17] McDougal and Burke, *The Public Order of the Oceans* (n 7) 207.
[18] International Law Commission 'Articles Concerning the Law of the Sea with Commentaries' (1956) *Yearbook of the International Law Commission*, vol 2, 273 in which Draft Article 17(4) provided: 'There must be no suspension of the innocent passage of foreign ships through straits normally used for international navigation between two parts of the high seas'.
[19] Ibid.

for international traffic 26 nm or less in width.[20] This study was clearly prepared in contemplation of the conference reaching conclusive agreement on the breadth of the territorial sea and its implications for straits which would have potentially become the subject of overlapping territorial sea claims. However, as UNCLOS I failed to settle the territorial sea issue the need for a more substantive regime dealing with international straits was circumvented, and ultimately the conference relied upon the ILC Draft Articles in adopting a provision dealing with international straits. Article 16(4) of the 1958 Convention on the Territorial Sea and Contiguous Zone[21] provided that:

> There shall be no suspension of the innocent passage of foreign ships through straits which are used for international navigation between one part of the high seas and another part of the high seas or the territorial sea or a foreign State.

Two points can be made regarding the final text of the Convention. The first is that the word 'normally' was deleted from the ILC draft article thereby removing any qualifier that may have suggested some regularity or long-standing usage of a strait for the purposes of international navigation. The second was that the scope of the right was extended not only to straits connecting two areas of the high seas, but also straits connecting the high seas with the territorial sea of a state, as would be the case with a strait leading to a gulf or a bay. In all other respects, however, the Convention adopted the ICJ's formulation on the rights of passage through international straits.

Another matter which was relevant at this time was navigation through straits within archipelagos. Following the ICJ's decision in the *Anglo-Norwegian Fisheries* Case,[22] which considered the special legal issues concerning the fringing islands along the Norwegian coast, there was growing support for recognition of the special status of states comprising groups of islands which made up an archipelago. Whilst the matter had not been given extensive consideration by the ILC, by the time of UNCLOS I some momentum had developed for more active review of the potential recognition under the law of the sea of archipelagic status. The Conference was provided in its preparatory documents with a paper by Jens Evensen which outlined the issues associated with the delimitation of the territorial waters of archipelagos,[23] which considered the issue of navigation within straits that fell within the internal waters of an archipelago. Evensen proposed recognition of 'free navigation' and innocent passage within such waters and drafted an article for inclusion to that effect.[24] Whilst Evensen's proposal did not win support during UNCLOS I, during First Committee negotiations there was active consideration given to the inclusion of a reference to 'other sealanes' in the draft of what eventually became Article 16(4).[25] However, the inclusion of this term was not adopted in the convention text.[26] The effect of this decision was to

---

[20] RH Kennedy, 'A Brief Geographical and Hydrographical Study of Straits which Constitute Routes for International Traffic' in *United Nations Conference on the Law of the Sea: Official Records*, vol 1 (Geneva, United Nations, 1958) 114.

[21] *Basic Documents* No 9.

[22] *Fisheries (United Kingdom v Norway)* [1951] ICJ Rep 116.

[23] Jens Evensen, 'Certain Legal Aspects Concerning the Delimitation of the Territorial Waters of Archipelagos' in *United Nations Conference on the Law of the Sea: Official Records*, vol 1 (Geneva, United Nations, 1958) 289.

[24] Ibid 302.

[25] *United Nations Conference on the Law of the Sea: Official Records*, ibid vol 3, 231; 'Netherlands, Portugal and United Kingdom of Great Britain and Northern Ireland: Proposal', UN Doc A/CONF.13/C.1/L.71.

[26] *United Nations Conference on the Law of the Sea: Official Records*, ibid vol 3, 96.

effectively stall the development for the time being of any distinctive body of law dealing with navigation within archipelagos.[27]

II. UNCLOS III Deliberations and the LOSC

UNCLOS III was pivotal to the development of the contemporary international regime dealing with navigation within straits, and within the waters of an archipelago. Two pivotal decisions at the Conference paved the way for the current LOSC regime. The first was the recognition of a 12 nm territorial sea. This provided certainty for the law and a clear indicator as to how the territorial sea regime would develop, but it also had immediate ramifications for potentially enclosing straits of 24 nm or less within overlapping territorial sea claims. Whilst this would not have precluded navigation within those waters as the regime of innocent passage would have applied, it was strongly asserted by major maritime powers at UNCLOS III, including the United Kingdom and Italy, that there was a need for a distinctive regime dealing with international straits, and that the ongoing application of an innocent passage regime as provided for in the Convention on the Territorial Sea and Contiguous Zone would not have been adequate. Spain, on the other hand, led a group of states that supported retention of the innocent passage regime.[28] This was a particularly important issue with respect to warships, whose freedom of navigation through straits that previously contained areas of high seas would potentially become subject to the regime of innocent passage and the vagaries of coastal state views as to the presence of foreign warships within their territorial sea.[29]

The second development was the recognition that states comprising a group or groups of islands have a distinctive status under the law of the sea as archipelagic states, with an entitlement to enclose their waters by the use of archipelagic baselines. This in turn raised important issues with respect to navigational rights through these archipelagic waters, in some cases through waters that were previously considered international straits.[30] The result of this development was the need for a distinctive navigational regime through archipelagos, built upon principles that were compatible with the other recognised navigational regimes in the Convention.

A. The Straits Regime

Early recognition of the need for such a passage regime through international straits emerged in negotiations prior to UNCLOS III.[31] In 1971 the United States proposed to the

---

[27] O'Connell was particularly critical of this development: DP O'Connell, 'Mid-Ocean Archipelagos in International Law' (1971) 45 *British Year Book of International Law* 1, 72.

[28] *Virginia Commentaries*, vol 2, 287–89.

[29] This point was particularly highlighted by the United States and the Soviet Union; KL Koh, *Straits in International Navigation* (London, Oceana, 1982) 102–109.

[30] This was especially the case for a number of the straits within the Indonesian archipelago, including Lombok Strait and Sunda Strait.

[31] See generally John Norton Moore, 'The Regime of Straits and the Third United Nations Conference on the Law of the Sea' (1980) 74 *AJIL* 77.

Ad Hoc Committee to Study the Peaceful Use of the Sea-Bed and the Ocean Floor Beyond the Limits of National Jurisdiction of the United Nations General Assembly that within straits used for international navigation between two parts of the high seas or the high seas and a part of the territorial sea 'all ships and aircraft in transit shall enjoy the same freedom of navigation and overflight, for the purpose of transit through and over such straits'.[32] In 1973 the Soviet Union put forward a similar proposal also using the term 'transit passage'.[33] This matter was the subject of extensive debate throughout UNCLOS III deliberations with some states forming negotiating groupings in order to advance various positions. The Second Committee debate in 1974 highlighted the difficulties faced in reaching agreement, with 13 states indicating their support for the continuation of innocent passage within straits, while 26 states supported a transit passage regime in certain straits.[34] Prominent contributors to the debate in addition to the United States and the Soviet Union, were Algeria, Denmark, Fiji, Finland, Malaysia, Spain and the United Kingdom.[35] Over the duration of UNCLOS III greater consensus was reached and each successive draft of the convention text began to reflect a coherent set of provisions in which a distinctive regime for international straits began to emerge. Notwithstanding some efforts at late amendment to the final convention text, the conference reached agreement on a new regime of transit passage and this was reflected in the final convention.[36]

B. The Archipelagic Regime

There was also significant debate during UNCLOS III regarding the status of archipelagic states, of which navigation rights within the waters of an archipelago were subject to particular scrutiny. This was because of the sensitivity associated with any proposal to restrict already existing rights of the high seas freedom of navigation though the waters found within the archipelago. As several straits of strategic importance could have been enclosed within baselines proclaimed by archipelagic states, resolution of this issue during UNCLOS III deliberations was seen as a priority by maritime powers.[37] In March 1973 the four key island states of Fiji, Indonesia, Mauritius and the Philippines put forward a draft proposal which expressly recognised a right of innocent passage through the waters of an

[32] 'Draft Articles on the Breadth of the Territorial Sea, Straits and Fisheries', Committee on the Peaceful Uses of the Sea-Bed and the Ocean Floor Beyond the Limits of National Jurisdiction, United Nations General Assembly, reprinted in S Houston Lay, Robin Churchill and Myron Nordquist (eds), *New Directions in the Law of the Sea*, vol 2 (Dobbs Ferry, NY, Oceana Publications, 1973) 552.

[33] 'Draft Articles on Straits Used for International Navigation', ibid 554.

[34] Koh, *Straits in International Navigation* (n 29) 143.

[35] Ibid 129–49; De Yturriaga, *Straits Used for International Navigation: A Spanish Perspective* (Dordrecht, Martinus Nijhoff, 1991) 99–144, who notes at 104 that the UK observed that the extension of the territorial sea would mean that in over 100 straits there would no longer be a high seas corridor.

[36] De Yturriaga, *Straits Used for International Navigation: A Spanish Perspective*, ibid 144–47. Nevertheless, some states were of the view that the final convention text represented a progressive development of the law concerning straits and that accordingly only 'state parties to the Law of the Sea Convention shall be entitled to benefit from the contractual rights created therein'; see Islamic Republic of Iran, 'Interpretative Declaration on the Subject of Straits' (10 December 1982) in United Nations Division for Ocean Affairs and the Law of the Sea, 'Declarations and Statements' at www.un.org/Depts/los/convention_agreements/convention_declarations.htm.

[37] Straits that would have been subject to possible enclosure as a result of archipelagic claims included Lombok, Macassar, Molucca, Ombai and Sunda: RP Anand, *Origin and Development of the Law of the Sea* (The Hague, Martinus Nijhoff, 1983) 208.

archipelago. However, this proposal was not equivalent to the existing right of innocent passage through straits found in Article 16(4) of the Convention on the Territorial Sea and Contiguous Zone, which was the conventional regime operating at that time for straits that fell within the boundaries of states.[38] However, an August 1973 proposal by the same group of island states saw significant development of a distinctive navigational regime within an archipelago, including express reference to the designation of sealanes, and this assisted in further promoting the debate.[39] Given that these debates were in parallel with those occurring regarding passage through international straits, it was inevitable that the proposals would eventually become joined and that key elements of the transit passage regime became reflected in the eventual archipelagic navigational regime.

III. International Straits

Unlike the 1958 Convention on the Territorial Sea and Contiguous Zone, the LOSC devotes considerable attention in Part III to the regime of straits used for international navigation. Reference is made to a 'regime of passage through straits used for international navigation'[40] established in Part III of the Convention, suggesting that the intention was to create a comprehensive legal framework for such straits. This is what is ultimately achieved by the transit passage regime, which is a separate regime within the LOSC for straits used for international navigation. However, there are many potential categories of straits which, depending on their history, geographical configuration and usage, may be subject to different characterisations for the purposes of the law of the sea. The ICJ in the *Corfu Channel* case hinted that a variety of factors may need to be taken into account in determining which navigational rights applied within a particular strait. Accordingly, one of the initial issues that needed to be addressed in the LOSC was distinguishing between various navigational regimes that apply in the different bodies of water that may comprise a strait. One of those factors is clearly the width of the strait and surveys have estimated that there are 52 international straits less than 6 nm in width, 153 international straits between 6 and 24 nm in width, and 60 other international straits in excess of 24 nm in width.[41]

A. Categories of Straits

The starting point for an analysis of Part III is its title—'Straits Used for International Navigation'—a descriptor repeated in various articles found within this part of the Convention. This immediately raises for consideration what the Convention classifies as a strait used for international navigation. Using terminology similar to that found in the *Corfu Channel* case, by the ILC, and in the Geneva Convention on the Territorial Sea and Contiguous

---

[38] CF Amerasinghe, 'The Problem of Archipelagoes in the International Law of the Sea' (1974) 23 *International and Comparative Law Quarterly* 539, 547–49.

[39] Ibid 549–52.

[40] LOSC, art 34(1).

[41] AR Thomas and James C Duncan (eds), 'Annotated Supplement to The Commanders Handbook on the Law of Naval Operations' (1999) 73 *International Legal Studies* 207–08, Table A2-5.

Zone, this phrase suggests both a geographical and functional element. The geographical element relates to a strait being a body of water which lies between two areas of land, either continental land masses,[42] a continent and an island,[43] or two islands.[44] However, there is no guidance as to how proximate the bodies of land must be to one another, or at which point the width of the body of water which separates the two areas of land is no longer considered a strait but rather a sea or an ocean.[45] For practical purposes this distinction may not be of great relevance as most bodies of water that separate sufficiently proximate areas of land are referred to as straits, or have equivalent titles.[46] Nevertheless, the recognition of a body of water as a strait is an important starting point in the application of the Part III legal regime.

In addition to the geographical criterion, in the *Corfu Channel* case the ICJ placed emphasis on the strait being one that was 'used for international navigation'.[47] While there was no analysis as to what volume of navigation through the strait would be required to meet the usage requirement, reference was made to the volume of navigation through the Strait between 1936 and 1937 which in the view of the Court assisted it in determining that the Corfu Channel had been 'a useful route for international maritime traffic'.[48] Therefore, while this functional element remains a feature of the LOSC, it is unclear as to what level of international navigation is required for a strait to be appropriately classified as an 'international strait'. However, it is doubtful whether infrequent or irregular use of a strait would suffice to meet the functional criterion. Likewise, the strait must have been used by foreign flagged vessels; and not only by through or cross-strait local vessel traffic.

The status of the Northwest Passage, a waterway that connects the Beaufort Sea with either Baffin Bay or the Labrador Sea and which runs between the islands of the Canadian Arctic Archipelago, raises issues as to whether it should be characterised as a single strait or a series of interconnected straits. In this regard, the Northwest Passage could be considered unique as both customary international law and the LOSC have focused on single straits, and not interconnected straits that in sum comprise a navigational route from one area of the high seas/EEZ to another. Nevertheless, it is not contested that the Northwest Passage meets the geographical requirement of a strait or a series of straits as reflected in decisions such as the *Corfu Channel* case, the LOSC or customary international law.[49]

The most significant requirement, and one that has been the principal point of contention between Canada and the United States over the status of the Northwest Passage, is the functional requirement that the strait actually be used for international navigation. Pharand's view has been that because of the low number of recorded transits of the strait it would not

---

[42]   An example is the Bering Strait separating continental Asia and North America.

[43]   The Dover Strait lies between the continent of Europe and the island of Great Britain.

[44]   The Cook Strait separates the North and South Island of New Zealand.

[45]   RR Baxter, *The Law of International Waterways* (Cambridge, Mass, Harvard University Press, 1964) 3–4. George K Walker, 'Definitions for the 1982 Law of the Sea Convention—Part II: Analysis of the IHO Consolidated Glossary' (2003) 33 *California Western International Law Journal* 219, 298 observes that: 'The geographic definition of a strait is a narrow passage of water between two land masses or islands, or groups of islands connecting two sea areas'.

[46]   Of which the term 'channel' is in state practice used as an alternative to 'strait', as in the Corfu Channel; other terms that are used include 'Belt', 'Mouth' and 'Sound'.

[47]   *Corfu Channel (United Kingdom v Albania)* [1949] ICJ Rep 4, 28.

[48]   Ibid.

[49]   See Donat Pharand, *Canada's Arctic Waters in International Law* (Cambridge, Cambridge University Press, 1988) 223–24.

be possible to classify the Northwest Passage as a 'strait used for international navigation'.[50] This clearly raises issues as to the actual recorded number of transits that have taken place, whether distinctions should be made between historical figures and more contemporary assessments, and the percentage of transits completed by non-Canadian flagged vessels.[51] Pharand identified 15 transits of the Northwest Passage by United States flagged vessels in the period to 2005, of which only two were by non-government vessels—the *Manhattan* (1969–70) and an adventure yacht, the *Belvedere* (1983–88).[52] More recent figures have indicated 18 transits of the Northwest Passage during the summer of 2010,[53] while Headland has identified 135 full transits of the Northwest Passage in the period 1903–2009.[54]

Relying upon the actual use of the Northwest Passage since the first successful navigation, Pharand has maintained that the passage is not an international strait.[55] He has argued that those who contend otherwise confused potential use with actual use and that what is required is not mere capacity but rather actual use.[56] The United States, however, as recently as May 2013, has reasserted its position that it enjoys the freedom of navigation through the Northwest Passage.[57] Two respected United States scholars with close links to the United States Department of State observed in 2012 that, on the basis of the statistics of usage of the strait, 'to deny, as Canada continues to do, that the Northwest Passage is not a strait used for international navigation … is simply not credible'.[58]

In addition to straits used for international navigation between one part of the high seas or EEZ and another part of the high seas or EEZ to which the regime of transit passage applies,[59] Part III also makes reference to other categories of straits. These include the following:

— straits which are regulated in whole or in part by long-standing international conventions;[60]
— straits where there exists a route through the high seas or EEZ of similar convenience;[61]
— straits which exist between the mainland and an island where there exists seaward of the island a route through the high seas or EEZ of similar convenience;[62] and
— straits used for international navigation between one part of the high seas or EEZ and the territorial sea of a foreign State.[63]

---

[50] Ibid 202–14.

[51] From the time of the very first transit of the passage in 1903–06 by Amundsen until 2005, Pharand identified 69 foreign transits: Donat Pharand, 'The Arctic Waters and the Northwest Passage: A Final Revisit' (2007) 38 *Ocean Development and International Law* 3, 32–33.

[52] Ibid 31–32.

[53] See discussion in J Ashley Roach and Robert W Smith, *Excessive Maritime Claims*, 3rd edn (Leiden, Martinus Nijhoff, 2012) 478.

[54] RK Headland, 'Ten Decades of Transits of the Northwest Passage' (2010) 33(1–2) *Polar Geography* 1, 3–9.

[55] Donat Pharand, 'Canada's Sovereignty over the Northwest Passage' (1989) 10 *Michigan Journal of International Law* 653, 669–70; Pharand, *Canada's Arctic Waters in International Law* (n 49) 225; Donat Pharand, 'The Northwest Passage in International Law' (1979) 17 *Canadian Yearbook of International Law* 99, 112–13.

[56] Pharand, *Canada's Arctic Waters in International Law* (n 49) 225; Pharand, 'The Northwest Passage in International Law', ibid 113.

[57] President of the United States, *National Strategy for the Arctic Region* (Washington, White House, May 2013) 9.

[58] Roach and Smith, *Excessive Maritime Claims* (n 53) 478–79.

[59] LOSC, art 37.

[60] Ibid art 35(c).

[61] Ibid art 36.

[62] Ibid art 38(1).

[63] Ibid art 45.

All of these categories of straits are ones in which the principal regime of transit passage as created under the LOSC does not apply, but in its place alternative navigation regimes are recognised.

In the case of straits that are subject to long-standing international conventions, there are a number of instances of such straits including the Aaland Straits, Danish Straits, Straits of Magellan and Turkish Straits,[64] some of which will be considered in more detail below. One of the issues which arise from the terminology used in the LOSC is how long-standing the convention must be. Both the Torres Strait[65] and the Strait of Tiran[66] are the subject of treaties that refer to navigational rights and freedoms but both were concluded in the late 1970s. In coming years if the treaties which regulate those straits remain operative and are respected not only by the parties themselves but by other user states it may be asserted that they may fall into this distinctive category envisaged under the LOSC.

Where there is a high seas or EEZ route through a strait, providing that the route is of similar convenience with respect to navigational and hydrographical circumstances, then Part III of the LOSC does not apply.[67] In theory this includes all straits that are broader than 24 nm, although in marginal cases such as where the breadth of the waters barely exceeds 24 nm at its narrowest point, it may be arguable as to whether a narrow channel through the EEZ is one of 'similar convenience'. This will especially be the case if the traffic through the strait is heavy and needs to be separated through the use of sea lanes for safety reasons. The related exemption applies in the case where the strait is formed by a mainland and an island and there exists a route of similar convenience with respect to navigational and hydrographical characteristics seaward of the island. In this instance the LOSC is essentially stating that if international navigation has a choice of route of similar convenience, then that which exists through the high seas or EEZ is to be preferred. If, on the other hand, international shipping prefers to pass between the mainland and the island then a right of innocent passage applies in the place of transit passage, though the right of innocent passage cannot be suspended.[68] Examples of straits that fall within this exception are Georgia (Canada), Hainan (China), the Strait of Messina (Italy), the Pemba Channel (Tanzania) and the Solent (United Kingdom).[69] However, care needs to be taken in applying this exception because even within a strait the presence of islands may create a number of navigational options with the effect that there exists a number of geographical straits within a much larger strait.[70]

---

[64] Hugo Caminos, 'Categories of International Straits Excluded from the Transit Passage Regime under Part III of the United Nations Convention on the Law of the Sea' in Tafsir Malick Ndiaye and Rüdiger Wolfrum (eds), *Law of the Sea, Environmental Law and Settlement of Disputes* (Leiden, Martinus Nijhoff, 2007) 583, 583–84; Thomas and Duncan (eds), 'Annotated Supplement to The Commanders Handbook on the Law of Naval Operations' (n 41) 205, Table A2-3 lists five straits: Bosporus, Dardanelles, Magellan, Oresund and Store Belt (Storebaelt).

[65] 1978 Treaty between Australia and the Independent State of Papua New Guinea concerning Sovereignty and Maritime Boundaries in the area between the two Countries, including the area known as Torres Strait, and Related Matters.

[66] 1979 Treaty of Peace between the Arab Republic of Egypt and the State of Israel.

[67] LOSC, art 36.

[68] Ibid art 45.

[69] Thomas and Duncan (eds), 'Annotated Supplement to The Commanders Handbook on the Law of Naval Operations' (n 41) 204–05, Table A2-2, listing 22 straits that fall into this category.

[70] An example is Bass Strait formed between the Australian continent and the island of Tasmania where within the strait there are two significant islands (Flinders Island and King Island) plus a number of smaller island chains which in themselves form straits: Donald R Rothwell, 'International Straits and UNCLOS: An Australian Case Study' (1992) 23 *Journal of Maritime Law and Commerce* 461.

Finally, in the case of those straits which connect an area of high seas or EEZ with a territorial sea, then even if the strait otherwise meets the characteristics of a strait used for international navigation, a regime of non-suspendable innocent passage will apply.[71] This category of straits, which are sometimes referred to as 'dead end' straits, include the Strait of Tiran, the Gulf of Bahrain and the Gulf of Honduras.

B. The Regime of Transit Passage

The regime of transit passage which exists between straits used for international navigation between one part of the high seas and EEZ and another part of the high seas and EEZ is one which all ships and aircraft enjoy.[72] That transit passage is also open to aircraft as well as ships is an important point of distinction with the regime of innocent passage in the territorial sea, and a contemporary recognition that freedom of overflight within an international strait has significant implications for the freedom of movement of peoples and for government aircraft. The right of transit passage is also one that is not to be 'impeded',[73] implying that the strait state must not bar or suspend transit passage or otherwise engage in activities that may have the practical effect of doing so.

i. The Act of Transit

Article 38(2) of the LOSC goes on to outline the physical act of transit passage which includes the freedom of navigation and overflight 'solely for the purpose of continuous and expeditious transit of the strait', which reflects the objective of ensuring that the regime facilitates the movement of vessels and aircraft physically through the strait from an entrance to an exit point. These provisions build upon the ICJ's notion in *Corfu Channel* of a strait being an 'international highway'.[74] Allowance is also made in the case where passage through the Strait is undertaken for the purpose of 'entering, leaving or returning from a State bordering the strait',[75] thereby facilitating ships or aircraft which are seeking to dock or land at a facility within a state adjoining a strait, of which Singapore is one of the most prominent examples.[76] Transit passage is therefore enjoyed by ships and aircraft which seek to pass through the strait, or which are entering or exiting the strait after having stopped at, or on their way to, a state which borders the strait.

ii. Duties of Ships and Aircraft in Transit

Once engaged in transit passage, under Article 39 of the LOSC ships and aircraft have certain duties that are reflective of some of the elements of innocent passage, though these are by no means as extensive. They include the requirement to proceed without delay,

---

[71] LOSC, art 45; Moore, 'The Regime of Straits and the Third United Nations' (n 31) 112.
[72] LOSC, art 38(1).
[73] Ibid art 38(1).
[74] *Corfu Channel (United Kingdom v Albania)* [1949] ICJ Rep 4, 29.
[75] LOSC, art 38(2).
[76] The only way in which Singapore can be approached by ship is via either the Straits or Malacca and Singapore, or the Straits of Jahore; similarly for an aircraft making an approach by sea and not overflying the territory of adjoining states, these Straits provide the only means of air access.

to refrain from any use or threat of force against the sovereignty, territorial integrity or political independence of the strait state, or in any other manner in violation of principles of international law found in the UN Charter, and to refrain from activities other than those which are incidental 'to their normal mode' of transit, unless rendered necessary by *force majeure* or distress.

These duties of ships and aircraft engaged in transit passage reflect an important balancing of rights and interests within the straits regime. On the one hand transit passage was developed to permit the free and unimpeded passage of ships and aircraft through international straits, thereby ensuring the continuation of important guarantees of the freedom of navigation and overflight that had historically developed through the law of the sea within certain bodies of water. On the other hand, strait states have legitimate security concerns relating to the presence of foreign ships and aircraft within or above their territorial sea in what may be relatively confined waters, and accordingly must be protected from any acts that may constitute a threat to their sovereignty or territorial integrity. Balancing those competing rights and objectives, especially in the case of military vessels and aircraft, has at times proved to be a major challenge. This has certainly been the case with respect to warships, in particular in interpreting what constitutes the 'normal modes of continuous and expeditious transit' for such vessels. In the case of submarines, it can be contended that their normal mode of transit would be via submerged passage rather than on the surface. However, in the alternative it can also be contended that submerged passage by a submarine within the territorial sea of a state would prima facie be considered a threat to the strait state. For aircraft carriers, their normal mode of operation extends to organic aircraft taking off and landing and in some instances receiving visiting aircraft. Setting aside the related air navigation issues that arise from such operations, clearly these activities may be considered by some strait states to be impermissible, on the basis that they may pose a threat to their national interests. Both of these examples highlight some of the sensitivities that arise from naval operations in international straits.[77]

In addition to these generic duties, ships in transit passage are to comply with generally accepted international regulations and procedures dealing with safety of life at sea and COLREG,[78] and also with generally accepted international regulations for the prevention, reduction and control of pollution.[79] Aircraft shall observe the Rules of the Air established by the International Civil Aviation Organization (ICAO), and related measures for the safety of air navigation, and also monitor radio frequencies for the purpose of air traffic control.[80]

iii. Obligations of Strait States

Article 44 of the LOSC makes clear that strait states are not to 'hamper' transit passage and are to give appropriate notification of any dangers to navigation or overflight within or over the strait of which they may be aware, which would extend to cases of shipwreck blocking parts of the strait or to severe weather conditions. It is also made clear that strait states are

---

[77] See detailed discussion in ch 12.
[78] 1972 Convention on the International Regulations for Preventing Collisions at Sea, *Basic Documents* No 20.
[79] LOSC, art 39(2).
[80] Ibid art 39(3); the later requirement is especially significant for state aircraft, in particular military aircraft, which may not otherwise be subject to such requirements.

not to suspend transit passage. Here, one of the important distinctions that exists between the regime of transit passage in an international strait and innocent passage within the territorial sea is made clear: while transit passage cannot be suspended by the strait state, a coastal state may temporarily suspend innocent passage.[81] Therefore, even if a strait state has concerns regarding its national security because of the potential for transiting traffic to be caught up in internal disturbances, it may not suspend the right of transit passage. However, it may issue a warning to ships of the potential hazards that exist within its waters at any particular point in time.[82] The obligation upon the strait state not to 'hamper' transit passage suggests that no obligations or requirements may be imposed upon ships or aircraft that create a burden for them. One traditional interpretation of this requirement is that the strait state may not impose tolls or any other fees in return for a right of passage.[83] However, some strait states have expressed concerns about the financial burdens they face in maintaining navigational aids and other safety and marine environmental protection measures within the waters of an international strait without receiving any recompense and have argued that there should be an entitlement to charge tolls or at least a fee-for-service that relates directly to the benefits they provide to international shipping that passes through the strait.[84]

Related issues have arisen with respect to whether the imposition of compulsory pilotage in some international straits is an imposition which amounts to the hampering or impairment of transit passage, or is instead a legitimate measure to reduce the risk of marine environmental damage.[85] Imposition of compulsory pilotage in an international strait raises issues with respect to the role of the IMO, which has responsibility for certain aspects of the LOSC concerning navigation within the territorial sea and international straits. As such, a coastal state seeking to designate sea lanes and traffic separation schemes within the territorial sea of an international strait must take into account the views of the IMO as the 'competent international organisation'.[86] Likewise, when seeking to regulate navigation and shipping, the coastal state is to take into account not only the provisions of the LOSC, but also 'other rules of international law',[87] which would include the Collision Regulations (COLREGs), SOLAS[88] and other IMO conventions, such as MARPOL.[89] The IMO is therefore directly engaged in coordinating with a coastal state, and in some instances authorising a coastal state, to undertake certain measures that regulate navigation and shipping within the territorial sea and in an international strait. This role in often performed by individual IMO committees, of which the Maritime Safety Committee is particularly important.[90]

---

[81] Ibid art 25(3).

[82] Note that ibid art 44 refers to 'any danger to navigation or overflight within or over the strait of which they have knowledge', which is a direct reference to the issues that arose in *Corfu Channel* regarding whether Albania did or did not have knowledge as to the existence of mines in the strait: see *Corfu Channel (United Kingdom v Albania)* [1949] ICJ Rep 4, 22–23.

[83] LOSC, art 26; *Virginia Commentaries*, vol 2, 161, 236.

[84] Mark J Valencia and Abu Bakar Jaafar, 'Environmental Management of the Malacca—Singapore Straits: Legal and Institutional Issues' (1985) 25 *Natural Resources Journal* 195–232.

[85] RC Beckman, 'PSSAs and Transit Passage—Australia's Pilotage System in the Torres Strait Challenges the IMO and UNCLOS' (2007) 38 *Ocean Development and International Law* 337.

[86] LOSC, arts 22(3)(a), 41(4).

[87] LOSC, arts 21(1), 43(1)(b), where the term 'applicable international regulations' is used.

[88] *Basic Documents* 22.

[89] 1973/1978 International Convention for the Prevention of Pollution from Ships, *Basic Documents* 21.

[90] Beckman, 'PSSAs and Transit Passage' (n 85) 327.

Therefore, while the coastal state has considerable latitude in adopting pilotage measures within its territorial sea or an international strait, it cannot do so unilaterally and must work within certain agreed frameworks, and in particular utilise IMO mechanisms.

iv. Regulation of Transit Passage

Subject to the constraints of Article 44, strait states enjoy the capacity to enact laws and regulations relating to transit passage. For ships such laws can extend to the safety of navigation and regulation of maritime traffic, the prevention, reduction and control of pollution by giving effect to applicable international regulations, the stowage of gear on fishing vessels, and the loading or unloading of any commodity, currency or person contrary to customs, fiscal, immigration or sanitary laws.[91] Such laws are not to have the effect of discriminating between foreign ships, which are expected to comply with such laws subject to appropriate publicity having been given to their enactment.[92] However, consistent with the limitations that are reflected in Article 44 such laws are also not to 'have the practical effect of denying, hampering or impairing the right of transit passage'.[93]

Closely related to these measures and the initiatives which the strait state can take to ensure the safety of navigation, Article 41 permits the designation of sea lanes and traffic separation schemes within straits. A strait state that wishes to designate a sea lane needs to take into account the views of a relevant international organisation, of which the IMO is considered to be the leading authority in this particular field. This will not only impact upon how a sea lane has been designated, but also the navigational rules and safety standards which will apply within the sea lane. The COLREGs deal with safety of navigation, and Rule 10 addresses the behaviour of vessels in or near a TSS within which certain sea lanes operate. The first formal TSS was established in the Dover Strait in 1967 on a voluntary basis, but following several maritime incidents in 1971 the IMO's Maritime Safety Committee recommended that the observance of all TSS become mandatory and this was endorsed by the IMO Assembly and is now reflected in the COLREGs. A TSS seeks to separate vessel traffic in opposite directions by the use of a separation zone, or a lane, or by other means. A sea lane which exists within a TSS is predominantly designed to facilitate safe one-way through traffic of shipping. The lanes or zones may or may not be marked by buoys or other navigational aids, though a coastal state does have the legal capacity to install such devices. The operation of the sea lane is principally divided between through traffic, 'local' or 'coastal traffic', and crossing vessels which are seeking to move from one sea lane to another. Vessels engaged in through traffic within a sea lane are to proceed in the general direction of the traffic flow, as far as practicable keep clear of a traffic separation line, only join the lane at designated points or in such a manner as to merge with the general flow of traffic, and avoid crossing traffic lanes. Compliance with navigational rules within a sea lane will depend upon the relevant laws of the strait state, which may extend its laws to all vessels, including those which are foreign-flagged. The modern day TSS within Dover Strait regulates over 400 commercial vessels a day, and in addition to being monitored by French and UK authorities is also subject to a Channel Navigation Information Service which provides a 24 hour radio and radar safety service for all shipping. Other prominent

---

[91]   LOSC, art 42(1).
[92]   Ibid arts 42(2), (3), (4).
[93]   Ibid art 42(2).

straits with a TSS in place include Bass Strait, the Straits of Malacca and Singapore, and the Strait of Hormuz.

v. Enforcement of Strait State Laws and Regulations

One aspect of the transit passage regime which is not made clear in the LOSC is the level of enforcement action a strait state may undertake against a delinquent vessel purportedly exercising a right of transit passage. One scenario arises when a vessel is not complying with the requirements of transit passage and its actions are in breach of Article 39 such that it is posing a threat to the strait state or it is not engaging in 'normal mode' passage. In these circumstances a strait state retains its capacity of self-defence under international law and could rely upon that right in the face of a hostile act by a transiting ship or aircraft. It also has the capacity, consistent with the LOSC, to prohibit passage by a ship or aircraft which is not engaged in transit passage in conformity with Part III. Accordingly, even if the ship or aircraft poses no threat to the national security of the strait state, a delinquent ship could be prevented from continuing its passage.

Another enforcement scenario arises when a ship, or an aircraft, legitimately engaging in transit passage in compliance with its Article 39 duties breaches the laws and regulations of the strait state. Part III is silent on the actual enforcement capacity of the strait state in such circumstances, which raises issues as to how a strait state may go about seeking to enforce its law in a manner that does not have the practical effect of hampering or impairing transit passage. Nevertheless, Article 34 of the LOSC makes clear that the Part III regime dealing with straits used for international navigation does not in other respects affect the legal status of the waters of the strait with regards to the coastal state's sovereignty and jurisdiction. This would extend to the coastal state's criminal and civil jurisdiction within the territorial sea of the strait. This view is supported by the text of Articles 27 and 28 which respectively deal with coastal state criminal and civil jurisdiction in the case of 'a foreign ship passing through the territorial sea'. These provisions make it clear that in the case of criminal jurisdiction the coastal state retains a right, subject to certain constraints, to board a ship and effect an arrest whist that ship is within the territorial sea, which would also extend to a ship engaged in transit passage.

If the infraction by the transiting ship relates to a marine environmental measure, other provisions in the LOSC will also apply. Article 233, which is found in Part XII dealing with the marine environment, makes clear that ships that commit violations of certain environmental laws and regulations while undertaking transit passage, and which are 'causing or threatening major damage to the marine environment of the straits' may be subject to 'appropriate enforcement measures' by the strait state.[94] The context of the provision suggests that law enforcement against delinquent foreign ships engaged in transit passage is permitted, which by implication would extend to stopping and barring further passage of a vessel to contain any threat to the marine environment. Spain indicated upon both its signature and ratification of the LOSC that it also interpreted Article 221 as providing a basis of intervention against international navigation following a maritime casualty.[95] In

---

[94] Erik Jaap Molenaar, *Coastal State Jurisdiction over Vessel-Source Pollution* (The Hague, Kluwer Law International, 1998) 295–98.

[95] Spain, 'Upon Ratification' (15 January 1997) in United Nations Division for Ocean Affairs and the Law of the Sea, 'Declarations and Statements' at www.un.org/Depts/los/convention_agreements/convention_declarations.htm.

the United States' response to the Spanish Declaration, it was agreed that 'in the event of maritime casualties, a coastal state of a strait used for international navigation may, within its territorial sea, take reasonable actions in response to pollution or a threat of pollution that may reasonably be expected to result in major harmful consequences'.[96]

C. Navigation in Specific International Straits

There are in the vicinity of 265 international straits,[97] and accordingly a full treatment of the particular geographical and legal regimes of each of those straits is not possible here. What follows is a discussion of selected examples of some of the major straits that seeks to highlight how the law of the sea applies to straits in practice.

1. Turkish Straits

The Turkish Straits are two related straits that connect the Black Sea to the Mediterranean and have been subject to a long-standing convention that pre-dated the LOSC, and accordingly fall into the category of straits referred to in Article 35. The straits comprise the Dardanelles, which connects the Aegean Sea and the Sea of Marmara, and the Bosphorus, which connects the Sea of Marmara with the Black Sea.[98] The straits are of great historical and commercial importance, effectively connecting eastern and western civilisations. Their strategic significance has been reflected in recurrent conflicts which have been fought between major powers over the centuries over the territory fronting the straits, and they were of critical military significance during World Wars I and II.

The 1936 Montreaux Convention[99] sought to reach a settlement over the status of the straits, and it has remained operative despite developments in the contemporary law of the sea. The Convention's preamble provides in part:

> Desiring to regulate transit and navigation in the Straits of the Dardanelles, the Sea of Marmora and the Bosphoros comprised under the general term 'Straits' in such manner as to safeguard, within the framework of Turkish security and of the security, in the Black Sea, of the riparian states[100]

Reflective of the issues at the time, the Convention has distinctive provisions dealing with navigation by merchant vessels, vessels of war, and aircraft. Article 1 recognises and affirms the 'freedom of transit and navigation by sea in the Straits', which were subsequently endorsed more generally in the LOSC, Part III. These navigational freedoms in the strait are particularly outlined in Article 2 with respect to merchant vessels which confirms the 'freedom of transit and navigation' for vessels under any flag and with any cargo. No taxes or charges are to be levied, other than those provided for under the Convention. Ships entering the straits are required to stop near the entrance for the purposes of sanitary control

---

[96] Roach and Smith, *Excessive Maritime Claims* (n 53) 291.
[97] Thomas and Duncan (eds), 'Annotated Supplement to The Commanders Handbook on the Law of Naval Operations' (n 41) 207–08, Table A2-5.
[98] Brüel, *International Straits* (n 2) vol 2, 252.
[99] 1936 Convention Regarding the Regime of Straits, *Basic Documents* No 3.
[100] Original parties to the Convention were Bulgaria, France, Great Britain, Greece, India, Japan, Romania, the Soviet Union, Turkey and Yugoslavia.

as prescribed under Turkish law.[101] Special provisions are made for dealing with merchant vessels during times of war, and when Turkey is and is not a belligerent, including allowance for compulsory pilotage.[102] The Montreaux Convention provisions dealing with naval vessels are detailed and provide for multiple instances of passage by warships, depending on their type, tonnage, flag, and whether navigation is taking place during a time of war.[103] Transit through the strait by warships is to be preceded by notification.[104] Allowance is also made for the establishment of air routes through the straits so that civil aircraft can cross between the Mediterranean and the Black Sea.[105]

Although Turkey was a participant at UNCLOS III, it ultimately voted against adoption of the Convention, and since 1982 has not joined the LOSC, thereby maintaining its rights under the Montreaux Convention. However, that Convention was adopted in another era, and unless it is capable of being modified to reflect contemporary navigational conditions, including those which apply with respect to the safety of shipping and marine environmental protection, its ongoing application may be questioned by user states.[106]

ii. Strait of Gibraltar

The Strait of Gibraltar is a body of water at the western extremity of the Mediterranean Sea which connects the Mediterranean with the Atlantic Ocean. It is one of the most significant international straits because it provides a means of seaborne transit for shipping between the Atlantic and Mediterranean, and via the Suez Canal into the Indian Ocean and beyond. Because of its strategic location and the access that it has granted to the adjacent coastal states in both southern Europe and Northern Africa, the strait has long-standing historic and strategic significance, which is partly reflected in the interests of the various littoral states and powers with interests in the adjoining coast.[107]

The strait lies between the southernmost tip of Spain and the northern tip of Morocco with the territory of Gibraltar, governed by the United Kingdom, at the north eastern edge of the strait. Whilst Britain has exercised effective control over Gibraltar since 1713, its status has been contested by Spain for many centuries. France asserted control over that part of Morocco that fronted the strait until 1956. Currently the states which have direct interests over the strait and assert maritime claims are Morocco, Spain and the United Kingdom. The Gibraltar Port Authority estimates that 71,000 vessels transit the strait annually, with approximately half that number of vessels engaged in cross strait North–South traffic. Until the opening of the Suez Canal in 1869, the Strait of Gibraltar was the only means of oceanic access to and from the Mediterranean Sea.[108]

---

[101] 1936 Convention Regarding the Regime of Straits, art 3.
[102] Ibid arts 4–7.
[103] Ibid arts 8–22.
[104] Ibid art 13.
[105] Ibid art 23.
[106] Nihan Ünlü, *The Legal Regime of the Turkish Straits* (The Hague, Martinus Nijhoff, 2002) 109–14, considering options for reform.
[107] For more details see Donald R Rothwell, 'Gibraltar, Strait of' in *Max Planck Encyclopaedia of Public International Law* (2009) at www.mpepil.com; and generally De Yturriaga, *Straits Used for International Navigation: A Spanish Perspective* (n 35).
[108] Brüel, *International Straits* (n 2) vol 2, 116–99; De Yturriaga, *Straits Used for International Navigation: A Spanish Perspective* (n 35) 85–91.

Spain predominantly exercised control over the Strait up until the late nineteenth century. Although rarely seeking to close the Strait, Spain did require merchant vessels to hoist their flags when passing through the Strait in order to identify themselves. This practice continued until as late as 1864 when the British vessel *Mermaid* was subject to canon fire as a result of a failure to hoist its ensign. Spain abolished its practice requiring ship identification by way of an 1865 Declaration with Great Britain. However, passage through the Strait remained a sensitive issue and in the 1904 Anglo-French Declaration, concluded at a time when France had control of the north African coast, it was provided that:

> In order to secure free passage of the Straits of Gibraltar, the two Governments agree not to permit the erection of any fortifications or strategic works on that portion of the coast of Morocco comprised between, but not including Melilla and the heights which command the right bank of the River Sebou.[109]

Italy and the Soviet Union asserted during UNCLOS III that the Strait of Gibraltar was a strait governed by a long-standing international convention and should not be subject to the regime of transit passage. This claim rested with an interpretation of the 1904 Anglo-French Declaration and the subsequent 1912 Franco-Spanish Convention under which the freedom of navigation through the Strait was guaranteed.[110] However, both Spain and Morocco rejected this interpretation during Conference deliberations and at best it remains a minority position and does not reflect the contemporary right of transit passage through the Strait. Nevertheless, Spain has been careful to ensure that its rights under the 1713 Treaty of Utrecht[111] with Great Britain dealing with the status of Gibraltar and associated issues, were not prejudiced by the LOSC and upon both signing and ratifying the Convention lodged a Declaration to the effect that 'this act cannot be construed as a recognition of any rights or status regarding the maritime space of Gibraltar that are not included in Article 10 of the Treaty of Utrecht'.[112]

iii. Straits of Malacca and Singapore

The Straits of Malacca and Singapore are some of the most heavily transited international straits on the world's oceans.[113] Connecting east with west, they have grown in prominence since the end of World War II with the rise of Japan as a major industrial power and its reliance upon supertankers for traffic between the Middle East and the Pacific.[114] The Straits also have considerable strategic and military significance as a 'choke' point for maritime

---

[109] Declaration between France and Great Britain respecting Egypt and Morocco (adopted 8 April 1904), art VII.

[110] Convention between France and Spain respecting Relations in Morocco (adopted 27 November 1912).

[111] Treaty of Peace and Friendship between Great Britain and Spain (Treaty of Utrecht) (adopted 13 July 1713, entered into force 4 August 1713).

[112] This was subject to a response in the Declaration upon accession of the United Kingdom: United Nations Division for Ocean Affairs and the Law of the Sea, 'Declarations and Statements' at www.un.org/Depts/los/convention_agreements/convention_declarations.htm; De Yturriaga, *Straits Used for International Navigation: A Spanish Perspective* (n 35) 150.

[113] Joshua H Ho, 'Enhancing Safety, Security, and Environmental Protection of the Straits of Malacca and Singapore: The Cooperative Mechanism' (2009) 40 *Ocean Development and International Law* 233. See generally Michael Leifer, *International Straits of the World: Malacca, Singapore and Indonesia* (Alphen aan den Rijn, Sijthoff & Noordhoff, 1978).

[114] O'Connell, *The International Law of the Sea* (n 8) vol 1, 318.

traffic, and are often cited as one of the primary reasons why the United States insisted upon the transit passage regime for international straits at UNCLOS III.

Indonesia, Malaysia and Singapore are the adjoining strait states and notwithstanding the troubled modern history between these three neighbours, they have in recent decades been able to assert a relatively common position on matters concerning the straits. Principal concerns have ranged from the maintenance of navigational safety, to marine environmental protection, to maritime security. At UNCLOS III, they increasingly shared a negotiating position on international straits, and took joint initiatives with the IMO to address navigational and maritime safety issues through the straits.[115] This level of cooperation was highlighted in April 1982 when Indonesia, Malaysia and Singapore indicated to the President of the Conference that they had reached agreement with certain major maritime states on the application of the Convention to the Straits of Malacca and Singapore, in particular with respect to the issue of laws and regulations with respect to traffic separation schemes in the Straits and also under keel clearance for certain ships.[116]

An upsurge of pirate attacks in Southeast Asia in the 1990s, followed by regional security concerns in the aftermath of the 2001 terrorist attacks upon New York and Washington, and the subsequent terrorist attacks in Bali and Jakarta highlighted the need to maintain security of shipping within the straits.[117] In response to some of these concerns over the significant burdens imposed upon the strait states by the provisions of the LOSC combined with the high volume of traffic through the straits, in 2005 to 2007, the IMO with the support of the strait states, held a series of meetings in order to broker an agreement on burden sharing. Relying upon the framework of Article 43 of LOSC, which provides that '[u]ser States and States bordering a strait should by agreement cooperate' with respect to maintenance of navigational and safety aids and the prevention, reduction and control of pollution, agreement was reached to enhance cooperation between the users and strait states.[118] Under the so-called 'Cooperative Mechanism' major user states, including Australia, Germany, India, Japan, Panama, South Korea and the United Kingdom, agreed to contribute to a range of projects relating to the safety and security of the straits.

iv. Torres Strait

The Torres Strait lies between Australia and Papua New Guinea and provides a sea route between the Indonesian archipelago and the South Pacific.[119] It is an especially significant navigation route between ports on the east coast of Australia and the Southeast Asian ports of Singapore, Port Dickson and beyond. The strait is the subject of a maritime boundary treaty between Australia and Papua New Guinea,[120] which delimits the fisheries and seabed

---

[115] Leifer, *International Straits of the World: Malacca, Singapore and Indonesia* (n 113) 141–48; Koh, *Straits in International Navigation* (n 29) 55–95, 175–94.

[116] De Yturriaga, *Straits Used for International Navigation: A Spanish Perspective* (n 35) 148–49. This 'understanding' was confirmed in letters of concurrence from representatives of Australia, France, the United Kingdom, the United States, Japan and the Federal Republic of Germany.

[117] Nihan Ünlü, 'Protecting the Straits of Malacca and Singapore Against Piracy and Terrorism' (2006) 21 *International Journal of Marine and Coastal Law* 539–49.

[118] Ho, 'Enhancing Safety, Security, and Environmental Protection of the Straits of Malacca and Singapore' (n 113) 237–42.

[119] See generally Stuart Kaye, *The Torres Strait* (The Hague, Martinus Nijhoff, 1997).

[120] 1979 Treaty between Australia and the Independent State of Papua New Guinea Concerning Sovereignty and Maritime Boundaries in the Area between the Two Countries, including the Area known as Torres Strait, and

boundary between the two countries. In recognition of the special cultural significance of the strait to the indigenous people of the region, the agreement provides for a protected zone that deals with environmental, cultural and management issues in the region. As the treaty was negotiated in the mid- to late 1970s and concluded in 1978, an issue arose as to how the developing transit passage regime in the LOSC should be accommodated. To that end, there are a number of references throughout the treaty to respect for the freedom of navigation through the strait and, relying upon the latest negotiating draft from UNCLOS III, direct reference to the right of transit passage applying within the waters of the strait.[121] The treaty also includes some significant reciprocal rights of navigation between and through the waters of the strait for Australian and Papua New Guinean vessels. There was also equivalent recognition of the rights of overflight.

A feature of the Torres Strait is that there are a number of reefs and shoals within the strait which significantly limit the number of shipping channels that can be safely used by large vessels. In addition, the strait is subject to tidal variation and storms which can make navigation hazardous. Concerned about the potential for a major maritime incident to occur in the strait, in 1987 Australia was successful in having the IMO recognise a voluntary pilotage regime for the strait, which was extended in 1991.[122] In 1997, Australia along with support from Papua New Guinea (PNG) was also able to obtain IMO endorsement of a mandatory ship reporting scheme in the Torres Strait and adjacent waters of the Great Barrier Reef.[123] While these initiatives were initially successful, in the late 1990s and early part of the 2000s there was a significant fall in compliance with the voluntary pilotage regime. In response, Australia and Papua New Guinea sought to have the waters of the strait declared part of a Particularly Sensitive Sea Area (PSSA).

The IMO responded to the Australian/PNG PSSA application with the adoption, through the Marine Environment Protection Committee on 22 July 2005, of Resolution MEPC.133(53), which designated the Torres Strait as part of a PSSA[124] and recognised the existence of a two-way route through the strait. The Resolution further stated:

> 3. Recommends that Governments recognize the need for effective protection of the Great Barrier Reef and Torres Strait region and inform ships flying their flag that they should act in accordance with Australia's system of pilotage for merchant ships 70 m in length and over or oil tankers, chemical tankers, and gas carriers irrespective of size …[125]

Related Matters; Henry Burmester, 'The Torres Strait Treaty: Ocean Boundary Delimitation by Agreement' (1982) 76 *AJIL* 321.

[121] Torres Strait Treaty, art 7(6).
[122] Sam Bateman and Michael White, 'Compulsory Pilotage in the Torres Strait: Overcoming Unacceptable Risks to a Sensitive Marine Environment' (2009) 40 *Ocean Development and International Law* 184, 191.
[123] Stuart Kaye, 'Regulation of Navigation in the Torres Strait: Law of the Sea Issues' in Donald R Rothwell and Sam Bateman (eds), *Navigational Rights and Freedoms and the New Law of the Sea* (The Hague, Martinus Nijhoff, 2000) 119, 127.
[124] At the time of its designation as a PSSA, the Torres Strait became one of only 11 recognised PSSAs around the world, the first of which was the Great Barrier Reef. The other recognised PSSAs at the time were: the Sabana-Camagüey Archipelago (Cuba), Malpelo Islands (Columbia), Florida Keys (USA), Wadden Sea (North Sea), Paracas National Reserve (Peru), Western Europe, Canary Island (Spain), Galapagos Islands (Ecuador) and the Baltic Sea. For the current list of PSSAs see IMO, 'Particularly Sensitive Sea Areas' at www.imo.org/en/OurWork/Environment/PSSAs/Pages/Default.aspx.
[125] IMO Resolution MEPC.133(53) [3]; the Resolution is formally an amendment of Resolution MEPC.45(30), which provided for compulsory pilotage in the Great Barrier Reef, with the effect that the pilotage regime is recognised for both the Great Barrier Reef and Torres Strait.

Details were then provided as to the precise area within the Torres Strait to which pilotage was to apply. The approval of the Torres Strait PSSA proposal provided a basis for the subsequent introduction of a compulsory pilotage regime within the strait in 2006, with it being put into effect under Australian law.[126]

However, Australia's implementation of compulsory pilotage in the Torres Strait resulted in a number of states and other bodies raising their concerns in both the IMO and the United Nations.[127] The principal focus of the criticism was that Resolution MEPC.133(53) was only recommendatory in nature, and did not provide a legal basis for the adoption by Australia of compulsory pilotage in the Torres Strait. At the 55th session of the MEPC in 2006, the Chair of the Committee observed that 'when the Committee adopts resolutions with an operative paragraph beginning with the word "RECOMMENDS", the content of the paragraph is of a recommendatory nature'.[128] The Committee agreed with the Chair that the resolution was of a recommendatory nature,[129] with Singapore asserting that Resolution MEPC.133(53) provided 'no international legal basis for mandatory pilotage for ships in transit in this or any other strait used for international navigation'.[130] Singapore continued its criticism of the Australian position in the United Nations, asserting in 2007 that:

> Unfortunately, Australia continues to operate the compulsory pilotage system in the Torres Strait ... In Singapore's view, this goes beyond what is permitted by Article 42 of the Convention. The requirement to take a pilot on board, which Australia will enforce using its criminal laws, seriously undermines the right of transit passage which all vessels enjoy under the Convention.[131]

In addition to these statements, Singapore and the United States sent diplomatic notes to Australia in 2006,[132] which in turn prompted an Australian reply later that year which was further responded to by the United States in 2007.[133] The extent of these exchanges, and the firm view that was being expressed by Singapore and the United States that Australia's actions were not consistent with the LOSC resulted in suggestions that international litigation may be one means of resolving what had clearly become a legal dispute.[134]

Despite this diplomatic tension, the Australian Maritime Safety Authority (AMSA) reported that for the period October 2006–September 2007 a total of 1,004 piloted transits had taken place through the Torres Strait, which not only reflected 100 per cent compliance, but also that Singapore flagged vessels had undertaken 94 transits during that time.[135]

---

[126] Navigation Act 1912 (Australia), ss 186I, 186J; see also Australian Maritime Safety Authority, *Marine Notices* 8/2006 and 16/2006 and *Marine Orders* 54, specifying the Torres Strait as a Compulsory Pilotage Area.

[127] As compulsory pilotage was provided for under Australian law and not PNG law as transiting vessels do not enter the PNG territorial sea, Australia's legislative actions were the principal focus of these responses.

[128] IMO, Report of the 55th Marine Environment Protection Committee (2006) [8.10].

[129] Ibid.

[130] Ibid, [8.12]; this position was supported by the delegations of the Bahamas, Chile, China, Cyprus, Greece, India, Iran, Israel, Italy, Japan, Latvia, Liberia, the Marshall Islands, Nigeria, Norway, Panama, Republic of Korea, Russian Federation, Thailand, UK, USA.

[131] Statement by Ambassador Vanu Gopala Menon, Permanent Representative of the Republic of Singapore to the United Nations, at the General Assembly Debate on Agenda Item 77 (A): Oceans and the Law of the Sea, 10 December 2007.

[132] Beckman, 'PSSAs and Transit Passage' (n 85) 337.

[133] Ibid 340.

[134] Ibid 337.

[135] Bateman and White, 'Compulsory Pilotage in the Torres Strait: Overcoming Unacceptable Risks to a Sensitive Marine Environment' (n 122) 188–89.

Nevertheless, in September 2011 it was revealed that Australia and the United States had reached an understanding with respect to the enforcement of the Torres Strait compulsory pilotage regime. In 2008 Australia had sought to reassure the United States that while the legislative regime would remain in place, in practice Australia would apply a voluntary pilotage scheme for those ships which passed through the strait and did not subsequently visit an Australian port.[136] The change in Australia's position was reflected in an April 2009 *Marine Notice* issued by AMSA, which provided:

> if a vessel passes through the Torres Strait and it does not comply with Australia's system of pilotage for merchant ships 70 metres in length and over or oil tankers, chemical tankers, and gas carriers, irrespective of size, the Government of Australia will notify the vessel's Flag State, Owner, Operator and Master that the vessel failed to take a pilot and henceforth cannot enter an Australian port without the risk of the Owner, Operator and/or Master of the vessel being subject to a non-custodial penalty under Australian law.[137]

v. Bering Strait

The Bering Strait is bordered by Russia to the west and the United States (Alaska) to the east, and is approximately 51 miles wide. The northern approach through the Chukchi Sea is relatively wide, before it gradually narrows on approach to the strait, while the southern approach has the Aleutian Islands (United States) as a barrier to the east. However, high seas navigation through the central Bering Sea presents no difficulties until St Lawrence Island (United States) is reached immediately to the south of the strait proper. St Lawrence Island straddles the southern entrance to the Bering Strait, forcing shipping to route to the east or to the west between the island and the Russian mainland. The distance between the southeast point of Cape Chukoski (Russia) and Northwest Cape on St Lawrence Island is approximately 38 nm, while the Alaskan mainland is approximately 124 nm at its closest point, allowing for navigation via a high seas corridor on either side of St Lawrence Island before the Bering Strait is entered. At the mid-point of the strait there are two islands—Big Diomede (Russia) and Little Diomede (United States)—effectively creating three navigational channels:

— Bering Strait—West, which lies between the Russian mainland and Big Diomede Island, and is approximately 22.5 nm wide;
— Bering Strait—East, which lies between the US mainland and Little Diomede Island, and is approximately 22.5 nm wide; and
— The Diomede channel,[138] which is a 2.4 nm channel separating Big Diomede and Little Diomede Islands.[139]

Bering Strait—East and Bering Strait—West are recognised by the US Navy as international straits for the purposes of the LOSC.[140]

---

[136] Philip Dorling, 'Reef Safeguard Cut Back', *The Age*, 12 September 2011.
[137] Australian Maritime Safety Authority, 'Bridge Resource Management (BRM) and Torres Strait Pilotage', *Marine Notice* 7/2009.
[138] There does not appear to be an official name for the body of water that separates the two islands, other than that the waters fall within the Bering Strait. Accordingly, it is referred to as the 'Diomede channel'.
[139] These measurements are taken from Roach and Smith, *Excessive Maritime Claims* (n 53) 479–80.
[140] Thomas and Duncan (eds), 'Annotated Supplement to The Commanders Handbook on the Law of Naval Operations' (n 41) 205, Table A2-3.

The Bering Strait meets all of the geographical requirements of a strait for the purposes of Part III of the LOSC. That technically there may exist three geographical straits within the body of water known as the Bering Strait (Bering Strait—East; Bering Strait—West and the Diomede channel) is irrelevant for the purposes of the LOSC, and there are many other international straits throughout the world which are formed by two opposite land masses within which they may be scattered small islands.[141] Whether the Bering Strait is one used for 'international navigation' in the *Corfu Channel* sense may have been contestable in the past, but it would appear clear on the basis of current usage that the strait is certainly considered useful for international navigation. For example, the 2009 *AMSA Report* noted that '150 large commercial vessels pass through the Bering Strait during the July–October open water period, with transits of these vessels most frequent at the beginning (spring) and end of the period (autumn)'.[142] While some caution needs to be exercised because of the usage of the strait by previously Soviet and currently Russian flagged shipping, it is clear that on current and future projections the strait will be used by many ships other than those which are Russian or United States flagged. On that basis, the Bering Strait would meet the requirements for an international strait under Part III of the LOSC, to which the regime of transit passage applies.[143]

A unique feature of the Bering Strait is that international shipping has effectively two viable routes through the strait: the 'Russian route', to the west of the Diomede Islands and through the Russian territorial sea; and the 'American route', to the east of the Diomede Islands and through the US territorial sea. The Diomede channel, at only 2.4 nm, does not appear to be wide enough to be attractive to commercial shipping when compared to the alternative routes. There is also the issue that the waters between the islands fall within the Russia/US maritime boundary, with the effect that shipping would be subject to both Russian and United States law at different times as they completed their transit. In principle, the existence of alternative American and Russian routes through the strait does not raise any significant international law issues given that the LOSC creates a set of standards which are equally applicable to each route and which are not dependent on the strait being a 'one state' or 'two state' strait. It does, however, highlight the fact that the United States has yet to become a party to the LOSC, and whilst United States state practice has been consistently to adhere to the transit passage regime and effectively accept its status as part of customary international law,[144] it still raises the potential for slight variations in state practice in the interpretation of transit passage on either side of the strait. It also raises the prospect of differing laws and regulations being applicable within the Russian and United States sides of the strait, once again consistent with Article 42 of the LOSC, although such laws are to be non-discriminatory and to not deny, hamper or impair the right of passage. Given the

---

[141] The Torres Strait (Australia/Papua New Guinea) and the Strait of Hormuz (Iran/Oman/UAE) are examples.

[142] Arctic Council, *Arctic Marine Shipping Assessment 2009 Report* (Tromsø, Arctic Council, 2009) 109 (*AMSA Report*).

[143] The view is also endorsed by the *AMSA Report*, which states that 'The Bering Strait region is an international strait for navigation and a natural chokepoint for marine traffic in and out of the Arctic Ocean from the Pacific Ocean': ibid 109.

[144] See United States Presidential Proclamation 5928 (27 December 1988), in which President Regan stated that 'In accordance with international law, as reflected in the applicable provisions of the 1982 United Nations Convention on the Law of the Sea, with the territorial sea of the United States ... the ships and aircraft of all countries enjoy the right of transit passage through international straits'; see generally Roach and Smith, *Excessive Maritime Claims* (n 53) 271–75.

environmental sensitivity associated with all aspects of Arctic shipping, some consideration may in due course be given to the establishment of sea lanes and a traffic separation scheme through the Bering Strait so as to facilitate 'one way' north–south and south–north traffic on either side of the Diomede Islands. Such measures would be consistent with Article 41, but would require cooperation between Russia and the United States in referring such a proposal to the IMO for adoption. The 2009 *AMSA Report* noted there were no vessel routing measures within the Bering Strait and few aids to navigation. Given the significant potential of this strait for increased maritime traffic and the difficult navigational conditions, it would be anticipated that in due course such arrangements will be put in place.[145]

In 2010 the US Coast Guard commenced a 'Port Access Route Study' in order to assess whether there was a need to create new vessel routing measures in the Bering Strait. While the area under review only encompasses US waters in the strait, the Coast Guard study does have the potential to facilitate appropriate bilateral arrangements with Russia if such are deemed appropriate.[146] In a further sign that the United States and Russia are giving attention to their shared interests in the Bering Strait region, in 2012 it was announced that the two neighbours would commence negotiations towards the finalisation of a 'Transboundary Area of Shared Beringian Heritage' that would link the national parks in Alaska and Russia.[147]

IV. Archipelagic Navigation

One of the principal goals of UNCLOS III once agreement was reached on the definition of an archipelago was to determine the various navigation regimes which existed within archipelagic waters. In this regard, it was important not only to focus upon waters on the landward side of the archipelagic baselines but also to consider waters that fell within the potential maritime zones that an archipelagic state could assert, of which the territorial sea was the most significant from a navigational perspective.

Whilst the LOSC provided that archipelagic states were able to claim sovereignty over the waters within the limits of the archipelagic baselines which also extended to the air space,[148] the sovereignty of the archipelagic state was to be exercised in conformity with Part IV of the Convention, which made express allowance for a range of navigational regimes within archipelagic waters. Article 50 makes clear that within archipelagic waters, subject to certain exceptions, the ships of all states enjoy the right of innocent passage and that this right is to be applied in accordance with the relevant articles found in Part II dealing with innocent passage.[149] Therefore, for the purposes of navigation within archipelagic waters the innocent passage regime effectively applies in the same way as it does within the territorial sea. Hence ships of all states have the right of passage through archipelagic waters irrespective of

---

[145] *AMSA Report* (n 142) 109.

[146] Department of Homeland Security: United States Coast Guard, 'Port Access Route Study: In the Bering Strait' 33 CFR Part 167, *Federal Register*, 75 (No 215), 8 November 2010.

[147] US Department of State, 'US–Russia Cooperation on Antarctica, Interregional Areas, and Beringia' Fact Sheet (8 September 2012) at www.state.gov/r/pa/prs/ps/2012/09/197523.htm.

[148] LOSC, art 49.

[149] Ibid arts 17–32.

whether they are calling at a local port, or simply passing through from an entry to an exit point, provided that the passage is innocent and not prejudicial to the peace, good order and security of the archipelagic state and in conformity with any relevant laws and regulations the archipelagic state may have adopted. Notwithstanding Article 23 of the LOSC, which permits innocent passage by foreign nuclear-powered ships or those which are carrying nuclear or other dangerous or toxic substances providing appropriate documentation is being carried and precautionary measures are being observed, a number of archipelagic states have objected to the presence of such vessels within their waters.[150]

A. Innocent Passage Within Archipelagic Waters

Innocent passage within archipelagic waters is the default navigation regime for those ships not otherwise undertaking archipelagic sea lanes passage and is subject to only two qualifications.[151] First, like the innocent passage regime within the territorial sea, the archipelagic state may temporarily suspend innocent passage within specified areas of the archipelagic waters 'if such suspension is essential for the protection of its security'.[152] Such suspension is to only take effect after having been duly published. Accordingly, an archipelagic state may from time to time, and with appropriate notice, completely close areas of its archipelagic waters to international shipping. The LOSC places few limitations on this right other than it be non-discriminatory, and a temporal and notification requirement, thereby providing the archipelagic state with considerable latitude in how it interprets this provision,[153] including its capacity to suspend navigation in waters which are at a considerable distance from any of the islands that fall within archipelagic baselines.

Secondly, the innocent passage regime is without prejudice to the right of the archipelagic state to draw closing lines for the delimitation of internal waters within the archipelago.[154] Nevertheless, innocent passage may still be enjoyed between archipelagic waters and the internal waters of the archipelago where a ship is proceeding to or from those internal waters, such as in the case of a port facility.[155] In addition to the right of innocent passage within archipelagic waters, innocent passage also applies within the territorial sea of an archipelagic state, which lies on the seaward side of the normal baselines and archipelagic baselines. Therefore, foreign ships which enter into the territorial sea of an archipelagic state would enjoy an ongoing right of innocent passage as they passed from the territorial

---

[150] Mohamed Munavvar, *Ocean States: Archipelagic Regimes in the Law of the Sea* (Dordrecht, Martinus Nijhoff, 1995) 166.

[151] This is made clear by LOSC, art 52(1) which states that the right of innocent passage is '[s]ubject to article 53 [right of archipelagic sea lanes passage] and without prejudice to article 50 [delimitation of internal waters]'. In the case of Indonesia, Government Regulation No 37 on the Rights and Obligations of Foreign Ships and Aircraft Exercising the Right of Archipelagic Sea Lanes Passage through Designated Sea Lanes (28 June 2002) (2003) 52 *Law of the Sea Bulletin* 20, art 13 contemplates the exercise of the right of innocent passage within an archipelagic sea lane.

[152] LOSC, art 52(2).

[153] The equivalent provision in LOSC, art 25(3) provides that the coastal state may temporarily suspend innocent passage 'if such suspension is essential for the protection of its security, including weapons exercises'. The omission of a reference to weapons exercises in art 52(2) does not appear significant.

[154] LOSC, arts 50, 52(1).

[155] Using the language and the provisions found in LOSC art 18(1)(b).

sea into archipelagic waters and then passed through the archipelago back out into the territorial sea.

B. Archipelagic Sea Lanes Passage

The most significant distinctive navigational regime that applies within archipelagic waters is that of archipelagic sea lanes passage (ASLP), which is outlined in Article 53 but which borrows heavily from the transit passage regime in Part III of the LOSC, even to the extent of applying some of the provisions of the transit passage regime *mutatis mutandis*.[156] ASLP is exercised within and above archipelagic waters, which is an area over which the archipelagic state enjoys sovereignty extending to both the air space, seabed and the subsoil.[157] Within archipelagic sea lanes all ships and aircraft enjoy a right of ASLP in sea lanes and air routes.[158] The right is one that can be exercised for the purpose of 'continuous, expeditious and unobstructed transit' between one part of the high seas or an EEZ and another part of the high seas or an EEZ.[159] The omission of a reference to transit through the territorial sea at the perimeter of the entrance and exit from archipelagic waters is intentional, as the sea lanes through which ASLP is enjoyed traverse through the archipelagic waters and the adjacent territorial sea.[160] ASLP therefore duplicates key aspects of the transit passage regime within international straits in that it is designed to facilitate the passage of both ships and aircraft through and over the waters of the archipelagic state so that they can freely move through the archipelago as they continue their journey. In this respect, emphasis is given to the regime being one which promotes continuous and expeditious transit. Vessels that seek to call at a port within archipelagic waters therefore do not exercise ASLP, but rather revert to the innocent passage regime noted above.[161] Indonesia, as the first archipelagic state to designate archipelagic sea lanes consistent with the processes outlined in Article 53 of the LOSC, in 2002 adopted Government Regulation No 37 dealing with the rights and obligations of foreign ships and aircraft in passage.[162] The Indonesian Regulation directly refers

---

[156] Ibid art 54.

[157] Ibid art 49. Upon signature and subsequent ratification of the LOSC, the Philippines lodged a Declaration under LOSC, art 310 which in part provided: 'The provisions of the Convention on archipelagic passage through sea lanes do not nullify or impair the sovereignty of the Philippines as an archipelagic State over the sea lanes and do not deprive it of authority to enact legislation to protect its sovereignty, independence and security', United Nations Division for Ocean Affairs and the Law of the Sea, 'Declarations and Statements' at www.un.org/Depts/los/convention_agreements/convention_declarations.htm.

[158] LOSC, art 53(2). Writing in 1991, Barbara Kwiatkowska and Etty R Agoes, *Archipelagic Waters Regime in the Light of the 1982 United Nations Law of the Sea Convention and State Practice* (Bandung, ICLOS, UNPAD, 1991) 43 asserted the right of 'non-suspendable archipelagic sea lanes passage of all ships and aircraft, … is alongside with the innocent passage of warships the most controversial element of [sic] archipelagic state regime'.

[159] LOSC, art 53(3).

[160] Ibid art 53(4).

[161] Ibid art 38(2) which anticipates a vessel or aircraft in transit passage entering, leaving or returning from a state which borders a strait, does not have an equivalent provision in the ASLP regime. This is understandable given that within archipelagic waters there exists a mixed regime of innocent passage for some ships and ASLP for other ships.

[162] Indonesian Government Regulation No 37 on the Rights and Obligations of Foreign Ships and Aircraft Exercising the Right of Archipelagic Sea Lanes Passage through Designated Sea Lanes (28 June 2002) (2003) 52 *Law of the Sea Bulletin* 20.

to the right of archipelagic sea lane passage by foreign ships and aircraft as being a right recognised under Indonesian law by Act No 6 regarding Indonesian Waters.[163]

i. Navigation in the 'Normal Mode'

The right of ASLP is one that is to be exercised in the 'normal mode' which again duplicates language found in the transit passage regime.[164] As in the case of transit through an international strait, ASLP in the normal mode through an archipelagic sea lane can raise significant issues especially in the case of warships,[165] where an archipelagic state may have a legitimate sensitivity to the presence of such ships within the waters which in effect comprise the state. Likewise, it is arguable that because passage through an archipelago along an archipelagic sea lane may be a lengthy voyage that could take many hours then 'normal modes' of operation for warships should be allowed a more flexible interpretation, especially in the case of submarines and aircraft carriers.

ii. Navigation within Archipelagic Sea Lanes

Unlike the transit passage regime, where the coastal state has little capacity to influence where ships and aircraft exercise the right of transit other than in designated sea lanes, the right of ASLP is one which the LOSC conferred significant rights upon the archipelagic state so as to designate sea lanes within which ASLP can be exercised. The sea lanes and air routes must include 'all normal passage routes used as routes for international navigation and overflight' and in the case of ships 'all normal navigational channels'.[166] Recognising that the waters within many archipelagic states would previously have been either high seas, or straits within which a right of international navigation prevailed, the clear intent of the LOSC is to preserve these previously existing navigation routes and this is emphasised by the repeated use of the word 'normal' in the context of the passage routes and channels. The effect of this foundational provision as to where ASLP may be enjoyed is that the LOSC sought to retain the status quo with respect to navigation routes that existed through some of the major archipelagos prior to the conclusion of the LOSC, and accordingly for major straits such as Sunda and Lombok within the Indonesian archipelago, the entry into force of ASLP provisions should not have had a major impact upon traditional navigation routes. Nevertheless, irregularly used routes such as those which may be selected by foreign yachts undertaking a pleasure cruise through an archipelago would not fall into the category of a 'normal' route. The archipelagic sea lanes are also to include 'all normal navigational channels' with an exception arising in the case where there may have previously existed a number of duplicate routes of similar convenience. The effect here is that only one

---

[163] Act No 6 of 8 August 1996 regarding Indonesian Waters (Indonesia); see also ibid art 2.

[164] LOSC, art 53(3); cf art 39(1)(c).

[165] Kwiatkowska and Agoes, *Archipelagic Waters Regime* (n 158) 44, 54; Munavvar, *Ocean States* (n 150) 168. Upon its signature of the LOSC in 1983, Sao Tome and Principe lodged a declaration consistent with LOSC, art 310 which in part provided: 'The Government of the Democratic Republic of Sao Tome and Principe reserves the right to adopt laws and regulations relating to the innocent passage of warships through its territorial sea or its archipelagic waters and to take any other measures aimed at safeguarding its security': United Nations Division for Ocean Affairs and the Law of the Sea, 'Declarations and Statements' at www.un.org/Depts/los/convention_ agreements/convention_declarations.htm.

[166] LOSC, art 53(4).

sea lane is required for designation within any one particular body of water. In addition, the designation of particular sea lanes may also need to take into account the harmonisation of foreign ships undertaking ASLP with local commercial navigation moving within the archipelago.[167]

iii. Designation of Archipelagic Sea Lanes

Article 53 of the LOSC envisages that the archipelagic state will designate sea lanes consistent with the procedures provided in the Convention, however, in recognition that sea lanes may not have been designated, there is a default provision that ASLP 'may be exercised through the routes normally used for international navigation'.[168] Not only could this be relied upon in instances where an archipelagic state delays its designation of sea lanes or air routes after becoming bound by the LOSC, thereby addressing some of the inevitable delays that may accompany the entry into force of the Convention for some states, but it also applies where an archipelagic state either refuses to designate sea lanes or is content to accept the default position imposed by the LOSC. Whilst these provisions guarantee an ongoing right of ASLP through an archipelago even in the absence of sea lanes designation, there is the potential for varying interpretations as to what are the routes which have been 'normally used for international navigation' through an archipelago. At the major entry and exit points into the archipelago which in most instances would be straits, it will be possible to rely upon previous state practice. However, in some instances, especially in the case of archipelagic states which have been able to gain recognition in reliance upon the *sui generis* archipelagic baselines provisions of Part IV, which may have resulted in baselines as long as 125 nm, there may be little clear state practice as to which routes had previously been utilised especially due to the fact that these waters would have been high seas and there would have been minimal obligations upon international shipping to use any particular route.[169]

It is therefore clearly beneficial for an archipelagic state to designate sea lanes and air routes, which are to be identified by a series of continuous axis lines from entry to exit points throughout the archipelago, and are to be clearly indicated on charts to which due publicity shall have been given.[170] Both ships and aircraft are required not to deviate more than 25 nm either side of the axis lines, with the effect that a sea lane may be up to 50 nm in width, subject to constraints which may be posed by islands or navigational hazards.[171] Archipelagic waters may contain islands of varying size and in some instances these inner islands may impinge upon the corridor within which ASLP can be exercised. In recognition of the sovereign interests of the archipelagic state, the LOSC provides that ships and aircraft are to not navigate closer to the coasts than 10 per cent of the distance between the

---

[167] Jay L Batongbacal, 'Barely Skimming the Surface: Archipelagic Sea Lanes Navigation and the IMO' in Alex G Oude Elferink and Donald R Rothwell (eds), *Oceans Management in the 21st Century: Institutional Frameworks and Responses* (Leiden, Martinus Nijhoff, 2004) 49, 65.

[168] LOSC, art 53(12). In contrast to LOSC, art 53(4) the words 'or overflight' are not included in LOSC, art 53(12), leading to some ambiguity, however as the sub-article also refers to the failure of the archipelagic state to 'designate … air routes' the necessary implication is that the provision also extends to air routes used for overflight as well as sea lanes.

[169] Munavvar, *Ocean States* (n 150) 168.

[170] LOSC, art 53(10).

[171] Ibid art 53(5).

nearest points of the islands bordering the sea lane.[172] The effect of this provision is that if an island is 18 nm distant from the axis coordinate points of the sea lane, then shipping may navigate no closer to the island than 1.8 nm, consequently having a narrowing impact upon the breadth of the sea lane. In addition to the designation of archipelagic sea lanes, the archipelagic state may also designate traffic separation schemes for the safe passage of ships through 'narrow channels' in the sea lanes.[173] This would have particular relevance in the case where a sea lane has been considerably narrowed as a result of islands within the archipelago and application of the 10 per cent rule.

iv. Obligations while Undertaking Archipelagic Sea Lanes Passage

Whilst Part IV outlines in some detail the regime of ASLP, many of the rights, duties and obligations of both the user state and archipelagic state are left silent. The exception is Article 54, which makes clear that the provisions of Articles 39, 40, 42 and 44 apply *mutatis mutandis* to ASLP, which is a further reinforcement of the linkage between the transit passage and ASLP regimes. Accordingly, both ships and aircraft engaged in ASLP are required to proceed without delay and to refrain from any threat or use of force against the sovereignty or territorial integrity of the archipelagic state.[174] Article 39(1)(c) reinforces that passage is to be undertaken in the normal mode. Ships and aircraft also have obligations to comply with appropriate safety at sea and marine environmental provisions, and for civil aircraft to comply with ICAO Rules of the Air and for state aircraft to have due regard to the safety of navigation, whilst also monitoring designated air traffic control authorities. Foreign ships engaged in ASLP are also not to undertake marine scientific research, including any survey activities, without prior authorisation.[175] There is likewise an obligation upon foreign ships and aircraft to comply with the relevant laws and regulations of the archipelagic state which may have been adopted which in the case of ships may deal with safety of navigation, pollution control, stowage of fishing gear, and activities contrary to customs, fiscal, immigration or sanitary laws and regulations.[176] That the same category of laws and regulations which apply to ships in transit passage also apply in ASLP is a significant concession to international maritime traffic given the comparative length of time ships may spend within archipelagic waters as opposed to the territorial sea whilst in transit passage. Of some note here is that no express provisions are included to deal with the case of warships, and like the Part III provisions dealing with transit passage, the ASLP provisions remain silent on whether any distinction can be made between warships and other ships exercising ASLP.[177] A further contrast can be made between the right of navigation by submarines within archipelagic waters which under the applicable innocent passage

---

[172] Ibid art 53(5).

[173] Ibid art 53(6).

[174] Ibid art 39(1)(a)(b). This is reflected also in Indonesian law; Indonesian Government Regulation No 37 on the Rights and Obligations of Foreign Ships and Aircraft Exercising the Right of Archipelagic Sea Lanes Passage through Designated Sea Lanes, arts 4, 6.

[175] LOSC, art 40.

[176] Ibid art 42(1). The safety of navigation and regulation of maritime traffic provisions cross-refer back to Article 41, which would also apply in the case of ASLP which makes allowance for the possible designation of a traffic separation scheme within an archipelagic sea lane.

[177] Under Indonesian Government Regulation No 37 on the Rights and Obligations of Foreign Ships and Aircraft Exercising the Right of Archipelagic Sea Lanes Passage through Designated Sea Lanes, art 4(4) purports to restrict the right of warships and aircraft engaged in ASLP from conducting war exercises.

regime are required to navigate on the surface,[178] yet whilst undertaking ASLP may navigate submerged on the grounds that this is their 'normal mode'.[179]

v. Obligations of the Archipelagic State

The obligations of the archipelagic state with respect to ASLP are likewise transposed from Article 44 within Part III and as such they are to not hamper transit passage, give appropriate publicity to any danger of which they have knowledge, or suspend ASLP. These obligations upon the archipelagic state are further reinforced with the Article 53 reference to ASLP being 'unobstructed'. Accordingly, other than for permissible laws and regulations which the archipelagic state may enact consistent with the LOSC, an archipelagic state must permit ASLP to be enjoyed by all vessels and aircraft other than those not acting in conformity with their Article 39 obligations, in which case they are not legitimately undertaking ASLP and could have their continued right of navigation or overflight revoked by intervention from the archipelagic state. The obligation to give publicity to any dangers to navigation and overflight is potentially significant, given the size of some archipelagic states, and is only qualified to the extent that it applies only to those dangers of which 'they have knowledge'. In the past 15 years both Indonesia and the Philippines have faced internal disruption as a result of the actions of insurgent groups and these have had the potential to pose dangers to navigation and overflight.[180] During the 1990s, throughout the 2000s and in 2015 there have also been reports of pirate attacks within the waters of both archipelagos.[181] Not only do these events trigger obligations to warn, but may also result in the need to adjust sea lanes in order to ensure safe passage. Bearing in mind that ASLP cannot be suspended, in the case of significant ongoing threats especially to ships, there may be a need to substitute designated sea lanes with other sea lanes on a temporary basis.[182]

One of the clearest obligations which archipelagic states have with respect to ASLP is not to suspend passage and this duplicates a similar obligation of strait states with respect to transit passage within international straits. The obligation is significant as it means that at all times the waters within the archipelago will be subject to navigation and overflight through the sea lanes such that there will always be a foreign presence within the waters of the archipelagic state. This dual nature of the non-suspendable ASLP regime and the suspendable innocent passage regime within archipelagic waters perhaps inevitably will lead to confusion as to which regime applies in essentially the same body of water, especially as ships engaging in innocent passage may legitimately have the need to enter and

---

[178] LOSC, art 20.

[179] This distinction between the two regimes is highlighted by Batongbacal, who notes that: '"Normal mode" navigation will have to comply fairly closely with standards for innocent passage, because it would not be acceptable for vessels transiting the very heartland of an archipelagic State to be able to undertake activities more liberally than vessels transiting up to 12 miles away from the coast of a continental coastal State': Batongbacal, 'Barely Skimming the Surface' (n 167) 62.

[180] In the case of the Philippines these incidents have included the 2000 bombing of the inter-island ferry *MV Our Lady of Mediatrix*, and bombing of the *MV SuperFerry 14* in Manila Bay in 2004: Mary Ann Palma, 'The Philippines as an Archipelagic and Maritime Nation: Interests, Challenges and Perspectives' (2009) *RSIS Working Paper* No 182, 21.

[181] Rendi A Witular, 'Java Sea, Lombok Strait Becoming More Dangerous, Government Says', *The Jakarta Post*, 3 August 2005, 13; 'Pirates in South-East Asia: Malacca Buccaneers', *The Economist*, 27 June 2015, 24.

[182] Some allowance is made for the need to substitute sea lanes in LOSC, art 53(7).

exit archipelagic waters via an archipelagic sea lane, or to intersect a sea lane whilst moving from one part of the archipelago to the other. In 1988 Indonesia temporarily closed the Sunda and Lombok Straits to navigation in order to conduct weapons exercises. This action attracted diplomatic protests from several countries, including Australia, West Germany and the United States.[183] Whilst Indonesia had ratified the LOSC, the Convention had yet to enter into force, creating challenges in assessing the content of Indonesia's obligations under both treaty law and customary international law to give effect to the ASLP regime. Whilst Indonesia has not attempted to close passage through these or other straits in recent years, this incident did highlight the sensitivity associated with how the LOSC sought to balance the interests of maritime states wanting to maintain the freedom of navigation in the Convention with the rights and interests of archipelagic states.[184]

C. State Practice Designating Archipelagic Sea Lanes

An important aspect of the operationalisation of the ASLP regime in Part IV is the designation of archipelagic sea lanes. No recognised archipelagic state under the LOSC had designated sea lanes at the time of the Convention's 1994 entry into force, with the effect that the default provisions of the Convention applied and ASLP was recognised through the routes within those archipelagic states that were 'normally used for international navigation'.[185] Although in effect this resulted in ongoing application of the status quo within the major navigation routes through archipelagos, it did create the potential for disputes to arise between user states and archipelagic states as to what those routes actually were.

Soon after the entry into force of the LOSC, Indonesia began a process to designate archipelagic sea lanes under the Convention. This created an immediate challenge, as Article 53 makes clear that there is no unilateral right of sea lanes designation but that the archipelagic state is to 'refer proposals to the competent international organization with a view to their adoption'.[186] However, as archipelagic sea lanes were a creature of the LOSC there was no previous experience for any international organisation in the designation of such sea lanes, and the Convention did not create any new organisation to fulfil that task. In 1996 Indonesia proposed to the IMO the adoption of archipelagic sea lanes, and as this referral was not met with objection by other LOSC parties, it was clear that a consensus view had developed that with respect to this matter the IMO was the most appropriate international organisation to fulfil this role.[187] At the IMO the Indonesian proposals were considered by the Maritime Safety Committee, and the Safety of Navigation Sub-Committee. Indonesia also held a series of bilateral meetings with key user states, including Australia and the United States.

---

[183] Nayan Chanda and Nigel Holloway, 'Troubled Waters: Indonesia's Neighbours Consider Responses to Closure of Straits', *Far Eastern Economic Review*, 10 November 1988, 18.

[184] Donald R Rothwell, 'The Indonesian Straits Incident: Transit or Archipelagic Sea Lanes Passage?' (1990) 14 *Marine Policy* 491.

[185] LOSC, art 53(12).

[186] Ibid art 53(9).

[187] Rosalie Balkin, 'The Role of the International Maritime Organization in the Settlement of International Disputes' in Donald R Rothwell and Sam Bateman (eds), *Navigational Rights and Freedoms and the New Law of the Sea* (The Hague, Martinus Nijhoff, 2000) 293, 310–13.

With no previous experience in considering the archipelagic sea lanes provisions of the LOSC, the IMO determined the need for internal procedures to be devised within the Organization for the designation process. This resulted in the 1998 adoption of the General Provisions on the Adoption, Designation and Substitution of Archipelagic Sea Lanes (GPASL). The GPASL not only sought to reflect the IMO experience in considering the Indonesian proposals, but were also designed to guide future deliberations under the Article 53 process.[188] The Philippines, however, made clear during the IMO deliberations that it did not consider the GPASL to represent a precedent for future archipelagic sea lane designations.[189]

Some of the main issues which arose with the Indonesian proposal were concerns expressed by major maritime states of the direction of the routes and whether there were adequate North-South and East-West sea lanes under consideration. In addition, there were issues as to the interpretation of the 10 per cent rule, the role of the ICAO with respect to overflight of the sea lanes, and whether the designated sea lanes could be subject to subsequent variation or modification. Following endorsement by the IMO in 1998 of Indonesia's proposed archipelagic sea lanes, Indonesia proceeded to proclaim the sea lanes. However, an understanding was reached with major user states such as Australia and the United States that the right of archipelagic sea lanes passage could continue to be exercised throughout routes normally used for international navigation.[190] Indonesia therefore completed a partial designation of its archipelagic sea lanes within which the right of ASLP applies, but there remain other routes within the Indonesian archipelago considered to be 'routes normally used for international navigation' within which ASLP rights still apply. Accordingly, user states are able to rely upon an interpretation of Article 53(12) to support their ongoing use of routes through the Indonesian archipelago which they previously used for international navigation. The Indonesian designation of these archipelagic sea lanes is now reflected in Indonesian law.[191]

While in 2015 the Philippines' House of Representatives and Senate were debating the 'Philippines Archipelagic Sea Lanes Act', which would permit the declaration of archipelagic sea lanes, no archipelagic sea lanes had yet been declared by the Philippines consistent with the Article 53 and IMO procedures noted above. Much of the delay for the Philippines has related to the finalisation of its archipelagic baselines, which were settled in 2009 with an appropriate notification made to the United Nations.[192] Matters to be considered by the Philippines as a part of the process of declaring archipelagic sea lanes will include assessing the already existing routes which are currently being used for international navigation, the existing multiple internal routes used for domestic trade and transport, and maritime safety and security.[193]

---

[188] Robin Warner, 'Implementing the Archipelagic Regime in the International Maritime Organization' in Donald R Rothwell and Sam Bateman (eds), *Navigational Rights and Freedoms* ibid 170, 174.

[189] Batongbacal, 'Barely Skimming the Surface' (n 167) 58.

[190] Warner, 'Implementing the Archipelagic Regime in the International Maritime Organization' (n 188) 176–84.

[191] Indonesian Government Regulation No 37 on the Rights and Obligations of Foreign Ships and Aircraft Exercising the Right of Archipelagic Sea Lanes Passage through Designated Sea Lanes, arts 11, 12.

[192] See the discussion in ch 8.

[193] Palma, 'The Philippines as an Archipelagic and Maritime Nation' (n 180) 7–9.

V. Further Reading

David Caron and Nilufer Oral (eds), *Navigating Straits: Challenges for International Law* (Leiden, Brill, 2014)

Ana G López Martin, *International Straits: Concept, Classification and Rules of Passage* (Berlin, Springer-Verlag, 2010)

SN Nandan and DH Anderson, 'Straits Used for International Navigation: A Commentary on Part III of the United Nations Convention on the Law of the Sea 1982' (1989) 60 *British Yearbook of International Law* 159

Graham Gerard Ong, *Piracy, Maritime Terrorism and Securing the Malacca Straits* (Singapore, Institute of Southeast Asian Studies, 2006)

Donald R Rothwell and Sam Bateman (eds), *Navigational Rights and Freedoms and the New Law of the Sea* (The Hague, Martinus Nijhoff, 2000)

Nihan Ünlü, *The Legal Regime of the Turkish Straits* (The Hague, Martinus Nijhoff, 2002)

12

Military Uses of the Oceans

I. Introduction

The law of the sea has always been highly relevant to naval strategy[1] and the linkages and tensions between and law and naval operations became more prominent as the law consolidated and was codified throughout the twentieth century. Alongside these developments, the international law regulating international armed conflict also went through a major codification process starting with the Hague Conferences in 1899 and 1907 and eventually resulting in the adoption of the four 1949 Geneva Conventions and the two 1977 Additional Protocols. As was the case with warfare more generally, the twentieth century saw some of the most extensive developments in the history of modern naval warfare ranging from the development of new warships—including submarines and aircraft carriers—to new weapons systems. The consequence of these developments was that while the oceans became subject to greater forms of regulation, with increasing restraints placed upon the freedom of navigation, new naval technologies meant that there was also greater potential to use the oceans as a theatre for modern warfare.

Any discussion of the military use of the oceans needs to make a clear distinction between the law as it applies during armed conflict and during peacetime. During an armed conflict Hague law, the 1949 Geneva Conventions, and the Protocols have application,[2] in addition to the distinctive international law that applies to the sea during these times, including the laws of naval warfare.[3] The LOSC applies during peacetime, and its provisions were crafted with that in mind, a point reinforced in both the Preamble and Article 301.[4] The LOSC was also designed to bring security to the oceans, and with it an enhancement of the peaceful uses of the oceans through maritime confidence building,[5] of which the certainty associated with maritime boundary limits and claims is an example. However, the distinction between war and peace in the twenty-first century is not always clear, especially

---

[1] Ken Booth, *Law, Force and Diplomacy at Sea* (Boston, George Allen & Unwin, 1985) 3.

[2] See generally Yoram Dinstein, *The Conduct of Hostilities under the Law of International Armed Conflict*, 2nd edn (Cambridge, Cambridge University Press, 2010).

[3] Louise Doswald-Beck (ed), *San Remo Manual on International Law Applicable to Armed Conflicts at Sea* (Cambridge, Cambridge University Press, 1995).

[4] LOSC, Preamble provides: 'Recognizing the desirability of establishing through this Convention, with due regard for the sovereignty of all States, a legal order for the seas and oceans which will facilitate international communication, and will promote the peaceful uses of the seas and oceans'.

[5] Donald R Rothwell, 'The Law of the Sea as a Maritime Confidence Building Measure' in Sam Bateman and Stephen Bates (eds), *Calming the Waters: Initiatives for Asia Pacific Maritime Cooperation* (Canberra, Strategic and Defence Studies Centre, Australian National University, 1996) 77–90.

given ongoing non-international armed conflicts and also certain internationalised armed conflicts arising from the ongoing global struggle against terrorism. The role of the United Nations Security Council in the contemporary law of the sea also needs to be acknowledged, especially in the light of its capacity under Chapter VII of the UN Charter to authorise peace-enforcement and peace-keeping operations which have both a land and a maritime dimension. The increasing concern of the United Nations over nuclear proliferation and associated WMD highlights additional issues for the oceans which ultimately go to global and regional maritime security but also raise issues of maritime regulation and enforcement.[6]

II. Historical Overview

As the seas and oceans were traditionally used predominantly for trade and assertion of power, the military use of the oceans has been associated with the seas since armed forces acquired a naval capacity. Predominantly these early uses of the oceans were for the purpose of asserting naval power with the objective of controlling the oceans. Early forms of naval power were exercised throughout the seas adjacent to Europe, especially the Baltic Sea, North Sea and Mediterranean Sea. There is also significant evidence of naval supremacy being established by the Chinese in the South China Sea, and Arab rulers and kings in the northern Indian Ocean, and eventually throughout South and Southeast Asia.[7] The historical connection between the law and sea power became evident when the modern international law of the sea began to develop in the seventeenth century, and was clearly related to aspects of the debates which arose between publicists such as Grotius and Selden regarding the future of the seas. The arguments in favour of a 'closed sea' were directly related to the security concerns of coastal states and the threats that were posed to them by foreign navies. The freedom of the sea promoted by Grotius on the other hand not only allowed for virtually unfettered access to the oceans for the purposes of trade and commerce but also allowed for the seas to be ruled by the strongest navies of the day. The ultimate endorsement of the Grotian view of the oceans not only cemented respect for the freedom of the seas, but also the capacity of naval powers to exercise considerable influence during peacetime.

This seventeenth-century perspective on law and naval power prevails today with the effect that the primary aim of most naval powers remains the assertion of the freedom of the seas.[8] Accordingly, one of the tensions associated with the development of the modern international law of the sea has been to ensure an appropriate balance between expanding coastal state rights over adjoining areas of ocean and the navigational freedoms applicable to both merchant and naval vessels. To that end, it is significant that the *Corfu Channel* case[9]—the very first case before the new International Court of Justice—directly addressed

---

[6] David D Caron and Harry N Scheiber (eds), *The Oceans in the Nuclear Age: Legacies and Risks* (Leiden, Martinus Nijhoff, 2010).

[7] RP Anand, *Origin and Development of the Law of the Sea* (The Hague, Martinus Nijohff, 1983) 22–28.

[8] DP O'Connell, *The Influence of Law on Sea Power* (Manchester, Manchester University Press, 1975) 1.

[9] *Corfu Channel (United Kingdom v Albania)* [1949] ICJ Rep 4.

issues of the naval freedom of the seas. These tensions have remained in recent decades, with the vigorous assertion by the United States of its Freedom of Navigation Program to ensure ongoing recognition of the navigational rights and freedoms of the United States Navy during peacetime being a prominent example.[10]

III. International Law and Naval Operations

The international law of naval operations is characterised by two streams of international law dealing with operations during armed conflict and peacetime. Whilst they are separate and distinct, each forms an important backdrop for the other and occasionally they overlap. The modern international law of armed conflict began its development in the mid nineteenth century and was characterised early in the twentieth century by the negotiation of a great number of treaties and conventions seeking to regulate various aspects of armed conflict. Given the history and traditions associated with naval warfare it is unsurprising that this area in particular was subjected to efforts to codify the law at the 1899 and 1907 Hague Conferences which paved the way for the development of the modern international law of naval warfare within the international law of armed conflict.[11] The law of the sea, on the other hand, sought to deal with peacetime, and the codification and development of the law throughout the twentieth century was characterised by a focus on the peaceful use of the oceans by coastal states and maritime navigation. On the entitlement to the use of force, and any limitations that may be applicable to it, the law of the sea has consistently deferred to general international law. This is reflected in Article 301 of the LOSC with its chapeau titled 'Peaceful uses of the seas' and its restatement of the obligation under Article 2(4) of the UN Charter requiring states to refrain from the threat or use of force against other states or in a manner inconsistent with the Charter. Yet while the modern law of the sea has been developed deliberately so as to avoid matters associated with war or armed conflict, many aspects of the law most certainly have an impact upon military operations at sea during peacetime, particularly the movement of foreign naval vessels through the territorial sea, international straits, and archipelagic waters. Two dimensions of general international law have particular relevance to military operations at sea: the law of naval warfare, and United Nations sanctioned naval operations.

A. Law of Naval Warfare

The law of naval warfare developed initially in customary international law, and then was subject to partial codification during the 1899 and 1907 Hague Conferences which resulted in conventions dealing with the status of enemy merchant ships,[12] the conversion

---

[10] J Ashley Roach and Robert W Smith, *Excessive Maritime Claims*, 3rd edn (Leiden, Martinus Nijohff, 2012) 6–13, 637–39.
[11] C John Colombos, *The International Law of the Sea*, 6th edn (London, Longmans, 1967) 481–91, outlining the general framework and historical development of the law.
[12] 1907 Hague Convention (VI) Relating to the Status of Enemy Merchant Ships at the Outbreak of Hostilities.

of merchant ships into warships,[13] the laying of submarine mines,[14] naval bombardment[15] and the right of capture.[16] These conventions sought to reflect customary international law and dealt with the important distinctions between belligerents and neutral states whilst also seeking to maintain certain freedoms of maritime commerce by merchant ships. There was also a recognition of the need to place constraints on unlimited naval warfare and as such Hague Convention IX Concerning Bombardment by Naval Forces in Time of War prohibited the bombardment by naval forces of undefended ports, town and villages.[17] Immediately following World War I, when submarine warfare had emerged as a significant issue especially with respect to the threat that it posed to merchant shipping, the 1922 Washington Treaty Relating to the Use of Submarines and Noxious Gases in Warfare was concluded; however, it failed to win the support of all the negotiating parties and never entered into force. Nevertheless, the 1930 International Treaty for the Limitation and Reduction of Naval Armament was successfully concluded amongst 11 states, and by a 1936 Procès-Verbal[18] was extended to a greater number of potential states parties.[19] Under the Rules established by the so-called 1936 London Protocol, submarines in relation to their engagement of merchant ships were required to 'conform to the rules of International Law to which surface vessels were subject'.

The outbreak of World War II halted the development of this aspect of the law, and also severely tested its implementation. The conclusion of the war brought about the development of new laws regulating armed conflict, not only via the UN Charter with its limitations on the use of force in Article 2, but also through new conventions regulating the conduct of armed conflict. The 1949 Geneva Conventions represented a radical rethink in the law and gave heavy emphasis to the humanitarian treatment of all persons involved in armed conflict, including seamen.[20] These provisions were further extended by the two 1977 Additional Protocols to the Geneva Conventions. These two strands of international law developed at The Hague and Geneva have now become recognised as 'international humanitarian law' reflecting a focus upon the law regulating the conduct of armed conflict and the protection of those persons affected by the conflict such as shipwrecked seamen, prisoners and civilians.[21] The law of naval warfare is therefore comprised of a mixture of the Hague Conventions, the 1949 Geneva Conventions and 1977 Additional Protocols, plus relevant state practice, but has not formally taken into account the parallel developments in the international law of the sea.[22]

---

[13] 1907 Hague Convention (VII) Relating to the Conversion of Merchant Ships into War-ships.

[14] 1907 Hague Convention (VIII) Relative to the Laying of Automatic Submarine Contact Mines.

[15] 1907 Hague Convention (IX) Concerning Bombardments by Naval Forces in Time of War.

[16] 1907 Hague Convention (XI) Relative to Certain Restrictions with Regard to the Exercise of the Right of Capture in Naval War.

[17] 1907 Hague Convention (IX) Concerning Bombardments by Naval Forces in Time of War, art 1, though art 3 did permit bombardment after due notice had been given.

[18] [1936] ATS 14.

[19] By 1939 and the outbreak of World War II the Procès-Verbal had a total of 50 state parties.

[20] See Geneva Convention (II) for the Amelioration of the Condition of Wounded, Sick and Shipwrecked Members of Armed Forces at Sea.

[21] Dinstein, *The Conduct of Hostilities under the Law of International Armed Conflict* (n 2) 18–19 discussing the development of the term 'international humanitarian law'.

[22] As to the contemporary state of the law of naval warfare, see J Ashley Roach, 'The Law of Naval Warfare at the Turn of the Two Centuries' (2000) 94 *AJIL* 64.

As a response, the *San Remo Manual on International Law Applicable to Armed Conflicts at Sea* was prepared between 1988 and 1994 in order to 'provide a contemporary restatement of international law applicable to armed conflicts at sea'.[23] The *San Remo Manual* updates the law of naval warfare and associated provisions of international humanitarian law to take into account the developments in the LOSC and the recognition that it gives to a number of maritime zones that did not exist early in the twentieth century. It makes clear that the rules concerning armed conflicts at sea and the hostile actions of naval forces may be conducted in the internal waters, territorial sea, EEZ and continental shelf of belligerent states, the high seas, and subject to certain limitations the EEZ and continental shelf of neutral states.[24] Care needs to be exercised when reflecting upon the *San Remo Manual* as it is not a treaty or official document of an international organisation or group of states, but instead is a restatement of the relevant international law. Nevertheless, as observed by Dinstein 'such restatements may at times be perceived even as accurate replicas of customary international law, and in their innovative parts may … pave the way for future treaties'.[25] The *San Remo Manual* has an exclusive focus upon armed conflict at sea conducted by hostile forces, and it does not purport to have any general application to peacetime military operations at sea, including maritime regulation and enforcement operations which may be engaged in by naval vessels.

B. United Nations-Sanctioned Naval Operations

The role of the United Nations Security Council in the law of the sea has significantly evolved since the end of the Cold War, and the 2001 terrorist attacks in New York and Washington. In the post-Cold War era the Council's main contributions had been through the authorisation of various enforcement actions, allowing for vessels to be stopped and inspected to ensure adherence of mandatory Security Council resolutions setting out arms embargos or seeking to prevent the passage of other goods and supplies to particular countries.[26] The Security Council authorised such interdictions under Chapter VII of the UN Charter in relation to the 1991 Gulf War and the action in Afghanistan in 2001,[27] as well as in connection with the 1991–93 war in Yugoslavia, the 1993–94 conflict in Haiti, and the 1997 civil war in Sierra Leone.[28] Because of the highly sensitive nature of these interdictions, they were inevitably carried out by naval forces operating under United Nations mandate, and by specially equipped government ships capable of such enforcement operations such as the Coast Guard.

---

[23] Doswald-Beck (ed), *San Remo Manual* (n 3) 5.

[24] Ibid 8, r 10. Some of these issues were relevant in the decision of the ICJ in *Oil Platforms (Islamic Republic of Iran v United States)* [2003] ICJ Rep 161.

[25] Dinstein, *The Conduct of Hostilities under the Law of International Armed Conflict* (n 2) 17.

[26] See Natalie Klein, *Maritime Security and the Law of the Sea* (Oxford, Oxford University Press, 2010) ch 6.

[27] MJ Valencia, 'The Proliferation Security Initiative: Making Waves in Asia', Adelphi Papers, 34, 2005 (referring to Maritime Interdiction Operation under resolutions relating to Iraq, and the Leadership Interdiction Operation and NATO's Operation Active Endeavour targeting the Taliban and al Qaeda operatives).

[28] Jon M Van Dyke, 'Perspective: Balancing Navigational Freedom with Environmental and Security Concerns' (2003) *Colorado Journal of International Environmental Law & Policy* (Yearbook) 19, 25.

In acting within its mandate to maintain international peace and security, the Security Council frequently operates with due regard to existing law of the sea principles.[29] For example, the Security Council has called upon states to act within existing international law to enforce its sanctions, as was the case with Resolution 1540 (2004) requiring states to prohibit and criminalise the transfer of WMD and their delivery systems to non-state actors but not going so far as to the authorise non-flag state high seas interdiction. Similar approaches were taken in Resolution 1718 (2006) regarding the movement of certain cargo in response to a North Korean nuclear test.[30] In 2011 the Security Council took a more expansive approach to high seas interdiction when seeking to enforce an arms embargo against Libya. Resolution 1973 (2011) authorised United Nations member states, acting individually or through regional organisations or arrangements, to undertake high seas inspections of vessels bound to or from Libya suspected of carrying items in contravention of the embargo. Member states of NATO undertaking inspections in the Mediterranean in reliance upon Resolution 1973 were required to immediately inform the United Nations Secretary-General and a Security Council Committee as to the result of an inspection.[31] United Nations Security Council responses to piracy off the coast of Africa have also highlighted not only the capacity of the United Nations to deal with this issue but also its impact upon aspects of the law of the sea such as the piracy provisions in Articles 100 to 107 of the LOSC.[32] In this respect it is noteworthy that Resolution 1851 (2008)[33] made clear that counter-piracy operations at sea were to be conducted consistently with international humanitarian law, thereby incorporating any relevant provisions of the law of naval warfare and international humanitarian law that may be applicable to those operations.

IV. Codification of the Law of the Sea

When the law of the sea began to be codified the principal early concerns were to reflect the developments which had taken place in customary international law with respect to the high seas and matters such as piracy and hot pursuit, whilst also clarifying the law as it related to the developing territorial sea. Little consideration was given to the law as it may have applied during a time of war, especially since there had already been developments in that field through The Hague and London Conventions. Nevertheless, the law of the sea could not ignore naval operations. Under customary international law sovereign immunities applied to warships and other naval vessels of states,[34] and nineteenth- and early

---

[29] See generally Rob McLaughlin, *United Nations Naval Peace Operations in the Territorial Sea* (Leiden, Martinus Nijhoff, 2009).

[30] Resolution 1718 (2006) prohibited the import and export of WMD and ballistic weapon technology to North Korea and called upon all member states to take 'in accordance with their national authorities and legislation, and consistent with international law, cooperative action including through inspection of cargo to and from the DPRK, as necessary'.

[31] Under 'Operation Unified Protector' NATO conducted 3,000 hailings at sea, with almost 300 boardings for inspection, and detained 11 vessels prior to transit to their next port of call: NATO, 'NATO and Libya' at www.nato.int/cps/en/natolive/topics_71652.htm.

[32] See the detailed discussion on this issue in chs 7 and 17.

[33] *Basic Documents* No 89.

[34] See *The Schooner Exchange v M'Faddon* (1812) 11 US 116 and discussion in Colombos, *The International Law of the Sea* (n 11) 264–68.

twentieth-century treaties concerning commerce, navigation and ports often distinguished between warships and other merchant ships,[35] including the 1936 Montreux Treaty dealing with the Turkish Straits which made significant distinctions between the rights of passage by warships and merchant ships through the straits.[36]

A. Work of the International Law Commission

The ILC's work on the codification and development of the law of the sea had several direct and indirect consequences for military operations at sea. With the Commission's work commencing just a few years after the ICJ's decision in *Corfu Channel*, the issue of navigational rights of warships during peacetime was clearly a key issue for determination and the ILC was certainly mindful of its import during their deliberations.[37] The final draft articles addressed a range of matters which had direct and indirect impact upon military operations at sea, and whilst there was no express reference in any draft article to the distinction between peace and wartime operation of the law, the Commission made it clear in its commentary to Section III dealing with the right of innocent passage as to its intention:

> The Commission wishes to point out that this section, like the whole of these regulations, is applicable only in time of peace. No provision of this section affects the rights and obligations of Members of the United Nations Organization under the Charter.[38]

The final draft articles contained a number of provisions with express application to warships and associated naval vessels, and to military operations during peacetime.[39] Of particular significance was the recommendation in Article 24 that the passage of warships through the territory may be subject to prior authorisation or notification. Mindful of the issues which arose in the *Corfu Channel* decision, the ILC was under pressure from states to recognise this right of coastal states. Acknowledging that 'the passage of warships through the territorial sea of another State can be considered by that State as a threat to its security' the ILC conceded that it was not really in a position to dispute the right of a state to take such a measure.[40] Article 32 proposed immunity from the jurisdiction of any state other than the flag state for warships on the high seas, and in doing so proposed a definition of 'warship' drawn from the 1907 Hague Convention (VII) Relating to the Conversion of Merchant Ships into Warships.[41] Also of interest to more general military uses of the oceans was the reference in the Commentary to the failure of the ILC to make direct reference to the freedom to undertake nuclear tests on the high seas. In that respect, the Commission merely

---

[35] See, eg, 1894 Treaty of Commerce and Navigation between the United Kingdom of Great Britain and Ireland and Japan; 1926 Convention and Statute on the International Regime of Maritime Ports, *Basic Documents* No 1, art 13.

[36] *Basic Documents* No 3.

[37] See comments at the 6th Session in 1954, by the Special Rapporteur, Mr Francois, and also Mr Lauterpacht (later Sir Hersch Lauterpacht): (1954) *Yearbook of the International Law Commission*, vol 1, 109 [24], 112 [62].

[38] 'Articles Concerning the Law of the Sea with Commentaries' (1956) *Yearbook of the International Law Commission*, vol 2, 272.

[39] See arts 15, 24, 25, 27, 32, 46, 47.

[40] 'Articles Concerning the Law of the Sea with Commentaries', 277.

[41] Ibid 280; referring to arts 2 and 3 of the Convention.

observed that: 'States are bound to refrain from any acts which might adversely affect the use of the high seas by nationals of other States'.[42]

B. UNCLOS I and the Geneva Conventions

In line with the ILC proposals, none of the four Geneva Conventions adopted at UNCLOS I sought to address military operations during a time of armed conflict, thus reflecting the developing *sui generis* nature of the then law of armed conflict and the significance of the UN Charter in this field. The conventions also had little impact upon the freedom of navigation of warships, or the right of overflight of military aircraft. This was mainly a result of the failure of UNCLOS I to agree upon the breadth of the territorial sea, which in addition to the multitude of views which existed on that topic was also influenced by Cold War rivalries. As Bowett observed, an overriding concern of Western powers at the time was that a 12 nm territorial sea 'would produce vast areas of "neutral" and therefore inviolable waters'.[43]

Notwithstanding the view of the ILC, the innocent passage provisions in the Convention on the Territorial Sea and Contiguous Zone[44] did not seek to draw a significant distinction between warships and other ships. The vessels of all states enjoyed the right of innocent passage, with particular limitations being imposed only upon fishing vessels and submarines,[45] with the latter being entitled to innocent passage if exercised on the surface whilst displaying their flag. Coastal states were not permitted to hamper innocent passage, and this could extend to any requirement that warships first give notification prior to passage. Article 23 of the Convention on the Territorial Sea and Contiguous Zone was the only provision that specifically mentioned warships, and then only in the context of where a warship which ignores coastal state regulations concerning passage may be requested to leave the territorial sea. The Convention on the High Seas[46] confirmed the freedom of navigation as being open to all nations,[47] and that every state had a right to sail its ships on the high seas.[48] The Convention confirmed the immunities of warships on the high seas, which were defined as:

> a ship belonging to the naval forces of a State and bearing the external marks distinguishing warships of its nationality, under the command of an officer duly commissioned by the government and whose name appears in the Navy List, and manned by a crew who are under regular naval discipline.[49]

It also clarified the rights of warships to engage in hot pursuit,[50] and to seize pirate ships on the high seas.[51]

---

[42] Ibid 278.
[43] DW Bowett, *The Law of the Sea* (Manchester, Manchester University Press, 1967) 9 referring to the practice of German U-boats in World War I and II seeking refuge in Norwegian territorial waters.
[44] *Basic Documents* No 9.
[45] Convention on the Territorial Sea and Contiguous Zone, art 14.
[46] *Basic Documents* No 10.
[47] Convention on the High Seas, art 2.
[48] Ibid art 4.
[49] Ibid art 8.
[50] Ibid art 23.
[51] Ibid art 21.

C. UNCLOS III and the LOSC

Given that UNCLOS III commenced during the height of the Cold War, and that the security implications of the law of the sea were acute, particularly in the context of settling the limits of existing and new maritime zones such as archipelagic waters, it is somewhat remarkable that the LOSC was able to be successfully concluded. This was possible because it became clear during the negotiations that while the Convention would inevitably have implications for maritime security, it would not directly impact upon military operations.[52] Instead, consistent with the way in which the law of the sea had been codified in the latter part of the twentieth century, the Convention focussed upon the peaceful uses of the oceans.[53] This is not only reflected in Article 301, but is restated in numerous provisions throughout the Convention, including that the high seas are reserved for peaceful purposes,[54] that the use of the Area is exclusively for peaceful purposes[55] and that marine scientific research is to be carried out exclusively for peaceful purposes.[56] Consistent with these articles and the Preamble, the Convention also emphasises that passage in the territorial sea which is 'prejudicial to the peace' is inconsistent with the LOSC and coastal states may respond accordingly.[57] The LOSC therefore goes to great lengths to ensure that the sea is used for peaceful ends, and in addition facilitates the peaceful settlement of international disputes through Part XV mechanisms.[58]

The direct and indirect references throughout the LOSC to military operations and uses of the oceans makes it clear that military operations are not incompatible with the peaceful uses of the oceans. Military assets may be used to undertake maritime regulation and enforcement so as to uphold coastal state rights and freedoms, to exercise the right of self-defence under general international law, and military operations either by individual states or in coalition to maintain international peace and security consistent with the UN Charter. Multiple provisions throughout the LOSC therefore seek to give greater certainty to military operations whilst also striving to achieve a balance between the interests of coastal states and those of maritime states which possess naval interests. To that end, it should be noted that the United States, a state with both significant coastal state and maritime state interests, did not reject the LOSC in 1982 because of concerns that its national security interests had not been adequately protected, but rather because of its concerns with the Part XI regime for the deep seabed.[59]

The LOSC duplicated the key provisions of the Geneva Conventions as they impacted upon military operations, whilst also making accommodations for the major adjustments

---

[52] See Donald R Rothwell and Natalie Klein, 'Maritime Security and the Law of the Sea' in Natalie Klein, Joanna Mossop and Donald R Rothwell (eds), *Maritime Security: International Law and Policy Perspectives from Australia and New Zealand* (London, Routledge, 2009) 22.

[53] Dale G Stephens, 'The Impact of the 1982 Law of the Sea Convention on the Conduct of Peacetime Naval/Military Operations' (1998–99) 29 *California Western International Law Journal* 283, 283.

[54] LOSC, art 88.

[55] Ibid art 141.

[56] Ibid art 240.

[57] Ibid art 19.

[58] Ibid art 279 providing that 'State Parties shall settle any dispute between them concerning the interpretation or application of this Convention by peaceful means'.

[59] See further Scott G Borgerson, *The National Interest and the Law of the Sea* (New York, Council on Foreign Relations, 2009) 22–27.

which were made to the law of the sea by the LOSC regime. The definition of a warship is found in Article 29 and provides a generic definition for the purposes of the Convention.[60] It substantially repeats the definition found in the 1958 Convention on the High Seas, expanding the control of the ship from 'naval forces' to 'armed forces' with consequential adjustments elsewhere in the text.[61] Transit passage and archipelagic sea lanes passage were particularly sensitive in terms of their potential impact upon military operations at sea and in the air,[62] and the recognition of the rights of transit in the 'normal mode' were significant.[63] Likewise, recognition of high seas freedoms of navigation, including overflight within the EEZ, was essential for the acceptance of that regime. The LOSC also reflected some important developments in international law as they applied to military operations in peacetime, including state responsibility for the loss or damage caused to a coastal state by non-compliance by a warship with coastal state laws and regulations.[64]

V. Navigational Rights and Freedoms

The foundation upon which military operations at sea rest is the freedom of navigation. Although growth in air power since the mid twentieth century has permitted an ever expanding range of military operations by air over the oceans, the extent of these operations cannot in any way be compared to the military power that can be projected by naval operations.[65] During this time there has not only been an expansion in the capability of navies, but also their capacity, raising a number of issues for the law of the sea of which nuclear-powered and armed warships is but one. It was because of the fundamental importance of the freedom of navigation to naval operations that the breadth of the territorial sea was so contentious, and the associated navigational regimes of innocent passage, transit passage, and archipelagic sea lanes passage were so crucial to the development of the international law of the sea at UNCLOS I and III. The outcomes of these negotiations are all reflected in the regimes agreed upon in the LOSC.

The influence of the *Corfu Channel* decision on the development of the law in this regard should not be underestimated. The ICJ was confronted in that case with a volatile peacetime situation arising only one year after the conclusion of World War II when security concerns for both coastal states and maritime powers such as the United Kingdom remained high. It is significant then that the Court did not rely upon the 1907 Hague Convention[66]

---

[60] See the brief discussion in *ARA Libertad (Argentina v Ghana)*, Provisional Measures, Order of 15 December 2012, [93]–[95].

[61] This definition is duplicated in Doswald-Beck (ed), *San Remo Manual* (n 3) r 13(g), with Commentary at 90 [13.21]. See also Bernard H Oxman, 'The Regime of Warships under the United Nations Convention on the Law of the Sea' (1984) 24 *Virginia Journal of International Law* 809.

[62] See generally Kay Hailbronner, 'Freedom of the Air and the Convention on the Law of the Sea' (1983) 77 *AJIL* 490.

[63] LOSC, arts 39, 53.

[64] Ibid art 31; cf art 236.

[65] McLaughlin, *United Nations Naval Peace Operations* (n 29) 46–47, referring to the 'manifest usefulness of navies'; and generally Charles E Pirtle, 'Military Uses of Ocean Space and the Law of the Sea in the New Millennium' (2000) 31 *Ocean Development and International Law* 7.

[66] 1907 Hague Convention (VIII) Relative to the Laying of Automatic Submarine Contact Mines.

in its findings against Albania regarding its responsibilities to notify users of the strait as to the existence of the minefield. Rather the Court relied upon what it referred to as 'general and well-recognized principles' being 'elementary considerations of humanity, even more exacting in peace than in war; the principle of the freedom of navigation; and the state's obligation not to allow knowingly its territory to be used for acts contrary to the rights of other States.'[67] The ICJ's finding that the freedom of navigation is enjoyed by warships in peacetime was subsequently reflected in deliberations at UNCLOS I and III and in both the Geneva Conventions and the LOSC.[68] That it was considered a general principle further elevates its significance and needs to be taken into account when interpreting the international law of the sea concerning navigation by warships.

In 2014, in an effort to reach some consensus amongst certain navies, the Western Pacific Naval Symposium[69] issued a 'Code for Unplanned Encounters at Sea' (CUES),[70] a non-legally binding document designed to deal with safety and communication procedures when naval forces had unplanned encounters at sea.[71] While CUES does not supersede applicable international law,[72] it has been drafted with a view to the COLREGs and relevant international law, such as the LOSC. To that end, CUES outlines a variety of safety procedures for navies following an unplanned encounter, including action to avoid collision, formations and conveys, manoeuvres in a traffic separation scheme, safe speeds and distance, exercises with submarines, and assurance measures for actions such as the simulation of attacks. In November 2014 the United States and China both adopted a Memorandum of Understanding regarding rules of behaviour for the safety of air and maritime encounters,[73] which emphasised that military vessels which encounter each other at sea were to abide by COLREG, COLREGs and CUES. Annex II of the memorandum contains a series of agreed 'rules' for 'Maritime Navigation Warning Areas', and for establishing mutual trust at sea. While not intended to be binding under international law, initiatives such as this demonstrate the way in which militaries are capable of reaching mutual agreement upon the conduct of naval operations at sea, which contributes to maritime confidence building.

Warships regularly visit foreign ports as part of good will missions, humanitarian operations such as those following a natural disaster, or whilst undertaking naval exercises and 'war games' with allies. As there is no automatic right of entry by a foreign warship into the port, harbour or internal waters of another state, diplomatic clearance is required. Entry of a warship into a foreign port raises issues as to the application of local coastal state laws and regulations. Whilst there may be a Status of Forces Agreement or equivalent international

---

[67] *Corfu Channel (United Kingdom v Albania)* [1949] ICJ Rep 4, 22.

[68] See also the discussion of these principles in the *Military and Paramilitary Activities in and Against Nicaragua (Nicaragua v United States)* (merits) [1986] ICJ Rep 14, 111–12 with respect to the freedom of communications and maritime commerce; Stephens 'The Impact of the 1982 Law of the Sea Convention' (n 53) 293–304 compares the ICJ decisions in *Corfu Channel* and *Nicaragua* on their observations regarding the freedom of navigation.

[69] The Western Pacific Naval Symposium is an annual meeting of navies active in the western Pacific, including those of Australia, Canada, China, France, Japan, South Korea, Russia and the United States.

[70] Western Pacific Naval Symposium, 'Code for Unplanned Encounters at Sea' Version 1.0 (22 April 2014) at news.usni.org/2014/06/17/document-conduct-unplanned-encounters-sea (CUES).

[71] Such an encounter is described as 'when naval ships or naval aircraft of one State meet casually or unexpectedly with a naval ship or naval aircraft of another State': CUES [1.3.2].

[72] CUES [1.5.2].

[73] Memorandum of Understanding between the Department of Defense of the United States of America and the Ministry of National Defense of the People's Republic of China Regarding the Rules of Behavior for Safety of Air and Maritime Encounters (Washington/Beijing, 9 and 10 November 2014).

instrument in place to deal with the visit of foreign naval personnel, the warship will continue to be sovereign immune whilst in port or in internal waters.[74] Nevertheless, when port visits are undertaken on this basis international comity suggests that the foreign warship will seek to comply with all reasonable coastal state requirements and restrictions. This would extend not only to navigational safety whilst within the port but also marine environmental protection standards.[75] Any efforts of law enforcement against a foreign warship in port will raise issues of great international sensitivity, as was emphasised when ITLOS granted provisional measures requiring the unconditional release of the Argentine warship *ARA Libertad* following its detention by Ghana at the port of Tema.[76]

A. Innocent Passage by Warships

Part II, Section 3 of the LOSC dealing with innocent passage in the territorial sea makes clear that the ships of all states enjoy the right of innocent passage. Whilst subsection C encompassing Articles 29 to 32 address some issues which are particular to warships, they do not go to the right of innocent passage. Accordingly, the LOSC is clear that warships enjoy a right of innocent passage which may be exercised in the same manner as merchant ships. Nevertheless, there are three particular types of constraints in the innocent passage regime that have relevance for warships. The first is that warships need to take particular care while in passage not to engage in acts which are considered non-innocent under Article 19. A number of limitations on passage found in Article 19(2) have particular application to warships, including that they do not engage in actions considered to constitute any threat or use of force against the coastal state; any form of weapons exercise; acts aimed at collecting information to the prejudice of the defence or security of the coastal state; acts of propaganda, research or survey activities; acts aimed at interfering with the communications systems of the coastal state; and the launching, landing or taking on board of any aircraft or military device.[77] This is clearly an extensive list of requirements, which if complied with will ensure that the possible security threats to coastal states posed by foreign warships are neutralised as far as possible whilst they are within the territorial sea. In contrast to the transit passage and archipelagic sea lanes passage regimes, there is no reference in the right of innocent passage to 'normal mode' of navigation, therefore precluding warships undertaking activities which would otherwise be permissible in other settings. A clear limitation in this respect is the prohibition on aircraft carriers launching or receiving aircraft or military devices (such as unmanned aerial vehicles) whilst undertaking innocent passage, as such activity conflicts with Article 19(2)(e) and (f). However, some aspects of warship

---

[74] This was confirmed by ITLOS in *ARA Libertad* (n 60) [95].

[75] See AR Thomas and James C Duncan (eds), 'Annotated Supplement to The Commanders Handbook on the Law of Naval Operations' (1999) 73 *International Legal Studies*, Annex A2-1 outlining the United States position that 'US Military Ships and Aircraft proceeding to and from a foreign port under diplomatic clearance shall comply with reasonable host country requirements and/or restrictions'.

[76] *ARA Libertad* (n 60) [99].

[77] In January 2014 the Government of Australia acknowledged that the actions of several state vessels (Navy and Customs) which had entered the territorial sea of Indonesia were not consistent with exercising the right of innocent passage, resulting in an apology from Australia to Indonesia: Scott Morrison (Minister for Immigration and Border Protection, Australia), 'Transcript: Press Conference—Operation Sovereign Borders Update' (17 January 2014) at newsroom.border.gov.au

operations remain ambiguous, such as the activation of radar whilst in passage. Radar is clearly an aid to navigation for all vessels and as such promotes safety at sea, but also may be used for defensive purposes.[78] By way of contrast, there is nothing in the innocent passage regime, the LOSC, or general international law which suggests that warships do not enjoy the right of self-defence whilst within the territorial sea of a foreign state.[79] This issue has been highlighted since the October 2000 terrorist attack on the USS *Cole* whilst in port at Aden, Yemen and the subsequent United States response to ensuring the security of its warships whilst within potentially hostile waters.[80]

The second constraint relates to compliance by warships with the laws and regulations of a coastal state relating to innocent passage that may have been adopted under Article 21 of the LOSC. In the case of warships, relevant provisions would be those relating to the safety of navigation and regulation of maritime traffic, the preservation of the environment and the prevention of pollution. The LOSC makes clear that '[f]oreign ships exercising the right of innocent passage ... shall comply' with such laws and regulations.[81] Whilst coastal states would encounter difficulty in applying their civil and criminal laws to warships because of the principles of sovereign immunity,[82] the LOSC in recognition of this legal reality makes clear in Article 30 that if a non-compliant warship disregards a request for compliance the coastal state may require the warship to leave the territorial sea with the effect that the right of innocent passage has been lost. The third restraint found in the LOSC relates to the particular situation of submarines, which under Article 20 are 'required to navigate on the surface and show their flag'.[83]

A number of issues arise from these provisions. One is the capacity of the coastal state to interpret the LOSC unilaterally and determine that either the mere presence of a warship within the territorial sea constitutes a threat to its security, or that the actions of the warship whilst engaged in passage are not innocent. There is a widely held view that a presumption of innocence exists, which can only be rebutted by proof from the coastal state, relying upon the objective and specific criteria in Article 19, of a non-innocent act.[84] While maintaining a balance between a coastal state's sovereign rights and its duty to respect innocent passage would suggest that only an objective standard would be acceptable when interpreting Article 19,[85] this is made challenging by the existence of terms such as 'propaganda' which are difficult to define and assess objectively when national interests are at stake. Even if such a wide discretion is acknowledged, commentators such as Ngantcha emphasise that the coastal state's subjective appraisal of passage as non-innocent should be limited by the

---

[78] John Astley and Michael N Schmitt, 'The Law of the Sea and Naval Operations' (1997) 42 *Air Force Law Review* 119, 131.

[79] See discussion in AV Lowe, 'Self-Defence at Sea' in William E Butler (ed), *The Non-Use of Force in International Law* (Dordrecht, Martinus Nijhoff, 1989) 185–202.

[80] See Department of Defense USS Cole Commission (United States), *USS Cole Commission Report* (Washington, Department of Defense, 2001).

[81] LOSC, art 21(4).

[82] Ibid art 32.

[83] *Virginia Commentaries*, vol 2, 183 observing the use of the term 'are required' is unusual, leaving open the possibility that the coastal state may waive the requirement.

[84] FD Froman, 'Uncharted Waters: Non-innocent Passage of Warships in the Territorial Sea' (984) 21 *San Diego Law Review* 625, 658; JW Rolph, 'Freedom of Navigation and the Black Sea Bumping Incident: How 'Innocent' must Innocent Passage Be?' (1992) 135 *Military Law Review* 137, 159.

[85] Gerald Fitzmaurice 'Some Results from the Geneva Conference on the Law of the Sea' (1959) 8 *International and Comparative Law Quarterly* 73, 96–97.

objective requirement that any violation which is alleged to have occurred have taken place while the vessel is in passage.[86]

Another contentious issue is whether coastal states may insist on authorisation or notification by warships prior to undertaking innocent passage through the territorial sea. Whilst there was debate on this issue at UNCLOS III,[87] it was never included in the LOSC, although a number of state parties made clear through Declarations their intention to require prior authorisation or prior notification.[88] State parties which require prior authorisation include Algeria, Antigua and Barbuda, Bangladesh, Barbados, Brazil, Cambodia, Cape Verde, China, Congo, Denmark, Grenada, Iran, Maldives, Myanmar, Oman, Pakistan, Philippines, Poland, Romania, St Vincent and the Grenadines, Somalia, Sri Lanka, Sudan, Syria, United Arab Emirates, Vietnam and Yemen.[89] Prior notification of the passage of warships is required by Bangladesh, Croatia, Denmark, Egypt, Estonia, Guyana, India, Libya, Malta, Mauritius, Nigeria, Serbia and Montenegro and South Korea.[90] A number of state parties responded to these claims in their LOSC Declarations, with Germany, Italy and the Netherlands all making clear that a requirement either for consent or notification of passage by warships was inconsistent with the Convention.[91] The United States, though a non-party to the LOSC, has also protested these consent and notification requirements for warships, and in some instances actively asserted the right of innocent passage as part of its freedom of navigation programme.[92]

There is some evidence to suggest these differing interpretations of the LOSC on prior notification and consent represent a divide between the West and Asia,[93] which with China's rise as an economic and military power has the potential to become a flashpoint. In 1989 the United States and Soviet Union, the two most significant naval powers of the time, issued a 'Joint Statement on the Uniform Interpretation of Rules of International Law Governing Innocent Passage'[94] which provided as follows:

> All ships, including warships, regardless of cargo, armament or means of propulsion, enjoy the right of innocent passage through the territorial sea in accordance with international law, for which neither prior notification nor authorization is required.[95]

---

[86] Francis Ngantcha, *The Right of Innocent Passage and the Evolution of the International Law of the Sea* (London, Pinter, 1990) 51.

[87] Roach and Smith, *Excessive Maritime Claims* (n 10) 239–42.

[88] See LOSC Declarations made by Bangladesh (2001), China (1996) Egypt (1983), Croatia (1995) Iran (1982), Malta (1993), Montenegro (2006), Oman (1983), United Nations Division for Ocean Affairs and the Law of the Sea (UNDOALOS), 'United Nations Convention on the Law of the Sea: Declarations Made upon Signature, Ratification, Accession or Succession or Anytime Thereafter', at www.un.org/Depts/los/convention_agreement/convention_declarations.htm.

[89] Robin R Churchill, 'The Impact of State Practice on the Jurisdictional Framework Contained in the LOS Convention' in Alex G Oude Elferink (ed), *Stability and Change in the Law of the Sea: The Role of the LOS Convention* (Leiden, Martinus Nijhoff, 2005) 112–13.

[90] Churchill, 'The Impact of State Practice', ibid 113; Roach and Smith, *Excessive Maritime Claims* (n 10) 250–51. Some states which previously required prior notification have now abandoned that practice: K Hakapää and EJ Molenaar, 'Innocent Passage—Past and Present' (1998) 23 *Marine Policy* 131, 138.

[91] See LOSC Declaration by Germany (1994), Italy (1995), and the Netherlands (1996) in UNDOALOS 'Declarations Made upon Signature, Ratification, Accession or Succession or Anytime Thereafter'.

[92] Roach and Smith, *Excessive Maritime Claims* (n 10) 243–51; William K Agyebeng, 'Theory in Search of Practice: The Right of Innocent Passage in the Territorial Sea' (2006) 39 *Cornell International Law Journal* 371, 398.

[93] Stephens, 'The Impact of the 1982 Law of the Sea Convention' (n 53) 306.

[94] *Basic Documents* No 42.

[95] Joint Statement on the Uniform Interpretation of Rules of International Law Governing Innocent Passage, [2].

This 1989 Statement, which also went on to address common interpretations of other key provisions of the LOSC dealing with innocent passage, reflects the United States and Russian position on these issues into the twenty-first century. The People's Republic of China, on the other hand, made clear at the time of its 1996 ratification of the LOSC that the Convention did not 'prejudice the right of a coastal State to request ... a foreign State to obtain advance approval from or give prior notification to the coastal State for the passage of its warships through the territorial sea.'[96] This position was consistent with Chinese practice prior to becoming a party to the LOSC, but has been the subject of criticism from Chinese scholars based outside China.[97]

One exception to the strict requirements upon warships whilst operating within the territorial sea, or adjacent to the territorial sea, is the exercise of the right of assistance to persons in distress at sea. The duty to render assistance at sea is well founded in the law of the sea and is outlined in Article 98 of the LOSC which applies to the EEZ and high seas. This has raised issues as to whether a foreign warship has a right to enter the territorial sea of another state to render assistance to persons in distress or whether it may do so only with notification and consent. The United States view is that there is an obligation to render assistance in these circumstances and United States warships can enter a foreign territorial sea without permission to undertake a bona fide rescue mission.[98] Provided that such a temporary entry into the territorial sea without exercising innocent passage poses no threat to the coastal state, the exercise of such a right would be consistent with long-standing traditions of the sea and general international law to provide humanitarian assistance to persons in distress.[99]

B. Transit Passage by Warships

Given the issues and sensitivities associated with innocent passage by warships, it is not surprising that similar and even more acute issues arise in the context of transit passage through international straits. This is illustrated by the pre-LOSC codification efforts in relation to straits, and the ongoing sensitivities associated with naval navigation through pivotal 'choke points' which have persisted. The 1936 Montreux Treaty[100] is a prominent illustration of a pre-LOSC initiative to address questions of navigation through an international strait by warships containing a range of measures which made distinctions between different types of naval vessels depending on their capacity and size, flag of origin, and overall maximum aggregate tonnage of a naval force exercising passage. A right of transit through the straits could be enjoyed with or without significant limitations and constraints,

---

[96] UNDOALOS, 'United Nations Convention on the Law of the Sea: Declarations'.

[97] Zou Keyuan, 'Innocent Passage for Warships: The Chinese Doctrine and Practice' (1998) 29 *Ocean Development and International Law* 195–223; Zou Keyuan, 'Navigation of Foreign Vessels within China's Jurisdictional Waters' (2002) 29 *Maritime Policy and Management* 351, 364.

[98] Thomas and Duncan (eds), 'Annotated Supplement to The Commanders Handbook' (n 75) 120, Annex 2-3; see also at 173 details on bilateral arrangements between the United States with Canada and Mexico regulating this activity.

[99] Ibid 120–21, where the United States concedes that a right of search can only be conducted with the consent of the coastal state.

[100] *Basic Documents* No 3.

though any transit was to be preceded by notification to Turkey.[101] The ICJ's decision in *Corfu Channel* is another prominent example in this respect, given that the Court directly endorsed the innocent passage by warships through an international strait without prior authorisation.[102] With an obvious reference to the Montreux Treaty, the Court observed that: 'Unless otherwise prescribed by an international convention, there is no right for a coastal State to prohibit such passage through straits in time of peace'.[103]

These pre-LOSC precedents need to be measured against the impact of the Convention recognising the legitimacy of a 12 nm territorial sea and the impact of that upon the high seas corridor which would have once existed through a number of international straits around the world. The effect of the 12 nm territorial sea was that 116 international straits potentially became enclosed within a territorial sea which even though subject to the regime of innocent passage had the potential to place considerable constraints upon the freedom of military operations and especially the capacity of navies to speedily move from one maritime domain to another.[104] Particularly sensitive strategic 'choke points' where maritime traffic converges to move from one ocean or sea to another include the Straits of Dover, Formosa (Taiwan), Gibraltar, Hormuz, Lombok, Malacca, and Sunda.[105]

The LOSC makes clear that transit passage is a right enjoyed by 'all ships' with respect to straits used for international navigation where warships pass through the territorial sea between one part of the high seas or EEZ and another part of the high seas or EEZ.[106] Warships whilst engaged in transit passage are bound by the same constraints as merchant ships. Two particular constraints apply to warships. The first is that they are to refrain from any activity constituting a threat or use of force against the coastal state, and likewise refrain from any activities not incidental to their normal mode. The second of these is that they are to comply with generally accepted international rules and regulations regarding safety of life at sea and pollution prevention.[107]

Of particular significance here is what constitutes 'normal mode' of operations for a warship and when would such operations be considered to cross the boundaries so as to constitute a threat to the coastal state? In the *Virginia Commentaries* to the LOSC, the observation has been made that 'it is clear from the context and from the negotiating history that the term was intended to refer to that mode which is normal or usual for navigation for the particular type of ship ... making the passage in given circumstances. In the case of surface ships, this means navigation on the surface in ordinary sailing conditions.'[108] Some guidance on this point can again be found in *Corfu Channel*, where the ICJ was satisfied that even when the British warships passed through the channel with crews at action stations, and ready to retaliate if fired upon, this was consistent given the tensions that then existed between Albania and the United Kingdom at the time with the right of passage.[109]

---

[101] Convention Regarding the Regime of the Straits, art 13; see further discussion in Nihan Ünlü, *The Legal Regime of the Turkish Straits* (The Hague, Martinus Nijhoff, 2002) 87–100.

[102] *Corfu Channel (United Kingdom v Albania)* [1949] ICJ Rep 4, 28.

[103] Ibid.

[104] Booth, *Law, Force and Diplomacy at Sea* (n 1) 97–119.

[105] Ibid 98–99.

[106] LOSC, art 38(1).

[107] See the discussion in ch 15.

[108] *Virginia Commentaries*, vol 2, 342.

[109] *Corfu Channel (United Kingdom v Albania)* [1949] ICJ Rep 4, 31.

It is doubtful, however, whether this would be an acceptable mode of navigation on all occasions as the Court gave weight to the context of when the passage was being exercised and its manner. At the other end of the spectrum, in the case of the actions of the British warships several weeks later when minesweeping operations were conducted in the strait, the ICJ did not accept those actions as being legitimate under either the law of the sea or other general principles of international law.[110] For modern warships, the normal mode for surface vessels would extend to the launching and recovering of aircraft (including unmanned aerial vehicles) and the deployment of radar, sonar and depth-finding devices. For submarines, navigation through the strait could be submerged.[111] The conduct of weapons exercises, however, would not be consistent with normal mode as such an activity would constitute a threat of the use of force against the coastal state.

The second constraint is the expectation that all ships, including by implication warships, also comply with legitimate coastal states laws and regulations relating to transit passage. Laws of particular relevance would be those relating to safety of navigation, including passage through sea lanes and traffic separation schemes, and pollution control.[112] In recognition of the immunities enjoyed by warships and the difficulties therefore associated with the enforcement of any coastal state laws against warships, the LOSC makes clear that the flag state will bear international responsibility for any loss or damage that may arise as a result of the warship acting in a manner contrary to those laws and regulations.[113]

Some international straits have particular military significance because of their strategic location and this has raised sensitivities regarding any limitations which may be placed upon transit through those straits. In the case of the Northwest Passage passing through the islands of the Canadian Arctic Archipelago, Canada has sought to impose a number of constraints on passage on environmental grounds.[114] Whilst none of these measures applied to sovereign immune warships, Canada has also been concerned over the potential undetected passage through these waters by nuclear submarines. If the waters of the passage are considered an international strait, their submerged passage is consistent with the Convention; if on the other hand the waters are considered Canadian internal waters such passage is impermissible.[115] Related conflicts have also arisen over the Northeast Passage along the northern Russian Arctic coastline, where United States submarines are reported to have undertaken submerged passage during the Cold War.[116] Other controversies that have arisen include demands by Yemen for prior consent of transit passage through Bab el Mandeb,[117] Iranian demands that only LOSC state parties were entitled to transit through

---

[110] Ibid 33–35; see comment in Stephens, 'The Impact of the 1982 Law of the Sea Convention' (n 53) 306–307.
[111] *Virginia Commentaries*, vol 2, 342–43; Astley and Schmitt, 'The Law of the Sea and Naval Operations' (n 78) 133.
[112] LOSC, art 42.
[113] Ibid art 42(5); see also art 236.
[114] See Donald R Rothwell 'The United States and Arctic Straits: The Northwest Passage and the Bering Strait' in Suzanne Lalonde and Ted L McDorman (eds), *International Law and Politics of the Arctic Ocean: Essays in Honor of Donat Pharand* (Leiden, Brill, 2015) 160, 166–71.
[115] Roach and Smith, *Excessive Maritime Claims* (n 10) 318–28, detailing the Canadian/United States diplomatic exchanges on this matter.
[116] See ibid 312–18; R Douglas Brubaker, *The Russian Arctic Straits* (Leiden, Martinus Nijhoff, 2005).
[117] Roach and Smith, *Excessive Maritime Claims* (n 10) 284–86; see the Yemen Declaration at UNDOALOS, 'United Nations Convention on the Law of the Sea: Declarations'.

the Strait of Hormuz,[118] and interpretations by Denmark and Sweden that the Baltic Straits which include the Little Belt, Great Belt and the Sound (Oresund) are governed by long-standing international conventions with the effect that warships may be subject to so-called 'Sound Dues'.[119]

C. Archipelagic Sea Lanes Passage by Warships

There is overlap in the issues which arise concerning the rights of passage by warships through international straits and archipelagic sea lanes due to the similarity of these two passage regimes. Given the strategic significance of straits that fell within archipelagic states such as Indonesia and the Philippines, and the very significant United States naval presence in East and Southeast Asia and the western Pacific, the negotiation of Part IV of the LOSC dealing with archipelagic states raised particular sensitivities for military operations. The outcome in Part IV sought to balance the rights and interests of archipelagic states and the naval powers, making the important concession in Article 53(3) that archipelagic sea lanes passage was the exercise in accordance with the Convention 'of navigation ... in the normal mode' for 'continuous, expeditious and unobstructed transit' through the archipelago from one part of the EEZ or high seas to another. This was a right enjoyed by all ships, without qualification. The use of the term 'normal mode' was crucial for warships and duplicates the entitlements enjoyed when undertaking transit passage through an international strait. Similar issues therefore arise as to what constitutes normal mode, including for aircraft carriers, the rights of submarines to navigate submerged, and 'security streaming' for a naval task force.[120]

There are three important aspects of archipelagic sea lanes passage for warships. The first is that the right is non-suspendable, and can therefore be enjoyed by warships without fear of closure.[121] The second is that the right can only be enjoyed within the designated sea lanes, or those sea routes which are 'normally used for international navigation'.[122] As the archipelagic state is entitled to designate traffic separation schemes for the purpose of safe passage through narrow channels within the archipelagic sea lane, an issue arises as to whether foreign warships are bound by these constraints given their entitlement to sovereign immunity or rather because of the practical importance of safe navigation through narrow shipping channels they elect to follow the designated shipping route. The third issue is that as the conduct of archipelagic sea lanes passage may see a foreign warship within the waters of an archipelagic state for a considerable period of time, not only would there be heightened sensitivity that the warship should not engage in any actions during that time

---

[118] UNDOALOS, 'United Nations Convention on the Law of the Sea: Declarations'; an assertion which was strongly rejected by the United States: Roach and Smith, *Excessive Maritime Claims* (n 10) 293–96.

[119] Roach and Smith, *Excessive Maritime Claims* (n 10) 328–32; see the Declaration by Sweden upon signature (1982) and ratification of the LOSC (1996): UNDOALOS, 'United Nations Convention on the Law of the Sea: Declarations'.

[120] Stephens, 'The Impact of the 1982 Law of the Sea Convention' (n 53) 291; Thomas and Duncan (eds), 'Annotated Supplement to The Commanders Handbook' (n 75) 127.

[121] Cf Indonesia's 1988 closure of the Sunda and Lombok Straits, discussed in ch 11; see also Kim Young Koo, 'The Law of the Sea, Archipelagoes, and User States: Korea' in Donald R Rothwell and Sam Bateman (eds), *Navigational Rights and Freedoms and the New Law of the Sea* (The Hague, Martinus Nijhoff, 2000) 158, 164.

[122] LOSC, art 53(12).

which would pose a threat to the archipelagic state, but also that the warship should not pollute the marine environment. Whilst a warship retains its rights of sovereign immunity within archipelagic waters, there remains an expectation that the warship comply with those generally accepted international regulations concerning the prevention, reduction and control of pollution.[123]

D. EEZ Navigation by Warships

The EEZ is a zone of coastal state resource sovereignty and jurisdiction, but it is not a zone which gives to a coastal state extensive capacity to regulate navigation. This is confirmed by Articles 58 and 90 of the LOSC which provide that every state has a right to sail ships flying its flag on both the high seas and adjacent EEZ, subject only to recognising the lawful uses by the coastal state of the EEZ. It therefore follows that warships enjoy a freedom of navigation within the EEZ of coastal states. However, at the time of the conclusion of the Convention some states took a position on the interpretation of Article 301 providing for the peaceful use of the oceans which suggested they may place some limitations on the activities of foreign warships. Brazil, for example, asserted in a Declaration lodged with its 1988 ratification of the LOSC that Article 301 applied 'in particular to the maritime areas under the sovereignty or jurisdiction of the coastal State',[124] whilst also asserting that within the EEZ other states were not to conduct 'military exercises or manoeuvres'. This is an interpretation which has been contested by the United States.[125] The United States likewise protested provisions of the Iranian Marine Areas Act 1993,[126] which sought to place limitations upon foreign warships within the EEZ on the grounds that the freedom of navigation by foreign warships was being constrained.[127]

i. Military Survey Activities

An aspect of naval operations in the EEZ which has been contentious has been military survey activities. These are surveillance or scientific research activities undertaken by military or naval auxiliary vessels within the EEZ of third states. Often these activities may be designed to gather oceanographic or other data, or they may be undertaken to secure other forms of intelligence with a national security dimension.[128] These activities raise a range of issues under the LOSC, including whether they constitute legitimate marine scientific research under Article 246, or whether they are generic research activities which fall within the reach of Article 87 high seas freedoms which are also enjoyed within the EEZ.

---

[123] J Ashley Roach and Robert W Smith, *United States Responses to Excessive Maritime Claims*, 2nd edn (The Hague, Martinus Nijhoff, 1996) 387–88.

[124] UNDOALOS, 'United Nations Convention on the Law of the Sea: Declarations'.

[125] Roach and Smith, *Excessive Maritime Claims* (n 10) 381–82.

[126] *Act on the Marine Areas of the Islamic Republic of Iran in the Persian Gulf and the Oman Sea 1993* (Iran), reprinted in (1993) 24 *Law of the Sea Bulletin* 10–15.

[127] Roach and Smith, *Excessive Maritime Claims* (n 10) 382–83; generally on military operations within the EEZ see Jon M Van Dyke, 'Military Ships and Planes Operating in the Exclusive Economic Zone of Another Country' (2004) 28 *Marine Policy* 29.

[128] See the general discussion in Roach and Smith, *Excessive Maritime Claims* (n 10) 416–17.

The United States has been involved in several incidents within China's claimed EEZ involving military survey operations. In March 2001 the unarmed hydrographic survey ship USNS *Bowditch* was confronted by a Chinese naval frigate and ordered to leave the EEZ. The *Bowditch* complied with the Chinese request, but returned to the area a few days later accompanied by an armed United States naval escort.[129] In a similar incident in March 2009, the USNS *Impeccable*, a United States navy ocean surveillance vessel operating 75 nm south of China's Hainan island within the Chinese claimed EEZ, was surrounded by five Chinese vessels, including a naval intelligence ship and a government-operated fisheries patrol vessel, and subjected to significant harassment necessitating the taking of avoidance action to avoid collision.[130] The *Impeccable* withdrew but returned to the area the next day under the escort of a United States guided-missile destroyer.[131] The United States protested to China following the 2009 incident; however, China responded by asserting that the *Impeccable* was operating illegally within the Chinese EEZ in violation of both international and Chinese law.[132] The point of distinction between the Chinese and United States position on these issues is whether a non-resource related activity in the EEZ such as military marine data collection is a form of marine scientific research subject to coastal state regulation or whether this is a legitimate freedom of the seas. Providing these military activities fall beyond the scope of Article 246 marine scientific research and there is no direct threat posed to the coastal state which would legitimately activate the right of self-defence by the coastal state, then military-related survey activities in the EEZ are consistent with the LOSC and international law.

VI. Naval Operations at Sea

A. United Nations Sanctioned Interdictions

An important dynamic in the law of the sea in the post-1945 period has been the capacity of the United Nations to intervene in matters which are a threat to international peace and security thereby having maritime implications. The United Nations Security Council's mandate in these matters is made clear in Chapter VII of the UN Charter. Once the Security Council makes a determination that certain events constitute a threat to international peace and security, recommendations may be made in Security Council resolutions under Articles 40, 41 and 42 of the Charter. Measures short of the use of armed force are contemplated in Article 41 and these can include measures directed towards the sea, such as the imposition of trade sanctions which are enforced at sea but also on land and in the air. Likewise, measures that include the use of force, including blockade, may be authorised under

---

[129] Raul Pedrozo, 'Close Encounters at Sea: The USNS *Impeccable* Incident' (Summer 2009) 62(3) *Naval War College Review* 101, 101.

[130] Pedrozo, 'Close Encounters at Sea', ibid 101; John R Crook (ed), 'Contemporary Practice of the United States Relating to International Law' (2009) 103 *AJIL* 349.

[131] Pedrozo, 'Close Encounters at Sea', ibid 102.

[132] Crook (ed), 'Contemporary Practice of the United States' (n 130) 350 51.

Article 42 which would extend to military operations at sea.[133] In both instances, the naval forces of United Nations member states would be engaged in the implementation and enforcement of these Security Council resolutions.

While there were some Security Council sanctioned maritime interdictions prior to the 1990s,[134] much of the United Nations' practice in this area developed following the conclusion of the Cold War and principally in the situations concerning Iraq (1990–2003), the Former Republic of Yugoslavia (1992–93),[135] and Haiti (1994). The case of conflict in Iraq is of particular significance because it was the first major exercise of United Nations Chapter VII powers following the conclusion of the Cold War, and the ongoing economic sanctions against Iraq both prior to the 1991 Gulf War and subsequently were pivotal to ensuring that the export of oil or petroleum products from Iraq took place only under very strict limitations. These measures had a broad maritime dimension. For example, Security Council Resolution 665 (1990):

> Call[ed] upon those member States cooperating with the government of Kuwait, which are deploying maritime forces to the area, to use such measures commensurate to the specific circumstances as may be necessary under the authority of the Security Council to halt all inward and outward shipping in order to inspect and verify cargoes and their destinations and to ensure the strict implementation of the provisions related to such shipping laid down in Resolution 661.

This resolution formed the basis for ongoing United Nations mandated operations against shipping in the vicinity of Iraq, including the Red Sea and Persian Gulf, for nearly 13 years and at one stage the interdiction force comprised 95 warships from 18 United Nations members.[136] The significance of this precedent is summed up by McLaughlin: 'Resolution 665 is thus the fundamental conceptual precedent for modern United Nations naval interdiction operations.'[137]

Another contemporary example of how the United Nations may authorise interdictions at sea has arisen with respect to nuclear non-proliferation and the concerns of the Security Council to engage in efforts to stop the spread of nuclear weapons. Following a nuclear weapons test by DPRK in 2006, the Security Council adopted Resolution 1718 (2006) which imposed limitations on the flagged vessels of United Nations member states supplying or transferring to North Korea certain military materials and nuclear-related technology. In 2009, these sanctions were taken a step further following the launch by North Korea of an unarmed rocket into the Sea of Japan, after which significant international concerns were raised as to North Korea's capacity to launch a nuclear-armed warhead. Security Council Resolution 1874 (2009) mandated states not only to take actions against their own flagged vessels that may be engaged in prohibited trade with North Korea, but to also 'inspect vessels, with consent of the flag state, on the high seas, if they have information that provides

---

[133]   UN mandated blockade under Chapter VII of the UN Charter should be contrasted with 'belligerent blockade' under the international law on the use of armed force: Rob McLaughlin, 'United Nations Mandated Naval Interdiction Operations in the Territorial Sea' (2002) 51 *International and Comparative Law Quarterly* 249, n 2; and generally LA Ivanashchenko, *Blockade at Sea and Contemporary International Law* (Seoul, Korea University, 1989).

[134]   See UN Security Council Resolution 221 (1966) which called upon the United Kingdom to 'prevent, by the use of force if necessary, the arrival at Beira of vessels reasonably believed to be carrying oil for Southern Rhodesia'.

[135]   See UN Security Council Resolution 787 (1992) [12]; UN Security Council Resolution 820 (1993) [22].

[136]   McLaughlin, 'United Nations Mandated Naval Interdiction Operations' (n 133) 261.

[137]   Ibid.

'reasonable grounds' that prohibited cargo was being carried.[138] Flag states which do not consent to inspection of their flagged vessels on the high seas, are to direct the ships to appropriate ports so that port state inspections can occur. The effect of these types of United Nations measures is therefore to give to United Nations member states a controlled right of visit based on flag state consent. As has been noted above, in the context of a United Nations mandated arms embargo against Libya in 2011, Security Council Resolution 1973 (2011) also authorised United Nations member states to carry out inspections on the high seas of vessels suspected of acting contrary to the embargo. In that instance, flag state consent was not a basis for the exercise of the right of inspection, which was closely monitored by the United Nations to ensure member states did not act beyond their authorisation.

B. Proliferation Security Initiative

United States President George W Bush launched the Proliferation Security Initiative (PSI) in May 2003 in response to security concerns arising from the spread of WMD and the potential for terrorists to gain access to such weapons.[139] Self-described as an 'activity' and not an 'organisation', considerable effort was expended to develop frameworks and mechanisms for implementing the PSI, including through numerous multilateral training exercises. In Paris in September 2003, 'Interdiction Principles for the Proliferation Security Initiative' were agreed upon[140] and these outline the basis and intent of the PSI, and some aspects of its operationalisation. Whilst the PSI has multiple operational dimensions and extends to land, sea and air, its principal focus has been on maritime operations and these have attracted significant analysis as to their legality.[141] The PSI revolves around a framework involving 102 states as of December 2012,[142] which through a combination of flag, coastal, and port state jurisdiction have sought to develop measures to counter the maritime proliferation of WMD. In addition, there is an 'Operational Experts Group' involving 21 PSI states who discuss proliferation concerns and plan future exercises.[143]

The PSI Interdiction Principles, which are stated to be 'consistent with national legal authorities and relevant international law' call upon states to take a range of measures, including at their own initiative or at the request of another state, to search their own flagged vessels suspected of carrying WMD, give consent for other states to search their flagged vessels suspected of carrying WMD, and to stop and search all vessels within

---

[138] UN Security Council Resolution 1874 (2009), [12].

[139] The catalyst was the December 2002 high seas interdiction by a Spanish warship of the North Korean-flagged *So San* which was carrying Scud missiles, warheads and missile fuel to Yemen. At the time of the boarding the *So San*'s details did not appear in the North Korean registry: Mary Beth Nikitin, 'Proliferation Security Initiative (PSI)', *Congressional Research Service* 7–5700 RL34327 (8 January 2010) 1.

[140] *Basic Documents* No 73.

[141] Douglas Guilfoyle, 'The Proliferation Security Initiative: Interdicting Vessels in International Waters to Prevent the Spread of Weapons of Mass Destruction' (2005) 29 *Melbourne University Law Review* 733; Michael Byers, 'Policing the High Seas: The Proliferation Security Initiative' (2004) 98 *AJIL* 526.

[142] 'The Proliferation Security Initiative' at www.psi-online.info; Nikitin, 'Proliferation Security Initiative (PSI)' (n 129) 2, though it has been noted that '[r]equirements for participation appear to be fairly weak'.

[143] Ibid; the members are Argentina, Australia, Canada, Denmark, France, Germany, Greece, Italy, Japan, the Netherlands, New Zealand, Norway, Poland, Portugal, Russia, Singapore, South Korea, Spain, Turkey, the United Kingdom and the United States.

internal waters, territorial sea or contiguous zones which are reasonably suspected of carrying WMD cargoes.[144] Building upon this framework, the United States has negotiated a number of ship-boarding agreements with certain flag of convenience states which pre-authorise boarding of suspect vessels with the proviso that the flag state has two hours to respond to a boarding request.[145]

C. Weapons Testing and Military Manoeuvres

One area of contention that has arisen under the LOSC relates to weapons testing and related military manoeuvres on the high seas and within the EEZ. Whilst the LOSC makes clear that the freedom of navigation is enjoyed within the high seas, and also within the EEZ subject only to some specific EEZ limitations, the Convention is silent as to what constitutes the freedom of navigation and whether that extends to the right of warships to conduct weapons exercises within these waters. The LOSC is not completely silent on weapons exercises per se, as direct reference is made to the right of the coastal state to conduct such exercises within its territorial sea,[146] although no direct reference is made to this right—by either the coastal state or other states—with respect to other maritime zones. If weapons exercises are to be conducted on the high seas, the LOSC does make clear that in the exercise of the high seas freedoms states are to 'have due regard to the interests of other States',[147] suggesting that it would be appropriate to declare a temporary exclusion zone so as to ensure the safety of surface and aerial navigation. Any such weapons testing would also need to be subject to the provisions of Part XII and the obligations of a flag state to ensure protection and preservation of the marine environment.

These issues become more problematic and contentious in the EEZ where although the coastal state only has limited sovereign rights, there is clearly the potential for heightened sensitivity when foreign military powers are seeking to conduct weapons testing and military manoeuvres as near as 13 nm from the coastal state. Again the LOSC is silent on this issue other than the broad reference in Article 58 to states having 'due regard to the rights and duties' of a coastal state when exercising their rights within the EEZ. In the case where there is genuine uncertainty as to the extent of the legal rights of the coastal state and that of other states within the EEZ, recourse can be had to Article 59 which provides that conflicts of this nature should be resolved on the 'basis of equity and in the light of all the relevant circumstances, taking into account the respective importance of the interests involved to the parties as well as to the international community as a whole'. This would suggest that a range of factors would be applicable in determining whether weapons testing and naval manoeuvres are permissible within the EEZ, including the distance from the coastal state's territorial sea, the length of these operations, their impact upon the general freedom of

---

[144] Interdiction Principles for the Proliferation Security Initiative, pt 4.

[145] See, eg, 2004 Agreement between the Government of the United States of America and the Government of the Republic of Liberia Concerning Cooperation to Suppress the Proliferation of Weapons of Mass Destruction, Their Delivery Systems, and Related Materials at Sea, *Basic Documents* No 74, art 4.

[146] LOSC, art 25(3), in the context of the ability of the coastal state being able to temporarily suspend innocent passage.

[147] Ibid art 87(2).

navigation within the area, and also potential implications for the marine environment, including marine living resources.[148]

A number of coastal states have made clear that foreign military exercises and manoeuvres, including the right to use weapons, are only permissible with the consent of the coastal state, in some instances seeking to support these claims by reference to Article 301. Bangladesh, Brazil, Cape Verde, India, Malaysia, Pakistan and Uruguay take this position in Declarations they appended either to their signature or to ratification of the Convention.[149] These interpretations have been contested by France, Italy, the Netherlands, and the United Kingdom,[150] whilst the United States considers military operations, exercises and activities are lawful uses of the seas.[151] There is also a small number of bilateral treaties principally concluded between western states and the former USSR which implicitly suggest there is an unfettered right to conduct weapons exercises and naval manoeuvres in the EEZ.[152] In light of this diversity in state practice, Churchill observed in 2005 that 'there is no agreed interpretation of the Convention nor a rule of customary international law' on whether there is an unfettered right to conduct these military operations in the EEZ.[153]

State practice with respect to military style operations dealing with asylum seekers and irregular migrants in various parts of the world has proven to be variable, with European states in the Mediterranean focusing more on safety of life at sea and bringing persons on board these boats ashore, while the United States (in the case of Cuba) and some states in South East Asia have adopted more assertive means and deployed their navies to stop these persons reaching landfall.[154] These practices have also seen the law of the sea intersect with the rights of persons to seek asylum.[155] Australia's conduct of 'Operation Sovereign Borders' from 2013 onwards, during which time naval and customs vessels undertook interdiction of boats bringing asylum seekers to Australia which were then turned back or towed back towards Indonesia, raised some novel questions with respect to the conduct of military operations within the EEZ of another state. The first was whether the towing of a boat carrying asylum seekers into the EEZ of another state as part of a military style operation to protect state borders was consistent with the freedom of navigation. While the towing of a distressed vessel across the EEZ by a military vessel as part of a safety of life at sea operation conducted under SOLAS would be permissible as ancillary to the freedom of navigation, it is doubtful whether towing a vessel through the EEZ of another state and then releasing that vessel within the EEZ and directing it towards the nearest landfall is consistent with the freedom of navigation. Likewise, any alternative characterisation as a military operation is also difficult to support as the Australian vessels were engaged in an operation directly to uphold territorial sovereignty by preventing the entry of asylum seekers' boats

---

[148] For comment see *Virginia Commentaries*, vol 2, 566–69; Churchill, 'The Impact of State Practice' (n 89) 134–35.

[149] UNDOALOS, 'United Nations Convention on the Law of the Sea: Declarations'.

[150] Ibid.

[151] Roach and Smith, *Excessive Maritime Claims* (n 10) 379–91.

[152] See, eg, 1986 United Kingdom and Union of Soviet Socialist Republics Agreement Concerning the Prevention of Incidents at Sea beyond the Territorial Sea.

[153] Churchill, 'The Impact of State Practice' (n 89) 135.

[154] 'Indonesia Turns Away Boat as Asian Migrant Crisis Escalates', *The Jakarta Post*, 18 May 2015.

[155] Guy S Goodwin-Gill, 'The Right to Seek Asylum: Interception at Sea and the Principle of Non-refoulment' [2011] *International Journal of Refugee Law* 443.

into the Australian territorial sea, and could not be characterised as being equivalent to a law enforcement type operation consistent with a hot pursuit as no effort was made to prosecute.[156]

D. Demilitarised and Nuclear Free Zones

A further aspect to consider with respect to naval operations at sea is the impact of demilitarised and nuclear free zones. Since the end of World War II there has been an increasing pressure to demilitarise certain areas that can be regarded as part of the global commons.[157] Antarctica has been subject to demilitarisation under the 1959 Antarctic Treaty which extends to the seas of the Southern Ocean as far north as 60° south latitude.[158] Article I of the Antarctic Treaty provides:

> Antarctica shall be used for peaceful purposes only. There shall be prohibited, *inter alia*, any measures of a military nature, such as the establishment of military bases and fortifications, the carrying out of military maneuvers, as well as the testing of any type of weapons.

This provision has been interpreted such that any form of belligerent military operations in the Southern Ocean is impermissible under the Antarctic Treaty, and Argentina and the United Kingdom, both parties to the treaty, honoured this interpretation during the 1982 Falklands War in which the area of operations extended close to the northern limits of the treaty area.

In an effort to prevent nuclear proliferation, there have also been several initiatives globally to adopt nuclear free zones and nuclear-weapon free zones and regional treaties have been concluded which cover parts of Latin America and the Caribbean, the South Pacific, Southeast Asia and Africa.[159] To varying degrees, these zones apply not only to the territorial seas and EEZs of the state parties, but also extend to the high seas, thereby creating issues as to the freedom of navigation of nuclear-powered and nuclear-armed warships. However, no significant issues have arisen with respect to these regimes because of an appreciation that a rigid enforcement of nuclear free status to both non-parties and those states from beyond the region would impact navigational freedoms. Accordingly, the 1985 Treaty of Raratonga creating the South Pacific Nuclear Free Zone sidesteps its potential impact upon the freedom of navigation by providing that: 'Nothing in this Treaty shall prejudice or in any way affect the rights, or the exercise of the rights, of any state under international law with regard to freedom of the seas.'[160] A similar provision is found in the 1995 Treaty of

---

[156] See discussion in Joyce Chia, Jane McAdam and Kate Purcell, 'Asylum in Australia: "Operation Sovereign Borders" and International Law' (2014) 32 *Australian Year Book of International Law* 33, 50–62; Natalie Klein, 'Assessing Australia's "Push Back the Boats" Policy under International Law: Legality and Accountability for Maritime Interceptions of Irregular Migrants' (2014) 15 *Melbourne Journal of International Law* 124.

[157] An example of these types of initiatives is the 1979 Agreement Governing the Activities of States on the Moon and other Celestial Bodies (Moon Treaty), art 3 of which forbids the placement of military installations or testing of any forms of military weapons, including nuclear weapons, on the moon.

[158] Antarctic Treaty, art VI.

[159] See generally Scott Parish, 'Nuclear-Weapon-Free Zones and Maritime Transit of Nuclear Weapons' in Caron and Scheiber (eds), *The Oceans in the Nuclear Age* (n 6) 337–51.

[160] South Pacific Nuclear Free Zone Treaty, art 2.

Bangkok creating the Southeast Asian Nuclear Weapon-Free Zone, though this Treaty only extends as far as the EEZs of the states within the region and does not purport to apply to the high seas. These regional initiatives are to be distinguished from the practices of some states which prohibit access to their ports by nuclear-armed or nuclear-powered vessels, which have particular implications for visiting foreign warships. For instance, the impact of the New Zealand Nuclear Free Zone, Disarmament and Arms Control Act 1987 has been that New Zealand port visits by United States warships have been suspended because of the refusal of the United States to confirm or deny whether those warships are nuclear armed.[161]

It is arguable that the Area is also a nuclear free zone given the objectives of the common heritage regime in Part XI of the LOSC and the clear statement in Article 141 that the Area is to be used 'exclusively for peaceful purposes'. Prior to the negotiation of the LOSC there was concern as to the possible militarisation of the seabed partly due to the strategic mineral resources that it was anticipated would be available following deep seabed mining.[162] Some of these concerns were put to rest by the 1970 Seabed Treaty,[163] Article I of which prohibited the emplacement of nuclear weapons or WMD on the seabed.[164] Consistent with the objectives of the LOSC in relation to the Area, it was important that these principles be reinforced in the Convention. The LOSC provides that all activities within the Area are to be carried out for the benefit of humankind,[165] and protection of the marine environment of the Area,[166] which lend further support to the denuclearisation of the Area and its exemption from weapons testing.

VII. Overflight by Military Aircraft

An increasingly important aspect of military operations at sea is the role played by aircraft. In contrast to the 1958 Geneva Conventions, a range of LOSC provisions address issues relating to the operations of military aircraft,[167] including overflight. In an important distinction between the operations of warships and military aircraft, the regime of innocent passage does not apply to overflight within the territorial sea. This is consistent with the recognised sovereignty the coastal state enjoys over its airspace,[168] and an acknowledgement that there has never been in customary international law any rights of overflight above the territorial sea by foreign military aircraft. Disputes which have arisen regarding overflight within this area are often founded upon excessive baseline claims resulting in certain waters

---

[161] Joanna Mossop, 'Maritime Security in New Zealand' in Klein, Mossop and Rothwell (eds), *Maritime Security* (n 52) 54, 61–62.

[162] Booth, *Law, Force and Diplomacy at Sea* (n 1) 120–24.

[163] 1970 Treaty on the Prohibition of the Emplacement of Nuclear Weapons and Other Weapons of Mass Destruction on the Seabed and the Ocean Floor and its Subsoil Thereof.

[164] See discussion in DP O'Connell, *The International Law of the Sea,* vol 2, (Oxford, Clarendon Press, 1984) 826–28.

[165] LOSC, art 140.

[166] Ibid art 145.

[167] See ibid art 111, addressing the role of military aircraft in the right of hot pursuit.

[168] Ibid art 2.

being deemed internal waters,[169] excessive territorial sea claims which are not recognised, or claims to regulate overflight beyond the territorial sea within international airspace in a manner inconsistent with the Article 87 freedom of overflight over the EEZ and high seas.[170]

The freedom of overflight is only directly addressed in the territorial sea in the context of overflight within an international strait where the right of transit passage applies equally to ships and aircraft.[171] Military aircraft therefore enjoy the same rights of transit through an international strait as do warships, subject only to the particular duties that apply to aircraft under Article 39(3), including the expectation that 'state aircraft' would 'normally' comply with ICAO safety measures, including having due regard for the safety of navigation, and monitoring either local air traffic control or international distress radio frequencies. These provisions raise issues with respect to the obligations of state aircraft, which include military aircraft, to comply with ICAO safety standards within what may be congested airspace above an international strait.[172] These issues have been highlighted by Spain's interpretation of the LOSC as it applies to the Strait of Gibraltar. Upon both signature and subsequent ratification of the Convention, Spain issued declarations which have implications for transit passage by military aircraft. The first was Spain suggesting an interpretation of Part III which permitted the coastal state to apply its own regulations with respect to air navigation, provided that the right of transit passage was not impeded. The second, related to Article 39(3)(a), where Spain indicated that the 'word 'normally' means 'unless by *force majeure* or by distress'.[173] The effect of this declaration was that Spain had an expectation that state aircraft transiting the Strait of Gibraltar were expected to comply with the ICAO Rules of the Air.[174] The United States has made clear to Spain its objections to these declarations as being incompatible with both customary international law and the LOSC.[175] The United States position is consistent with the law of the sea.

The overflight provisions that apply to transit passage are effectively duplicated for the purposes of overflight of an archipelagic sea lane under Part IV of the LOSC. Aircraft, without distinction between civilian or state aircraft, enjoy the right of archipelagic sea lanes passage within designated air routes, or through such routes as may be normally used for international navigation.[176] When the archipelagic state has designated air routes, aircraft are not to deviate more than 25 nm either side of the of the axis lines of those routes subject to limitations on navigating certain distances from the coastline. As the provisions of Article 39 also apply within archipelagic sea lanes, the same issues arise with respect to the obligations of military aircraft to comply with ICAO air rules. None of the recognised

---

[169] The United States has raised this as a concern in response to Libya's baselines across the Gulf of Sidra based on a claim that it is an historic bay, and has asserted its rights of overflight above the waters of the bay, which in 1981 resulted in clashes between United States and Libyan aircraft in air-to-air combat: Roach and Smith, *Excessive Maritime Claims* (n 10) 46–47, and see the discussion regarding baselines in ch 2.

[170] Ibid 353–61.

[171] LOSC, art 38.

[172] *Virginia Commentaries*, vol 2, 344–48.

[173] UNDOALOS, 'United Nations Convention on the Law of the Sea: Declarations'.

[174] See discussion in José A de Yturriaga Straits, *Used for International Navigation: A Spanish Perspective* (Dordrecht, Martinus Nijhoff, 1991) 227–32.

[175] Roach and Smith, *Excessive Maritime Claims* (n 10) 290–93.

[176] LOSC, art 53.

archipelagic states have lodged any distinctive Declarations under LOSC relating to aspects of archipelagic sea lanes passage that have particular application to military aircraft.

As the right of overflight applies within the international airspace of the EEZ, one area of dispute that has arisen has been the different interpretations of the LOSC as to the capacity of a coastal state to regulate certain types of overflight by military aircraft. This has been particularly contentious with respect to overflight conducted in association with military manoeuvres which is inevitably undertaken in parallel with equivalent operations of warships, but also more distinctive operations such as surveillance, ordinance testing and firing, and intelligence gathering.[177] These issues were highlighted in 2001 when a United States Navy surveillance aircraft collided with a Chinese Navy fighter jet over the South China Sea above the Chinese EEZ. The incident resulted in the death of a Chinese airman, and the need for the United States aircraft to make an emergency landing on Hainan Island where the crew were detained for some days. China lodged strong protests with the United States over this incident especially against the United States practice of conducting surveillance missions adjacent to the territorial sea.[178] Whilst there was considerable debate regarding certain military operations such as weapons exercises within the EEZ during the LOSC negotiations, a fact reflected in Declarations lodged upon signature or ratification, no state parties sought to address the issue of aerial surveillance or reconnaissance. Iran's 1993 Marine Areas Act claimed the right to prohibit 'collection of information' within the EEZ, and this assertion has been subject to protest from the United States.[179] Subject to the capability of aircraft to conduct aerial surveillance, a coastal state may be able to assert constructive presence if the foreign military aircraft is operating adjacent to territorial sea limits.[180]

A. Air Defence Identification Zones

Some states have established Air Defense Identification Zones (ADIZ), which extend beyond the territorial sea of the state to an area conterminous with or beyond the EEZ.[181] An ADIZ has been characterised as an area of airspace over land or water where a state 'requires the immediate and positive identification, location, and air traffic control of aircraft in the interests of the country's national security'.[182] The United States has been proactive in the proclamation of such zones, which first commenced in 1948 during the Cold

---

[177] See generally Van Dyke, 'Military Ships and Planes' (n 127).

[178] Ivan Shearer 'Military Activities in the Exclusive Economic Zone: The Case of Aerial Surveillance' [2003] 17 *Ocean Yearbook* 548, 548–49. The United States position as to overflight of the high seas within international airspace is outlined in Thomas and Duncan (eds), 'Annotated Supplement to The Commanders Handbook' (n 75) 140.

[179] Roach and Smith, *Excessive Maritime Claims* (n 10) 382–83.

[180] See discussion of constructive presence in ch 17.

[181] See generally Peter A Dutton, '*Caelum Liberum*: Air Defense Identification Zones Outside Sovereign Airspace' (2009) 103 *AJIL* 691.

[182] Ian E Rinehart and Bart Ellias, 'China's Air Defense Identification Zone' *Congressional Research Service* R43894 (30 January 2015) at www.crs.gov 1; for US practice see United States Naval War College, *Maritime Operational Zones* (Newport, RI, United States Naval War College, 2015) 1-18–19 at usnwc.edu/Departments---Colleges/International-Law/References/Maritime-Operational-Zones-Manual-May-2015.aspx.

War, and, alongside an equivalent zone claimed by Canada, are monitored and enforced by the North American Air Defense Command.[183] A number of East and South Asian states have also claimed an ADIZ, including Japan, South Korea, Republic of China (Taiwan), the Philippines, Myanmar and India.[184] A feature of many of these ADIZs, including that of the United States, is that de jure or de facto they do not apply to state aircraft, thereby recognising the freedom of overflight enjoyed by state aircraft consistent with the LOSC.[185] The more significant impact of an ADIZ is therefore upon civil aircraft en route to or from the sovereign airspace of a state. However, for these civil aircraft the provision of basic details relating to their identification, flight data and flight path assist in contributing to their safety, which is consistent with the spirit of the 1944 Chicago Convention. States also have declared Flight Information Regions (FIRs), which relate to the provision of air traffic services over both land and sea. The effect of FIRs is that civil aircraft will always have a designated air traffic controller even when that aircraft is over the high seas, which for commercial airlines contributes to the safety of air navigation.[186] In 2013 China declared an 'East China Sea Air Defense Identification Zone', which extended beyond the FIR managed by China, overlapped the declared ADIZs of Japan and Korea, and included the airspace above the Senkaku/Diaoyu Islands, which are claimed by both China and Japan.[187] The East China Sea ADIZ was the first declared by China and sought to apply to both state and civil aircraft. A number of China's regional neighbours were critical of the East China Sea ADIZ, as were the United States and Australia.[188] In November 2013 and August 2014 United States military aircraft entered the East China Sea ADIZ without notification,[189] making clear the United States' position that it does not recognise the application of an ADIZ to state aircraft exercising the freedom of overflight.

VIII. Further Reading

Louise Doswald-Beck, *San Remo Manual on International Law Applicable to Armed Conflicts at Sea* (Cambridge, Cambridge University Press, 1995)

Douglas Guilfoyle, *Shipping Interdiction and the Law of the Sea* (Cambridge, Cambridge University Press, 2009)

---

[183] Rinehart and Ellias, 'China's Air Defense Identification Zone' (n 182) 2–3.

[184] Ibid 3.

[185] Dutton, *'Caelum Liberum'* (n 181) 700 observes 'although US regulations appear to reflect ambiguity about the sovereign immunity of foreign state aircraft operating in an American ADIZ, US practice reflects respect for the right of foreign military aircraft to exercise traditional high seas freedoms in the airspace above the EEZ'.

[186] The United States has had occasion to protest efforts by Myanmar and India to extend their FIRs to US military aircraft when those aircraft did not enter territorial airspace; see Roach and Smith, *Excessive Maritime Claims* (n 10) 348–50.

[187] Ministry of National Defense (PRC), 'Announcement of the Aircraft Identification Rules for the East China Sea Air Defense Identification Zone of the PRC' (23 November 2013), reproduced at news.xinhuanet.com/english/china/2013-11/23/c_132911634.htm.

[188] Rinehart and Ellias, 'China's Air Defense Identification Zone' (n 182) 15–22; Department of Foreign Affairs and Trade (Australia), 'Media Release: China's Announcement of an Air-Defence Identification Zone over the East China Sea' (26 November 2013) at foreignminister.gov.au/releases.

[189] Rinehart and Ellias, 'China's Air Defense Identification Zone' (n 182) 15–16.

Natalie Klein, *Maritime Security and the Law of the Sea* (Oxford, Oxford University Press, 2010)

James Kraska, 'Military Operations' in Donald R Rothwell, Alex G Oude Elferink, Karen N Scott and Tim Stephens (eds), *The Oxford Handbook of The Law of the Sea* (Oxford, Oxford University Press, 2015) 866

Rob McLaughlin, *United Nations Naval Peace Operations in the Territorial Sea* (Leiden, Martinus Nijhoff, 2009)

DP O'Connell, *The Influence of Law on Sea Power* (Manchester, Manchester University Press, 1975)

13

Marine Resource Management

I. Introduction

The world's oceans contain extensive natural resources, many of which have been explored and exploited only to a limited extent by comparison with terrestrial resources. Although fisheries in many regions are under pressure as a result of overfishing, pollution and climate change, other living resources, such as the marine organisms being targeted by bioprospectors, hold substantial untapped potential. Moreover, many marine non-living resources are underutilised, mainly because of their relative inaccessibility. This is especially the case with respect to deposits of oil and gas in deep water areas of continental shelves, and mineral deposits on and under the deep seabed beyond national jurisdiction (the Area). However, this situation is rapidly changing as demand for mineral resources increases, and new frontiers for resource exploitation are opened as a result of improved mining technologies.

For most of the history of the law of the sea, the management of living and non-living resources has been pursued on an exclusively zonal basis, with coastal states having sole rights over resources in a narrow band of adjacent waters, and with high seas resources then subject to the freedom of resource exploitation, a freedom enjoyed in principle by all states.[1] The LOSC radically expanded coastal state resource zones for living and non-living resources through the continental shelf and EEZ regimes, created a new common heritage regime for the non-living resources of the Area, and established new rules to safeguard fisheries and the marine environment more generally. As a result, nearly 40 per cent of ocean space that was high seas is now within the 200 nm zones of coastal states.[2]

While the conclusion of LOSC substantially transformed the global regime for marine resource management, in particular by introducing new duties of cooperation in relation to fisheries conservation, it also remained animated to a large degree by a zonal approach, and therefore did not itself establish a truly holistic and 'integrated' system for marine resource management. However, very substantial progress towards this objective has been achieved through developments in treaty law and state practice in the post-LOSC period, most notably in the context of high seas and transboundary fisheries. The most important of these was the conclusion of an implementing agreement under the LOSC, the 1995 Agreement for the Implementation of the Provisions of the United Nations Convention on the Law of the Sea of 10 December 1982 Relating to the Conservation and Management of Straddling

---

[1] Yoshifumi Tanaka, *A Dual Approach to Ocean Governance: The Cases of Zonal and Integrated Management in the International Law of the Sea* (Farnham, Ashgate, 2008) 1–6.
[2] AV Lowe, 'Reflections on the Waters: Changing Conceptions of Property Rights in the Law of the Sea' (1986) 1 *International Journal of Estuarine and Coastal Law* 1, 4.

Fish Stocks and Highly Migratory Fish Stocks (the FSA).[3] Designed to ensure the long-term conservation and sustainable use of transboundary and high seas fisheries stocks that have historically been poorly managed, the FSA is built around the precautionary principle, and seeks to protect marine ecosystems as a whole, rather than particular fisheries, irrespective of maritime boundaries. The FSA, and the regional fisheries management organisations (RFMOs) brought within its auspices have therefore heralded a significant transition from a resource-focussed to an ecosystemic approach to fisheries management.[4]

Despite these significant additions to the legal framework, many commercial fisheries and by-catch species[5] are in serious crisis, confirming the continuing need for further improvements to international fisheries law to ensure the availability of fish for human consumption, and to maintain the integrity of marine ecosystems.[6] In particular, there is a need to strengthen further the response to illegal, unreported and unregulated (IUU) fishing, which poses a threat to the sustainability of a number of fisheries.[7] Assessments by the FAO estimate that the maximum wild capture fisheries potential throughout the world's oceans has probably been reached, and that 90 per cent of fisheries are being harvested up to or beyond their sustainable limits.[8] Only around 10 per cent of stocks are underexploited.[9] Maintaining sustainable fisheries is not only important from an ecological perspective, it is also vital for achieving food security,[10] and to support the livelihoods of between 660 and 820 million people globally.[11]

The FAO was established in 1945[12] to raise levels of nutrition and standards of living worldwide, by securing improved productivity of agriculture and fisheries, and to better the condition of rural populations. A key programme area for the FAO is fisheries, including both capture fisheries and aquaculture, the latter now supplying a record 42 per cent of the 158 million tonnes of fish produced by wild fisheries.[13] The Fisheries and Aquaculture Department of the FAO is tasked with securing the long-term sustainable development of fisheries, and to that end collects, analyses and distributes fisheries data, monitors the state of fisheries, supports RFMOs and national governments, and develops legal and policy instruments to achieve responsible and sustainable fisheries production.

---

[3] *Basic Documents* No 56.

[4] See David Freestone, 'International Fisheries Law since Rio: The Continued Rise of the Precautionary Principle' in Alan Boyle and David Freestone (eds), *International Law and Sustainable Development: Past Achievements and Future Challenges* (Oxford, Oxford University Press, 1999).

[5] By-catch are marine or other living organisms that are incidentally caught in fishing nets or other fishing gear. Some by-catch species have been threatened by poor fishing practices and have been subject to specific conservation initiatives. See, eg, the 1992 Agreement for the Reduction of Dolphin Mortality in the Eastern Pacific Ocean and the 2001 Agreement on the Conservation of Albatrosses and Petrels.

[6] Colin W Clark, *The Worldwide Crisis in Fisheries: Economic Models and Human Behaviour* (Cambridge, Cambridge University Press, 2006) 7.

[7] For a full definition of IUU fishing see Art 3 of the FAO International Plan of Action on Illegal, Unreported and Unregulated Fishing, *Basic Documents* No 67. See also Rachel J Baird, *Aspects of Illegal, Unreported and Unregulated Fishing in the Southern Ocean* (Dordrecht, Springer, 2006).

[8] FAO, *The State of World Fisheries and Aquaculture 2014* (Rome, FAO, 2014) 37.

[9] Ibid 37.

[10] *Report of the Secretary-General on the Oceans and the Law of the Sea*, UN Doc A/69/71 (2014), [143].

[11] *Report of the Secretary-General on the Oceans and the Law of the Sea*, UN Doc A/70/74 (2015), [15]

[12] 1945 Constitution of the Food and Agriculture Organization of the United Nations.

[13] FAO, *The State of World Fisheries* (n 8) 19.

II. Non-Living Marine Resources

A. Resource Potential

The oceans, seabed and subsoil contain a variety of non-living resources, but these have been far less accessible for exploitation than those found on the continental landmasses.[14] Today, however, familiar features of many seascapes are drilling and petroleum production platforms both near to the coast and in open ocean areas.

Oil and gas exploitation constitutes the most important offshore non-living resource sector.[15] Since the first industrial-scale oil wells were sunk off the coast of Louisiana in the United States in the 1940s, there has been a steady increase in offshore production of hydrocarbons.[16] In 2015 offshore oil production constituted around 30 per cent of world oil production.[17] Offshore gas production increased between the 1980s and the 1990s by almost 30 per cent, and by the 1990s comprised 50 per cent of world gas production.[18] The areas of most concentrated offshore oil and gas activity are the Gulf of Mexico, the North Sea, and offshore West Africa and South-East Asia, and increasingly in deeper waters as deposits close to shore are exhausted.[19]

As the most readily exploitable offshore stocks of oil and gas begin to be depleted, attention is turning to new marine resource frontiers, such as the Arctic Ocean, which is likely to be nearly ice-free in the summer within decades, potentially making its hydrocarbon resources accessible.[20] The United States Geological Survey estimates that 30 per cent of the world's undiscovered gas and 13 per cent of the world's undiscovered oil may be found north of the Arctic Circle.[21] However, all Arctic hydrocarbon resources are considered to be unburnable if the global temperature rise is to be kept below 2°C, the officially agreed global warming 'guardrail'.[22] Similarly, untapped hydrocarbon resources such as methane hydrates will need to remain undisturbed.[23] It is estimated that ocean-floor hydrates contain twice the amount of hydrocarbon resources as those found in all of the unrecovered oil, gas and coal deposits elsewhere on earth,[24] and that methane hydrates contain almost 30 times the amount of carbon dioxide in the atmosphere.[25] However, as presently configured, the law

---

[14] For an overview of oceanic mineral resources see Fillmore CF Earney, *Marine Mineral Resources* (London, Routledge, 1990). See also Ronán J Long, *Marine Resource Law* (Dublin, Thomson Round Hall, 2007).

[15] *Report of the Secretary-General on the Oceans and the Law of the Sea*, UN Doc A/57/57 (2002), [229].

[16] *Report of the Secretary-General on the Oceans and the Law of the Sea*, UN Doc A/51/645 (1996), [245].

[17] *Report of the Secretary-General on the Oceans and the Law of the Sea*, UN Doc A/70/74 (2015), [41].

[18] *Report of the Secretary-General on the Oceans and the Law of the Sea*, UN Doc A/57/57 (2002), [229].

[19] Ibid [231].

[20] IPCC, Climate *Change 2014: Synthesis Report. Contribution of Working Groups I, II and III to the Fifth Assessment Report of the Intergovernmental Panel on Climate Change* (Geneva, IPCC, 2014) 62.

[21] Donald L Gautier et al, 'Assessment of Undiscovered Oil and Gas in the Arctic' (2009) 324(5931) *Science* 1175.

[22] Christophe McGlade and Paul Ekins, 'The Geographical Distribution of Fossil Fuels Unused When Limiting Global Warming to 2°C' (2015) 517 *Nature* 187, 190.

[23] Myles R Allen et al, 'Warming Caused by Cumulative Carbon Emissions towards the Trillionth Tonne' (2009) 458 *Nature* 1163.

[24] *Report of the Secretary-General on the Oceans and the Law of the Sea*, UN Doc A/51/645 (1996), [276].

[25] *Report of the Secretary General on the Oceans and the Law of the Sea*, UN Doc A/52/487 (1997), [253]. Methane is a greenhouse gas that has a heat trapping effect many times more powerful than carbon dioxide and global

of the sea is not concerned in any way with limiting the exploitation of oil, gas or any other non-living resource that has associated environmental impacts, and instead leaves the regulation of the human impact on the carbon cycle to the international climate change regime founded upon the 1992 United Nations Framework Convention on Climate Change.[26]

In addition to hydrocarbons, the oceans have also been exploited for other mineral resources, such as precious stones, including diamonds (there have been diamond mines offshore South Africa since the 1960s). Seawater itself also contains many minerals, including gold, magnesium and cobalt, and it is technically possible, though not economically feasible, to extract these by processing very large volumes of water.[27]

B. Internal Waters and Territorial Sea

Within internal waters and the territorial sea, the coastal state has exclusive competence to regulate access to non-living resources. Access by foreign nationals, for prospecting, exploration or exploitation, is therefore only possible where the coastal state has granted its express consent. This is reaffirmed in the case of the territorial sea by Article 19(2)(j) of the LOSC which provides that a foreign ship in the territorial sea engaging in 'research or survey activities', which would include exploratory activities for minerals, will be engaged in passage that is prejudicial to the peace, good order, or security of a coastal state, and therefore not able to enjoy the privileges of innocent passage.[28]

In relation to the territorial sea and internal waters there has been no change from the rights enjoyed by coastal states under the pre-LOSC regime, except that these now apply out to the 12 nm territorial sea.[29] Coastal states regularly grant licences to foreign companies to engage in oil and gas prospecting, exploration and exploitation, in the territorial sea, with coastal states setting the terms of such contracts, including making provision for the collection of royalties. The subsequent regulation by the coastal state of this foreign investment then often comes within the terms of bilateral investment treaties.

C. Continental Shelf and Exclusive Economic Zone

The LOSC recognised and further developed the doctrine of the continental shelf, a zone that is concerned primarily with coastal state sovereign rights over non-living resources. The 1945 proclamation by United States President Harry S Truman[30] was the first major statement of entitlement to these resources, and was the culmination of demands made by

---

warming will be exacerbated by the release of gaseous methane to the atmosphere from ocean hydrates if they are exploited, and if they escape as sea temperatures rise: David Archer, 'Methane Hydrate Stability and Anthropogenic Climate Change' (2007) 4 *Biogeosciences* 52.

[26] See Rachel Baird, Meredith Simons and Tim Stephens, 'Ocean Acidification: A Litmus Test for International Law' (2009) 3 *Carbon and Climate Law Review* 459.

[27] *Report of the Secretary General on the Oceans and the Law of the Sea*, UN Doc A/52/487 (1997), [255].

[28] See further ch 14.

[29] LOSC, art 3.

[30] Proclamation 2667, 'Policy of the United States With Respect to the Natural Resources of the Subsoil and Seabed of the Continental Shelf' 28 September 1945, *Basic Documents* No 5.

the oil industry, from as early as 1918, for offshore mining permits outside the territorial sea.[31] In addition to recognising the continental shelf, the LOSC also established a new resource zone, the EEZ, which applies to both living and non-living resources and therefore overlaps to a considerable extent with the continental shelf regime. However, some non-living resource-related activities, such as the production of energy from the water, currents and the wind, fall only within the purview of the EEZ regime in Part V of the LOSC.[32] As most accessible offshore mineral resources are found within 200 nm zones, the LOSC resource regime means that coastal states are effectively accorded exclusive responsibility for the management of the majority of marine non-living resources in the world's oceans.

One characteristic of non-living resource management in the law of the sea that very clearly distinguishes it from the management of fisheries is that it is not premised upon any duty of conservation. In the EEZ, and on the high seas, states are bound by extensive conservation duties in relation to fisheries.[33] However, for non-living resources there are no such duties in any maritime zone. Hence minerals and hydrocarbons may be exploited without regard to climate protection goals or any object of rational use that would extend their availability for human consumption until such time as alternatives can be developed.[34] Nonetheless, in seeking to exploit mineral resources states must adhere to the obligations of marine environmental protection found in Part XII of the LOSC, which among other things require states to prevent, reduce and control pollution of the marine environment.[35]

There are other treaties and soft-law instruments operating in tandem with the LOSC that are relevant to the offshore mining industry in the EEZ and the continental shelf. These include instruments that deal with matters such as the prevention of pollution,[36] the removal of offshore installations and structures,[37] and the protection of such platforms from terrorist activities and other acts of violence.[38]

D. The High Seas and Deep Seabed

Although reducing the area of seabed that was regarded as high seas, the emergence of the continental shelf and EEZ did not affect the legal status of the high seas as a *res communis* area in which non-living resources were open to be used by all states. Initially the actual enjoyment of such rights was impractical, given the technical difficulties involved in gaining access to seabed resources at a substantial distance from coastlines. However, mining on the high seas became a real possibility from the 1960s onwards with rising mineral prices

[31] Lawrence Juda, *International Law and Ocean Use Management: The Evolution of Ocean Governance* (London, Routledge, 1996) 94–95.

[32] LOSC, art 56(1)(a).

[33] Ibid arts 61, 117–19. These provisions are discussed below.

[34] David M Ong, 'Towards and International Law for the Conservation of Offshore Hydrocarbon Resources within the Continental Shelf?' in David Freestone, Richard Barnes and David M Ong (eds), *The Law of the Sea: Progress and Prospects* (Oxford, Oxford University Press, 2006) 93, 118.

[35] See, eg, LOSC, art 194(3)(c).

[36] See, eg, the 1980 Protocol for the Protection of the Mediterranean Sea against Pollution from Land-Based Sources and Activities, *Basic Documents* No 25.

[37] See, eg, the 1989 Guidelines and Standards for the Removal of Offshore Installations and Structures on the Continental Shelf and in the Exclusive Economic Zone, *Basic Documents* No 41.

[38] See, eg, the 1988 Protocol for the Suppression of Unlawful Acts against the Safety of Fixed Platforms located on the Continental Shelf.

and improvements in marine resource extraction technologies. The realisation that high seas mining was technically feasible (if not economically viable) led to developments in the law of the sea that resulted in the designation of the Area and its resources as the 'common heritage of mankind'.[39] This common heritage regime in Part XI of the LOSC replaced the high seas freedom of non-living resource exploitation with a new conceptualisation of the deep seabed, which vested its resources in the international community as a whole, and established a system for administering prospecting, exploration and exploitation through the ISA.[40]

The deep seabed regime under LOSC applies only to solid, liquid or gaseous mineral resources in or beneath the seabed, including polymetallic nodules.[41] Therefore it does not apply to other non-living resources potentially exploitable on the high seas, such as energy that could be harvested from currents, waves and wind. Such resources continue to be subject to the freedom of the high seas, and may be utilised freely by states subject only to the requirement to have due regard for the interests of other states in their exercise of the freedom of the high seas.[42]

E. Joint Development

Non-living resources generally present fewer management challenges for the law of the sea than do living resources, as their fixed location means that their exploitation can normally be regulated by a single state or, in the case of the Area, by the ISA. However, management on this zonal basis is obviously contingent on the clear demarcation of maritime zones, and this has not been achieved in many regions where overlapping EEZ and continental shelf areas have not been delimited, or where there remains doubt as to the outer limits of a coastal state's continental shelf. Moreover, in some places oil and gas deposits straddle the maritime zones of two or more states, such that the extraction activities authorised by one state can impact upon a shared resource such as a single pool of hydrocarbons found within a basin.

Joint development arrangements have proven to be helpful in sidestepping resource disputes arising from competing claims to maritime jurisdiction, and in facilitating the development of common mineral resources.[43] Agreements of this character had been concluded many years prior to the LOSC; however, they have become much more common since 1982. This is primarily because Articles 74(3) and 83(3) of the LOSC provide that pending agreement on a boundary where there are overlapping EEZ and continental shelf areas, states 'in a spirit of understanding and cooperation, shall make every effort to enter into provisional arrangements of a practical nature'. It is made clear, however, that such arrangements amount to nothing more than *modi vivendi*, as they 'shall be without prejudice to the final delimitation'.

---

[39] LOSC, arts 1(1), 136.
[40] See further ch 6.
[41] LOSC, art 133(a).
[42] Ibid art 87(2).
[43] David M Ong, 'Joint Development of Common Offshore Oil and Gas Deposits: "Mere" State Practice or Customary International Law' (1999) 93 *AJIL* 771.

The first maritime joint development agreement was concluded between Bahrain and Saudi Arabia in 1958,[44] and provides that the exploitation of oil deposits in a joint zone is to be conducted in a manner determined by Saudi Arabia on the condition that one half of the net revenue is remitted to Bahrain. Other joint development agreements have had to address not only non-living resources but also fisheries, as is the case with the 1978 Agreement between Australia and Papua New Guinea concerning the Torres Strait. This complex agreement draws separate water column and seabed boundaries to take account of the fact that most islands in the Torres Strait are under Australian sovereignty, and that several of these lie close to the coast of Papua New Guinea. While fisheries jurisdiction accrues to Australia around islands near to the Papua New Guinea coast, the seabed boundary lies further south in the centre of the strait between the main landmasses of the two states.[45]

Another innovative joint development zone in the Asia Pacific is that found in the Timor Sea lying between Australia, Timor-Leste and Indonesia. Australia and Indonesia had negotiated seabed boundaries in the Timor Sea in 1972 at a time in which East Timor was under Portuguese sovereignty. Following Indonesia's occupation and annexation of East Timor in 1975 there was a need for a new agreement, to address the 'Timor Gap', a section of the boundary necessarily omitted from the Australia/Indonesia delimitation in 1972.[46] Regarding the 1972 agreement, which set the seabed boundary close to the Indonesian coastline, as unjust and wrongly based on the natural prolongation theory, Indonesia pressed for a median line boundary in the Timor Gap. Australia did not accept this proposal, and instead in 1989 the two states concluded a creative agreement to establish a joint development zone in the Timor Gap pending delimitation of the seabed boundary through the 1989 Treaty On the Zone of Cooperation in an Area Between the Indonesian Province of East Timor and Northern Australia (the Timor Gap Treaty). The Timor Sea joint development area was divided into three zones, to the north, abutting the centre, and to the south of the median line. When Timor-Leste gained independence in 2002 a new agreement became necessary. Following a transitional period in which the terms of the Timor Gap Treaty continued to be given effect,[47] negotiations with Australia led to the 2002 Timor Sea Treaty[48] which established a joint petroleum development area that coincided with the central zone of the 1989 Timor Gap Treaty. However, whereas under the Timor Gap Treaty revenues in this zone were split 50:50, under the 2002 Timor Sea Treaty they are divided 90:10 in favour of Timor-Leste.[49]

---

[44] 1958 Bahrain-Saudi Arabia Boundary Agreement.

[45] Stuart B Kaye, *Australia's Maritime Boundaries*, 2nd edn (Wollongong, NSW, Centre for Maritime Policy, 2001).

[46] 1972 Agreement Between Australia and Indonesia Establishing Certain Seabed Boundaries in the Area of the Timor and Arafura Seas.

[47] See Gillian Triggs, 'Legal and Commercial Risks of Investment in the Timor Gap' (2000) 1 *Melbourne Journal of International Law* 5.

[48] *Basic Documents* No 70.

[49] See also the 2003 International Unitisation Agreement for Greater Sunrise, and the 2006 Treaty on Certain Maritime Arrangements in the Timor Sea (CMATS), *Basic Documents* No 71, which are also interim arrangements, designed to bring certainty to a particular reservoir in the Timor Sea that falls partly inside, and partly outside, of the Joint Development Petroleum Area. The CMATS treaty is the subject of international arbitration, with Timor-Leste contending that it is invalid, alleging Australia spied on the Timorese delegation during the treaty negotiation: *Arbitration under the Timor Sea Treaty (Timor-Leste v Australia)*, Permanent Court of Arbitration, proceedings commenced 23 April 2013.

Another example of a joint development zone is found in the East China Sea, where in 2008 China and Japan reached an in principle agreement to develop jointly an identified area of the seabed, around 2,700 square kilometres.[50] This arrangement allows the cooperative development of an area of the East China Sea that remains hotly contested between the two states. While China argues for a seabed boundary on the basis of natural prolongation of the continental margin to the Okinawa Trough, Japan has maintained a claim based on equidistance.[51]

III. Living Resources

A. Fisheries and the 'Tragedy of the Commons'

'Picture a pasture open to all …'. So began the vignette used by Garrett Hardin in his landmark essay 'The Tragedy of the Commons' to explain how open access resources are prone to over-exploitation.[52] Hardin's well-known argument is that where a pasture is freely accessible, individual herders will rationally expand their flocks because the environmental costs are shared among all resource users. However, eventually this individually rational behaviour will lead to a collective tragedy caused by overgrazing, which in some places will cause permanent damage to the landscape through erosion and desertification.

Although much challenged, especially as few commons are completely open and unregulated, Hardin's analysis remains influential, and of obvious application to many marine living resources from fisheries through to marine mammals such as whales and seals. Indeed Hardin made specific mention of the 'shibboleth of the "freedom of the seas"', with its concomitant freedom to fish, as leading inexorably to the extinction of species of fish and marine mammals.[53] Hardin's prediction has come to pass in many fisheries; not only those requiring management by two or more states but also in poorly regulated EEZ fisheries. As Grafton et al explain, the cause of the 'all too common tragedy' of overfishing is 'not the rapaciousness of fishers' but rather 'arises from the characteristics of fisheries—harvests are rivalrous, fish are fugitive and thus are difficult to "own" and manage, and fisheries are subject to irreducible uncertainties'.[54]

B. Pre-LOSC Developments

Hugo Grotius regarded the living resources of the oceans as being practically inexhaustible, and argued on this basis that there could be no limits on the rights of nation to fish.[55]

---

[50] See http://au.china-embassy.org/eng/fyrth/t466632.htm.

[51] See Gao Jianjun, 'Joint Development in the East China Sea: Not an Easier Challenge Than Delimitation' (2008) 23 *International Journal of Marine and Coastal Law* 39, 61–66.

[52] Garrett Hardin, 'The Tragedy of the Commons' (1968) 162 (No 3859) *Science* 1243, 1244.

[53] Ibid 1245.

[54] R Quentin Grafton, James Kirkley, Tom Kompas and Dale Squires, *Economics for Fisheries Management* (Aldershot, Ashgate, 2006) 2.

[55] Hugo Grotius, *The Freedom of the Seas: or the Right Which Belongs to the Dutch to Take Part in the East Indian Trade* (Ralph van Deman Magoffin trans, original publication 1609, 1916) 57.

The living fruits of the sea were a common resource, and could be appropriated by anyone, with no need to place restrictions on fishing activities. This may have been appropriate in the seventeenth century, but it was a position that could not be sustained by the middle of the nineteenth century, when it became apparent that important fisheries were over-exploited. During this period the term 'overfishing' was coined, and there was concerted scientific interest in the health of ocean fisheries.[56] Conservation measures were made necessary by the increase in fishing fleets and fishing effort through changes in fishing technology, especially the advent of trawl fishing from the 1830s onwards. Fishing enterprises became even more efficient in the 1890s when steam powered vessels that could spend weeks at sea were commissioned, and new light cotton nets were developed and deployed.[57]

Increased fishing capacity and effort in particular marine regions led to significant conflicts between fishing states, and it was this problem, rather than the sustainability of fisheries, that prompted some of the earliest fisheries agreements. To address increasingly volatile conflicts in the North Sea, Belgium, Britain, Denmark, France, Germany and the Netherlands concluded the 1882 Convention for Regulating the Police of the North Sea Fisheries.[58] That convention provided for a three mile territorial sea limit, the registration of vessels of the contracting parties, the marking of vessels with the port of registry, the minimisation of interference among fishing operations in the same area, and the monitoring of infractions of the regulations by the navies of the parties. Significantly, however, the Convention did not impose any limits upon catch levels, it being thought that the critical issue to be resolved was the conflict between competing fishing fleets. The British and French governments also maintained that catch limits were unnecessary because the supply of fish could not realistically be exhausted.[59] This was an increasingly marginalised view, particularly in respect of the North Sea. Overfishing was recognised by international legal bodies as a problem requiring legal regulation: the Institute of International Law in 1894 noted that the three mile territorial sea, which was expressly recognised in the North Sea Fisheries Convention, was 'insufficient for the protection of coastwise fishing'.[60]

Overfishing began to generate significant disputes between some coastal states that wished to safeguard offshore fisheries found beyond the territorial sea, and fishing states, that sought to preserve the greatest area of ocean space as high seas subject to the freedom to fish. An early case that illustrates such tensions is the *Bering Sea Fur Seals* case[61] between Britain and the United States. The dispute arose following the arrest by the United States of British-flagged Canadian sealing schooners that were hunting Alaskan fur seals near the Pribilof Islands in Alaska, part of United States territory. The United States had arrested the vessels on the high seas, pursuant to domestic legislation that prohibited the taking of marine wildlife from Alaskan territory or the waters thereof. Britain contended that the arrests were unlawful as the Canadian vessels were exercising the high seas freedom

---

[56] Tim D Smith, 'A History of Fisheries and Their Science and Management' in Paul JB Hart and John B Reynolds (eds), *Handbook of Fish Biology and Fisheries*, vol 2 (London, Blackwell, 2002) 61, 65.

[57] Juda, *International Law and Ocean Use Management* (n 31) 18.

[58] See the discussion in CJ Colombos, *The International Law of the Sea*, 5th rev edn (London, Longmans, 1962) 374.

[59] Juda, *International Law and Ocean Use Management* (n 31) 20.

[60] Henry G Crocker (ed), *The Extent of the Marginal Sea: A Collection of Official Documents and Views of Representative Publicists* (Washington, DC, United States Government Printing Office, 1919) 116.

[61] *Bering Sea Fur Seals (Great Britain v United States)* (1898) 1 Moore 755.

of fishing. The United States justified its actions on the basis, among other reasons, that it had property in the seals which were begotten and born on its territory, that it was entitled to protect a seal herd in which it had an interest in harvesting, and, most innovatively, that it was acting as trustee for future generations in protecting seals that were a 'gift in common' to mankind.[62] The tribunal did not address these arguments, finding simply that the United States had no rights to fisheries on the high seas beyond the three nm limit of the territorial sea. Accordingly the tribunal strictly upheld the *mare liberum* doctrine, even in the face of clear evidence that unregulated sealing would lead to the collapse of the seal fishery.

One more promising aspect of the *Bering Sea Fur Seal* case from the perspective of fisheries conservation was the sealing regulations devised by the tribunal at the request of the parties. These were set out in nine detailed articles, and included the kinds of measures that continue to be used today in fisheries management, including an initial moratorium on sealing; a vessel licensing system; a requirement for catch records; provision for closed areas and closed seasons; limitations on vessel size; limitations on the types of fishing gear that could be used; and also exceptions from these regulations to protect indigenous subsistence hunting. These regulations provided the basis for subsequent agreement among the sealing states, including Japan and Russia, on a regional treaty.[63]

Several other regional fisheries agreements were concluded in the first half of the twentieth century, as was an important global species-specific agreement: the 1946 International Convention for the Regulation of Whaling.[64] However, most of the treaty-making activity in relation to fisheries took place after World War II, by which time there was considerable alarm at the depletion of fisheries, a problem which was now better understood because of improved data on catches landed, the extent of fishing effort, and the stock dynamics of individual fisheries.[65] In this period coastal states sought more concrete assurances that their interests in adjacent fisheries would be protected, and to this end began to make a series of unilateral claims that would ultimately lead to the widespread recognition of the notion of an exclusive fisheries zone, and subsequently the EEZ.

An important development in this regard was the 1945 Truman Proclamation on Fisheries,[66] issued at the same time as the Truman Proclamation on the Continental Shelf. The Proclamation on Fisheries acknowledged the need for better management of coastal fisheries, and asserted 'the special rights and equities of the coastal state and of any other state which may have established a legitimate interest therein'.[67] It went on to provide that the United States 'regards it as proper to establish conservation zones in those areas of the high seas contiguous to the coasts of the United States wherein fisheries activities have been or in the future may be developed and maintained on a substantial scale'. The Proclamation on Fisheries did not, however, seek to disturb the international consensus on the three mile territorial sea, in that the United States was not asserting sovereignty or jurisdiction in

[62] For discussion see Tim Stephens, *International Courts and Environmental Protection* (Cambridge, Cambridge University Press, 2009) 200–206.
[63] 1911 Convention Respecting Measures for the Preservation and Protection of Fur Seals in the North Pacific Ocean.
[64] *Basic Documents* No 7. Issues concerning the conservation and management of marine mammals are discussed below.
[65] Juda, *International Law and Ocean Use Management* (n 31) 107.
[66] United States Presidential Proclamation No 2668, Policy of the United States with Respect to Coastal Fisheries in Certain Areas of the High Seas, *Basic Documents* No 6.
[67] Ibid.

high seas areas beyond this limit. Rather it stressed that agreement on conservation zones would have to be reached between the United States and other states active in high seas fishing grounds. One of the reasons for the caution of the Proclamation on Fisheries in this respect, in comparison with the Continental Shelf Proclamation, which claimed exclusive rights in the non-living resources of the continental shelf, is that the United States did not wish other states to close their adjacent high seas areas to distant water fishing fleets from the United States.[68]

C. 1958 Geneva Conventions

Fisheries management issues were addressed to some extent in the four 1958 Geneva Conventions that were the outcome of UNCLOS I. The 1958 Convention on the Territorial Sea and the Contiguous Zone codified the customary position in relation to resource sovereignty in the territorial sea, which included unfettered control over fisheries resources, subject to no limitation of conservation. The 1958 Convention on the Continental Shelf gave to coastal states rights over sedentary fisheries on the continental shelf, again accompanied by no duty of conservation. The 1958 Convention on the High Seas affirmed the freedom of fishing as a core high seas freedom,[69] and imposed no limitations on fishing activities beyond the territorial sea, other than the vague stipulation that the freedom to fish must be exercised 'with reasonable regard to the interests of other states in their exercise of the freedom of the high seas'.[70]

Nonetheless, at UNCLOS I there was some awareness of overfishing and conflicts between coastal states and other fishing nations, and, in response, agreement was reached on a further convention making up the Geneva Regime: the 1958 Convention on Fishing and Conservation of the Living Resources of the High Seas. The ILC, in its commentary to the draft articles on which the Geneva regime was based, recognised that existing law provided no effective protection of marine fauna 'against waste or extermination',[71] and that this constituted 'a danger to the food supply of the world'.[72] Moreover, the absence of an international legal framework also operated as a powerful incentive to coastal states to take 'unilateral measures of self-protection', even though several of these were unlawful in so far as they purported to exclude foreign nationals from access to certain high seas areas.[73]

The 1958 Convention on Fishing emphasised the need for high seas fisheries to be conserved to ensure optimum sustainable yield, to as to ensure maximum supply of food and other marine products.[74] This was a reference to the notion of 'maximum sustainable yield' (MSY), which, until relatively recently, was the overriding objective of fisheries management. The concept of MSY is based on the biological characteristics of many fish stocks, which respond to a certain level of harvesting by rapidly increasing in size. In principle it is possible for the level of harvest to match the level of yield so that the fish population

---

[68]   Juda, *International Law and Ocean Use Management* (n 31) 111.
[69]   LOSC, art 2(2).
[70]   1958 Convention on the High Seas, art 2.
[71]   [1956] *Yearbook of the International Law Commission*, vol 1, 286.
[72]   Ibid.
[73]   Ibid.
[74]   1958 Convention on Fishing, art 2.

remains stable, with the biomass at a volume that is approximately the same as it was prior to being fished.[75] In reality, however, ecologically sustainable management of fisheries cannot be achieved by stock-specific MSY formulae, and the MSY concept has been subject to significant criticism.[76] Hence while MSY remains a helpful starting point for fisheries management, with the advent of the ecosystem and precautionary approaches it has given ground to more integrated techniques for the management of the resources supplied by marine ecosystems.

In several provisions the 1958 Convention on Fishing laid down a duty upon states to ensure that their nationals engaged in fishing any stock on the high seas follow appropriate conservation measures.[77] While recognising that coastal states have 'a special interest' in maintaining the productivity of high seas fisheries adjacent to their territorial seas,[78] it expressly ruled out any entitlement on the part of coastal states to take enforcement action in such areas against foreign nationals,[79] and instead established a convoluted procedure allowing unilateral measures of conservation in zones adjacent to the territorial sea to be adopted in circumstances where negotiations with other states broke down,[80] and which could be subject to endorsement or overrule by a special fisheries commission with the power to make binding decisions.[81]

The 1958 Convention on Fishing did not successfully address the concerns of coastal states, and was perceived as being too favourable to distant water fishing nations. It was not until 1966 that it entered into force, and it never attracted widespread ratification.[82] Moreover international fisheries conservation was not significantly advanced at UNCLOS II in 1960, even though the conference had been convened specifically to reach agreement on the breadth of the territorial sea, and the extent of coastal state fisheries jurisdiction. The proposal at the conference for a six mile territorial sea and a further six mile exclusive fishing zone, with a 10 year grace period for foreign fishing in this outer zone, fell short of the required two thirds majority by a single vote.[83] The 'six-plus-six' proposal had attracted criticism from a number of states, including Iceland and Mexico, which were deeply unhappy with the rider that preserved foreign fishing rights.[84]

Neither UNCLOS I or UNCLOS II was therefore able to forestall unilateral assertions of fisheries jurisdiction seawards of the territorial sea limit. Several Latin American states that had made claims in the late 1940s to 200 nm maritime zones that included sovereignty rights over living and non-living resources, showed no signs of relinquishing their claims.[85] Iceland was another notable claimant to fisheries jurisdiction. Although more modest in the extent of its claim to adjacent fisheries, Iceland was resolute in giving it effect,

---

[75] R Quentin Grafton et al, *Economics for Fisheries Management* (n 54) 5–7; Stuart Kaye, *International Fisheries Management* (The Hague, Kluwer, 2001) 49–60.

[76] For an early and landmark critique see PA Larkin, 'An Epitaph for the Concept of Maximum Sustained Yield' (1977) *Transactions of the American Fisheries Society* 106.

[77] 1958 Convention on Fishing, arts 1(2), 3, 4(2).

[78] Ibid art 6(1).

[79] Ibid art 6(4).

[80] Ibid art 7.

[81] Ibid arts 9–11.

[82] As of 1 July 2015 the Convention had 39 parties.

[83] Juda, *International Law and Ocean Use Management* (n 31) 161.

[84] Ibid.

[85] William T Burke, *The New International Law of Fisheries* (Oxford, Clarendon Press, 1994) 14–18.

sparking controversy when it arrested foreign fishing vessels in the so-called 'cod war' with the United Kingdom. Pursuant to a 1948 law that permitted the establishment of conservation zones within Iceland's continental shelf, Iceland extended its exclusive fisheries zone in progressive stages: from three to four miles in 1952, to 12 nm in 1958, and eventually to 50 nm in 1971. The United Kingdom and Germany objected to these claims, and in 1972 they commenced proceedings against Iceland in the ICJ in the *Fisheries Jurisdiction* case (proceedings in which Iceland refused to take part).[86] The ICJ handed down a decision on the merits in 1974, finding that a 12 nm EFZ could be claimed consistent with international law (a finding that was significantly aided by the 1964 European Fisheries Convention, which permitted 12 nm EFZs).[87] The Court also developed a novel doctrine, concluding that Iceland had 'preferential fishing rights' beyond 12 nm to a distance not specified, on the basis that such rights of a coastal state arise 'when the intensification in the exploitation of fishery resources makes it imperative to introduce some system of catch-limitation and sharing of those resources' so as 'to preserve the interests of their rational and economic exploitation'.[88] The Court also emphasised the importance of cooperation when managing fisheries in which multiple states have an interest.[89]

D. LOSC Regime

The findings of the ICJ in the *Fisheries Jurisdiction* case were quickly overtaken by developments at UNCLOS III, which led to the recognition of the 200 nm EEZ. Claims by coastal states to fisheries zones of 200 nm were becoming increasingly widespread, and this reality had to be acknowledged in the text that was being negotiated. From early in the proceedings at UNCLOS III it was apparent that a 200 nm EEZ was supported by the majority of states.[90]

Hence the LOSC sought to address the problem of overfishing primarily by arrogating to states large areas of ocean space previously part of the high seas. As around 95 per cent of commercially exploitable fish stocks are found within the 200 nm EEZ, it was expected that by enclosing the commons, and bringing fisheries within national jurisdiction, coastal states would have an economic incentive to adopt effective conservation measures.[91] Having the strong support of newly independent states in the global South which were not seeing economic returns from fishing by distant water fleets in the waters off their coasts, the enclosure approach prevailed over functional, species-based proposals for fisheries management. Under such proposals, which were put by the United States and a number of other states, coastal fisheries with a range extending to the high seas would have fallen under coastal state jurisdiction, whereas access to migratory fisheries would be regulated by RFMOs.[92] Although clearly rejected in the LOSC as an overarching framework for fisheries

---

[86] *Fisheries Jurisdiction (United Kingdom v Iceland)* (jurisdiction) [1973] ICJ Rep 3 (merits) [1974] ICJ Rep 3; *(Germany v Iceland)* (jurisdiction) [1973] ICJ Rep 49 (merits) [1974] ICJ Rep 175.
[87] 1964 European Fisheries Convention, arts 2, 3.
[88] *Fisheries Jurisdiction (United Kingdom v Iceland)* (merits) [1974] ICJ Rep 3, 27.
[89] Ibid 32.
[90] *Virginia Commentaries*, vol 2, 550.
[91] Juda, *International Law and Ocean Use Management* (n 31) 258.
[92] *Virginia Commentaries*, vol 2, 598–99, 619–20.

management in preference for a zonal approach, aspects of this species-specific approach find expression in the treatment by the LOSC of anadromous species (such as salmon that spawn in rivers but then migrate to the sea), catadromous species (such as eels that spawn at sea but then migrate to rivers) and marine mammals.

The fisheries regime in the LOSC is actually a complex collection of nine sub-regimes.[93] The first three of these take a zonal approach: there is coastal state sovereignty over fisheries in internal waters, the territorial sea and archipelagic waters, coastal state sovereign rights and jurisdiction in the EEZ and the continental shelf, and then flag state jurisdiction on the high seas. In addition, there are six sub-regimes that are functional in nature. Two of these relate to shared and straddling stocks, and a further four deal with highly migratory fish, marine mammals, anadromous species, and catadromous species. Each of these will now be considered in turn.

i. *Internal Waters, the Territorial Sea and Archipelagic Waters*

Within internal waters and the territorial sea the coastal state has complete sovereignty over living resources, and may adopt whatever measures it sees fit dealing with the management and conservation of fisheries. Foreign vessels have no right of access to territorial sea fisheries, and may not engage in fishing when exercising the right of innocent passage.[94] In regulating innocent passage, coastal states may enact and enforce laws relating to the conservation of the living resources of the sea, and the prevention of infringement of fisheries laws and regulations.[95] Much the same situation pertains in archipelagic waters, that is those waters enclosed within archipelagic baselines drawn between the outer islands of an archipelago. However, within archipelagic waters, unlike the territorial sea, archipelagic states are required to respect any existing agreement with other states and to recognise 'traditional fishing rights and other legitimate activities of the immediately adjacent neighbouring States in certain areas falling within archipelagic waters'.[96]

Although there are no requirements for sustainable management of fisheries in the territorial sea or archipelagic waters, the important conservation duties imposed by the EEZ regime in many cases effectively extend landwards, given that many commercially important inshore stocks move between these zones and can only be effectively managed in the EEZ through regulations also applicable in the territorial sea or archipelagic waters.

ii. *Exclusive Economic Zone*

The most extensive fisheries provisions in the LOSC are found in Part V that establishes the EEZ and sets out the rights and duties of coastal states and other states within this unique maritime zone. In essence, the LOSC fisheries regime for the EEZ seeks to achieve a balance between exclusive coastal state sovereign rights in the living resources of the EEZ and duties of conservation and optimum utilisation that will ensure that these living resources are sustainably exploited.

---

[93] See Ellen Hey, 'The Fisheries Provisions of the LOS Convention' in Ellen Hey, *Developments in International Fisheries Law* (The Hague, Kluwer, 1999) 19.

[94] LOSC, art 19(2)(i).

[95] Ibid art 21(1)(d), (e).

[96] Ibid art 51.

In the EEZ coastal states are given 'sovereign rights for the purpose of exploring and exploiting, conserving and managing' living resources of the water column, the seabed and subsoil.[97] In this respect it is a matter for the coastal state alone to determine the allowable catch for living resources in its EEZ.[98] The allowable catch is to be set having regard to the best scientific evidence, so as to prevent overexploitation of fisheries.[99] However, at the same time, the coastal state is to adopt measures designed to maintain or restore fisheries at levels that can produce the MSY.[100] Coastal states are also to take into account the impact of fishing on the broader marine ecosystem, by factoring in the effects upon associated or dependent species to protect these from being seriously threatened.[101] And conservation measures may be qualified by relevant environmental and economic factors, such as the economic needs of coastal fishing communities, and the special requirements of developing states.[102]

In addition, and without prejudice to the duty of conservation, coastal states are to promote the objective of 'optimum utilisation'.[103] This entails a requirement that the coastal state is to determine its capacity to harvest fisheries within the EEZ, and where it is not able to harvest the entire allowable catch, then it is to provide other states with access to the surplus.[104] The notion of optimum utilisation is not necessarily synonymous with full utilisation—the coastal state may legitimately set an allowable catch that would be less than exploitation of the MSY.[105] In this regard various factors are to be taken into account by coastal states in deciding whether to grant access to other states to the surplus, and a non-exhaustive list of these are set out in Article 62(3). These include the significance of the living resources of the area to the economy of the coastal state and its other national interests; the requirements of developing states; and the need to minimise economic dislocation in states whose nationals have historically fished in the zone. Coastal states are also to take into account the special interests of landlocked and geographically disadvantaged states.

If access is granted to foreign fishers to a coastal state's EEZ, the coastal state may impose conservation measures and other terms and conditions that must be complied with.[106] The laws and regulations dealing with these matters must be consistent with the LOSC, and may relate, among other things, to (a) the licensing of fishing vessels and the collection of access fees; (b) the species that may be targeted, and catch quotas; (c) fishing seasons and areas of fishing, fishing gear, and the number of vessels; (d) the age and size of fish that may be caught; (e) the data that fishing vessels must collect such as size of catch and vessel position reports; (f) the conduct of fisheries research; (g) the placing of observers on board vessels; (h) where catches are to be landed in the coastal state; (i) terms and conditions concerning joint ventures with local enterprises; (j) requirements for training of crew and the transfer of fisheries technology; and (k) enforcement procedures. Coastal state laws and

---

[97] Ibid art 56(1)(a).
[98] Ibid art 61(1).
[99] Ibid art 61(2).
[100] Ibid art 61(3).
[101] Ibid art 61(4).
[102] Ibid art 61(3).
[103] Ibid art 62(1).
[104] Ibid art 62(2).
[105] Patricia Birnie, Alan Boyle and Catherine Redgwell, *International Law and the Environment*, 3rd edn (Oxford, Oxford University Press, 2009) 717.
[106] LOSC, art 62(4).

regulations dealing with such matters of conservation and management are required to be publicised.[107]

Coastal states not only have an entitlement to exercise prescriptive or legislative jurisdiction in passing such laws, but are also given the power to enforce them by Article 73. Under Article 73(1) coastal states may in the exercise of their sovereign rights to manage the living resources of the EEZ take such measures as may be necessary to ensure compliance with EEZ laws and regulations, including boarding, inspection, arrest and judicial proceedings. However, this is subject to the caveat that arrested vessels and their crew are to be promptly released upon the posting of a reasonable bond or other security.[108] Moreover, penalties for breaching fisheries regulations must not include imprisonment, unless there are agreements between states concerned that permit incarceration.[109]

The prompt release requirement is subject to the compulsory dispute settlement provisions of the LOSC under Article 292, which gives ITLOS jurisdiction to determine disputes concerning Article 73, unless the parties have agreed to submit the dispute to another court or tribunal. It is significant that many of the cases brought to ITLOS since it was established have related to the prompt release of detained vessels, and the scope and application of Article 73 of the LOSC.[110] These cases have assisted in particular in explaining what is meant by reasonable bond or other financial security as those terms are used in Articles 73(2) and 292(1).

The extent of a coastal state's power to enact and enforce laws in the EEZ concerning fishing has been considered by ITLOS in several cases, beginning with the *M/V Saiga* case.[111] That case was instituted in ITLOS after authorities from Guinea arrested the *M/V Saiga*, an oil tanker that was flagged to St Vincent and the Grenadines, for violating Guinean customs laws by supplying gas oil to fishing vessels licensed to operate within the 200 nm Guinean fishing zone. In considering an application by St Vincent and the Grenadines in relation to the release of the vessel, ITLOS examined the reach of Article 62(4), which allows coastal states to enact laws and regulations on a non-exhaustive list of subjects to apply to foreign vessels in their EEZs. Bunkering is not included in that list, and while ITLOS found that it did not have to rule on the point, it was said that refuelling could 'arguably be classified' as a subject within coastal state legislative jurisdiction in the EEZ.

In its decision on the merits in *M/V Saiga (No 2)*,[112] ITLOS concluded that a coastal state is entitled to apply customs laws and regulations in its territorial sea, and that it also

---

[107] Ibid art 62(5). For a compendium of coastal state legislation see FAO, *Coastal State Requirements for Foreign Fishing* at faolex.fao.org/fishery/.

[108] LOSC, art 73(1).

[109] Ibid art 73(3).

[110] *M/V Saiga (No 1) Case (Saint Vincent and the Grenadines v Guinea)* (prompt release) (1997) 110 ILR 736; *Camouco (Panama v France)* (prompt release) (2000) 125 ILR 151; *Monte Confurco (Seychelles v France)* (prompt release) (2000) 125 ILR 203; *Grand Prince (Belize v France)* (prompt release) (2001) 125 ILR 251; *Chasiri Reefer 2 (Panama v Yemen)* (prompt release) (proceedings discontinued 13 July 2001) www.itlos.org; *Volga (Russian Federation v Australia)* (prompt release) (2003) 42 ILM 159; *Juno Trader (St Vincent and the Grenadines v Bissau)* (prompt release) (2004) 44 ILM 498; *Hoshinmaru (Japan v Russian Federation)* (prompt release) 6 August 2007 www.itlos.org; *Tomimaru (Japan v Russia)* (prompt release) (2007) 46 ILM 1185.

[111] *M/V Saiga (No 1) Case (Saint Vincent and the Grenadines v Guinea)* (prompt release) (1997) 110 ILR 736; *M/V Saiga (No 2) (Saint Vincent and the Grenadines v Guinea)* (provisional measures) (1998) 117 ILR 111 (admissibility and merits) (1999) 120 ILR 143.

[112] *M/V Saiga (No 2) (Saint Vincent and the Grenadines v Guinea)* (provisional measures) (1998) 117 ILR 111 (admissibility and merits) (1999) 120 ILR 143.

has enforcement jurisdiction in the contiguous zone to ensure that these laws are complied with.[113] In the EEZ, however, there was no such entitlement. Guinea had argued that under Article 58(3) it could apply 'other rules of international law' not incompatible with LOSC, which enabled it to apply and enforce domestic laws directed at securing the 'public interest' of Guinea, which extends to preventing economic activities such as bunkering, which has impacts on fisheries and environmental matters. The tribunal rejected this argument, finding that reference to a principle of 'public interest' to justify laws within the EEZ would 'curtail the rights of other States' and would be incompatible with Articles 56 and 58 of the LOSC.[114] Once again the tribunal did not, however, venture a definitive view as to whether bunkering within the EEZ could be regulated by coastal states, holding that it was unnecessary to consider the issue because of the particular circumstances of the case. Nonetheless, despite this equivocal analysis, both state practice and a plain reading of the LOSC strongly suggested that coastal state powers of fisheries regulation do extend to include incidental matters such as bunkering or processing fish caught within the EEZ.[115]

The matter was directly considered by ITLOS in *M/V Virginia G*,[116] a case which arose from the arrest of a Panamanian registered tanker that was supplying oil to fishing vessels in Guinea-Bissau's EEZ. Referring to Article 56, which accords to coastal states sovereign rights for the purpose of managing fisheries, ITLOS held that coastal states may control bunkering activities in their EEZs that support fishing activities:

> The Tribunal is of the view that the regulation by a coastal State of bunkering of foreign vessels fishing in its exclusive economic zone is among those measures which the coastal State may take in its exclusive economic zone to conserve and manage its living resources under article 56 of the Convention read together with article 62, paragraph 4, of the Convention. This view is also confirmed by State practice which has developed after the adoption of the Convention.[117]

The EEZ regime therefore gives coastal states very extensive powers of fisheries management, subject only to limited obligations to grant access to other states. It also imposes duties on both coastal and flag states to ensure the sustainable management of fisheries, including shared and straddling stocks. In *Request for an Advisory Opinion Submitted by the Sub-Regional Fisheries Commission (SRFC Advisory Opinion)*,[118] ITLOS provided an Advisory Opinion on the obligations of states to combat IUU fishing and, more generally, in relation to the content of their fisheries management obligations in the EEZ. The Opinion was sought by the Sub-Regional Fisheries Commission (SRFC), a fisheries commission comprising seven West African nations, against the backdrop of the serious problem of IUU fishing in the EEZs of SRFC members. With most fisheries in the region fully exploited or overexploited, IUU fishing is undermining the capacity of SRFC members to maintain their

---

[113] *M/V Saiga (No 2) (Saint Vincent and the Grenadines v Guinea)* (admissibility and merits) (1999) 120 ILR 143, [127].

[114] Ibid [131].

[115] See WT Burke, 'Coastal State Fishery Regulation Under International Law: A Comment on the *La Bretagne* Award of July 17, 1986' (1988) 25 *San Diego Law Review* 495; Richard Barnes, 'The Convention on the Law of the Sea: An Effective Framework for Domestic Fisheries Conservation?' in David Freestone, Richard Barnes and David M Ong (eds), *The Law of the Sea: Progress and Prospects* (Oxford, Oxford University Press, 2006) 233, 255–56. But cf *Filleting within the Gulf of St Lawrence* (1986) 90 *Revue General de Droit International Public* 713.

[116] *M/V Virginia G (Panama v Guinea Bissau)* (2014) 53 ILM 1164.

[117] Ibid [217].

[118] Advisory Opinion of 2 April 2015.

fishing industries and provide fish protein for their populations. The SRFC has expressed frustration over a series of violations of fisheries laws in the SRFC area, including the use of bunkering vessels to support IUU fishing. The SRFC request for an Advisory Opinion was made under the 2012 Convention on the Definition of the Minimum Access Conditions and Exploitation of Fisheries Resources Within the Maritime Zones under the Jurisdiction of SRFC Member States (MAC Convention), which provides in Article 33 that the SRFC may 'bring a given legal matter before [ITLOS] for an advisory opinion'.

ITLOS found that, in light of the 'special rights and responsibilities' of the coastal state in the EEZ, 'the primary responsibility for taking the necessary measures to prevent, deter and eliminate IUU fishing rests with the coastal State'.[119] It is the coastal state's responsibility to adopt necessary laws and regulations, including enforcement procedures, consistent with the LOSC, to conserve and manage the living resources in the EEZ.[120] The fishing activities that coastal states may regulate, consistent with Article 62 of the LOSC and the tribunal's decision in *M/V Virginia G*, must be 'directly' connected to fishing.[121] However, this does not relieve other states of their obligations to control IUU fishing. Under Articles 58(3), 62(4) and 192 of the LOSC and the MCA Convention, flag states have the 'responsibility to ensure that vessels flying their flag do not conduct IUU fishing activities within the [EEZs] of SRFC Member States'.[122]

In the *SRFC Advisory Opinion*, ITLOS also set out at length the responsibility of coastal states in managing their fisheries. ITLOS observed that Article 61(2) of the LOSC provides that coastal states, taking into account the best scientific evidence, must ensure through proper conservation and management measures the maintenance of the living resources of the EEZ. Such measures are to be designed to maintain or restore fish stocks at levels which can produce the maximum sustainable yield (Article 61(3)), and coastal states shall take into consideration effects of measures on associated and dependent species (Article 61(4)). ITLOS considered that the ultimate goal of sustainable management of fisheries 'is to conserve and develop them as a viable and sustainable resource,' and that therefore 'sustainable management' meant 'conservation and development' as referred to in Article 63(1) of the LOSC.[123] ITLOS also elaborated the various obligations on SRFC member states to ensure the sustainable management of shared stocks as including obligations: to cooperate through competent international organisations (see Article 61(2)), to seek agreement on measures to coordinate and ensure the conservation and development of such stocks (see Article 61(3)) and, in relation to tuna species, to cooperate directly or through the SRFC to ensure conservation and to promote the objective of optimum utilisation of such species.[124] ITLOS noted that conservation and management measures should be based on the best scientific evidence available and, when such evidence is insufficient, the precautionary approach should apply.[125]

To a significant extent the creation of the EEZ was motivated by a desire to secure some degree of distributive justice of oceanic resources for disadvantaged states. However, it is

[119] Ibid [106].
[120] Ibid [104].
[121] Ibid [100].
[122] Ibid [124].
[123] Ibid [190]–[191].
[124] Ibid [207].
[125] Ibid [208].

open to question whether this has been achieved, given the relatively low fees paid by many distant water nations for access to coastal state EEZs and the persistent problem of IUU fishing highlighted in the *SRFC Advisory Opinion*.[126] For many developing states it is a significant challenge to meet their duties of conservation and management under the LOSC, especially for those states with very large EEZs. Capacity constraints are evident not only in the surveillance of EEZs and enforcement of fisheries law, but also the collection of fisheries data and the development of fisheries management plans. For instance, Kiribati, a Pacific microstate, has a population of under 100,000 people, living on land area around 800 square kilometres in total across 33 islands, yet its EEZ is around 3.5 million square kilometres. As with many other small island developing states it has faced great difficulties in adopting and implementing fisheries policies to utilise effectively the extensive living resources of its seas, particularly tuna fisheries.[127]

In an effort to pool resources and improve fisheries management, especially in the areas of surveillance and enforcement, Kiribati joined with other South Pacific island states in the 1992 Niue Treaty on Cooperation in Fisheries Surveillance and Law Enforcement. Concluded under the auspices of the Forum Fisheries Agency (FFA),[128] the Niue Treaty requires its parties to cooperate in harmonising fisheries laws, to develop regionally agreed procedures for surveillance and law enforcement, and to conclude subsidiary agreements which would allow the enforcement of fisheries laws by vessels in the EEZs of other parties to the Niue Treaty.[129] The Niue Treaty has been significantly strengthened by a multilateral subsidiary agreement, the 2012 Agreement on Strengthening the Implementation of the Niue Treaty on Fisheries Surveillance and Law Enforcement in the South Pacific Region, which establishes a system of flexible cooperation for fisheries surveillance and law enforcement, including aerial surveillance, sea patrols, and inspections and investigations in port. The agreement includes provision for one party to request another to undertake fisheries enforcement on its behalf, and the use of reliable technical means to maintain hot pursuits. The agreement even prescribes a distinctive flag that is to be displayed by authorised vessels when operating outside waters under the jurisdiction of the flag state.

There are numerous other examples of states seeking to cooperate in fisheries enforcement, such as the 2007 Agreement on Cooperative Enforcement of Fisheries Laws between Australia and France in relation to their nearby sub-Antarctic island territories Kerguelen Island, and Heard and McDonald Islands. These waters have witnessed extensive IUU fishing by vessels flying flags of convenience targeting the Patagonian toothfish, a threatened and highly prized species.[130] Supplementing a 2003 agreement between the two states on cooperation in combating illegal foreign fishing,[131] the 2007 treaty allows cooperative

---

[126] Douglas Johnston, 'Is Coastal State Fishery Management Successful or Not?' (1991) 22 *Ocean Development and International Law* 199, 202; Tim Stephens, 'Fisheries-Led Development in the South Pacific: Charting a "Pacific Way" to a Sustainable Future' (2008) 39 *Ocean Development and International Law* 257, 267.

[127] Kate Barclay and Ian Cartright, *Capturing Wealth from Tuna: Case Studies from the Pacific* (Canberra, Asia Pacific Press, Australian National University, 2007) 117–47.

[128] The FFA was established by the 1979 South Pacific Forum Fisheries Convention, and has 17 members: Australia, Cook Islands, Federated States of Micronesia, Fiji, Kiribati, Marshall Islands, Nauru, New Zealand, Niue, Palau, Papua New Guinea, Samoa, Solomon Islands, Tokelau, Tonga, Tuvalu, Vanuatu.

[129] 1992 Niue Treaty, arts III, IV and VI.

[130] For a popular account of the problem see G Bruce Knecht, *Hooked: A True Story of Pirates, Poaching and the Perfect Fish* (Emmaus, Rodale, 2006).

[131] 2003 Treaty on Cooperation in the Maritime Areas Adjacent to the French Southern and Antarctic Territories, Heard Island and the McDonald Islands.

enforcement of fisheries laws in the EEZs of the islands, including through boarding, inspection and hot pursuit. One of the novel provisions of the agreement is that which allows hot pursuit to be maintained by each state in the other's maritime zones, including the territorial sea. It has been questioned whether this right would be opposable to the flag state of a pursued vessel as Article 111(3) of the LOSC makes clear that the right of hot pursuit ceases as soon as the ship being pursued enters the territorial sea of third state.[132]

Not only does the LOSC give coastal states very wide discretionary powers in managing EEZ fisheries according to their own particular needs, but the exercise of some of these powers is effectively scaled off from supervision under Part XV of the LOSC. Under Article 297(3)(a) coastal states are not obliged to submit to judicial settlement disputes relating to sovereign rights with respect to EEZ living resources, including the exercise of discretionary powers for determining the allowable catch, its harvesting capacity, the allocation of surpluses, and the terms and conditions established in its conservation and management laws and regulations. Hence it prevents both the exercise of sovereign rights, and accompanying duties of conservation, from being the basis of a complaint by another state under the Part XV regime.[133] Nonetheless, in serious cases, where a coastal state has manifestly failed to adopt conservation and management measures to protect EEZ living resources, has arbitrarily refused to determine an allowable catch, or has arbitrarily refused to grant access to any available surplus, then compulsory conciliation under Annex V of the LOSC may be invoked. To date this has not occurred.

Fish are no respecters of jurisdictional boundaries, and the migratory characteristics of many fishes are such that they move between the EEZs of multiple states (these are known as shared stocks), or between EEZs and the high seas (these comprise both straddling, and highly migratory fish stocks).[134] This underscores the biological arbitrariness of the 200 nm EEZ which, although politically desirable for coastal states, and coincident with many major fisheries, does not reflect the ecological divisions of the oceans.[135] In recognition of this the LOSC contains provisions that provide a framework for cooperation for managing transboundary stocks.

The LOSC deals fairly summarily with the phenomenon of shared stocks, that is those occurring in two or more EEZs. Under Article 63(1) the states concerned must 'seek, either directly or though appropriate subregional or regional organizations, to agree upon the measures necessary to co-ordinate and ensure the conservation and development of such stocks'. Hence the LOSC is non-specific about the duties that attach to the management of shared stocks, and there has been a marked tendency for states, even when cooperating through RFMOs, to continue to take a national property approach to shared EEZ fisheries, allowing business as usual harvesting to continue within their EEZs.[136]

---

[132] Warwick Gullett and Clive Schofield, 'Pushing the Limits of the Law of the Sea Convention: Australian and French Cooperative Surveillance and Enforcement in the Southern Ocean' (2007) 22 *International Journal of Marine and Coastal Law* 567. For discussion of the right of hot pursuit see ch 17.

[133] Robin Churchill, 'The Jurisprudence of the International Tribunal for the Law of the Sea: Is There Much in the Net?' (2007) 22 *International Journal of Marine and Coastal Law* 383, 389.

[134] Ellen Hey, *The Regime for the Exploitation of Transboundary Marine Fisheries Resources* (Dordrecht, Martinus Nijhoff, 1989) 53–60.

[135] Juda, *International Law and Ocean Use Management* (n 31) 243.

[136] Birnie, Boyle and Redgwell, *International Law and the Environment* (n 105) 719.

iii. Continental Shelf

The waters of the continental margins of coastal states support an abundance of commercially important species, and the harvesting of these from the water column within 200 nm is regulated by the EEZ regime. What remains for the continental shelf regime so far as living resources are concerned is sedentary species, that is organisms, which at the harvestable stage, either are immobile on or under the seabed, or are unable to move except in constant physical contact with the seabed or the subsoil.[137] There are no duties of conservation or management that apply directly to these species under the continental shelf regime (nor an obligation to grant access to other states to the surplus from any fishing that takes place). The only protection that they may possibly enjoy is via the general requirements of the EEZ regime that coastal states take into account associated and dependent species when managing EEZ fisheries.[138]

iv. The High Seas

Although EEZ fisheries are the most commercially important, many fisheries on the high seas are being increasingly exploited as various fishing grounds closer to shore are depleted. Moreover, many species of fish migrate between EEZs and the high seas, and these straddling stocks can only be managed effectively if all states engaged in fishing for them cooperate. To this end Article 63(2) of the LOSC lays down an obligation upon coastal states, and other states fishing for straddling stocks, to seek either directly or through appropriate subregional or regional organisations, to agree upon the measures necessary for the conservation of these stocks. Similar obligations of cooperation attach to highly migratory species, marine mammals, and anadromous and catadromous species all of which move between EEZs and the high seas.[139]

Problems in effectively managing straddling stocks have been highlighted in several regions by 'holes' of high seas surrounded by the EEZs of coastal states. These include the Bering Sea 'doughnut hole' which was extensively fished in the 1980s by distant water states, placing pressure on fisheries that straddled the neighbouring EEZs of the United States and Russia. This prompted the conclusion of the 1994 Convention on the Conservation and Management of Pollock Resources in the Central Bering Sea to address management problems in this region.[140] Similar agreements have not been reached to supply a sustainable fisheries management framework for the 'Peanut Hole' in the Sea of Okhotsk or the 'Loop Hole' in the Barents Sea.

As far as fisheries occurring exclusively on the high seas are concerned, the LOSC by itself adds little to the obligations under the 1958 Convention on Fisheries. On the high seas states have the freedom of fishing,[141] subject to general duties of conservation and cooperation. All states have the duty to take alone, and in cooperation with other states, measures applicable to their nationals necessary for the conservation of high seas living resources.[142] States are to cooperate with each other in conserving and managing high seas

---

[137] LOSC, art 77(4).
[138] Ibid art 61(4).
[139] Ibid arts 64–67.
[140] See further Kaye, *International Fisheries Management* (n 75) ch 9.
[141] LOSC, arts 87(1)(e), 116.
[142] Ibid art 117.

living resources, and to this end should, as appropriate, establish regional or subregional fisheries organisations.[143] In language that mirrors that applicable to the EEZ, Article 119 provides that states should determine an allowable catch for high seas fisheries and take measures to maintain or restore fish populations at levels that can produce the MSY.[144]

Unlike the EEZ fisheries provisions, those applicable to high seas fishing are subject to the dispute settlement system under Part XV, and so states could be held to account for falling short of their cooperation obligations. However, these are cast in such general and discretionary terms that it may prove difficult to secure a finding that a state has violated the LOSC.[145] Moreover, in respect of fishing within the EEZ of valuable transboundary stocks that move between the EEZ and the high seas (straddling, highly migratory, anadromous and catadromous stocks), the Article 297(3) exception would apply, which means that disputes over many of the most significant high seas stocks could be the subject of litigation through the Part XV system.[146]

The high seas fisheries provisions of the LOSC were considered by ITLOS in the *Southern Bluefin Tuna* cases.[147] Australia and New Zealand sought provisional measures from ITLOS pending the establishment of an Annex VII tribunal to hear the merits of a dispute with Japan concerning the conduct by Japan of an experimental fishing programme for southern bluefin tuna on the high seas. The context of the dispute was that the RFMO charged with managing southern bluefin tuna, the Commission for the Conservation of Southern Bluefin Tuna,[148] had failed for some time to establish an allowable catch, or set national allocations. Australia and New Zealand contended that through its experimental fishing programme, Japan had violated obligations under Articles 64 and 116 to 119 of the LOSC, because it was neglecting to take conservation measures for its nationals so as to maintain or restore stocks of southern bluefin tuna. ITLOS granted provisional measures to restrain the programme, and in its order the tribunal made several important statements concerning the fisheries provisions of the LOSC. The tribunal observed that 'the conservation of the living resources of the sea is an element in the protection and preservation of the marine environment'[149] which drew an important link between the fisheries conservation provisions of the LOSC, and the more general provisions in Part XII which concern marine environmental protection. Here stocks of southern bluefin tuna, which was and remains listed as 'critically endangered' on the International Union for Conservation of Nature (IUCN) Red List of threatened species, were clearly at risk. This was relevant to ITLOS's jurisdiction under Article 290 to prescribe provisional measures to 'prevent serious harm to the marine environment'. Not only did ITLOS encourage the parties to 'act with prudence and caution in order to ensure that effective conservation measures are taken',[150] but it went on to apply the precautionary approach in prescribing detailed provisional measures. The tribunal's decision to issue provisional measures was later overturned by the Annex VII

[143] Ibid art 118.
[144] Ibid art 119(1)(a).
[145] Churchill, 'The Jurisprudence of the International Tribunal for the Law of the Sea' (n 133) 387.
[146] Ibid 389–90.
[147] *Southern Bluefin Tuna (New Zealand v Japan; Australia v Japan)* (provisional measures) (1999) 117 ILR 148.
[148] Established by the 1993 Convention for the Conservation of Southern Bluefin Tuna, *Basic Documents* No 55.
[149] *Southern Bluefin Tuna (New Zealand v Japan; Australia v Japan)* (provisional measures) (1999) 117 ILR 148, [70].
[150] Ibid [77].

Tribunal established to determine the merits of the case, on the basis that Part XV of LOSC did not apply because the parties had agreed to settle the dispute by an alternative means.[151] However, this decision did not challenge the reasoning of ITLOS in relation to substantive issues of fisheries conservation.

There are several RFMOs mandated to address high seas fisheries in general (as opposed to particular species, as is the case with the 1993 Convention for the Conservation of Southern Bluefin Tuna). These include the Commission for the Conservation of Antarctic Marine Living Resources formed by the 1980 Convention on the Conservation of Antarctic Marine Living Resources (CCAMLR) under the Antarctic Treaty System. The negotiation of CCAMLR was prompted by the need to manage the Antarctic krill fishery, which began to be exploited from the 1950s onwards.[152] Concluded before LOSC, CCAMLR was a pioneering agreement in that it was designed to protect and conserve all Antarctic marine living resources rather than particular species, and to this end adopted a whole ecosystem approach.[153] CCAMLR is an integral part of the Antarctic Treaty System, and applies to Antarctic marine living resources of the area south of 60 degrees South latitude, and to the Antarctic marine living resources of the area between that latitude and the Antarctic convergence.[154] CCAMLR therefore applies to areas of the high seas, and also to areas within the EEZs of several coastal states with sub-Antarctic island possessions. In this regard one of the distinctive features of CCAMLR is its 'bi-focal' approach which allows these states to implement conservation measures that are more (or less) strict than those set by the CCAMLR Commission.[155]

Initiatives taken by the CCAMLR Commission include the use of the precautionary principle in setting catch limits, a management regime for Antarctic krill that addresses the impact on dependent species, the establishment of an ecosystem monitoring programme, the adoption of rules to mitigate by-catch of seabird, and the collection of data on by-catch more generally.[156] The most serious challenge facing CCAMLR is continued IUU fishing, despite robust enforcement efforts in the EEZs of subantarctic islands within the CCAMLR Area. In response, CCAMLR has adopted a Catch Documentation Scheme for toothfish, the main species targeted by IUU operations. CCAMLR has also been proactive in relation to bottom-trawling, instituting and maintaining a ban on this damaging fishing practice.

There has been considerable recent progress in the creation of high seas regional fisheries bodies. These include the South East Atlantic Fisheries Organisation (SEAFO), set up by the 2001 Convention on the Conservation and Management of Fishery Resources in the South-East Atlantic Ocean.[157] The SEAFO superseded the defunct International Commission for

---

[151] *Southern Bluefin Tuna (Australia & New Zealand v Japan)* (jurisdiction and admissibility) (2000) 119 ILR 508.

[152] Donald R Rothwell, *The Polar Regions and the Development of International Law* (Cambridge, Cambridge University Press, 1996) 124.

[153] See 1980 CCAMLR, art II(3)(b).

[154] Ibid art I(1).

[155] See Alan D Hemmings and Tim Stephens, 'The Extended Continental Shelves of Sub-Antarctic Islands: Implications for Antarctic Governance' (2010) 46 *Polar Record* 312.

[156] See the discussion in Adriana Fabra and Virginia Gascón, 'The Convention on the Conservation of Antarctic Marine Living Resources and the Ecosystem Approach' (2008) 23 *International Journal of Marine and Coastal Law* 567, 576; Howard S Schiffman, 'CCAMLR Fisheries: Challenges to Effective Conservation and Management' (2009) 12 *Journal of International Wildlife Law and Policy* 180.

[157] *Basic Documents* No 66.

the Southeast Atlantic Fisheries, and takes account of developments since the conclusion of LOSC, and implements the ecosystem and precautionary approaches. The fisheries that SEAFO regulate include red crab and orange roughy, a threatened bottom-dwelling fish.[158] Another recently established high seas regional fisheries body is the South Pacific Regional Fisheries Organisation (SPRFMO), created by the 2009 Convention on the Conservation and Management of High Seas Fishery Resources in the South Pacific Ocean. Taking an ecosystem approach, and guided by the precautionary principle, SPRFMO seeks to manage non-highly migratory fisheries in South Pacific marine areas beyond national jurisdiction, such as Chilean jack mackerel, alfonsino and orange roughy.[159]

However, beyond these and several other high seas RFMOs,[160] the regime for managing high seas fisheries remains relatively weak, as the freedom of fishing and the exclusivity of flag state jurisdiction preserved by the LOSC constitute major impediments to sustainable resource management.[161] Awareness of these limitations has led to a suite of post-LOSC developments that have sought to provide a more effective legal framework, and to resolve the fundamental management conundrum in this commons area: providing governance in the absence of government.[162] We consider these post-LOSC developments below.

v. Deep Seabed

The 1970 United Nations Declaration of Principles Governing the Sea-Bed and Ocean Floor, and the Subsoil Thereof, beyond the Limits of National Jurisdiction[163] referred to 'resources' generally, suggesting that they may also include living resources. By contrast under Part XI of the LOSC the resources of the Area are defined only to include minerals.[164] As a result the LOSC regime for the deep seabed does not regulate the harvesting of marine living organisms on, in or under the Area. This means not only that sedentary species such as molluscs may be freely exploited consistent with the freedom of high seas fishing, but also that there are no limitations on bioprospecting for marine genetic resources from seabed organisms. Such organisms and the habitats in which they are found enjoy only a limited degree of incidental protection by virtue of the responsibility of the ISA to adopt rules, regulations and procedures for the protection of the marine environment of the deep seabed.[165] Such rules apply to prospecting, exploring and exploiting the mineral resources of the Area.[166]

---

[158] See the discussion in Tore Henriksen, Geir Hønneland and Are Sydnes, *Law and Politics in Ocean Governance: The UN Fish Stocks Agreement and Regional Fisheries Management Regimes* (Leiden, Martinus Nijhoff, 2006) ch 6.

[159] See www.sprfmo.int.

[160] Such as the Mediterranean General Fisheries Council (established in 1949), Northwest Atlantic Fisheries Organization (established in 1978), the Northeast Atlantic Fisheries Commission (established in 1980).

[161] See Rosemary Rayfuse, *Non-Flag State Enforcement in High Seas Fisheries* (Boston, Martinus Nijhoff, 2004) ch 1.

[162] Olav Schram Stokke, 'Conclusions' in Olav Schram Stokke (ed), *Governing High Seas Fisheries: The Interplay of Global and Regional Regimes* (Oxford, Oxford University Press, 2007) 329, 329. See also ch 19.

[163] UNGA Res 2749 (XXV), *Basic Documents* No 17.

[164] LOSC, art 133.

[165] Ibid art 145.

[166] See further ch 6.

E. Species-Specific Rules

In addition to promoting conservation and management within maritime zones, the LOSC also includes rules that deal with particular species, categorised mostly according to their migratory behaviour. These specific rules are also reflective of the fact that some species such as marine mammals tend to be more vulnerable than others to overfishing because of biological characteristics such as low reproduction rates.

i. Highly Migratory Species

Under Article 64 of the LOSC, coastal states and other interested states engaged in fishing for highly migratory species within a region are to cooperate either directly or through an appropriate international organisation to ensure and promote the objective of optimum utilisation of such species. In regions where there is no appropriate international organisation, states are to cooperate in establishing such an organisation, and then participate in its work. The highly migratory species to which the obligation in Article 64 attaches, are listed in Annex I of the LOSC, and include species such as tuna, marlin, swordfish and sharks and also marine mammals which are impacted in particular by the tuna fishing industry. Additional rules apply specifically to the protection of cetaceans, as discussed below. The list of 17 species or family groups in Annex I is extensive, but it is not exhaustive and is now in need of updating (a task made difficult by the fact that it is subject to the amendment procedure applicable to the LOSC as a whole).[167] The fairly generic obligations under Article 64 have now been supplemented by the more detailed FSA, which fleshes out the obligations applicable to straddling and highly migratory fish stocks, and mandates greater levels of international cooperation to protect such fisheries.[168]

ii. Marine Mammals

There are around 120 species of marine mammals, the largest of which are the cetaceans (including whales, dolphins and porpoises), pinnipeds (seals and walrus), and sirenians ('sea cows' or dugong). Some marine mammals are highly migratory, and those that are, and which are listed in Annex I to LOSC, have a basic level of protection under Article 64. They also have the benefit of the more far-reaching Article 65, which provides that nothing in Part V restricts the rights of coastal states or an international organisation 'to prohibit, limit or regulate the exploitation of marine mammals more strictly than provided for' in Part V. In addition, the application of Article 65 is extended to the high seas by Article 120.

The main import of Article 65 is that marine mammals are not subject to the obligation of optimum utilisation. Hence while the LOSC itself does not forbid whaling, it does give states and international organisations a right to do so. Many states have enacted legislation prohibiting the taking of whales in their EEZs, and on the high seas whaling (for large whales) is substantially limited by 1946 International Convention for the Regulation of Whaling (ICRW), that established the International Whaling Commission (IWC) and

---

[167] LOSC, arts 312–13.
[168] See in particular the FSA, art 8.

equipped it with the capacity to adopt binding regulations for whaling via amendments to the Schedule to the ICRW.

The ICRW is the main international regime for the regulation of whaling, although there are also several regional agreements.[169] The ICRW has assumed responsibility only for large whales, comprising 15 of the approximately 70 species of whales. As Couzens has noted, '[s]taggeringly, there is no legal instrument of global scope that effectively covers these [other] species.'[170] There is no equivalent to the ICRW for small marine mammals; however, there are several treaties that apply on a regional basis to marine mammals such as dolphins[171] and seals.[172]

The IWC was initially a resource-focussed body, designed to promote the continued hunting of whales by ensuring that heavily depleted species such as blue whale, which were hunted close to extinction, were given an opportunity to recover from collapse. However, the IWC has since been transformed from an economic to a primarily conservation regime.[173] This was in large part a response to the failure of the IWC to prevent overfishing, and was formally effected by amendments to the Schedule to the ICRW in 1982, which imposed a moratorium on commercial whaling that took effect from 1985.[174]

By operation of Article 1(1) of the ICRW, the Schedule forms an 'integral part' of the IWC, and is therefore binding in full upon the parties. However, it is subject to the objection procedure, which allowed members who wish to opt-out of the moratorium to do so.[175] Japan, Norway, Peru and the Soviet Union initially lodged objections to the moratorium on this basis, and were therefore not bound by it; however, Japan and the Soviet Union later withdrew their objections. In 1994 Norway resumed commercial whaling. Iceland, another significant whaling state, did not lodge an objection to the moratorium and abided by it. However, in 1992 it withdrew from the IWC with a view to resuming commercial whaling. It later rejoined the IWC in 2002, this time registering its objection to the moratorium (the legal effect of which is not accepted by a number of IWC members). Iceland recommenced commercial whaling in 2006.

Permitted to continue under the moratorium is aboriginal subsistence whaling, which occurs under permits that are granted by Denmark, the Russian Federation, St Vincent and the Grenadines, and the United States. Also permissible is 'special permit' whaling under Article VIII of the ICRW, which allows whaling for scientific purposes. Iceland, Japan and Norway have all undertaken scientific whaling programmes in reliance on Article VIII. In the case of Japan the scientific whaling programmes in the North Pacific and in the

---

[169] 1992 Agreement on Research, Conservation and Management of Marine Mammals in the North Atlantic (NAMMCO), 1992 Agreement on the Conservation of Small Cetaceans of the Baltic and North Seas (ASCOBANS) and the 1996 Agreement on the Conservation of Cetaceans of the Baltic Sea, Mediterranean Sea and Contiguous Atlantic Area (ACCOBAMS).

[170] Ed Couzens, 'Size Matters, Although it Shouldn't: The ICRW and Small Cetaceans: A Reply to Stephenson, Mooers and Attaran' (2014) 3 *Transnational Environmental Law* 265, 270. See further Ed Couzens, *Whales and Elephants in International Conservational Law and Politics: A Comparative Study* (Abingdon, Routledge, 2014).

[171] See, eg, the 1992 Agreement on the Conservation of Small Cetaceans and the 1996 Agreement on the Conservation of Cetaceans of the Black Sea, Mediterranean Sea and Contiguous Atlantic Area.

[172] See, eg, the 1972 Convention for the Conservation of Antarctic Seals and the 1990 Agreement on the Conservation of Seals in the Wadden Sea.

[173] Alexander Gillespie, *Whaling Diplomacy: Defining Issues in International Environmental Law* (Northhampton, Mass, Edward Elgar, 2005) ch 1.

[174] 1946 ICRW, sch, [10(e)].

[175] Ibid art V(3).

Southern Ocean have been extensive, with Japan taking each year for research a greater number of whales that it had previously taken for research in the period between the establishment of the IWC and the establishment of the moratorium.[176]

The scientific whaling exception also allows states to take whales within the two whale sanctuaries declared by the IWC where commercial whaling is prohibited independently of the moratorium: the Indian Ocean Sanctuary (established in 1970) and the South Ocean Sanctuary (established in 1994). Proposals for the establishment of additional sanctuaries in the South Atlantic and South Pacific have failed to attract the three-quarters majority of votes required to amend the Schedule to establish them.

The controversy surrounding scientific whaling, especially that conducted by Japan, has led to efforts to reform the IWC so as to reach a compromise position that would satisfy the interests both of pro-whaling and anti-whaling states. Since 1982 voting patterns within the IWC have shifted substantially, so that the membership of the IWC is fairly evenly divided between states that oppose and states that support whaling. This has meant that the IWC has become effectively deadlocked. In an effort to break the stalemate, at the sixtieth meeting of the IWC in June 2008, the Commission established the Small Working Group on the Future of the International Whaling Commission (SWG), which was mandated to assist the Commission reach a consensus position on whale conservation and management. In May 2009 the SWG delivered its report to the IWC, which presented a 'package deal' set of reforms to the ICRW which would, if it had been adopted, lead to the substantial reduction in research whaling while allowing the resumption of Japanese small-type commercial whaling.[177]

The lawfulness of scientific whaling was considered by the International Court of Justice in the *Whaling in the Antarctic* case[178] between Australia and Japan (with New Zealand intervening). The Court found by 12 votes to four that Japan's whaling programme in the Southern Ocean (known as JARPA II) was not undertaken 'for purposes of scientific research' as required by Article VIII of the ICRW. By the same margin, the Court held that JARPA II violated the moratorium on whaling for commercial purposes, a ban that has been in place under the ICRW since 1985.[179] The ICJ did not rule out the practice of scientific whaling altogether. It emphasised that Article VIII of the ICRW expressly allows for the conduct of scientific whaling programmes, including those that are lethal and that 'pursue an aim other than either conservation or sustainable exploitation of whale stocks'.[180] The Court further held that while Article VIII 'gives discretion to a State party to the ICRW' to issue special permits to take whales, whether such permits are issued 'for purposes of scientific research cannot depend simply on that State's perception'.[181] Rather, the Court identified an objective standard of review, which involved considering first whether Japan's programme

---

[176]   Christopher C Joyner, 'Challenges to the Antarctic Treaty: Looking Back to See Ahead' (2008) 6 *New Zealand Yearbook of International Law* 25, 52.

[177]   *Report of the Small Working Group on the Future of the International Whaling Commission*, 18 May 2009. See further Mike Iliff, 'The Hogarth Initiative on the Future of the International Whaling Commission' (2010) 34 *Marine Policy* 360 and Mike Iliff, 'Contemporary Initiatives on the Future of the International Whaling Commission' (2010) 34 *Marine Policy* 461.

[178]   *Whaling in the Antarctic (Australia v Japan; New Zealand intervening)*, Judgment of 31 March 2014.

[179]   Ibid [247].

[180]   Ibid [58].

[181]   Ibid [61].

'involves scientific research' and, secondly, whether 'the killing, taking and treating of whales is "for purposes of" scientific research' having regard to 'whether, in the use of lethal methods, the programme's design and implementation are reasonable in relation to achieving its stated objectives'.[182] In assessing Japan's research programme, the Court found that it involved activities that 'can broadly be characterised as "scientific research"', thus relieving the ICJ of the need to consider generally the meaning of 'scientific research'.[183] However, the Court did not find in favour of Japan on the second limb of its standard of review—namely whether JARPA II was conducted 'for purposes of scientific research'. There were a number of reasons given for this. First, Japan did not consider the feasibility of using non-lethal methods.[184] Secondly, the Court identified a number of deficiencies in the way in which Japan set sample sizes for the three whale species targeted: minke whales, fin whales and humpback whales. The sample sizes 'were not driven by strictly scientific considerations' as Japan's 'priority was to maintain whaling operations without any pause',[185] and there was a lack of information and transparency in relation to the selection of particular sample sizes.[186] Moreover, there was a significant discrepancy between the target sample sizes and the actual number of whales taken. The Court observed that:

> [t]he fact that the actual take of fin and humpback whales is largely, if not entirely, a function of political and logistical considerations, further weakens the purported relationship between JARPA II's research objectives and the specific sample sizes for each species—in particular, the decision to engage in the lethal sampling of minke whales on a relatively large scale.[187]

The Court identified further deficiencies in the implementation of JARPA II, namely the limited scientific output (only two peer-reviewed papers to date)[188] and limited evidence of cooperation with other research institutions.[189] In conclusion, the Court:

> considers that JARPA II involves activities that can broadly be characterized as scientific research (see paragraph 127 above), but that the evidence does not establish that the programme's design and implementation are reasonable in relation to achieving its stated objectives. The Court concludes that the special permits granted by Japan for the killing, taking and treating of whales in connection with JARPA II are not 'for purposes of scientific research' pursuant to Article VIII, paragraph 1, of the Convention.[190]

Following the ICJ's decision, Japan developed a revised research plan for the Southern Ocean known as NEWREP-A, which sought to address the Court's judgment, and proposed a significantly reduced quota in terms of both species to be caught (only minkes) and sample size (333 per annum).[191] NEWREP-A is proposed to run from 2015 to 2027. In June 2015 the Scientific Committee of the IWC released its report of its annual

---

[182] Ibid [67].
[183] Ibid [127].
[184] Ibid [144].
[185] Ibid [156].
[186] Ibid [181] and [188].
[187] Ibid [212].
[188] Ibid [219].
[189] Ibid [222].
[190] Ibid [227].
[191] *Proposed Research Plan for New Scientific Whale Research Program in the Antarctic Ocean (NEWREP-A)*, at http://www.jfa.maff.go.jp/j/whale/pdf/newrep--a.pdf.

meeting, in which it was concluded that the committee could not reach a consensus view on NEWREP-A, and a majority of scientists on the committee joined an annex to the report which stated that 'the need for lethal sampling has not been demonstrated'.[192] This indicates potential grounds for a fresh challenge to Japan's planned Southern Ocean whaling activities, as one key reason why the Court found that JARPA II was not 'for purposes' of scientific research was because of the failure to provide a compelling justification for the use of lethal sampling methods.

iii. Anadromous Species

The special interests of coastal states in salmon and other anadromous species such as sturgeon that spawn in freshwater rivers but later migrate to the high seas are addressed in Article 66 of the LOSC. As with the framework applicable to marine mammals, this provision permits conservation regulations to be given a preservationist rather than utilisation emphasis.

States in whose rivers anadromous stocks originate have the primary interest in, and responsibility for, such stocks.[193] As such, these states are to ensure the conservation of anadromous fisheries by establishing appropriate regulatory measures in their EEZs.[194] This may involve the setting of total allowable catches, and the involvement of foreign fishers,[195] but unlike fisheries in the EEZ generally this is not required. Hence coastal states may impose a total ban on fishing for anadromous species in the EEZ.

Fishing for anadromous species on the high seas is subject to a general prohibition. Article 66(3) provides that fishing should be restricted to the EEZ except in cases where this would result in economic dislocation for another state. In such cases it is a matter for the states concerned to enter into consultations to achieve agreement on terms and conditions for the fishing, having due regard to conservation requirements and the needs of the state of origin. There is nothing, however, which would prohibit the taking of anadromous fish within the EEZ of a state other than the originating state. In such cases, however, the states concerned are to cooperate in the conservation and management of the stock.[196]

In relation to salmon, the provisions of Article 66 have been further implemented in the North Atlantic and North Pacific Oceans by the 1982 Convention for the Conservation of Salmon in the North Atlantic Ocean and the 1992 Convention for the Conservation of Anadromous Stocks in the North Pacific Ocean. Subject only to very narrow exceptions, these agreements prohibit fishing for salmon on the high seas in these regions, and have also sought to facilitate steps to prevent flags of convenience being used by non-members.[197]

iv. Catadromous Species

Catadromous species such as eels have the opposite life cycle to anadromous species, and reproduce at sea before migrating to rivers and lakes where they spend the majority of their

---

[192] Dennis Normille, 'Scientists Renew Objections to Japan's Whaling Program', *ScienceInsider*, 19 June 2015.
[193] LOSC, art 66(1).
[194] Ibid art 66(2).
[195] Ibid.
[196] Ibid art 66(4).
[197] See further Ted L McDorman, *Salt Water Neighbors: International Ocean Law Relations Between the United States and Canada* (New York, Oxford University Press, 2009) 289–311.

lives. Under Article 67 of the LOSC it is coastal states in whose waters catadromous species spend the greater part of their life that have responsibility and management of these species. They are to ensure the ingress and egress of these migrating fish,[198] and may regulate the harvesting of these species within the EEZ in accordance with the general regime for EEZ fishing.[199] Where catadromous fish migrate through the EEZs of multiple states, then their management is to be regulated by agreement between all relevant states. This agreement is to ensure the rational management of the species.[200] In contradistinction to anadromous species, catadromous species are not exempted from the objective of optimum utilisation. However, more clearly than for anadromous species, high seas fishing for catadromous species is prohibited.

F. Post-LOSC Developments

The LOSC was concluded in the early 1980s in an era in which the concept of integrated management of ocean ecosystems had some years to gain currency. However, by 1992, when the United Nations Convention on Environment and Development was convened, and which led to the conclusion of the Rio Declaration and Agenda 21, it was clear that international law relating to fisheries required significant development to address persistent management problems, especially for high seas fisheries. Agenda 21 recognised the LOSC as providing the foundational obligations for fisheries conservation, but exhorted states to adopt a more effective legal framework for straddling and highly migratory fish stocks. In this regard Chapter 17 of Agenda 21 addresses the oceanic environment, and in Programme Area C identified inadequacies in the protection of high seas fisheries because of the lack of regulation, overcapitalisation, large fishing fleets, flags of convenience, and use of fishing gear that is insufficiently selective.[201]

More recently the United Nations Secretary-General has made regular statements calling for further enhancements to the legal and policy framework, for states and RFMOs to adopt measures to ensure long-term sustainability of fisheries on the basis of the best scientific studies, and in conformity with the precautionary and ecosystem approaches.[202] The United Nations General Assembly has catalogued the main causes of the fisheries crisis as being 'illegal, unreported and unregulated fishing, inadequate flag State control and enforcement, including monitoring, control and surveillance measures, harmful fisheries subsidies and overcapacity'.[203]

i. High Seas Fishing

In the 1980s a number of states began to deploy large drift nets, particularly in the South Pacific, to catch tuna and several other species.[204] However, drift net fishing was and remains a highly indiscriminate method of fishing—these nets are often described by the environment

---

[198] LOSC, art 67(1).
[199] Ibid art 67(2).
[200] Ibid art 67(3).
[201] Agenda 21, *Basic Documents* No 48, [17.45].
[202] *Oceans and the Law of the Sea: Report of the Secretary General*, UN Doc A/64/66/Add.1 (2009), [176].
[203] UNGA Resolution 63/112, UN Doc A/RES/63/112 (2009).
[204] See Ellen Hey et al, *The Regulation of Driftnet Fisheries on the High Seas* (Rome, FAO, 1991).

movement as 'walls of death' because of their tendency to snare a range of by-catch species, including dolphins and turtles. The LOSC does not prohibit the use of any particular type of fishing gear on the high seas, and instead refers only to a general requirement that states take measures as are necessary for the conservation of high seas living resources.

Concern over drift-net fishing, especially in the South Pacific where the use of the gear was criticised not only for its effects on non-targeted species but also in driving overfishing, led to a resolution of the United Nations General Assembly in 1989.[205] The resolution called for the end of large-scale pelagic driftnet fishing in the South Pacific no later than July 1991, with a global moratorium to take effect by June 1992. The moratorium has since been restated in subsequent resolutions of the General Assembly, and until 2002 was the subject of reports of the Secretary-General summarising state initiatives to implement the moratorium.[206] The Secretary-General's 2002 report concluded that 'the problem of large-scale pelagic drift-net fishing is abating owing to the continued resolve by the international community to ensure implementation of the global moratorium'.[207] Because of the broad support that the General Assembly's drift-net resolutions attracted from a very early stage, and having regard to the high levels of compliance with them, they are widely regarded as having established a binding rule of customary international law.[208]

There have been some regional initiatives to implement the moratorium in both high seas areas and waters within national jurisdiction. States in the South Pacific concluded the 1989 Wellington Convention for the Prohibition of Fishing with Long Driftnets in the South Pacific, which obliges members to prevent the use of long drift-nets by their nationals, and to restrict access to ports by vessels which use drift-nets. And in 2002 a European Community drift net ban came into effect.[209] Compliance with the ban has been problematic in the Mediterranean, and in response in 2003 the International Commission for the Conservation of Atlantic Tuna adopted a measure prohibiting the use of driftnets for fisheries of large pelagic species.[210]

A more recent concern relating to the use of fishing gear is in relation to bottom trawling, which is damaging a number of vulnerable marine ecosystems such as seamounts, being undersea mountains that are of tectonic or volcanic origin, and hydrothermal vents which support an array of unique species of marine life.[211] In 2007 the General Assembly, in its now annual resolution on the subject of sustainable fisheries, called upon RFMOs with the competence to regulate bottom fisheries, to implement measures to regulate bottom trawling consistent with the precautionary and ecosystem approaches, by the end of 2008.[212] Specifically, the resolution required the closure of vulnerable marine ecosystems, including

---

[205] UNGA Resolution 44/225 (1991), UN Doc A/RES/46/215 (1991), *Basic Documents* No 47.

[206] For the 2002 report see *United Nations Secretary General, Large-scale Pelagic Drift-net Fishing, Unauthorized Fishing in Zones of National Jurisdiction and on the High Seas, Illegal, Unreported and Unregulated Fishing, Fisheries By-catch and Discards, and other Developments*, UN Doc A/57/459 (2002).

[207] Ibid [218].

[208] See further Grant J Hewison, 'The Legally Binding Nature of the Moratorium on Large-Scale High Seas Driftnet Fishing' (1994) 25 *Journal of Maritime Law and Commerce* 557, 578–79.

[209] European Council Regulation 1239/98, [60]. This regulation did not extend the ban to the Baltic Sea. A subsequent European Council Regulation (812/2004), which took effect in 2007, removed this exemption.

[210] See Elizabeth M De Santo and Peter JS Jones 'Offshore Marine Conservation Policies in the North East Atlantic: Emerging Tensions and Opportunities' (2007) 31 *Marine Policy* 336, 345.

[211] See Johannes Imhoff and Michael Hügler, 'Deep Sea Hydrothermal Vents—Oases Under Water' (2009) 24 *International Journal of Marine and Coastal Law* 201.

[212] UNGA Resolution 61/205, UN Doc A/RES/61/105 (2007).

seamounts, hydrothermal vents and cold water corals to bottom trawling unless conservation and management measures are adopted to prevent significant adverse impacts upon
them.[213] In August 2008 the FAO adopted the International Guidelines for the Management
of Deep-Sea Fisheries in the High Seas, which provide tools for fishers to ensure the sustainable use of deep-sea fisheries, and the protection of vulnerable deep-sea ecosystems.

Beyond global initiatives to deal with poor fishing practices involving the use of specific
types of fishing gear, there have also been efforts made to promote more sustainable high
seas fishing generally. Much of this activity has taken place under the auspices of the FAO.
There is no world fisheries organisation for international fisheries management in the same
way that international trade, for instance, is supervised by the World Trade Organization.
However, the FAO has spearheaded important developments in international fisheries law
to fill gaps in the legal framework. In particular the FAO has sought to establish regional
fisheries advisory bodies in regions of the seas where there are no regulatory commissions.
These bodies have a much more limited role than a fully formed fisheries commission, and
deal with issues such as the promotion of scientific research, the gathering of fisheries data
and the facilitation of training. More concretely, the FAO has been pivotal in the conclusion
of post-LOSC agreements addressing straddling, highly migratory, and high seas stocks and
issues surrounding compliance with fisheries agreements.

A particular focus of the FAO has been on compliance and enforcement,[214] to ensure
that fishing regulations are not circumvented. In 1993 the Conference of the FAO approved
the Agreement to Promote Compliance with International Conservation and Management Measures by Fishing Vessels on the High Seas.[215] The Compliance Agreement, which
entered into force in 2003, seeks to improve the regulation of fishing vessels on the high
seas by strengthening the obligations of flag states. Parties are required to maintain an
authorisation and recording system for high seas fishing vessels, and flag states must take
such measures as may be necessary to ensure that vessels flying their flag do not engage in
any activity that undermines the effectiveness of international conservation and management measures.[216] Specifically, flag states are to prohibit their vessels from high seas fishing in the absence of authorisation, with such authorisation only to be granted where the
flag state is able effectively to exercise its responsibilities under the Agreement in respect
of the vessel.[217] Moreover flag state regulation of vessels is to be backed up by enforcement measures—contraventions of provisions of the Agreement are to be made an offence
under national legislation, with sanctions to be sufficient to deprive offenders of the benefits of illegal activities.[218] The Agreement also took some tentative steps towards greater
port-state control to prevent illegal fishing. Under Article V, port states with reasonable
grounds for believing that a fishing vessel has undermined the effectiveness of conservation
and management measures is to notify the flag state promptly, and the parties may make

---

[213] Ibid [83(c)].
[214] Compliance refers to the conformity by a state with its international legal obligations, while enforcement
refers to the process of compelling compliance: Christopher C Joyner, 'Compliance With and Enforcement of
International Fisheries Law' in Ellen Hey (ed), *Developments in International Fisheries Law* (The Hague, Kluwer,
1999) 327, 329.
[215] *Basic Documents* No 54.
[216] 1993 FAO Compliance Agreement, art III(1).
[217] Ibid art III(3).
[218] Ibid art III(8).

arrangements for port state investigation to establish whether the vessel has indeed been used contrary to the Agreement.

Subsequent to the Compliance Agreement the Conference of the FAO adopted a further instrument: the Code of Conduct for Responsible Fisheries. Unlike the Compliance Agreement, the Code of Conduct is non-binding; however, it is broader in its application in that it applies to fishing in all maritime zones, not only the high seas. Under the auspices of the Code of Conduct four voluntary plans of action have been adopted: an International Plan of Action to Prevent, Deter and Eliminate Illegal, Unreported and Unregulated Fishing; International Plan of Action for Reducing Incidental Catch of Seabirds in Longline Fisheries; International Plan of Action for the Conservation and Management of Sharks; and International Plan of Action for the Management of Fishing Capacity.

The most recent FAO instrument concerning sustainable fisheries aims to strengthen port-state control, which holds significant promise as the most effective means of enforcing international fisheries laws.[219] CCAMLR, the General Fisheries Commission for the Mediterranean, the North East Atlantic Fisheries Commission and the Northwest Atlantic Fisheries Organization have adopted port-state measures targeting IUU activities which include the prohibition on entry to and use of ports and port services such as landing and trans-shipment.[220] In November 2009 FAO's governing conference sought to broaden port state controls through a new multilateral treaty, the 2009 Agreement on Port State Measures to Prevent, Deter and Eliminate Illegal, Unreported and Unregulated Fishing. The treaty, which is yet to enter into force, requires parties to request information of foreign fishing vessels prior to their entry into port, allowing port states to identify suspect vessels in advance, to conduct regular inspections of vessels in port according to standard procedures, and to take follow-up action against IUU vessels.

More could still be done to improve compliance, one practical measure being the establishment of a comprehensive global register of fishing vessels maintained by the FAO. Such a register was recommended by an expert consultation by the FAO, for reasons that it can prevent, deter and eliminate IUU fishing by rendering it more difficult and costly for illegal fishing enterprises.[221] In 2013 the IMO Assembly agreed to a proposal (co-sponsored by the FAO) to include large (100 gross tonnage and above) fishing vessels in the IMO Ship Identification Number Scheme. This will serve as the 'Unique Vessel Identifier' assigned to a vessel throughout its life, and will be recorded in the FAO's 'Global Record' in order to provide reliable identification of fishing vessels and assist in curtailing IUU fishing.

ii. Fish Stocks Agreement

The LOSC establishes fairly generic requirements that states cooperate in respect of straddling and highly migratory species.[222] It does not specify in any detail what form this

---

[219] On port state control generally see EJ Molenaar, 'Port State Jurisdiction: Towards Comprehensive, Mandatory and Global Coverage' (2007) 38 *Ocean Development and International Law* 225. See also Report of the Expert Consultation to Draft a Legally-Binding Instrument on Port-State Measures, FAO Fisheries Report 2007, 846.

[220] For discussion of practice in the General Fisheries Commission for the Mediterranean see Nicola Ferri, 'Current Legal Developments: General Fisheries Commission for the Mediterranean' (2009) 24 *International Journal of Marine and Coastal Law* 163.

[221] Gail Lugten, 'Current Legal Developments Food and Agriculture Organization' (2008) 23 *International Journal of Marine and Coastal Law* 761.

[222] LOSC, arts 63(2), 64.

cooperation should take, nor does it set out what legal consequences should flow from a failure to cooperate. It is these omissions that the FSA seeks to remedy.[223]

The negotiations which led to the conclusion of the FSA were prompted by the 1992 United Nations Conference on Environment and Development. Shortly after the Conference the United Nations General Assembly called on states to convene a conference under the auspices of the United Nations to address straddling and highly migratory fish stocks, and more generally better cooperation within RFMOs.[224] The United Nations Conference on Straddling Fish Stocks and Highly Migratory Fish Stocks took place between 1993 and 1995, and the FSA was adopted by consensus in August 1995.

The conference took place against a backdrop of growing tension between some coastal and other states over access to straddling fisheries. In an echo of the preferential fishing doctrine stated by the ICJ in the *Fisheries Jurisdiction* case,[225] several coastal states, most notably Canada, maintained that they retained primary responsibility for maintaining straddling stocks, and could implement measures beyond their EEZs where the health of stocks were seriously endangered. This was certainly the case with respect to turbot being extensively fished on the Grand Banks in the Atlantic by vessels from the European Community, authorised to do so under overly generous quotas granted by the North Atlantic Fisheries Organization. In 1995 Canada seized a Spanish-flagged fishing vessel, the *Estai*, on the high seas pursuant to the Coastal Fisheries Protection Act 1994 (Can) which enabled Canadian authorities to take action to protect endangered straddling stocks.[226] This arrest prompted Spain to commence proceedings against Canada in the ICJ.[227] The Court did not, however, decide the case on the merits, finding that Canada's optional clause declaration excluded the Court's jurisdiction in relation to disputes arising out of or concerning conservation and management measures taken by Canada with respect to vessels fishing in the Grand Banks area. Canada and Spain were not at the time parties to the LOSC.[228]

Another state to make broad claims to fisheries jurisdiction on the high seas is Chile, through the concept of the 'presential sea'.[229] Under legislation passed in 1991, Chile adopted conservation measures for high seas straddling stocks, and reserved the right to impose bans on the landing of fish taken contrary to these measures in Chilean ports. Such bans imposed in relation to swordfish led the European Community in 2000 to commence proceedings against Chile under the World Trade Organization dispute settlement system,[230] and in what was effectively a counterclaim, Chile launched proceedings against the European Community under Part XV of the LOSC for the failure to cooperate with

---

[223] Francisco Orrego Vicuña, *The Changing International Law of High Seas Fisheries* (Cambridge, Cambridge University Press, 1999) 201.

[224] UNGA Resolution 47/192 (1992), UN Doc A/RES/47/192 (1992).

[225] *Fisheries Jurisdiction (United Kingdom v Iceland)* (jurisdiction) [1973] ICJ Rep 3 (merits) [1974] ICJ Rep 3; *(Germany v Iceland)* (jurisdiction) [1973] ICJ Rep 49 (merits) [1974] ICJ Rep 175.

[226] McDorman, *Salt Water Neighbors* (n 197) 111.

[227] *Fisheries Jurisdiction (Spain v Canada)* (jurisdiction and admissibility) [1998] ICJ Rep 431. See further Robin Churchill, 'Fisheries Jurisdiction Case (Spain v Canada)' (1999) 12 *Leiden Journal of International Law* 597.

[228] Spain ratified the LOSC in January 1997, and Canada in November 2003.

[229] José A De Yturriaga, *The International Regime of Fisheries: From UNCLOS 1982 to the Presential Sea* (The Hague, Martinus Nijhoff, 1997), 228–38.

[230] *Chile—Measures Affecting the Transit and Importation of Swordfish* (2000) WTO Doc WT/DS1931/1 (request for consultations by the European Communities) (2000) WTO Doc WT/DS193/2 (request for the establishment of a panel by the European Communities).

Chile under Articles 64 and 117 to 119 of the LOSC.[231] The matter was eventually settled by the parties, and removed from the ITLOS docket in 2009.

It is clear that this approach—the creeping of coastal state jurisdiction further seawards—is not compatible with the LOSC, and only likely to generate further conflict between coastal and distant water fishing states.[232] Instead there is a need for greater cooperation, especially among RFMOs, and this is the fundamental objective of the FSA. It not only supplements the provisions of LOSC addressing straddling and highly migratory stocks, but introduces a number of key reforms that fundamentally change the international law of fisheries.

The FSA is an implementing agreement under LOSC, and is to be interpreted and applied as consistent with the LOSC.[233] Unlike the 1994 Implementing Agreement in relation to Part XI of the LOSC it is a stand-alone agreement, and hence states may be party to either the LOSC or the FSA and not both (the United States for instance is a party to the FSA but not the LOSC). The basic approach of the FSA is to provide foundational rules and principles for the effective operation of regional fisheries agreements. Unlike the LOSC which places primary emphasis on MSY, the FSA places an objective of optimum utilisation within a precautionary and ecosystem-focussed approach to marine living resource conservation.

The FSA is based upon the 12 fundamental principles contained in Part II which require all states to adopt measures to ensure the long-term sustainability and optimum utilisation of straddling and highly migratory fish stocks, take measures according to the best scientific evidence, apply the precautionary and ecosystem approaches, minimise pollution and by-catch, protect marine biodiversity, eliminate overfishing and overcapacity, collect and share fisheries data, and implement and enforce conservation measures by effective monitoring, control and enforcement.[234] The precautionary approach attracts additional treatment in Article 6, which requires states to apply the approach widely to straddling and highly migratory stocks to protect both marine resources and the marine environment generally.[235] Furthermore, Annex II to the FSA includes seven guidelines for the application of the precautionary approach which establishes a fairly precise methodology for determining 'precautionary reference points', which if exceeded trigger conservation and management action to facilitate stock recovery. Freestone has commented that this strong emphasis on precaution amounts to 'the introduction for the first time of a truly environmental dimension into international fisheries law'.[236]

Also attracting detailed treatment in Part II is the principle of compatibility—that is the requirement that measures adopted in the EEZ are compatible with those adopted for the high seas.[237] To this end coastal states and states fishing on the high seas are under a duty to cooperate in devising compatible measures, which are to be determined according to an extensive list of criteria. These include a requirement that measures adopted for the

---

[231] *Conservation and Sustainable Exploitation of Swordfish Stocks in the South-East Pacific Ocean (Chile/European Community)* (removed from docket 17 December 2009) www.itlos.org.

[232] Birnie, Boyle and Redgwell, *International Law of the Environment* (n 105) 732.

[233] FSA, art 4.

[234] Ibid art 5.

[235] Ibid art 6(1).

[236] David Freestone, 'Implementing Precaution Cautiously: The Precautionary Approach in the Straddling and Highly Migratory Fish Stocks Agreement' in Ellen Hey (ed), *Developments in International Fisheries Law* (The Hague, Kluwer, 1999) 287, 287.

[237] FSA, art 7.

high seas do not undermine the effectiveness of measures adopted for the EEZ,[238] take into account the biological unity of the stocks,[239] and ensure that the measures do not result in harmful impact on marine living resources as a whole.[240] The requirement that states cooperate to devise compatible conservation measures is backed up by the entitlement of states to invoke the dispute settlement procedures of the LOSC, which apply *mutatis mutandis* to the FSA, if no agreement can be reached within a reasonable period of time.[241]

In Part III the FSA details the mechanisms that are to form the basis of international cooperation for conserving and managing straddling and highly migratory fish stocks. Where there is an RFMO with competence to establish conservation and management measures, then states shall give effect to their duty of cooperation by becoming members, or by agreeing to apply the measures adopted by the RFMO.[242] Only those states which do so shall have access to the fishery resources.[243] Hence RFMO non-members are effectively excluded from the fishery. Where there is no RFMO, then coastal and other states fishing in the high seas shall cooperate to establish such an organisation.[244] The FSA therefore seeks to ensure that existing governance frameworks are used, or if they do not exist then they are to be established. The agreement lays down basic requirements that new RFMOs should meet,[245] and the functions that new or existing RFMOs should discharge.[246] Particular emphasis is given to transparency in decision-making.[247]

Part V of the FSA addresses the duties of the flag state, which are similar to, but more detailed than, the FAO Compliance Agreement. These measures are also designed to ensure that flag states exercise an appropriate level of supervision of vessels flying their flag, and above all do not engage in any activity that undermines the effectiveness of measures adopted by RFMOs.[248] Part VI addresses compliance and enforcement, requiring flag states to enforce measures adopted by RFMOS against vessels flying their flag,[249] and requiring states to assist flag states in this task.[250] It also sets out an innovative system for improved regional cooperation in enforcement in high seas areas. This allows a party to the FSA which is a member of an RFMO to use duly authorised inspectors to board and inspect fishing vessels flying the flag of another party to the FSA.[251] Such boarding is to take place according to procedures adopted by the RFMO;[252] however, if after two years of the adoption of the FSA no such procedures have been established, then it may occur in accordance with the basic procedures set out in Article 22. Rounding out the compliance provisions of the FSA is Article 23, which affords port states the right to inspect documents, fishing gear and

---

[238] Ibid art 7(2)(a).
[239] Ibid art 7(2)(d).
[240] Ibid art 7(2)(f).
[241] Ibid arts 7(4), 30.
[242] Ibid art 8(3).
[243] Ibid arts 8(4), 17.
[244] Ibid art 8(5).
[245] Ibid art 9.
[246] Ibid art 10.
[247] Ibid art 12.
[248] Ibid art 18.
[249] Ibid art 19.
[250] Ibid art 20.
[251] Ibid art 21.
[252] Ibid art 21(2).

catch of vessels of any nationality.[253] Port states may also prohibit landings and transhipments in circumstances where it is established that the catch has been taken in a manner which undermines the effectiveness of conservation measures.[254] Port state capacity and responsibility to take action has since been further strengthened by the 2009 Agreement on Port State Measures to Prevent, Deter and Eliminate Illegal, Unreported and Unregulated Fishing, discussed above. Such measures should close the gap that applies to non-members to the FSA which are not bound by its requirements, including the prohibition on fishing for high seas stocks, when not a member of the appropriate regional body.

The FSA is a major improvement to the international framework for sustainable fishing, and has been widely ratified.[255] Although it addresses most of the major commercially valuable stocks crossing over the EEZ and high seas boundary, it does not deal with all high seas fish stocks—only those that are straddling or highly migratory—and hence other instruments such as the FAO Compliance Agreement which apply to high seas fishing generally, will continue to have an important role to play in promoting sustainable fishing. Also of importance are fisheries commissions with competence extending to non-highly migratory high seas fisheries, such as the newly created South Pacific Regional Fisheries Management Organisation, established by the 2009 Convention on the Conservation and Management of the High Seas Fishery Resources of the South Pacific Ocean.

Since the FSA entered into force there have been efforts made to establish new RFMOs, and to improve existing regimes,[256] to implement the agreement's new approach to marine resource management. An example is the Western and Central Pacific Fisheries Commission (WCPFC), which was established by the 2000 Convention for the Conservation and Management of Highly Migratory Fish Stocks in the Western and Central Pacific Ocean[257] which entered into force in 2004.[258] The WCPFC brings together Pacific small island developing states and major distant water fishing nations with the objective of ensuring—through effective regional management—the long-term conservation and sustainable use of the tuna resources of the region. This is significant as the WCPFC area[259] includes the world's most important tuna fishery by value and volume, and one that has not yet been fully exploited. As such the WCPFC will be an important test as to whether the new approach to fisheries management adopted in the FSA is able to succeed in establishing sustainable fishing industries where previous efforts have failed.

iii. Biodiversity Beyond National Jurisdiction

In the post-LOSC era there has been increasing concern at the failure to regulate the exploitation of marine living resources in areas beyond national jurisdiction. Much of the focus has been upon deficiencies in high seas fisheries management (as discussed above). Also featuring in international discussion and debate is how research for, and exploitation of, marine organisms for pharmaceutical and other applications should be regulated. There is

---

[253] Ibid art 23(2).

[254] Ibid art 23(3).

[255] As of 1 July 2015 there were 82 parties.

[256] See, eg, the Inter-American Tropical Tuna Commission (IATTC) which was recently undertaken a review of the 1949 Inter-American Tropical Tuna Convention in light of the Fish Stocks Agreement.

[257] *Basic Documents* No 63.

[258] See further Transform Aqorau, 'Current Legal Developments: Western and Central Pacific Fisheries Commission' (2009) 24 *International Journal of Marine and Coastal Law* 737.

[259] WCPFC, art 3.

currently no regulatory framework for such activities (known as bioprospecting) in areas beyond national jurisdiction. As regards marine genetic resources identified in living organisms in the water column, such as fish, plants and bacteria, it is possible to argue that bioprospecting should be regulated in much the same way as high seas fishing, and that under Article 117 all states have a duty to take cooperative measures to conserve these resources. However, in relation to organisms on and under the seabed, it seems highly improbable that these could be assimilated to the mineral resources of the Area such that Part XI of the LOSC would apply to them, and thereby mandate an equitable distribution of the economic benefits derived from their use. A commitment was made at the 2012 United Nations Conference on Sustainable Development (Rio+20):

> to address, on an urgent basis … before the end of the sixty-ninth session of the General Assembly, the issue of the conservation and sustainable use of marine biological diversity beyond areas of national jurisdiction, including by taking a decision on the development of an international instrument under the [LOSC].[260]

In June 2015 the General Assembly initiated the negotiating process for a new protocol to the LOSC that would seek both to protect biodiversity on the high seas and provide clarity on the legal status of bioprospecting on the high seas and in the Area.[261] The matters to be addressed are:

> the conservation and sustainable use of marine biological diversity of areas beyond national jurisdiction, in particular, together and as a whole, marine genetic resources, including questions on the sharing of benefits, measures such as area-based management tools, including marine protected areas, environmental impact assessments and capacity-building and the transfer of marine technology.[262]

This is a highly significant development, and appears very likely to produce a third implementing agreement to the LOSC. The process and anticipated outcome of the deliberations on marine biodiversity beyond national jurisdiction illustrates how the LOSC as a framework for marine resource management can be elucidated and supplemented to respond to newly identified challenges to sustainable oceans governance.

IV. Further Reading

Rachel J Baird, *Aspects of Illegal, Unreported and Unregulated Fishing in the Southern Ocean* (Dordrecht, Springer, 2006)

William T Burke, *The New International Law of Fisheries* (Oxford, Clarendon Press, 1994)

Ellen Hey, *Developments in International Fisheries Law* (The Hague, Kluwer, 1999)

Douglas Johnston, *The International Law of Fisheries: A Framework for Policy-Oriented Inquiries* (Dordrecht, Martinus Nijhoff, 1987)

Stuart Kaye, *International Fisheries Management* (The Hague, Kluwer, 2001)

Rosemary Rayfuse, *Non-Flag State Enforcement in High Seas Fisheries* (Boston, Martinus Nijhoff, 2004)

---

[260] UN Doc A/CONF.216/L.1 (2012), [162].

[261] UNGA RES 69/269, UN Doc A/69/L.65 (2015). See generally Robin M Warner, 'Conserving Marine Biodiversity in Areas Beyond National Jurisdiction' in Donald R Rothwell, Alex G Oude Elferink, Karen N Scott and Tim Stephens (eds), *The Oxford Handbook of the Law of the Sea* (Oxford, Oxford University Press, 2015) 752.

[262] UNGA RES 69/269, UN Doc A/69/L.65 (2015), [2].

14

Marine Scientific Research

I. Introduction

It is often said that humankind knows less about the oceans than the heavens. While it is certainly the case that much remains unknown, progress in MSR, especially in recent decades, has greatly enhanced our understanding of the oceanic environment. This is well demonstrated by advances in climate science that have provided insights into the role of the oceans in the global climate system. Beyond the study of ocean circulation, a staple oceanographic concern, scientific research in ocean space is directed towards a multitude of topics. These include seabed topography (that is bathymetry, which is critical for drawing nautical charts); the geology and geomorphology of the seabed (for locating hydrocarbon resources, and to understand tectonic processes); and fisheries and marine ecosystems (for improving fisheries management, and for biological prospecting ('bioprospecting') for genetic resources both for pure research and for commercial purposes).[1] Improved scientific understanding of the human influence on many aspects of the oceanic environment has been a particularly important impetus for giving the law of the sea an increasing environmental focus. In this regard Chapter 17 of Agenda 21,[2] emphasises throughout its plan for integrated management and sustainable development of the oceans, that scientific capacity should be enhanced, particularly in developing states, and that sound science should be at the centre of assessments of environmental risks, and the making of management decisions.

The subjects of marine scientific inquiry are seldom discrete, in that research on one phenomenon (such as the distribution of a fishery) often sheds important light on another (such as the biological effects of pollutants). Likewise, the purposes to which scientific research may be put often overlap. For instance, the geomorphology of continental margins is of interest not only because it is relevant to the study of the seismic activity responsible for catastrophes such as the 2004 Indian Ocean tsunami,[3] or in the Indian Ocean search for Malaysian Airlines Flight 370 lost in 2014,[4] but also because such physical oceanographic data must be gathered in order for a coastal state to establish the outer limits of

---

[1] See generally David Leary et al, 'Marine Genetic Resources: A Review of Scientific and Commercial Interest' (2009) 33 *Marine Policy* 183.

[2] *Basic Documents* No 48.

[3] The Indian Ocean tsunami resulted in the death of a quarter of a million people in landmasses surrounding the Indian Ocean, and was caused by an exceptionally large undersea earthquake that struck off the west coast of Sumatra on 26 December 2004.

[4] WHF Smith and KM Marks, 'Seafloor in the Malaysian Airlines Flight MH370 Search Area' (2014) 95 *Eos, Transactions, American Geophysical Union* 173.

its continental shelf beyond 200 nm, pursuant to Article 76 of the LOSC.[5] This latter point highlights the difficulty in drawing a distinction between 'pure' or 'fundamental' research on the one hand, and 'applied' research on the other. The reality is that there is considerable cross-over between the two, with pure science often forming the basis for practical oceans management decisions, and for further, commercially oriented, research. The law of the sea has nonetheless sought to make something of a distinction in privileging the conduct of pure research in the EEZ and the continental shelf, while allowing coastal states discretion in granting or withholding approval for the conduct of resource-related research in these zones.

Compared to the 1958 Geneva regime, the LOSC is a major advance in the promotion and regulation of MSR. The Preamble to the LOSC makes clear that one of its key purposes is to promote the '*study*, protection and preservation of the marine environment' (emphasis added), a formulation that highlights the critical linkages between MSR and the sustainable development of ocean space. The body of the LOSC sets out in Part XIII an 'exceptionally comprehensive'[6] body of rules to facilitate and regulate MSR, and in Part XIV a similarly extensive system for developing and transferring marine technology.

The term MSR is not defined in the LOSC; however, international law has in recent years begun to consider in more detail the parameters of 'scientific research', and accordingly the interaction between science and international law. In 2014 the International Court of Justice for the first time considered the meaning of the term in the specific context of the 1946 International Convention for the Regulation of Whaling.[7] In the *Whaling in the Antarctic* case,[8] the Court declined to offer a general definition of scientific research,[9] preferring to focus on the meaning of the phrase 'for the purposes of scientific research' in order to determine whether Japan's conduct of its Southern Ocean 'special permit' whaling programme was consistent with Article VIII of the Convention.[10] The findings of the Court accordingly provide some general guidance on the interpretation of the term MSR under the LOSC.

During UNCLOS III, various possible definitions of MSR had been mooted, some of which sought to restrict the term only to pure research while others encompassed all scientific studies in the oceans, including research connected with the exploitation of natural resources.[11] No definition was ultimately included in the LOSC because it was considered that the provisions in Part XIII adequately gave meaning to the concept.[12] In its ordinary sense, and the one adopted in this chapter, MSR means 'any form of scientific investigation, fundamental or applied, concerned with the marine environment, i.e. that has the

---

[5] See further ch 5.

[6] Patricia Birnie, 'Law of the Sea and Ocean Resources: Implications for Marine Scientific Research' (1995) 10 *International Journal of Marine and Coastal Law* 229.

[7] *Basic Documents* No 7.

[8] *Whaling in the Antarctic (Australia v Japan; New Zealand intervening)*, Judgment of 31 March 2014.

[9] Ibid [86].

[10] Ibid [87]–[97], [223]–[227]. Some members of the ICJ cast doubt over whether the Court could properly define 'scientific research', observing the differences of opinion that existed over the term within the scientific community: see *Whaling in the Antarctic (Australia v Japan; New Zealand intervening)*, Dissenting Opinion of Judge Owada, [25]; Separate Opinion of Judge Cançado Trindade [74], who observed that '"Scientific research" is surrounded by uncertainties; it is undertaken on the basis of uncertainties'.

[11] *Virginia Commentaries*, vol 4, 444–49.

[12] AHA Soons, 'Marine Scientific Research Provisions in the Convention on the Law of the Sea: Issues of Interpretation' in ED Brown and RR Churchill (eds), *The UN Convention on the Law of the Sea: Impact and Implementation* (Honolulu, Law of the Sea Institute, 1989) 365, 366.

marine environment as its object',[13] which is carried out in the oceans. As such, MSR will include physical oceanography, marine chemistry and biology, scientific ocean drilling and coring, geological and geophysical research, and other activities that have a scientific purpose.[14] So defined, MSR must be distinguished from research conducted at sea that has as its object non-marine environments, such as atmospheric or astronomical observation. Such research is not subject to the LOSC regime for MSR. Also not encompassed by the LOSC is MSR undertaken outside of the surface, water column, subsoil or seabed in the marine environment.[15] Despite the extensive use of *ex situ* research techniques, such as remote sensing from satellites that are increasingly displacing *in situ* ship-based methods for obtaining data on the marine environment, these are not addressed by Part XIII of the Convention, nor do they fall within the reach of coastal state jurisdiction. Similar considerations apply to remote sensing from satellites over internal waters, the territorial sea and archipelagic waters.

A distinctive feature of contemporary MSR is the way in which it is being pursued by three main protagonists: independent marine scientists engaged in pure research (eg in respect of ocean acidification), commercially backed scientific programmes (eg fisheries researchers and marine 'bioprospectors'; ocean fertilisation projects), and governments and their navies (eg geoscience expeditions identifying continental shelf limits, or naval hydrographers surveying seafloor features to inform naval tacticians). An immediate challenge for the MSR regime is to bring clarity to the application or not of Part XIII of the LOSC to military surveying, and the extent to which coastal states have an entitlement to exclude such activities from their EEZs.

II. Development of the Regime for Marine Scientific Research

A. Early History of Marine Scientific Research

The history of MSR is extensive, extending from ancient times. Herodotus, writing around 450 BCE, addressed oceanographic issues such as the tides in the Red Sea, and silting in the Nile Delta.[16] Later Aristotle was to devote a substantial portion of *Meteorologica* to subjects of marine biology and ocean topography, considering such fundamental questions as to sources of the oceans and their chemistry.[17] However, it was not until the seventeenth and eighteenth centuries, following the Age of Discovery, that MSR began to acquire a truly systematic and professional basis. The field was advanced by naturalists such as Charles Darwin, who during the voyages of the HMS *Beagle* gathered extensive scientific data on topics as diverse as the formation of corals and the classification of marine living organisms

---

[13]   Birnie, 'Law of the Sea and Ocean Resources' (n 6) 242.

[14]   J Ashley Roach and Robert W Smith, *Excessive Maritime Claims*, 3rd edn (Leiden, Martinus Nijhoff, 2012) 414.

[15]   For a US position on activities that are encompassed by MSR, see ibid 415.

[16]   Herodotus, *The Histories*, Book 2 (GC Macaulay trans, New York, Barnes and Noble, 2004) 11.

[17]   Aristotle, *Meteorologica*, Book 2 (HDP Lee trans, London, Heinemann, 1952) pts 1–3.

such as barnacles.[18] Forty years later the voyage of the HMS *Challenger* undertook a systematic investigation of the world's oceans, and led to the publication of an extensive set of reports that, among other things, identified for the first time the existence of polymetallic nodules on the deep seabed.[19] Many further expeditions followed in the twentieth century, and developments such as the establishment of the Scripp's Institution of Oceanography in 1924,[20] led to science assuming far greater importance in the development of national and international policies and laws to address marine matters, most notably in the management of fisheries.

B. Marine Scientific Research and North–South Tensions in the Post-WW II Period

In the period following the Second World War there was a substantial expansion in MSR effort, directed not only to scientific inquiry for its own sake, but also to manage fisheries, to locate oil and gas resources, and to protect the marine environment. The heavy investment in pure and applied scientific research in the 1950s and 1960s, primarily by industrialised states, took place at a time in which there was a substantial increase in the number and influence of newly independent developing states. These states were concerned that unrestricted MSR by technologically advanced states on the high seas, which then extended over most ocean space, would place them at a considerable disadvantage when it came to locating and exploiting living and non-living resources. There was also a concern that scientific research could be used to justify unreasonable restrictions on marine pollution that would hinder economic development, and that MSR could also have military repercussions.[21] As a result, several developing states argued at UNCLOS III not only for sovereign rights and jurisdiction in the resources of the continental shelf and the EEZ, but also for the right to regulate MSR, including a capacity to refuse consent for it to be undertaken in their resource zones.[22] On the other hand, major researching states, including the United States, contended that the adoption of an EEZ regime that did not allow the free pursuit of scientific research would mean that they would be excluded from large areas of ocean of especial interest to the scientific community.

C. The Pre-LOSC Regime for Marine Scientific Research

The views of developing states expressed at UNCLOS III brought a new perspective to debates over MSR that had been absent at UNCLOS I or II, and was therefore not reflected either in the 1958 Geneva Conventions, or at customary international law.

---

[18] See, eg, Darwin's first book: *The Structure and Distribution of Corals* (London, Smith, 1899).
[19] Challenger Office, *Report on the Scientific Results of the Voyage of HMS Challenger 1873–76* (London, HMSO, 1880–95) vols 1–40.
[20] See scripps.ucsd.edu.
[21] Barbara Kwiatkowska, *The 200 Mile Exclusive Economic Zone and the Law of the Sea* (Dordrecht, Martinus Nijhoff, 1989) 135.
[22] Such as the proposals by Trinidad and Tobago, and by Colombia for the Group of 77 Developing States for an absolute consent regime: Alfred HA Soons, *Marine Scientific Research and the Law of the Sea* (The Hague, Kluwer, 1982) 160.

The 1958 Convention on the Territorial Sea and the Contiguous Zone[23] did not deal with MSR, but it necessarily followed from the definition of the territorial sea as a zone in which the coastal state enjoyed sovereignty in the seabed, subsoil, water column and airspace,[24] that MSR could only be conducted by foreign states with coastal state approval. The same conclusion also applied in relation to internal waters where coastal state sovereign rights are complete. By contrast, the 1958 Convention on the High Seas[25] effectively preserved the freedom of scientific research to the fullest extent. Although the Convention made no reference to MSR, it did define high seas freedoms in Article 2 in a broad, and non-exhaustive, way that implicitly protected the free pursuit of this long-standing practice beyond the limits of coastal state jurisdiction, which at the time meant ocean space beyond a narrow territorial sea.[26] In relation to living resources, the 1958 Convention on Fishing and Conservation of the Living Resources of the High Seas[27] encouraged greater levels of research, in emphasising the importance of MSR to fisheries management. It referred to the importance of 'scientific findings' in devising and implementing measures to achieve optimum sustainable yield.[28] While the High Seas and Fisheries Conventions sought to protect high seas scientific research, in practice this was limited over time because of the emergence of claims to EFZs most of which post-dated these treaties. A necessary incident of EFZs was an assertion of sovereign rights over fisheries, and jurisdiction to regulate their taking, whether for economic or for research purposes.[29]

At UNCLOS I, Indonesia and other developing states proposed that scientific research on the continental shelf should be subject in all cases to coastal state consent.[30] However, a compromise position was ultimately reached which allowed the scientific community to continue MSR in a fairly broad range of circumstances. The 1958 Convention on the Continental Shelf[31] sought on the one hand to safeguard the interests of coastal states by requiring that 'the consent of the coastal State shall be obtained in respect of any research concerning the continental shelf and undertaken there'.[32] On the other hand it promoted fundamental research in providing that 'the coastal State shall not normally withhold its consent if the request is submitted by a qualified institution with a view to purely scientific research into the physical or biological characteristics of the continental shelf', subject to the right of the coastal state, 'if it so desires, to participate or to be represented in the research'.[33] Moreover, it was made clear to coastal states that activities directed at exploring or exploiting resources on the continental shelf should not result 'in any interference with fundamental oceanographic or other scientific research carried out with the intention of open publication'.[34]

---

[23] *Basic Documents* No 9.

[24] 1958 Convention on the Territorial Sea and the Contiguous Zone, art 2.

[25] *Basic Documents* No 10.

[26] In its commentary on the draft article that was to become this provision, the ILC observed that MSR was an accepted freedom of the high seas even though not specifically referred to in the text: [1956] *Yearbook of the International Law Commission* vol 2, 278.

[27] *Basic Documents* No 11.

[28] 1958 Convention on Fishing and Conservation of the Living Resources of the High Seas, art 7(2).

[29] Coastal state fisheries legislation applicable in the EEZ often requires foreign fishers to obtain licenses for the taking of any fish, whether for commercial or research purposes. See, eg, *Fisheries Act 1996* (NZ), ss 83, 89, 97.

[30] See UN Doc A/CONF.13/C.4/L.53 in *First Conference*, 4th Comm, 140.

[31] *Basic Documents* No 12.

[32] 1958 Convention on the Continental Shelf, art 5(8).

[33] Ibid.

[34] Ibid art 5(1).

The 1958 Convention on the Continental Shelf therefore provided some capacity to coastal states to control MSR, but its overall value as a legal framework was constrained because the definition of the continental margin was imprecise (the outer limits were defined by reference to the exploitability of seabed resources),[35] and also limited the breadth of the continental shelf in most places to a relatively narrow band of seabed. Therefore MSR relevant to resource exploitation could be conducted relatively close to the shorelines of coastal states. Uncertainty also surrounded the extent of coastal state jurisdiction to subject research within the continental shelf to oversight. This was because the consent regime was applicable only in relation to research 'concerning the continental shelf *and* undertaken there',[36] which suggested that any research, for any purpose, that did not involve physical disturbance of the seabed could proceed without coastal state consent. An example of such research would be marine seismic studies used to locate undersea resources through the use of sound waves emitted from underwater explosions or the firing of pneumatic guns.

III. The LOSC Regime for Marine Scientific Research

The LOSC made a number of significant changes to the existing customary and conventional regime relating to MSR. These resulted in an expansion in the geographical extent and scope, and the content of coastal state jurisdiction over marine scientific activities.[37] A broader territorial sea, the 200 nm and outer continental shelf, and the new EEZ and archipelago regimes brought with them coastal state jurisdiction over MSR in a far larger geographical area. The scope of jurisdiction was also increased in that coastal states were given not only rights to withhold consent for MSR in the new EEZ, but also in relation to the continental shelf in an additional set of circumstances. Furthermore, the content of the jurisdiction was made more detailed in provisions regulating the rights and duties of coastal and researching states.

A. General Provisions

Part XIII of the LOSC opens with Article 238, which provides that all states (and not only parties to the LOSC), regardless of their geographical circumstances, and also competent international organisations, have the right to conduct MSR subject to the rights and duties of other states under the LOSC. This is an important general statement of the right to conduct MSR not found in the Geneva regime. It is significant also in recognising the right of intergovernmental organisations with particular competence in marine science, such as the Intergovernmental Oceanographic Commission of UNESCO (IOC), to undertake and to promote MSR.[38]

The IOC was established in 1960 to promote international cooperation and to coordinate programmes in MSR in order to improve knowledge of the nature and resources

---

[35] Ibid art 1.
[36] Ibid art 5(8).
[37] Soons, *Marine Scientific Research* (n 22) 261.
[38] See also LOSC, art 239.

of the oceans and coastal areas, and to provide a sound basis for oceans management, sustainable development of marine resources and marine environmental protection.[39] UNESCO, through the IOC, is the recognized competent international organisation for the purposes of Parts XIII and XIV of the LOSC. In 2015 it had a total of 147 member states. Programmes being undertaken by the IOC in the past decade have included assessing climate change, ocean health, coastal research and management; improving scientific capacity; the Global Ocean Observing System to develop an observation capacity for all of the world's oceans; the International Oceanographic Data and Information Exchange, which is designed to enhance MSR by facilitating the exchange of data between members; the International Ocean Carbon Coordination Project, which is examining the role of the oceans in the carbon cycle, including the acidification effects of increased absorption of carbon dioxide from the atmosphere; and maintaining tsunami warning systems for the Pacific and Indian Oceans. The IOC has also sought to assist members in implementing three elements of the LOSC concerning MSR: Part XIII, Part XIV and Article 76. To this end, the IOC has, among other things, generated criteria and guidelines for the transfer of marine technology, a procedure for the operation of Article 247 relating to MSR undertaken by international organisations. In 2009 the IOC began consideration of an 'IOC Legal Framework for the Collection of Oceanographic Data' which, among other things, would seek to clarify the meaning of MSR for the purposes of the LOSC. However, progress on this initiative has been slow.

The right to engage in MSR is supplemented by general principles set out in Article 240 and Article 241 of the LOSC that apply to oceanic research in all maritime zones. Article 240 requires that MSR shall (a) be conducted exclusively for peaceful purposes, (b) be conducted with appropriate scientific methods,[40] (c) not unjustifiably interfere with other legitimate uses of the sea and shall be duly respected in the course of such uses, and (d) be conducted in compliance with all relevant regulations adopted consistent with the LOSC, including those for the protection and preservation of the marine environment.

Although the requirement that research be conducted for peaceful purposes suggests that research serving military objectives is prohibited, Article 240(a) adds no additional disciplines to other similar provisions of the Convention, such as Article 88 which provides that the high seas 'shall be reserved for peaceful purposes'. Rather than imposing a blanket ban on the use of the oceans for military purposes, the effect of these provisions is to apply the general prohibition on the use of force except in self-defence, or where authorised by the United Nations Security Council under its Chapter VII powers.

The other three general principles referred to in Article 240 serve simply to reaffirm that the right to undertake MSR for legitimate scientific ends must be balanced against other lawful ocean activities, and must respect coastal state laws adopted consistently with the Convention, especially, but not only, those dealing with environmental protection. Also somewhat otiose is Article 241, which provides that MSR cannot be the legal basis for any claim to the marine environment or its resources. This reaffirms not only that areas beyond the limits of national jurisdiction (the high seas and the seabed) cannot be subject to

---

[39] See ioc-unesco.org.
[40] This was a matter considered in the *Whaling in the Antarctic* case in considerable detail, albeit in the context of the 1946 International Convention for the Regulation of Whaling: *Whaling in the Antarctic (Australia v Japan: New Zealand intervening)*, Judgment of 31 March 2014, [127]–[227].

appropriation on the basis of MSR conducted there, but is also protective of the sovereign rights of coastal states in the resources of the continental shelf and EEZ.[41]

The remaining provisions that round out the opening general principles for the conduct of MSR (Articles 242 to 244) are directed primarily to promoting international cooperation, especially in enhancing the flow of scientific knowledge gained from research to developing states where there is less capacity to fund and administer oceanographic programmes. One of the key purposes of international cooperation in MSR is outlined in Article 242(2), which provides that states should allow other states a reasonable opportunity to obtain information necessary to prevent and control damage to the health and safety of persons and to the marine environment. As was noted by the United States during UNCLOS III, cooperation which allows states to understand ocean-driven processes such as the South Asian Monsoon can be vital not only to economic development, but to the very survival of societies dependent upon them.[42] This observation has added resonance today in the context of human induced climate change which is having a variety of effects on the oceans, and has the potential to shift ocean circulation systems, leading to major changes in regional climate and weather patterns.[43]

Further articles of a general character are found towards the conclusion of Part XIII. These include a provision addressing the issue of liability, which makes researching states or international organisations liable for damage caused by measures contrary to the LOSC,[44] and for pollution of the marine environment arising out of MSR.[45] There is also a provision that highlights the special arrangements applicable to the settlement of disputes concerning MSR.[46] Whereas most controversies concerning the LOSC are subject to compulsory arbitration or judicial settlement, coastal states are not obliged to accept submission to dispute settlement in relation to any dispute arising out of the exercise by a coastal state of a right or discretion to grant or withhold consent to conduct MSR in its continental shelf or EEZ,[47] or a decision to order suspension or cessation of a research project.[48] The only possibility for compulsory dispute settlement in such circumstances is reserved by Article 297(2)(b) which allows a researching state to invoke compulsory conciliation of a dispute with a coastal state if the latter is not complying with the LOSC in relation to a request to carry out research, unless that research is of direct significance for the exploration and exploitation of natural resources.

Against the backdrop of these general provisions, the LOSC addresses MSR more specifically in relation to each of the maritime zones.

B. Internal Waters, Archipelagic Waters and the Territorial Sea

The position as regards the territorial sea is addressed in Article 245, which gives coastal states complete control over MSR in these waters. Research may be conducted here only

---

[41] *Virginia Commentaries*, vol 4, 464.
[42] Ibid 469.
[43] See D Herr and GR Galland, *The Ocean and Climate Change: Tools and Guidelines for Action* (Gland, IUCN, 2009) 12.
[44] LOSC, art 263(2).
[45] Ibid art 263(3).
[46] Ibid art 264.
[47] Ibid art 297(2)(i).
[48] Ibid art 297(2)(ii).

with the express consent of the coastal state, and subject to any conditions it imposes. The same position applies by necessary implication in internal waters and archipelagic waters.[49]

Coastal state control over research in the territorial sea is further reinforced by Article 19(2)(j), which provides that passage will be prejudicial to the peace, good order and security of the coastal state, and will therefore become non-innocent, if it involves any research or survey activities. Article 21(g) further stipulates that coastal states may adopt laws and regulations relating to innocent passage in respect of MSR. While this would allow the coastal state to prevent the conduct of any MSR, including hydrographic surveying during the exercise of innocent passage in both the territorial sea and archipelagic waters,[50] it would not affect the use of sonar for depth sounding, the use of radar, or the monitoring of ocean and wind currents, where necessary for the safe navigation of a vessel.[51] Similarly, the gathering of such data would also be a permissible exception to the prohibition on research and surveying undertaken during the exercise of transit passage through international straits,[52] or while exercising the similar right of archipelagic sea lanes passage.[53] These conclusions would apply not only to research and survey vessels, but also to military vessels, the passage of which would be rendered neither non-innocent in the territorial sea, nor outside the 'normal mode' of navigation in straits or archipelagic sea lanes,[54] by the gathering of such information, even though it could potentially be used for tactical purposes.

C. Continental Shelf and Exclusive Economic Zone

The EEZ regime makes reference in Article 56(1)(b)(ii) to the exclusive jurisdiction of coastal states with regard to MSR, and this right must be read in light of Article 246 in Part XIII. The LOSC addresses MSR in the continental shelf and the EEZ in a combined set of provisions in Article 246. Coastal states are accorded a general right to regulate, authorise and conduct MSR in both of these zones in accordance with relevant provisions of the Convention. The overriding rule is that MSR in the EEZ and on the continental shelf is only to be conducted with the consent of the coastal state.[55]

As MSR is not defined in the LOSC, Part XIII potentially encompasses a very wide range of scientific activities. However, the Convention limits the impacts of its broad-based consent regime on the freedom of scientific research by stipulating in Article 246(3) that coastal states shall 'in normal circumstances' grant consent for research carried out 'exclusively for peaceful purposes and in order to increase scientific knowledge of the marine environment for the benefit of all mankind'. In addition, it mandates that coastal states must 'establish rules and procedures ensuring that such consent will not be delayed or denied unreasonably'. In this way the LOSC grants important privileges to MSR projects conducted by the scientific community in the public interest. By contrast, under Article 246(5)(a) coastal states are given absolute discretion to withhold consent for MSR which is 'of direct significance for the exploration and exploitation of natural resources, whether living or

---

[49] Ibid art 2(1).
[50] Ibid art 52(1).
[51] Soons, *Marine Scientific Research* (n 22) 149.
[52] LOSC, art 40.
[53] Ibid art 54.
[54] Ibid arts 39, 53
[55] Ibid art 246(2).

non-living'. Consent may also be withheld at the discretion of coastal states in relation to research, whether pure or applied, if it involves drilling into the continental shelf; the use of explosives; the introduction of harmful substances into the marine environment; or the construction, operation or use of artificial islands and structures.[56]

The triggers for enlivening the qualified consent regime in the LOSC provide a much clearer basis for determining when consent may be withheld than those set out in the 1958 Convention on the Continental Shelf which drew a distinction between pure and applied research in a way that left much room for subjective interpretation. However, there are areas where further clarification is needed. The 'direct significance' test in Article 246(5)(a) may have functioned satisfactorily at the time the LOSC was negotiated in relation to the natural resources then of interest, but today the reach of the provision is not as clear when one considers advances in biotechnology which allows organisms recovered as part of a 'pure' research programme to be the subject of commercial development well after they have been located in, and collected from, the marine environment.[57] Bioprospecting in the marine environment involves a wide range of activities, including the search for valuable compounds and genetic materials, their extraction and analysis, and research and commercial development.[58] In terms of process surrounding the actual collection of samples, bioprospecting does not differ from pure MSR, and it might therefore be argued that it should normally be consented to by coastal states. However, later steps in the bioprospecting process which involve the commercialisation of a discovery has the practical effect of transforming the activity into one that is of direct significance to the exploitation of a natural resource. Hence sampling that is conducted within the continental shelf or the EEZ for the express purpose of later commercialisation should only proceed where the advance consent of the coastal state has been sought and granted.[59]

Special provision is made in Part XIII for the outer continental shelf, that is those parts of the seabed where the continental margin extends beyond 200 nm. In these areas the water column is high seas but seabed resources come within the sovereign rights of coastal states. Article 246(6) provides that coastal states may not withhold consent to other states to undertake MSR except in relation to specific areas publicly designated by coastal states as areas in which exploration or exploitation is occurring, or is about to occur.

Several other provisions place important limits on the capacity of coastal states to withhold consent for research within the EEZ or on the juridical, 200 nm, continental shelf. Coastal state consent will be implied where the research is being undertaken by an international organisation of which the coastal state is a member, and where it has not expressed an objection to the project within four months of notification.[60] There will also be implied

---

[56] Ibid art 246(5)(b), (c).

[57] David Leary, *International Law and the Genetic Resources of the Deep Sea* (Leiden, Martinus Nijhoff, 2007) 49. Note that the 1992 Convention on Biological Diversity and the 2010 Nagoya Protocol on Access to Genetic Resources and the Fair and Equitable Sharing of Benefits Arising from their Utilization have sought to resolve this gap within the LOSC.

[58] Alan Hemmings and Michele Rogan-Finnemore, 'Access, Obligations and Benefits' in Michael I Jeffery, Jeremy Firestone and Karen Bubna-Litic (eds), *Biodiversity Conservation, Law + Livelihoods: Bridging the North-South Divide* (Cambridge, Cambridge University Press, 2008) 539, 537.

[59] Salvatore Arico and Charlotte Salpin, *Bioprospecting of Genetic Resources in the Deep Seabed: Scientific, Legal and Policy Aspects*, UNU-IAS Report 2005, 33–34. For further analysis see Joanna Mossop, 'Protecting Marine Biodiversity on the Continental Shelf Beyond 200 Nautical Miles' (2007) 38 *Ocean Development and International Law* 283, 292–94; David Leary, *Bioprospecting in the Arctic*, UNU-IAS Report 2008, 25–26.

[60] LOSC, art 247.

consent where a coastal state fails to inform a researching state or international organisation of its decision to grant or withhold consent within six months of a valid request containing all of the required information.[61]

The duty of researchers to provide information is contained in Article 248. States or international organisations intending to conduct MSR in the EEZ or on the continental shelf must provide, at least six months in advance of the expected project start date, full details relating to (a) the nature and objectives of the project; (b) the method and means to be used; (c) the area where it will be conducted; (d) the time period during which the research will take place; (e) details as to the body sponsoring the project, and the person in charge; and (f) consistent with the spirit of scientific cooperation, the extent to which the coastal state could potentially participate in the project. Compliance with this duty to provide information is critical for any research project as it is the very basis for coastal states assessing whether consent should be given to the proposed project, and the consequences for providing inaccurate information may be significant. Under Article 246(5)(d) one of the grounds upon which a coastal state may withhold or withdraw consent is where the nature or objectives of a marine science project has been inaccurately documented in the information dossier provided. Consent may also be refused or revoked if the researching state or competent international organisation has outstanding obligations to the coastal state from a prior research project.

If a coastal state grants consent to MSR the permission need not be on a *carte blanche* basis. In relation to fundamental research, researchers must respect the right of coastal states to participate or be represented in the project,[62] and be provided with both preliminary and final reports and conclusions arising from the research.[63] Researching states are also under a duty to make the results internationally available as soon as practicable,[64] and to remove scientific research installations or equipment once the research project is complete, unless the coastal state agrees otherwise.[65] For pure research it is only these specified conditions that may be laid down by the coastal state, in conformity with the intent of Part XIII to promote free scientific inquiry as far as possible. As such coastal states could not require payment for granting consent to a marine scientific project, although a fee for assessing an application to conduct research could be levied.

When it comes to research of direct significance for the exploration and exploitation of natural resources a different situation pertains. Coastal states may impose conditions by its laws and regulations in relation to the granting or withholding of research.[66] Although such conditions that may be laid down are not limited, only one receives specific mention: a coastal state may insist that its agreement be obtained before the results of any resource-related research is made internationally available.[67]

---

[61] Ibid art 252.
[62] Ibid art 249(1)(a).
[63] Ibid art 249(1)(b).
[64] Ibid art 249(1)(e).
[65] Ibid art 249(1)(g).
[66] Ibid art 249(2).
[67] Ibid.

i. Hydrographic Surveying

A significant disagreement has arisen between some maritime powers and coastal states over whether Part XIII extends to all forms of data collection in the EEZ.[68] The United States and the United Kingdom argue that surveying of a hydrographic[69] and military[70] nature is a freedom that may be exercised in the EEZ, free from coastal state regulation, just as is the case on the high seas. The legal basis for this contention is that the LOSC refers to MSR and surveying (including hydrographic surveying) in separate provisions. Both MSR and surveying of any kind are clearly referred to as activities not permitted in the territorial sea during the exercise of innocent passage, transit passage, and archipelagic sea lanes passage.[71] However, surveying is not mentioned at all in Part XIII, which prompts the conclusion that hydrographic and military surveying would be neither pure nor applied research subject to the coastal state consent regime. The United States has taken the view that in addition to hydrographic and military surveys, activities not taken up by Part XIII include environmental monitoring and assessment of marine pollution (carried out pursuant to Part XII), activities related to submerged wrecks or objects of an archaeological character,[72] and operational oceanography.

Several coastal states disagree with this interpretation of Part XIII, most notably India and China both of which have lodged a series of protests over the survey activities of United States and United Kingdom vessels in their EEZs. China enacted legislation in 2002 requiring authority from the Chinese government for all surveying and mapping carried out within China's EEZ.[73] The maritime security dimension of the issue was highlighted in March 2009 by an encounter involving the USNS *Impeccable*. While undertaking ocean surveillance activities within China's EEZ 75 nm to the south of Hainan Island, five Chinese vessels surrounded the *Impeccable* and sought to block its path.[74] The event highlighted how China's active interpretation of its EEZ rights such as to limit navigation, MSR, and the conduct of surveillance, could flare into a major international incident.[75]

One argument that may be made in support of China's assumption of jurisdiction is that hydrographic and military surveying is essentially MSR, concerned as it is with much the same type of phenomena as oceanographers have always been interested in. The only real difference stems from the motivation for the activity, with hydrographic and military surveying tending to serve different purposes from either pure or applied research. Hydrographic surveying is carried out primarily to improve the safety of navigation for all maritime users, including navies, while military surveying is relevant for a range of non-classified

---

[68] Sam Bateman, 'Hydrographic Surveying in the EEZ: Differences and Overlaps with Marine Scientific Research' (2005) 29 *Marine Policy* 163.

[69] Hydrography is the science of surveying and charting bodies of water and is concerned with properties including depth, configuration of the bottom, direction and force of currents, and heights and times of tides.

[70] Military surveys involve not only the gathering of hydrographic data but a range of other oceanographic information including chemical, biological and acoustic data: Bateman, 'Hydrographic Surveying' (n 68) 167.

[71] See LOSC, arts 19(j), 21(1)(g), 40, 54.

[72] On this see Sarah Dromgoole, 'Revisiting the Relationship between Marine Scientific Research and the Underwater Cultural Heritage' (2010) 25 *International Journal of Marine and Coastal Law* 33, 44–54.

[73] Surveying and Mapping Law (2002) arts 2, 7, 10, 32 at en.sbsm.gov.cn/article//LawsandRules/Laws/200710/20071000003241.shtml.

[74] D Sevastopulo, 'White House Protests to Beijing over Naval Incident', *Financial Times*, 10 March 2009, 3.

[75] F Ching, 'China will Avoid Military Showdown with the US', *Business Times Singapore*, 18 March 2009.

and classified military purposes from tactical and strategic planning in relation to potential theatres of conflict, through to the testing and development of military equipment such as underwater acoustic sensor systems. In relation to hydrographic surveys an appropriate response to the apparent lacuna in Part XIII would be to allow foreign states to conduct these with the permission of the coastal state, with the caveat that consent should normally be granted given the high value of accurate hydrography for the safety of navigation.[76] The situation for military information gathering is potentially different, because most of the data gathered by navies in the EEZs is not publicly released and therefore has less value as a tradable commodity in the same sense as mapping data obtained through hydrographic surveying.[77] In both cases, the capacity of the coastal state to regulate these activities must be balanced against the rights of other states within the EEZ to exercise 'other internationally lawful uses of the sea' as recognised in Article 58. This issue in particular will also be seen against the backdrop of concerns from maritime states over the creeping jurisdiction of coastal states regarding the regulation of an expanding array of activities within the EEZ, which, in the case of hydrographic and military surveys, also have a significant security dimension.

ii. *Scientific Research Installations and Equipment*

Specific provisions in Part XIII apply to the deployment and use of any type of scientific research installations or equipment, in any area of the marine environment. The basic principle, set out in Article 258, is that this activity is governed by the same rules as are prescribed in Part XIII for the conduct of MSR in any area in which such installations or equipment are deployed or used. However, a distinction can be drawn between equipment that is not fixed to the ocean floor (such as floating buoys) and 'artificial islands, installations and structures' that are. Coastal states should not normally withhold consent for the deployment and use of floating devices for the purposes of pure research.[78] Conversely, the use of such technologies for resource-focussed research can only proceed with coastal state consent.[79] In addition, if the research involves the construction, operation or use of artificial islands, installations and structures then the coastal state may withhold consent regardless of the purpose or character of the research being proposed.[80]

A number of unresolved questions surround the use of floating objects, vehicles and other devices for MSR, and these are attracting increasing scrutiny because of the growing use of these technologies for monitoring marine conditions.[81] Many thousands of floats have been deployed across the world's oceans to measure a range of variables, including wave height, ocean temperature, salinity and currents. These include the several thousand Argo floats launched from ships or aircraft that periodically sink to, and rise from, determined depths to collect data which is transmitted via satellite to shore where it is used by

---

[76] Bateman, 'Hydrographic Surveying in the EEZ' (n 68) 172.

[77] Ibid 170, 173.

[78] LOSC, art 246(3).

[79] Ibid art 246(5)(a).

[80] Ibid art 246(5)(c).

[81] Katharina Bork et al, 'The Legal Regulation of Floats and Gliders—In Quest of a New Regime?' (2008) 39 *Ocean Development and International Law* 298.

the Argo Project to better understand the role of the oceans in the climate system.[82] More recently, use has been made of autonomous submersible vehicles known as gliders, which can be pre-programmed or controlled from shore to navigate to designated waypoints in order to collect data not only at various depths but over a wide geographical area.

One difficulty that arises in applying Part XIII to these devices is that once they are set loose in the marine environment it is impossible to maintain complete control over them, as they may be carried by currents a considerable distance from their original place of deployment, into the EEZs and territorial seas of foreign states. The strict application of Part XIII would mean that the deploying state must seek coastal state consent before this occurs, yet this is impractical as researching states would need to obtain approval from a potentially large number of states.[83] In so doing, researching states would need to provide information on the matters listed in Article 248, including the precise geographical area in which the equipment will be used, at least six months in advance, which is a difficult if not impossible task given the uncertainties involved.

Another question that arises is which state or states may exercise jurisdiction over floating objects. The position in the territorial sea (where the coastal state would have complete jurisdiction) and the high seas (where the deploying flag state would have complete jurisdiction) is clear enough. However, for the EEZ and the continental shelf, the matter is not resolved by Part XIII. The placement of research infrastructure on or connected to the seabed would clearly be covered by Article 60 and Article 80 which gives coastal states exclusive jurisdiction over the construction and use of installations and structures. For floats and gliders there is no guidance in the LOSC precisely on this point. If utilised for applied research then Article 249(2), which allows the coastal state to impose a wide range of conditions, probably means that the coastal state would have jurisdiction.

Novel law of the sea issues surrounding the use of floats and gliders were anticipated to some extent in a convention drafted in 1972 at the instigation of the IOC and the IMO to deal with 'ocean data acquisition systems'.[84] However, the treaty has never been completed, as negotiations were placed on hold during UNCLOS III, and work that was restarted on the project in 1982 was ultimately brought to an end in 1993 without agreement on a finished text. The last iteration of the text dealt more comprehensively with ocean data acquisition systems than does the LOSC, including issues concerning jurisdiction over, and the recovery and return, of floating research devices.[85] It would require deploying states to take steps to monitor the position of devices to prevent unauthorised entry into coastal state jurisdictional zones, require coastal states to notify the deploying state of a device found in its jurisdiction and facilitate its return, and give the deploying state the same rights in, and jurisdiction over, devices as they have over vessels flying its flag. In the absence of

---

[82] Deployment of Argo floats (named after the ship in Greek mythology captained by Jason) began in 2000 and the array was completed in 2007 (although deployments continue to be made to maintain the total array at around 3,000 floats). This array permits real-time and continuous monitoring temperature, salinity and currents in the upper 2000 m of the oceans. See www-argo.ucsd.edu; Bork et al, 'The Legal Regulation of Floats and Gliders' (ibid) 305–06; Roach and Smith, *Excessive Maritime Claims* (n 14) 446–47.

[83] Bork et al, 'The Legal Regulation of Floats and Gliders' (ibid) 311–12.

[84] Preliminary Draft Convention on Ocean Data Acquisition Systems, UN Doc SC-72/CONF.85/3, Annex III (1972).

[85] Draft Convention on the Legal Status of Ocean Data Acquisition Systems, Aids and Devices, UN Doc IOC-XVII/Inf. 1 (1993).

a concluded text, the IOC has sought to fill the gap in regulation through the adoption of non-legally binding guidelines as part of its work on a 'Legal Framework Within the Context of [the LOSC] for the Collection of Oceanographic Data'.[86]

D. High Seas

Whereas the 1958 Continental Shelf Convention implicitly guaranteed the freedom of high seas MSR, the right is made express by the LOSC in Article 257 which provides that all states, irrespective of their geographical circumstances, and competent international organisations may conduct MSR in the water column beyond the EEZ. However, there are some potential limitations on this freedom stemming from the need to accommodate other high seas uses. Hence if research installations or equipment is deployed on the high seas then they must not interfere with established international shipping routes.[87] Additionally the infrastructure is to bear identification markings and adequate warning signals to ensure safety at sea.[88]

While coastal states exercise oversight over MSR conducted within the EEZ and on the continental shelf, MSR on the high seas is largely left to self-regulation, although it would be possible for the dispute settlement provisions of Part XV to be invoked if there was a breach of the general principles of Part XIII set out in Article 240. At UNCLOS III Malta submitted a proposal for the establishment of an International Ocean Space Institution, which would have been competent to regulate MSR in areas beyond national jurisdiction, and would have been responsible for issuing permits for conducting MSR.[89] However, there were strenuous objections by the United Kingdom, the United States and other states which maintained that MSR should be as free from regulation as possible, consistent with the objective of increasing scientific knowledge.[90]

E. Deep Seabed

Research on the deep seabed has given rise to some of the most significant scientific findings of the last century. These include the discovery of chemosynthetic-based ecosystems at hydrothermal vents, which are found at ocean ridges where superheated and mineral-rich water streams are driven by sub-surface volcanism. They sustain a multitude of species, most of which are endemic to specific vents, and these organisms are notable for producing energy from chemical compounds (chemosynthesis) rather than sunlight and for being able to tolerate extreme water temperatures. Heavy concentrations of sulphides found around hydrothermal vents also contain valuable minerals, including precious metals, and are the subject of growing interest from the mining industry.

---

[86] For discussion see Philomène A Verlaan, 'Current Developments: Intergovernmental Oceanographic Commission of the United Nations Educational, Scientific and Cultural Organization (IOC/UNESCO)' (2009) 24 *International Journal of Marine and Coastal Law* 173.

[87] LOSC, art 261.

[88] Ibid art 262.

[89] Leary, *International Law and the Genetic Resources of the Deep Sea* (n 57) 190–96.

[90] Ibid 194.

All states and competent international organisations are entitled to conduct MSR on the deep seabed, that is the area beyond the continental shelf (the Area); however, this research must be conducted in conformity with the provisions of the LOSC relating to the deep seabed set out in Part XI.[91] The primary provision of relevance there is Article 143, which emphasises that MSR in the Area must be carried out for peaceful purposes and for the benefit of humankind as a whole. State parties may carry out such research,[92] as may the ISA.[93] The ISA is the organisation established by the LOSC to organise and control mineral resource activities in the Area. However, the ISA has no general competence to regulate MSR conducted in the Area. For instance, although 'pure' MSR at hydrothermal vent sites poses the most immediate and significant risk to the environment of these areas it does not come under the oversight of the ISA, unless conducted by the body itself.[94] Research involving the actual prospecting or exploring for mineral resources would be applied research that could only occur with the approval of the ISA, as MSR of this character would constitute 'activities in the Area'.[95] However, pure MSR, MSR for mineral resources at a more preliminary stage, and MSR for non-mineral resources such as genetic materials are not matters subject to ISA control.[96]

IV. Marine Scientific Research Under Other Regimes

Although the LOSC is the principal global regime for MSR, there are other instruments at both regional and global level that are of relevance to the conduct of scientific research in ocean space as they relate to research being conducted in the context of a particular activity. Examples include fisheries treaties, which commonly speak of the need for using the 'best scientific evidence available' when taking measures to ensure the long-term sustainability of fish stocks,[97] and which may establish scientific committees for the purpose of advising fisheries commissions on the status and trends of stocks, to coordinate ongoing research, and to make recommendations on matters relating to conservation, management and optimum utilisation.[98] Marine living resources conventions may also include provisions privileging scientific research, as is the case with Article VIII of the 1946 International Convention on the Regulation of Whaling, which allows parties to issue special permits in relation to the taking of whales for research purposes. Article VIII was contested following the moratorium on commercial whaling that commenced in 1985/86, after which Japan

---

[91] See further ch 6.

[92] LOSC, art 143(3).

[93] Ibid art 143(2).

[94] Lyle Glowka, 'Putting Marine Scientific Research on a Sustainable Footing at Hydrothermal Vents' (2003) 27 *Marine Policy* 303, 305.

[95] LOSC, art 1(3).

[96] Leary, *International Law and the Genetic Resources of the Deep Sea* (n 57) 50.

[97] See, eg, 1995 Agreement for the Implementation of the Provisions of the United Nations Convention on the Law of the Sea Relating to the Conservation and Management of Straddling Fish Stocks and Highly Migratory Fish Stocks, *Basic Documents* No 56, arts 5(b), 6(3) and (7), 10(f), 16(1). These provisions are generally consistent with the provisions of the LOSC that contemplate reliance upon scientific information in fisheries management: LOSC, arts 61, 119.

[98] See, eg, 1993 Convention for the Conservation of Southern Bluefin Tuna, *Basic Documents* No 55, art 9.

began issuing special permits to conduct whaling for research purposes in the Southern Ocean. In 2014 the ICJ ruled in favour of Australia that Japan was not undertaking whaling activities 'for the purposes of scientific research' via its special permit whaling programme but rather was undertaking commercial whaling, and in doing so assessed the meaning of that term in the context of Article VIII.[99]

In the context of marine pollution, the parties to relevant IMO conventions have been particularly active in promoting scientific research, and monitoring new forms of research that may be damaging to the marine environment. A watching brief, for example, has been maintained on scientific research involving iron fertilisation of the oceans, a technique to stimulate plankton blooms and thereby result in greater ocean absorption of carbon dioxide from the atmosphere. The parties to the 1972 Convention on the Prevention of Marine Pollution by Dumping of Wastes and Other Matter[100] and its 1996 London Protocol[101] adopted a resolution in 2010 adopting an 'Assessment Framework for Scientific Research Involving Ocean Fertilization' to be used to assist in determinations as to whether 'proposed ocean fertilization activity constitutes legitimate scientific research' not contrary to the London Protocol.[102] This interim measure will eventually be replaced by two new Annexes and associated amendments to the London Protocol adopted in 2013.[103] Annex 4 introduces a definition for Marine Geoengineering Activities in the context of ocean fertilization, while Annex 5 establishes a legally binding assessment framework for such activities. The effect of these London Protocol amendments is that ocean fertilisation is prohibited unless it is 'assessed as constituting legitimate scientific research taking into account any specific placement assessment framework'.[104] Considerations that will be assessed in determining the MSR activity include whether it will answer questions that will add to scientific knowledge, if the research methodology is appropriate and based on best available scientific knowledge and technology, whether the activity is subject to scientific peer review, and whether economic interests have influenced the design of the proposed activity.[105] The 2013 Annexes had yet to enter into force in 2015.

An ocean area where there is substantial overlap between the regime for MSR supplied by the LOSC and another system for regulating MSR is the Southern Ocean, which lies within the purview of the Antarctic Treaty System built upon the 1959 Antarctic Treaty, a fundamental objective of which is to promote scientific investigation within Antarctica. The 1959 Antarctic Treaty itself imposes few controls on the conduct of research, other than to promote international cooperation in scientific investigation in Antarctica through the transfer of plans for scientific research, the exchange of personnel, and the exchange and publication of scientific observations and results.[106] By contrast, the 1991 Environmental Protocol to the Antarctic Treaty has broad application to activities within the Antarctic Treaty

---

[99] *Whaling in the Antarctic Case (Australia v Japan; New Zealand intervening)*, Judgment of 31 March 2014.
[100] *Basic Documents* No 18.
[101] 1996 Protocol to the Convention on the Prevention of Marine Pollution by Dumping of Wastes and Other Matter, *Basic Documents* No 19.
[102] Resolution LC-LP.2 (2010).
[103] Resolution LP.4 (8) (2013).
[104] Resolution LP.4 (8) (2013), Annex 4 (1.3).
[105] Resolution LP.4 (8) (2013), Annex 5 (8).
[106] 1959 Antarctic Treaty, art 3.

Area, that is the land and sea areas below 60 degrees South latitude, that may have effects on the Antarctic environment, including scientific research. As regards other activities, the Environmental Protocol requires scientific research to be planned to minimise adverse environmental impacts[107] and to establish a system for the granting of permits involving interference with wildlife.[108] However, because of the unique status of territorial claims in Antarctica, and the constraints placed upon the active assertion of coastal state jurisdiction by the provisions of the Antarctic Treaty, an unusual dynamic exists in the Southern Ocean with respect to the limited capacity of coastal states to regulate MSR within the maritime zones adjoining their Antarctic claims, the freedoms to conduct MSR under the LOSC and the active promotion of the freedom of scientific research under the Antarctic Treaty. This gap in the regulatory regime could be overcome if the Antarctic Treaty parties exercised a form of 'collective jurisdiction' over MSR, but to date state practice indicates a reluctance on the parties to do so.[109]

V. Coastal State Legislation Concerning Marine Scientific Research

State practice when it comes to coastal state regulation of MSR is far from being uniform.[110] A compilation of the relevant municipal laws of coastal states in 1989 indicated that most had not enacted detailed legislation specifically applicable to MSR, and that the most common approach was simply to assert jurisdiction over research in quite general terms.[111] This position has not changed markedly, despite the very substantial increase in MSR activities worldwide. A 2003 survey of coastal states legislation on MSR conducted by the IOC at the request of the United Nations General Assembly[112] drew responses from 31 coastal states, 21 of which reported having some type of regulation. These differ substantially in their specificity; some legislation such as that of Canada[113] and Australia[114] is quite general in nature and does not seek to mirror the relevant provisions of the LOSC, whereas other regimes are more detailed and largely replicate Part XIII, as is the case for the Polish legislation concerning its maritime zones and maritime administration.[115]

---

[107] 1991 Protocol to the Antarctic Treaty on Environmental Protection, arts 3, 8.
[108] Ibid art 3 and Annex II.
[109] René Lefeber, 'Marine Scientific Research in the Antarctic Treaty System' in Erik Jaap Molenaar, Alex G Oude Elferink and Donald R Rothwell (eds), *The Law of the Sea and the Polar Regions: Interactions between Global and Regional Regimes* (Leiden, Martinus Nijhoff, 2013) 323, 327–31.
[110] See further Montserrat Gorina-Ysern, *An International Regime for Marine Scientific Research* (Ardsley, Transnational Publishers, 2003) pt I.
[111] United Nations, *The Law of the Sea: National Legislation, Regulations and Supporting Documents on Marine Scientific Research in Areas Under National Jurisdiction* (New York, United Nations, 1989).
[112] UN Doc A/RES/56/12 (2001).
[113] See the Oceans Act 1996 (Canada), ss 14, 42 ff.
[114] See the Fisheries Management Act 1991 (Australia), s 3; Offshore Petroleum and Greenhouse Gas Storage Act 2006 (Australia), pt 2.6; Offshore Minerals Act 1994 (Australia), s 315. See also the Australian Foreign Research Vessel Guidelines.
[115] See the 'Act Concerning the Maritime Areas of the Polish Republic and Marine Administration (1991)', arts 28–32 in United Nations, *The Law of the Sea: National Legislation on the Exclusive Economic Zone* (New York, United Nations, 1993) 270.

Recognising these variations in state practice, the United Nations Division on Ocean Affairs and the Law of the Sea in 2010 published a guide to the implementation to the relevant LOSC MSR provisions.[116] The guide, which revised an earlier 1991 publication, takes into account trends in MSR, including marine data acquisition, marine data dissemination and large-scale international collaborative research programmes.[117] It highlights the increasing engagement by coastal states with the MSR regime and the development of legislative frameworks and policy regimes to give effect to the relevant provisions of Part XIII of the LOSC.[118] Nevertheless, the guide contains a general statement that 'States are strongly encouraged to harmonize their national legislation with the provisions of the Convention, and where applicable, relevant agreements and instruments, to ensure the consistent application of those provisions'.[119] Several states have expressed no intention to regulate MSR, such as the Netherlands and the United States. The Proclamation issued by United States President Ronald Reagan in 1983 in relation to the EEZ did not assert jurisdiction over MSR, as the Reagan administration took the view that this would be contrary to the encouragement of MSR both within the United States EEZ and in the EEZs of other states. The United States Department of State requires researching states to apply for advance consent only if the research (a) is conducted within its territorial sea; (b) is conducted within a national marine sanctuary or other marine protected area; (c) involves the study of cetaceans or endangered species; (d) involves the taking of commercial quantities of marine resources; or (e) involves contact with its continental shelf.[120]

VI. Further Reading

Montserrat Gorina-Ysern, *An International Regime for Marine Scientific Research* (Ardsley, Transnational Publishers, 2003)

David Leary, *International Law and the Genetic Resources of the Deep Sea* (Leiden, Martinus Nijhoff, 2007)

Tullio Treves, 'Marine Scientific Research' *Max Planck Encyclopaedia of Public International Law* (2009), at www.mpepil.com.

United Nations, *The Law of the Sea: National Legislation, Regulations and Supporting Documents on Marine Scientific Research in Areas Under National Jurisdiction* (New York, United Nations, 1989)

---

[116] UNDOALOS, *Marine Scientific Research: A Revised Guide to the Implementation of the Relevant Provisions of the United Nations Convention on the Law of the Sea* (2010) at www.un.org/Depts/los/doalos_publications/publicationstexts/msr_guide%202010_final.pdf.

[117] Ibid v.

[118] Ibid 29–35.

[119] Ibid 37 [129].

[120] Roach and Smith, *Excessive Maritime Claims* (n 14) 425–27.

15

Marine Environmental Protection

I. Introduction

One of the signal achievements of UNCLOS III was the development of a global legal architecture for the protection and preservation of the marine environment. Environmental issues had not been a major focus at UNCLOS I or UNCLOS II, and the 1958 Geneva Conventions include few provisions addressing pollution or other threats to marine ecosystems.[1] By contrast, the LOSC establishes a unifying framework for marine environmental protection that seeks to address all sources of marine pollution, incorporates by reference the latest international rules and standards, strengthens the enforcement capacity of port and flag states, and gives coastal states extensive jurisdiction with regard to the protection and preservation of the marine environment within their territorial seas and EEZs. Moreover, the LOSC has provided a legal framework for the implementation of contemporary principles of environmental protection such as the ecosystem approach, the precautionary approach, and ecologically sustainable development.

It was apparent by the time UNCLOS III was convened in 1973 that there was a need for more comprehensive regulation of marine pollution. Major maritime disasters, such as the sinking of the Liberian oil tanker the *Torrey Canyon* off the Cornish coast of England in 1967, and the construction of supertankers with unprecedented shipping capacity, raised public awareness of the risks of accidental pollution. There was also growing appreciation of the less dramatic, but nonetheless insidious, effects of incidental marine pollution from the normal operations of a growing number of merchant vessels plying the seas, from the intentional dumping of nuclear and other wastes in the oceans, and from land-based pollutants such as sewage and industrial and agricultural effluent.

As a result of the LOSC, and a suite of regional and global treaties several of which predate LOSC, the regime for preventing marine pollution and protecting the marine environment is now very detailed and comprehensive. It is also generally judged to be successful, particularly in limiting accidental and operational vessel-source pollution,[2] and in curbing

---

[1] See, eg, 1958 Convention on the High Seas, *Basic Documents* No 10, arts 24, 25.

[2] Gini Mattson, 'MARPOL 73/78 and Annex I: An Assessment of its Effectiveness' (2006) 9 *Journal of International Wildlife Law and Policy* 175; Ronald Mitchell et al, 'International Vessel-Source Oil Pollution' in Oran R Young (ed), *The Effectiveness of International Environmental Regimes: Casual Connections and Behavioral Mechanisms* (Cambridge, MA, MIT Press, 1999) 33.

the intentional dumping of wastes such as radioactive materials.[3] However, it needs to be recognised that ship-borne pollution and dumping remain relatively minor sources of marine pollution by comparison with pollution from land-based industries and from the atmosphere. Taken together, land-based and air pollution account for almost 80 per cent of the marine pollution entering the seas annually.[4] It is in this context where there has been markedly less success in curbing marine pollution.

II. Sources and Type of Marine Pollution

There is a wealth of studies that reveal the nature and extent of marine pollution,[5] although there is a need for more systematic monitoring of global marine environmental health. Recognising this, the 2002 World Summit on Sustainable Development agreed to establish 'a regular process under the United Nations for global reporting and assessment of the state of the marine environment'.[6] The 'World Oceans Assessment' that is being produced as a part of this process will provide the first global integrated marine assessment, and will include an assessment of the sources and effects of marine pollution.[7]

Authoritative assessments of the sources and types of marine pollution are produced by the Joint Group of Experts on the Scientific Aspects of Marine Environmental Protection (GESAMP), an advisory body established in 1969 to provide scientific advice to the United Nations on marine environmental protection. GESAMP has since issued a number of reports that have estimated the volume of pollutants entering the marine environment. In 1990 GESAMP provided a rough estimate of the relative contributions of pollutants from human activities that enter the marine environment. It was concluded that most marine pollution comes from land-based discharges (44 per cent), followed by atmospheric sources (33 per cent), while vessel pollution (12 per cent) and dumping (10 per cent) were much smaller contributors, and each of similar volumes. Offshore production of oil and gas made a minor contribution to marine pollution (at 1 per cent).[8] GESAMP has not updated these estimates; however, there are good reasons to think that the relative contributions of these pollution sources have changed, particularly as more stringent rules have been developed and implemented to control operational pollution and dumping.

In terms of vessel-source pollution, the marine pollutant that has been the main focus of the law of the sea has been oil. Accidental oil spills from tankers such as the *Torrey Canyon*, the *Exxon Valdez* in Prince William Sound, Alaska, in 1989, and the *Prestige* off the Galician coast in 2002, have attracted a great deal of attention. However, such oil spills account for only about 10 per cent of the oil released into the environment each year, and tend

---

[3] Edward L Miles, 'Sea Dumping of Low-Level Radioactive Waste, 1964 to 1982' in Edward L Miles et al (ed), *Environmental Regime Effectiveness: Confronting Theory with Evidence* (Cambridge, MA, MIT Press, 2002) 87.

[4] GESAMP, *The State of the Marine Environment* (Oxford, Blackwell Scientific Publication, 1990) 88; *Oceans and the Law of the Sea: Report of the Secretary General*, UN Doc A/64/66/Add.1 (2009), [225].

[5] See, eg, UNEP and Global Programme of Action, *The State of the Marine Environment: Trends and Processes* (The Hague, UNEP/GPA, 2006).

[6] See UNGA Resolution 57/141 (2002) and UNGA Resolution 60/30 (2005).

[7] See http://www.worldoceanassessment.org/.

[8] GESAMP, *The State of the Marine Environment* (n 4) 88.

to be mostly localised in their impacts. Moreover, although some local effects from these casualties may be evident across many decades, a major proportion of the initial pollution is relatively quickly biodegraded in the marine environment.[9] A much greater volume of oil entering the marine environment comes from discharges from the normal operation of vessels, such as from oil in bilge and ballast water, and oil that is released when operators clean the tanks of oil tankers.

In a 2007 study, GESAMP estimated that the annual input of oil entering the environment was 1,245,200 metric tonnes.[10] Of this, 457,000 tonnes came from vessels, with 163,200 tonnes from accidental releases, and the remainder from operational discharges.[11] Offshore oil and gas installations release relatively small amounts of oil from accidents or in normal operation, at around 17,000 tonnes per year.[12] There have nonetheless been several very large spillages, such as the 1979 *Ixtoc I* incident in the Gulf of Mexico, the 1983 incident involving the Nowruz Oil Field in Iran, the leak from the *West Atlas* wellhead platform in the Timor Sea in 2009 and the *BP Deepwater Horizon* oil spill in the Gulf of Mexico in 2010.[13] Coastal facilities such as refineries release a large volume of oil into the marine environment, at around 115,000 tonnes per annum. There is also a significant amount of oil leaking into the oceans from natural seeps—at 600,000 tonnes, it is close to half of the total average annual input of oil.[14] As seeps are normally old, spread across large areas and release oil and gas at a slow rate, they have far less environmental impact than large, sudden and localised discharges of oil from human activities.

Other chemicals entering the marine environment in smaller concentrations are of more serious concern than oil because of their toxic, persistent and bio-accumulative properties. However, these are not as closely regulated as oil, as they come mainly from land-based sources. Some persistent organic chemicals used in industry and agriculture can cause long-term damage to marine organisms and ecosystems, including by disrupting reproduction and by causing genetic mutations.[15] Toxic heavy metals, such as mercury and lead, though persistent, are now judged to be a less serious concern than originally thought, especially when discharged in the open seas.[16] Similarly, artificial radionuclides, which enter the environment from nuclear power plants and processing facilities that are often located in coastal settings, are understood to cause relatively minor pollution of the marine environment. This is at odds with the public concern surrounding the risk of nuclear pollution, anxiety which was made manifest in the 2002 *MOX Plant* case between Ireland and the United Kingdom relating to the latter's commissioning of a nuclear reprocessing plant on the Cumbrian coast of the Irish Sea.[17] Even the March 2011 accident at the Fukushima Daiichi Nuclear Power Plant in Japan, which resulted in a large discharge of radioactive

[9] GESAMP, *A Sea of Troubles* (The Hague, UNEP, 2001) 7.
[10] GESAMP, *Estimates of Oil Entering the Marine Environment from Sea-Based Activities* (London, IMO, 2007) viii.
[11] Ibid.
[12] Ibid vii.
[13] The *West Atlas* leak was the subject of a Commission of Inquiry established by the Australian Government; the *BP Deepwater Horizon* spill was considered in multiple inquiries, including the National Commission on the BP Deepwater Horizon Oil Spill and Offshore Drilling.
[14] GESAMP, *Estimates of Oil Entering the Marine Environment* (n 10) viii.
[15] GESAMP, *A Sea of Troubles* (n 9) 7.
[16] Ibid.
[17] *MOX Plant (Ireland v United Kingdom)* (provisional measures) (2002) 41 ILM 405.

isotopes in the Pacific marine ecosystem, released radiation at levels below those necessary to cause measurable impacts on populations of marine wildlife (except for seaweed near the point of discharge).[18]

Other pollutants from land-based sources are of more pressing concern. Around a third of the world's population live within 100 kilometres of the coast, and this places tremendous pressure on coastal and estuarine habitats and the broader marine environment, and has led to increased flows of various pollutants. Sewage pollution is identified in the scientific literature as an increasing problem, affecting fisheries, recreation and tourism, and also damaging human health by contaminating seafood and causing increasingly frequent outbreaks of gastrointestinal diseases, including cholera and typhoid.[19] Discharges of sewage, fertilisers and nitrous oxides from burning fossil fuels are the main drivers of the eutrophication (an excess of nutrients). Nutrient-rich waters promote the growth of algae (phytoplankton), which in turn can deplete oxygen levels and generate large 'dead zones' devoid of marine life, such as those regularly seen in the Gulf of Mexico.[20] Algae blooms or 'red tides' may produce toxins that damage coastal fisheries, other marine wildlife and human health.[21] Other toxins in effluent from agriculture and industry such as heavy metals and persistent organic pollutants (such as DDT and PCBs)[22] can have more lingering and diffuse effects, not least because they may accumulate in living organisms and can cause genetic damage.

Land-based pollution also includes garbage and other solid debris, especially plastics, notably polyethylene and polypropylene. Plastics are also discarded from ships, including fishing vessels that regularly dump nylon fishing nets. Although many plastic solids separate into smaller fragments (microplastics), they are not broken down rapidly in the marine environment, and often remain buoyant.[23] Plastics can strangle marine birds, mammals and turtles, block the intestinal tracts of fish and other marine wildlife, smother sea floors, and cause damage to corals.[24] The seriousness of the problem of plastic debris in the marine environment has been highlighted by the discovery of the 'Plastic Vortex'—a large patch of ocean-borne plastics, around the size of Texas and with a volume of around four million tonnes, in the North Central Pacific Ocean.[25] Subsequent studies have shown that this is but one of many ocean zones in which plastic debris is accumulating.[26] Between five and 13 million metric tons of plastic waste enter the world's oceans each year, and it is

---

[18] Jordi Vives I Batlle et al, 'The Impact of the Fukushima Nuclear Accident on Marine Biota: Retrospective Assessment of the First Year and Perspectives' (2014) 487 *Science of the Total Environment* 143.

[19] GESAMP, *A Sea of Troubles* (n 9) 5.

[20] Ibid 8.

[21] Ibid.

[22] DDT, or dichlorodiphenyltrichloroethane, is a synthetic pesticide that has been used since the 1940s to control mosquitoes and other insects that are vectors for disease, and later as an agricultural insecticide. PCBs, or polychlorinated biphenyls, are organic compounds once used in a range of applications including as coolants and in paint, but are now effectively banned by the 2001 Stockholm Convention on Persistent Organic Pollutants.

[23] Julia Resser et al, 'Millimeter-Sized Marine Plastics: A New Pelagic Habitat for Microorganisms and Invertebrates' (2014) 9 *PLoS ONE* e100289.

[24] GESAMP, *Pollution in the Open Oceans: A Review of Assessments and Related Studies* (Nairobi and Paris, UNEP and UNESCO, 2009) 40. See also UNEP, *Marine Litter: a Global Challenge* (Nairobi, UNEP, 2009).

[25] Brian Morton, 'Editorial' (2009) 58 *Marine Pollution Bulletin* 1097, 1097.

[26] Andrés Cózar et al, 'Plastic Debris in the Open Ocean' (2014) 111 *Proceedings of the National Academy of Sciences* 10239.

predicted that the cumulative volume of plastic waste available to enter the world's oceans from land will increase by an order of magnitude by 2025.[27]

Atmospheric pollution accounts for a growing proportion of marine pollution. Sulphur and nitrogen oxides emitted from industry and from transportation not only causes acid rain that is damaging to terrestrial plant life such as forests and crops, but is also absorbed by the oceans. Although it has been the subject of increasingly strict and successful regulation in the Northern Hemisphere since the 1970s, it remains a major problem in China and Asia more generally. One of the largest sources of atmospheric pollution of the marine environment is now carbon dioxide released from human activities, including the burning of fossil fuels, industrial processes (such as the manufacture of cement) and land use change (such as deforestation). The oceans absorb around one-third of the carbon dioxide produced by human activities, and this gives rise to the chemical process known as ocean acidification. Alongside the direct effects of climate change such as rising sea levels and warmer water temperatures which affects ocean circulation and generates ocean dead zones,[28] ocean acidification poses one of the most serious threats to the health of the marine environment.[29]

Another pollutant gaining increasing attention is noise generated by human activities in the marine environment. It is estimated that noise levels in the oceans are ten times higher than they were a few decades ago.[30] Shipping, oil and gas exploration, dredging, fishing and military activities (such as the use of new forms of sonar) generate acoustic pollution that can travel considerable distances, and cause damage to marine wildlife for example by disrupting the natural behaviour of cetaceans which rely on sound to navigate and communicate.[31]

III. The Legal Framework: LOSC and Regional Treaties

A. LOSC

The LOSC supplies the overarching legal framework for marine environmental protection, which is supplemented by a multitude of other treaties and soft-law instruments. As a result of LOSC, and the development of mutually supporting rules in global and regional treaties, there has been a significant shift in the approach to regulating marine pollution. Rather than pollution and dumping being regarded as legitimate and permissible uses of the seas,

---

[27] Jenna R Jambeck et al, 'Plastic Waste Inputs from Land into the Ocean' (2015) 347 *Science* 768.

[28] See Gary Shaffer et al, 'Long-Term Ocean Oxygen Depletion in Response to Carbon Dioxide Emissions from Fossil Fuels' (2009) 2 *Nature Geoscience* 105.

[29] See generally Jean-Pierre Gattuso and Lina Hansson (eds), *Ocean Acidification* (Oxford, Oxford University Press, 2011).

[30] GESAMP, *Pollution in the Open Oceans* (n 24) 39.

[31] Ibid. See also JM Van Dyke, EA Gardner and JR Morgan, 'Whales, Submarines and Active Sonar' (2004) 18 *Ocean Yearbook* 330.

subject to certain restrictions, there is now a presumption that pollution that damages the marine environment is, or should be, prohibited.[32]

The core provisions of the LOSC relevant to marine environmental protection are found in Part XII; however, there are references made throughout the Convention to the need to protect the marine environment. There are also obvious linkages to the provisions of the LOSC addressing marine living resources. As ITLOS observed in the *Southern Bluefin Tuna* cases, 'the conservation of the living resources of the sea is an element in the protection and preservation of the marine environment'.[33] The Preamble and 46 of the LOSC's 320 articles make some mention of marine environmental protection. Of pivotal importance is Article 1(1)(4), which provides a definition of marine pollution:

> 'pollution of the marine environment' means the introduction by man, directly or indirectly, of substances or energy into the marine environment, including estuaries, which results or is likely to result in such deleterious effects as harm to living resources and marine life, hazards to human health, hindrance to marine activities, including fishing and other legitimate uses of the sea, impairment of quality for use of sea water and reduction of amenities.

This formulation is significant in two key respects. First, it is inclusive of all sources of marine pollution. Hence it encompasses not only the traditional concern of marine pollution control—vessel-source pollution—but also pollution from land-based activities and from the atmosphere. Secondly, it adopts an open definition to include any type of pollution where it results in harmful effects. This allows the LOSC to have ongoing relevance as new pollutants, such as acoustic pollution, are identified by the marine scientific community, and become issues of concern for policy makers.

Article 192, the first provision in Part XII, establishes the fundamental duty of parties to protect and preserve the marine environment. This duty is elevated above the sovereign right of states to exploit their natural resources, as Article 193 provides that this right must be exercised by states 'in accordance with their duty to protect and preserve the marine environment'. The reach of the Article 192 obligation is significant in that it applies to the entirety of the marine environment. This is confirmed in Article 194(1) which provides that states shall take, individually or jointly as appropriate, all measures necessary to prevent, reduce and control pollution of the marine environment from any source. Article 194(2) provides further that states are to ensure that activities under their jurisdiction or control do not cause damage to other states or their environment, or that pollution spreads beyond the areas where they exercise sovereign rights. The Seabed Disputes Chamber of ITLOS in *Responsibilities and Obligations of States Sponsoring Persons and Entities with Respect to Activities in the Area (Seabed Mining Advisory Opinion)*[34] observed that Article 194(2) is an example of a 'due diligence' obligation, requiring states to take reasonable and appropriate measures to prevent damage to the marine environment.[35] The obligation in Article 194(2) expands upon the customary obligation of states not knowingly to permit the use of their

---

[32] Catherine Redgwell, 'From Permission to Prohibition: The 1982 Convention on the Law of the Sea and Protection of the Marine Environment' in David Freestone, Richard Barnes and David M Ong (eds), *The Law of the Sea: Progress and Prospects* (Oxford, Oxford University Press, 2006) 180.

[33] *Southern Bluefin Tuna (New Zealand v Japan; Australia v Japan)* (provisional measures) (1999) 117 ILR 148, [70].

[34] (2011) 50 ILM 458.

[35] Ibid, [113].

territory in such a way as to cause serious injury by pollution in the territory of another state, as expressed in the *Trail Smelter* case,[36] by incorporating the responsibility referred to in the 1972 Stockholm Declaration[37] and 1992 Rio Declaration[38] to prevent damage to the environment of areas beyond national jurisdiction.[39] Additionally, Article 194(3) specifies the need for measures to address all sources of pollution, to minimise release of toxic substances, pollution from vessels and pollution from installations. Special emphasis is placed by Article 194(5) on the importance of protecting and preserving rare or fragile ecosystems, and the habitat of threatened marine species.[40]

In order to achieve the goal of marine environmental protection, Part XII requires states to cooperate on a global and, as appropriate, regional basis, directly or through competent international organisations in formulating international rules, standards, and recommended practices and procedures.[41] In the 2002 *MOX Plant* case, ITLOS recognised that 'the duty to cooperate is a fundamental principle in the prevention of pollution of the marine environment under Part XII of the Convention and general international law'.[42] It was on this basis that ITLOS went on to prescribe provisional measures under Article 290 of the LOSC requiring Ireland and the United Kingdom to enter into consultations to exchange additional information with regard to possible consequences for the Irish Sea arising out of the commissioning of the MOX plant, monitor the risks or the effects of the operation of the MOX plant for the Irish Sea, and devise measures to prevent pollution of the marine environment which might result from the operation of the MOX plant.[43]

The rather generic provisions in Part XII relating to cooperation on matters of marine environmental protection are supplemented by more specific articles addressing pollution from land-based sources, from seabed activities subject to national jurisdiction, pollution from activities in the deep seabed (the Area), pollution from vessels, and pollution from the atmosphere.[44] What these seek to do is to incorporate by reference the very latest 'internationally agreed, rules, standards and recommended practices and procedures' established through 'competent international organizations'. This is a classic illustration of the framework nature of the LOSC. What it achieves is the application, via the LOSC, of standards adopted through global pollution control conventions and soft-law instruments under the auspices of the IMO and other competent international organisations, such as the International Atomic Energy Agency which has adopted regulations relating to the safe transport of nuclear materials.[45]

---

[36] *Trail Smelter (Canada/United States)* (1938 and 1941) 3 RIAA 1911.

[37] Declaration of the United Nations Conference on the Human Environment, UN Doc A/CONF.48/14/Rev 1 (1973), Principle 21.

[38] United Nations Declaration on Environment and Development, UN Doc A/CONF.151/5/Rev.1 (1992), Principle 2. See Leslie-Anne Duvic-Paoli and Jorge E Viñuales, 'Principle 2: Prevention' in Jorge E Viñuales (ed), *The Rio Declaration on Environment and Development. A Commentary* (Oxford, Oxford University Press, 2015) 107.

[39] For a comprehensive analysis of the duties applicable to protect the marine environment of the high seas and the Area see Robin Warner, *Protecting the Oceans Beyond National Jurisdiction: Strengthening the International Law Framework* (Leiden, Martinus Nijhoff, 2009).

[40] LOSC, art 194(5).

[41] Ibid art 197.

[42] *MOX Plant (Ireland v United Kingdom)* (provisional measures) (2002) 41 ILM 405, [82].

[43] Ibid [89].

[44] LOSC, arts 207–12.

[45] See, eg, 2009 IAEA Regulations for the Safe Transport of Radioactive Material.

The IMO was established by the 1948 Convention on the International Maritime Organization[46] as a specialised agency of the United Nations. Its primary task is to develop a detailed set of regulations for international shipping, addressing efficiency of navigation, maritime safety, prevention of marine pollution, and maritime security. These regulations are developed through formal diplomatic conferences convened by the IMO, which can lead to the adoption of conventions and protocols, of which there are now 53 (see Table 15.1, below, for the key IMO instruments).[47] It also takes place through the work of the organisation's specialised committees, particularly the Maritime Safety Committee, the Legal Committee, and the Marine Environment Protection Committee, which may make recommendations to the IMO's executive body, the IMO Council, which comprises 40 elected members representing key maritime states, including those with the largest interest in providing shipping services.[48] The Council then refers regulations to the IMO's plenary body, the IMO Assembly, which may adopt them. While not themselves legally binding, such recommendations are made mandatory if they relate to subjects over which the LOSC defers to the IMO for formulating internationally agreed rules and standards. In the same way, a widely ratified convention adopted under IMO auspices become binding on parties to the LOSC, even when these states are not parties to the instrument concerned.[49] As Boyle has noted, if the objective of Part XII is 'to bring about the widest possible application of international rules, this conclusion seems inescapable'.[50]

B. Regional Treaties

Another category of framework treaties that seek to address marine pollution in its various forms and sources are regional agreements. In several provisions the LOSC makes reference to the need to adopt 'regional rules', and this has been achieved primarily through regional arrangements under the umbrella of the UNEP's Regional Seas Programme (RSP). The RSP was established in the wake of the 1972 United Nations Conference on the Human Environment and establishes action plans, many of which are made binding through conventions or protocols, to address pollution and other environmental management issues.[51] There are 13 RSPs covering the Black Sea, Wider Caribbean, East Asian Seas, Eastern Africa, South Asian Seas, Persian Gulf, Mediterranean, North-East Pacific, North-West Pacific, Red Sea and Gulf of Aden, South-East Pacific, Pacific, and Western Africa. There are also five areas regarded as 'partners' to the RSP: the Antarctic, Arctic, Baltic Sea, Caspian Sea and the North East-Atlantic. Notably there is no regional seas convention for South East Asia.

In relation to enclosed or semi-enclosed seas, which are defined in Article 122 of the LOSC, as gulfs, basins or seas surrounded by two or more states and connected to another sea or the ocean by a narrow outlet, the LOSC specifically requires the states concerned to coordinate measures for the protection and preservation of the marine environment.[52]

---

[46] *Basic Documents* No 8.
[47] These conventions and protocols are listed on the IMO website: www.imo.org.
[48] 1948 Convention on the International Maritime Organization, art 17.
[49] Alan Boyle, 'Marine Pollution Under the Law of the Sea Convention' (1985) 79 *AJIL* 347, 356.
[50] Ibid.
[51] See www.unep.org/regionalseas/.
[52] LOSC, art 123.

Table 15.1: Status of Select IMO Conventions as at 27 April 2015

Instrument	Entry into force	No of parties	Percentage of world tonnage
IMO Convention	17 Mar 1958	171	96.53
SOLAS	25 May 1980	162	98.60
SOLAS Protocol 1978	1 May 1981	119	96.86
SOLAS Protocol 1988	3 Feb 2000	105	95.03
Load Lines (LL) 1966	21 Jul 1968	161	98.39
LL Protocol 1988	3 Feb 2000	98	95.22
COLREGs	15 Jul 1977	156	98.59
Standards of Training, Certification and Watchkeeping (STCW) 1978	28 Apr 1984	158	98.62
Search and Rescue (SAR) 1979	22 Jun 1985	105	82.13
MARPOL 73/78 (Annex I/II)	2 Oct 1983	153	98.52
MARPOL 73/78 (Annex III)	1 Jul 1992	141	97.79
MARPOL 73/78 (Annex IV)	27 Sep 2003	134	90.74
MARPOL 73/78 (Annex V)	31 Dec 1988	147	98.03
MARPOL Protocol 1997 (Annex VI)	19 May 2005	80	95.23
London Dumping Convention (LC) 1972	30 Aug 1975	87	61.76
LC Protocol 1996	24 Mar 2006	45	36.60
Intervention on High Seas in Cases of Oil Pollution (INTERVENTION) 1969	6 May 1975	88	74.38
INTERVENTION Protocol 1973	30 Mar 1983	56	51.48
Civil Liability (CLC) 1969	19 Jun 1975	35	2.70
CLC Protocol 1976	8 Apr 1981	53	59.29
CLC Protocol 1992	30 May 1996	133	96.70
Fund For Compensation of Oil Pollution Damage (FUND) Protocol 1976	22 Nov 1994	31	49.69
FUND Protocol 1992	30 May 1996	114	94.16
FUND Protocol 2003	3 Mar 2005	31	18.26
Bunkers Convention 2001	21 Nov 2008	78	91.46
Anti-Fouling Systems Convention 2001	17 Sep 2008	70	84.85
Ballast Water Management Convention 2004	Not yet in force	44	32.86

Source: www.imo.org

Agreements for such enclosed or semi-enclosed seas have been concluded for the Baltic,[53] the Black Sea,[54] the Persian Gulf,[55] and the Mediterranean.[56] Regional cooperation in these settings is essential because of the ecological distinctiveness of enclosed and semi-enclosed seas, and their greater susceptibility to pollution problems. Beyond these obvious subjects of regional cooperation, agreements have also been adopted in other areas where there is a sufficient level of political integration among states to sustain a regional approach to pollution and other environmental management challenges. Examples include the 1983 Convention for the Protection and Development of the Marine Environment of the Wider Caribbean and the 1986 Convention for the Protection of the Natural Resources of the Environment of the South Pacific Region.

These and other regional seas agreements have seldom stood still, and have been supplemented over time by protocols addressing matters such as environmental impact assessment, transboundary movement of hazardous materials, dumping from ships and aircraft, pollution from land-based sources, pollution from maritime casualties, and pollution from seabed activities. As a result, many regional regimes have evolved in a dynamic way to address new environmental threats and to incorporate contemporary principles of oceans governance as called for in Agenda 21,[57] adopted at the 1992 United Nations Conference on Environment and Development in Rio. Agenda 21 emphasised the need for a precautionary and anticipatory rather than reactive approach, one which integrates marine environmental protection objectives into social and economic policies, and which addresses marine ecosystems in a holistic manner, addressing pollution, resource management and habitat protection objectives.

Two main approaches have been taken in the revision of regional regimes. The first has involved the conclusion of a new and more comprehensive treaty. An example is the 1992 Convention for the Protection of the Marine Environment and Coastal Region of the Baltic Sea Area (Helsinki Convention),[58] which replaced an earlier 1974 convention. While it is formally outside the UNEP RSP, this convention nonetheless provides an example of an innovative regional arrangement that has been reshaped to incorporate contemporary standards in an aim to achieve the ecological restoration of the Baltic Sea. The Convention requires parties to apply the precautionary and polluter pays principles;[59] eliminate the introduction of harmful substances from land-based sources;[60] engage in environmental impact assessment of activities or projects which are likely to cause significant adverse impact on the marine environment of the Baltic Sea;[61] prevent pollution from ships;[62]

---

[53] 1992 Convention for the Protection of the Marine Environment of the Baltic Sea Area, *Basic Documents* No 49.

[54] 1992 Convention on the Protection of the Black Sea Against Pollution.

[55] 1978 Regional Convention for Cooperation on the Protection of the Marine Environment from Pollution.

[56] 1976 Convention for the Protection of the Marine Environment and the Coastal Region of the Mediterranean, *Basic Documents* No 23.

[57] *Basic Documents* No 48.

[58] *Basic Documents* No 49.

[59] Helsinki Convention, arts 3(2), 3(4).

[60] Ibid art 6.

[61] Ibid art 7.

[62] Ibid art 8.

prohibit dumping[63] and incineration;[64] take measures to conserve natural habitats and biological diversity and protect ecological processes;[65] and make information available to the public.[66] It also establishes a commission, the Baltic Marine Environment Protection Commission, to monitor continuously the implementation of the Convention.[67]

The second approach has involved the conclusion of implementing protocols, and this is the approach taken in most of the UNEP RSP agreements. An example is the 1995 Convention for the Protection of the Marine Environment and the Coastal Region of the Mediterranean.[68] This convention updated a 1978 agreement that had focussed only on pollution, but unlike the Helsinki Convention remains an umbrella regime that includes few specific rules and standards. These are instead addressed in protocols addressing dumping,[69] land-based marine pollution,[70] pollution from the exploration and exploitation of seabed mineral resources,[71] protected areas and biological diversity,[72] transboundary movement of hazardous wastes,[73] pollution from ships and in cases of emergency,[74] and integrated coastal zone management.[75]

Because of such developments, there has been a significant shift from the primary and original focus of the LOSC and regional agreements on preventing polluting to more integrated regional oceans management.[76] Whereas in other fields of international environmental law there has been a concern that the adoption of regional agreements might lead to the phenomenon of 'fragmentation' in which universal environmental protection standards are weakened,[77] quite the opposite has occurred in relation to marine pollution where there has been a strong integrative tendency, while addressing the particular ecological circumstances of individual regions.[78] This is in large part due to the coordinating role played by UNEP through the RSP, and this is a function that could be further enhanced to prevent conflicts between environmental rules on regional and global scales.[79]

---

[63] Ibid art 11.

[64] Ibid art 10.

[65] Ibid art 15.

[66] Ibid art 17.

[67] Ibid arts 19–23.

[68] *Basic Documents* No 23.

[69] 1976 Protocol for the Prevention and Elimination of Pollution of the Mediterranean Sea by Dumping from Ships and Aircraft or Incineration at Sea, *Basic Documents* No 24.

[70] 1980 Protocol for the Protection of the Mediterranean Sea against Pollution from Land-Based Sources and Activities, *Basic Documents* No 25.

[71] 1994 Protocol for the Protection of the Mediterranean Sea against Pollution Resulting from Exploration and Exploitation of the Continental Shelf and the Seabed and Its Subsoil, *Basic Documents* No 26.

[72] 1995 Protocol Concerning Specially Protected Areas and Biological Diversity in the Mediterranean, *Basic Documents* No 27.

[73] 1996 Protocol on the Prevention of Pollution of the Mediterranean Sea by Transboundary Movements of Hazardous Wastes and Their Disposal, *Basic Documents* No 28.

[74] 2002 Protocol Concerning Cooperation in Preventing Pollution from Ships, and in Cases of Emergency, Combating Pollution of the Mediterranean Sea, *Basic Documents* No 29.

[75] 2008 Protocol on Integrated Coastal Zone Management in the Mediterranean, *Basic Documents* No 30.

[76] Alan Boyle, 'Further Development of the 1982 Convention on the Law of the Sea: Mechanisms for Change' in David Freestone, Richard Barnes and David M Ong (eds), *The Law of the Sea: Progress and Prospects* (Oxford, Oxford University Press, 2006) 41, 53–54.

[77] See generally Tim Stephens, 'Multiple International Courts and the "Fragmentation" of International Environmental Law' (2006) 25 *Australian Year Book of International Law* 227.

[78] Boyle, 'Further Development of the 1982 Convention on the Law of the Sea' (n 76) 53.

[79] Rüdiger Wolfrum and Nele Matz, *Conflicts in International Environmental Law* (Berlin, Springer-Verlag, 2003) 191.

IV. Operational Vessel-Source Pollution

Shipping introduces many pollutants to the marine environment, as a result of the normal operation of vessels, and also from marine casualties following collisions and groundings. The shipping industry has grown immensely in the last 60 years, in line with increasing world trade. In 2012 global seaborne trade exceeded 9 billion tons for the first time, and carried approximately 80 per cent of global merchandise trade.[80] Without improvements in international rules and standards addressing the construction and operation of vessels and safety at sea, this growth would inevitably have led to substantial increases in volumes of pollution being released into the marine environment.

A. Operational and Accidental Vessel Pollution Distinguished

Operational vessel-source pollution occurs when substances are discharged from the normal working of vessels, or from seafaring practices, such as when fuel oil is released from engine rooms, when there are discharges of sewage or ballast water, or when cargo holds for substances carried in bulk are cleaned. Depending on the type of cargo being carried, these wastes can be problematic, as is the case with oil-tankers which once used to be cleaned by flushing with seawater, with the resulting effluent then released into the ocean. Improved cleaning methods such as the 'load on top' and 'crude oil washing' systems adopted from the 1960s onwards have all but eliminated this problem. The load on top system involves washing oil compartments with seawater, but then pumping the oily mixture into a slops tank where the oil floats to the surface, allowing the water below to be safely pumped into the sea. The crude oil washing method uses the cargo itself as a solvent to clean oily residues from the walls of tanker compartments, and is now mandatory for oil tankers 20,000 tonnage and above.[81]

B. LOSC and the IMO

The LOSC addresses vessel-source pollution in Article 211, a lengthy provision that serves two main purposes. First, it requires states acting through a 'competent international organization', which in this context means the IMO,[82] to 'establish international rules and standards to prevent, reduce and control pollution … from vessels'.[83] Secondly, it establishes a sophisticated jurisdictional framework so that such standards can be effectively enforced not only by flag states but also port states and coastal states. Flag states cannot always be relied upon to apply pollution control standards to their vessels; shipping operators understand this and will seek to utilise so called 'flags of convenience' or

---

[80] *Oceans and the Law of the Sea: Report of the Secretary General*, UN Doc A/69/71/Add.1 (2014), [19].
[81] 1973 International Convention for the Prevention of Pollution from Ships, as Modified by the Protocol of 1978 Relating Thereto, *Basic Documents* No 21, Annex I, reg 13(6).
[82] *Virginia Commentaries*, vol 4, 201.
[83] LOSC, art 211(1).

'open registers', particularly of states where the regulations are least strict and operating costs are the lowest.[84] Under Article 91 of the LOSC, states may fix conditions for the grant of nationality to ships, and there must be a genuine link between the state and the ship. However, this nexus will be satisfied by the fact of bare registration alone, and need not be accompanied by more substantive links between the vessel and the flag state.[85] In *M/V Virginia G*, ITLOS found that

> [O]nce a ship is registered, the flag State is required, under article 94 of the Convention, to exercise effective jurisdiction and control over that ship in order to ensure that it operates in accordance with generally accepted international regulations, procedures and practices. This is the meaning of 'genuine link'.[86]

The majority of merchant vessels by tonnage are now registered in open registries, including in landlocked states such as Bolivia and Mongolia. This means that there has been a significant shift within the IMO, whereby flag of convenience states have gained influence at the expense of the ship-owning states, which are predominantly Western European. This has had an impact on voting within IMO bodies, including the Marine Environment Protection Committee, where two-thirds of parties, representing at least 50 per cent gross tonnage of the world's merchant fleet, are required to agree to adopt new, or amend existing, pollution control regulations. In some cases it has slowed the adoption of stricter standards, as seen by the length of time it has taken for some IMO instruments to enter into force. On average it takes around five years for IMO conventions to gain sufficient ratifications to become operative.

C. International Standards

The primary source of international standards for controlling incidental vessel-source pollution is MARPOL,[87] which replaced the earlier 1954 International Convention for the Prevention of Pollution of the Sea by Oil (OILPOL). The ambitious objective of MARPOL is 'to achieve the complete elimination of intentional pollution of the marine environment by oil and other harmful substances and the minimization of accidental discharge of such substances'.[88] It applies to the discharge of all harmful substances, except those from dumping, seabed exploration and exploitation, and from legitimate scientific research into pollution abatement.[89] MARPOL is the most important, but not the only, multilateral convention under IMO auspices designed to reduce pollution from ships. Among these is SOLAS, which incorporates detailed provisions addressing matters such as the stowage, packing, marking, labelling and documentation for dangerous goods.

The structure of MARPOL combines a relatively compact convention, which contains provisions dealing with national laws, certificates, inspections, and enforcement of

---

[84] See generally Boleslaw Adam Boczek, *Flags of Convenience: An International Legal Study* (Cambridge, MA, Harvard University Press, 1962).
[85] *M/V Saiga (No 2) (St Vincent and the Grenadines v Guinea)* (merits) (1999) 120 ILR 143, [83].
[86] *M/V Virginia G (Panama v Guinea Bissau)* (2014) 53 ILM 1164.
[87] *Basic Documents* No 21.
[88] MARPOL, Preamble, 4th Recital.
[89] Ibid art 2(3)(b).

standards, with six detailed annexes: the Prevention of Pollution by Oil (Annex I), the Control of Pollution by Noxious Liquid Substances (Annex II), the Prevention of Pollution by Harmful Substances in Packaged Form (Annex III), the Prevention of Pollution by Sewage from Ships (Annex IV), the Prevention of Pollution by Garbage from Ships (Annex V) and the Prevention of Air Pollution from Ships (Annex VI). Of these, only Annexes I and II are mandatory.

When it appeared that MARPOL might never enter into force because of the low number of ratifications by major maritime states, a 1978 protocol introduced an amendment making only Annex I mandatory, with Annex II to become binding three years after the protocol had entered into force. In addition to the 1978 protocol, the MARPOL regime has been subject to extensive amendment. The core of the MARPOL regime has achieved close to universal acceptance. As of 27 April 2015 there were 153 parties to MARPOL, and therefore also to Annexes I and II, representing 99 per cent of merchant tonnage. The other annexes, which are now all in force, have not been quite so widely ratified. Nonetheless, with participation rates of 98 per cent of world tonnage for Annex III, 91 per cent for Annex IV, 98 per cent for Annex V and 95 per cent for Annex VI, these additional standards bind a very substantial majority of shipping states.

MARPOL is a more comprehensive set of rules and standards than that found in OILPOL, with Annex I more far-reaching and including technical regulations that limit discharges of oil from machinery and cargo spaces. For instance, Regulation 34 specifies that any discharge into the sea of oil or oily mixtures from the cargo area of an oil tanker is prohibited unless it meets six strict conditions which include that the tanker is not within a special area,[90] is more than 50 nm from the nearest coast, and is proceeding en route, and the instantaneous rate of discharge of oil content does not exceed 20 litres per nautical mile. Rather than discharging oily wastes at sea, vessels are instead to take advantage of reception facilities which parties are required to provide at oil loading terminals, repair ports, and other ports in which ships have oily residues to discharge.

Annex I also contains regulations addressing construction standards for the cargo area of oil tankers, which require double hulls for new and most existing vessels. The high risk attending the use of single-hull tankers was highlighted by the *Exxon Valdez* disaster, and more recently by the *Erika* and *Prestige* incidents. Following the latter two casualties, the IMO moved to phase out single-hull tankers through revisions to Annex I,[91] so that from 2010 all oil tankers were required to have double hulls. This became necessary because the European Union moved unilaterally to ban single-hull tankers from the ports of EU members.[92] Regular amendments to the MARPOL regime have ensured that it is highly responsive, and have been made possible because of the tacit acceptance amendment procedure, which deems amendments to be accepted unless they are objected to by not

---

[90] Ibid Annex I, reg 1(11) defines 'special area' as 'a sea area where for recognized technical reasons … the adoption of special mandatory methods for the prevention of sea pollution by oil is required', and lists enclosed and semi-enclosed seas (such as the Mediterranean, the Baltic, the Black Sea and the Red Sea) along with other sensitive areas such the Antarctic.

[91] See ibid Annex I, reg 20.

[92] See Alan Khee-Jin Tan, *Vessel-Source Marine Pollution: The Law and Politics of International Regulation* (Cambridge, Cambridge University Press, 2006) 139–55.

less than one third of the parties, or by the parties the combined merchant fleets of which constitute not less than 50 per cent of the gross tonnage of the world's merchant fleet.[93]

The five other annexes to MARPOL contain pollution control standards, tailored to the particular pollutants to which they relate. As with Annex I, these address technical, techno-logical, and operational practices. Annex II sets out measures for the control of pollution by noxious liquid substances carried in bulk. A revised Annex II entered into force in 2007, and sets out a four-category system, with the most hazardous substances (category X) subject to a complete prohibition on discharge, while less hazardous substances (categories Y and Z) may be discharged in limited quantities in certain circumstances, and a final category of 'other substances' (harmless products such as clay slurry, and glucose solution) that may be discharged when cleaning tanks, or releasing bilge and ballast water. One significant result of these revisions is that vegetable oils (such as palm oil, used in the food industry, and also as a biofuel) are placed in category Y, and must be transported in double-hull chemical tankers.

Annex III, the first optional annex, contains regulations for the prevention of pollution by harmful substances in packaged form. It includes standards concerning packaging, mark-ing, labelling, documentation, stowage and quantity limits. Harmful substances are those defined as marine pollutants in the International Maritime Dangerous Goods Code, first adopted by the IMO in 1965 and subsequently updated, which lists several hundred types of dangerous goods.[94] No jettisoning of harmful substances in packaged form from vessels is permitted under Annex III, except where this is necessary for the purpose of securing the safety of the ship or saving life at sea.[95]

In Annex IV there are regulations relating to sewage which apply to ships undertaking international voyages, which are 400 gross tonnage or above, or that are certified to carry more than 15 persons. It requires these ships to be equipped with a sewage treatment plant, a sewage disinfecting and comminuting (that is diminishing or minimising) system, or a sewage holding tank. Sewage discharges from ships are required to be limited. More than three nm from the nearest land, sewage may be discharged at a moderate rate if it is from an approved sewage treatment plant, or has been comminuted and disinfected.[96] Beyond 12 nm ships may discharge untreated sewage.[97] Parties undertake to ensure the provision of facilities at ports and terminals for the reception of sewage, without causing undue delay to ships.[98]

The prevention of pollution of the sea by garbage from ships is addressed in Annex V. 'Garbage' here means all kinds of food, domestic and operational refuse generated during the normal operation of the ship.[99] The disposal into the sea of all plastics, from synthetic fishing nets to plastic garbage bags, is prohibited.[100] Dunnage (that is wood and matting holding cargo in position), lining and packing materials that will float are to be disposed as

---

[93] MARPOL, art 16(f)(ii)–(iii).

[94] Ibid annex III, reg 1. See further Meltem Deniz Güner-Özbek, *The Carriage of Dangerous Goods by Sea* (Berlin, Springer-Verlag, 2007) 16ff.

[95] MARPOL, annex III, reg 7.

[96] Ibid annex IV, reg 8.

[97] Ibid.

[98] Ibid annex IV, reg 10.

[99] Ibid annex V, reg 1.

[100] Ibid annex V, reg 3.

far as practicable from the nearest land, but not less than 25 nm. Victual wastes and other garbage, including paper, rags, glass, metal, bottles, crockery and the like, may be disposed of no less than 12 nm from the nearest land. In special areas such as the Mediterranean and the Gulfs area, the disposal of all garbage except food wastes is prohibited.[101]

The final set of regulations for vessel-source pollution is found in Annex VI which addresses air pollution from ships. Annex VI was added to MARPOL by a specific protocol in 1997, and set limits on the volumes of sulphur oxide and nitrous oxide that may be emitted from ship engines, and prohibits the release of ozone depleting substances. Sulphur and nitrogen emissions from vessels have historically been high because of the poor grade heavy fuel oil used in the engines of ocean-going ships. A new chapter adopted in 2011 introduced new technical and operational measures to reduce greenhouse gas emissions from shipping. Shipping is one of the most fuel-efficient forms of transport, but the growth of the merchant fleet means that shipping emissions accounts for around 2.7 per cent of total global carbon dioxide emissions, and shipping emissions are predicted to rise by up to 300 per cent by 2050.[102] As with aviation emissions, these emissions from the use of bunker fuel are not included in the targets agreed under the 1997 Kyoto Protocol to the 1992 United Nations Framework Convention on Climate Change.

As extensive as the standards in MARPOL are, they have not addressed all sources of incidental pollution. In particular, it is widely recognised that more needs to be done to control releases of ballast water, which is taken on board ships to aid stability. To this end, the IMO concluded the 2004 International Convention for the Control and Management of Ships' Ballast Water and Sediments as a stand-alone instrument (in preference to the original proposal to add a further Annex to MARPOL). This treaty, which has not yet entered into force, is designed to reduce the movement of harmful invasive aquatic organisms through ballast water.[103] It is estimated that around 10 billion tons of ballast water are transferred globally each year, and that more than 3,000 species of plants and animals are relocated through this process daily.[104] There are numerous examples where the failure to adopt ballast water management measures have resulted in the transboundary movement of harmful species, including microorganisms such as various strains of cholera, and animals such as American comb jelly which has pushed anchovy and sprat fisheries close to extinction in the Black and Azov Seas.

Another field where there have been efforts to tighten the rules relating to operational pollution is in relation to vessel anti-fouling systems. Anti-fouling paints are applied to the hulls of vessels to prevent the attachment of organisms such as algae and molluscs; however, the contents of these paints are often highly toxic. The 2001 International Convention on the Control of Harmful Anti-fouling Systems on Ships, which entered into force in 2008, aims to minimise this problem. Under the Convention, ships are not permitted to apply or reapply biocidal organotin compounds (that is chemicals based on tin and hydrocarbons) unless they are covered by a coating that will prevent them leaching into the sea. The objective of the Convention is the complete phase out of organotins, and their substitution with safe alternatives.

---

[101] Ibid annex V, reg 5.

[102] *Oceans and the Law of the Sea: Report of the Secretary General*, UN Doc A/64/66/Add.1 (2009), [349].

[103] As at 27 April 2015, the Convention had 44 parties, representing 33% of gross merchant shipping tonnage—just shy of the 35% required under art 18(1) for the Convention to enter into force.

[104] *Oceans and the Law of the Sea: Report of the Secretary General*, UN Doc A/64/66/Add.1 (2009), [244].

D. The MARPOL Jurisdictional Framework

MARPOL relies on a mixture of flag state, port state, and coastal state jurisdiction for the enforcement of its pollution control standards. In giving competence to port and coastal states, it marked an important development from the traditional reliance on flag state jurisdiction.

i. Flag States

At customary international law, flag states enjoy the capacity to prescribe laws relating to pollution control applicable to their vessels, wherever those vessels may be. They may also enforce these laws not only in their ports and in their territorial seas, but also on the high seas. Flag state capacity and flag state responsibility are of course quite different things; the existence of an entitlement to exercise jurisdiction over vessels is no guarantee that this competence will utilised. MARPOL seeks to strengthen flag state duties, requiring flag states to adopt laws to ensure that the regulations are extended to vessels that it registers.[105] Any violation of MARPOL, wherever it occurs, is to be prohibited, sanctions are to be established under the law of the flag state and in the event of a breach criminal proceedings must be taken.[106] The penalties are to be adequate in severity to discourage violations of MARPOL, and are to be equally severe irrespective of where the violations occur.[107] Hence flag states must apply and enforce sanctions of equal gravity to pollution violations in whatever maritime space they occur, including on the high seas. Additional flag state duties relate to the inspection of vessels and the issuing of certificates. Under MARPOL, Annex I, flag states are required to ensure that oil tankers of 150 gross tonnage and above, and every other ship of 400 gross tonnage and above, is subject to initial and then periodic surveys of the structure, equipment, systems, fittings and arrangement of the vessel.[108] An International Oil Pollution Prevention Certificate is to be issued after an initial or renewal survey.[109]

ii. Port States

The inspection and certification rules form the basis of the system of port state jurisdiction under MARPOL. A certificate issued in accordance with MARPOL is to be accepted by other parties as having the same validity as a certificate issued by them.[110] While in a port or at a terminal a ship required to hold a certificate is subject to inspection by port state authorities.[111] Such inspection should be limited to verifying that there is a valid certificate on board, unless there are clear grounds for believing that the condition of the ship, or its equipment, does not correspond substantially with the particulars of the certificate.[112] In such a case, or if the ship does not carry a valid certificate, then the port state must ensure that the ship does not sail until it can proceed to sea without presenting an unreasonable threat of harm to the marine environment.[113] A similar requirement applies where port

[105] MARPOL, art 3.
[106] Ibid arts 4(1), 4(2).
[107] Ibid art 4(4).
[108] Ibid Annex I, reg 6.
[109] Ibid Annex I, reg 7.
[110] Ibid art 5(1).
[111] Ibid art 5(2).
[112] Ibid.
[113] Ibid.

state inspection reveals clear grounds for believing that the master or crew are not familiar with essential shipboard procedures relating to the prevention of pollution.[114] When inspection detects violation of MARPOL or its Annexes, then the port state is to forward a report to the flag state, which must then take action.[115]

In principle, the system of port state control should be the optimal approach for detecting violations of the MARPOL regime; regardless of its flag, a vessel will need to call at ports to load and unload cargo. Moreover, it entails the effective extension of MARPOL standards to the vessels of non-parties because MARPOL requires parties to apply the regime in such a way that no more favourable treatment is given to the ships registered by states that are not parties to the regime.[116] Hence port states must apply MARPOL standards to all ships calling at their ports or terminals, a broad requirement but one which is entirely consistent with the plenary capacity of port states to set conditions on the entry into their ports.

In recent years the IMO has encouraged the adoption of a raft of soft-law Memoranda of Understanding (MoU) relating to port state inspection in maritime regions throughout the world's oceans. These are designed to lift the rate and rigour of inspections to ensure that vessels do not evade MARPOL rules by calling at ports where the chance of being inspected is small, or where the inspection regime is lax. Port state control MoUs have been signed in respect of all sea areas globally: Europe and the North Atlantic (the Paris MoU); Asia and the Pacific (Tokyo MoU); Latin America (Viña del Mar MoU); the Caribbean (Caribbean MoU); West and Central Africa (Abuja MoU); the Black Sea (Black Sea MoU); the Mediterranean (Mediterranean MoU); the Indian Ocean (Indian Ocean MoU); and the Gulf Region (Riyadh MoU). In Europe, the Paris MoU is complemented by a binding measure, a European Community Directive of 1995 on Port State Control of Shipping.[117]

The number of inspections being carried out under these MoU arrangements is considerable. In 2013 there were 17,687 inspections by the 27 members of the Paris MoU, which identified 49,074 deficiencies and gave rise to 668 detentions (around half as many as in 2008).[118] For three successive years there has been no increase in the number of deficiencies detected. The worst-performing flag states were United Republic of Tanzania, Honduras, Dominica and Togo, whilst the best performing were France, Norway, Sweden, Denmark and Italy.[119] Overall, the average detention rate appears to be stabilised, and is around four per cent of inspections.[120]

E. The LOSC Jurisdictional Framework

i. Flag States

Under the LOSC, the jurisdictional competence of flag states was not changed; they have always enjoyed the capacity to pass pollution control laws for their vessels. However, the

---

[114] See ibid Annex I, reg 11(1), and Annex II, reg 9(1).
[115] Ibid art 6.
[116] Ibid art 5(4).
[117] *Basic Documents* No 59.
[118] Paris MoU, *Annual Report* (2013), 24.
[119] Ibid, 8 and 19.
[120] Ibid 24.

LOSC does seek to harmonise the exercise of flag state jurisdiction, with Article 211(2) requiring flag states to adopt laws and regulations to prevent marine pollution that at least have the same effect as that of generally accepted international rules and standards, as established through the competent international organisation, or general diplomatic conference. Widely accepted rules, such as MARPOL, and all of its annexes which have entered into force, and have attracted high participation, would be regarded as generally accepted international standards. Less clear is whether nascent rules, such as those adopted in the 2004 Ballast Water Convention, which has yet to enter into force, would meet the threshold.

In relation to enforcement jurisdiction, the LOSC does not alter the capacity of flag states to take action to enforce pollution control standards. What is significant, however, is that the LOSC transforms the customary law capacity into a positive obligation—if a vessel violates international pollution control standards, then the flag state shall provide for immediate investigation and where appropriate institute proceedings, irrespective of where the violation occurred, or where the pollution caused by such violation has occurred.[121] Flag states are to take appropriate measures to ensure that vessels flying their flag are prohibited from sailing unless they can proceed to sea in compliance with international pollution control standards.[122] They must also ensure that vessels carry on board the required certificate, and are subject to periodic inspection.[123]

ii. Port States

Under the LOSC port states retain the capacity to legislate for the prevention, reduction and control of pollution of the marine environment as a condition for the entry of foreign vessels into their ports or internal waters.[124] They must give due publicity to such requirements, and communicate them to the IMO.[125] However, the LOSC greatly expands the powers of port states to enforce pollution standards, and a major attraction of this approach is that it involves no interference with navigational rights and freedoms that would be entailed by greater reliance on coastal state jurisdiction.

Port states may take administrative measures to prevent a vessel from sailing, where it is in violation of international standards relating to seaworthiness, and thereby threatens damage to the marine environment.[126] More significantly, the LOSC extends the capacity of port states to take proceedings against delinquent vessels. Whereas previously this was confined to taking action for breaches of port state regulations within the port itself, or the internal waters, territorial sea or EEZ of the port state,[127] the LOSC gives port states the ability to take action against vessels for breaches of international pollution standards wherever these breaches have taken place.[128] However, no proceedings are to be instituted in respect of a discharge violation in the internal waters, territorial sea, or EEZ of another state unless requested by that state, the flag state, or a state damaged or threatened by the discharge violation.[129]

---

[121] LOSC, art 217(4).
[122] Ibid art 217(2).
[123] Ibid art 217(3).
[124] Ibid art 211(3).
[125] Ibid.
[126] Ibid art 219.
[127] This right is preserved in ibid art 220(1).
[128] Ibid art 218(1).
[129] Ibid art 218(2).

iii. Coastal States

The most significant reforms in the jurisdictional regime relating to pollution control made by the LOSC were for coastal states.[130] Through the 200 nm EEZ, the LOSC greatly extended the sovereign rights of coastal states over adjacent living and non-living resources, and also gave coastal states jurisdiction with regard to the protection and preservation of the marine environment.[131] At UNCLOS III, a number of developed, and most developing, states advocated a significant broadening of coastal state powers to prescribe and enforce pollution control laws over vessels in EEZ areas as a concomitant of the creation of the EEZ regime.[132] However, this ran headlong into the desire by the major maritime states to retain navigational rights and freedoms within the territorial sea and the EEZ, rights that gained express recognition in Article 17 and Article 58(1) of LOSC. A compromise on jurisdiction between these two positions was achieved, so that while the geographical reach of coastal state jurisdiction was enlarged, the content of coastal state laws was limited so as to prevent 'creeping' coastal state jurisdiction.

In the territorial sea, coastal states may legislate to control pollution by foreign vessels so long as they give effect to generally accepted international rules or standards.[133] These laws must not hamper the exercise of innocent passage. For the EEZ, Article 211(5) provides that coastal states may legislate in the EEZ to implement international rules and standards. As a result, coastal states do not have unfettered power to pass pollution control laws in the territorial sea and EEZ that would, for instance, ban the movement of hazardous waste, or prevent navigation by certain vessels such as oil tankers. In all cases, coastal state laws must be in conformity with IMO rules; they may not be less demanding than international standards, but nor may they be more stringent. The effect of this ceiling on the stringency of coastal state laws was highlighted in 2003 when the United Nations Secretary-General noted that measures by France, Portugal and Spain to ban single-hull oil supertankers from their EEZs in response to the *Prestige* disaster fell foul of Article 58 of the LOSC.[134] There are a number of other states that have enacted legislation infringing Article 211(5) by asserting a general jurisdiction to prevent pollution in the EEZ.[135]

There are two exceptions to the general requirement of coastal states to adhere to international standards. First, in ecologically sensitive sea areas in their EEZs coastal states may under Article 211(6) pass additional laws and regulations relating to discharges or navigational practices following appropriate consultations with the IMO (although they may not adopt stricter rules relating to design, construction, manning or equipment standards than the generally accepted international rules).[136] Coastal states are increasingly relying on

---

[130] See Erik Jap Molenaar, *Coastal State Jurisdiction Over Vessel Source Pollution* (The Hague, Kluwer, 1998) 99.

[131] LOSC, art 56.

[132] *Virginia Commentaries*, vol 4, 188.

[133] LOSC, art 21(2).

[134] *Report of the Secretary-General on the Oceans and the Law of the Sea*, UN Doc A/58/65 (2003), [57].

[135] Bangladesh: Territorial Waters and Maritime Zones Act 1974, s 8; Cape Verde: Law No 60/IV/92, art 16; Cote d'Ivoire: Law No 77–926, art 6; Haiti: Decree No 38 of 1977, art 7; Malaysia: Exclusive Economic Zone Act 1984, ss 10(1), 15(1), 24(1); Sri Lanka: Maritime Zones Law No 27 (1976), s 7; Sweden: Act on Measures Against Vessel Source Water Pollution, ch 7, s 1. See Robin Churchill, 'The Impact of State Practice on the Jurisdictional Framework Contained in the LOS Convention' in Alex G Oude Elferink (ed), *Stability and Change in the Law of the Sea: The Role of the LOS Convention* (Leiden, Martinus Nijhoff, 2005) 91, 129–30.

[136] LOSC, art 211(6).

this provision in implementing Associated Protective Measures in Particularly Sensitive Sea Areas (PSSAs) designated by the IMO.[137] A PSSA is defined as 'an area that needs special protection through action by IMO because of its significance for recognised ecological, socio-economic or scientific reasons and because it may be vulnerable to damage by international shipping activities'.[138]

Secondly, in ice-covered areas that are within a coastal state's EEZ, the coastal state may adopt pollution control laws that are stricter than the international standards, in recognition that pollution in such areas could cause 'major harm to or irreversible disturbance of the ecological balance'.[139] Such laws must be adopted and enforced on a non-discriminatory basis.[140] The IMO has sought to contribute to improved regulation of shipping in ice-covered waters in both the Arctic and the Antarctic through the adoption in 2014 of the binding International Code for Ships Operating in Polar Waters (Polar Code).[141] In recent years there has been a marked increase in the number of tourist and other vessels operating within the Antarctic Treaty Area, and a corresponding increase in maritime casualties, such as the grounding of the *MV Nordkapp* and the sinking of the *MV Explorer*, both of which occurred in 2006. The Polar Code builds upon non-binding guidelines that had been in development for over a decade, and is given effect through MARPOL and SOLAS. It is the culmination of the IMO's involvement in polar shipping matters over a lengthy period, beginning in 1990, when the Antarctic was designated a MARPOL special area. The Polar Code includes provisions going to the construction of vessels, equipment, operations, crewing, training, search and rescue, and measures for environmental protection and damage control. The IMO expects the Polar Code to enter into force in 2017, with amendments to SOLAS and MARPOL aligned to take effect at the same time.

iv. Enforcement Jurisdiction

The enforcement jurisdiction of coastal states in the territorial sea and EEZ in relation to pollution issues is not unlimited under the LOSC. Where there are clear grounds for believing that a vessel navigating in the territorial sea of the coastal states has violated laws and regulations consistent with international standards, then the coastal state may undertake a physical inspection of the vessel relating to the violation and may institute proceedings, including the detention of the vessel.[142] Moreover, under the innocent passage regime in Part II of the LOSC, 'wilful and serious pollution' is considered to be prejudicial to the peace, good order or security of the coastal state, disentitles a foreign ship to innocent passage, and enlivens the coastal state's enforcement capacity.[143]

In the EEZ, the coastal state may only arrest and prosecute a vessel where there is clear objective evidence that the vessel has committed a violation resulting in a discharge causing

---

[137] See Julian Roberts et al, 'The Western European PSSA Proposal: A "Politically Sensitive Sea Area"' (2005) 29 *Marine Policy* 431, 438–39.

[138] IMO Assembly Resolution A.927(22), Annex 2, [1.2].

[139] LOSC, art 234. See further Donald R Rothwell, *The Polar Regions and the Development of International Law* (Cambridge, Cambridge University Press, 1996) 294–95.

[140] LOSC, art 234.

[141] For discussion see Julia Jabour, 'Progress Towards the Mandatory Code for Polar Shipping' (2014) 6 *Australian Journal of Maritime and Ocean Affairs*, 64.

[142] LOSC, art 220(2).

[143] Ibid art 19.

major damage or threat of major environmental damage.[144] Where instead the violation has resulted in a substantial discharge causing or threatening significant pollution, then the coastal state may undertake physical inspection of the vessel.[145] In lesser cases of violation, where there is neither substantial discharge, nor a discharge causing major damage, then all that coastal states may do is require the vessel to give information regarding its identify, and port of registry, its last and its next port of call.[146] This regime leaves to coastal states some degree of discretion in characterising the seriousness of a discharge violation, and therefore the extent of enforcement action that may be taken.

The LOSC also lays down a number of safeguards in relation to the exercise of enforcement jurisdiction by port and coastal states. These are found in Part XII, Section 7. Under Article 224, powers of enforcement against foreign vessels may only be exercised by government ships or aircraft, and under Article 225 enforcement action is not to endanger the safety of navigation, or create any hazard to any vessel, or expose the marine environment to an unreasonable risk. Enforcement action must also be non-discriminatory.[147] Significantly, flag states enjoy a right of pre-emption in all criminal proceedings except where the discharge violation results in major damage to the coastal state, or where the flag state has repeatedly disregarded its obligation to enforce effectively the applicable international rules and standards.[148]

In practice, the regime of coastal state jurisdiction over pollution violations does not appear to have been extensively used. Not only are there few instances of coastal state legislation addressing pollution in detail in the territorial sea and the EEZ, but there are no examples of coastal states arresting vessels while navigating in the EEZ for violations of such laws. Port state control has been far more important for implementation and compliance.[149]

V. Accidental Vessel-Source Pollution

While operational discharges of oil and other substances account for most vessel-source pollution, spillage of pollutants as a result of maritime casualties continues to be a concern. The magnitude of the risk posed by such accidents is a function, among other things, of the type of commodity being shipped. Oil tankers and ships carrying noxious chemicals in bulk are rightly the targets of the most attention because of the likelihood of severe damage being caused in the local marine environment should they become shipwrecked. Major casualties regularly occurred from the 1960s until the 1980s, with 19 of the 20 largest spills occurring before 2000. In recent years the occurrence of large spills has fallen dramatically, with only one spill greater than 700 tonnes in 2014 (the sinking of a small tanker in the South China Sea). There were around 25 large spills each year in the 1970s, 10 each year in the 1980s and 1990s, three each year in the 2000s and two each year since 2010.[150]

---

[144] Ibid art 220(6).
[145] Ibid art 220(5).
[146] Ibid art 220(3).
[147] Ibid art 227.
[148] Ibid art 228.
[149] See Tan, *Vessel-Source Marine Pollution* (n 92) ch 5.
[150] International Oil Tanker Owners Pollution Federation, *Oil Tanker Spill Statistics 2014* (2015), 4.

There are three areas of the law of the sea relevant to efforts to reduce the risks associated with accidental vessel-source pollution. First there are the rules found in MARPOL, already considered, that relate to the construction of vessels, and their ongoing inspection and certification, which have resulted in more seaworthy ships being used to transport oil and noxious chemical cargoes. Secondly, there are rules that concern the safety of shipping more generally, that range beyond construction standards and deal also with the safety of navigation. The primary source of these rules is SOLAS. Thirdly, there are customary and conventional rules addressing the rights and duties of flag and coastal states in responding to pollution emergencies at sea.

A. Safety of Shipping

Under Article 94(3) of the LOSC, flag states are under an obligation to take such measures as are necessary to ensure safety at sea with regard to the construction, equipment and seaworthiness of ships, the manning of ships, labour conditions and the training of crews, the use of signals, the maintenance of communications and the prevention of collisions. These measures are to ensure that ships are regularly surveyed by qualified inspectors; have on board the necessary charts and navigational equipment; are in charge of a qualified master and crew which are conversant with and required to observe standards for safety of life at sea, the prevention of collisions and the prevention, reduction and control of marine pollution.[151] These are not generic requirements, as Article 94(5) makes clear that states are required to conform to generally accepted international regulations, procedures and practices. This incorporates into the LOSC the rules of SOLAS, and the other IMO conventions, codes and guidelines concerned with maritime safety.

i. SOLAS

The origins of SOLAS lie in an early convention concluded in 1914 in response to the *Titanic* disaster.[152] There were several subsequent incarnations of the instrument, and a thoroughly revised and updated convention was adopted in 1974. Since that time SOLAS has been extensively amended via a tacit amendment procedure, and for this reason is referred to as 'SOLAS, 1974, as amended'. Amendments may be made by a two-thirds majority of present and voting members of the IMO's Maritime Safety Committee, or by a Conference of Contracting Governments. Amendments may then be taken to be adopted at the end of a period of not less than one year unless more than one-third of parties, or parties the combined merchant fleets of which constitute more than 50 per cent of the gross tonnage of the world's merchant fleet, notify the IMO Secretary-General that they object to the amendment.[153] SOLAS has been ratified by 162 states, representing over 98 per cent of world merchant shipping tonnage, and is therefore, like MARPOL, effectively a universal regime.

---

[151] LOSC, art 94(4).
[152] 1914 International Convention for the Safety of Life at Sea.
[153] SOLAS, art VIII.

The primary purpose of SOLAS is to set down standards for the construction, equipment and operation of ships that will promote their seaworthiness. In a similar fashion as MARPOL, which relies upon a headline convention and six annexes, the structure of SOLAS is a short (13 article) convention containing general provisions, with a single lengthy Annex divided into 12 chapters, several of which are made up of sub-chapters: I: General Provisions, II-1: Construction, II-2: Fire Protection, III: Life Saving Appliances, IV: Radio Communications, V: Safety of Navigation, VI: Carriage of Cargoes, VII: Carriage of Dangerous Goods, VIII: Nuclear Ships, IX: Management of Ships, X: High Speed Craft, XI-1: Special Measures to Enhance Maritime Safety, XI-2: Special Measures to Enhance Maritime Security, XII: Bulk Carriers.

The core of SOLAS is the responsibility of flag states to ensure that ships under their flag comply with the requirements of the Convention and its annex, including by promulgating all laws, decrees, orders and regulations that are necessary to do so.[154] In much the same way as MARPOL, SOLAS requires flag states to inspect and survey ships, and issue certificates of seaworthiness.[155] In addition, every ship when in port is subject to the control of port authorities which are to verify that certificates issued are valid.[156] Certificates, if valid, shall be accepted unless there are clear grounds for believing that the condition of the ship or of its equipment does not correspond substantially with the certificate.[157] If there are such grounds, then the port state is to take steps to ensure that the ship does not sail until it can proceed to sea, or leave the port for the purpose of proceeding to a repair yard, without danger to the ship or its crew.[158]

In addition to SOLAS, there are several further conventions agreed under IMO auspices that address maritime safety issues. These include conventions going to questions of ship construction and safe operation, such as the 1966 International Convention on Load Lines which aims to prevent overloading by setting limits on the draught to which a ship may be loaded, and the 1993 Protocol to the 1977 Convention for the Safety of Fishing Vessels which specifies rules concerning the design and operation of fishing vessels. Such vessels had not been included in the SOLAS and 1966 Convention on Load Lines because of the significant differences in the design and working of these vessels compared with cargo ships. The 1993 Protocol, which updates, amends, and absorbs the 1977 Convention was concluded in an effort to encourage ratification of the regime. Further changes to this end were agreed in the 2012 Cape Town Agreement. Although now streamlined, the regime has still not entered into force.

ii. Qualifications and Working Conditions for Seafarers

A further category of IMO conventions relating to maritime safety addresses the qualifications and training of ship crews, which are drawn from around 1.5 million active seafarers worldwide.[159] The IMO is not the only international organisation to have concerned itself with these issues, with the International Labour Organization, which was established in 1919 with the task of improving working conditions also active in the area, setting out

---

[154] Ibid art I.
[155] Ibid Annex, ch I, reg 6.
[156] Ibid Annex, ch I, reg 19(a).
[157] Ibid Annex, ch I, reg 19(b).
[158] Ibid Annex, ch I, reg 19(c).
[159] *Oceans and the Law of the Sea: Report of the Secretary General*, UN Doc A/64/66/Add.1 (2009), [103].

the rights of seafarers to safe and decent conditions of work in the 2006 Maritime Labour Convention. It has been described as the 'fourth pillar' for achieving safe shipping, alongside MARPOL, SOLAS and the STCW Convention. The 2006 Maritime Labour Convention, its Regulations, and Code, consolidate the standards contained in more than 60 instruments adopted by the ILO on the subject since 1920. They set minimum requirements for seafarers to work on a ship such as medical fitness, conditions of employment, standards of onboard accommodation, occupational health and safety, and compliance and enforcement. Significantly, the 2006 Convention, which is known as the 'seafarers' bill of rights', permits port state inspections.

The LOSC imposes a general obligation on flag states to ensure that each ship is 'in charge of a master and officers who possess appropriate qualifications, in particular in seamanship, navigation, communications and marine engineering' and furthermore that 'the crew is appropriate in qualification and numbers for the type, size, machinery and equipment of the ship'.[160] Through two conventions the IMO has elaborated technical standards that give clear guidance to states on the personnel requirements to ensure safe sailing: the STCW Convention and the 1995 Convention on Standards of Training, Certification and Watchkeeping for Fishing Vessel Personnel. Only the SCTW Convention has entered into force, and is as widely supported as MARPOL and SOLAS.[161]

The SCTW Convention, its annex, and the extensive STCW Code which expands upon the general regulations, require flag states to certify that masters and crew meet defined training and qualification standards, and specifies the level of watchkeeping to be maintained. Flag states have the main responsibility for ensuring that these standards are met. However, port state control is also utilised by the SCTW Convention, allowing port states to prevent ships from sailing where it is found that there are serious deficiencies which pose a danger to persons, property or the environment.[162]

iii. Preventing Collisions at Sea

Additional IMO rules concerning maritime safety relate to preventing collisions at sea. COLREG updates and replaces the 1960 Collision Regulations. It was a collision at sea which led to the *Lotus* case.[163] The PCIJ's conclusion, based on the since discredited theory that the Turkish vessel was the 'floating territory' of Turkey, was subsequently overridden by the 1958 High Seas Convention which provides in Article 11 that in the event of a collision or any other incident of navigation concerning a ship on the high seas, no penal or disciplinary proceedings may be instituted against the master or crew of a vessel except by the flag state, or the state of which the accused is a national. This provision was repeated in Article 97 of the LOSC.

COLREG does not modify this rule. Instead it is concerned to specify rules regarding such matters as look out, safe speed, use of radar and other equipment to reduce risk of collisions, action to be taken to avoid collision, navigation through narrow channels, conduct during poor visibility and rules concerning lights, shapes and signals. One of the most important aspects of COLREG relates to traffic separation schemes which regulate traffic in

---

[160] LOSC, art 94(4)(b).
[161] As at 29 July 2015 there were 159 parties, representing 99% of total world merchant vessel tonnage.
[162] STCW Convention, art X(2).
[163] *Lotus (France v Turkey)* [1927] PCIJ Rep ser A no 10. See the discussion in ch 7.

busy and confined waterways by requiring vessels to travel in the same direction in designated lanes, and to cross lanes at right angles.

Traffic separation schemes and other systems for routeing ships have been adopted by the IMO in most major congested shipping areas, resulting in significantly fewer collisions and casualties.[164] Under SOLAS, the IMO is 'recognised as the only international body for developing guidelines, criteria and regulations on an international level for ships' routeing systems'. Under COLREG, Rule 10, vessels from states parties to the Convention must observe the requirements of IMO traffic separation schemes. Many of these extend within the territorial seas of coastal states, where they have the capacity to require foreign ships exercising the right of innocent passage to use sea lanes and traffic separation schemes they prescribe having regard to the recommendations of the IMO.[165]

VI. Pollution Emergencies

Maritime disasters resulting in the release of oil and other pollutants have brought to light three main sets of legal issues surrounding the control of pollution emergencies at sea: first, how states can cooperate in responding to such events in order to minimise pollution damage to the marine environment; secondly, what positive obligations should attach to states to control pollution in the event of an emergency within their jurisdiction or control; and thirdly, what steps coastal states may take unilaterally to abate pollution threats from casualties involving foreign-flagged vessels on the high seas.

A. Responding to Pollution Emergencies

The LOSC stipulates that when a state becomes aware of a situation in which the marine environment is in imminent danger of being damaged, or has been harmed by pollution, it must immediately notify other states that are likely to be affected by such pollution.[166] This is an obligation that applies to all states, in respect of all maritime areas. Furthermore, states in the area affected must, in accordance with their capabilities, cooperate in eliminating the effects of pollution and in preventing or minimising the damage.[167] In this respect, states are required jointly to develop and promote contingency plans for responding to pollution incidents.[168] In addition, where a pollution emergency occurs within the jurisdiction or control of a state, and there is a possibility that it will result in damage to another state, then there is an obligation to take reasonable steps to prevent this transboundary effect from occurring.[169]

These general obligations under the LOSC are elaborated and extended by the 1990 Convention on Oil Pollution Preparedness, Response and Cooperation (OPPRC

---

[164] See further ch 11.
[165] LOSC, art 22.
[166] Ibid art 198. See also MARPOL, art 8.
[167] LOSC, art 199.
[168] Ibid.
[169] Ibid art 194(2).

Convention), and the 2000 Protocol on Preparedness, Response and Co-operation to Pollution Incidents by Hazardous and Noxious Substances (OPRC-HNS Protocol). The OPPRC Convention was concluded by the IMO after the *Exxon Valdez* disaster in an effort to bolster flag and coastal state readiness and planning for potential pollution incidents, and to require parties to provide assistance to states affected by pollution. To this end, the OPPRC Convention, which takes account of both the precautionary approach and the polluter pays principle, requires states to formulate oil pollution plans for their vessels and for their ports and offshore terminals.[170] States must also establish a national system for responding promptly and effectively to oil pollution incidents, including as a minimum the designation of a competent national authority with responsibility for oil pollution preparedness and response.[171] Masters must report without delay any event on their ship or offshore unit involving a discharge or possible discharge of oil to the nearest coastal state.[172] On receiving an oil pollution report the coastal state is to assess the seriousness of the event, and then inform, without delay, all states whose interests are affected or are likely to be affected.[173] To respond to oil pollution incidents parties commit, subject to their capacities, and the availability of resources, to provide assistance, when the severity of the incident justifies, by way of advice, technical support and equipment.[174] The costs incurred in the provision of such assistance are to be defrayed in accordance with the Annex to the OPPRC Convention, which provides that if action is taken by one party at the express request of another, the latter shall reimburse the assisting party. The OPPRC-HNS Protocol applies the rules of the OPPRC Convention to pollution incidents involving hazardous and noxious substances, and entered into force in 2007.

In addition to global obligations to respond to pollution emergencies, there have also been regional mechanisms, such as the 2013 Agreement on Cooperation on Marine Oil Pollution, Preparedness and Response in the Arctic, which was adopted under the auspices of the Arctic Council (an intergovernmental forum for the eight Arctic states).[175] The Agreement requires parties to maintain effective national oil pollution preparedness response systems, to cooperate in response operations (including assuring free and prompt movements across boundaries of necessary vehicles and equipment) and to promote joint exercises and training programmes.

B. Coastal State Rights of Intervention

Coastal states are under a positive obligation to respond to pollution emergencies within their jurisdiction and control, and also enjoy a right to intervene in incidents occurring beyond their territorial sea, including if these involve foreign vessels. In the *Torrey Canyon* disaster, the United Kingdom bombed the sinking tanker on the high seas in an effort to

---

[170] OPPRC, art 3.
[171] Ibid art 6.
[172] Ibid art 4.
[173] Ibid art 5.
[174] Ibid art 7.
[175] Canada, Denmark (including Greenland and the Faroe Islands), Finland, Iceland, Norway, Russia, Sweden and the United States. Six international organisations that represent Arctic Indigenous Peoples have permanent participant status.

incinerate and dissipate its cargo of oil. However, the British government advanced no legal justification for its conduct, and questions surrounded its legality as it appeared to offend the exclusivity of flag state jurisdiction on the high seas, where vessels enjoy freedom of navigation, free from interference by the all authorities except those of their state of nationality, with only limited exceptions.[176] At customary international law, intervention would prima facie be unlawful; however, the internationally wrongful act may be excused on the basis of necessity, that is where the act of intervention is the only means for the coastal state to safeguard an essential interest against grave and imminent peril.[177]

The question of coastal state intervention rights to control pollution was referred to the IMO following the grounding of the *Torrey Canyon*, and resulted in the conclusion of the 1969 Convention on the High Seas in Cases of Oil Pollution Casualties (1969 Intervention Convention).[178] This convention was supplemented by a protocol to cover other forms of pollution: the 1973 Protocol Relating to Intervention on the High Seas in Cases of Pollution by Substances Other than Oil. The 1969 Intervention Convention allows parties to take such measures on the high seas as may be necessary to prevent, mitigate, or eliminate 'grave and imminent danger' to their coastline or related interests from pollution or threat of pollution of the sea.[179] The matter is also addressed in the LOSC, which in Article 221(1) provides in similar terms that nothing in Part XII shall prejudice the right of states pursuant to customary and conventional law to take and enforce measures beyond the territorial sea proportionate to the actual or threatened damage to protect their coastline or related interests, including fishing, from pollution. The formulation in Article 221(1) of the LOSC sets a lower threshold than the 1969 Intervention Convention, in that it includes no reference to 'grave and imminent danger', but rather allows intervention where there is 'actual or threatened damage' that 'may reasonably be expected to result in major harmful consequences'.

Both the 1969 Intervention Convention and the LOSC recognise the rights of coastal states to intervene in emergencies following a 'maritime casualty', which is defined as a collision of vessels, stranding, or other incident of navigation, or other occurrence resulting in material damage or imminent threat of material damage to a vessel or cargo.[180] As a result, the right of intervention may only be invoked in the event of a true emergency, and could not be relied upon in order to respond to a pollution incident resulting from dumping, or from operational pollution.

C. The Role of Salvors

Coastal states now have a fairly well-defined right of intervention. However, in addressing marine pollution emergencies there is also a role for private maritime salvors in assisting

---

[176]   See LOSC, art 110.

[177]   2001 Draft Articles on the Responsibility of States for Internationally Wrongful Acts, art 25. See further James Crawford, *The International Law Commission's Articles on State Responsibility: Introduction, Text and Commentaries* (Cambridge, Cambridge University Press, 2002) 178–86. In *Gabčíkovo-Nagymaros Project (Hungary/Slovakia)* [1997] ICJ Rep 7 the ICJ accepted that the environment could constitute an 'essential interest' for the purposes of the necessity defence (at [53]).

[178]   *Basic Documents* No 14.

[179]   1969 Intervention Convention, art 1(1).

[180]   1969 Intervention Convention, art 2(1); LOSC, art 221(2).

vessels in distress, and in preventing and reducing environmental damage. Traditionally, maritime salvage has proceeded on the basis of the 'no cure, no pay' rule which meant that the salvor would receive no payment or other reward unless the vessel was saved. Hence efforts that substantially reduced pollution, but nonetheless were unsuccessful in salvaging a vessel in its entirety, would go unrewarded. This rule, which was a disincentive to salvors to protect the marine environment, was modified by the 1989 International Convention on Salvage.[181] Salvage operations which have a 'useful result' give right to a reward,[182] with the reward being fixed by reference, among other things, to the skill and efforts of the salvors in preventing or minimising damage to the environment.[183]

VII. Liability for Vessel-Source Pollution

Despite best efforts to prevent pollution of the marine environment, maritime casualties continue to occur, and when they do there is a need to address liability issues so that victims of vessel-source pollution do not go uncompensated. In this respect, there are now detailed rules relating to state responsibility and operator liability for vessel-source pollution. These rules not only serve a corrective function, but they also act as a powerful incentive for all those involved in the shipping industry to adopt measures to safeguard against pollution casualties.

A. State Responsibility

When damage is caused as a result of vessel-source pollution (or indeed from marine pollution from any source), an immediate issue arises as to whether the flag state or the state from which the pollution orginates may be held internationally responsible. The LOSC in Article 194(2) requires states to take all measures necessary to ensure that activities under their jurisdiction or control are conducted so as not to cause pollution damage to other states, or to areas beyond national jurisdiction. Furthermore, Article 235(1) provides that states are responsible for the fulfilment of their international obligations concerning the protection and preservation of the marine environment, and that they 'shall be liable in accordance with international law'.

Both of these provisions are restatements in the law of the sea context of the customary law rules of state responsibility for pollution damage, which have been developed since the *Trail Smelter* case.[184] Important recent developments in this regard include the International

---

[181] *Basic Documents* No 40.
[182] 1989 International Convention on Salvage, art 12(1).
[183] Ibid art 13(1)(b).
[184] *Trail Smelter (Canada/United States)* (1938 and 1941) 3 RIAA 1911. See generally Brian Smith, *State Responsibility and the Marine Environment: The Rules of Decision* (Oxford, Oxford University Press, 1988). See also Stuart B Kaye, 'The Impact of the *Trail Smelter* Arbitration on the Law of the Sea' in Rebecca M Bratspies and Russell A Miller (eds), *Transboundary Harm in International Law: Lessons from the Trail Smelter Arbitration* (Cambridge, Cambridge University Press, 2006) 209.

Law Commission's Draft Articles on State Responsibility,[185] and Draft Articles on the Prevention of Transboundary Harm from Hazardous Activities.[186] As there has been no resolution of any inter-state claims in relation to transboundary marine pollution damage on the basis of state responsibility rules, this area of international law has not been put to the test. However, the ITLOS Seabed Disputes Chamber provided some guidance on the question in the *Seabed Mining Advisory Opinion*.[187] The Seabed Disputes Chamber referred to Article 194(2) and observed that

> The expression 'to ensure' is often used in international legal instruments to refer to obligations in respect of which, while it is not considered reasonable to make a State liable for each and every violation committed by persons under its jurisdiction, it is equally not considered satisfactory to rely on mere application of the principle that the conduct of private persons or entities is not attributable to the State under international law (see ILC Articles on State Responsibility, Commentary to Article 8, paragraph 1).[188]

If there is a breach of Article 194 of the LOSC, then under Article 42 of the Articles on State Responsibility 'injured' states will be able to invoke the responsibility of the state that has breached the obligation. For breaches of a multilateral treaty such as the LOSC, a state will be injured if it is 'specially affected', and the ILC in its commentaries on the Articles on State Responsibility gave Article 194 of the LOSC as an example of a provision that could be invoked by a coastal state affected by pollution from a vessel on the high seas.[189] Even if no state is 'specially affected', state responsibility may still be invoked under Article 48 of the Articles on State Responsibility if the relevant obligation is owed to a group of states, including that state, and is established for the protection of a collective interest, or the obligation is owed to the international community as a whole. In the *Seabed Mining Advisory Opinion*, the Seabed Disputes Chamber referred to Article 48 as supporting the view that any state party to the LOSC would be entitled to claim compensation in respect of damage to the marine environment of the high seas or the Area.[190]

B. Civil Liability

Article 235(2) of the LOSC requires states to take steps to provide domestic legal remedies to ensure that there is prompt and adequate compensation for pollution of the marine environment by natural or juridical persons under their jurisdiction. Article 235(2) complements and goes further than an earlier provision of Part XII, Article 229, which provides that nothing in the LOSC affects the institution of civil proceedings in respect of any claim for loss or damage resulting from pollution of the marine environment. The purpose of Article 235(2) is to allow victims of pollution to take civil proceedings in the courts of

---

[185]   *Report of the International Law Commission*, 53rd Session, UN Doc A/56/10 (2001).
[186]   Ibid. See also the Draft Principles on the Allocation of Loss in the Case of Transboundary Harm Arising out of Hazardous Activities, *Report of the International Law Commission*, 56th Session, UN Doc A/59/10 (2004).
[187]   (2011) 50 ILM 458.
[188]   Ibid, [112].
[189]   *Articles on Responsibility of States for Internationally Wrongful Acts, Report of the International Law Commission, 53rd Session*, UN Doc A/56/10 (2001), 43–59.
[190]   *Seabed Mining Advisory Opinion* (2011) 50 ILM 458, [180].

the state which has jurisdiction over natural or juridical persons responsible for the pollution damage. Once those proceedings are exhausted, or if there is no available remedy, then the state of the victim may exercise the right of diplomatic protection on the victim's behalf. There are now a suite of regimes establishing civil liability for marine pollution in the courts of the state in whose territory, territorial sea or EEZ such pollution damage has been suffered.

i. Liability for Oil Pollution Damage

Civil proceedings for compensation for oil pollution can be complex, costly and slow, as demonstrated clearly by the protracted litigation following the *Exxon Valdez* disaster in 1989. The proceedings were only resolved following the 2008 decision of the United States Supreme Court in *Exxon Shipping Co v Baker*,[191] in which the Court substantially reduced the quantum of punitive damages awarded against Exxon Mobil (from US$2.5 billion to US$500 million). However, this US$500 million is in addition to the US$3.4 billion in cleanup costs, compensatory payments and fines already paid by Exxon. The proceedings in the *Exxon Valdez* matter were taken in accordance with United States maritime law, which was revised by the 1990 Oil Pollution Act that was enacted in response to the disaster. That legislation significantly raised, and in some cases removed, limits on liability for oil pollution damage, and allowed compensation to be obtained for 'natural resource damage'.[192]

The United States regime for oil pollution liability is more advanced than that which has been adopted internationally under IMO auspices, although the latter has been strengthened considerably in recent years. The key instruments are the CLC and the 1971 Convention on the Establishment of an International Fund for Compensation for Oil Pollution Damage. The CLC was concluded at an international conference convened in the aftermath of the *Torrey Canyon* incident, and seeks to ensure that coastal states and their nationals obtain appropriate compensation in the result of pollution from oil tankers. It does so by overcoming some of the hurdles faced in transnational litigation, namely establishing jurisdiction, the applicable law, the standard of liability, and, most importantly, the limits of that liability. Both conventions were substantially reformed in 1992 through protocols to each treaty, and the amended texts are referred to as the 1992 Civil Liability Convention (1992 CLC) and the 1992 Fund Convention.

ii. 1992 Civil Liability Convention

This regime applies to sea-going vessels or craft constructed or adapted for the purpose of carrying persistent hydrocarbon mineral oil in bulk as cargo.[193] It allows claims for pollution damage caused in the territory, territorial sea, or EEZ of a coastal state, or up to 200 nm from the territorial sea baselines if no EEZ has been claimed, to be brought in the courts of

---

[191] 128 S Ct 2605 (2008). For discussion see Tanya Paula de Sousa, 'Oil Over Troubled Waters: *Exxon Shipping Co v Baker* and the Supreme Court's Determination of Punitive Damages in Maritime Law' (2009) 24 *Villanova Environmental Law Journal* 247.

[192] See James Boyd, 'Compensation for Oil Pollution Damages: The American Oil Pollution Act as an Example for Global Solutions?' in Michael G Faure and James Hu (eds), *Prevention and Compensation of Marine Pollution Damage* (Alphen aan den Rijn, Kluwer, 2006).

[193] 1992 CLC, art 1.

that state if it is a party to the 1992 CLC. This jurisdiction is territorial—an entitlement to take proceedings exists regardless of the flag of the vessel involved in the incident. 'Pollution damage' is defined as 'loss or damage caused outside the ship by contamination resulting from the escape or discharge of oil from the ship, wherever such escape or discharge may occur, provided that compensation for impairment of the environment other than loss of profit from such impairment shall be limited to the costs of reasonable measures of reinstatement actually undertaken or to be undertaken'.[194] Anyone sustaining pollution damage may bring a claim for compensation, including individuals, businesses and governments. Compensation is payable for costs incurred in reasonable clean-up measures and to combat the oil and defend sensitive resources, for reasonable costs incurred in the capture, cleaning and rehabilitation of wildlife, and for cleaning, repairing or replacing property contaminated by oil. Compensation is also available for loss of earnings from owners of contaminated property, or where uses are impaired, such as when fishers are prevented from fishing.

In relation to damage to the environment, compensation is only payable for the loss of profit from the impairment of the environment, and the costs of reasonable reinstatement measures.[195] This limitation has not always been respected by governments or domestic courts. In the 1985 *Patmos* and the 1991 *Haven* cases, the Italian government sought compensation for damage to the marine environment per se.[196] More recently, in proceedings arising from the *Erika* disaster, which led to the spillage of 19,800 tonnes of heavy fuel oil off the coast of Brittany, the Criminal Court in Paris, which considered both criminal and civil claims, assessed civil liabilities to include damages for moral damages and damage to the environment.[197] This is not consistent with Article 1(6)(a) of the 1992 CLC, which gives no redress for pure environmental harm. The Court assessed the total damages in the amount of €192.8 million, which included €153.9 million for the French government. This amount was subsequently paid in full by Total SA, and as a result the French government withdrew all civil actions in respect of the disaster.[198]

Under the 1992 CLC, claims for compensation are to be made against the registered owner of the ship, or the owner's insurer, and not the operator of the ship, or the owner of the oil cargo. Hence no proceedings may normally be instituted against other potential parties who may have had a hand in the incident such as the operator, the charterer, master, crew, pilot or salvor.[199] This 'channelling provision' of the 1992 CLC permits such claims only if the damage was a result of their personal act or omission which was committed with intent to cause the damage, or recklessly with the knowledge that such damage would probably result. However, the 1992 CLC does not preclude the shipowner from seeking recourse against third parties.

The liability of shipowners is strict, and hence they will be liable to pay compensation for pollution damage caused by the escape or discharge of persistent oil from a ship, even if

---

[194] Ibid art 1(6).
[195] See generally International Oil Pollution Compensation Fund, *Claims Manual* (IOPCF, 2008).
[196] Louise de La Fayette, 'The Concept of Environmental Damage in International Liability Regimes' in Michael Bowman and Alan Boyle (eds), *Environmental Damage in International and Comparative Law* (Oxford, Oxford University Press, 2002) 149, 156.
[197] See IOPC/OCT09/3/4 (2009) 2.
[198] International Oil Pollution Compensation Funds, *Annual Report 2008*, 81.
[199] 1992 CLC, art 3(4).

the pollution was not due to any fault on their part. However, liability is not absolute, and exceptions to liability apply where it can be established that the damage resulted from an act of war, hostilities, civil war, insurrection, or a national phenomenon of an exceptional, inevitable or irresistible character; was wholly caused by an act or omission by a third party with intent to cause damage (that is sabotage or terrorism); or was wholly caused by the negligence of any government or other authority responsible for the maintenance of navigational aids.[200]

Shipowners of vessels that carry more than 2,000 tonnes of oil as cargo are required to hold insurance or other financial security to cover liability. This liability is limited to an amount determined by reference to the size of the vessel. Before 2003 the limit was 59.7 million Special Drawing Rights[201] (SDR) for the very largest vessels, those 140,000 units of tonnage or over. However, by amendments agreed in 2000, for incidents after 2003 the limits were raised to 89.77 million SDR for the largest tankers, which is equivalent to around US$65 million. Lesser limits apply to ships of lower tonnage—for ships not exceeding 5,000 gross tonnage, 4.51 million SDR, and for ships 5,000 to 140,000 gross tonnage, 4.51 million SDR plus 631 SDR for each gross tonne over 5,000.

iii. The 1992 Fund Convention

The 1992 CLC liability amounts are not always sufficient to cover the damage incurred in very serious pollution incidents. The *Erika* incident is illustrative of this, in that compensation claims were made by nearly 700 claimants, including the French government, totalling more than €200 million even though only around €13 million was available under the 1992 CLC.[202] Hence there is a need for additional funds to satisfy liabilities, and to this end the International Oil Pollution Compensation Fund (IOPCF), established by the 1992 Fund Convention, may be drawn upon where there is compensable damage that exceeds the liability limits for shipowners.

The IOPCF is financed by companies and other entities of member states which receive oil that is carried by sea. In essence the establishment of the IOPCF serves to distribute liability between the two main economic beneficiaries of the transport of oil—the ship owners, and the owners of the oil cargo. Under the 1992 Fund Convention, recourse may be had against the IOPCF to satisfy liability, up to a maximum of 203 million SDR, which equates to around US$225 million, for events occurring on or after 1 November 2003. For incidents before that date the maximum was 135 million SDR. In 2003 a Supplementary Fund was established by a protocol to the 1992 Fund Convention, increasing the limit for any one incident to 750 million SDR, or around US$540 million, inclusive of liability under the 1992 CLC.[203] However, the 2003 Protocol to the 1992 Fund Convention has not yet attracted widespread support.[204]

---

[200] Ibid art 3(1) and art 3(2).
[201] SDR are a reserve of international assets created by the International Monetary Fund based on four key international currencies (the Euro, Japanese Yen, Pound Sterling, and US Dollar). As of 28 July 2015 one SDR was valued at US$0.72.
[202] International Oil Pollution Compensation Funds, *Annual Report 2008*, 77.
[203] Ibid 17.
[204] Although it has entered into force, there are only 31 parties, representing around 18% of total world tonnage.

The IOPCF can be called on where the damage exceeds the shipowners' liability limit under the 1992 CLC. However, it can also be used to provide compensation when the shipowner is not liable because the damage was caused by natural disaster, by intentional wrongdoing by a third party, or by the negligence of a public authority in maintaining navigational aids. It is also available if the shipowner is financially incapable of meeting the liability under the 1992 CLC, or if the insurance taken out is insufficient. However, the IOPCF cannot be asked to pay compensation if the pollution resulted from an act of war, hostilities, civil war or insurrection, or if the claimant is unable to establish that the damage resulted from an accident involving a ship as defined by the 1992 CLC and 1992 Fund Convention, that is a vessel carrying oil in bulk as cargo. By the end of 2008, the IOPCF had been involved in the settlement of claims arising out of over 130 incidents, and had disbursed over £500 million.[205]

The liability regime established by the 1992 CLC and the 1992 Fund Convention does not affect the entitlement of government authorities to institute criminal proceedings in relation to oil pollution incidents. In such cases the defendants may include not only ship owners and operators, but also others such as private classification societies that are increasingly being outsourced to inspect and certify the seaworthiness of vessels.[206]

iv. Liability for Other Pollution Damage

The 1992 CLC and the 1992 Fund Convention apply only to oil pollution, and not to other noxious cargoes. To fill the gap in the liability regime, the IMO adopted the 1996 Convention on Liability and Compensation for the Carriage of Hazardous and Noxious Substances by Sea (HNS Convention). The HNS Convention never entered into force, and was superseded by the 2010 Protocol to the International Convention on Liability and Compensation for Damage in Connection with the HNS Convention (known as the 2010 HNS Convention). The 2010 HNS Convention, if and when it enters into force, will enable victims to claim up to 100 million SDR for accidents involving bulk chemicals and other noxious substances. The maximum liability of shipowners is increased to 115 million SDR in respect of damage from packaged hazardous substances, or from a combination of both bulk and packaged substances. Beyond these limits to liability, compensation is available from the HNS Fund, up to a limit of 250 million SDR. The regime is modelled on the 1992 CLC and 1992 Fund Convention in its two-tier system of limited liability and then recourse to a fund which is financed from contributions on enterprises in contracting states that receive a certain minimum quantity of HNS cargo.

Strict liability attaches to shipowners, rather than other potential parties such as the crew of vessels. The hazardous and noxious substances to which the 2010 HNS Convention applies are those defined in MARPOL, Annex II, and the pollution column of chapters 17 and 18 of the International Bulk Chemical Code. These include oils, other noxious or dangerous liquids, liquefied gases such as liquefied natural gas, dangerous, hazardous and harmful materials and substances carried in packaged form, and solid bulk materials that constitute a chemical hazard. The 2010 HNS Convention does not apply to damage by oil pollution covered by the 1992 CLC.

---

[205] International Oil Pollution Compensation Funds, *Annual Report 2008*, 51.

[206] There are around 50 marine classification societies, including the Lloyd's Register of Shipping, Registro Italiano Navale, the American Bureau of Shipping, and Det Norske Veritas. These four and several other societies are members of the International Association of Classification Societies: www.iacs.org.uk.

Also of relevance is the 2001 Convention on Civil Liability for Bunker Oil Pollution Damage (2001 Bunkers Convention), which entered into force in late 2008 and now has close to 80 parties, representing over 90 per cent of world tonnage. Neither the 1992 CLC nor the 2010 HNS Convention addresses pollution from oil spills from fuel carried in ships' bunkers. The 2001 Bunkers Convention follows the model of the other two regimes, and further covers the field of pollution damage. It is significant because it takes away a potential area of liability that is currently covered by the 1976 Convention on Limitation of Liability for Maritime Claims, which provides for circumstances in which shipowners may limit their liability.

It should be noted that none of the IMO liability regimes apply to civil liability for nuclear damage of the marine environment. Instead the key treaties are those agreed under the auspices of the International Atomic Energy Agency (the 1963 Vienna Convention on Civil Liability for Nuclear Damage), and the Organisation for Economic Co-operation and Development (the 1960 Paris Convention on Third Party Liability in the Field of Nuclear Energy). The two treaties were linked by a joint protocol in 1988, and are stronger than the IMO liability conventions in that they impose absolute rather than strict liability. In other respects they are very similar to the IMO conventions, as they provided the basic model for the IMO civil liability regime.

A further addition to the regime for civil liability was made in 2007 with the conclusion of the 2007 International Convention on the Removal of Wrecks.[207] This convention, which entered into force in 2015, is designed to promote the removal of shipwrecks and lagan that constitute a hazard to navigation or the marine environment. The Convention subjects the registered owner to liability for the costs of locating, marking and removing such wrecks, with such liability to be covered by compulsory insurance or other financial security maintained in respect of ships 300 gross tonnage and above.[208]

The 1992 CLC and the 1992 Fund Convention apply only to pollution from vessels, and as such do not regulate pollution from offshore wells. This gap in the regulatory framework was highlighted by the 2009 *West Atlas* and 2010 *BP Deepwater Horizon* blow-outs of offshore wells that resulted in major oil spills. While both incidents have attracted the ongoing application of national law frameworks,[209] there is no global regime to address the liabilities of offshore hydrocarbon exploration and exploitation. This has prompted calls for a new convention,[210] and the IMO's Legal Committee has included in its programme of work an assessment of the liability and issues arising from transboundary pollution from such incidents.

VIII. Seabed Pollution

Exploring and exploiting the hydrocarbon and other non-living resources of the seabed inevitably results in some level of disturbance of the ocean-bottom environment, and can

[207] *Basic Documents* No 83.
[208] 2007 International Convention on the Removal of Wrecks, arts 10, 12.
[209] Thomas J Schoenbaum, 'Liability for Damages in Oil Spill Accidents: Evaluating the USA and International Law Regimes in the Light of Deepwater Horizon' (2012) 24 *Journal of Environmental Law* 395.
[210] Steven Rares, 'An International Convention on Off Shore Hydrocarbon Leaks?' (2012) 26 *Australian and New Zealand Maritime Law Journal* 10.

also lead to the intentional or accidental release of pollutants. This includes the release of harmful chemicals used in routine processes of drilling, the discharge of 'produced water' from oil platform operations, and the emission of airborne pollutants from activities such as 'flaring' of excess gas.

Unlike vessel-source pollution, neither operational pollution from seabed activities nor the risk of accidental pollution has attracted sufficient attention to generate a detailed global agreement. Hence with the exception of some regional regimes and in relation to the Mining Code in force in the Area (discussed in Chapter 6) beyond national jurisdiction, most of the applicable rules are of a fairly general character. While MARPOL and the dumping regime (discussed below) have some application to pollution and the discarding of wastes from offshore installations such as oil and gas rigs and platforms, they do not apply to harmful substances released directly from the exploration, exploitation and associated offshore processing of seabed mineral resources.[211]

A. Territorial Sea, EEZ and Continental Shelf

Article 208(1) of the LOSC requires coastal states to adopt laws and regulations to prevent, reduce and control pollution of the marine environment arising from seabed activities subject to their jurisdiction, and from artificial islands, installations and structures. These laws are to be no less effective than international rules, standards and recommended practices and procedures.[212] Such rules are few and far between. There are for instance none of the detailed prescriptions for the construction and operation of seabed installations as are applicable to vessels under MARPOL.[213] Under Article 214 of the LOSC states are required to enforce the laws and regulations adopted in accordance with Article 208.

A related provision of the LOSC, Article 60(3), addresses the responsibility of states to remove any abandoned or disused installations or structures in order to ensure the safety of navigation. Such removal is to take account of any generally accepted international standards established by the competent international organisation, the IMO. Here the IMO has been active, having adopted Guidelines and Standards in 1989 which reiterate that states should generally remove such installations, except where non-removal, or partial removal, is consistent with the guidelines.[214] The decision to allow an offshore installation, structure or part thereof to remain on the seabed must be based on a consideration of a number of matters, including the rate of deterioration of the material, and its present and possible future effects on the marine environment and living resources. No installation or structure may be placed on any continental shelf or in any EEZ unless its design or construction is such that entire removal upon abandonment or permanent disuse would be feasible.

Article 208(4) encourages states to harmonise national policies in relation to pollution from seabed installations at an appropriate regional level, and to this end several regional

---

[211] MARPOL, art 2(b)(ii), 1996 Protocol, art 1(4)(c).

[212] LOSC, art 208(3).

[213] Although in relation to mobile drilling rigs see the non-binding 1989 IMO Code for the Construction and Equipment of Mobile Offshore Drilling Units, IMO Assembly Resolution A.649(16).

[214] IMO Assembly, Guidelines and Standards for the Removal of Offshore Installations and Structures on the Continental Shelf and in the Exclusive Economic Zone, Resolution A.672(16), *Basic Documents* No 41.

regimes have developed rules to address the problem. Hence in the Persian Gulf, the 1989 Protocol Concerning Marine Pollution resulting from Exploration and Exploitation of the Continental Shelf adds to the general regime for controlling marine pollution in the region under the UNEP RSP convention for the area.[215] Similarly, there is a protocol dedicated to pollution from seabed activities in the Mediterranean.[216]

In relation to the North Sea and North East Atlantic, the regional regime is the 1992 Convention for the Protection of the Marine Environment of the North-East Atlantic (OSPAR Convention),[217] which consolidates and updates two earlier regimes: the 1972 Oslo Convention and the 1974 Paris Convention. The OSPAR Convention is the main regime by which 15 states of the western coasts and catchments of Europe, together with the European Union, cooperate to protect the marine environment of the North-East Atlantic. Article 5 of the Convention requires parties to take all possible steps to prevent and eliminate pollution from offshore sources in accordance with the provisions of the Convention, in particular as provided for in Annex III. The region is an important one for offshore oil and gas exploitation—although production of hydrocarbons has peaked in fields in the North Sea, there are other basins within the OSPAR maritime area,[218] such as the Barents Sea, where there is potential for much greater production. Annex III to OSPAR addresses both dumping of wastes and offshore installations themselves.[219] In 1995, British proposals to dump the disused *Brent Spar* oil storage buoy in the Rockall Trough generated a high profile protest from Greenpeace and other groups, and was one catalyst for an OSPAR decision making permanent a moratorium on the dumping of offshore installations, subject to limited exceptions.[220]

The use and discharge of substances that may reach the maritime area are to be strictly subject to authorisation or regulation by national authorities, and they are to implement applicable decisions and recommendations adopted under the OSPAR Convention.[221] Competent authorities must also establish a system of monitoring and inspection to assess compliance with the authorisation or regulation procedures.[222] The OSPAR Commission is also charged with the task of collecting information about the substances which are used in offshore activities, and agree lists of substances for which authorisation or regulation is required, list substances which are toxic, persistent and likely to bioaccumulate, and draw up plans for their reduction and phase out.[223]

In 2003 the Ministerial Meeting of the OSPAR Commission adopted a strategy for the offshore oil and gas industry which is designed to prevent and ultimately eliminate pollution from offshore sources, and, where practical, to restore marine areas that have been damaged by such pollution. The OSPAR Convention parties have also adopted a string

---

[215] 1978 Kuwait Regional Convention for Cooperation on the Protection of the Marine Environment from Pollution.

[216] 1994 Protocol for the Protection of the Mediterranean Sea against Pollution Resulting from Exploration and Exploitation of the Continental Shelf and the Seabed and its Subsoil, *Basic Documents* No 26.

[217] *Basic Documents* No 50.

[218] OSPAR Convention, art 1(a).

[219] Ibid Annex III, art 3(1).

[220] OSPAR Decision 98/3 on the Disposal of Disused Offshore Installations, *Basic Documents* No 51.

[221] OSPAR Convention, Annex III, art 4(1).

[222] Ibid Annex III, art 4(2).

[223] Ibid Annex III, arts 10(a), (b).

of recommendations concerning issues such as a pre-screening scheme for chemicals used by the offshore industry,[224] for replacing wherever possible toxic chemicals with safe substitutes,[225] for limiting discharges of chemicals,[226] and the management of produced water from offshore installations.[227]

IX. Dumping at Sea

Covering two-thirds of the surface of the planet, and with a seemingly limitless capacity to assimilate wastes from human activities, the oceans present an obvious dumping ground for many substances that are costly or difficult to process or dispose of on land. Unregulated dumping and incineration activities increased in the post-Second World War period, and gained particular intensity in the late 1960s and early 1970s, and involved the dumping of large quantities of industrial effluents and sludges, sewage, nuclear wastes and decommissioned military hardware.

Dumping at sea was discussed at the 1972 Stockholm Conference on the Human Environment, and was a major leitmotif of environmental concern in the 1970s. This concern catalysed legal developments on regional and global scales. At a global level, the 1972 Convention on the Prevention of Marine Pollution by Dumping of Wastes and Other Matter[228] (1972 London Convention) was concluded, and this was supplemented by regional agreements in a number of sea areas, mostly under the auspices of the UNEP RSP. These were major advances, as the only rule at the time was supplied by the 1958 High Seas Convention, which required states to take measures to prevent pollution of the seas from the dumping of radioactive waste.[229]

A. 1972 London Convention

In its initial guise, the 1972 London Convention adopted a permissive approach to the regulation of dumping. Hence dumping, defined as the deliberate disposal at sea of wastes or other matter but not discharges from the normal operation of ships or from accidents, was permitted unless the substances concerned were established to be harmful.[230] The original convention divided wastes into three categories: (1) the 'black list' in Annex I such as oil and high-level nuclear waste, the dumping of which was prohibited outright; (2) the 'grey list' in Annex II such as certain metals, pesticides and low-level nuclear waste, the dumping of which was allowed under permit from the national authority; and (3) other substances that may be dumped, again under a permitting system, which served only to provide a level of

---

[224] OSPAR Recommendation 2000/4 on a Harmonised Prescreening Scheme for Offshore Chemicals.

[225] OSPAR Recommendation 2006/3 on Environmental Goals for the Discharge by the Offshore Industry of Chemicals that Are, or Which Contain Substances Identified as Candidates for Substitution.

[226] OSPAR Decision 2000/2 on a Harmonised Mandatory Control System for the Use and Reduction of the Discharge of Offshore Chemicals.

[227] OSPAR Recommendation 2001/1 for the Management of Produced Water from Offshore installations.

[228] *Basic Documents* No 18.

[229] 1958 High Seas Convention, art 25(1).

[230] 1972 London Convention, art III(1).

supervision of the dumping industry. This regime was not altered by the LOSC, which has fairly generic provisions concerning dumping that encourage states to prevent, reduce and control dumping, but allows the practice to continue.[231] The LOSC does provide, however, that states should adopt and enforce national laws, regulations and measures which are no less effective in preventing, reducing and controlling pollution than global rules and standards, opening the way for the implementation of a stricter system.[232]

B. 1996 Protocol

The permissive approach was reversed following major revision of the 1972 London Convention by the 1996 Protocol to the Convention on the Prevention of Marine Pollution by Dumping of Wastes and Other Matter[233] (1996 Protocol), which modernises and supersedes the original regime for those states which were also parties to the 1972 London Convention.

The 1996 Protocol adopts a prohibitionist approach such that dumping of any substance is generally outlawed, unless it can be demonstrated that it is not damaging to the marine environment. In this respect the Protocol requires parties to apply 'a precautionary approach to environmental protection from dumping ... whereby appropriate preventative measures are taken when there is reason to believe that wastes ... are likely to cause harm even when there is no conclusive evidence to prove a casual relation between inputs and their effects'.[234]

The objective of the 1996 Protocol is considerably stronger than the 1972 London Convention in that it aims for the elimination, where practicable, of pollution caused by dumping or incineration of wastes at sea.[235] The 1996 Protocol entered into force in 2006, and now has 45 parties. As the 1972 London Convention is more widely ratified (with 87 parties), the two instruments continue to operate side-by-side. In practice, however, the general prohibition on dumping at the heart of the 1996 Protocol, and in a number of regional agreements, appears to be respected by states, whether or not they are parties to one or both of the anti-dumping instruments.

Under the 1996 Protocol, dumping is defined as the deliberate disposal into the sea of wastes or other matter from vessels, aircraft, platforms or other man-made structures at sea, any deliberate disposal of vessels, aircraft, platforms, or other man-made structures, any storage of wastes or other matter in the seabed and the subsoil.[236] It does not include the disposal of wastes or other matter incidental to the normal operations of vessels, aircraft and platforms.[237] Incineration at sea is defined as the combustion of wastes on board a vessel, platform or other man-made structure at sea for the purpose of their deliberate disposal.[238]

---

[231] LOSC, art 210.
[232] Ibid arts 210(6), 216.
[233] *Basic Documents* No 19.
[234] 1996 Protocol, art 3(1).
[235] Ibid art 2.
[236] Ibid art 1(4)(a).
[237] Ibid art 1(4)(b).
[238] Ibid art 1(5)(a).

States are required to prohibit the incineration of all wastes at sea.[239] They must also prohibit the dumping of any wastes or other matter with the exception of those listed in Annex I. Those wastes are dredged material (which makes up the bulk of wastes dumped at sea); sewage sludge, fish waste, vessels and platforms; inert geological material (for example mine tailings); organic material of natural origin; bulky items primarily comprising iron, steel, concrete and similar mostly harmless materials (but only where there are no practicable alternatives to dumping); and carbon dioxide streams from carbon capture and storage processes.[240] Exceptions do, however, apply when it is necessary to secure the safety of human life or of vessels, aircraft, or platforms in situations of *force majeure* caused by adverse weather.[241]

Dumping of those substances listed in Annex I, though allowed, must still be subject to permitting and reporting obligations. Dumping may only proceed on obtaining a permit from a national authority, with governments paying attention to the opportunities to avoid dumping 'in favour of environmentally preferable alternatives'.[242] Parties must keep a record of the nature and volumes of wastes for which dumping permits have been issued, and the actual quantities of materials dumped, their location, time and method of dumping.[243] The 1996 Protocol is supplemented by Guidelines for the Assessment of Wastes or Other Matter that May be Considered for Dumping. These provide guidance to national authorities in evaluating applications for permits to dump waste, and encourage authorities to consider waste management options other than dumping such as re-use, recycling or treatment.

Significant amendments to the 1996 Protocol were made in 2006, the year it entered into force. At the First Meeting of the Contracting Parties, in November 2006, amendments to the 1996 London Protocol were adopted which permitted the storage of carbon dioxide under the seabed.[244] These amendments have now been implemented in domestic legislation in a number of jurisdictions.[245] The amendments allow for the regulation of sub-seabed sequestration of carbon dioxide, with carbon dioxide streams from carbon capture processes added to Annex I as a waste or other matter that may be considered for dumping. The amendments have been supplemented by Specific Guidelines for Assessment of Carbon Dioxide Streams for Disposal into Sub-Seabed Geological Formations.[246]

The 1996 Protocol does not permit water column sequestration of carbon dioxide, which can occur through the dumping of materials such as iron compounds to promote the growth of plankton which absorb carbon dioxide. This is the process known as ocean fertilisation.[247] In light of the significant environmental risks associated with ocean fertilisation, in 2008

---

[239] Ibid art 5.

[240] Ibid Annex I, [1].

[241] Ibid art 8(1).

[242] Ibid art 4(b).

[243] Ibid art 9(1)(b).

[244] IMO Doc LC-LP.1/Circ.5 (2006).

[245] See, eg, the Offshore Petroleum and Greenhouse Gas Storage Act 2006 (Australia) and the Energy Act 2008 (United Kingdom).

[246] IMO Doc LC 34/15 (2012), Annex 8.

[247] See further Robin Warner, 'Marine Snow Storms: Assessing the Environmental Risks of Ocean Fertilization' (2009) 3 *Carbon and Climate Law Review* 426; Rosemary Rayfuse, Mark G Lawrence and Kristina M Gjerde, 'Ocean Fertilization and Climate Change: The Need to Regulate Emerging High Seas Uses' (2008) 23 *International Journal of Marine and Coastal Law* 1.

the parties agreed to impose a moratorium on the practice, unless carried out for the purposes of legitimate scientific research.[248] This resolution expressly acknowledged similar decisions by parties to the 1992 Convention on Biological Diversity.[249] In 2010, the parties adopted a subsequent resolution setting out an 'Assessment Framework for Scientific Research Involving Ocean Fertilization', which guides parties in the assessment of ocean fertilisation research proposals.[250]

Subsequently, in Resolution LP.4(8) in 2013, the parties to the London Protocol agreed on a new Article 6bis, which provides that parties shall not allow the placement of matter into the sea from vessels, aircraft, platforms or other man-made structures at sea for marine geo-engineering purposes unless the activity is authorised under a permit. Marine geo-engineering is defined as 'a deliberate intervention in the marine environment to manipulate natural processes, including to counteract anthropogenic climate change', and a new Annex 4 to the London Protocol on marine geo-engineering lists and defines ocean fertilisation as 'any activity undertaken by humans with the principal intention of stimulating primary productivity in the oceans'. Ocean fertilisation activities may only be permitted if assessed to constitute legitimate scientific research.

C. Jurisdiction and Enforcement

The responsibility for issuing permits for dumping lies with the state party in which the waste is loaded, except where the loading occurs in a state which is not a party, in which case the flag state is to issue permits.[251] Parties are required to apply the measures to implement the 1996 Protocol to vessels and aircraft flying their flag, and vessels and aircraft loading in their territory wastes to be dumped or incinerated.[252] They must take appropriate measures to prevent and if necessary punish acts contrary to the provisions of the 1996 Protocol.

The LOSC provides an additional level of enforcement capacity. Under Article 210(5), dumping within the territorial sea, the EEZ, or onto the continental shelf shall not occur without the express prior approval of the coastal state. The coastal state 'has the right to permit, regulate and control such dumping after due consideration of the matter with other States which by reason of their geographical situation may be adversely affected thereby'. National laws and regulations, and applicable international rules and standards for controlling dumping, are to be enforced by the coastal state in the territorial sea, the EEZ, and the continental shelf, by the flag state with regard to its vessels, and by states in which the wastes are loaded onto vessels.[253]

While national laws are to be no less effective than global rules and standards,[254] there is nothing preventing coastal states from prescribing and enforcing stricter standards. This would be the case even in respect of a vessel granted a licence to dump wastes by another

---

[248] Resolution LC-LP.1, 31 October 2008.
[249] See COP IX/20 (2008).
[250] Resolution LC-LP.2 (2010) (IMO Doc LC 32/15 (2010), Annex 6).
[251] 1996 Protocol, art 9(2).
[252] Ibid art 10.
[253] LOSC, art 216(1).
[254] Ibid art 210(6).

state pursuant to the 1996 Protocol. Hence the rules in relation to dumping are more favourable for coastal states than those relating to operational vessel-source pollution, and this is essentially because allowing coastal state jurisdiction over dumping does not raise the freedom of navigation sensitivities surrounding coastal state regulation of incidental pollution from foreign vessels.

The 1972 London Convention, as amended over time, and the 1996 Protocol have had a significant impact upon state practice. The reductions in the volume of dumping were most extensive from the mid-1980s, as the regime became more stringent. The regime has since achieved the effective elimination of dumping of environmentally damaging materials, and for this reason it is frequently cited as one of the most successful regimes for regulating marine pollution. Around 1,000 permits to dump waste are issued by parties annually, primarily for the dumping of dredged materials (both maintenance and capital), sewage sludge, bulky items, fish wastes and spoilt cargo.[255]

D. Ship Scrapping and Recycling

Permits are also issued by a number of states to dispose of decommissioned vessels, in some cases so as to establish artificial reefs for use by recreational divers. Ships may only be dumped when they will not cause damage to the marine environment, and hence states will need to ensure that such vessels are stripped of environmentally hazardous substances such as heavy metals, oils and asbestos. Most ships are scrapped rather than dumped, and the processing of hazardous substances by ship recyclers pose risks to human health among workers in scrapyards, particularly in some developing states where there are lax or non-existent occupational health and safety standards. To remedy this, in May 2009 the IMO concluded the 2009 Hong Kong Convention for the Safe and Environmentally Sound Recycling of Ships, which addresses a host of issues surrounding ship recycling processes. The Convention, which is yet to enter into force, includes regulations addressing the design, construction and preparation of ships that will facilitate safe and environmentally sound recycling, the safe and environmentally sound operation of ship recycling facilities, and a certification and reporting system to promote compliance. The Convention puts into binding law many of the provisions of the 2003 IMO Guidelines on Ship Recycling.

E. Regional Agreements

Regional agreements are less important than they once were in regulating dumping because of the stringency of the global rules. These regional treaties for the most part follow the approach of the 1972 London Convention, and in many cases have been updated to reflect the 1996 Protocol. Such regimes apply in the Baltic, the Black Sea, the Mediterranean, the North-East Atlantic and the South Pacific.[256]

---

[255] See Convention on the Prevention of Marine Pollution by Dumping of Wastes and Other Matter, 1972 and its 1996 Protocol, *Final Report on Permits Issued in 2010*, IMO Doc LC-LP.1/Circ.63 (2014).

[256] See respectively the 1992 Convention on the Protection of the Marine Environment of the Baltic Sea, *Basic Documents* No 49, the 1992 Convention on the Protection of the Black Sea Against Pollution, the 1976 Protocol

One of the most active regimes has been that under the OSPAR Convention. The regime mirrors the 1996 Protocol in most material respects, but has a more supervisory character by virtue of the OSPAR Commission. At the 2007 meeting of the Commission, amendments to the Annexes to the Convention were adopted to allow carbon sequestration in geological formations under the seabed. In association with these, a decision was adopted to ensure environmentally safe storage of liquefied carbon dioxide in geological formations pursuant to OSPAR Guidelines for Risk Assessment and Management.[257] Mindful of the acidification impacts of carbon dioxide, the Commission also adopted a decision to prohibit placement of carbon dioxide on or above the seabed.[258] This practice illustrates that while the OSPAR Commission is committed to carbon capture and storage to reduce atmospheric concentrations of carbon dioxide, it is also aware of the need to ensure that this mitigation strategy does not itself contribute to ocean pollution.

X. Land-Based and Atmospheric Pollution

It was observed at the beginning of this chapter that land-based and atmospheric pollution make up the lion's share of harmful substances entering the marine environment. Yet unlike the other sources of pollution, these have proved to be the most difficult to regulate, in large part because this would require significant restrictions on industrial and other activities within the territory of all states, and coastal states in particular. Although land-based and atmospheric pollution is undoubtedly contributing significantly to the declining health of ocean environments, the sources of this pollution and its environmental effects are highly diffuse. Moreover, in the case of point-source land-based pollution such as sewage from coastal or ocean outfalls, many coastal states have neither the capacity nor the inclination to implement stringent pollution control standards. Land- and atmosphere-based pollution of the oceans is therefore an obvious and acute 'tragedy of the commons'.

The LOSC contains several provisions applicable to land-based and atmospheric pollution of the marine environment and in this respect is an improvement on the Geneva regime that imposed no obligation to control such pollution. Under Article 207(1), states are required to adopt laws and regulations to prevent, reduce and control pollution from land-based sources, including rivers, estuaries, pipelines and outfall structures, taking into account internationally agreed rules. A similar obligation applies to pollution from or through the atmosphere by dint of Article 212(1). Specific mention is made of the requirement to control atmospheric pollution from vessels and aircraft. As we have seen, the IMO has made significant headway in relation to the reduction of some airborne pollutants from merchant shipping through MARPOL, Annex VI. Targeted substances include ozone

for the Prevention of Pollution of the Mediterranean by Dumping from Ships and Aircraft or Incineration at Sea, *Basic Documents* No 24, the 1992 OSPAR Convention, *Basic Documents* No 50, and the 1986 Noumea Protocol for the Prevention of Pollution from Dumping.

[257] OSPAR Decision 2007/2 on the Storage of Carbon Dioxide Streams in Geological Formations, *Basic Documents* No 53.

[258] OSPAR Decision 2007/1 to Prohibit the Storage of Carbon Dioxide Streams in the Water Column or on the Sea-Bed, *Basic Documents* No 52.

depleting gases, used principally in vessel refrigeration systems, and nitrous and sulphur oxides emitted from the operation of marine diesel engines.

The obligation to take measures to deal with land-based and atmospheric pollution in Articles 207 and 214 of the LOSC is supplemented by the obligation in Articles 213 and 222 to enforce them. However, this scheme is clearly less demanding than that applicable to vessel-source pollution and dumping, in that it does not mandate the application of international standards, but requires only that states take these into account. This gives coastal states considerable latitude in determining whether to adopt pollution abatement measures, and whether particular substances should be considered to be polluting within the meaning of Article 1(4) of the LOSC. This flexibility is further emphasised as regard pollution from land-based sources by Article 207(4), which provides that in establishing global and regional rules, states should take into account 'characteristic regional features, the economic capacity of developing States and their need for economic development'.

Land-based and atmospheric marine pollution has been subject to some attention in proceedings before international courts and tribunals. In the *MOX Plant* case[259] ITLOS issued an important provisional measures order, which required the two states to cooperate in order, among other things, to devise measures to prevent pollution of the marine environment of the Irish Sea from a nuclear fuel reprocessing plant. In *Land Reclamation by Singapore in and Around the Straits of Johor*,[260] ITLOS repeated its statement in the *MOX Plant* case that 'the duty to cooperate is a fundamental principle in the prevention of pollution of the marine environment'[261] under the LOSC, observed that it could not be excluded that Singapore's land reclamation works may have adverse effects on the marine environment, including within Malaysia's territorial sea,[262] and directed Singapore not to conduct land reclamation in such a way that might cause serious harm to the marine environment.[263]

Thirty years earlier, in response to French atmospheric nuclear testing in the Pacific that had a number of impacts on the marine environment of the region, Australia and New Zealand commenced proceedings against France in the ICJ in the *Nuclear Tests* cases.[264] Both applicants contended that the nuclear testing generating radioactive fallout constituted an infringement of high seas freedoms by interfering with the freedom of navigation and overflight, and interfering with the freedom to explore and exploit the living and non-living resources of the sea. To this end, Australia and New Zealand sought interim orders in relation not only to potential pollution on each respective metropolitan land mass, but also ocean space. However, the Court did not consider the issue of marine pollution, and ordered France to refrain from nuclear tests causing deposit of radioactive substances on Australian or New Zealand territory. The arguments relating to marine pollution were also not considered on the merits, with the Court finding that the dispute had

---

[259] *MOX Plant (Ireland v United Kingdom)* (provisional measures) (2002) 41 ILM 405.
[260] *Land Reclamation by Singapore in and Around the Straits of Johor (Malaysia v Singapore)* (provisional measures) 8 October 2003 www.itlos.org.
[261] *MOX Plant* (provisional measures) (2002) 41 ILM 405, [82].
[262] *Land Reclamation by Singapore in and Around the Straits of Johor (Malaysia v Singapore)* (provisional measures) 8 October 2003 www.itlos.org, [96].
[263] Ibid [106].
[264] *Nuclear Tests (Australia v France)* (interim measures) [1973] ICJ Rep 99, (merits) [1974] ICJ Rep 253; *(New Zealand v France)* (interim measures) [1973] ICJ Rep 135, (merits) [1974] ICJ Rep 457.

become moot following France's public undertaking to cease atmospheric tests. An effort by New Zealand to reopen the case in 1995 following French resumption of testing, this time underground, involved a claim that France was polluting the marine environment contrary to international law. As with the proceedings in the 1970s, these were brought to an end by the ICJ when it found that there was no basis for the proceedings, as the underground testing did not did not disturb the original decision which concerned atmospheric testing.[265]

A. 1995 Global Programme of Action

Prior to the 1992 United Nations Conference on Environment and Development in Rio, there were calls for a global treaty to address land-based sources of marine pollution in order to replace the non-binding 1985 Montreal Guidelines. No such treaty was agreed, but in the wake of the Rio Earth Summit, 108 states and the European Commission adopted the 1995 Washington Declaration on the Protection of the Marine Environment from Land-based Activities, and the 1995 Global Programme of Action for the Protection of the Marine Environment from Land-Based Activities (GPA).[266]

Adopting a soft-law approach, the GPA provides guidance for national and regional authorities in devising and implementing measures to prevent, reduce, control and eliminate marine degradation from land-based activities. The GPA reflects an effort to provide some coherence to an area of global environmental policy where there has been a proliferation of regional agreements that, while independently successful, are not always well co-ordinated. Among other things, the GPA exhorts states to establish national programmes of action, and recommends that states establish specific targets for nine categories of pollutant—sewage, persistent organic pollutants (POPs), radioactive materials, heavy metals, oils, nutrient, sediments, litter, and physical alteration or destruction of habitats.[267]

Much of the GPA is fairly general and hortatory in calling for integrated coastal area management; however, in other respects it is relatively prescriptive. Some of the recommended targets for pollutant categories are fairly specific, as seen in the passages of the GPA addressing sewage, where it adopts the Agenda 21 target of ensuring that by 2025 all sewage, waste waters and solid wastes are disposed of in conformity with national or international environmental quality guidelines.[268] Regrettably it is in relation to sewage that there has probably been the least progress among the nine land-based threats that are the focus of the GPA. For instance, in East Asia up to 90 per cent of waste water discharged into the marine environment is untreated.[269] Also problematic is the ongoing failure of efforts to prevent pollution of the seas from persistent debris, especially plastics. It is estimated that such materials introduce substantial quantities of persistent toxics into the marine environment,

---

[265] *Nuclear Tests, Request for an Examination of the Situation in Accordance with Paragraph 63 of the Court's Judgment of 20 December 1974 in Nuclear Tests (New Zealand v France)* [1995] ICJ Rep 288.

[266] UN Doc UNEP(OCA)/LBA/IG.2/7 (1995). See generally Daud Hassan, *Protecting the Marine Environment from Land-based Sources of Pollution: Towards Effective International Cooperation* (Burlington, VT, Ashgate Publishing Company, 2006) 96ff.

[267] GPA, [21(b)].

[268] Ibid [96].

[269] UNEP/GPA, *The State of the Marine Environment: Trends and Processes* (The Hague, UNEP/GPA, 2006), 4.

and are responsible for the deaths of more than one million seabirds and 100,000 marine mammals each year through ingestion, suffocation and entanglement.[270]

As VanderZwaag and Powers have noted, the main challenges facing the effective implementation of the GPA include limited national participation and implementation, limited reporting by national authorities, limited coverage of pollution categories, limited financing, and the non-binding character of the instrument.[271] One particular weakness of the GPA is in relation to atmospheric pollution of the marine environment, one of the most serious of impacts of which is ocean acidification caused by ocean uptake of carbon dioxide from the atmosphere. While, as noted above, the GPA sets specific targets for nine source categories, which cover a majority of land-based marine pollutants, carbon emissions from land-based sources are not included in any of these.

The present atmospheric concentration of carbon dioxide is higher than it has been for the past 420,000 years, and possibly for the last 15 million years.[272] While the effects of this change to the carbon concentration of the atmosphere on the global climate system is widely acknowledged and increasingly well understood,[273] the impact of carbon dioxide on the chemistry of the oceans has only relatively recently attracted attention from scientists and policy-makers. Between 1800 and 1994 the world's oceans absorbed about one-third of the carbon dioxide released from all human activities.[274] As atmospheric concentrations of carbon dioxide increase, a larger quantity of carbon dioxide is absorbed by the oceans and over the next few millennia the oceans will absorb approximately 90 per cent of carbon dioxide emitted into the atmosphere.[275] Climate change and the related process of ocean acidification undoubtedly pose the most serious threat to the integrity of the global marine environment.[276]

The chemical process of ocean acidification is relatively straightforward, although there is substantial regional and seasonal variability in ocean pH.[277] As the term 'ocean acidification' suggests, when carbon dioxide dissolves in the oceans it reacts with water to form carbonic acid.[278] This process results in substantial changes to the carbon chemistry of the oceans. Hydrogen ions released in the formation of carbonic acid combine with carbonate ions in the water to form bicarbonate, removing substantial amounts of carbonate ions from the water which are essential for the formation of a range of marine organisms.

---

[270] Ibid 27.

[271] David VanderZwaag and Anne Powers, 'The Protection of the Marine Environment from Land-Based Pollution and Activities: Gauging the Tides of Global and Regional Governance' (2008) 23 *International Journal of Marine and Coastal Law* 423, 437ff.

[272] SCOR/IOC, 'The Ocean in a High CO_2 World' (2004) 17 *Oceanography* 72, 72.

[273] See Intergovernmental Panel on Climate Change, *Climate Change 2014: Synthesis Report* (Cambridge, Cambridge University Press, 2014).

[274] CL Sabine et al., 'The Oceanic Sink for Anthropogenic CO_2' (2004) 305 *Science* 367.

[275] SCOR/IOC, 'The Ocean in a High CO_2 World', 72.

[276] Intergovernmental Panel on Climate Change, *Climate Change 2013: Impacts, Adaptation and Vulnerability. Contribution of Working Group II to the Fifth Assessment Report of the Intergovernmental Panel on Climate Change* (Cambridge, Cambridge University Press, 2013) vol I, ch 6 'Ocean Systems'.

[277] See BI McNeil and RJ Matearb, 'Southern Ocean Acidification: A Tipping Point at 450-ppm Atmospheric CO_2' (2008) 105 *Proceedings of the National Academy of Sciences* 18860. pH refers to the 'potential for hydrogen' and is a measure of the acidity or alkalinity of a solution.

[278] JC Orr et al, 'Anthropogenic Ocean Acidification over the Twenty-first Century and Its Impact on Calcifying Organisms' (2005) 437 *Nature* 681.

Many marine photosynthetic organisms and animals, such as molluscs, corals, echino-derms, foraminifera and calcareous algae, make shells and plates out of calcium carbonate.[279] This is only possible when the seawater contains a sufficient concentration of calcium carbonate. Increased concentrations of carbon dioxide will increase acidity, which impedes the process of calcification. Calcifying organisms will be negatively affected in the present century,[280] with estimates suggesting that calcification rates will decrease by as much as 50 per cent by 2100 due to the fall in calcium carbonate concentration, with potentially devastating consequences for coral reefs, and the broader marine ecosystems which they support.[281]

XI. Further Reading

Alan Boyle, 'Marine Pollution Under the Law of the Sea Convention' (1985) 79 *American Journal of International Law* 347

Jean-Pierre Gattuso and Lina Hansson (eds), *Ocean Acidification* (Oxford, Oxford University Press, 2011)

Daud Hassan, *Protecting the Marine Environment from Land-based Sources of Pollution: Towards Effective International Cooperation* (Burlington, VT, Ashgate Publishing Company, 2006)

Aleka Mandaraka-Sheppard, *Modern Maritime Law* 2nd edn (London, Routledge-Cavendish, 2007) pts III and IV

Erik Jap Molenaar, *Coastal State Jurisdiction Over Vessel Source Pollution* (The Hague, Kluwer, 1998)

Brian Smith, *State Responsibility and the Marine Environment: The Rules of Decision* (Oxford, Oxford University Press, 1988)

Alan Khee-Jin Tan, *Vessel-Source Marine Pollution: The Law and Politics of International Regulation* (Cambridge, Cambridge University Press, 2006)

Robin Warner, *Protecting the Oceans Beyond National Jurisdiction: Strengthening the International Law Framework* (Leiden, Martinus Nijhoff, 2009)

---

[279] Royal Society, *Ocean Acidification Due to Increasing Atmospheric Carbon Dioxide* (London, Royal Society, 2005) 20.

[280] OSPAR Commission, *Effects on the Marine Environment of Ocean Acidification Resulting from Elevated Levels of CO_2 in the Atmosphere* (2006).

[281] O Hoegh-Guldberg, 'Coral Reefs Under Rapid Climate Change and Ocean Acidification' (2007) 318 *Science*, 1737, 1740.

16

Delimitation of Maritime Boundaries

I. Introduction

The development of the international law of the sea has had an important impact upon the oceans in many ways with perhaps the most significant being the capacity of coastal states to establish a range of different maritime zones. Initially the claims to the territorial sea were so restricted in their extent that limited consideration needed to be given to the issues which arose from overlap between the maritime entitlements of multiple states. However, as territorial sea claims expanded further into the oceans and as new maritime zones were added, there was an increasing need to settle upon methods for maritime boundary delimitation. This need arose in two instances. The first was in the case of adjacent states which shared a land boundary which terminated at a point on the coast from which maritime claims were then asserted into the adjacent sea. Techniques therefore needed to be developed to address how the adjoining territorial sea claims of these states would be delimited. The second instance was that of opposite states which faced one another across a maritime domain, whether as narrow as a strait or as wide as an ocean. The delimitation of relatively narrow territorial seas did not pose insurmountable difficulties; however, the scale and complexity of the task of maritime boundary delimitation was multiplied when broad continental shelves and the EEZ were recognised in the law of the sea.

The twentieth century witnessed a very significant growth in international law and relevant state practice associated with maritime boundary delimitations, and these issues were tackled at both UNCLOS I and III. While the law in this field is now well developed, and there are many examples of concluded maritime boundaries which have been settled as a result of agreement between the states or following international adjudication or arbitration, there remain instances where neighbouring states have yet to settle their maritime boundaries.[1] This area of the law has received further impetus in recent years as a result of the submission of outer continental shelf claims to the CLCS, which has been a catalyst for some coastal states to determine their maritime boundaries and take into account respective overlapping continental shelf entitlements beyond 200 nm.[2]

---

[1] A prominent example is the unresolved maritime boundaries between Canada and the United States; see discussion in Ted L McDorman, *Salt Water Neighbors: International Ocean Law Relations between the United States and Canada* (New York, Oxford University Press, 2009).

[2] See the discussion in ch 5.

The law of the sea has developed principles, processes and institutions to assist in the determination of maritime boundaries in a peaceful and methodical manner, in the service of an overriding objective to bring stability and order to maritime affairs. The importance of this value was highlighted in the recent *Bay of Bengal Arbitration (Bangladesh/India)*, in which Bangladesh contested the selection of basepoints on unstable features on the Indian coast, noting that they will disappear or change as a consequence of sea level rise caused by climate change. The tribunal found that the issue of future change was irrelevant, as its task was to achieve a delimitation at the present time,[3] and concluded that 'neither the prospect of climate change nor its possible effects can jeopardize the large number of settled maritime boundaries throughout the world. This applies equally to maritime boundaries agreed between States and to those established through international adjudication.'[4] Although correct in principle, the conclusion is difficult to reconcile with the rapidly changing coastline conditions in the Bay of Bengal (and elsewhere) driven by sea level rise. This affirmation of stability in the context of maritime boundaries also sits in stark contrast to the manner in which rising sea levels are addressed in the context of baselines, where the LOSC, as it currently stands, adopts an ambulatory approach, with territorial sea baselines shifting landwards as the seas encroach.[5]

As soon as coastal states began to contemplate some form of offshore maritime claims it was inevitable that there would be a need to determine maritime boundaries between states, and this prompted consideration as to the relevance of territorial borders, and the modalities for settling them, to the resolution of overlapping maritime domains. Although there was long established state practice concerning the drawing of land boundaries, this had little application to maritime boundaries except the practices which had developed in the case of rivers. The principle of the mid-channel or *thalweg* had some currency in the case where two states shared a river and there was a need to determine the international boundary through the river.[6] The principle had its foundation in Roman law and had been adopted by Anglo-Saxons as early as the seventh century where it had particular application in wide rivers and estuaries.[7] As Fulton observed, by applying these principles to the seas the effect was that 'the mid-line in the sea lying between the coasts of two states was held to be the boundary of their respective maritime jurisdiction or sovereignty'.[8] There were also examples of state practice applying this principle in concluded boundary treaties which encompassed rivers, lakes, and adjacent maritime areas of which the practice adopted between Great Britain and the United States regarding their North American boundaries between Canada and the United States was particularly extensive.[9]

[3] *Bay of Bengal Maritime Boundary Delimitation Arbitration (Bangladesh/India)*, Award of 7 July 2014, [214] (*Bay of Bengal Arbitration (Bangladesh/India)*).
[4] Ibid [217].
[5] See the discussion in ch 2.
[6] See the discussion of this principle in *Iowa v Illinois* (1893) 147 US 1, 7–8; C John Colombos, *The International Law of the Sea*, 6th edn (London, Longman, 1967) 224.
[7] Thomas Wemyss Fulton, *The Sovereignty of the Sea* (Edinburgh, Blackwood, 1911) 541–42.
[8] Ibid 542, pointing to examples as ancient as 1023 in support of the use of this approach.
[9] See 1783 Definitive Treaty of Peace between Great Britain and the United States, art II with respect to the boundary in the western Gulf of Maine; and 1846 Oregon Boundary Treaty between Great Britain and the United States with respect to the Pacific boundary through the Juan de Fuca.

A. *Grisbådarna Arbitration*

By the turn of the twentieth century state practice had become sufficiently developed with respect to the territorial sea that some coastal states began to give active consideration to the delimitation of their adjacent or opposite maritime boundaries. Where these could not be concluded by way of treaty, states began to resort to international arbitration, thereby setting a precedent which has continued into the current century.

The most significant of these early cases was the 1909 *Grisbådarna Arbitration* between Norway and Sweden.[10] In that case the parties agreed to submit to arbitration a dispute as to the direction of their joint maritime boundary as it ran between Norwegian islands and the Swedish mainland into the Grisbådarna fishing bank, which at that time was an area fished by both countries. Whilst a 1661 treaty had been concluded which partly resolved these issues,[11] the task for the arbitrators was to determine whether the boundary had been conclusively settled or whether a further delimitation should take place. After reviewing the facts, the arbitrators formed the view that the 'delimitation should be made today by tracing a line perpendicularly to the general direction of the coast'.[12] The arbitrators then went on to consider that lobster fishing had been conducted for a much longer period of time in the area by Swedish fishermen than Norwegians; that Sweden had performed certain acts in the area such as the erection of navigation beacons; and that whilst the Swedish fishermen had a longer history in the area, the Norwegians had never been excluded. In light of these facts the arbitrators provided for a boundary line to pass midway between the Swedish mainland and Norwegian islands until it reached the high seas.[13] The importance of the decision is that whilst the arbitrators did take into account the conventional technique of delimiting boundaries by way of a mid-line, they also considered the special circumstances of the region and the fact that both states had exploited the fishing banks and that to have awarded the fishing banks to one state alone would not have been consistent with the history of the area. The arbitrators were therefore mindful of the 'special circumstances' of the area in question in reaching their decision.[14]

B. Influence of Boggs

The scholar who had the most influence upon the early debates on the techniques of maritime boundary delimitation was the Geographer to the United States Department of State, S Whittemore Boggs, who was a member of the United States delegation to the 1930 Hague Conference and led its submissions on the methods for territorial sea delimitation.[15]

---

[10] *Arbitral Award in the Question of the Delimitation of a Certain Part of the Maritime Boundary between Norway and Sweden* (1910) AJIL 226 (*Grisbådarna Arbitration*).

[11] Convention between Denmark and Sweden (1660–61) 6 Consolidated Treaty Series 495.

[12] *Grisbådarna Arbitration* (1910) AJIL 226, 232.

[13] Ibid 235–36.

[14] This aspect of the decision had continuing relevance, see Edward Collins and Martin A Rogoff, 'The International Law of Maritime Boundary Delimitation' (1982) 34 *Maine Law Review* 1, 56–58.

[15] S Whittemore Boggs, 'Delimitation of the Territorial Sea: The Method of Delimitation Proposed by the Delegation of the United States at the Hague Conference for the Codification of International Law' (1930) 24 *AJIL* 541.

In 1937 Boggs had argued that it was important to determine a 'triple point' when dealing with offshore maritime boundaries of adjacent states, defining that point as being one at which three boundaries should meet: 'namely the boundary between the territorial seas of the two contiguous countries and, for each of the two countries, the boundary between its territorial sea and the high sea.'[16] Boggs did not favour an approach which resulted in the continuation of the land boundary, noting the distinction between land and maritime boundaries, but supported the use of a straight line which would be 'equidistant' so as to take into account various offshore features so that the line is 'constructed on the chart exactly as the median line in a lake or river is constructed.'[17]

Boggs further developed these views at around the same time as the ILC was commencing its work on the law of the sea. It was at this stage that Boggs began to expand upon the notion of a 'median line' which was to be a 'line every point of which is equidistant from the nearest point or points on opposite shores.'[18] Mindful of the impact of the expanding scope of coastal state sovereignty resulting from claims being made at that time to the continental shelf, Boggs suggested that 'the lateral jurisdiction limit should be developed progressively from the outer limit of sovereignty, which is the seaward limit of the territorial sea. In this progressive development or extension of the line of lateral jurisdiction, greater and greater stretches of the coasts of the two adjacent states are taken into consideration, thus taking into account all of the sinuosities of the coast, including gulfs and peninsulas, large and small.'[19]

II. Work of the International Law Commission

The ILC commenced its work on the law of the sea in 1949 and almost immediately recognised the need to address the question of maritime boundaries. However, the Commission was confronted with the challenge of there being no body of existing international law on point, as there was little state practice or decisions of international courts and tribunals to consider. The early reports of the Special Rapporteur, JPA François, were influenced by the work of Boggs, but the ILC quickly realised that there was a need for expert input into the matter and in 1953 a Committee of Experts met in The Hague to consider a number of questions which had been put to them. In the case of the territorial sea between opposite states, the Committee of Experts recommended that the general rule should be a median line boundary 'every point of which is equidistant from the base-lines of the States concerned.'[20] It was acknowledged that islands would need to be taken into account in the delimitation process, as would drying rocks and shoals within a defined distance of the

---

[16] S Whittemore Boggs 'Problems of Water-Boundary Definition: Median Lines and International Boundaries Through Territorial Waters' (1937) 27 *Geographical Review* 445, 453.

[17] Ibid 456.

[18] S Whittemore Boggs, 'Delimitation of Seaward Areas under National Jurisdiction' (1951) 45 *AJIL* 240, 256–58.

[19] Ibid 262.

[20] 'UN Doc No A/CN 4/61/Add 1, Annex' (1953) *Yearbook of the International Law Commission*, vol 2, 77.

coastal state. In the case of delimitation for adjacent states, the principle of equidistance was recommended which could be circumvented by the states through agreement to negotiate a boundary in order to reach an equitable solution.[21] The Committee of Experts recommended that these techniques could also be applied in the case of continental shelf boundary delimitations.[22]

These proposals were actively considered by the ILC in its subsequent deliberations and their influence can be seen in the draft Articles adopted by the Commission in 1956 which contained three provisions dealing with maritime boundary delimitation.[23] In the case of the territorial sea, two draft articles were proposed dealing with the case of opposite states, including within a strait, and adjacent states. Article 12 dealing with delimitation in straits and between opposite states provided that the boundary was to be fixed by agreement, in the absence of which, and unless special circumstances existed, the boundary was to be 'a median line every point of which is equidistant from the nearest points on the baselines'.[24] In its accompanying commentary the ILC observed that whilst its work had been influenced by the Committee of Experts it considered that 'it would be wrong to go into too much detail and that the rule should be fairly flexible'.[25] With respect to the application of the proposed rule in the absence of agreement having been reached, the ILC observed that 'special circumstances would probably necessitate frequent departures from the mathematical median line'.[26]

In the case of the boundary between adjacent states, Article 14 of the ILC draft proposed a similar formula, though in this instance providing that in the absence of agreement or special circumstances, the boundary was to be drawn on the basis of equidistance 'from the nearest points on the baseline from which the breadth of the territorial sea of each country is measured'. In its accompanying commentary to Article 14, the ILC observed the number of options it was confronted with in this instance, including extending the land frontier into the sea, and drawing a line at right angles to the coast as was considered in the *Grisbådarna Arbitration*. Ultimately the ILC noted that it endorsed the views of the Committee of Experts and this was reflected in the drafting of Article 14. However, the rule was one that needed to be applied flexibly.[27] With respect to the continental shelf, draft Article 72 essentially recommended duplicate provisions to those which had been endorsed in the case of the territorial sea, with the only distinction being favouring the median line in the case of opposite states and an equidistance line in the case of adjacent states. The ILC observed once again that these rules needed to be 'fairly elastic' to take into account a range of coastal features, including islands and navigable channels.[28]

---

[21] Ibid.

[22] Ibid.

[23] International Law Commission, 'Articles Concerning the Law of the Sea with Commentaries' (1956) *Yearbook of the International Law Commission*, vol 2, 265–301. Notwithstanding that the ILC proposed the creation of a contiguous zone in the draft articles, no allowance was made for the delimitation of contiguous zone boundaries between opposite or adjacent states.

[24] Ibid 271.

[25] Ibid 271.

[26] Ibid 271.

[27] Ibid 272.

[28] Ibid 300.

III. Codification of the Law

When the ILC's draft articles were considered at UNCLOS I there was a risk that as the conference progressed differing approaches would be taken with respect to the delimitation of territorial sea and continental shelf boundaries because each question was considered by separate committees. Nevertheless, because the work of the Fourth Committee in considering the continental shelf was concluded relatively early in the conference deliberations, it was possible to take its discussions into account when the First Committee looked at the territorial sea.

A. Convention on the Territorial Sea and Contiguous Zone

Mindful of the discussions which had taken place in the Fourth Committee, the First Committee when considering the territorial sea sought to adopt complementary provisions, although there was debate on whether the reference to 'special circumstances' was appropriate and if there was a need to retain the ILC's proposed two articles. Eventually a decision was made to maintain the reference to 'special circumstances' whilst also merging draft Articles 12 and 14 to form a single convention article on territorial sea boundary delimitation. The outcome was Article 12 of the 1958 Convention on the Territorial Sea and Contiguous Zone,[29] which sought to address the situation of opposite and adjacent states in a single provision in which, in the absence of agreement, the territorial sea was to be determined 'beyond the median line every point of which is equidistant from the nearest points on the baselines from which the breadth of the territorial sea ... is measured'.[30] An exception to this rule was permitted in the case of historic title or other special circumstances. The Convention also required states to mark their agreed boundaries on charts.[31] In an interesting departure from the ILC's draft articles, UNCLOS I also endorsed in Article 24(3) of the Convention a provision dealing with the delimitation of the contiguous zone between opposite and adjacent states in which absent agreement between them, the contiguous zone was not to extend beyond a median line which was to be equidistant from the nearest points on the baseline.

B. Convention on the Continental Shelf

Article 6 of the 1958 Convention on the Continental Shelf[32] sought to address the issue of continental shelf boundaries between opposite and adjacent states in the one provision and essentially provides for a similar mechanism, with one distinction. Both provisions emphasise that the boundaries are to be determined by agreement, thereby giving to the relevant coastal states the opportunity to negotiate a settlement of the maritime

---

[29] *Basic Documents* No 9.
[30] Convention on the Territorial Sea and Contiguous Zone, art 12(1).
[31] Ibid art 12(2).
[32] *Basic Documents* No 13.

boundary. In the absence of agreement, and 'unless another boundary line is justified by special circumstances',[33] the boundary in the case of opposite states was to be based on a median line while that for adjacent states was an equidistance line. In both instances, the drawing of the boundaries should be referenced against charts and geographical features as they exist at a particular date and 'reference should be made to fixed permanent identifiable points on the land'.[34]

Following the conclusion and entry into force of the Convention, six states made declarations or reservations which expressly referred to Article 6. Yugoslavia, which unsuccessfully sought to have removed from the draft convention reference to 'special circumstances', indicated its rejection of that provision,[35] whilst Venezuela lodged an express reservation to the whole article.[36] China, Greece and Iran also lodged reservations and declarations, as did France which refused to accept the equidistance principle in three instances, one of which was where special circumstances existed as in the case of the Bay of Biscay, Bay of Granville, parts of the Straits of Dover and in the North Sea adjacent to the French coast.[37]

IV. Early Cases

In the wake of UNCLOS I there was considerable commentary with respect to the maritime boundary delimitation provisions of both the Convention on the Territorial Sea and Contiguous Zone, and the Convention on the Continental Shelf. With the growing interest, however, in continental shelf claims and the impetus given to this developing regime at UNCLOS I, in addition to the greater potential for overlapping claims requiring delimitation of new boundaries because of the greater extent of this maritime zone, more attention was given to the continental shelf provisions. Of particular concern was the 'special circumstances' exception and the instances in which coastal states would be able to rely upon that provision to justify a departure from a median or equidistance line boundary.[38] Gutteridge, a member of the United Kingdom delegation to UNCLOS I, wrote following the conference that the 'special circumstances' criterion would be of particular use 'Where the continental shelf underlies an area of shallow sea, such as the Persian Gulf, which has many islands and is surrounded by the coasts of opposite or adjacent states, the drawing of the boundary on the strict principle of the median line could, it is clear, result in many curious and inequitable deflections of the median line'.[39] These observations on the implementation of the Convention on the Continental Shelf formed some context to judicial consideration of these issues in some important post-UNCLOS I decisions.

---

[33] Convention on the Continental Shelf, art 6(1) and art 6(2).

[34] Ibid art 6(3).

[35] UN Doc No ST/LEG/SER. E/2, 627.

[36] Ibid 627; Venezuela also made a reservation/declaration to the Convention on the Territorial Sea and Contiguous Zone, arts 12, 24 (3): at 611.

[37] UN Doc No ST/LEG/SER. E/2, 626–27; the United Kingdom lodged an objection to this French reservation: UN Doc No ST/LEG/SER. E/2, 628.

[38] DW Bowett, *The Law of the Sea* (Manchester, Manchester University Press, 1967) 40.

[39] JAC Gutteridge, 'The 1958 Convention on the Continental Shelf' (1959) 35 *British Year Book of International Law* 102, 120.

A. *North Sea Continental Shelf* Cases

The first test for judicial interpretation of Article 6 of the Convention on the Continental Shelf arose in the *North Sea Continental Shelf* cases[40] between the Federal Republic of Germany (West Germany), and the Netherlands and Denmark over their respective continental shelf boundaries in the North Sea. Whilst West Germany had been able to reach separate agreements with both the Netherlands and Denmark over the partial delimitation of the continental shelf based on the principle of equidistance,[41] it had proved impossible to reach agreement on the further extension of those two boundaries into the North Sea with the effect that it was mutually agreed by all three states to refer their dispute to the International Court of Justice. The Court was asked to determine the 'principles and rules of international law' applicable between the parties with respect to the delimitation of the continental shelf in the North Sea.[42] Of relevance to this task was that whilst both Denmark and the Netherlands had ratified the Convention, West Germany had not.[43]

The ICJ, faced with the fact that one of the parties to the dispute had not ratified the Convention, gave due consideration to whether Article 6 of the Convention reflected customary international law. The Court identified a number of difficulties with the principle of equidistance in Article 6 and observed that 'the notion of equidistance as being logically necessary, in the sense of being an unescapable a priori accompaniment of basic continental shelf doctrine, is incorrect.'[44] It supported this conclusion by reference to the work of the ILC Committee of Experts, and the manner in which UNCLOS I had given emphasis to reaching delimitation by agreement through the use of equitable principles.[45] The Court concluded that the ILC had proposed the adoption of equidistance 'with considerable hesitation, somewhat on an experimental basis, at most de lege ferenda, and not at all de lege lata or as an emerging rule of customary international law'.[46] The Court then proposed a set of rules which states were to follow in all delimitations. These being: (1) that the parties were obliged to enter into negotiations with a view to arriving at agreement; (2) that equitable principles were to be applied; and (3) that the continental shelf was the natural prolongation of a coastal state's land territory and it could not encroach upon the natural prolongation of the territory of another state.[47] Whilst the Court was prepared to accept that in certain cases where equity was applied the equidistance principle would be acceptable, in some geographical circumstances the use of that principle caused an inequitable result, as would occur in this case.[48] The Court then considered the factors to be taken into account by the parties so as to obtain an equitable delimitation, accepting as being relevant the need to consider the geographical configuration of the coastline, the unity of any seabed

---

[40] *North Sea Continental Shelf (Federal Republic of Germany v Denmark; Federal Republic of Germany v The Netherlands)* [1969] ICJ Rep 3 (*North Sea Continental Shelf*).
[41] Ibid [6].
[42] Ibid [6].
[43] West Germany had signed the Convention on the Continental Shelf on 30 October 1959 but had not ratified it by the time proceedings were instituted before the ICJ.
[44] *North Sea Continental Shelf* [1969] ICJ Rep 3, [46].
[45] Ibid [50]–[55].
[46] Ibid [62].
[47] Ibid [85].
[48] Ibid [89].

mineral deposits, and the need for a reasonable degree of proportionality between the length of the coastline and the extent of the continental shelf claimed.[49] Following the ICJ's decision, treaties were concluded by the respective parties in 1971 which provided for the delimitation of their continental shelves based upon the principles outlined by the Court.[50]

B. *Anglo-French Arbitration*

The second decision of relevance during this period was the 1977 *Anglo-French Arbitration* between the United Kingdom and France with respect to their continental shelf boundaries in an area encompassing the English Channel and those waters of the Atlantic Ocean to the south and west of both countries.[51] Unlike the *North Sea Continental Shelf* cases, both France and the United Kingdom were parties to the Convention on the Continental Shelf, although France had made reservations to Article 6 of the Convention which had been the subject of a United Kingdom objection. A significant feature in the area under delimitation were the Channel Islands, which were British islands located near the Golfe de St-Malo adjacent to the French Normandy coast. There was also a seabed feature known as the 'Hurd Deep' which had a width of between one to three nm and a depth of over 100 metres. In this case the tribunal was immediately faced with an important question of treaty law, and it was concluded that the Convention on the Continental Shelf was inapplicable to the extent of the reservation which resulted in the exclusion of its provisions to Granville Bay and the adjacent Channel Islands with the effect that the rules of customary international law applied within that area.[52]

Upon reviewing the effects of the Convention and relevant customary international law the tribunal concluded that Article 6 provided for a combined equidistant–special circumstances rule,[53] in which a boundary based on an equidistance line was the general principle unless another was justified by special circumstances.[54] The tribunal noted that the criteria of special circumstances was 'to ensure an equitable delimitation; and the combined "equidistance-special circumstances rule" in effect gives particular expression to a general norm that, failing agreement, the boundary between States abutting on the same continental shelf is to be determined on the basis of equitable principles'.[55] Stressing that the rules of delimitation of both Article 6 and customary international law strive for the goal of an equitable result,[56] the tribunal also went on to review the customary law principles referred to by the ICJ in *North Sea Continental Shelf*.[57] In applying these principles to the three distinct areas under consideration, the tribunal first delimited the continental shelf boundary through the English Channel on the basis of a median line after having found

[49] Ibid [96]–[98].
[50] 1971 Treaty between the Federal Republic of Germany and Kingdom of Denmark relating to the Delimitation of the Continental Shelf under the North Sea; 1971 Treaty between the Kingdom of the Netherlands and the Federal Republic of Germany on the delimitation of the Continental Shelf under the North Sea.
[51] *Anglo-French Continental Shelf Arbitration* (1979) 18 ILM 397.
[52] Ibid [74].
[53] Ibid [68].
[54] Ibid [70].
[55] Ibid [70].
[56] Ibid [75].
[57] Ibid [76]–[86].

that the Hurd Deep did not constitute a special circumstance as it did not disrupt the essential unity of the continental shelf in the area.[58] In the case of the Atlantic sector, which was the most extensive area of the continental shelf under consideration, the tribunal concluded that the Scilly Isles had a distorting effect upon an equidistance line such as to create a special circumstance. In response, the tribunal elected to give the islands 'half-effect' such that the boundary was drawn midway between two different equidistance lines, one which took into account the existence of the islands and the other which did not.[59] Finally, in the case of the Channel Islands it was concluded that considerations of geography, law and equity demanded consideration when the islands of one state lay within the continental shelf of another state. As a result, a median line was drawn which disregarded the islands, whilst also recognising their right to a 12 nm seabed within what had become the French continental shelf.[60]

V. LOSC

During the negotiation of the LOSC at UNCLOS III it quickly became apparent that the key delimitation issues would revolve around the provisions applying to the delimitation of the continental shelf and the new EEZ—both of which at a minimum extended to 200 nm. The territorial sea, on the other hand, did not have the same resource implications as the other zones, and that fact, in combination with the more limited extent of territorial sea boundaries, saw the conference focus its attention upon the delimitation formula for the continental shelf and EEZ. The Second Committee of the conference was allocated the responsibility for dealing with these issues and it quickly became apparent that the topic was controversial given the emergence of many maritime boundary disputes, and the not surprising attempt by some states to use the conference to promote views that were favourable to their cause. It was not until the Tenth session of UNCLOS III in 1981 that a breakthrough was reached in the negotiations with a proposed text put forward by Ireland and Spain,[61] and this paved the way for eventual acceptance of the boundary delimitation provisions as part of the 'package deal' agreed upon at the conference.

There are in essence two LOSC provisions dealing with maritime boundary delimitation. The first is found in Article 15 dealing with the delimitation of the territorial sea between states with opposite or adjacent coasts. Other than minor modifications, Article 15 duplicates the equivalent provision in the Convention on the Territorial Sea and Contiguous Zone. It provides:

> Where the coasts of two States are opposite or adjacent to each other, neither of the two States is entitled, failing agreement between them to the contrary, to extend its territorial sea beyond the median line every point of which is equidistant from the nearest points of the baselines from which the breadth of the territorial seas of the two States is measured. The above provision does not apply,

---

[58] Ibid [107]–[110].
[59] Ibid [245]–[251].
[60] Ibid [188]–[202].
[61] Bernard H Oxman, 'The Third United Nations Conference on the Law of the Sea: The Tenth Session (1981)' (1982) 76 *AJIL* 1, 14.

however, where it is necessary by reason of historic title or other special circumstances to delimit the territorial seas of the two States in a way which is at variance therewith.

Article 16 is a complementary provision requiring states to have drawn on charts those boundaries settled via the Article 15 process. These charts are to be given due publicity and deposited with the Secretary-General of the United Nations.

The second key provision is that relating to the EEZ and continental shelf and these can be found in Articles 74 and 83 respectively. The key component of both articles is paragraph 1 which provides:

> The delimitation of the [exclusive economic zone] [continental shelf] between States with opposite or adjacent coasts shall be effected by agreement on the basis of international law, as referred to in Article 38 of the Statute of the International Court of Justice, in order to achieve an equitable solution.

In the absence of agreement within a reasonable period of time, Articles 74(2) and 83(2) provide that the states 'shall resort' to the Part XV dispute resolution procedures. However, in recognition that final maritime boundary delimitation arrangements may take some time to settle, provision is also made in paragraph 3 for states to 'enter into provisional arrangements of a practical nature' which are to be without prejudice to any final delimitation of the boundary. Recognition is also granted to any pre-existing arrangements for the delimitation of the EEZ or continental shelf, with paragraph 4 providing for delimitation to be determined in accordance with those agreements. Articles 74(1) and 83(1) are substantially less clear than Article 15, and this reflects the efforts at UNCLOS III to avoid controversy over the role of equidistance. The consequence is that the LOSC provides little guidance on continental shelf and EEZ delimitation, and effectively defers to customary international law as articulated in a succession of international judicial and arbitral decisions.

Following the conclusion of the LOSC, a number of states lodged declarations upon signature or ratification which provided an interpretation of some of the above provisions. Malaysia and Malta separately provided in their declarations that in the absence of agreement, for an equitable solution to be achieved consistent with Articles 74 and 83 the boundary was to be a median line.[62] Yemen lodged a similar declaration, though it had broader effect so as to apply to all maritime boundaries.[63] Romania lodged a specific declaration regarding Articles 74 and 83 which was directed towards uninhabited islands without economic life, which in Romania's view of the requirements of equity could not affect maritime boundary delimitations.[64]

VI. The ICJ and Maritime Boundary Delimitation

Commencing with the 1969 *North Sea Continental Shelf* cases, the ICJ has had occasion to consider a significant number of maritime boundary delimitation cases, and the

---

[62] Malaysia (14 October 1996), Malta (20 May 1993): 'Declarations and Statements' at www.un.org/Depts/los/convention_agreements/convention_declarations.htm.

[63] Yemen (21 July 1987): 'Declarations and Statements' at www.un.org/Depts/los/convention_agreements/convention_declarations.htm.

[64] Romania (17 December 1996): 'Declarations and Statements' at www.un.org/Depts/los/convention_agreements/convention_declarations.htm.

Court's jurisprudence has made a major contribution to the development of the law, with consequential impacts upon state practice.[65] Indeed, given the activity of the ICJ, ITLOS and arbitral tribunals, judicial decisions have become the dominant influence on this area of the law of the sea, raising the spectre of potential fragmentation in the law should divergent approaches be taken by the multiple fora now engaged in settling delimitation disputes (a threat that has not, as yet, materialised).[66] The ICJ's jurisprudence can be broadly divided into three phases. The first is pre-LOSC decisions between 1969 and 1982, in which the Court relied principally upon delimitation provisions in the Convention on the Territorial Sea and Contiguous Zone, the Convention on the Continental Shelf or relevant customary international law. There were three cases commenced during this period, and although only two judgments on the merits were delivered[67] they nonetheless established an initial methodology for the Court's approach to the task of maritime boundary delimitation. Four judgments were handed down in the period between 1983 and 1992, and in this period the Court showed considerable circumspection towards equidistance as a guiding principle for delimitation. Subsequently, in the period between 1993 and 2015 there were a further eight judgments, in which the ICJ has significantly softened its attitude towards equidistance, accepting that, prima facie, it can provide an equitable solution to the delimitation of boundaries between opposite or adjacent states.[68] There are currently three pending maritime boundary cases before the ICJ.[69]

The ICJ is by no means the exclusive source of international jurisprudence in the field of maritime boundary delimitation, and there is also a significant body of arbitral jurisprudence on the topic, including now ITLOS. Nonetheless, the decisions of the ICJ are clearly looked to as being the most authoritative (and innovative) in the field. This can be seen clearly in the first boundary delimitation case of ITLOS, *Bay of Bengal (Bangladesh/ Myanmar)*,[70] in which ITLOS approved and adopted the ICJ's three-stage approach to delimitation first set out in the *Black Sea* case.[71] Before turning to consider the main principles of delimitation, several ICJ decisions are worthy of brief review to highlight the role of the conventional law in the decision-making process.

---

[65] See Robert Kolb *Case Law on Equitable Maritime Delimitation: Digest and Commentaries* (The Hague, Martinus Nijhoff, 2003).

[66] Malcolm D Evans, 'Maritime Boundary Delimitation' in Donald R Rothwell, Alex G Oude Elferink and Tim Stephens (eds), *The Oxford Handbook of the Law of the Sea* (Oxford, Oxford University Press, 2015) 254, 255.

[67] In *Aegean Sea Continental Shelf (Greece v Turkey)* [1978] ICJ Rep 3, the Court determined that it lacked jurisdiction and therefore did not proceed to deliver a judgment on the merits; DNII Johnson, 'The International Court of Justice Declines Jurisdiction Again (the Aegean Sea Continental Shelf Case)' [1981] 7 *Australian Year Book of International Law* 309.

[68] *Maritime Delimitation in the Area between Greenland and Jan Mayen (Denmark v Norway)* [1993] ICJ Rep 38, [64]; *Maritime Delimitation and Territorial Questions Between Qatar and Bahrain (Qatar v Bahrain)* [2001] ICJ Rep 40, [230]. See Evans, 'Maritime Boundary Delimitation' (n 66), 258–59.

[69] *Question of the Delimitation of the Continental Shelf between Nicaragua and Colombia beyond 200 nautical miles from the Nicaraguan Coast (Nicaragua v Colombia); Maritime Delimitation in the Caribbean Sea and the Pacific Ocean (Costa Rica v Nicaragua); Maritime Delimitation in the Indian Ocean (Somalia v Kenya)*. See www. icj-cij.org.

[70] *Delimitation of the Maritime Boundary in the Bay of Bengal (Bangladesh/Myanmar)* [2012] ITLOS Rep 12 (*Bay of Bengal (Bangladesh/Myanmar)*).

[71] *Maritime Delimitation in the Black Sea (Romania v Ukraine)* [2009] ICJ Rep 61 (*Black Sea*). A Special Chamber of ITLOS has been seised of a further delimitation case: *Dispute Concerning Delimitation of the Maritime Boundary between Ghana and Côte d'Ivoire in the Atlantic Ocean (Ghana/Côte d'Ivoire)*, Case No 23. In April 2015, the Special Chamber issued provisional measures in the case requiring Ghana to refrain from drilling for oil in an area disputed between the parties, pending the final decision on the boundary: Order of 15 April 2015.

Table 16.1: ICJ Judgments on Maritime Boundary Delimitations 1969–2015

Year	Case Name	Parties	Boundary	Reported
1969	North Sea Continental Shelf	Federal Republic of Germany v Denmark; Federal Republic of Germany v Netherlands	Continental Shelf	[1969] ICJ Rep 3
1978	Aegean Sea Continental Shelf	Greece v Turkey	Continental Shelf	[1978] ICJ Rep 3
1982	Continental Shelf	Tunisia v Libya Arab Jamahiriya	Continental Shelf	[1982] ICJ Rep 18
1984	Gulf of Maine	Canada v United States	Single Maritime Boundary	[1984] ICJ Rep 246
1985	Continental Shelf	Libyan Arab Jamahiriya v Malta	Continental Shelf	[1985] ICJ Rep 13
1992	Land, Island and Maritime Frontier Dispute	El Salvador/Honduras; Nicaragua intervening	Territorial Sea and Continental Shelf	[1992] ICJ Rep 351
1993	Maritime Delimitation in the Area between Greenland and Jan Mayen	Denmark v Norway	Continental Shelf and Fisheries Jurisdiction	[1993] ICJ Rep 38
1995	Maritime Delimitation between Guinea-Bissau and Senegal	Guinea-Bissau v Senegal	Single Maritime Boundary	[1995] ICJ Rep 423
2001	Maritime Delimitation and Territorial Questions between Qatar and Bahrain	Qatar v Bahrain	Single Maritime Boundary	[2001] ICJ Rep 40
2002	Land and Maritime Boundary between Cameron and Nigeria	Cameroon v Nigeria; Equatorial Guinea intervening	Single Maritime Boundary	[2002] ICJ Rep 303
2007	Territorial and Maritime Dispute between Nicaragua and Honduras in the Caribbean Sea	Nicaragua v Honduras	Single Maritime Boundary	[2007] ICJ Rep 659
2009	Maritime Delimitation in the Black Sea	Romania v Ukraine	Single Maritime Boundary	[2009] ICJ Rep 61
2012	Territorial and Maritime Dispute	Nicaragua v Colombia	Single Maritime Boundary	[2012] ICJ Rep 624
2014	Maritime Dispute	Peru v Chile	Single Maritime Boundary	Judgment of 27 January 2014

As noted above, in *North Sea Continental Shelf* the ICJ determined that the 1958 Convention on the Continental Shelf did not apply between the parties and therefore set about determining the relevant customary international law of maritime boundary delimitation. In 1982, however, when the Court came to determine the *Tunisia/Libya Continental Shelf* case,[72] UNCLOS III was nearing conclusion and the LOSC was in its final draft. Libya was also not a party to the Convention, with the effect that the judgment was based upon custom. Whilst clearly the Court was not bound to apply the LOSC (indeed, the Court noted that any observation as to 'trends' in the developing law would need to be confined to the legal relations between the states)[73] the ICJ did give some important guidance as to how an 'equitable solution' could be achieved in maritime boundary delimitations. The Court observed that: 'It is clear that what is reasonable and equitable in any given case must depend on particular circumstances. There can be no doubt that it is virtually impossible to achieve an equitable solution in any delimitation without taking into account the relevant circumstances of the area.'[74] The Court then proceeded to take into account a variety of circumstances which were considered to be relevant, including the length of the coastlines of both states, the direction of the coastlines, the presence of islands and previously established colonial boundaries.[75] Prior to delimiting the boundary, the Court also made some observations with respect to the principle of equidistance. Commenting that: 'Treaty practice, as well as the history of Article 83 of the draft convention on the law of the sea, leads to the conclusion that equidistance may be applied if it leads to an equitable solution; if not, other methods should be employed.'[76]

Whilst both Canada and the United States were parties to the 1958 Convention on the Continental Shelf, in the 1984 *Gulf of Maine* case[77] the Court was asked to define the direction of a single maritime boundary taking into account continental shelf and fisheries issues and as such the Convention did not strictly apply.[78] The ICJ could find no rule of international law making it impossible to draw a single boundary,[79] and it proceeded to delimit the area on the basis of the law and practice at the time but without significant reference to the LOSC.[80] The third case decided in this period was the 1985 *Libya/Malta Continental Shelf* case.[81] However, only Malta was a party to the 1958 Convention on the Continental

---

[72] *Continental Shelf (Tunisia/Libyan Arab Jamahiriya)* [1982] ICJ Rep 18 (*Tunisia/Libya Continental Shelf*).

[73] Ibid [24].

[74] Ibid [72].

[75] Ibid [75]–[95].

[76] Ibid [109]; for discussion see Mark B Feldman 'The Tunisia-Libya Continental Shelf Case: Geographic Justice or Juridical Compromise?' (1983) 77 *AJIL* 219. In 1985 the ICJ delivered a judgment following a request by Tunisia for revision of its 1982 judgment; whilst the Court refused to do so it did provide additional interpretation of its judgment: *Application for Revision and Interpretation of the Judgment of 24 February 1982 in the Case Concerning the Continental Shelf (Tunisia v Libyan Arab Jamahiriya)* [1985] ICJ Rep 192.

[77] *Delimitation of the Maritime Boundary in the Gulf of Maine Area (Canada/United States)* [1984] ICJ Rep 246 (*Gulf of Maine*).

[78] Ibid [5].

[79] Ibid [27].

[80] As to the ongoing impact of this decision see Stuart Kaye, 'Lessons Learned from the Gulf of Maine Case: The Development of Maritime Boundary Delimitation Jurisprudence since UNCLOS III' (2008) 14 *Ocean and Coastal Law Journal* 73; and for an analysis soon after the judgment see Jan Schneider, 'The Gulf of Maine Case: The Nature of an Equitable Result' (1985) 79 *AJIL* 539.

[81] *Continental Shelf (Libyan Arab Jamahiriya/Malta)* [1985] ICJ Rep 13 (*Libya/Malta Continental Shelf*).

Shelf, and whilst both states had signed the LOSC they had not ratified the Convention, which, in any event, had not entered into force. Nevertheless, both parties had indicated to the Court that they agreed that relevant provisions of LOSC were applicable as customary international law.[82] The Court noted that the provisions of the LOSC dealing with the definition of the continental shelf in Article 76 and its delimitation in Article 83 were not 'only distinct but are also complementary'.[83] In this respect, the Court observed as to the LOSC delimitation criteria that: 'The Convention sets a goal to be achieved, but is silent as to the method to be followed to achieve it. It restricts itself to setting a standard, and it is left to states themselves, or to the courts, to endow this standard with specific content.'[84] In an important jurisprudential development, and recognising the impact of the LOSC, the Court commented that following the development of the law so as to broaden continental shelf claims to 200 nm, the previous influence that geological or geophysical factors may have had with respect to verifying legal title for one state or the other was now diminished. Libyan claims as to the significance of a 'rift zone' in the continental shelf area under consideration were therefore not a special circumstance for the purposes of delimitation.[85] Consistent with its earlier decisions, the Court also noted that there was nothing in the law which required as either a preliminary or provisional step that the equidistance method was one which '*must* be used',[86] and that rather the goal of an equitable result was what the Court was predominantly concerned with.[87]

Two other judgments highlight the difficulty in precisely applying and interpreting treaty law with respect to maritime boundary delimitation. In the 1993 *Greenland/Jan Mayen* case between Denmark and Norway,[88] the Court commented that this was the first occasion that it had to apply, as a matter of treaty law, the 1958 Convention on the Continental Shelf.[89] However, the Court was mindful that any interpretation of the Convention would still require consideration of appropriate customary international law. Finally, and somewhat remarkably, it was 20 years after the LOSC was concluded, in the *Land and Maritime Boundary* case between Cameroon and Nigeria (Equatorial Guinea intervening),[90] that the ICJ determined a maritime boundary case in which the LOSC was binding upon both parties.[91] Nevertheless, there is little variation in the Court's treatment of the law in this case when compared to those noted above, which highlights how closely aligned the treaty law and customary international law is in this area.

---

[82] Ibid [26].
[83] Ibid [27].
[84] Ibid [28].
[85] Ibid [39]–[41].
[86] Ibid [43].
[87] Ibid [45].
[88] *Maritime Delimitation in the Area between Greenland and Jan Mayen (Denmark v Norway)* [1993] ICJ Rep 38 (*Greenland/Jan Mayen*).
[89] Ibid [45]; see discussion in Robin R Churchill, 'The Greenland-Jan Mayen Case and Its Significance for the International Law of Maritime Boundary Delimitation' (1994) 9 *International Journal of Marine and Coastal Law* 1.
[90] *Land and Maritime Boundary between Cameroon and Nigeria (Cameroon v Nigeria; Equatorial Guinea intervening)* [2002] ICJ Rep 303 (*Cameroon/Nigeria*).
[91] Ibid [285].

VII. Principles of Maritime Boundary Delimitation

At the conclusion of UNCLOS III in 1982 it was estimated that there were 376 potential maritime boundaries throughout the world, of which at that time only 90 had been negotiated.[92] Whilst many delimitations have taken place since 1982, both by way of negotiation and through judicial determination by way of arbitration or adjudication, many boundaries still remain to be settled. In addition, an important new dynamic has emerged since this time, with states asserting entitlements to continental shelves beyond 200 nm resulting in overlapping outer continental shelves. This will require the delimitation of new outer continental shelf boundaries either before or after submission of claims to the CLCS. In these various ways the law on maritime boundary delimitation remains dynamic, and of ongoing relevance and importance to the law of the sea.

Determining the contemporary principles of maritime boundary delimitation is made difficult by the imprecise terminology used in the LOSC. While there is considerable jurisprudence in the field, the legal basis (in either treaty law or custom) upon which those judgments have been delivered has also been variable. Cases have been determined on the basis of customary international law, the Geneva Conventions, the LOSC, or a mixture of both custom and treaty law. During this time the jurisprudence has evolved, but so too has the international law of the sea as there has been a gradual transition from the Geneva Conventions to the LOSC with relevant customary international law on fisheries zones also bound up in that process. One of the most important impacts upon the law of maritime boundary delimitation during this time has been the changing nature of the juridical continental shelf. The Geneva emphasis upon 'natural prolongation', reflected in submissions made in cases such as the *Anglo-French Arbitration*, has now been replaced by an acceptance that geomorphology has less significance under the Article 76 regime, which grants coastal states a minimum 200 nm continental shelf.[93] International courts and tribunals have throughout this time been in search of objective criteria to apply in maritime boundary delimitation.[94] In light of their collective jurisprudence, state practice, and the delimitation methods laid down in Articles 15, 74 and 83 of the LOSC, it is now possible to identify with reasonable clarity the key elements of contemporary maritime boundary delimitation, although it must be cautioned that delimitations often turn on their unique geographical circumstances.

A. Delimitation Methodology

As international courts and tribunals have become more experienced in dealing with maritime boundary delimitation they have been able to develop certain techniques to assist in drawing delimitation lines. These techniques have become more sharply focussed since

---

[92] Robert W Smith, 'A Geographical Primer to Maritime Boundary-Making' (1982) 12 *Ocean Development and International Law* 1, 3.

[93] *Barbados v Trinidad and Tobago* (2006) 45 ILM 798, [224]–[226].

[94] Ibid [230].

the adoption of the LOSC and the jurisprudence interpreting Articles 74 and 83 has evolved. The ICJ first began to identify different stages of the delimitation process in the *Libya/ Malta Continental Shelf* case,[95] and since that time the approach has gradually become more refined. In its more recent judgments, the Court has referred to a 'methodology' to be applied in maritime boundary delimitation and this represents a significant advance in the jurisprudence. Because of the difference in the language of Article 15 and Articles 74 and 83, there are variations in the approach taken with respect to a territorial sea delimitation and that for an EEZ or continental shelf delimitation; however, in post-LOSC decisions there has been a strong tendency to emphasise the importance of the equidistance or median line in delimitations in respect of all three zones.

i. Territorial Sea

In the 2007 *Caribbean Sea* case between Nicaragua and Honduras the ICJ considered a methodology to be applied to the areas to be delimited in the context of an Article 15 territorial sea boundary.[96] The Court observed that '[t]he methods governing territorial sea delimitations have needed to be, and are, more clearly articulated in international law than those used for the other, more functional maritime areas'.[97] First, consideration should be given to the drawing of a provisional equidistance line.[98] Secondly, if this proves impossible because of certain features on the coastline or within the area of delimitation, an equidistance line can be abandoned due to special circumstances.[99] Thirdly, the Court may consider alternative methods of delimitation proposed by the parties or elect to apply its own methods. In *Caribbean Sea* the Court found that an equidistance line could not be applied in the first instance because of geographical and geological difficulties associated with the nature of the coastline and unstable coastal features, including the identification of basepoints from which an equidistance line could be drawn.[100] As an alternative to equidistance, the Court sought to apply a 'bisector' line.[101] Finally, as noted in *Caribbean Sea*, the Court will also need to take into account relevant coasts which will include reference to the geographical configuration of the coastline and, when the territorial sea of adjacent states is being delimited, the geomorphological features of the area adjacent to the endpoint of a land boundary.[102] The *Caribbean Sea* case indicates that while the equidistance or median line is the starting point for territorial sea delimitation, it is not necessarily conclusive and may be displaced by the special circumstances of the case.

---

[95] [1985] ICJ Rep 13, [60].

[96] *Territorial and Maritime Dispute between Nicaragua and Honduras in the Caribbean Sea (Nicaragua v Honduras)* [2007] ICJ Rep 659 (*Caribbean Sea*).

[97] Ibid [269].

[98] Ibid [268].

[99] Ibid [281]. In *Maritime Delimitation and Territorial Questions between Qatar and Bahrain (Qatar v Bahrain)* (merits) [2001] ICJ Rep 40, [176] (*Qatar v Bahrain*) the Court observed that: 'The most logical and widely practised approach is first to draw provisionally an equidistance line and then to consider whether that line must be adjusted in the light of the existence of special circumstances.'

[100] *Caribbean Sea*, [2007] ICJ Rep 659, [273]–[280].

[101] Ibid [287].

[102] Ibid [292]; this would be an especially important factor in instances where a river mouth is part of the land boundary.

ii. EEZ, Continental Shelf and Single Maritime Boundaries

In the 2009 *Black Sea* case between Romania and Ukraine,[103] the Court for the first time referred generically to a 'delimitation methodology' that could be applied in cases dealing with the delimitation of the EEZ, continental shelf, or a single maritime boundary line.[104]

This approach involves three stages. The first is the establishment of a provisional delimitation line which in the case of adjacent coasts will be an equidistance line, and in the case of opposite coasts a median line,[105] unless, as occurred in *Caribbean Sea*, there are compelling reasons which make such a line unsuitable. The second stage is a consideration as to whether there are any factors which call for an adjustment of the provisional line in order to achieve an equitable result.[106] Finally, and after having made any adjustments to the provisional line as a result of the second stage, the Court will seek to verify that the line does not lead to an inequitable result 'by reason of any marked disproportion between the ratio of the respective coastal lengths and the ratio between the relevant maritime area of each State by reference to the delimitation line'.[107] This process thereby ensures that there is no great disproportionality between the division of the maritime area under delimitation and the relevant coastal lengths. A crucial element of this methodology is the determination of the 'relevant area' which the Court has referred to as a 'legal concept'.[108] This area will depend upon the configuration of the relevant coasts within their geographical context and a consideration of the seaward projections of those coasts which will differ depending on whether a territorial sea or much longer maritime boundary is being delimited, and the interests of any third states.[109] Likewise, different considerations will apply in the case of convex and concave coastlines, significant indentations such as gulfs, and when islands are within the area of delimitation.[110] The determination of the relevant area is crucial for the application of proportionality which is undertaken at the third stage of the delimitation process.[111] Accordingly, a court will need to make a determination as to the relevant area under consideration prior to commencing the process of delimiting a boundary line. In *Bay of Bengal (Bangladesh/Myanmar)* ITLOS adopted the ICJ's three-stage approach, noting its development 'in the most recent case law on the subject'.[112]

iii. Delimitation Beyond 200 nm

The *Bay of Bengal (Bangladesh/Myanmar)* case is significant in several respects, including being the first time in which an international court had addressed the question of continental shelf delimitation beyond 200 nm. The issue was raised but not resolved in the ICJ in 2012 in *Territorial and Maritime Dispute*,[113] in which Nicaragua sought a delimitation taking into account the potential extent of its continental shelf beyond 200 nm. The Court

---

[103] *Maritime Delimitation in the Black Sea (Romania v Ukraine)*, [2009] ICJ Rep 61.
[104] Ibid [115]–[122].
[105] Ibid [116].
[106] Ibid [120].
[107] Ibid [122].
[108] Ibid [110].
[109] *Caribbean Sea*, [2007] ICJ Rep 659, [262].
[110] *Black Sea*, [2009] ICJ Rep 61, [110].
[111] Ibid.
[112] *Bay of Bengal (Bangladesh/Myanmar)* [2012] ITLOS Rep 12, [240].
[113] *Territorial and Maritime Dispute (Nicaragua v Colombia)* [2012] ICJ Rep 624.

considered that, as Nicaragua had not yet established an extended continental shelf through the CLCS process, the Court did not need to address 'the argument as to whether a delimitation of overlapping entitlements which involves an extended continental shelf of one party can affect a 200-nautical-mile entitlement to the continental shelf of another party'.[114] In late 2013, Nicaragua instituted new proceedings in the ICJ against Colombia, asking the Court to delimit the boundary between its outer continental shelf beyond 200 nm and the Colombian continental shelf.[115]

The matter was addressed differently in the *Bay of Bengal (Bangladesh/Myanmar)* case, in which both Bangladesh and Myanmar had made submissions to the CLCS, but in circumstances in which the CLCS had deferred consideration of the submissions as Bangladesh objected to the CLCS considering Myanmar's submission. But Myanmar contended that ITLOS did not have jurisdiction to delimit the outer limits of the continental shelf until the CLCS had made its recommendations. ITLOS sought to overcome this 'Catch 22' situation, noting that 'it would be contrary to the object and purpose of the Convention not to resolve the existing impasse',[116] and proceeded to delimit the continental shelf beyond 200 nm 'without prejudice to the establishment of the outer limits of the continental shelf' in accordance with Article 76(8) of the LOSC.[117] Unlike *Territorial and Maritime Dispute*, in *Bay of Bengal (Bangladesh/Myanmar)* both parties accepted, and the evidence before ITLOS clearly showed, the existence of a continental shelf beyond 200 nm. The floor of the Bay of Bengal was covered by a thick layer of sediments up to 22 kilometres deep, originating in the Himalayas and Tibetan Plateau, and accumulating in the Bay of Bengal over thousands of years.[118] ITLOS was therefore satisfied as to the existence of a 'continuous and substantial layer of sedimentary rocks extending from Myanmar's coast to the area beyond 200 nm'.[119] As for the method to be deployed in delimiting the extended continental shelf, ITLOS found that it should not differ from that applicable within 200 nm, and

> Accordingly, the equidistance/relevant circumstances method continues to apply for the delimitation of the continental shelf beyond 200 nm. This method is rooted in the recognition that sovereignty over the land territory is the basis for the sovereign rights and jurisdiction of the coastal State with respect to both the exclusive economic zone and the continental shelf.[120]

Not unsurprisingly, the approach taken by ITLOS was followed by the Annex VII arbitral tribunal in the *Bay of Bengal Arbitration (Bangladesh/India)*.[121] Specifically referencing the ITLOS judgment, the arbitral tribunal saw no reason why it should refrain from exercising jurisdiction to decide the delimitation of the continental shelf beyond 200 nm even though the outer limits were yet to be conclusively established.[122]

---

[114] Ibid [130].
[115] *Question of the Delimitation of the Continental Shelf between Nicaragua and Colombia beyond 200 nautical miles from the Nicaraguan Coast (Nicaragua v Colombia)*, International Court of Justice, Application of 16 September 2013. Nicaragua subsequently submitted a further set of proceedings, contending that Colombia has not complied with the 2012 decision: *Alleged Violations of Sovereign Rights and Maritime Spaces in the Caribbean Sea (Nicaragua v Colombia)*, International Court of Justice, Application of 26 November 2013.
[116] *Bay of Bengal (Bangladesh/Myanmar)* [2012] ITLOS Rep 12, [392].
[117] Ibid [394].
[118] Ibid [444].
[119] Ibid [447].
[120] Ibid [455].
[121] *Bay of Bengal Arbitration (Bangladesh/India)*, Award of 7 July 2014.
[122] Ibid [76].

iv. 'Grey Zones'

An important feature of the Bay of Bengal delimitations between Bangladesh, India and Myanmar beyond 200 nm is the phenomenon of 'grey zones' or 'grey areas' created where a single delimitation line 'which is not an equidistance line reaches the outer limit of one State's [EEZ] and continues beyond it in the same direction, until it reaches the outer limit of the other State's EEZ'.[123] In the Bay of Bengal there are several grey areas falling within the continental shelf of Bangladesh as delimited by ITLOS and the Annex VII arbitral tribunal, but within the 200 nm of India and Myanmar and therefore those states' EEZs. In *Bay of Bengal (Bangladesh/Myanmar)*, ITLOS noted that in the area beyond Bangladesh's EEZ within Myanmar's EEZ the boundary delimits the rights of the parties over the continental shelf, but did not otherwise limit Myanmar's rights in the superjacent waters in the EEZ.[124] The tribunal noted that 'the legal regime of the continental shelf has always coexisted with another legal regime in the same area. Initially that other regime was that of the high seas and the other States concerned were those exercising high seas freedoms.'[125] Similarly, in the *Bay of Bengal Arbitration (Bangladesh/India)* the arbitral tribunal observed that it only had the capacity to delimit respective entitlements of the parties where they overlap, and that in the grey area this means that it may only delimit the continental shelf,[126] with the parties to determine what measures they consider appropriate to facilitate their respective enjoyment of continental shelf and EEZ rights.[127]

B. Territorial Sea Delimitations

A characteristic of contemporary territorial sea delimitations is that many have now been settled given the long-standing nature of the territorial sea regime, and when they are settled they are often delimited within the context of a single maritime boundary which encompasses related EEZ and continental shelf areas.[128] The law in the field has also acquired stability, given the continuity which exists between the key delimitation provisions of Article 12 of the Convention on the Territorial Sea and Contiguous Zone and Article 15 of the LOSC. Nevertheless, there are distinctive issues which arise in the case of territorial sea boundary delimitations, the great majority of which are between adjacent states, due to the different delimitation methods allowed for under Article 15 of the LOSC and

---

[123] *Bay of Bengal (Bangladesh/Myanmar)* [2012] ITLOS Rep 12, [464]. On grey zones see generally Alex G Oude-Elferink, 'Does Undisputed Title to a Maritime Zone Always Exclude its Delimitation: The Grey Area Issue' (1998) 13 *International Journal of Marine and Coastal Law* 143.

[124] *Bay of Bengal (Bangladesh/Myanmar)* [2012] ITLOS Rep 12, [474].

[125] Ibid [475].

[126] Ibid [503].

[127] Ibid [508].

[128] *Guyana/Suriname Arbitration* (2007) 139 ILR 566 (*Guyana/Suriname Arbitration*) is an example where a tribunal was to first delimit the territorial sea, and then to delimit the continental shelf and EEZ. (Note that there is minimal state practice with respect to contiguous zone maritime boundaries, primarily because in the case of lateral boundaries between adjacent states these boundaries are absorbed into the single lines drawn for an EEZ or continental shelf: David Colson, 'The Legal Regime of Maritime Boundary Arrangements' in Jonathan I Charney and Lewis M Alexander (eds), *International Maritime Boundaries*, vol 1 (Dordrecht, Martinus Nijhoff, 1993) 41, 42).

the potential for a greater range of geographical and geomorphological factors to influence the boundary. Also, because of the close connection between land and territorial sea boundaries, there may be a need to take into account historical boundary arrangements.[129]

The LOSC emphasises the capacity of states to determine their territorial sea boundaries by agreement, and that in the absence of agreement, claims of historic title, or special circumstances, a median line that is equidistant from the nearest points on the baselines is to be employed. Through decisions such as *Qatar v Bahrain*[130] and *Caribbean Sea* the courts have developed a clear delimitation methodology in interpreting Article 15. Whilst concerns exist over the potential distorting effects of an equidistance line, this is minimised within the comparatively small areas of the territorial sea under delimitation.[131] As to what may constitute 'special circumstances' nothing in Article 15 suggests that certain features are excluded from consideration or that there is 'a finite list of special circumstances'.[132]

In two separate 2007 decisions international courts had occasion to refer to the ILC commentary to the 1956 draft articles in order to obtain insights into what may constitute 'special circumstances'. In the *Guyana/Suriname Arbitration*, where a territorial sea had to be delimited immediately adjacent to the mouth of a large coastal river, the tribunal took note of the ILC's observation that a navigable channel could make a boundary based on equidistance inequitable.[133] In that case, the tribunal concluded after reviewing established practice between the parties that they were prepared to take the special circumstances of navigation into account in adjusting the boundary to deviate from the median line.[134] Likewise, in the *Caribbean Sea* case the ICJ was prepared to find that the presence of unstable islands at the mouth of a river creating geomorphological problems was a 'special circumstance' impacting upon the delimitation of the territorial sea.[135]

A further distinctive factor that may arise in some territorial sea delimitations is where a previous three nm territorial sea is extended to 12 nm, consistent with the provisions of the LOSC. In the *Guyana/Suriname Arbitration* the tribunal was of the view that in these cases there should not be an automatic extension of the existing three nm boundary line and that additional factors may require consideration. These included the more extensive coastal state control over navigation, pollution and customs matters in addition to its general criminal laws.[136] Accordingly, factors that may have constituted special circumstances closer to the coast such as to have an impact upon the initial direction of the maritime boundary become less significant as the boundary runs further into the ocean where general sovereign rights over the territorial sea may have greater weight.

---

[129] Ibid [323]. See, eg, some of the issues arising for Croatia with respect to its territorial sea delimitations following the breakup of the former Yugoslavia: Damir Arnaut, 'Stormy Waters on the Way to the High Seas: The Case of the Territorial Sea Delimitation between Croatia and Slovenia' in David D Caron and Harry N Scheiber (eds), *Bringing New Law to Ocean Waters* (Leiden, Martinus Nijhoff, 2004) 427.

[130] See discussion in Maurice Mendelson, 'The Curious Case of Qatar v Bahrain in the International Court of Justice' (2001) 72 *British Yearbook of International Law* 183.

[131] *Caribbean Sea*, [2007] ICJ Rep 659, [269].

[132] *Guyana/Suriname Arbitration* (2007) 139 ILR 566, [302].

[133] Ibid [301].

[134] Ibid [306].

[135] *Caribbean Sea*, [2007] ICJ Rep 659, [280].

[136] *Guyana/Suriname Arbitration* (2007) 139 ILR 566, [311]–[316].

C. Equitable Solution/Equitable Result

The adoption of Articles 74 and 83 of the LOSC ushered in a new era in maritime boundary delimitation with respect to the longest and most significant of the boundaries coastal states delimit. In distinction to the methodology formulated in Article 6 of the 1958 Convention on the Continental Shelf, with its technical distinction between opposite and adjacent states and reliance upon equidistance, the LOSC favoured the application of general international law as reflected in Article 38 of the Statute of the International Court of Justice in order to reach an equitable solution, which is also often referred to as an 'equitable result'.[137] This invites states engaged in boundary delimitation, and the courts and tribunals called to adjudicate boundary disputes, to refer to the rich variety of sources of international law in order to achieve the desired outcome. Nevertheless, as was observed in the 1999 *Eritrea/Yemen Arbitration*, although Articles 74 and 83 were 'designed to decide as little as possible' it was clear that 'both Articles envisage an equitable result'.[138]

The ICJ in *Tunisia/Libya Continental Shelf* gave initial guidance as to how this may be achieved, emphasising the importance of taking into account the relevant circumstances of the case.[139] This approach has been followed in subsequent decisions and is illustrated by consideration given to a wide range of relevant geographical factors in order to ensure they are taken into account in the final delimitation lines. However, there are constraints in seeking to achieve an equitable result, and, as was noted in the *Barbados v Trinidad and Tobago Arbitration*, legal principle needs to be accounted for 'in particular in respect of the factors that may be taken into account', including that of the decided cases.[140] In this respect, the ICJ has drawn a distinction between achieving an equitable result and 'delimiting in equity'. In the 2002 *Cameroon/ Nigeria* case it was observed that: 'The Court's jurisprudence shows that, in disputes relating to maritime delimitation, equity is not a method of delimitation, but solely an aim that should be borne in mind in effecting delimitation.'[141] Similarly, in *Bay of Bengal (Bangladesh/Myanmar)*, ITLOS observed that '[t]he goal of achieving an equitable result must be the paramount consideration guiding the action of the Tribunal in this connection'.[142] A common method used to achieve an equitable result/solution is an adjustment to the maritime boundary after the second stage of the delimitation process in order to ensure proportionality.[143]

D. Equidistance and Median Lines

It is clear from the development of the law and the decisions of the ICJ,[144] that the principle of equidistance which was so influential in the initial development of the international law on maritime boundary delimitation has subsequently surrendered its dominant position.

---

[137] *Black Sea*, [2009] ICJ Rep 61, [120].

[138] *Eritrea v Yemen*, Award of the Arbitral Tribunal in the Second Stage of the Proceedings (Maritime Delimitation), 17 December 1999, [116] (*Eritrea/Yemen Arbitration*).

[139] *Tunisia/Libya Continental Shelf* [1982] ICJ Rep 18, [72].

[140] *Barbados v Trinidad and Tobago* (2006) 45 ILM 798, [243]; see also the discussion in Barbara Kwiatkowska, 'The 2006 Barbados/Trinidad and Tobago Award: A Landmark in Compulsory Jurisdiction and Equitable Maritime Boundary Delimitation' (2007) 22 *International Journal of Marine and Coastal Law* 7, 38–43.

[141] *Cameroon/Nigeria* [2002] ICJ Rep 303, [294].

[142] *Bay of Bengal (Bangladesh/Myanmar)* [2012] ITLOS Rep 12, [235].

[143] *Black Sea*, [2009] ICJ Rep 61, [122]; *Libya/Malta Continental Shelf* [1985] ICJ Rep 13, [71].

[144] See especially *North Sea Continental Shelf* [1969] ICJ Rep 3, [46]–[56] rejecting equidistance.

This is due to the distorting effect that an equidistance line may have upon the direction of a maritime boundary the further that boundary extends from the coast, and its inability to address certain geographical features.[145] In some instances, as occurred in *Caribbean Sea*, there may be a number of geological or geomorphological factors which make it impossible even to plot an equidistance line because of the absence of viable basepoints.[146] Nevertheless, at least as a starting point for maritime boundary delimitation, equidistance and median lines have retained a central place in law and practice as reflected in the LOSC, decisions of the courts and tribunals, and state practice.[147]

Equidistance and median lines may be utilised in the case of territorial sea delimitations consistent with Article 15, subject to special circumstances or the parties reaching agreement on another method. Likewise, notwithstanding some different approaches taken by courts and tribunals as to the relevance of an equidistance/median line,[148] there remain contemporary examples where an equidistance/median line has been applied as a provisional line, only to have been modified or adjusted in order to achieve an equitable solution.[149] This approach was endorsed by the ICJ as the first stage of a boundary delimitation in the 2009 *Black Sea* decision when the Court upheld this approach.[150] In some instances, as occurred in the *Cameroon/Nigeria* case,[151] or the *Guyana/Suriname Arbitration*,[152] a conclusion may even be reached that an equidistance line represents an equitable result and that no circumstances exist which require modification of the line. There is also significant state practice to the effect that where maritime boundaries have been settled by agreement, states have relied upon a partial equidistance line, modified equidistance line, or in some case a line drawn only by reference to equidistance.[153]

E. Relevant and Special Circumstances

A feature of the law of maritime boundary delimitation has been the ongoing reference to 'special circumstances' as factors to be taken into account in the delimitation process. Reference to special circumstances as a justification for departing from the median/equidistant line appeared in the 1958 Geneva Conventions and was noted in the early boundary cases. Whilst now only expressly referred to in the LOSC in the context of territorial sea delimitations, there is a large body of jurisprudence identifying and applying

---

[145] Ibid [59].

[146] *Caribbean Sea*, [2007] ICJ Rep 659, [281].

[147] Alex G Oude Elferink, 'Maritime Delimitation between Denmark/Greenland and Norway' (2007) 38 *Ocean Development and International Law* 375 referring to the use of a median line in the delimitation of the maritime boundary between Denmark and Norway in the area between Greenland and Svalbard.

[148] *Gulf of Maine* [1984] ICJ Rep 246, [107].

[149] *Barbados v Trinidad and Tobago* (2006) 45 ILM 798, [350]; *Maritime Delimitation and Territorial Questions between Qatar and Bahrain (Qatar v Bahrain)* (merits) [2001] ICJ Rep 40, [230].

[150] *Black Sea*, [2009] ICJ Rep 61, [116], where it was also observed that: 'No legal consequences flow from the use of the terms "median line" and "equidistance line" since the method of delimitation is the same for both.'

[151] *Cameroon/Nigeria* [2002] ICJ Rep 303, [306].

[152] *Guyana/Suriname Arbitration* (2007) 139 ILR 566, [392].

[153] An example can be found in the 2004 Treaty between the Government of Australia and the Government of New Zealand Establishing Certain Exclusive Economic Zone Boundaries and Continental Shelf Boundaries, in which the Australian government 'National Interest Analysis' associated with this treaty makes direct reference to the use of equidistance: [2004] ATNIA 8.

various 'special circumstances' in continental shelf and EEZ delimitations. More recently, international courts and tribunals have preferred to refer to 'relevant circumstances'. For instance, in *Bay of Bengal (Bangladesh/Myanmar)*, ITLOS observed that the 'jurisprudence has developed in favour of the equidistance/relevant circumstances method' and this method is adopted 'in the majority of delimitation cases'.[154]

i. Special Circumstances

Whilst now only expressly referred to in Article 15 of the LOSC, there is extensive jurisprudence by international courts and tribunals referring to the impact of special circumstances or equivalent factors upon the placement of a maritime boundary. The factors which may be taken into account are extensive and predominantly geographical, and there is some limited scope for consideration to be given to historical factors which extends to relevant practice by the parties. The ICJ has observed that 'special circumstances are those circumstances which might modify the result produced by an unqualified application of the equidistance principle. ... This concept can be described as a fact necessary to be taken into account in the delimitation process.'[155] Islands have traditionally been one special circumstance which the courts have been prepared to consider because of the impact they may have upon the direction of a maritime boundary, and the need to take into account the maritime zones the islands generate consistent with Article 121 of the LOSC.

In the early jurisprudence, the natural prolongation of the continental shelf was a factor that was often considered in continental shelf delimitations;[156] however, with the redefinition of the judicial continental shelf under Article 76 to encompass a minimum seabed limit of 200 nm, this factor has faded from influence.[157] Beginning with *Libya/Malta Continental Shelf* and restated in *Territorial and Maritime Dispute*, the ICJ has held that 'geological and geomorphological considerations are not relevant to the delimitation of overlapping entitlements within 200 nm of the coasts of States'.[158] Whether natural prolongation is relevant in the delimitation of the continental shelf beyond 200 nm was considered by ITLOS in the *Bay of Bengal (Bangladesh/Myanmar)*, in which Bangladesh argued that Myanmar's continental shelf was affected by a discontinuity around 50 nm from the Myanmar coast. ITLOS rejected this argument, finding that:

> the reference to natural prolongation in article 76, paragraph 1, of the Convention, should be understood in light of the subsequent provisions of the article defining the continental shelf and the continental margin. Entitlement to a continental shelf beyond 200 nm should thus be determined by reference to the outer edge of the continental margin, to be ascertained in accordance with article 76, paragraph 4.[159]

---

[154] *Bay of Bengal (Bangladesh/Myanmar)* [2012] ITLOS Rep 12, [238].

[155] *Greenland/Jan Mayen* [1993] ICJ Rep 38, [55].

[156] *Anglo-French Continental Shelf Arbitration* (1979) 18 ILM 397, [107]–[110]; *Libya/Malta Continental Shelf* [1985] ICJ Rep 13, [39]–[41]; Malcolm D Evans, *Relevant Circumstances and Maritime Delimitation* (Oxford, Clarendon Press, 1989) 99–118.

[157] *Barbados v Trinidad and Tobago* (2006) 45 ILM 798, [224].

[158] *Territorial and Maritime Dispute (Nicaragua v Colombia)* [2012] ICJ Rep 624, [214].

[159] *Bay of Bengal (Bangladesh/Myanmar)* [2012] ITLOS Rep 12, [437].

Any pre-existing boundaries which extend into the maritime area under consideration, whether they be colonial or contemporary boundaries, will have relevance.[160] Likewise, any pre-existing exercise of sovereign rights or jurisdiction will be relevant, such as the issuance of fishing licences.[161] The Court has also indicated that the legitimate security considerations of the parties may be a factor to be taken into account in adjusting a provisional delimitation line.[162]

The ICJ has emphasised that in taking into account special circumstances it does not have the capacity to 'refashion geography' but rather, as was noted in *North Sea Continental Shelf*, the intention is to abate 'the effects of an incidental special feature from which an unjustifiable difference of treatment could result'.[163] More recently the ICJ observed in the *Cameroon/Nigeria* case that the Court 'is not required to take all such geographical peculiarities into account in order to adjust or shift the provisional delimitation line'.[164] Nevertheless, in some instances certain geographical factors may be impossible to ignore, such as a significant disparity in the lengths of the coasts of the respective parties.[165] Likewise, even after an exhaustive assessment of the relevant coastal geography it may be found that there are no features or related factors which qualify as a special circumstance.[166]

ii. Relevant Circumstances

In recent cases international courts and tribunals have begun to refer to the concept of 'relevant circumstances'.[167] In the *Barbados/Trinidad and Tobago Arbitration* the tribunal noted that: 'The identification of the relevant circumstances becomes accordingly a necessary step in determining the approach to delimitation'[168] and this refers to an identification of the maritime domain, particularly geographical features such as the length and configurations of the respective coastlines. Likewise, in the *Black Sea* case, the ICJ referred to identification of the 'relevant maritime area' as being an essential aspect of the delimitation process.[169] This step encompasses not only a physical identification of the outer limits of the area under delimitation but also relevant circumstances within that area which may be important in the delimitation process. Accordingly, the length of the relevant coastal fronts, their general direction and configuration, and associated coastal and geographical features such as islands, reefs, atolls, bays and peninsulas will need to be identified.[170] The presence of ice within the area subject to delimitation may also be relevant.[171] Whether 'relevant circumstances' are then considered to be 'special circumstances' that need to be accounted for in the delimitation process will become a matter for determination.

---

[160]   *Black Sea*, [2009] ICJ Rep 61, [43]–[76]; *Maritime Dispute (Peru v Chile)*, Judgment of 27 January 2014, [183].

[161]   A factor considered in the *Grisbådarna Arbitration* (1910) AJIL 226, 233–34.

[162]   *Libya/Malta Continental Shelf* [1985] ICJ Rep 13, [51]; *Black Sea* [2009] ICJ Rep 61, [202]–[204]; *Territorial and Maritime Dispute (Nicaragua v Colombia)* [2012] ICJ Rep 624, [222]. See further Evans, *Relevant Circumstances and Maritime Delimitation* (n 156) 172–78.

[163]   *North Sea Continental Shelf* [1969] ICJ Rep 3, [91].

[164]   *Cameroon/Nigeria* [2002] ICJ Rep 303, [295].

[165]   *Greenland/Jan Mayen* [1993] ICJ Rep 38, [68]–[70], where the ICJ held that the disparity in the length of the coastlines of Greenland and Jan Mayen were so significant as to constitute a special circumstance.

[166]   *Guyana/Suriname Arbitration* (2007) 139 ILR 566, [377].

[167]   See generally Evans, *Relevant Circumstances and Maritime Delimitation* (n 156).

[168]   *Barbados v Trinidad and Tobago* (2006) 45 ILM 798, [233].

[169]   *Black Sea*, [2009] ICJ Rep 61, [106]–[114].

[170]   *Cameroon/Nigeria* [2002] ICJ Rep 303, [290]; *Caribbean Sea*, Judgment of 8 October 2007, [132]–[227].

[171]   *Greenland/Jan Mayen* [1993] ICJ Rep 38, [77]–[78].

iii. Islands

Issues arising from the delimitation of maritime boundaries associated with islands have a long and significant history in the modern international law of the sea starting with the 1951 *Anglo-Norwegian Fisheries* case.[172] The LOSC clarified the status of islands in Article 121 by confirming they enjoy a territorial sea, contiguous zone, EEZ and continental shelf, which has had implications for maritime boundary delimitations where islands are involved. In some instances, maritime boundary delimitations cannot proceed until sovereignty over islands has been settled.[173] Depending on the size of the islands these matters may be addressed in the larger context of maritime boundary delimitation,[174] or may require separate determination.[175] Whilst in other cases, such as the contested sovereignty over the Malvinas/Falkland Islands by Argentina and the United Kingdom the assertion of maritime claims by one state has the potential to reawaken a dispute with the other claimant state. A distinction needs to be drawn between islands, which may generate basepoints and/or be a relevant factor in delimitation, and low-tide elevations. For example, in the *Bay of Bengal Arbitration (Bangladesh/India)*, the Annex VII arbitral tribunal found that delimitation basepoints could not be selected on low tide elevations (although they may still be relevant to the generation of maritime zones).[176]

With respect to delimitation, islands can have a direct impact in two instances. The first is where the delimitation involves an island state or the territory of an island in which case all of the entitlements envisaged by Article 121 are applicable.[177] The other is where islands are present within the area subject to delimitation between two coastal states. In these instances consideration will need to be given to whether the islands have a distorting effect upon a maritime boundary, especially if they are relatively small and located in the vicinity of the other state, or whether they enjoy all their Article 121 entitlements.[178] These issues were especially significant in the *Eritera/Yemen Arbitration* where the area of the Red Sea under delimitation contained scattered islands of various sizes.[179]

Various techniques have been adopted by the courts and tribunals and in agreed boundary treaties to take into account the impact of islands. One approach has been to limit the entitlement of islands to only a territorial sea so that they are effectively disregarded for the purposes of the overall delimitation process. Australia and Papua New Guinea relied upon this approach in the 1978 Torres Strait Treaty where certain Australian islands which lay to the north of the seabed (continental shelf) boundary were only granted a three nm territorial sea,[180] which has remained intact even following Australia's declaration of a 12 nm

---

[172] *Fisheries (United Kingdom v Norway)* [1951] ICJ Rep 116.

[173] *Sovereignty over Pulau Ligitan and Pulau Sipadan (Indonesia/Malaysia)* [2002] ICJ Rep 625.

[174] *Caribbean Sea*, Judgment of 8 October 2007, [132]–[227].

[175] *Sovereignty over Pedra Branca/Pulau Batu, Middle Rocks and South Ledge (Malaysia/Singapore)*, Judgment of 23 May 2008 [2008] ICJ Rep 12.

[176] *Bay of Bengal Arbitration (Bangladesh/India)*, Award of 7 July 2014, [261].

[177] Examples are *Barbados v Trinidad and Tobago* (2006) 45 ILM 798; *Libya/Malta Continental Shelf* [1985] ICJ Rep 13; *Greenland/Jan Mayen* [1993] ICJ Rep 38.

[178] Evans, *Relevant Circumstances and Maritime Delimitation* (n 156) 135, who asks whether every island must be considered in order to determine whether it is a relevant circumstance.

[179] *Eritrea/Yemen Arbitration*, 17 December 1999, [138]–[157].

[180] 1978 Treaty between Australia and the Independent State of Papua New Guinea Concerning Sovereignty and Maritime Boundaries in the Area between the Two Countries, Including the Area Known as Torres Strait, and Related Matters.

territorial sea.[181] The enclave approach was also adopted in the *Anglo-French Arbitration* where the Channel Islands were granted a 12 nm territorial sea to the north and west, thereby leaving France access to seabed and fishing rights within the central Channel to the north and west of the islands.[182] Another delimitation dispute involving the island of one state close to the metropolitan territory of another state arose in the *Bay of Bengal (Bangladesh/ Myanmar)*[183] case, in which Bangladesh and Myanmar sought the delimitation of the territorial sea, continental shelf and EEZ in the Bay of Bengal. ITLOS gave consideration to the relevance of St Martin's Island, an island around 8 km^2 in area belonging to Bangladesh situated close to the coast of Myanmar and to the termination of the land border of the two states where the Naaf River discharges into the Bay of Bengal. ITLOS observed that '[w]hile it is not unprecedented in case law for islands to be given less than full effect in the delimitation of the territorial sea, the islands subject to such treatment are usually "insignificant maritime features"',[184] but that in this case St Martin's island was a 'significant maritime feature by virtue of its size and population and the extent of economic and other activities'[185] and therefore 'there are no compelling reasons that justify treating St. Martin's Island as a special circumstance'[186] that would lead to a modification of the equidistance line.

A different approach has often been taken when delimitating EEZ and continental shelf boundaries, in which islands have been accorded modified or no effect. An early example of this approach was adopted in 1968 by Iran and Saudi Arabia with respect to the Iranian island of Kharg in the Gulf of Iran.[187] The first apparent use of this technique by a court occurred in the *Anglo-French Arbitration* where the Scilly Isles, which lie to the south-west of Land's End in the United Kingdom, were only given half-effect so as not to have an ongoing distorting impact upon the maritime boundary as it proceeded into the Atlantic Ocean.[188] Similarly, the ICJ applied this approach with respect to the Kerkennah Islands off the Tunisian coastline in *Tunisia/Libya Continental Shelf*.[189] As to the circumstances in which such an approach is adopted, much will depend on how much of a distortion the island will cause to a provisional equidistance line. If its effect is considerable so as to create a gross disproportionality, then principles of equity and the objective of an equitable solution would inevitably require some modification of the boundary. In the 2002 *Cameroon/Nigeria* case the ICJ was confronted with the presence of the Equatorial Guinea island of Bioko within the maritime domain of Cameroon and Nigeria subject to delimitation. However, as Equatorial Guinea was not a party to the proceedings, the Court was of the view that the effect of Bioko on the Cameroon maritime claim was a matter between Cameroon and Equatorial Guinea and not a matter for its determination.[190] In the 2009

---

[181]   Brian R Opeskin and Donald R Rothwell, 'Australia's Territorial Sea: International and Federal Implications of its Extension to 12 Miles' (1991) 22 *Ocean Development and International Law* 395.

[182]   *Anglo-French Continental Shelf Arbitration* (1979) 18 ILM 397, [201]–[202].A modified enclave approach was adopted by the ICJ in *Caribbean Sea*, Judgment of 8 October 2007, [299]–[305].

[183]   *Bay of Bengal (Bangladesh/Myanmar)* [2012] ITLOS Rep 12.

[184]   Ibid [151].

[185]   Ibid.

[186]   Ibid [152].

[187]   Richard Young, 'Equitable Solutions for Offshore Boundaries: The 1968 Saudi Arabia—Iran Agreement' (1970) 64 *AJIL* 152, 154.

[188]   *Anglo-French Continental Shelf Arbitration* (1979) 18 ILM 397, [251].

[189]   *Tunisia/Libya Continental Shelf* [1982] ICJ Rep 18, [129].

[190]   *Cameroon/Nigeria* [2002] ICJ Rep 303, [299].

Black Sea case the Court elected to give no effect to Serpents' Island, a Ukrainian island in the Black Sea located close to the line of delimitation. This was due to the fact that part of the EEZ and continental shelf claim generated off the island was subsumed within that generated from the Ukraine coast, and that by a prior agreement between Romania and Ukraine the island had been granted a 12 nm territorial sea.[191] Similarly, in *Bay of Bengal (Bangladesh/Myanmar)*[192] ITLOS did not use St Martin's Island as a basepoint, given that it was located immediately adjacent to Myanmar's mainland and would result in a line blocking the seaward projection from Myanmar's coast.[193] Then, when it came to drawing the single continental shelf and EEZ delimitation line, ITLOS acknowledged that St Martin's Island was an important feature which could conceivably be considered a relevant circumstance, but that, given its location, to give it effect in the delimitation would cause 'an unwarranted distortion of the delimitation line'.[194] It was therefore disregarded.

iv. Fishing

There has been a history, starting with the *Grisbådarna Arbitration*, of international courts and tribunals being asked to consider access to fish stocks and fishing grounds as a relevant factor in the delimitation process. In some instances, as occurred in the *Greenland/Jan Mayen* case where the ICJ was asked to determine the limits of a fishery zone,[195] this is a legitimate consideration. In that instance the Court took into account the impact of a median line delimitation upon equitable access to a stock of capelin which migrated through the area.[196] However, with the emergence of the EEZ and its focus on distance from the coast as the basis for the maritime zone entitlement, rights of access to fish stocks have diminished. Nevertheless, traditional access by fisherfolk to a certain body of water may be a relevant circumstance to be taken into account as a special circumstance which justifies modification of a provisional equidistance line or other form of arrangement. However, it has been emphasised that strict evidentiary standards will need to be met to make out this type of claim which is 'altogether exceptional'.[197] Greater recognition has been accorded to 'artisanal fishing' as opposed to 'industrial fishing', which the tribunal described in the *Eritrea/Yemen Arbitration* as 'diving carried out by artisanal means, for shells and pearls' and 'the use of islands for drying fish, for way stations, for the provision of temporary shelter, and for the effecting of repairs'.[198]

---

[191] *Black Sea*, [2009] ICJ Rep 61, [187]–[188]. It had also been argued that Serpents' Island was no more than a rock not capable of sustaining human habitation with the effect that Article 121 LOSC became applicable in the context of an EEZ/continental shelf claim, however the ICJ did not expressly rule on that point. In the *Eritrea/Yemen Arbitration*, 17 December 1999, [147] the tribunal also elected to give no effect to certain islands.
[192] *Bay of Bengal (Bangladesh/Myanmar)* [2012] ITLOS Rep 12.
[193] Ibid [265].
[194] Ibid [318]. For critique of this aspect of the decision see Robin Churchill, 'The *Bangladesh/Myanmar* Case: Continuity and Novelty in the Law of Maritime Boundary Delimitation' (2012) 1 *Cambridge Journal of International and Comparative Law* 137, 144.
[195] *Greenland/Jan Mayen* [1993] ICJ Rep 38, [47].
[196] Ibid [75]–[76].
[197] *Barbados v Trinidad and Tobago* (2006) 45 ILM 798, [266]–[269]; and discussion in Kwiatkowska, 'The 2006 Barbados/Trinidad and Tobago Award' (n 140) 45–48; see also *Eritrea/Yemen Arbitration*, 17 December 1999, [72]–[73], where the tribunal rejected arguments presented by both parties that the line of delimitation should be adjusted to take into account historical practices of fishing.
[198] *Eritrea/Yemen Arbitration*, 17 December 1999, [103].

v. Oil Concessions

In areas of disputed continental shelf, consideration has been given in a number of cases to the impact of 'oil concessions' involving the issuing of licences for petroleum exploration and exploitation.[199] This will be an inevitable issue in instances where there have been delays in reaching agreement on a final delimitation of a maritime boundary during which time the parties have issued licences for exploration and exploitation of oil and gas within the area of continental shelf that is the subject of delimitation.[200] In the *Cameroon/Nigeria* case, Nigeria asked the ICJ to take into account oil concessions which had been granted in the area under delimitation. The Court reviewed the relevant jurisprudence and noted that 'although the existence of an express or tacit agreement between the parties on the siting of their respective oil concessions may indicate a consensus on the maritime areas to which they are entitled' they were not to be considered a relevant circumstance that would justify the shifting of a provisional delimitation line.[201] Only in instances where concessions were 'based on express or tacit consent between the parties'[202] would they be taken into account. This approach was endorsed by the tribunal in the *Guyana/Suriname Arbitration*.[203]

F. Single Maritime Boundaries

One phenomenon which may not have been anticipated during the drafting of the LOSC has been the tendency of states to favour the delimitation of a single maritime boundary which in some instances will encompass a territorial sea and then a joint EEZ/continental shelf boundary. In the case of opposite states separated by more than the breadth of their territorial sea but less then 400 nm apart, it may have been anticipated that a joint EEZ/continental shelf boundary may have been preferred. Indeed, during the midst of the UNCLOS III negotiations Australia and Papua New Guinea reached agreement on a joint fisheries/seabed boundary through a part of the Torres Strait.[204] What has perhaps been more surprising is that adjacent states have also favoured this approach, notwithstanding that different considerations may apply to the delimitation of a strict EEZ boundary as opposed to a continental shelf boundary. No provision is made in the LOSC for a single maritime boundary and the ICJ was well aware of the precedent that it was setting in this area when it was requested in the *Gulf of Maine* case to set a single fisheries/continental shelf boundary line,[205] especially given that up till that point in time most of the jurisprudence related to continental shelf delimitations and doubts were raised as to whether techniques adopted in those cases could be equally applied to a fisheries boundary.[206] Ultimately in that instance the ICJ resolved

---

[199] *Tunisia/Libya Continental Shelf* [1982] ICJ Rep 18, [129]; *Gulf of Maine* [1984] ICJ Rep 246, [149]–[152].

[200] This is an issue for Canada and the United States in the area of the Beaufort Sea where the maritime boundary has yet to be delimited: McDorman, *Salt Water Neighbors* (n 1) 187.

[201] *Cameroon/Nigeria* [2002] ICJ Rep 303, [304].

[202] Ibid where the ICJ found that there was no agreement to that effect. See also *Black Sea*, [2009] ICJ Rep 61, [189]–[198].

[203] *Guyana/Suriname Arbitration* (2007) 139 ILR 566, [390]; see also *Barbados v Trinidad and Tobago* (2006) 45 ILM 798, [364].

[204] 1978 Treaty Concerning Sovereignty and Maritime Boundaries in the Area between the Two Countries, Including in the Area Known as the Torres Strait, and Related Matters.

[205] *Gulf of Maine* [1984] ICJ Rep 246, [192].

[206] Ibid [193].

the matter by determining that it had to apply criteria, or a combination of criteria, which did not give preferential treatment to one or the other maritime areas and was 'equally suitable' to both.[207] All subsequent cases concerning a single maritime boundary have therefore required the courts and tribunals to be guided by precedent rather than the LOSC.[208]

Where the Court has been asked to draw a single line commencing with a territorial sea boundary, additional considerations need to be taken into account given the variation in delimitation techniques between the zones and the different sovereign rights at stake. The approach in those cases has been to deal separately with the territorial sea delimitation and, once that line has been established, then to address the joint EEZ/continental shelf.[209] Beyond the territorial sea, a single maritime boundary for the EEZ/continental shelf does raise distinctive issues which may require a court or tribunal to take into account different relevant circumstances and factor in different special circumstances in order to achieve an equitable result. This may involve some juggling of the relevant factors. However, as cautioned in the *Barbados/Trinidad and Tobago Arbitration*: 'There will rarely, if ever, be a single line that is uniquely equitable.'[210]

While state practice clearly indicates a preference for a single maritime boundary, no doubt due to practical convenience and the benefits associated with management and enforcement of a harmonised EEZ/continental shelf area rather than two distinctive areas, this approach will not be possible in all instances. There is state practice emerging of conterminous EEZ/continental shelf boundary lines diverging in instances where outer continental shelf claims beyond 200 nm have been asserted which follow from the distinctive rights over the continental shelf which exist within that area.[211] In those instances of maritime boundary delimitation, the particular features associated with Article 76 continental shelf claims beyond 200 nm need to be taken into account.[212]

VIII. Maritime Boundary Delimitation by Agreement

A. Settled Maritime Boundaries

Notwithstanding the reliance by some states upon formal dispute resolution processes for the settlement of their overlapping maritime claims with neighbouring states, Articles 74

---

[207] Ibid [194].

[208] *Guyana/Suriname Arbitration* (2007) 139 ILR 566, [334]; see the general discussion in Malcolm D Evans, 'Delimitation and the Common Maritime Boundary' (1993) 64 *British Yearbook of International Law* 283; Surya P Sharma, 'The Single Maritime Boundary Regime and the Relationship between the Continental Shelf and the Exclusive Economic Zone' (1987) 2 *International Journal of Estuarine and Coastal Law* 203.

[209] *Guyana/Suriname Arbitration* (2007) 139 ILR 566, [281], [330]; *Caribbean Sea*, Judgment of 8 October 2007, [265]–[266]; *Qatar v Bahrain* [2001] ICJ Rep 94, [173]–[174].

[210] *Barbados v Trinidad and Tobago* (2006) 45 ILM 798, [243].

[211] Stuart Kaye, 'The Use of Multiple Boundaries in Maritime Boundary Delimitation Law and Practice' (1998) 19 *Australian Year Book of International Law* 49.

[212] See the comment in *Barbados v Trinidad and Tobago* (2006) 45 ILM 798, [367]–[368]; and as an example of state practice the 2004 Treaty between the Government of Australia and the Government of New Zealand Establishing Certain Exclusive Economic Zone Boundaries and Continental Shelf Boundaries.

and 83 of the LOSC make clear that states are to engage in delimitation by agreement. This process can be effected directly by negotiation between the parties, or they may elect to refer the matter to a third party for mediation, conciliation, arbitration or adjudication consistent with the mechanisms available to them under Part XV of the LOSC. If the states elect to settle their boundaries bilaterally by agreement then they have open to them a great array of options to accommodate their individual and joint interests in the maritime area under consideration.[213] This has resulted in some particularly innovative approaches, often brought about by particular geographical, historical and other factors at play. For example, in the Torres Strait Treaty between Australia and Papua New Guinea, allowance was made for a protected zone in the middle of the boundary which took into account the interests of the indigenous peoples of the area, including their traditional fishing practices and their movement between the islands within the strait.[214]

What has occurred as a result of these bilateral boundary delimitations is somewhat variable state practice which has reflected different stages in the development of the international law of the sea. Accordingly, some maritime boundaries delimited via these processes prior to the conclusion of the LOSC appear inconsistent not only with contemporary delimitation practices but also the current law regarding entitlements to maritime claims. Examples can be found in continental shelf/seabed boundaries having been settled by agreement based on pre-LOSC legal criteria in which distinctive continental shelf features were decisive at the time.[215] Nevertheless, consistent with the provisions of international treaty law,[216] these boundaries remain in place.

B. Joint Development Zones

An innovative aspect of Articles 74(3) and 83(3) is the obligation states have to 'make every effort' to enter into 'provisional arrangements of a practical nature' pending a permanent maritime boundary settlement.[217] In the *Guyana/Suriname Arbitration*, the tribunal commented that 'this obligation constitutes an implicit acknowledgement of the importance of avoiding the suspension of economic development in a disputed maritime area, as long as such activities do not affect the reaching of a final agreement'.[218] Whilst the language

---

[213] See the exhaustive analysis of state practice contained in Jonathan I Charney et al (eds), *International Maritime Boundaries*, vols 1–5 (Dordrecht, Martinus Nijhoff, 1993–2005).

[214] 1978 Treaty Concerning Sovereignty and Maritime Boundaries in the Area between the Two Countries, Including in the Area known as the Torres Strait, and Related Matters, arts 10–16; see discussion in Dennis Renton, 'The Torres Strait Treaty after 15 Years: Some Observations from a Papua New Guinea Perspective' in James Crawford and Donald R Rothwell (eds), *The Law of the Sea in the Asian Pacific Region* (Dordrecht, Martinus Nijhoff, 1995) 171; KW Ryan and MWD White, 'The Torres Strait Treaty' [1981] 7 *Australian Year Book of International Law* 87.

[215] This particularly applies in the case of the Australian/Indonesia maritime boundaries in the Timor Sea and Indian Ocean; RD Lumb, 'The Delimitation of Maritime Boundaries in the Timor Sea' [1981] 7 *Australian Year Book of International Law* 72.

[216] 1969 Vienna Convention on the Law of the Treaties, art 62(2)(a) bars application of the rule of fundamental change of circumstances in the case of a treaty which establishes a boundary.

[217] Natalie Klein, 'Provisional Measures and Provisional Arrangements in Maritime Boundary Disputes' (2006) 21 *International Journal of Marine and Coastal Law* 423; Ranier Lagoni, 'Interim Measures Pending Maritime Delimitation Agreements' (1984) 78 *AJIL* 345.

[218] *Guyana/Suriname Arbitration* (2007) 139 ILR 566, [460].

of the obligation gives to states some flexibility, it has been emphasised that an obligation exists to negotiate in good faith.[219]

One approach that has been adopted is for states to agree upon provisional boundaries which remain in place until such time as a permanent boundary delimitation has been settled.[220] Another is where a joint development regime has been adopted for an area subject to overlapping claims and where the relevant states wish to ensure that their actions are 'sovereignty-neutral' and will not have a long-term effect upon the direction of a final boundary. A number of states have concluded joint development zone arrangements, including Thailand—Malaysia, South Korea—Japan, Saudi Arabia—Kuwait, Iceland—Norway, Australia—Indonesia, and Australia—Timor-Leste.[221] This approach has also been endorsed by international conciliators in the 1981 *Iceland/Jan Mayen* case.[222] More recently in the 1999 *Eritrea/Yemen Arbitration* the tribunal encouraged the states to consider joint development of any shared resources which may be discovered to straddle a delimited maritime boundary.[223] Model agreements for joint development of oil and gas have been proposed which states can adopt and modify to their particular circumstances.[224]

The two joint development zones which Australia has concluded with respect to the Timor Sea are illustrative of the effectiveness and flexibility which can be associated with joint development regimes. In 1989 Australia concluded with Indonesia the so-called 'Timor Gap Treaty'.[225] The treaty dealt with a disputed area of continental shelf over which Australia and Indonesia had been unable to reach a permanent settlement due to differing interpretations on the law of the sea and their heightened interest in the resource potential of the area. Accordingly, the area in dispute was delimited as a 'Zone of Cooperation' to encompass the outer points of each country's respective 200 nm continental shelf claims and some related areas, and then divided into Areas A, B and C. Within Area A—the central area—revenue was equally shared between Australia and Indonesia, whilst in Areas B and C the revenue was based on a 90/10 split with the northern area in favour of Indonesia and the southern area in favour of Australia. The management of the zone of cooperation was undertaken on a daily basis by a Joint Authority with oversight by a Ministerial Council. The treaty importantly provided in Article 3 that nothing which occurred whilst it was in force 'shall be interpreted as prejudicing the position of either Contracting State on a permanent continental shelf delimitation' and was not to affect the sovereign rights of either state within the area.

---

[219] Ibid [461].

[220] See Agreement between the Government of Australia and the Government of the Republic of Indonesia relating to Cooperation in Fisheries.

[221] See Mark J Valencia 'Taming Troubled Waters: Joint Development of Oil and Mineral Resources in Overlapping Claim Areas' (1986) *San Diego Law Review* 661; others remain under consideration, see Gao Jianjun, 'Joint Development in the East China Sea: Not an Easier Challenge than Delimitation' (2008) 23 *International Journal of Marine and Coastal Law* 39.

[222] *Continental Shelf Between Iceland and Jan Mayen (Iceland/Norway)* (1981) 20 ILM 797 (*Iceland/Jan Mayen*).

[223] *Eritrea/Yemen Arbitration*, 17 December 1999, [86]; which is also reflected in state practice when straddling mineral deposits may be discovered subsequent to a permanent boundary delimitation: Oude Elferink, 'Maritime Delimitation Between Denmark/Greenland and Norway' (n 147) 376.

[224] Hazel Fox et al, *Joint Development of Off-shore Oil and Gas: A Model Agreement for State for Joint Development with Explanatory Commentary*, vols 1–2 (London, British Institute of International and Comparative Law, 1989)'.

[225] 1989 Treaty between Australia and the Republic of Indonesia on the Zone of Cooperation in an Area between the Indonesian Province of East Timor and Northern Australia.

These arrangements lapsed following the Indonesian withdrawal from East Timor in October 1999. However, they were revived through an Exchange of Notes entered into between Australia and the United Nations Transitional Administration in East Timor (UNTAET),[226] which permitted the ongoing operation of the joint development regime until Timor-Leste achieved independence in 2002. Subsequently, Australia and Timor-Leste entered into a number of agreements which dealt with a virtually identical area of the Timor Sea continental shelf allowing for joint development for a period of 30 years or until such time as a permanent seabed boundary is delimited.[227] The 2002 treaty, which also does not impact upon any final permanent delimitation of the maritime boundary between the two states, provides for a 90/10 split in royalties in favour of Timor Leste.[228]

IX. Further Reading

Faraj Abdullah Ahnish, *The International Law of Maritime Boundaries and the Practice of States in the Mediterranean Sea* (Oxford, Clarendon Press, 1993)

Jonathan I Charney et al (eds), *International Maritime Boundaries*, vols 1–5 (Dordrecht, Martinus Nijhoff, 1993–2005)

Alex G Oude Elferink, *The Law of Maritime Boundary Delimitation: A Case Study of the Russian Federation* (Dordrecht, Martinus Nijhoff, 1994)

Malcolm D Evans, *Relevant Circumstances and Maritime Delimitation* (Oxford, Clarendon Press, 1989)

Malcolm D Evans, 'Maritime Boundary Delimitation' in Donald R Rothwell, Alex G Oude Elferink and Tim Stephens (eds), *The Oxford Handbook of the Law of the Sea* (Oxford, Oxford University Press, 2015) 254

Seoung-Yong Hong and Jon M Van Dyke (eds), *Maritime Boundary Disputes, Settlement Processes and the Law of the Sea* (Leiden, Martinus Nijhoff, 2009)

Douglas M Johnston, *The Theory and History of Ocean Boundary-Making* (Kingston, Ontario, McGill-Queen's University Press, 1988)

Robert Kolb, *Case Law on Equitable Maritime Delimitation: Digest and Commentaries* (The Hague, Martinus Nijhoff, 2003)

JRV Prescott and Clive H Schofield, *The Maritime Political Boundaries of the World*, 2nd edn (Leiden, Martinus Nijhoff, 2005)

Yoshifumi Tanaka, *Predictability and Flexibility in the Law of Maritime Delimitation* (Oxford, Hart Publishing, 2006)

---

[226] Exchange of Notes constituting an Agreement between the Government of Australia and the United Nations Transitional Administration in East Timor (UNTAET) concerning the continued Operation of the Treaty between Australia and the Republic of Indonesia on the Zone of Cooperation in an Area between the Indonesian Province of East Timor and Northern Australia of 11 December 1989.

[227] 2002 Timor Sea Treaty between the Government of East Timor and Government of Australia; 2006 Treaty between Australia and the Democratic Republic of Timor-Leste on Certain Maritime Arrangements in the Timor Sea.

[228] Timor Sea Treaty, art 4.

17

Maritime Regulation and Enforcement

I. Introduction

As the international law of the sea has developed through the centuries, coastal states have exercised increasing controls over the waters which fall within their sovereign reach and jurisdiction. Initially this extended only to those waters which incontrovertibly fell within their territory, such as ports, harbours, bays and estuaries. However, with the development of the territorial sea with its dominant focus upon security, the enforcement of coastal state laws and regulations became paramount. For some states, the territorial sea raised a number of fundamental legal issues concerning the extent of sovereignty and jurisdiction beyond land territory, extra-territorial legal competency, and the capacity of law enforcement agencies to undertake seizure and arrest. As the territorial sea became important in the eighteenth and nineteenth centuries for the control of the flow of goods in and out of a state, and customs laws became more sophisticated, an additional layer was added to coastal state interests in the application and enforcement of laws and regulations within that zone.[1] This in turn highlighted the importance of developing special laws to deal with ships which sought to escape the jurisdiction of the coastal state by fleeing from the territorial sea into the high seas. The response in customary international law was the right of hot pursuit, and then, through enactment of the Hovering Acts principally by Britain and the United States,[2] recognition of the right of coastal states also to claim a contiguous zone where additional rights of maritime jurisdiction for enforcement purposes could be exercised.

By the twentieth century there was in place a mix of customary international law and a variety of municipal coastal state laws and regulations concerning the exercise of sovereignty over the territorial sea. However, new challenges were confronted during the codification and development of the international law of the sea in the latter part of the century. This was particularly evident from the early efforts to proclaim and then enforce Fisheries Zones which not only were contested as to their legality, as occurred in the so-called 'Cod Wars' between Iceland and the United Kingdom,[3] but also raised issues as to the enforcement capacity of coastal states that were now asserting controls over vast areas of ocean space

---

[1] William E Masterton, *Jurisdiction in Marginal Seas with Special Reference to Smuggling* (Port Washington, NY, Kennikat Press, 1929).

[2] DP O'Connell, *The International Law of the Sea*, vol 2 (Oxford, Clarendon Press, 1984) 1034–39.

[3] Which proved to be part of the catalyst for the dispute in *Fisheries Jurisdiction* (*United Kingdom v Iceland*) (merits) [1974] ICJ Rep 3.

without accompanying enforcement assets such as naval craft, a coast guard or fisheries inspection vessels capable of fulfilling their jurisdictional designs or responsibilities. This in turn compromised the sovereignty and jurisdiction of the coastal state seeking to proclaim such zones.[4]

When it came to the negotiation of the LOSC,[5] these issues had been helpfully highlighted by state practice in areas such as hot pursuit, which had become well established in both customary international law and also in the 1958 Geneva Conventions.[6] Nevertheless, the LOSC did pose additional issues for resolution such as the extent of the enforcement capacity of coastal states over the EEZ and continental shelf especially with respect to expanded rights to regulate offshore fishing, the intermingling of *sui generis* high seas enforcement mechanisms such as hot pursuit and the right of visit with coastal states rights and interests over the EEZ, the development of completely new mechanisms for protection and preservation of the marine environment in Part XII, and the balancing of the rights and interests of coastal states with those of flag and maritime states in ensuring freedoms of navigation in newly-recognised international straits and archipelagic sea lanes. The LOSC is therefore littered with a variety of measures which seek to identify clearly the extent and capacity of coastal state enforcement jurisdiction, whilst also ensuring certain safeguards against abuse of those powers.

Against this backdrop, the international law of the sea has also witnessed a new phenomenon which has gathered momentum since the conclusion of the LOSC. Multilateral law enforcement authorised by the United Nations Security Council was envisaged under the 1945 UN Charter, and, whilst the United Nations mandated enforcement operations in Korea in the early 1950s and peacekeeping operations highlighted the capacity of the United Nations to engage in international peace and law enforcement, it was not until the end of the Cold War that this potential began to be fully recognised. The actions of the United States and its allies in the 1991 Persian Gulf War, authorised by several resolutions of the Security Council, demonstrated the capacity of United Nations members to engage in multilateral maritime operations in support of the enforcement of a sanctions regime. Since that time, the United Nations has further explored the extent of its Chapter VI and VII powers, and has given express or tacit consent to maritime enforcement regimes dealing with matters such as piracy,[7] nuclear non-proliferation,[8] and targeted trade and economic sanctions directed against several states,[9] such as the arms embargo imposed on Libya in 2011.[10]

The other development which the law of the sea has witnessed during this time has been the distinctive role of flag, coastal and port states. International law has traditionally recognised the exclusive jurisdiction of flag states over shipping on the high seas.[11] However,

---

[4] See generally the discussion in Ann L Hollick, 'The Origins of 200-Mile Offshore Zones' (1977) 71 *AJIL* 494.

[5] *Basic Documents* No 36.

[6] Especially the Convention on the High Seas, *Basic Documents* No 10; see further the discussion in ch 7.

[7] UN Security Council Resolution 1851 (2008), *Basic Documents* No 89.

[8] See generally David D Caron and Harry N Scheiber (eds), *The Oceans in the Nuclear Age: Legacies and Risks* (Leiden, Martinus Nijhoff, 2010).

[9] See, eg, Rob McLaughlin, 'United Nations Mandated Naval Interdiction in the Territorial Sea' (2002) 51 *International and Comparative Law Quarterly* 249.

[10] UN Security Council Resolution 1973 (2011), calling on United Nations members to inspect in their territory and on the high seas vessels and aircraft bound for Libya holding cargoes of arms.

[11] Cf *Lotus (France v Turkey)* [1927] PCIJ Rep ser A no 10 and discussion in ch 7.

the effect of the LOSC has been to expand significantly the extent of coastal state jurisdiction with respect to the activities that take place within the maritime zones adjacent to the state, and accordingly not only has there been a larger area of ocean over which coastal state jurisdiction can now be exercised but the subject matter of that regulation has also broadened. Given increasing activities in the oceans, this has raised its own challenges with respect to the effective enforcement of both coastal state and flag state laws and regulations. To that end, the LOSC and related international instruments have increasingly recognised the important role that port states can play in maritime regulation and enforcement, notwithstanding those states may only have a remote interest in the actions of delinquent ships.

II. International Law Regarding Enforcement Powers at Sea

With the early law of the sea maintaining exclusive flag state jurisdiction on the high seas, the debate in customary international law over the legitimacy of the territorial sea as a zone of coastal state sovereignty and jurisdiction was pivotal in the eventual recognition of coastal state rights to undertake maritime regulation and enforcement within these waters against ships of any nationality. This required not only an acceptance in customary international law of the territorial sea, but also an acceptance of the prescriptive and enforcement jurisdiction of the coastal state over those waters. The prescriptive jurisdiction of the coastal state was intimately associated with the recognised sovereignty of the coastal state over the territorial sea, such that it was possible to regulate activities of concern, such as smuggling and fishing.[12] In developing a more assertive approach to the enforcement of their laws, coastal states did have to contend with the doctrine of sovereign immunity, effectively barring the application of laws against the government ships of foreign states, and also doctrines which had long associated the flag state as having exclusive jurisdiction over shipping.[13] Gradually, as the sovereign rights of coastal states over the territorial sea gained greater recognition and acceptance, so too did the extent of the coastal State's prescriptive jurisdiction over ships within those waters. The law developed through state practice based on municipal law applying to the territorial sea;[14] the decisions of the municipal courts confirming coastal state jurisdiction;[15] and occasionally international courts and tribunals also upholding emerging coastal state jurisdiction and control over the territorial sea.[16] There was also limited state practice early in the twentieth century of cooperation between

---

[12] Masterton, *Jurisdiction in Marginal Seas* (n 1) 72–252 refers extensively to developments in state practice in Great Britain (as it was then) and the United States seeking to combat smuggling along the coast.

[13] See generally O'Connell, *The International Law of the Sea*, vol 2 (n 2) 919–53.

[14] Principally though various versions of the 'Hovering Act' enacted in Great Britain, and then subsequently the Customs Consolidation Act 1876 (UK) and Territorial Waters Jurisdiction Act 1878 (UK); DP O'Connell, *The International Law of the Sea*, vol 1 (Oxford, Clarendon Press, 1982) 96–98; C John Colombos, *The International Law of the Sea*, 6th edn (London, Longmans, 1967) 137–40 discussing the position in Great Britain and the United States.

[15] O'Connell, *The International Law of the Sea*, vol 1, ibid 84–106 reviewing the development of the common law and decisions of courts with respect to the territorial sea in Great Britain and the United States, and at 121–23 reviewing French practice.

[16] See a review of authorities, state practice and relevant treaties in *North Atlantic Coast Fisheries (Great Britain/ United States)* (1910) 11 RIAA 167.

flag and coastal states, in which flag states granted limited consent for high seas boarding of their ships on the high seas.[17]

The effect of these developments was that there was beginning to emerge a distinctive international law with respect to enforcement jurisdiction at sea by coastal states that took into account the particular issues arising from law enforcement at sea, in particular that delinquent ships were able to flee from the territorial sea and effectively escape capture by reaching the high seas, and that limitations on the use of force had to be applied in policing actions on the sea because of the potential for loss of life. It was from this practice that specific doctrines emerged with respect to hot pursuit and the use of force at sea.

A. Hot Pursuit

The contemporary international law of hot pursuit has its foundation in the ILC's draft articles and commentaries, the 1958 Convention on the High Seas, and in the LOSC.[18] Given the significance of hot pursuit for coastal state maritime enforcement, it is also reflected in the municipal laws of many coastal states.[19] The main features of hot pursuit as outlined in Article 111 of the LOSC are as follows:

— pursuit may be undertaken if the competent authorities of the coastal state believe that a ship has violated the laws and regulations of the state;
— the pursuit must commence when the foreign ship is within either the archipelagic or internal waters of the coastal state, or one of its maritime zones, and must cease once the pursued ship enters the territorial sea of another state;
— the pursuit can only be continued beyond the coastal states' maritime zones if it has been continuous and not subject to interruption;
— pursuit can only be commenced if the pursuing ship has given to the foreign ship a visual or auditory signal to stop;
— pursuit can only be undertaken by warships or military aircraft, or other ships or aircraft clearly marked and identifiable as being on government service; and
— pursuit initially commenced by an aircraft can be transferred to pursuit by a ship providing that the foreign ship was ordered to stop and the pursuit has been carried out without interruption.

Subject only to the expansion of the right of hot pursuit to take into account violations by the foreign ship of laws and regulations of the coastal state within the EEZ and continental shelf, the definition of hot pursuit has essentially remained the same since the ILC's attempts as codification in the 1950s.[20] However, new practices and technologies in

---

[17] See, eg, 1924 Convention respecting the Regulation of Liquor Traffic (United States of America and Great Britain), art II.

[18] Maidment argues that it is doubtful whether the right could be said to have been 'fully received into the body of international law' until the adoption of the 1958 Geneva Convention: Susan Maidment, 'Historical Aspects of the Doctrine of Hot Pursuit' (1972–73) 46 *British Yearbook of International Law* 365, 365.

[19] See, eg, Maritime Powers Act 2013 (Australia), ss 41–45; Maritime Drug Law Enforcement Act, 46 USC 70501 (US); Criminal Code, RSC 1985, C-46 (Canada).

[20] The ILC commented at the time that: 'In the main, this article is taken from article 11 of the regulations adopted by the Second Committee of The Hague Codification Conference in 1930. The right concerned is not contested in international law': International Law Commission, 'Articles Concerning the Law of the Sea with Commentaries' (1956) *Yearbook of the International Law Commission*, vol 2, 285.

maritime enforcement have demanded the reinterpretation of several elements of the right of hot pursuit.

i. Case Law

Hot pursuit has been considered by a number of international tribunals, both prior to and since the conclusion of the LOSC.[21] The leading decision of the International Tribunal for the Law of the Sea on hot pursuit is the *M/V Saiga (No 2)* case.[22] The *Saiga*, an oil tanker registered in Saint Vincent and the Grenadines, was the subject of an alleged hot pursuit within the EEZ of Guinea in October 1997. The ship was engaged in selling gas oil as bunker to fishing and other vessels off the coast of West Africa and during the relevant period had, over 24 hours, relocated from within the Guinean contiguous zone to the Guinean EEZ beyond 24 nm. Guinea asserted that it had commenced the hot pursuit at the time it received certain information regarding the activities of the *Saiga* and that the pursuit was commenced within the EEZ with the arrest effected on the high seas. Guinea alleged that the sale of gas oil by the *Saiga* constituted crimes of contraband, fraud and tax evasion, and the master of the ship was charged with such offences. Saint Vincent and the Grenadines challenged the legal basis of the arrest and the purported exercise of the right of hot pursuit.

ITLOS reviewed the terms of Article 111, and observed that the conditions for the exercise of hot pursuit were 'cumulative' and that 'each of them has to be satisfied for the pursuit to be legitimate under the Convention'.[23] The tribunal found that there were a number of important omissions from the Article 111 requirements in the way in which Guinea had sought to undertake pursuit of the *Saiga*, including the lack of basis for asserting violation of its laws, failure to give visual or auditory signals to stop, and an interruption of the alleged hot pursuit. ITLOS concluded that there was no legal basis under the law on hot pursuit for Guinea to stop and arrest the *Saiga*[24] and ordered that reparation be paid to Saint Vincent and the Grenadines.[25] Hot pursuit was also raised before ITLOS in the 2002 case of the *Volga*, but was not considered by the tribunal in its judgment.[26]

ii. State Practice

The contemporary right of hot pursuit, though now firmly grounded in conventional law and the LOSC, continues to raise a number of important issues in its implementation in practice. Fundamental to the right of the coastal state to undertake the pursuit is the existence of a 'good reason to believe' that a foreign ship has violated coastal state laws and regulations having a legitimate basis under the Convention. Therefore, identifying the character of the alleged unlawful conduct of the foreign ship, and the maritime zone within which that conduct has occurred, is crucial. This can be especially significant in cases of illegal fishing where the activity is occurring on the cusp of the EEZ and high seas. Pursuit cannot commence until a clear visual or auditory direction has been given to the foreign ship and it

---

[21] See *I'm Alone (Canada/United States)* 3 RIAA 1609.

[22] *M/V Saiga (No 2) (Saint Vincent and the Grenadines v Guinea)* (admissibility and merits) (1999) 120 ILR 143 ('*M/V Saiga (No 2)*').

[23] Ibid [146].

[24] Ibid [149].

[25] Ibid [167]–[177]; the total amount ordered to be paid was a sum of US$2,123,357.

[26] *Volga (Russian Federation v Australia)* (prompt release) (2003) 42 ILM 159.

has been ordered to stop.[27] The effect of this is that the pursuing ship must be in the vicinity of the foreign ship such that it is actually able to observe a violation of the coastal state's laws. The pursuit may also only be undertaken by certain state ships and aircraft which are authorised by the coastal state to undertake enforcement action. In addition to naval ships, this would also extend to include Coast Guard, customs, fisheries and police vessels, including those operated by provincial authorities within federal states.

The LOSC and the *M/V Saiga (No 2)* confirm that the pursuit must not be interrupted;[28] however, when a pursuit occurs in challenging weather and sea conditions, as has been the case in hot pursuits undertaken in the Southern Ocean in response to the infringement of EEZ fisheries laws, mere transitory interruption should not terminate the right of hot pursuit.[29] Technical means may be deployed to initiate and continue a pursuit, so that tracking by remote means, including radio, radar, satellite or sonar, would be consistent with the right. It is also clear that the pursuit may be transferred between an aircraft and ship of the coastal state as occurred in the *Volga* case,[30] whilst state practice also confirms that hot pursuit can be transferred between ships.[31]

iii. Multilateral Hot Pursuit

A related issue is whether it is consistent with the LOSC to utilise 'multilateral hot pursuit' or 'baton changes', in which the ships of two or more coastal states are engaged in the pursuit of a delinquent vessel.[32] Several prominent examples of this type of hot pursuit have both occurred in the Southern Ocean. In 2001 the Togo-registered *South Tomi* was pursued from within the Australian EEZ adjacent to Heard Island in the Southern Ocean by the Australian-flagged *Southern Supporter* for a total of 14 days over 3,300 nm until two South African naval vessels with Australian personnel aboard were eventually able to effect an arrest 320 nm south of Cape Town. In the case of the Uruguayan-flagged *Viarsa I*, it was pursued in 2003 by the *Southern Supporter* for 21 days over a total of 3,900 nm until the pursuit was brought to an end with the aid of South African and United Kingdom flagged vessels.[33] Although the LOSC is silent as to the capacity of third states to join in to assist with

---

[27] This matter was emphasised by the ILC in 1956 when it observed that 'To prevent abuse, the Commission declined to admit orders given by wireless, as these could be given at any distance; the words 'visual or auditory signal' exclude signals given at a great distance and transmitted by wireless': International Law Commission, 'Articles Concerning the Law of the Sea with Commentaries' (1956) *Yearbook of the International Law Commission*, vol 2, 285.

[28] *M/V Saiga (No 2)* (1999) 120 ILR 143 [147].

[29] Tim Stephens, 'Enforcing Australian Fisheries Laws: Testing the Limits of Hot Pursuit in Domestic and International Law' (2004) 15 *Public Law Review* 12, 15.

[30] LOSC, art 111(6); see *The Volga Case* 'Statement in Response of Australia' (7 December 2002) [5]–[13] where the pursuit was conducted jointly by ship and organic helicopter from that ship with the boarding party inserted onto the *Volga* via a fast rope from the helicopter.

[31] See *I'm Alone (Canada/United States)* 3 RIAA 1609 where two United States Coast Guard ships were engaged in the hot pursuit; whilst in the *South Tomi* (2001) and *Viarsa I* (2003) hot pursuits multiple ships from different countries were engaged in the hot pursuit: Erik Jaap Molenaar, 'Multilateral Hot Pursuit and Illegal Fishing in the Southern Ocean: The Pursuits of the Viarsa I and South Tomi' (2004) 19 *International Journal of Marine and Coastal Law* 19.

[32] Molenaar, 'Multilateral Hot Pursuit', ibid 41 defines this as 'a multilateral exercise of a coastal State right that involves pursuing vessels, aircraft or officials with different nationalities, that is authorized by the relevant coastal State where necessary and is consistent with the main substantive and procedural conditions in Article 111'.

[33] Ibid 19–23.

a hot pursuit, no protests were lodged by either Togo or Uruguay following the Southern Ocean pursuits and as the final arrest in each instance was effected by Australian officials the principle of coastal state enforcement of its laws and regulations was maintained.[34] Both of these cases also raised issues with respect to the escort and treatment of arrested ships over the high seas to Australia, where legal proceedings were brought against the crew and owners. Article 111(7) of the LOSC directly addresses this point, and makes clear that ships arrested following a hot pursuit and then escorted across the high seas or EEZ to a port of the coastal state have no grounds for release.[35]

Clearly in the case of a lengthy hot pursuit, or even one that has commenced adjacent to the maritime zones of another coastal state, there is every prospect that a delinquent ship may seek to flee to the territorial sea of another coastal state and thereby gain the protection of Article 111(3) requiring the hot pursuit to cease. However, coastal states engaging in cooperative measures to combat common threats such as illegal fishing or drug trafficking may elect to waive their sovereign rights in specific instances and permit the hot pursuit to continue. An example of such an approach can be found in a 2003 Australia France Treaty[36] applicable in the Southern Ocean which allows each state to request assistance from the other when engaged in a hot pursuit,[37] and also for hot pursuit to continue through the territorial sea of the other state provided they are informed and no physical law enforcement or other coercive action is taken against the pursued vessel whilst in those waters.[38] These types of cooperative maritime enforcement arrangements have particular application in remote regions where there are vast oceans to patrol and limited capacity to do so.[39] In the absence of such measures, the right of hot pursuit ceases as soon as the delinquent ships enters the territorial sea of its flag state or of a third state, even if that is a mere temporary entry before returning to waters beyond the territorial sea.

B. Use of Force

Accounts of the use of force in the maritime context[40] usually draw a distinction between force used in policing or constabulary operations and force used in military operations, including during armed conflict (such as in the exercise of the inherent right of self-defence under the UN Charter).[41] Coastal state maritime regulation and enforcement is predominantly concerned with policing functions directed at ensuring law and order within a

---

[34] See further comment in ibid 19–23.

[35] *Virginia Commentaries*, vol 3, 259.

[36] 2003 Treaty between the Government of Australia and the Government of the French Republic on cooperation in the maritime areas adjacent to the French Southern and Antarctic Territories (TAAF), Heard Island and the McDonald Islands ('2003 Australia France Treaty').

[37] Ibid art 3(3).

[38] Ibid art 4.

[39] See comment in Warwick Gullett and Clive Schofield, 'Pushing the Limits of the Law of the Sea Convention: Australia and French Cooperative Surveillance and Enforcement in the Southern Ocean' (2007) 22 *International Journal of Marine and Coastal Law* 545.

[40] The discussion under this heading should be read alongside ch 12; see also AV Lowe, 'Self-Defence at Sea' in WE Butler (ed), *The Non-Use of Force in International Law* (Dordrecht, Kluwer, 1989) 185, and more generally Christine Gray, *International Law and the Use of Force*, 2nd edn (Oxford, Oxford University Press, 2004).

[41] Ken Booth, *Law, Force and Diplomacy at Sea* (London, George Allen & Unwin, 1985) 3 describes this as the problem of 'between law and war'.

coastal state's maritime zones. This may involve the investigation of crimes and the arrest of suspected perpetrators, in much the same way as police operate ashore. However, given that maritime offences may occur many miles from shore, in circumstances where offending vessels may evade arrest, and detention and arrest may involve risk to a boarding party,[42] distinctive practices have developed in the use of force against ships at sea during policing operations, such as the firing of warning shots 'across the bow'. The use of force within maritime zones is closely regulated under international law and creates additional dimensions not normally present ashore. Account must be taken of the rights of other legitimate users in the area, such as local maritime commerce, foreign ships exercising a right of innocent passage within the territorial sea, or fishers going about their lawful business. Some forms of maritime regulation may also directly require the engagement of military forces, such as the enforcement of a United Nations sanctions regime, and whilst this is a situation short of armed conflict, fundamental principles regulating the use of force will continue to apply.

i. The LOSC and the Use of Force

The LOSC is mostly silent on issues associated with the use of force. This partly arises from the fact that the body of law dealing with the use of force is long standing, founded in customary international law and partly outlined in the UN Charter, and remains contentious. The Convention was also overwhelmingly concerned with peaceful uses of the oceans and did not directly address the status of the law of the sea during times of armed conflict. This is reaffirmed in Article 301, which emphasises that in exercising rights and performing their duties under the Convention, states parties are to 'refrain from any threat or use of force against the territorial integrity or political independence of any state, or in any manner inconsistent with the principles of international law embodied in the Charter of the United Nations'. Article 301 effectively reaffirms Article 2(4) of the Charter, but also recognises the application to the law of the sea of those other principles of international law embodied in the Charter, including Article 51, dealing with self-defence.[43] Article 225 of the LOSC, found in Part XII dealing with protection and preservation of the marine environment indicates that states '[i]n the exercise under this Convention of their powers of enforcement' are not to endanger safety of navigation or create any hazard to a vessel. Read in the context of Part XII, this apparent limitation on the use of force is consistent with measures for the protection and preservation of the marine environment, and more general obligations for the safety of life at sea. However, it is doubtful whether Article 225 operates so as to remove the inherent right of self-defence recognised under international law. Shearer has observed that: 'The only sensible construction of Article 225 is to read it subject to the customary law principles of necessity and proportion, and not as a blanket prohibition against the use of force in any circumstances.'[44] Commenting on these issues concerning the use of

---

[42] Molenaar, 'Multilateral Hot Pursuit' (n 31) 35.

[43] This is also reaffirmed in LOSC, art 293(1) providing that a court or tribunal having jurisdiction under Part XV shall apply 'other rules of international law not incompatible with this Convention'.

[44] IA Shearer, 'Problems of Jurisdiction and Law Enforcement against Delinquent Vessels' (1986) 35 *International and Comparative Law Quarterly* 320, 342.

force, the law of the sea, and international law, ITLOS observed in *M/V Saiga (No 2)* that 'the use of force must be avoided as far as possible and, where force is unavoidable, it must not go beyond what is reasonable and necessary in the circumstances. Considerations of humanity must apply in the law of the sea, as they do in other areas of international law'.[45]

The manner in which the use of force at sea is contemplated and the government agency engaged in that use of force may prove vital as to the characterisation of the use of force. Not only will intent be an important factor, but likewise capacity to use force will be relevant. Fisheries or Customs vessels often would carry only small arms for individual self-defence, whilst a Coast Guard vessel may be equipped with heavier weapons capable of being used in a hot pursuit, and also in its defence if it came under attack. Military ships engaged in maritime regulation and enforcement activities will have aboard weapons systems consistent with their individual capability and to that end there is the scope for considerable variation in capacity between naval patrol boats which may engage in constabulary type operations relatively close to shore, and larger patrol vessels, frigates or destroyers more suited to distant water operations within the EEZ. Likewise, the capacity of the alleged delinquent ship to defend itself may also be an important factor, as is the manner in which an enforcement operation is actually carried out.

In the 2007 *Guyana/Suriname Award*,[46] the arbitral tribunal was asked amongst a number of matters, to consider the conduct of the Suriname Navy which approached an oil-drilling rig, the *C.E. Thornton*, which was operating consistent with an oil concession granted by Guyana in disputed waters between Guyana and Suriname. The rig was directed to leave the area within 12 hours otherwise 'the consequences will be yours'. The rig withdrew from the concession area shadowed by Surinamese patrol boats. The tribunal concluded that this conduct 'constituted an explicit threat that force might be used if the order was not complied with'.[47] Whilst it was accepted that force may be used in maritime law enforcement activities providing that 'such force is unavoidable, reasonable and necessary',[48] it was concluded on the basis of the facts that what occurred in this instance 'seemed more akin to a threat of military action rather than a mere law enforcement activity'.[49] Suriname's actions were held to have been a direct threat of the use of force contrary to the LOSC, the UN Charter and general international law.[50]

ii. General Principles Regarding the Use of Force at Sea During Peacetime

As to the general principles which have been developed regarding the use of force in maritime regulation and enforcement operations, in the 1933 case of the *I'm Alone*, the Commissioners referred to the use of 'necessary and reasonable force for the purpose of effecting the objects of boarding, searching, seizing and bringing into port the suspected vessel'.[51]

---

[45]   *M/V Saiga (No 2)* (1999) 120 ILR 143 [155].
[46]   *Guyana/Suriname Arbitration* (2007) 139 ILR 566.
[47]   Ibid [439].
[48]   Ibid [445].
[49]   Ibid.
[50]   However, the tribunal rejected a claim for compensation arising from this incident: Ibid [452]; see the discussion in Patricia Jimenez Kwast, 'Maritime Law Enforcement and the Use of Force: Reflections on the Categorisation of Forcible Action at Sea in the Light of the *Guyana/Suriname* Award' (2008) 13 *Journal of Conflict and Security Law* 49.
[51]   *I'm Alone (Canada/United States)* 3 RIAA 1609, 1615.

In 1999 in the *M/V Saiga (No 2)*, ITLOS emphasised the importance of a graduated response when seeking to stop a suspected delinquent ship. This involved first the giving of a visual or auditory signal to stop, similar to that which would apply in the case of a hot pursuit, after which if the ship fails to stop then a variety of actions may be taken, including the firing of shots across the bow. Only if these measures have failed, and appropriate warnings have been issued may force be used as a last resort, although as the tribunal observed: 'Even then, appropriate warning must be issued to the ship and all efforts should be made to ensure that life is not endangered'.[52] As to the actual use of arms against a ship, O'Connell observed along similar lines that 'fire is not to be opened until every other tactical expedient to effect arrest or resist threat has been tried, and patiently pursued, in vain; and even then only the minimum degree of firepower is to be used.'[53]

The firing of weapons and direct use of force against foreign ships at sea is a significant matter with the potential for serious diplomatic consequences between the states involved. International courts and tribunals have been asked to resolve a number of these cases. In the 1961 *Red Crusader* incident[54] a Danish fishery protection vessel the *Niels Ebbesen* put a boarding party aboard a United Kingdom flagged fishing trawler, the *Red Crusader*. The party was promptly detained and the *Red Crusader* attempted to escape to the high seas. Following a 30 minute pursuit, the *Niels Ebbesen* fired warning shots across the bow and stern of the *Red Crusader* before directing fire using solid shot at its radar scanner and lights. The matter was referred to a Commission of Enquiry, which observed that the captain of the *Neils Ebbesen* 'exceeded legitimate use of armed force on two counts: (a) firing without warning of solid gunshot; (b) creating danger to human life on board the *Red Crusader* without proved necessity, by the effective firing at the *Red Crusader*'.[55] The Commission emphasised the importance of using other means to stop the *Red Crusader*.[56] Similar views were expressed by ITLOS in *M/V Saiga (No 2)*,[57] where the tribunal heavily criticised the actions of Guinea and its patrol boat which, without issuing signals or warnings, directly fired live ammunition into an almost fully laden oil tanker that was low in the water and only capable of a top speed of 10 knots.[58] The tribunal concluded that Guinea had used excessive force and endangered human life contrary to international law.[59]

It follows that the sinking of a delinquent ship would only be permissible in the most exceptional of circumstances. The *I'm Alone* involved the sinking in 1929 of a British flagged, and Canadian registered, ship that was engaged in the smuggling of liquor (rum running) to various parts of the United States coast along the Gulf of Mexico. The *I'm Alone* had been the object of a hot pursuit first involving the United States Coast Guard cutter *Wolcott* which was later joined by the *Dexter*. Fire was eventually opened which resulted in the sinking of the *I'm Alone*. Whilst not ruling out that the sinking of a delinquent ship the object of a hot pursuit may in some instances be justifiable, the Commissioners in this instance observed that the 'the admittedly intentional sinking of the suspected vessel

---

[52] *M/V Saiga (No 2)* (1999) 120 ILR 143 [156].
[53] DP O'Connell, *The Influence of Law on Sea Power* (Manchester, Manchester University Press, 1975) 65.
[54] *Red Crusader* (1962) 35 ILR 485.
[55] Ibid 499.
[56] Ibid.
[57] *M/V Saiga (No 2)* (1999) 120 ILR 143 [156].
[58] Ibid [157].
[59] Ibid [158].

was not justified',[60] and could not be justified by any principle of international law.[61] The actions of the United States were held to be unlawful, and the United States was required to acknowledge its illegality and pay a sum by way of compensation.[62]

III. Enforcement Operations Within Particular Maritime Zones

Each of the maritime zones within the LOSC raise their own distinctive issues with respect to maritime regulation and enforcement. With the expanding rights of coastal states to exercise sovereignty and jurisdiction in adjacent maritime zones, there have likewise been efforts made within the conventional law to ensure appropriate safeguards so that there is no undue impact upon the rights of other states, particularly freedoms of navigation. Part XII of the LOSC, for example, contains a range of measures designed to ensure that the coastal state does not overreach its enforcement jurisdiction with respect to the EEZ marine environment.[63] When states go beyond the limits of what is permissible, reparations may be ordered under general international law, as occurred in *I'm Alone*, and liability may arise under the LOSC.[64]

Occasionally, states will seek to exercise a form of extra-territorial law enforcement beyond the limits of their maritime zones. The LOSC gives some limited recognition to the legitimacy of this approach through the doctrine of constructive presence.[65] Hot pursuit may lawfully be undertaken by coastal states against ships beyond the limits of some maritime zones if they are 'mother' ships launching smaller craft that enter coastal state maritime zones to undertake illegal acts.[66] This issue arose on the facts in the *Arctic Sunrise* case,[67] following Russia's arrest and detention of the Greenpeace vessel *Arctic Sunrise* after persons from the vessel, using several inflatable craft, attempted to board a Russian oil rig, the *Prirazlomnaya*, as part of a protest to draw attention to risks of oil and gas exploitation in the Arctic. The *Arctic Sunrise* was arrested within Russia's EEZ, but did not come within 500 metres of the *Prirazlomnaya*, the maximum radius of a safety zone that Russia was permitted to establish under Article 60(5) of the LOSC.[68] However, the smaller protest vessels did enter the 500 m zone, raising the possibility that Russia could mount a lawful hot pursuit of the craft and the *Arctic Sunrise* as the mother ship, as permitted under Article 111. In its request for provisional measures, the Netherlands, as the flag state of the *Arctic Sunrise*,

---

[60] *I'm Alone (Canada/United States)* 3 RIAA 1609, 1615.

[61] Ibid 1617.

[62] Ibid 1618; the sum of US$25,000 was ordered to be paid.

[63] LOSC, arts 223–33, 235–36.

[64] See ibid arts 106, 111(8).

[65] O'Connell, *The International Law of the Sea*, vol 2 (n 2) 1092–93; Douglas Guilfoyle, *Shipping Interdiction and the Law of the Sea* (Cambridge, Cambridge University Press, 2009) 13–14; William C Gilmore, 'Hot Pursuit and Constructive Presence in Canadian Law Enforcement' (1988) 12 *Marine Policy* 105.

[66] LOSC, art 111(4) which expressly refers to a 'mother ship' located beyond certain maritime zones still being subject to hot pursuit.

[67] *The Arctic Sunrise Case (Netherlands v Russia)* (2014) 53 ILM 607.

[68] Russia had, in fact, purported to establish a three nm safety zone.

contended that even if the right of hot pursuit were open to Russia, it was not validly commenced (no signal to stop was given) nor continued uninterrupted.[69] Russia refused to appear in the proceedings, and the matter was not determined on the facts. Nor did ITLOS engage with the substantive legal issues involved. Instead, as appropriate for interlocutory proceedings, pending determination on the merits by an Annex VII tribunal, ITLOS confined itself to ordering the release of the vessel and its crew on the posting of a bond or other financial security by the Netherlands.[70]

Enforcement action taken beyond 200 nm has often been controversial, as seen in the heavy criticism of Canada when it amended the Coastal Fisheries Protection Act to prohibit foreign flagged fishing vessels from operating in a prescribed area of the high seas adjacent to the Canadian EEZ. Canadian government vessels subsequently intercepted, boarded and arrested the Spanish flagged *Estai* some 245 nm from the Canadian coast. Spain challenged Canada's actions in the International Court of Justice, but the Court found that it had no jurisdiction to deal with the dispute.[71] Canada's actions were influential, however, in prompting the international community to improve the protection of straddling fish stocks.[72]

Any maritime regulation and enforcement operation conducted by a coastal state must be founded in a right to do so based on international law and also municipal law, particularly if following the arrest and detention of a vessel criminal or civil proceedings are to arise. However, if a coastal State's municipal laws go beyond what is permissible under the LOSC and general international law, arrest, detention and prosecution may be without foundation. This fundamental point was emphasised by ITLOS in the *M/V Saiga (No 2)* case, where the tribunal found that Guinea's customs laws which it sought to apply within its EEZ had no basis in the LOSC.[73] As the tribunal observed, it 'needs to determine whether the laws applied or the measures taken by Guinea against the *Saiga* (are compatible with the Convention'.[74] This threshold question as to whether the exercise of prescriptive jurisdiction is consistent with the law of the sea must be considered in the context of each enforcement action and the answer is dependent on the maritime zone where the allegedly unlawful act by a foreign vessel has occurred.

A. Internal Waters

Coastal states possess absolute sovereignty over their internal waters, being those waters on the landward side of their baselines. Accordingly, a coastal state has very extensive sovereign rights to undertake maritime regulation and enforcement operations against foreign ships which lawfully enter their internal waters. Whilst the right of innocent passage anticipates foreign ships in some instances entering the internal waters of a coastal state, the right of

[69] Around 36 hours elapsed before the *Arctic Sunrise* was boarded by Russian authorities.
[70] *The Arctic Sunrise Case (Netherlands v Russia)* (2014) 53 ILM 607, [95]–[97].
[71] *Fisheries Jurisdiction (Spain v Canada)* [1998] ICJ Rep 432.
[72] Anthony Bergin et al, 'Marine Living Resources' in Lorne K Kriwoken et al (eds), *Oceans Law and Policy in the Post-UNCED Era: Australian and Canadian Perspectives* (London, Kluwer Law International, 1996) 173, 193–200.
[73] *M/V Saiga (No 2)* (1999) 120 ILR 143 [127].
[74] Ibid [126]. See also *M/V Virginia G (Panama v Guinea Bissau)* (2014) 53 ILM 1164, [209]–[213].

innocent passage does not extend to general navigation within internal waters. Nevertheless, foreign ships which are sovereign immune enjoy that privilege whilst within internal waters.[75] Accordingly, a foreign visiting warship which discharges pollutants whilst at dock would enjoy sovereign immunity unless that immunity had been expressly waived.[76] Given the status of internal waters, the LOSC has little to say on coastal state enforcement powers therein, other than to make clear in Article 220 that a vessel voluntarily within a port may be subject to proceedings arising from a pollution incident which took place in the coastal State's territorial sea or EEZ.

B. Territorial Sea

Foreign ships within the territorial sea enjoy the right of innocent passage subject to the requirements contained in Articles 17 to 19 of the LOSC.[77] In very limited cases, navigation through the territorial sea may also be subject to restrictions imposed under United Nations Security Council resolutions allowing for the inspection of certain merchant vessels or those suspected of engaged in piracy.[78] Ships undertaking innocent passage do not, however, enjoy any general exemption from laws and regulations enacted by the coastal state, and Article 21 makes clear that these ships may be subject to a range of laws, including those relating to the safety of navigation, conservation of living resources, and customs, fiscal or immigration matters. The immunities enjoyed by warships and government ships operated for non-commercial purposes, however, remain in place within the territorial sea.[79] The LOSC does make clear that coastal state laws and regulations relating to marine pollution within the territorial sea must not hamper the innocent passage of foreign vessels;[80] however, this needs to be read with Article 19(2)(h) which identifies an act of 'wilful and serious pollution' as being inconsistent with the right of innocent passage with the consequence that passage may be denied. Balanced against the safeguards provided for ships engaged in innocent passage, the coastal state nevertheless retains a range of enforcement options under Article 220 with respect to foreign vessels within the territorial sea which have polluted the marine environment. This includes the undertaking of a physical inspection of a vessel that has polluted the marine environment whilst within the territorial sea,[81] requiring a vessel navigating the territorial sea to provide certain information with respect to a pollution incident that occurred in the EEZ,[82] and the commencement of proceedings

---

[75] This right exists under general international law; see *The ARA Libertad Case (Argentina v. Ghana)*, Provisional Measures, Order of 15 December 2012, [95]; *The Schooner Exchange v M'Faddon* (1812) 11 US 116, and discussion in O'Connell, *The International Law of the Sea*, vol 2 (n 2) 944.

[76] The United States Commander's Handbook on the Law of Naval Operations observes in this respect that 'a failure of compliance is subject only to diplomatic complaint or to coastal nation orders to leave its territorial sea immediately': AR Thomas and James C Duncan (eds), 'Annotated Supplement to The Commanders Handbook on the Law of Naval Operations' (1999) 73 *International Legal Studies* 110.

[77] Discussed in more detail in ch 10.

[78] McLaughlin, 'United Nations Mandated Naval Interdiction Operations in the Territorial Sea?' (n 9).

[79] LOSC, art 32; *The ARA Libertad Case (Argentina v Ghana)*, Provisional Measures, Order of 15 December 2012, [95].

[80] LOSC, art 211(4).

[81] Ibid art 220(2).

[82] Ibid art 220(3), which may result in a physical inspection of the vessel if it refuses to cooperate: ibid art 220(5).

against a delinquent vessel whilst within the territorial sea relating to a 'substantial discharge causing or threatening significant pollution' which occurred in the EEZ.[83] Ships undertaking innocent passage may therefore be subject to the enforcement jurisdiction of the coastal state with respect to these matters, subject only to some particular limitations which arise with respect to criminal and civil jurisdiction, with distinctions being made between outward-bound and inward-bound ships.

With respect to foreign ships within the territorial sea which are not engaging in innocent passage consistently with Article 19 such that their actions are 'non-innocent', Article 25 makes clear that the coastal state may take 'necessary steps' to prevent that passage. The LOSC is silent as to how the coastal state may respond in this situation and by implication customary international law applies.[84] Any response would therefore need to be proportionate to the circumstances and may range from a request that a vessel refrain from undertaking a certain activity, to arrest and detention for a major infringement of its laws, removal of the vessel from its waters, physical prevention of the passage continuing, or, in the case where the coastal state feels sufficiently imperilled by the actions of the foreign ship, use of force may be deployed.[85]

i. Criminal Jurisdiction

Whilst the criminal laws of the coastal state are capable of applying within the territorial sea, Article 27 of the LOSC imposes important limitations as to the reach of those laws to ensure that there is no undue interference with navigation. Accordingly, the coastal state's criminal jurisdiction 'should not be exercised on board a foreign ship' passing through the territorial sea so as to effect the arrest of a person or to conduct an investigation in connection with a crime unless the consequences of the crime extend to the coastal state; the crime is one which disturbs the 'peace of the country or good order of the territorial sea'; relates to drug trafficking; or where the assistance of the coastal state has been sought by the master of the ship or officials of the flag state.[86] In recognition of the coastal state's sovereignty over its internal waters, these limitations do not apply to outward-bound ships which have departed internal waters and are within the territorial sea.[87] Further limitations apply with respect to the coastal state taking into account the interests of navigation in seeking to effect an arrest,[88] and also in the case of where a crime is alleged to have been committed prior to the entry of the ship into the territorial sea (other than from internal waters) and where that ship is only passing through the territorial sea without entering internal waters.[89]

ii. Civil Jurisdiction

Stricter limitations exist with respect to civil jurisdiction against foreign ships within the territorial sea. There is no capacity on the part of a coastal state to stop and divert a ship so

---

[83] Ibid art 220(6).

[84] Shearer, 'Problems of Jurisdiction and Law Enforcement' (n 44) 325.

[85] See, eg, John W Rolph, 'Freedom of Navigation and the Black Sea Bumping Incident: How "Innocent" must Innocent Passage Be?' (1992) 135 *Military Law Review* 137.

[86] LOSC, art 27(1).

[87] Ibid art 27(2).

[88] Ibid art 27(4).

[89] Ibid art 27(5).

as to exercise civil jurisdiction against persons on board ships within the territorial sea,[90] or to levy execution against or arrest of a ship with respect to civil proceedings other than with respect to matters which have arisen during the course of 'its voyage through the waters of the coastal State'.[91] This is broad enough to encompass civil proceedings that may have arisen whilst the foreign ship was within the EEZ prior to reaching the territorial sea. These limitations do not arise, however, with respect to civil proceedings against outward-bound ships arising from matters which occurred within internal waters, in which case execution against the ship or arrest can occur within the territorial sea.[92]

iii. Territorial Sea of an International Strait

As to the particular issues which arise with respect to foreign ships within the territorial sea of an international strait exercising transit passage, Part III of the LOSC applies and makes clear the duties of the coastal state and foreign ships within those waters. Whilst the coastal state is required to ensure that its actions shall not hamper transit passage, including not suspending transit passage,[93] activities which are not consistent with the exercise of the right of transit passage remain subject to the other applicable provisions of the LOSC.[94] Accordingly, a foreign ship within an international strait would remain subject to enforcement action by the coastal state consistent with the other provisions of the LOSC and general international law.[95]

C. Archipelagic Waters

Archipelagic states possess sovereignty over their archipelagic waters, and consistent with this have the capacity to engage in maritime regulation and enforcement within these waters. The great majority of the waters of an archipelagic state are those within which the right of innocent passage may be exercised, consistent with the relevant provisions of Articles 17 to 32 of the LOSC. Accordingly, an archipelagic state has as much capacity to control and regulate innocent passage of foreign ships within its archipelagic waters as does the coastal state within the territorial sea. This extends to the stopping, detention, arrest and prosecution of vessels engaging in actions which are contrary to the legitimate laws and regulations of the archipelagic state, and also taking necessary steps to prevent passage which is not innocent. The only limitations which may exist upon the archipelagic state in this regard would arise from the recognition of traditional fishing rights and other legitimate activities of neighbouring states within the archipelagic waters.[96]

With respect to archipelagic sea lanes passage, the rights of the archipelagic state to engage in regulation and enforcement within those waters is equated with the rights of the coastal

---

[90]   Ibid art 28(1).
[91]   Ibid art 28(2).
[92]   Ibid art 28(3).
[93]   Ibid art 44.
[94]   Ibid art 38(3).
[95]   Confirmed by ibid art 34, which makes clear that the legal status of the waters of a strait used for international navigation is not affected by their status as such under Part III.
[96]   Ibid art 51.

state within an international strait.[97] Because of the distinction which exists between innocent passage within archipelagic waters, and archipelagic sea lanes passage within the sea lanes, an archipelagic state will need to exercise particular care in any enforcement operation against a foreign ship, or aircraft exercising a right of passage via an air route, to ensure the location of that foreign ship or aircraft is not contested. There are no direct references in the LOSC to enforcement by an archipelagic state within its archipelagic waters of measures relating to the protection and preservation of the marine environment. However, archipelagic states will also have a territorial sea beyond the limits of their archipelagic baselines, permitting them the same rights as other coastal states in regulating ship-sourced pollution within that area.[98]

D. Contiguous Zone

Within the contiguous zone, the coastal state under Article 33 only has limited and distinctive rights of maritime regulation and enforcement. Coastal states may not establish or enforce offences applicable specifically to the contiguous zone; rather, it is a zone in which coastal states enjoy rights of extraterritorial enforcement over certain offences committed in the territory or territorial sea, and also have the right to prevent ships which enter the contiguous zone from committing such offences. However, account does need to be taken of conterminous EEZ and continental shelf rights which will apply between 12 nm and 24 nm. In the contiguous zone the coastal state's rights extend to preventing and punishing customs, fiscal, immigration or sanitary matters, and are consistent with the contiguous zone being a zone of *sui generis* jurisdiction and not of sovereign rights.[99] The ILC considered and ultimately rejected proposals that the contiguous zone recognise the distinctive security rights of the coastal state, although in its Commentary to the 1956 draft articles made express reference to the rights of self-defence recognised under the UN Charter.[100]

In the case of outward bound ships which have sailed from internal waters or the territorial sea, the coastal state has the capacity in the contiguous zone to 'punish infringement' of customs, fiscal, immigration or sanitary laws and regulations which have occurred within those areas. This extends not only directly to the ship, but also its crew and any passengers aboard. Accordingly, the coastal state may stop, board and arrest outward bound ships within the contiguous zone if such infringements have taken place. Importantly, there is no need for hot pursuit of the foreign ship from the territorial sea and accordingly the strict conditions of hot pursuit need not be followed.[101]

In the case of inward bound foreign ships, the coastal state has a capacity to 'prevent infringement' of customs, fiscal, immigration or sanitary laws and regulations which might

---

[97] Ibid art 54.

[98] Ibid art 220; subject to the limitation that an archipelagic sea lane which passes through the archipelagic waters also extends to territorial sea entry and exit points within which archipelagic sea lanes passage is exercised: Ibid art 53(4).

[99] Though the contiguous zone will in most instances be conterminous with the EEZ and continental shelf within which the coastal state does exercise certain sovereign rights, these rights are distinctive from those which the coastal state enjoys within the contiguous zone.

[100] International Law Commission, 'Articles Concerning the Law of the Sea with Commentaries' (1956) *Yearbook of the International Law Commission*, vol 2, 295.

[101] A distinctive right of hot pursuit can arise from within the contiguous zone, but only in relation to those laws and regulations which have ongoing enforcement capacity within the contiguous zone: LOSC, art 111(1).

occur within its territory or the territorial sea.[102] This gives to the coastal state a degree of discretion as to how it would seek to exercise this right. It certainly extends to the issuing of warnings, the stopping and inspecting of ships, and any other peaceful actions which would assist in deterring foreign ships continuing their voyage into the territorial sea.[103] However, Article 33 does not give to the coastal state a general right of inspection of all foreign ships which are approaching its territorial sea, and the rights which exist over the contiguous zone also need to be read consistently with the freedoms of navigation which extend over the high seas and EEZ up to the edge of the territorial sea.[104] The rights under Article 33 must therefore be exercised reasonably, having regard to the character and seriousness of the apprehended violation of coastal state laws.

One area of particular controversy is whether it is consistent with the rights of the coastal state within the contiguous zone to turn back or tow foreign ships beyond that area to prevent them from approaching the territorial sea. This practice has been applied by several states with respect to vessels carrying asylum seekers attempting to enter the territory of the coastal state.[105] Some coastal states assert that even if these persons may be eligible to claim status as refugees consistent with international law, their entry into the territory of the state without authorisation under domestic law amounts to an immigration offence, thereby providing a basis for the removal of these people from the territorial sea and contiguous zone. The preventive power would permit a coastal state to stop, detain and inspect such vessels to investigate whether immigration law may be breached by its continued passage, but Article 33 does not provide a general authority to coastal states to treat such vessels in any manner they wish, such as by detaining all those on board, or towing the vessel from the contiguous zone and through the EEZ onto the high seas.[106] It cannot be in dispute that under the law of the sea coastal states have a capacity to remove foreign vessels from the territorial sea and contiguous zone and direct them to the EEZ. However, absent flag state consent, what is unclear is the extent to which continuing control can be exercised over those vessels within the EEZ. Nonetheless, any such actions would need to be consistent with respect for the safety of life at sea, and unseaworthy vessels cannot be towed from the contiguous zone and abandoned at sea.[107]

---

[102] Ibid art 33(1)(a).

[103] Shearer, 'Problems of Jurisdiction and Law Enforcement' (n 44) 330.

[104] LOSC, arts 58 (1), 87.

[105] Such as Australia's 'Operation Sovereign Borders' (OSB), described by the Australian government as 'a military-led, border security operation'. Operational details relating to OSB have been withheld, making it difficult to identify with precision what activities have been undertaken by Australian authorities: see Natalie Klein, 'Assessing Australia's Push Back the Boats Policy Under International Law: Legality and Accountability for Maritime Interceptions of Irregular Migrants' (2014) 15 *Melbourne Journal of International Law* 1. In the 1980s the United States implemented the 'Haitian Migrant Interdiction Program' with the objective the United States Coast Guard interdicting vessels on the high seas suspected of carrying Haitian asylum seekers en route to the United States: Stephen H Legomsky, 'The USA and Caribbean Interdiction Program' (2006) 18 *International Journal of Refugee Law* 677; Arthur C Helton, 'The United States Government Program of Intercepting and Forcibly Returning Haitian Boat People to Haiti: Policy Implications and Prospects' (1993) 10 *New York Law School Journal of Human Rights* 325.

[106] See the discussion by Hayne and Bell JJ in *CPCF v Minister for Immigration and Border Protection* [2015] HCA 1 (High Court of Australia), [79]: 'whether, for the purposes of international law, Art 33 permits the coastal state to take persons on the vessel into its custody or to take command of the vessel or tow it out of the contiguous zone remains controversial'.

[107] See discussion in Andreas Fischer Lescano, Tillman Lohr and Timo Tohidipur, 'Border Controls at Sea: Requirements under International Human Rights and Refugee Law' (2009) 21 *International Journal of Refugee*

E. EEZ

The EEZ is perhaps the most complex of the maritime zones with respect to maritime regulation and enforcement. This is because of the unique but limited sovereign rights and jurisdiction coastal states possess over this area; the potential for creeping jurisdiction on the part of the coastal state to occur in this maritime zone more so than others; the interaction of the EEZ with the contiguous zone and particularly the high seas, which permits certain high seas rights of interdiction to be exercised within the EEZ; and the need to balance the rights and interests of the coastal state with those of the international community to enjoy certain freedoms of which the freedom of navigation is the most significant. To achieve a balance between all of these competing but equally valid rights and interests, the LOSC seeks to legitimate the rights of the coastal state to undertake maritime regulation and enforcement, whilst also safeguarding the rights of foreign ships, especially with respect to matters related to marine living resource management such as fisheries and marine pollution.

The rights of the coastal state to regulate a range of activities in the EEZ are made clear in Article 56 of the LOSC, being divided between sovereign rights over living and non-living resources and related activities, and jurisdiction with respect to artificial islands and installations, scientific research, and the marine environment. In its management and regulation of the EEZ, the coastal state needs to be mindful of the rights and duties of other states under the LOSC, and it is to act in a 'manner compatible' with the Convention. Accordingly, coastal states do not have plenary regulatory and enforcement powers in the EEZ, and their actions must be based upon those rights attributed under Article 56, subject also to the possible exercise of unattributed rights under Article 59. This point was clearly emphasised in *M/V Saiga (No 2)*, where ITLOS rejected the attempt by Guinea to apply its customs laws to the EEZ as being contrary to the Convention, with the effect that the arrest and detention of the *Saiga*, prosecution and conviction of the master of the ship, and confiscation of the cargo and seizure of the ship were held to be contrary to the LOSC.[108] *M/V Saiga (No 2)* also highlights that enforcement within the EEZ is likewise subject to general principles on the use of force and related relevant provisions found in the Convention.[109]

i. Matters Subject to EEZ Sovereign Rights

There is considerable state practice with respect to maritime regulation and enforcement of coastal state rights over marine living resources beyond the territorial sea which is reflected in the EEZ enforcement regime of the LOSC. Partly highlighted by some of the issues that had arisen with respect to the enforcement of pre-LOSC fisheries zones, Article 73 identifies both the rights of the coastal state with respect to enforcement balanced against certain

---

Law 256; Richard Barnes, 'Refugee Law at Sea' (2004) 53 *International and Comparative Law Quarterly* 47; Martin Davies, 'Obligations and Implications for Ships Encountering Persons in Need of Assistance at Sea' (2003) 12 *Pacific Rim Law & Policy Journal* 109.

   [108] *M/V Saiga (No 2)* (1999) 120 ILR 143 [136].
   [109] Rob McLaughlin, 'Coastal State Use of Force in the EEZ under the Law of the Sea Convention 1982' (1999) 18 *University of Tasmania Law Review* 11.

safeguards ensuring against abuse of rights. In order to ensure compliance with its laws and regulations relating to conservation and management of marine living resources, the coastal state may undertake boardings, inspections, arrests and commence judicial proceedings against delinquent ships, their masters and their crew. These provisions are sufficiently broad, when coupled with satellite and aerial surveillance capacity of coastal states, to be able to counter illegal fishing within the EEZ providing there exists an equivalent enforcement capacity. The right of hot pursuit further extends that right if foreign fishers seek to flee onto the high seas. These rights of the coastal state are balanced against the requirement to notify the flag state once an arrest or detention occurs, limitations on the penalties which may be applied for violations of fisheries laws, and prompt release of vessels and their crews upon the posting of a 'reasonable bond or security'.[110]

Following the entry into force of the LOSC, the interpretation of Article 73 has proven contentious. There is now a sizeable collection of ITLOS cases where the tribunal has been asked to assess in some detail coastal state practices, laws and regulations dealing with illegal fishing, and to determine the consistency of those actions with the LOSC.[111] These ITLOS cases reflect the growth in IUU fishing carried out by significant commercial fisheries interests which exploit gaps in the international legal framework, domestic legal loopholes, and weak enforcement mechanisms,[112] and the challenges faced by ITLOS in seeking to achieve a balance between the respective rights and interests of coastal states and flag states with respect to fisheries enforcement in the EEZ. The 2002 *Volga* case involving Russia and Australia saw ITLOS consolidate its prompt release jurisprudence. The tribunal confirmed that whether a bond or other financial security is 'reasonable' for the purposes of Article 292 (which expands upon the general provision in Article 73) will depend upon a number of factors, including (but not limited to) the gravity of alleged fishing offences, possible penalties for these offences under the coastal state's domestic law, the value of the vessel seized and the amount and form of the bond set. In line with previous decisions, the tribunal also confirmed that the purpose of Articles 73 and 292 of the LOSC is to balance the interests of coastal and flag states.[113]

ii. Matters Subject to EEZ Jurisdiction

With respect to the maritime regulation and enforcement rights of the coastal state over EEZ matters in which they possess jurisdiction, those relating to the protection and presentation of the marine environment need to be read alongside the detailed provisions

---

[110] LOSC, art 73(2).

[111] See in particular the following eight cases: (1) *M/V Saiga (No 1) Case (St Vincent and the Grenadines v Guinea)* (prompt release) (1997) 110 ILR 736; (2) *Camouco (Panama v France)* (prompt release) (2000) 125 ILR 151; (3) *Monte Confurco (Seycelles v France)* (prompt release) (2000) 125 ILR 203; (4) *Grand Prince (Belize v France)* (prompt release) (2001) 125 ILR 251; (5) *Volga (Russian Federation v Australia)* (prompt release) (2003) 42 ILM 159; (6) *Juno Trader (St Vincent and the Grenadines v Guinea-Bissau) (prompt release)* (2004) 44 ILM 498; (7) *Hoshinmaru (Japan v Russian Federation) (prompt release)* [2005–07] ITLOS Rep 18; (8) *Tomimaru (Japan v Russian Federation) (prompt release)* [2005–07] ITLOS Rep 74.

[112] Rachel Baird, 'Illegal, Unreported and Unregulated Fishing: An Analysis of the Legal, Economic and Historical Factors Relevant to Its Development' (2004) 5 *Melbourne Journal of International Law* 299; and see the discussion in ch 13.

[113] See further Donald R Rothwell and Tim Stephens, 'Illegal Southern Ocean Fishing and Prompt Release: Balancing Coastal and Flag State Rights and Interests' (2004) 53 *International and Comparative Law Quarterly* 171.

of Part XII of the LOSC.[114] Articles 210 to 212 outline the broad extent of coastal state jurisdiction to regulate aspects of marine pollution by foreign ships in the EEZ consistent with coastal state EEZ jurisdiction and related international marine pollution conventions. Directly related to this are the enforcement provisions found in Part XIII, Section III which outline the particular capacities of flag, port and coastal states, subject to rights of sovereign immunity recognised in Article 236. Article 220 is an extensive provision dealing with the enforcement capacity of the coastal state with respect to the prevention, reduction and control of pollution from vessels within the EEZ.[115] These rights extend to requiring a vessel to give information as to its identity and port of registry and next port of call, and if there has been a substantial discharge causing or threatening pollution within the EEZ and the delinquent ship has failed to provide the requested information, then the coastal state may order a physical inspection of that vessel, and may subsequently institute proceedings, including the detention of the ship. All of these rights of the coastal state are balanced against safeguards outlined in Part XIII, Section 7, which includes requirements that the investigation of foreign ships is not to result in undue delay,[116] non-discrimination,[117] suspension of proceedings following corresponding charges by the flag state[118] or limitations with respect to monetary penalties.[119] Enforcement operations within the EEZ against foreign ships for marine environmental infringements can only be undertaken by warships and military aircraft, or other clearly identifiable and authorised ships and aircraft on government service.[120] Coastal states that undertake unlawful enforcement measures or which exceed those permissible under the LOSC, shall be liable for any damage or loss attributable to their actions.[121] Finally, outlined in Article 60, is the jurisdiction with respect to artificial islands and installations over which the coastal state may establish safety zones and place some limitations upon navigation, subject to generally accepted international standards.[122] Coastal state jurisdiction with respect to marine scientific research within the EEZ needs to be read alongside Part XIII of the LOSC.

F. Continental Shelf

As the continental shelf is conterminous with EEZ out to the 200 nm limit, many of the maritime regulation and enforcement issues associated with the continental shelf are subsumed within the EEZ regime in the overlapping areas. Whilst Part VI of the LOSC does not contain as many detailed provisions regarding maritime regulation and enforcement as other parts of the Convention, the sovereign rights of the coastal state over the continental shelf are of great significance and, importantly, are exclusive with the result that no other

---

[114] See Alan Khee-Jin Tan, *Vessel-Source Marine Pollution* (Cambridge, Cambridge University Press, 2006) 212.
[115] LOSC, art 220. LOSC also contains dual provisions which have application in the territorial sea.
[116] Ibid art 226.
[117] Ibid art 227.
[118] Ibid art 228.
[119] Ibid art 230.
[120] Ibid art 224.
[121] Ibid art 232.
[122] See Stuart B Kaye, 'International Measures to Protect Oil Platforms, Pipelines and Submarine Cables from Attack' (2007) 31 *Tulane Maritime Law Journal* 377.

state can undertake activities for the purposes of exploring or exploiting the continental shelf without the 'express consent' of the coastal state.[123] The sensitivity of these issues was highlighted in the 2007 *Guyana/Suriname* Award following the actions of the Suriname navy warning off the oil-drilling rig *C.E. Thornton* from undertaking exploratory drilling in the contested area of continental shelf claimed by Guyana and Suriname.[124] Other distinctive aspects of the continental shelf regime extend to the regulation and management of sedentary species, including their harvesting;[125] matters associated with submarine cables and pipelines and their security and protection;[126] and artificial islands, installations and structure.[127]

G. High Seas

Within the high seas coastal states enjoy no specific rights of maritime regulation and enforcement, other than the continuing right of hot pursuit under that *sui generis* regime, and the capacity to intervene in the case of a maritime disaster resulting in actual or threatened damage to the coastline or related interests of the coastal state, including fishing.[128] Rather, on the high seas, the rights of the flag state are supreme.[129] Accordingly, warships and other authorised government vessels have a right to stop and inspect ships on the high seas flying the same flag. However, Part VII of the LOSC does recognise that certain ships on the high seas may be subject to universal jurisdiction by non-flag states thereby giving to all states a capacity to stop and inspect certain ships. This extends to ships engaged in the slave trade,[130] piracy,[131] and unauthorised broadcasting.[132] The LOSC gives content to this right of non-flag states to undertake a high seas boarding via the 'right of visit' outlined in Article 110. The right of visit also extends to ships without nationality or which, though flying a foreign flag, are actually of the same nationality as the warship seeking to undertake the boarding. Ships subject to this form of high seas inspection in addition to being boarded, may have their documentation checked and be subject to inspection.[133] The right of visit may be exercised by warships, military aircraft, and other duly authorised ships or aircraft on government service.[134] Ships which have been improperly subject to visit may be compensated for any loss or damage sustained.[135] The right of visit on the high seas may

---

[123] LOSC, art 77(2); art 81 making clear that the coastal state has the 'exclusive authority to authorize and regulate drilling on the continental shelf'.

[124] Kwast, 'Maritime Law Enforcement and the Use of Force' (n 50) 49–50.

[125] LOSC, art 77(4).

[126] Ibid art 79.

[127] Ibid art 80, applying art 60 *mutatis mutandis*; see also Kaye, 'International Measures to Protect Oil Platforms' (n 128) with respect to protection of submarine cables, pipelines and artificial islands.

[128] LOSC, art 221; see also 1969 International Convention Relating to Intervention on the High Seas in Cases of Oil Pollution Casualties *Basic Documents* No 14.

[129] Ibid art 92(1) makes clear that 'Ships shall sail under the flag of one State only and ... shall be subject to its exclusive jurisdiction'.

[130] Ibid art 99.

[131] Ibid art 100.

[132] Ibid art 109.

[133] Ibid art 110(2).

[134] Ibid art 110(1), (4), (5).

[135] Ibid art 110(3); aspects of the high seas right of visit have been further extended by the 2005 SUA Convention discussed below.

also be conducted in reliance upon bilateral or other agreements between flag states permitting reciprocal rights of visit and inspection of their flagged ships which are suspected of engaging in certain acts.[136]

IV. Specialist Regimes Relating to Maritime Regulation and Enforcement

A. Piracy

There is considerable history in the international law of the sea with respect to counter-piracy operations by coastal states;[137] however, since the 1990s there have been a number of new developments in this field.[138] The first was in response to the upsurge of pirate attacks in Southeast Asia in the 1990s, particularly within the Straits of Malacca and the Indonesian archipelago. The littoral states of Indonesia, Malaysia and Singapore responded to this threat through development of the 2004 Regional Cooperation Agreement on Combating Piracy and Armed Robbery against Ships in Asia (ReCAAP) which sought to enhance information sharing and capacity-building principally amongst the Association of Southeast Asian Nations (ASEAN), and neighbouring North East Asian and South Asian states.[139] This initiative demonstrated the capacity of regional states directly impacted upon by piracy to respond to the maritime regulation and enforcement issues.

The second development took the response to piracy from a regional level to multilateral United Nations engagement, following a dramatic upsurge in piratical activities off the coast of East Africa in the first decade of this century.[140] Of the attacks off the East African coast, Somalia was a particular concern due to the breakdown of law and order in that failed state.[141] Since the early 1990s the United Nations had been working with the Transitional Federal Government (TFG) to bring about a restoration of law and order not only within Somalia itself but also in its offshore waters. In June 2008 the Security Council adopted Resolution 1816 (2008),[142] which directly sought to address the threat posed by Somali pirates. Recognising the incapacity of the TFG to interdict pirates and secure offshore shipping lanes, and that pirate attacks were a threat to international peace and security in the region, the Security Council authorised states acting in cooperation with the TFG to enter

---

[136] See, eg, 2004 Agreement between the Government of the United States of American and the Government of the Republic of Liberia Concerning Cooperation to Suppress the Proliferation of Weapons of Mass Destruction, Their Delivery Systems, and Related Materials at Sea, *Basic Documents* No 74.

[137] Barry Hart Dubner, *The Law of International Sea Piracy* (The Hague, Martinus Nijhoff, 1980).

[138] Portions of the discussion under this heading are adapted from Donald R Rothwell, 'Maritime Piracy and International Law' Crimes of War Project at www.crimesofwar.org/onnews/news-piracy.html.

[139] Joshua Ho, 'Combating Piracy and Armed Robbery in Asia: The ReCAAP Information Sharing Centre' (2009) 33 *Marine Policy* 432.

[140] Report of the Secretary-General, *Oceans and the Law of the Sea* (25 November 2009), UN Doc A/64/66/Add.1, [119].

[141] See generally Bibi van Ginkel and Frans-paul Van Der Putten (eds), *The International Response to Somali Piracy* (Martinus Nijhoff, Leiden, 2011).

[142] *Basic Documents* No 86.

the 'territorial waters' of Somalia to undertake enforcement actions against piracy and armed robbery, including the use of 'all necessary means'.[143] This was a significant development as it was the first occasion the Security Council had recognised that piracy and armed robbery constituted a threat to international peace and security, requiring the Council to act under Chapter VII of the UN Charter. In doing so the Council was careful to reaffirm that the LOSC provided the legal framework for dealing with piracy, and that its actions only related to the situation in Somalia and were not to be considered as establishing 'customary international law'.[144] In recognition of some of the difficult jurisdictional issues these events had highlighted, especially with respect to the arrest and prosecution of suspected pirates, the Security Council also called upon flag, port, and coastal states, states of the nationality of victims and perpetrators, and also states with relevant jurisdiction 'to cooperate in determining jurisdiction' in the investigation and prosecution of persons responsible for pirate acts.[145] Resolution 1816 (2008) has been extended by a succession of further resolutions, renewing the Security Council's authorisation for counter-piracy operations.[146]

In response to these developments, in December 2008 the European Union launched 'Operation Atlanta'. NATO member states also commenced operations 'Allied Protector' and 'Ocean Shield', whilst other states contributed to 'Combined Task Force 151', or made individual contributions. In addition to key European Union and NATO states, others which contributed to these operations included Australia, China, India, Iran, Japan, Malaysia and Russia. States within the Western Indian Ocean and the Gulf of Aden also launched their own regional initiative in January 2009 aimed at repressing piracy.[147] A related development was United Nations Security Council Resolution 1851 (2008)[148] which authorised 'shiprider' agreements to facilitate more effective law enforcement capability. The resolution permitted the international community to operate not only within Somali waters but also ashore within Somali territory where activities occur to plan, facilitate or undertake acts of piracy and armed robbery at sea. In response to this initiative, the United States in 2008 formed a 'Contact Group on Somali piracy' so as to establish a mechanism for the sharing of intelligence, coordination of activities, and co-operation with partners in the shipping and insurance industries.[149] Following the seizure of the United States-flagged *Maersk Alabama* in April 2009, the United States announced further counter-piracy measures directed towards the tracking and freezing of pirate assets.[150] Multilateral enforcement measures, under the mandate of the Security Council, have had a significant impact, resulting in the frequency of piratical incidents declining very significantly in recent years. Globally, there were 245 actual and attempted piracy attacks in 2014 (down from 445 in 2010), and there were fewer

---

[143] UN Security Council Resolution 1816 (2008), [7].

[144] Ibid [9].

[145] Ibid [11].

[146] UN Security Council Resolutions 1838 (2008), 1846 (2008), 1851 (2008), 1897 (2009), 1918 (2010), 1950 (2010), 1976 (2011), 2015 (2011), 2020 (2011), 2077 (2012), 2125 (2013) and 2184 (2014).

[147] 2009 Code of Conduct Concerning the Repression of Piracy and Armed Robbery Against Ships in the Western Indian Ocean and the Gulf of Aden, *Basic Documents* No 90.

[148] *Basic Documents* No 89.

[149] Condoleezza Rice (United States Secretary of State), 'Combating the Scourge of Piracy', United States State Department (18 December 2008).

[150] Matthew Lee, 'Clinton Says US will Try to Target Pirate Assets', Associated Press (16 April 2009); James Kraska and Brian Wilson, 'The Pirates of the Gulf of Aden: The Coalition is the Strategy' (2009) 45 *Stanford Journal of International Law* 243.

attacks in the Gulf of Aden (four in 2014) than in a number of other regions, such as Bangladesh, Indonesia and Nigeria.[151]

One of the legal challenges the Somali counter-piracy operations highlighted was that jurisdiction with respect to most crimes at sea, such as piracy, is based predominantly on nationality or territoriality. Multinational maritime forces operating offshore Somali rarely had the necessary jurisdictional link to prosecute pirates, unless they chose to exercise universal jurisdiction which can raise contentious issues in some domestic legal systems. This also raised significant logistical issues for the multilateral maritime forces with respect to the collection of evidence, preparation of prosecution briefs, detention of alleged pirates awaiting trial, and determinations as to their place of trial. One response to this was an arrangement entered into between the European Union and Kenya allowing for the transfer of pirate suspects and associated seized property from European Union naval forces to Kenya whereupon those persons would await trial.[152] A relatively large number of prosecutions have taken place within Somalia itself, predominantly within Puntland and Somaliland, with other regional states also placing several hundred suspects on trial, although it should be noted that the conviction rate varies significantly from jurisdiction to jurisdiction.[153]

B. Maritime Terrorism and Related Unlawful Acts

Whilst terrorism at sea was understood as a concern during the twentieth century, it was not given serious consideration at UNCLOS I, II or III. However, the 1985 highjacking of the Italian cruise ship *Achille Lauro* in the Mediterranean, which resulted in the murder of an American passenger, saw the international community resolve to address the issue in a comprehensive fashion, modelled on other responses to international terrorism.[154] The result was the rapid adoption of the SUA Convention and an accompanying Protocol for the Suppression of Unlawful Acts against the Safety of Fixed Platforms Located on the Continental Shelf (SUA Fixed Platforms Protocol), both of which entered into force in 1992.[155] The Convention provided for parties to create criminal offences, establish jurisdiction, and accept into their custody those persons responsible for acts of violence at sea against ships. Following the 2001 terrorist attacks in New York and Washington, there was a heightened concern with respect to all forms of international terrorism, including in the maritime context,[156] and this led to a review of the SUA Convention with the aim of expanding its

---

[151] International Maritime Bureau, *Piracy and Armed Robbery Against Ships: Report for 2014* (2015) 5.

[152] Exchange of Letters between the European Union and the Government of Kenya on the conditions and modalities for the transfer of persons suspected of having committed acts of piracy and detained by the European Union-led Naval Force (EUNAVFOR), and seized property in the possession of the EUNAVFOR, from EUNAVFOR to Kenya for their treatment after such transfer, *Official Journal of the European Union* L79/49 (25 March 2009).

[153] Report of the Secretary-General on Specialized Anti-Piracy Courts in Somalia and Other States in the Region, UN Doc S/2012/50 (2012), [10].

[154] Malvina Halberstam, 'Terrorism on the High Seas: The Achille Lauro, Piracy and the IMO Convention on Maritime Safety' (1988) 82 *AJIL* 269; George R Constantinople, 'Towards a New Definition of Piracy: The Achille Lauro Incident' (1986) 26 *Virginia Journal of International Law* 723.

[155] Glen Plant, 'The Convention for the Suppression of Unlawful Acts against the Safety of Maritime Navigation' (1990) 39 *International and Comparative Law Quarterly* 27; David Freestone, 'The 1988 International Convention for the Suppression of Unlawful Acts against the Safety of Maritime Navigation' (1988) 3 *International Journal of Estuarine and Coastal Law* 305.

[156] See generally Natalie Klein, Joanna Mossop and Donald R Rothwell (eds), *Maritime Security: International Law and Policy Perspectives from Australia and New Zealand* (London, Routledge, 2009).

scope. Adjustments were concluded in 2005, resulting in the 2005 SUA Convention[157] and accompanying 2005 Protocol,[158] which both entered into force in 2010.[159] The Convention is clearly drafted to deal with certain acts of violence and terror at sea, and does not impact upon other rules of international law permitting states to exercise maritime regulation and enforcement against ships from other states.[160]

The 2005 SUA Convention is principally focussed upon acts occurring beyond the territorial sea.[161] It is directed towards the actions of persons who seek to seize control of a ship, perform acts of violence against a ship, seek to endanger the safe navigation of the ship, or to use a ship in a manner with the purpose of intimidating a population or compelling a government or international organisation to abstain from certain acts.[162] Jurisdiction is conferred upon flag and coastal states to respond and cooperate in the suppression of these acts, whilst enforcement capacity extends to both flag, coastal and port states in addition to the state of nationality of alleged offenders. The 2005 SUA Convention contains expanded rights of boarding and search beyond the territorial sea by non-flag states acting with flag state consent where there are reasonable grounds to suspect that the ship, or a person on board, is about to or has committed an offence.[163] In an attempt to streamline the process of gaining flag state consent for a high seas boarding, the Convention anticipates that state parties may give prior consent for a boarding to take place without advance notification or upon receipt of four hours notice.[164] Article 8bis(9) makes clear that 'the use of force shall be avoided' except when necessary to protect officials of the boarding state or persons on board the suspect ship. Caution on the use of force is provided and 'it shall not exceed the minimum degree of force which is necessary and reasonable in the circumstances'. These provisions are reinforced by certain safeguards, including not endangering the safety of life at sea, taking due account of the safety and security of the ship and its cargo, and the treatment of persons in accordance with international human rights law.[165]

C. Fisheries

Whilst the LOSC in Part V contains detailed mechanisms for the enforcement of fisheries laws, the past 30 years has seen the growth in regional fisheries regimes which have sought to develop distinctive approaches to the regulation and enforcement of fisheries laws and regulations within the EEZs of member states and adjoining high seas areas. An early approach is reflected in the CCAMLR, which applies in the Southern Ocean, and over

---

[157] *Basic Documents* No 79; amendments made to the 1988 SUA Convention result it becoming known as the 2005 SUA Convention.

[158] *Basic Documents* No 80; amendments made to the 1988 Protocol result it becoming known as the 2005 SUA Fixed Platforms Protocol.

[159] And as at 17 July 2015 had 36 and 31 states parties respectively.

[160] 2005 SUA Convention, art 9.

[161] Ibid art 4.

[162] Ibid arts 3, 3bis.

[163] Ibid art 8bis.

[164] Ibid art 8bis (5)(d)(e).

[165] Ibid art 8bis (10); for more extensive discussion of the 2005 SUA Convention see Natalie Klein, 'The Right of Visit and the 2005 Protocol on the Suppression of Unlawful Acts Against the Safety of Maritime Navigation' (2006–07) 35 *Denver Journal of International Law and Policy* 287.

time has adopted a number of innovative mechanisms to ensure compliance amongst the state parties combining a mixture of flag and coastal state jurisdiction.[166]

Subsequently within the LOSC framework, the Fish Stocks Agreement[167] contained significantly enhanced mechanisms for high seas fisheries enforcement directly related to straddling and highly migratory fish stocks. Part VI of the Fish Stocks Agreement is expressly directed to compliance and enforcement and whilst the primary enforcement obligation rests with the flag state,[168] the Agreement also recognises the capacity of an 'inspecting state', that is another state party to the Agreement or an RFMO,[169] to undertake the boarding and inspection of suspected delinquent fishing vessels within the EEZ or the high seas.[170] Article 22 outlines the basic procedures for boarding and inspection of fishing vessels by an inspecting state under the Fish Stocks Agreement framework, including notification to the flag state, and authorisation to inspect licence, gear, equipment and fish aboard fishing vessels. Clear limitations are laid down on the use of force which may only be resorted to in case of threat to the safety of inspectors or where they are obstructed in their duties. Any use of force shall not exceed that which is 'reasonably required in the circumstances'.[171] Complementary measures on compliance and enforcement, including the boarding and inspection of fishing vessels, can be found in a number of post-Fish Stocks Agreement instruments, including the 2000 Convention on the Conservation and Management of Highly Migratory Fish Stocks in the Western and Central Pacific Ocean,[172] and the 2001 Convention on the Conservation and Management of Fishery Resources in the South-East Atlantic Ocean.[173]

D. Transnational Crime

States have increasingly become concerned with transnational crime in recent decades and have sought to develop global, regional and bilateral frameworks to counter this problem more effectively. Two aspects of transnational crime with a maritime component that have attracted particular attention are the trafficking in illicit drugs and people smuggling. The LOSC directly refers to the illicit traffic of narcotic drugs and psychotropic substances in Article 108, and contemplates that flag states will call upon other states to

---

[166] Stuart Kaye, *International Fisheries Management* (The Hague, Kluwer Law International, 2001) 399–442; Rosemary Rayfuse, 'Enforcement of High Seas Fisheries Agreements: Observation and Inspection under the Convention on the Conservation of Antarctic Marine Living Resources' (1998) 13 *International Journal of Marine and Coastal Law* 579. See also the enforcement mechanisms in the 1994 Convention on the Conservation and Management of Pollock Resources in the Central Bering Sea; discussed by Kaye, *International Fisheries Management*, 342–45.

[167] *Basic Documents* No 56.

[168] Fish Stocks Agreements, art 19.

[169] Ibid art 21.

[170] Rosemary Rayfuse, *Non-flag State Enforcement in High Seas Fisheries* (Boston, Martinus Nijhoff, 2004) 82; Moritaka Hayashi, 'Enforcement by Non-flag States on the High Seas under the 1995 Agreement on Straddling and Highly Migratory Fish Stocks' (1996) 9 *Georgetown International Environmental Law Review* 1.

[171] Fish Stocks Agreement, art 22(1)(f). In *M/V Saiga (No 2)* (1999) 120 ILR 143 [156], ITLOS referred to this as being the 'basic principle concerning the use of force in the arrest of a ship at sea'; see also discussion of these provisions in *Fisheries Jurisdiction (Spain v Canada)* [1998] ICJ Rep 432, [81]–[84].

[172] *Basic Documents* No 63; Part VI especially art 26.

[173] *Basic Documents* No 66, art 16.

suppress the trafficking of such substances, which may be achieved via regional or bilateral frameworks.[174] Building upon this framework and extending the capacities of both flag and non-flag states is the 1988 United Nations Convention against Illicit Traffic in Narcotic Drugs and Psychotropic Substances.[175] The Convention is a specific multilateral response to this issue which, in addition to promoting general cooperation amongst the state parties in dealing with the problems associated with drug trafficking, in Article 17 directly addresses illicit trafficking by sea. Flag states are given primary responsibility to suppress drug trafficking, but they are able to request assistance from other parties. Individual state parties who have 'reasonable grounds to suspect that a vessel exercising freedom of navigation' and flying the flag of another state party is engaged in illicit trafficking, may request authorisation from the flag state to board and search the vessel.[176] Certain safeguards are to be applied, including not endangering safety of life at sea, and the security of the vessel or its cargo.[177] Ad hoc arrangements are therefore put in place which respect flag state jurisdiction but facilitate inspection of suspect vessels beyond the territorial sea.[178] A co-related agreement is the 1995 Agreement on Illicit Traffic by Sea, implementing Article 17 of the United Nations Convention against Illicit Traffic in Narcotic Drugs and Psychotropic Substances adopted by the Council of Europe.[179]

People smuggling has become a major transnational criminal enterprise in recent decades as a result of the impacts of globalisation, civil wars and other intra-state conflicts, natural disasters and the economic opportunities which draw migrants to parts of the developed world. The movement of asylum seekers and economic migrants by sea has prompted a range of responses by coastal states, and implicates not only the law of the sea, but also search and rescue obligations, refugee law and human rights.[180] Seaborne people smuggling has raised particular issues in the Caribbean, in parts of Southeast Asia, and in the Mediterranean following the 'Arab Spring' and the conflicts in Libya, Syria and elsewhere, and is seen by many states as being an issue closely connected with transnational organised crime.[181] The 2000 Protocol Against the Smuggling of Migrants by Land, Sea and Air Supplementing the United Nations Convention against Transnational Organized Crime[182] seeks to suppress the 'smuggling of migrants by sea' in accordance with the law of the sea.[183]

---

[174] See, eg, 1981 Agreement to Facilitate the Interdiction by the United States of Vessels of the United Kingdom Suspected of Trafficking in Drugs; Guilfoyle, *Shipping Interdiction and the Law of the Sea* (n 65) 82; William C Gilmore, 'Narcotics Interdiction at Sea: US–UK Co-operation' (1989) 13 *Marine Policy* 218.

[175] *Basic Documents* No 39; as of 17 July 2015 the Convention had a total of 189 parties; see discussion in William C Gilmore, 'Drug Trafficking by Sea: The 1988 United Nations Convention Against Illicit Traffic in Narcotic Drugs and Psychotropic Substances' (1991) 15 *Marine Policy* 183.

[176] 1988 United Nations Convention against Illicit Traffic in Narcotic Drugs and Psychotropic Substances, art 17(3), (4).

[177] Ibid art 17(5).

[178] Klein, 'The Right of Visit' (n 165) 304–05; for examples of state practice see Vicenta Gualde, 'Suppression of the Illicit Traffic in Narcotic Drugs and Psychotropic Substances on the High Seas: Spanish Case Law' (1996) 4 *Spanish Yearbook of International Law* 91.

[179] *Basic Documents* No 57.

[180] Natalie Klein, 'A Case for Harmonizing Laws on Maritime Interceptions of Irregular Migrants' (2014) 63 *International and Comparative Law Quarterly* 787.

[181] Guilfoyle, *Shipping Interdiction and the Law of the Sea* (n 65) 187–226, discussing the state practice of some of the relevant states in this area.

[182] *Basic Documents* No 64.

[183] 2000 Protocol against the Smuggling of Migrants by Land, Sea and Air supplementing the United Nations Convention against Transnational Organized Crime, art 7.

To that end, the Protocol borrows some of the procedures under the 1988 United Nations Convention against Illicit Traffic in Narcotic Drugs and Psychotropic Substances and anticipates ad hoc arrangements between flag states and other state parties permitting the latter states to undertake boarding and inspections of vessels suspected of engaging in people smuggling.[184] There are safeguards provided for, including the particular obligation under Article 9 to ensure 'the safety and humane treatment of the persons on board'. Some states have sought to enter into bilateral arrangements which provide for cooperative frameworks to address people smuggling at sea, including the interdiction of suspect vessels.[185]

V. Further Reading

Ken Booth, *Law, Force and Diplomacy at Sea* (London, George Allen & Unwin, 1985)

WE Butler (ed), *The Non-Use of Force in International Law* (Dordrecht, Martinus Nijhoff, 1989)

Christine Gray, *International Law and the Use of Force*, 2nd edn (Cambridge, Cambridge University Press, 2004)

Douglas Guilfoyle, *Shipping Interdiction and the Law of the Sea* (Cambridge, Cambridge University Press, 2009)

Natalie N Klein, *Maritime Security and the Law of the Sea* (Oxford, Oxford University Press, 2011)

DP O'Connell, *The Influence of Law on Sea Power* (Manchester, Manchester University Press, 1975)

---

[184] Ibid art 8.

[185] 2006 Agreement Between Australia and the Republic of Indonesia on the Framework for Security Cooperation, art 3.

18

Dispute Settlement in the Law of the Sea

I. Introduction

Among the most distinctive features of the LOSC is its system for the resolution of disputes. This sophisticated regime, set out in Part XV, is unusual in public international law because it is comprehensive and compulsory, subject only to limited exceptions. It may therefore be invoked unilaterally by any party to the LOSC in relation to most disputes, without the consent of the respondent party. The system is also noteworthy for the institutional framework that it establishes, the most prominent component of this being ITLOS, a permanent tribunal that has its seat in Hamburg, Germany. The ICJ also has a prominent role under the Part XV mechanisms, in addition to arbitral tribunals, which can be established under either Annex VII or Annex VIII of the LOSC.

The Part XV system is integral to the modern law of the sea, playing a critical role in ensuring that parties comply with the LOSC. The comprehensive coverage of Part XV in terms of the subject-matter of the disputes to which it applies, and its generally mandatory character, was considered at UNCLOS III to be critical for holding the package-deal LOSC together. Without authoritative interpretation by an independent adjudicatory process, it was feared that the LOSC could be unravelled by divergent application of its provisions by the parties. In this vein, the first President of UNCLOS III, Hamilton Shirley Amerasinghe, remarked that 'the provision of effective dispute settlement procedures is essential for sta- bilizing and maintaining the compromises necessary for the attainment of agreement on a convention'.[1] He observed further that: 'Dispute settlement will be the pivot upon which the delicate equilibrium must be balanced.'[2]

The mechanisms for dispute settlement in the law of the sea can be divided into two categories. First there is the 'endogenous' system provided for in Part XV of the LOSC, which applies to disputes concerning the Convention, and has subsequently been applied *mutandis mutatis* to other agreements that seek to implement aspects of the LOSC, most notably by the FSA.[3] Under the Part XV system, parties to the LOSC may refer disputes to judicial settlement to a new body, ITLOS, to ad hoc arbitration, or to the ICJ. Secondly

---

[1] UN Doc A/CONF.62/WP.9/ADD.1, Off Rec V, 122.
[2] Ibid.
[3] *Basic Documents* No 56, pt VIII.

there are the 'exogenous' or general means for dispute settlement available under public international law,[4] such as negotiation, arbitration, and judicial settlement, including by the ICJ.

Given the widespread ratification of the LOSC, the exogenous machinery is now less important for the resolution of most law of the sea disputes. However, there are some mandatory and optional exceptions to the coverage of the LOSC dispute settlement system, which means that the parallel regime outside the LOSC remains important in some circumstances.[5] An example is the resolution of maritime boundary disputes that parties to the LOSC may opt to exclude from the application of Part XV.[6] Only five such disputes have been submitted for settlement under the LOSC system.[7] Instead parties have preferred to utilise ad hoc arbitration or the ICJ independently of the LOSC regime.[8] Significantly, however, while the jurisdiction of the ICJ was not founded on Part XV, the LOSC is nonetheless referred to by the ICJ as supplying the applicable law,[9] a position that the Court took even when the LOSC had yet to enter into force.[10]

II. Dispute Settlement in International Law: General Mechanisms

Under the UN Charter, states are required to settle their disputes peacefully, in such a way that international peace and security and justice are not threatened.[11] The means available to states for resolving disputes are set out in Article 33 of the UN Charter and include negotiation, enquiry, mediation, conciliation, arbitration and judicial settlement. Most of these have been utilised to varying degrees in the settlement of law of the sea disputes.

Ordinarily the making of a claim by one state against another on the basis of the law of the sea results in a negotiated settlement, with third party procedures very rarely invoked.[12] Negotiation is often preferred over third party settlement, for the reason that

---

[4] On this endogenous/exogenous distinction see Cesare PR Romano, 'International Dispute Settlement' in Daniel Bodansky, Jutta Brunnée and Ellen Hey (eds), *The Oxford Handbook of International Environmental Law* (Oxford, Oxford University Press, 2007) 1036.

[5] LOSC, arts 297, 298.

[6] Ibid art 298(1)(a)(i).

[7] *Barbados v Trinidad and Tobago* (2006) 45 ILM 798; *Guyana/Suriname Arbitration* (17 September 2007) www.pca-cpa.org; *Delimitation of the Maritime Boundary between Bangladesh and Myanmar (Bangladesh/Myanmar)* (judgment) 14 March 2012 www.itlos.org; *Bay of Bengal Maritime Boundary Arbitration between Bangladesh and India (Bangladesh v India)* (7 July 2014) www.pca-cpa.org; *Dispute Concerning Delimitation of the Maritime Boundary between Ghana and Côte D'Ivoire in the Atlantic Coast (Ghana/Côte D'Ivoire)* (dispute submitted 3 December 2014) www.itlos.org.

[8] See eg *Territorial and Maritime Dispute between Nicaragua and Honduras in the Caribbean Sea (Nicaragua v Honduras)*, Judgment of 8 October 2007. Both Honduras and Nicaragua are parties to the LOSC. See also *Maritime Delimitation in the Black Sea (Romania v Ukraine)*, Judgment of 3 February 2009. Both Romania and Ukraine are parties to the LOSC.

[9] See further ch 16.

[10] See *Tunisia/Libya Continental Shelf* [1982] ICJ Rep 18.

[11] UN Charter, art 2(3).

[12] See Ted McDorman, 'Global Ocean Governance and International Adjudicative Dispute Resolution' (2000) 43 *Ocean and Coastal Management* 255, 257.

the involvement of a third party entails significant uncertainty as to the outcome of the proceedings.[13] Negotiation can also be used even when the dispute is escalated to another dispute settlement option such as adjudication. In the *Fisheries Jurisdiction* cases for example, which related to the 'cod war' between Iceland and Germany and the United Kingdom, the ICJ stated that 'the most appropriate method for the solution of the dispute' over access to fisheries around Iceland 'is clearly that of negotiation'.[14]

Whereas negotiation is conducted by the parties themselves, the other options for dispute settlement catalogued in Article 33 of the UN Charter involve a third party. In mediation a third party is on hand essentially to guide the negotiations, and the mediator will not normally reach an independent assessment of the factual and legal issues at dispute. By contrast, inquiry (or 'fact-finding') and conciliation may involve the third party examining the issues in contention, and issuing a report to the parties that seeks to resolve issues of fact and law. An example of inquiry in the law of the sea is the commission established to investigate the *Red Crusader* incident in 1961, which involved a confrontation between the British trawler and a Danish fisheries protection vessel, the *Niels Ebbesen*.[15] The British and Danish governments agreed to establish a three-member commission of inquiry to examine the facts surrounding the incident. This inquiry adopted an essentially arbitral process, and reached a number of legal conclusions, in relation to matters such as the use of force by the Danish commander.[16] An example of conciliation in the law of the sea is the 1992 OSPAR Convention,[17] the regime that seeks to protect the marine environment of the North East Atlantic, and provides that disputes under the Convention should in the first instance be settled by means of inquiry or conciliation.[18] Another example in a related context is the conciliation procedure in the 1992 Convention on Biological Diversity,[19] which New Zealand considered utilising in response to French nuclear testing in the Pacific in the 1990s, because of concerns that this activity would seriously damage the marine environment of the region.[20] Independently of these treaty-based mechanisms, states may also opt for conciliation of their law of the sea disputes consistently with Article 33 of the UN Charter. For example, in 1981 Iceland and Norway resorted to conciliation in order to settle the maritime boundary between Iceland and Jan Mayen.[21]

Arbitration and judicial settlement also involve a third party, but in a more formal role than other forms of third party dispute settlement, and one that usually requires the third party to resolve the dispute according to exclusively legal criteria through a decision that

---

[13] Andrew Serdy, 'The Paradoxical Success of UNCLOS Part XV: A Half-Hearted Reply to Rosemary Rayfuse' (2005) 36 *Victoria University of Wellington Law Review* 713, 715.

[14] *Fisheries Jurisdiction (United Kingdom v Iceland)* (merits) [1974] ICJ Rep 3; *(Germany v Iceland)* (merits) [1974] ICJ Rep 175, [73].

[15] See further ch 17.

[16] See John Merrills, *International Dispute Settlement*, 5th edn (Cambridge, Cambridge University Press, 2011) 48–51.

[17] 1992 Convention for the Protection of the Marine Environment of the North-East Atlantic, *Basic Documents* No 50.

[18] OSPAR Convention, art 32(1).

[19] 1992 Convention on Biological Diversity, art 27.

[20] Philippe Sands and Ruth MacKenzie, 'Guidelines for Negotiating and Drafting Dispute Settlement Clauses for International Environmental Agreements' in International Bureau of the Permanent Court of Arbitration (ed), *International Investments and Protection of the Environment* (The Hague, Permanent Court of Arbitration, 2001) 305, 314.

[21] *Continental Shelf between Iceland and Jan Mayen (Iceland/Norway)* (1981) 20 ILM 797.

is binding on the parties.[22] For most of the history of international law, when arbitration has been used it has been on an ad hoc basis, that is it has involved the establishment of an arbitral tribunal to address a specific dispute at hand. Arbitration was placed on a more institutionalised footing at the turn of the twentieth century when the Permanent Court of Arbitration (PCA) was established.[23] The PCA has been used in a number of historical and contemporary law of the sea cases under Part XV of the LOSC, and has more recently acted as the registry for LOSC Annex VII arbitrations, including the *MOX Plant* case,[24] the *Guyana/Suriname Arbitration*[25] and, in 2015, in *Chagos Marine Protected Area Arbitration*.[26]

Judicial settlement is closely similar to arbitration, but formalised to a greater extent in that it takes place in a permanent international court or tribunal. The international judicial settlement of law of the sea disputes was, until the establishment of ITLOS, pursued exclusively through the World Court—the PCIJ and its successor, the ICJ. The ICJ has jurisdiction over law of the sea disputes where that jurisdiction is conferred on a one-off basis (via a special agreement, a *compromis*) under Article 36(1) of the Statute of the ICJ, or through a dispute settlement clause in a treaty (including the LOSC).[27] Another method for conferring jurisdiction is via the ICJ's compulsory procedure, set out in Article 36(2) of the Statute of the ICJ. This allows states to lodge declarations in advance of a dispute indicating that they accept the Court's jurisdiction generally, or in relation to disputes involving certain subject-matter. As of 1 July 2015, there are 72 such 'optional clause' declarations, many of which extend to law of the sea disputes. However, several declarations seek to exclude the jurisdiction of the ICJ in relation to some maritime matters.[28]

There has been extensive use of arbitration and judicial settlement in the law of the sea, far more so than in most other areas of public international law. This has especially been the case in relation to maritime boundary delimitations. The ICJ has been central to the settlement of oceans disputes since its establishment as highlighted by the Court's first case, *Corfu Channel*, submitted in 1947.[29] Law of the sea proceedings have constituted a sizeable proportion of the ICJ's caseload,[30] with maritime boundary cases alone accounting for 17 of the 161 contentious cases in the ICJ.

---

[22] In its early history arbitration was a diplomatic or quasi-diplomatic procedure, but it has since become highly 'legalised'. The ICJ has the capacity to resolve disputes on the basis of equity (*ex aequo et bono*) if the parties request this (Statute of the ICJ, art 38(2)), but this has never occurred.

[23] By the 1899 International Convention for the Pacific Settlement of International Disputes.

[24] *MOX Plant (Ireland v United Kingdom)* (suspension of proceedings on jurisdiction and merits and request for further provisional measures) (order 3) (2003) 42 ILM 1187 (orders 1–2, 4–6) www.pca-cpa.org.

[25] *Guyana/Suriname Arbitration* (17 September 2007) www.pca-cpa.org.

[26] *In the Matter of the Chagos Marine Protected Area Arbitration (Mauritius v United Kingdom)*, Annex VII Arbitral Tribunal, 18 March 2015 www.pca-cpa.org.

[27] LOSC, art 287(1)(b).

[28] See, eg, the declarations of Australia (2002), which exclude maritime boundary disputes; Canada (1994), which excludes certain fisheries disputes; and New Zealand (1977), which excludes EEZ disputes. The text of these and other art 36(2) declarations are available at www.icj-cij.org/jurisdiction.

[29] *Corfu Channel (United Kingdom v Albania)* [1949] ICJ Rep 4.

[30] See generally Barbara Kwiatkowska, 'The International Court of Justice and the Law of the Sea—Some Reflections' (1996) 11 *International Journal of Marine and Coastal Law* 491. See also Barbara Kwiatkowska, *Decisions of the World Court Relevant to the UN Convention on the Law of the Sea: A Reference Guide* (The Hague, Kluwer, 2002).

III. Dispute Settlement in the Law of the Sea: Pre-LOSC Developments

There is a long history of law of the sea dispute settlement through both diplomatic channels and adjudicative bodies. Early arbitrations included the *Alabama Claims Arbitration*[31] in 1872 relating to neutrality and warfare at sea, the *Araunah* case[32] in 1888 concerning illegal fishing, the *Bering Sea Fur Seals* case[33] in 1893 concerning the enforcement of fisheries jurisdiction, and the *I'm Alone* case[34] in 1935 which related to the right of hot pursuit. These disputes were decided on an ad hoc basis, as a general system for law of the sea dispute settlement did not then exist, and was not to emerge fully formed until the LOSC. Nonetheless there were several developments in the interim that foreshadowed a more comprehensive range of mechanisms for the arbitration and judicial settlement of maritime disputes.

A. ILC Draft Articles on the Law of the Sea

In the work of the ILC on its Draft Articles Concerning the Law of the Sea, which were compiled in anticipation of UNCLOS I, some consideration was given to the issue of dispute settlement. Significantly, the ILC's draft articles, which were completed and submitted to the United Nations General Assembly in 1956, contained several provisions that would have made certain categories of law of the sea disputes subject to compulsory settlement by a seven-member arbitral commission, or by the ICJ. However, the ILC rejected the proposal that all law of the sea disputes should be subject to compulsory third party settlement, for several reasons. One was that the task of the ILC was to codify the substantive law of the sea, not to provide safeguards for enforcing that law. Another rationale given was that a new regime for dispute resolution in the law of the sea was not needed, with several members of the Commission arguing that it was sufficient to rely on the existing consensual system for resolving disputes by diplomatic and legal means.[35]

Although there were objections within the ILC to an overarching dispute settlement system for the law of the sea, arbitration was regarded by the Commission as essential for resolving disputes relating to fisheries shared by two or more states, and fisheries conservation measures, and provision for binding arbitration of disputes over these matters was made in draft Articles 57 to 59. The justification proffered for including this mechanism was that as coastal states had considerable discretion under the draft articles in deciding whether or not to admit other states to coastal fisheries, there was a prospect of serious controversies arising between coastal and fishing states.[36]

The draft articles also made provision for the ICJ to have compulsory jurisdiction in relation to disputes relating to the continental shelf. Under draft Article 73 (the final article

---

[31] *(United States v Great Britain)* (1872) 1 Moore 495.
[32] (1888) 1 Moore 824.
[33] *(Great Britain v United States)* (1898) 1 Moore 755.
[34] *(Canada/United States)* (1935) 3 RIAA 1609.
[35] [1956] *Yearbook of the International Law Commission*, vol 2, 288.
[36] Ibid 291ff.

of the ILC text) the matters that could be referred unilaterally to the ICJ included: disputes over the extent of the continental shelf of coastal states;[37] the sovereign rights exercised by coastal states in the continental shelf;[38] coastal state interference with high seas freedoms in the water column above the continental shelf[39] (including the right to lay submarine cables,[40] navigation and fishing);[41] and the delimitation of overlapping continental shelves for adjacent and opposite territories.[42] The Commission preferred the legal authority and expertise of the permanent ICJ over ad hoc arbitration on the grounds that continental shelf disputes would go to fundamental issues relating to the balance of rights between coastal and other states, and would not be of a predominantly technical nature, as were many fisheries disputes.[43] The ILC commentaries note that the referral of continental shelf disputes to the ICJ was also appropriate because of the novel issues surrounding this relatively new maritime zone. To ensure that the continental shelf regime did not 'endanger the higher principle of the freedom of the seas', it was 'essential that States which disagree concerning the exploration and exploitation of the continental shelf should be required to submit any dispute arising on this subject to an impartial authority'.[44]

B. UNCLOS I

The discussions at UNCLOS I drew extensively on the draft articles and commentaries produced by the ILC. However, the ILC's proposals regarding dispute settlement were only partially accepted. None of the four conventions adopted at UNCLOS I included provisions for compulsory arbitration or judicial settlement. In the 1958 Convention on Fishing and Conservation of the Living Resources of the High Seas, provision was made for a limited number of fisheries disputes to be submitted for settlement by a 'special commission' of five members.[45] Several delegates also strongly supported a dispute settlement mechanism at least as regards the continental shelf, in the absence of clearly defined limits of the continental shelf, and clear articulation of the rights of coastal and other states. Whereas the novelty of the continental shelf was considered by the ILC as a reason for subjecting disputes regarding the zone to compulsory jurisdiction, most delegates at UNCLOS I took the opposite view, concerned that an arbitral or judicial body would not be in a position to apply settled law.[46] In the result, the 1958 Convention on the Continental Shelf did not include any provision relating to dispute settlement, and the same was true of the 1958 Convention on the Territorial Sea and the Contiguous Zone and the 1958 Convention on the High Seas.

---

[37] 1956 Draft Articles Concerning the Law of the Sea, art 67.
[38] Ibid art 68.
[39] Ibid art 69.
[40] Ibid art 70.
[41] Ibid art 71.
[42] Ibid art 72.
[43] [1956] *Yearbook of the International Law Commission* vol 2, 300.
[44] Ibid 301.
[45] 1958 Convention on Fishing and Conservation of the Living Resources of the High Seas, *Basic Documents* No 11, art 9.
[46] Natalie Klein, *Dispute Settlement in the UN Convention on the Law of the Sea* (Cambridge, Cambridge University Press, 2005) 14–16.

Rather than adopting comprehensive dispute settlement provisions as part of each of the four Geneva Conventions, the delegates to UNCLOS I instead decided to conclude the 1958 Optional Protocol of Signature Concerning the Compulsory Settlement of Disputes Arising from the Law of the Sea Conventions[47] alongside the four substantive treaties. The Optional Protocol applies to all disputes relating to the interpretation or application of the Geneva regime, with the exception of controversies within the jurisdiction of the 'special commission' under the 1958 Convention on Fishing and Conservation.[48] It provides that disputes lie within the compulsory jurisdiction of the ICJ, and may be brought to the Court by an application made by any party to a dispute that is a party to the protocol.[49]

In reality, the Optional Protocol added little to the ICJ's optional clause system. Klein has noted that in adopting this opt-in system of law of the sea dispute settlement, the states at UNCLOS I 'maintained their traditional stance on consent-based, non-compulsory methods of dispute settlement', an attitude that was to continue for some time 'despite the growing awareness of the demands of interdependence in the international system'.[50] The Optional Protocol has not been widely supported, has only 38 parties, and has never been invoked to resolve a dispute.

C. UNCLOS III

The prospects for a comprehensive system for settling law of the sea disputes were not improved at UNCLOS II in 1960, which failed to produce any concrete outcomes because of disagreements on the breadth of the territorial sea. However, dispute settlement issues were considered very thoroughly from an early stage at UNCLOS III.[51] Progress on what was to become Part XV was advanced to a large extent by the work of an informal group, rather than in each of the three main negotiating committees. The informal group based its work on four main principles: that oceans disputes were to be settled by law, that compulsory procedures should apply wherever possible to guarantee uniform and consistent interpretation of the convention, that few exceptions would be permitted to the regime, and that the system should be integrated in the convention being drafted, rather than be an optional regime.[52] In large measure these principles were faithfully adhered to, and are now expressed in Part XV of the LOSC.

IV. Dispute Settlement Under the LOSC

Part XV comprises three Sections that seek both to utilise an existing international court, the ICJ, and to establish new institutions for the resolution of disputes concerning the LOSC,

---

[47] *Basic Documents* No 13.
[48] Optional Protocol Concerning the Settlement of Disputes, art II.
[49] Ibid art I.
[50] Klein, *Dispute Settlement* (n 46) 17.
[51] See AO Adede, *The System for Settlement of Disputes Under the United Nations Convention on the Law of the Sea* (Dordrecht, Martinus Nijhoff, 1987) chs II–VII.
[52] Klein, *Dispute Settlement* (n 46) 20–21.

including ITLOS. In overview, Section 1 of Part XV sets out prerequisites or conditions for activating the regime, Section 2 contains the core compulsory dispute settlement provisions, and Section 3 provides for several mandatory and optional exclusions from the Part XV system.

A. Jurisdictional Conditions

Article 279, the first provision in Section 1, reaffirms the obligation to resolve disputes peacefully consistent with the UN Charter. Article 280 emphasises that nothing in the LOSC prevents states from resolving disputes concerning the interpretation or application of the Convention through peaceful means of their choosing. Article 281(1) goes on to provide that the compulsory dispute settlement mechanisms contained in Section 2 of Part XV will only operate where the parties to a dispute have not reached a settlement by their agreed means and that agreement does not exclude any further procedure. In addition, in recognition that parties to a dispute concerning the LOSC may also be parties to other agreements that provide for the binding settlement of such a dispute, Article 282 states that those procedures will apply in lieu of Part XV. Rounding out the key provisions of Section 1, Article 283 stipulates that parties in dispute should proceed expeditiously to an exchange of views regarding the settlement of the dispute by negotiation or other peaceful means, and Article 283 states that a party may invite the other party to a dispute to utilise conciliation pursuant to Annex V, Section 1, or another conciliation procedure. The obligation to exchange views applies equally to both parties to the dispute,[53] and the practice of ITLOS when dealing with provisional measures applications has been to review whether the obligation has been met.[54] However, there is no obligation to continue to seek to exchange views where the possibility of reaching an agreement has been exhausted,[55] such as when efforts by one party to exchange views have been rebuffed by the other party and met with silence.[56]

As seen in the *Southern Bluefin Tuna* case[57] and *MOX Plant* case,[58] the companion Articles 281 and 282 may be significant procedural impediments to the operation of Part XV. The *Southern Bluefin Tuna* case related to a unilateral experimental fishing programme undertaken by Japan, which Australia and New Zealand contended was contrary to fisheries conservation provisions of the 1993 Convention for the Conservation of Southern Bluefin Tuna (CCSBT)[59] and the LOSC, to which the three states were parties. Following extensive efforts to reach a negotiated settlement of the dispute, Australia and New Zealand

---

[53] *Land Reclamation by Singapore in and Around the Straits of Johor (Malaysia v Singapore)* (provisional measures) 8 October 2003 www.itlos.org, [38].

[54] See *Arctic Sunrise (Netherlands v Russian Federation)* (2014) 53 ILM 607 [73]–[77].

[55] *MOX Plant (Ireland v United Kingdom)* (provisional measures) (2002) 41 ILM 405, [60].

[56] This was the case in *M/V Louisa (Saint Vincent and the Grenadines v Kingdom of Spain)* (provisional measures) 23 December 2010 www.itlos.org, [55]–[65], where the efforts of Saint Vincent and the Grenadines to exchange views with Spain were met with silence.

[57] *Southern Bluefin Tuna (New Zealand v Japan; Australia v Japan)* (provisional measures) (1999) 117 ILR 148 (jurisdiction and admissibility) (2000) 119 ILR 508.

[58] *MOX Plant (Ireland v United Kingdom)* (provisional measures) (2002) 41 ILM 405 (orders 1 to 6) www.pca-cpa.org/.

[59] *Basic Documents* No 55.

commenced proceedings against Japan under Part XV. At the provisional measures stage ITLOS found in favour of Australia and New Zealand, taking a precautionary approach in ordering Japan not to engage in its experimental fishing programme pending a determination of the merits.[60] However, the Annex VII arbitral tribunal subsequently established to consider the merits held that the proceedings could not continue because it did not have jurisdiction. It concluded that the consensual dispute settlement system of the CCSBT[61] prevailed over the compulsory system of Part XV by operation of Article 281. According to a majority of the tribunal, the CCSBT constituted an agreement for the settlement of a dispute concerning the LOSC within the meaning of Article 281.[62]

The arbitration in the *Southern Bluefin Tuna* case has received substantial criticism from many commentators, who have pointed out the difficulty in reconciling the conclusion of the tribunal with a plain reading of Article 281 and the object and purpose of Part XV, which is to establish a comprehensive dispute settlement system.[63] As Sir Kenneth Keith, observed in his Separate Opinion, clear wording is required to exclude the obligations of states to submit to binding procedures under the LOSC.[64] Such clarity is not supplied by the CCSBT which includes a dispute settlement clause that goes no further than Article 33 of the UN Charter.

Another case that highlighted difficulties that can arise in the interaction between the endogenous LOSC system and exogenous mechanisms for resolving law of the sea disputes was the *MOX Plant* case.[65] That case stemmed from a dispute between Ireland and the United Kingdom over potential marine pollution in the Irish Sea from a nuclear fuel reprocessing plant in Cumbria, in the United Kingdom. The dispute concerned not only the LOSC, but also a regional marine pollution regime, OSPAR, and European Community law. As a result it led to the invocation of the LOSC dispute settlement system and arbitration under OSPAR by Ireland,[66] and litigation in the European Court of Justice (ECJ) commenced by the European Commission against Ireland for violating European Community Law by invoking the LOSC, Part XV procedures.[67]

---

[60] *Southern Bluefin Tuna (New Zealand v Japan; Australia v Japan)* (provisional measures) (1999) 117 ILR 148, [90(c)–(d)]. See Tim Stephens, *International Courts and Environmental Protection* (Cambridge, Cambridge University Press, 2009) 220–28.

[61] Under art 16(1) of the CCBST, the parties were required to 'consult among themselves with a view to having the dispute resolved by negotiation, inquiry, mediation, conciliation, arbitration, judicial settlement or other peaceful means of their own choice'.

[62] *Southern Bluefin Tuna (New Zealand v Japan; Australia v Japan)* (jurisdiction and admissibility) (2000) 119 ILR 508, [59]. See Stephens, *International Courts* (n 60) 291–95.

[63] See David A Colson and Peggy Hoyle, 'Satisfying the Procedural Prerequisites to the Compulsory Dispute Settlement Mechanisms of the 1982 Law of the Sea Convention: Did the *Southern Bluefin Tuna* Tribunal Get it Right?' (2003) 34 *Ocean Development and International Law* 59. But cf Barbara Kwiatkowska, 'The Southern Bluefin Tuna Arbitral Tribunal Did Get it Right: A Commentary and Reply to the Article by David A Colson and Dr Peggy Hoyle' (2003) 34 *Ocean Development and International Law* 369.

[64] *Southern Bluefin Tuna (New Zealand v Japan; Australia v Japan)* (jurisdiction and admissibility) (2000) 119 ILR 508, Separate Opinion of Judge Sir Kenneth Keith, [19].

[65] *MOX Plant (Ireland v United Kingdom)* (provisional measures) (2002) 41 ILM 405; *MOX Plant (Ireland v United Kingdom)* (suspension of proceedings on jurisdiction and merits and request for further provisional measures) (order 3) (2003) 42 ILM 1187 (orders 1–2, 4–6) www.pca-cpa.org. See Stephens, *International Courts* (n 60) 232–39, 295–302.

[66] *OSPAR Arbitration (Ireland v United Kingdom)* (final award) (2003) 42 ILM 1118.

[67] *Commission of the European Communities v Ireland* C-182/189 (2006) 45 ILM 1051.

As with the *Southern Bluefin Tuna* case, the *MOX Plant* case was not decided on the merits under the Part XV system, notwithstanding an interim decision by ITLOS on Ireland's request for provisional measures that there was a prima facie basis for a view that an Annex VII arbitral tribunal would have jurisdiction.[68] Having regard to ongoing proceedings in the ECJ, the Annex VII arbitral tribunal of the LOSC suspended hearings pending the resolution of the issues concerning European Community law. The arbitral tribunal took the view that if the ECJ found that it had exclusive jurisdiction, then Article 282 of the LOSC would apply.[69] This was what ultimately occurred, which vindicated the arbitral tribunal's cautious approach. The ECJ determined that members of the European Community must bring disputes relating to the environmental protection provisions of the LOSC before the ECJ, and not the Part XV dispute settlement system.[70]

The *Southern Bluefin Tuna* case and *MOX Plant* case illustrate the significant difficulties that can arise in the interaction of multiple dispute settlement systems in the law of the sea. Where there are multiple instruments, each with its own procedure for dispute settlement, there are prospects for forum shopping, with litigants selecting the court or tribunal offering the greatest procedural and substantial advantages. In a sense both of these cases involved forum shopping in that the applicants sought to commence proceedings under the LOSC framework because of advantages presented to them in terms of the compulsory nature of Part XV and the capacity of ITLOS to issue provisional measures. Ultimately, however, the competition between Part XV and alternative dispute settlement systems were resolved in both cases in favour of the alternatives. Whether this is desirable is questionable, as in both cases the merits of the disputes were left unresolved, although in the *Southern Bluefin Tuna* case it has nonetheless been argued that the Annex VII jurisdictional decision was positive in encouraging the parties to cooperate afresh, and reach agreement on managing the fishery on a cooperative basis.[71]

Another set of proceedings which illustrates related difficulties in coordinating dispute settlement mechanisms in the law of the sea is the *Swordfish Stocks* case,[72] arising out of a dispute between Chile and the European Community when Chile imposed port bans on Spanish vessels targeting swordfish near the Chilean EEZ. In response to these bans the European Community initiated consultations in the WTO, and requested the establishment of a panel.[73] For its part Chile commenced what were effectively counterclaim proceedings under Part XV of the LOSC, contending that the European Community had violated provisions of the LOSC relating to the conservation of high seas fisheries.[74] The dispute was eventually resolved by negotiation before a hearing took place in either ITLOS or in a

---

[68]   *MOX Plant (Ireland v United Kingdom)* (provisional measures) (2002) 41 ILM 405, [52].

[69]   *MOX Plant (Ireland v United Kingdom)* (order 3) (2003) 42 ILM 1187, [22].

[70]   See the discussion by Karen N Scott, 'The MOX Plant Case Before the European Court' (2007) 22 *International Journal of Marine and Coastal Law* 303.

[71]   Bill Mansfield, 'The Southern Bluefin Tuna Arbitration' (2001) 16 *International Journal of Marine and Coastal Law* 361; Natalie Klein, 'Whales and Tuna: The Past and Future of Litigation between Australia and Japan' (2009) 21 *Georgetown International Environmental Law Review* 143, 210–14.

[72]   *Conservation and Sustainable Exploitation of Swordfish Stocks in the South-East Pacific Ocean (Chile/European Community)* (removed from docket 17 December 2009) www.itlos.org.

[73]   *Chile—Measures Affecting the Transit and Importation of Swordfish* (2000) WTO Doc WT/DS1931/1 (request for consultations by the European Communities) (2000) WTO Doc WT/DS193/2 (request for the establishment of a panel by the European Communities).

[74]   In particular LOSC, arts 116, 119.

WTO panel. The litigation does, however, indicate the prospects for two dispute settlement systems to operate side by side in relation to the same law of the sea dispute. Although each would have had a particular jurisdiction, and be limited to apply determined applicable law specific to each regime, it was possible that the two dispute settlement systems might have reached divergent conclusions on some legal issues, and upon factual matters, a clearly undesirable result.[75]

The prospects for problems to be encountered in the future in law of the sea disputes in the interaction between multiple dispute settlement systems remains high, because of the uncertainties that surround the interpretation of Articles 281 and 282. The law of the sea is not unusual in this respect, as jurisdictional competition is an increasingly well-recognised problem in international dispute settlement more generally, in an era where there has been a proliferation of international courts and tribunals and other dispute settlement mechanisms.[76] There is only a very limited and underdeveloped range of jurisdictional regulating rules that can be applied in order to resolve such difficulties,[77] and in the law of the sea they will only be addressed by decisions, including by ITLOS, that reach a concluded and accepted view about how the specific jurisdictional regulating rules in the LOSC can and should function.

B. Compulsory Dispute Settlement

Article 286, the first in Section 2 of Part XV, provides that the compulsory procedures apply only where the parties have failed to settle their dispute by recourse to the procedures set out in Section 1. This means among other things that the parties must make an effort to resolve their dispute through negotiations and exchanging views.[78] It is not necessary for the negotiations to proceed over a lengthy period, provided that they are serious and in good faith.[79]

The pivotal provision in Section 2 is Article 287, which outlines the various compulsory dispute settlement procedures that are available. At any time parties to the LOSC may declare a preference for one or more of four procedures, namely ITLOS, the ICJ, an arbitral tribunal established under Annex VII to the LOSC, or a special arbitral tribunal established under Annex VIII. Rather than relying exclusively on a single body such as the ICJ, Part XV of the LOSC presents states with a 'cafeteria'[80] or 'smorgasbord'[81] of options for resolving

---

[75] Alan E Boyle, 'The World Trade Organization and the Marine Environment' in Myron H Nordquist, John Norton Moore and Said Mahmoudi (eds), *The Stockholm Declaration and the Law of the Marine Environment* (The Hague, Kluwer, 2003), 109, 116; Marcos A Orcellana, 'The Swordfish Dispute Between the EU and Chile at the ITLOS and the WTO' (2002) 71 *Nordic Journal of International Law* 55, 65.

[76] Chester Brown, *A Common Law of International Adjudication* (Oxford, Oxford University Press, 2007), ch 1; Stephens, *International Courts* (n 60) ch 9.

[77] See generally Yuval Shany, *The Competing Jurisdictions of International Courts and Tribunals* (Oxford, Oxford University Press, 2003).

[78] LOSC, art 283.

[79] *Southern Bluefin Tuna (New Zealand v Japan; Australia v Japan)* (jurisdiction and admissibility) (2000) 119 ILR 508, [55].

[80] Alan E Boyle, 'Dispute Settlement and the Law of the Sea Convention: Problems of Fragmentation and Jurisdiction' (1997) 46 *International and Comparative Law Quarterly* 37, 40.

[81] Jonathan I Charney, 'The Implications of Expanding International Dispute Settlement Systems: The 1982 Convention on the Law of the Sea' (1996) 90 *AJIL* 69, 71.

law of the sea disputes. This reflects the importance of consent to international dispute settlement, and the reticence of states to accept one body as the definitive means for resolving law of the sea disputes.[82]

The ICJ, ITLOS and Annex VII arbitral tribunals are all given broad jurisdiction under Article 288 to address (1) any dispute concerning the application or interpretation of the LOSC submitted consistently with Part XV and (2) any dispute concerning the interpretation or application of an international agreement related to the purposes of the LOSC submitted consistently with that agreement. As of 1 January 2013, there were 15 such agreements.[83] The jurisdiction of Annex VII special arbitration is not as broad as that of the other Article 287 bodies. It is to deal only with disputes relating to (1) fisheries, (2) the protection and preservation of the marine environment, (3) marine scientific research, and (4) navigation, including pollution from vessels and by dumping.[84]

In relation to disputes concerning the exploration and exploitation of the seabed and ocean floor and subsoil beyond the limits of national jurisdiction (the Area)[85] there is a special regime that refers such disputes to a Sea-Bed Disputes Chamber of ITLOS, a special chamber of ITLOS, an ad hoc chamber of the Sea-Bed Disputes Chamber, or binding commercial arbitration.[86] The parties to disputes before the Sea-Bed Disputes Chamber of ITLOS or binding commercial arbitration may include not only states parties to the LOSC, but also the ISA,[87] the Enterprise,[88] state enterprises, natural or juridical persons and prospective contractors. The Sea-Bed Disputes Chamber also has the capacity to render an Advisory Opinion, as occurred in the 2011 *Responsibilities and Obligations of States Sponsoring Persons and Entities with Respect to Activities in the Area.*[89]

Anticipating variable preferences, Article 287 provides that Annex VII arbitration is the default procedure where no declaration has been made by a party to a dispute,[90] or where the parties have accepted different procedures.[91] As of 1 January 2015, there are 166 parties to the LOSC, and 43 of these have indicated a preferred procedure pursuant to Article 287. Thirty-one of these states have expressed confidence in ITLOS by selecting it as their preferred (or equally preferred) body for dealing with LOSC disputes (see Table 18.1). Some states, such as Cuba and Guinea-Bissau, have made declarations under Article 287

[82] Ted L McDorman, 'An Overview of International Fisheries Disputes and the International Tribunal for the Law of the Sea' (2002) XL *Canadian Yearbook of International Law* 119, 127.

[83] Robin Churchill, 'Dispute Settlement in the Law of the Sea: Survey for 2013' (2015) 30 *International Journal of Marine and Coastal Law* 1, 34. These include, amongst others, the 1993 Agreement to Promote Compliance with International Conservation and Management Measures by Fishing Vessels on the High Seas, *Basic Documents* No 54, the FSA, *Basic Documents* No 56, the 2000 Convention on the Conservation and Management of Highly Migratory Fish Stocks in the Western and Central Pacific Ocean, *Basic Documents* No 63, the 2001 Convention on the Protection of the Underwater Cultural Heritage, *Basic Documents* No 65, and the 2012 Convention on the Determination of the Minimal Conditions for Access and Exploitation of Marine Resources within the Maritime Areas under Jurisdiction of the Member States of the Sub-Regional Fisheries Commission (SRFC), as discussed in the *Request for an Advisory Opinion submitted by the Sub-Regional Fisheries Commission (SRFC)* (Advisory Opinion) 2 April 2015 www.itlos.org.

[84] LOSC, annex VIII, art 1.

[85] Ibid art 1(1).

[86] Ibid arts 186–91.

[87] Ibid arts 156–58.

[88] Ibid art 170.

[89] (2011) 50 ILM 458.

[90] LOSC, art 287(3).

[91] Ibid art 287(5).

Table 18.1: Summary of declarations under Article 287 of the LOSC indicating party preference(s) for method of dispute settlement

STATE PARTY	PREFERRED FORUM(S), IN ORDER OF PREFERENCE
Algeria	No choice made, except indication that does not consider itself bound by Article 287(1)(b) to submit disputes to ICJ
Angola	(a) ITLOS
Argentina	(a) ITLOS (b) Annex VIII special arbitration
Australia	(a) ITLOS/ICJ*
Austria	(a) ITLOS (b) Annex VIII special arbitration (c) ICJ
Bangladesh	(a) ITLOS
Belarus	(a) Annex VII arbitration (b) Annex VIII special arbitration
Belgium	(a) ITLOS/ICJ
Canada	(a) ITLOS/Annex VII arbitration
Cape Verde	(a) ITLOS (b) ICJ
Chile	(a) ITLOS (b) Annex VIII special arbitration
China	No choice made
Croatia	(a) ITLOS (b) ICJ
Denmark	(a) ICJ
Ecuador	(a) ITLOS (b) ICJ (c) Annex VIII special arbitration
Egypt	(a) Annex VII arbitration
Estonia	(a) ICJ/ITLOS
Finland	(a) ICJ/ITLOS
Gabon	No choice made
Germany	(a) ITLOS (b) Annex VII arbitration (c) ICJ
Greece	(a) ITLOS
Guinea-Bissau	No choice made, except indication that rejects jurisdiction of the ICJ
Honduras	(a) ICJ
Hungary	(a) ITLOS (b) ICJ (c) Annex VIII special arbitration
Iceland	No choice made
Italy	(a) ITLOS/ICJ
Latvia	(a) ITLOS (b) ICJ
Lithuania	(a) ITLOS (b) ICJ
Madagascar	(a) ITLOS
Mexico	(a) ITLOS/ICJ/Annex VIII special arbitration
Netherlands	(a) ICJ
Nicaragua	(a) ICJ
Norway	(a) ICJ

(continued)

Table 18.1: *(Continued)*

STATE PARTY	PREFERRED FORUM(S), IN ORDER OF PREFERENCE
Oman	(a) ITLOS/ICJ
Portugal†	(a) ITLOS (b) ICJ (c) Annex VII arbitration (d) Annex VIII special arbitration
Republic of Korea	No choice made
Russian Federation‡	(a) Annex VII arbitration/Annex VIII special arbitration
Saint Vincent and the Grenadines	(a) ITLOS
Saudi Arabia	No choice made
Slovenia	(a) Annex VII arbitration
Spain	(a) ITLOS/ICJ
Sweden	(a) ICJ
Switzerland	(a) ITLOS
Tanzania	(a) ITLOS
Thailand	No choice made
Timor-Leste	(a) ITLOS/ICJ/Annex VII arbitration
Trinidad and Tobago	(a) ITLOS (b) ICJ
Tunisia	(a) ITLOS (b) Annex VII arbitration
Ukraine	(a) Annex VII arbitration/Annex VIII special arbitration
United Kingdom	(a) ICJ
Uruguay	(a) ITLOS

* ITLOS/ICJ indicates that ITLOS and the ICJ have both been chosen, and no preference has been expressed for one forum over the other.
† Portugal's declaration does not appear to express any order of preference for these procedures, notwithstanding that they are listed in this order.
‡ The Russian Federation declaration also indicates the acceptance of ITLOS in matters of prompt release of detained vessels and crews.

Source: www.un.org/Depts/los/settlement_of_disputes/choice_procedure

indicating that they do not accept the jurisdiction of the ICJ and consequently will not accept the Court's jurisdiction with respect to matters arising under Articles 297 and 298, but are otherwise silent on their position regarding ITLOS and arbitral tribunals.

Beyond the LOSC, Part XV also applies to an additional suite of treaties because of the operation of the FSA,[92] which is designed to implement the general provisions of the LOSC in relation to straddling and highly migratory fisheries.[93] Under Article 30(2) of the FSA, Part XV applies *mutatis mutandis* to any dispute concerning the interpretation or application of a regional or global agreement relating to straddling or highly migratory fish stocks, where the parties to the dispute are parties to the FSA and to the regional or global fisheries

---

[92] *Basic Documents* No 56.
[93] See further ch 13.

agreement. This provision has been described as an 'innovative twist' that brings, for the first time, many disputes arising within regional fisheries management organisations under a compulsory procedure.[94] There are now over 20 agreements to which Article 30(2) of the FSA applies,[95] illustrating that the reach of the dispute settlement system of the LOSC continues to expand. This has been said to confirm that Part XV is the 'centrepiece' of the new law of the sea, and is 'envisaged as universal even by those States that are not parties to it'[96] such as the United States, which is a party to the FSA, and many regional fisheries agreements.

i. Applicable Law

In terms of the law that is to govern a dispute, Article 293(1) provides that a court or tribunal with jurisdiction under Part XV, section 2, is to apply the LOSC 'and other rules of international law not incompatible' with the LOSC. There is no provision setting out in detail the sources of law to which ITLOS may refer, unlike the Statute of the ICJ which specifies in detail in Article 38(1) the sources of international law applicable to disputes brought before the ICJ. However, as with the ICJ, which under Article 38(2) has jurisdiction to decide disputes on an equitable basis, a court or tribunal under Article 287 of the LOSC may decide a case *ex aequo et bono*, if the parties so agree.[97]

A distinction needs to be drawn between jurisdiction and applicable law. The Annex VII arbitral tribunal in the *MOX Plant* case found that there was a 'cardinal distinction' between the scope of the tribunal's jurisdiction under Article 298 'and the law to be applied by the Tribunal under Article 293'.[98] The Part XV dispute settlement mechanisms have jurisdiction only over disputes concerning the LOSC, and additional treaties as provided for in Article 288(2). Hence they do not have jurisdiction over disputes arising under general international law. In the *Chagos Marine Protected Arbitration*, the Annex VII arbitral tribunal found that 'where a dispute concerns the interpretation or application of the Convention, the jurisdiction of a court or tribunal pursuant to Article 288(1) extends to making such findings of fact or ancillary determinations of law as are necessary to resolve the dispute presented to it'.[99] However, where the real issue, or object of claim, does not relate to the interpretation or application of the LOSC, such as a dispute primarily about territorial sovereignty, then the dispute does not fall within Article 288(1).[100] On this basis, the tribunal found that it lacked jurisdiction to rule on the dispute between Mauritius and the United Kingdom concerning sovereignty over the Chagos Archipelago (although the tribunal did decide other aspects of the dispute between the parties). Nonetheless, in deciding disputes within their jurisdiction, Article 287 bodies may apply general international law where

---

[94] Peter Örebach, Ketil Sigurjonsson and Ted L McDorman, 'The 1995 United Nations Straddling and Highly Migratory Fish Stocks Agreement: Management, Enforcement and Dispute Settlement' (1998) 13 *International Journal of Marine and Coastal Law* 119, 136.

[95] Robin Churchill, 'Dispute Settlement under the UN Convention on the Law of the Sea: Survey for 2008' (2009) 24 *International Journal of Marine and Coastal Law* 603, 615.

[96] Tullio Treves, 'A System for Law of the Sea Dispute Settlement' in David Freestone, Richard Barnes and David M Ong (eds), *The Law of the Sea: Progress and Prospects* (Oxford, Oxford University Press, 2006) 417, 431–32.

[97] LOSC, art 293(2).

[98] *MOX Plant Case (Ireland v United Kingdom)*, Order No 3 (2003) 126 ILR 310, 19.

[99] *In the Matter of the Chagos Marine Protected Area Arbitration (Mauritius v United Kingdom)*, Annex VII Arbitral Tribunal, 18 March 2015 www.pca-cpa.org, [220].

[100] Ibid.

this is compatible with the LOSC, or with other treaties if the jurisdiction is based upon Article 288(2).[101] In the *M/V Saiga (No 2)*[102] case and the *Guyana/Suriname Arbitration*,[103] this enabled general international law relating to the use of force to be applied by the respective tribunals in assessing the legality of enforcement action taken by coastal states.

ii. Provisional Measures

Article 290 allows for the prescription of provisional measures either by an agreed court or tribunal or, failing agreement, by ITLOS,[104] in order 'to preserve the respective rights of the parties to the dispute or to prevent serious harm to the marine environment, pending the final decision'.[105] It is noteworthy that Article 290 says that an Article 287 body has the capacity to 'prescribe' provisional measures, a term which confirms that such measures are legally binding.[106] This is in contrast with the somewhat ambiguous term 'indicate' which is used in Article 41 of the Statute of the ICJ in relation to the power of the ICJ to issue provisional measures.[107]

Article 290 has proven to be an important source of jurisdiction for ITLOS, which has issued provisional measures on eight occasions (see Table 18.3) and declined a request to issue provisional measures on one occasion.[108] ITLOS practice in provisional measures applications is provided for in Article 290(5), whereby it must first be determined whether prima facie the tribunal to be constituted would have jurisdiction, and that the urgency of the situation requires the prescription of provisional measures. This can lead to the situation where ITLOS is requested to prescribe provisional measures pending the constitution of an Annex VII arbitral tribunal, as occurred in the *Southern Bluefin Tuna* case and more recently in the *Arctic Sunrise* case. As was demonstrated in *Southern Bluefin Tuna*, ITLOS and the Annex VII arbitral tribunal may take differing positions on whether there is jurisdiction. However, as ITLOS observed in *Arctic Sunrise*, where Russia's Article 298 declaration raised issues as to whether the dispute with the Netherlands was one that had been excluded from Part XV, Section 2 dispute resolution procedures, 'the Tribunal is not called

---

[101]   See the discussion in Michael Wood, 'The International Tribunal for the Law of the Sea and General International Law' (2007) 22 *International Journal of Marine and Coastal Law* 351. See also Klein, *Dispute Settlement* (n 46) 58.

[102]   *M/V Saiga (No 2) (Saint Vincent and the Grenadines v Guinea)* (admissibility and merits) (1999) 120 ILR 143.

[103]   *Guyana/Suriname Arbitration* (2007) 139 ILR 566.

[104]   LOSC, Annex VI, art 25; this capacity also extends to Special Chambers of ITLOS; see the decision in *Dispute Concerning Delimitation of the Maritime Boundary between Ghana and Côte D'Ivoire in the Atlantic Coast* (Ghana/ Côte D'Ivoire) (provisional measures) 25 April 2015 www.itlos.org.

[105]   Described in 2015 by the ITLOS Special Chamber as a capacity to 'prescribe provisional measures if it finds that there is a real and imminent risk that irreparable prejudice could be caused to the rights of the parties to the dispute': *Dispute Concerning Delimitation of the Maritime Boundary between Ghana and Côte D'Ivoire in the Atlantic Coast (Ghana/Côte D'Ivoire)* (provisional measures) 25 April 2015 www.itlos.org, [74].

[106]   Francisco Orrego Vicuña, 'The International Tribunal for the Law of the Sea and Provisional Measures: Settled Issues and Pending Problems' (2007) 22 *International Journal of Marine and Coastal Law* 451, 452.

[107]   It was decided by the ICJ in the *LaGrand (Germany v United States)* [2001] ICJ Rep 466 that its interim orders were in fact legally binding despite the use of the term 'indicate'. See Tim Stephens, 'The Right to Information on Consular Assistance under the Vienna Convention on Consular Relations: A Right for What Purpose?' (2002) 3 *Melbourne Journal of International Law* 143, 155–61.

[108]   *M/V Louisa (Saint Vincent and the Grenadines v Kingdom of Spain)* (provisional measures) 23 December 2010 www.itlos.org, [71]–[72].

upon to establish definitively the existence of the rights claimed by the Netherlands' and 'the provisions of the Convention invoked by the Netherlands appear to afford a basis on which the jurisdiction of the arbitral tribunal might be founded'. As such, ITLOS found that it had jurisdiction to prescribe provisional measures.[109]

Moreover, the formulation in Article 290 is particularly significant by virtue of the emphasis it places on marine environmental protection. The reference in Article 290 to the avoidance of 'serious harm to the marine environment' indicates the specific design of the Part XV system to respond effectively to situations of potential environmental damage, and not only to protect the rights of the parties to the dispute.[110] This approach was reinforced in 2015, when an ITLOS Special Chamber prescribed provisional measures after expressing its concern that exploration and exploitation activities conducted by Ghana in an area of the continental shelf also claimed by Côte D'Ivoire would 'result in a modification of the physical characteristics of the continental shelf'.[111] As Judge Treves noted in the *Southern Bluefin Tuna* case, there is a strong conceptual affinity between the precautionary principle and this provisional measures procedure.[112]

iii. Prompt Release

An additional and important head of jurisdiction is contained in Article 292 which relates to the prompt release of vessels and crews. While the LOSC conferred significant jurisdictional capacity upon coastal states in relation to their EEZs, there was an appreciation at UNCLOS III of the potential for enforcement processes to be abused when coastal states arrested flag state fishing vessels for breaches of fishing regulations unless there were procedural safeguards in place.[113] The LOSC also accords to coastal states expanded powers to detain foreign vessels that have violated laws and regulations with respect to the prevention, reduction and control of pollution in the coastal state's EEZ or territorial sea resulting in a discharge causing major damage or the threat of major damage to the marine environment.[114]

Specifically in relation to the enforcement of fisheries jurisdiction, Article 73 of the LOSC seeks to reconcile the competing interests of coastal and flag states. Article 73(1) provides that coastal states may, in the exercise of their sovereign rights to explore, exploit, conserve, and manage the living resources in the EEZ, take such enforcement action against vessels as is necessary to ensure conformity with its fishing regulations. However, the safeguard for flag states is the requirement in Article 73(2) that arrested vessels and their crews be 'promptly released upon the posting of reasonable bond or other security'.

Article 292 was included in Part XV in order to provide procedural safeguards for flag states, and a counterweight to excessive application of enforcement jurisdiction by coastal

---

[109] *Arctic Sunrise (Netherlands v Russian Federation)* (2014) 53 ILM 607; see also Joint Separate Opinion of Judge Wolfrum and Judge Kelly [9].

[110] Alan Boyle, 'The Environmental Jurisprudence of the International Tribunal for the Law of the Sea' (2007) 22 *International Journal of Marine and Coastal Law* 369, 380.

[111] *Dispute Concerning Delimitation of the Maritime Boundary between Ghana and Côte D'Ivoire in the Atlantic Coast (Ghana/Côte D'Ivoire)* (provisional measures) 25 April 2015 www.itlos.org, [88].

[112] *Southern Bluefin Tuna (New Zealand v Japan; Australia v Japan)* (provisional measures) (1999) 117 ILR 148, Separate Opinion of Judge Treves, [9].

[113] *Virginia Commentaries*, vol 5, 67.

[114] LOSC, art 220(6).

states in relation to fisheries and pollution matters.[115] Article 292 establishes a procedure by which coastal states may seek the resolution of any dispute concerning such arrests by either an agreed tribunal or, in all other situations, by ITLOS. Article 292 therefore confers residual compulsory jurisdiction on ITLOS in relation to prompt release cases if at the time of the arrest or detention there is no other court or tribunal having jurisdiction.[116]

Prompt release cases have dominated the tribunal's docket. The very first case in ITLOS, the *M/V Saiga* involved an application by a flag state, Saint Vincent and the Grenadines, for prompt release of an oil tanker that was operating as a bunkering vessel supplying fuel oil for fishing and other vessels offshore Guinea, that had been arrested within the Guinean EEZ.[117] A further eight such cases have been taken to the tribunal, including the 2007 decisions in the *Tomimaru*[118] and *Hoshinmaru* cases,[119] which involved applications by Japan for the prompt release of two Japanese flagged fishing vessels arrested by Russia in its EEZ in the Bering Sea for infringements of Russian fisheries laws.[120] However, the majority of the prompt release cases have related to illegal, unreported and unregulated fishing in the Southern Ocean for Patagonian toothfish and have followed arrests by Australia and France of vessels flying flags of convenience.

These cases have led to important developments in ITLOS jurisprudence on issues concerning the jurisdiction over and admissibility of prompt release applications (which includes issues surrounding the nationality of vessels), and what constitutes a 'reasonable bond'.[121] In several decisions the tribunal has confirmed that whether a bond or other financial security is 'reasonable' for the purposes of Article 292 will depend upon a number of factors, including (but not limited to) the gravity of alleged fishing offences, possible penalties for these offences under the coastal state's domestic law, the value of the vessel seized and the amount and form of the bond set. ITLOS has also repeatedly confirmed that the purpose of Articles 73 and 292 of the LOSC is to balance the interests of coastal and flag states.

ITLOS prompt release decisions have generally not met with the approval of arresting states, on the grounds that they have set relatively undemanding bond conditions that do not pay adequate regard to the international concern surrounding illegal fishing.[122] In particular, ITLOS has not accepted the argument that a 'bond or other financial security' under Article 292(4) and Article 73(3) can extend to non-financial conditions for the release of a vessel, such as the requirement that the vessel carry a Vessel Monitoring System by which a coastal state can track the position of the vessel at all times, and ascertain whether there have been future breaches of coastal state fisheries laws.[123] What has become increasingly

---

[115]   Klein, *Dispute Settlement* (n 46) 86.

[116]   *Virginia Commentaries*, vol 2, 794.

[117]   *M/V Saiga (No 1) Case (Saint Vincent and the Grenadines v Guinea)* (prompt release) (1997) 110 ILR 736.

[118]   *Tomimaru (Japan v Russia)* (2007) 46 ILM 1185.

[119]   *Hoshinmaru (Japan v Russian Federation)* (prompt release) 6 August 2007 www.itlos.org.

[120]   See Philip Bender, 'The *Tomimaru* and *Hoshinmaru* Cases before ITLOS' (2008) 23 *International Journal of Marine and Coastal Law* 349.

[121]   See Thomas A Mensah, 'The Tribunal and the Prompt Release of Vessels' (2007) 22 *International Journal of Marine and Coastal Law* 425.

[122]   R Rayfuse, 'The Future of Compulsory Dispute Settlement in the Law of the Sea Convention' (2010) 36 *Victoria University of Wellington Journal* 683, 692–93.

[123]   *Volga (Russian Federation v Australia)* (prompt release) (2003) 42 ILM 159, [55]–[80]. See Donald R Rothwell and Tim Stephens, 'Illegal Southern Ocean Fishing and Prompt Release: Balancing Coastal and Flag State Rights and Interests' (2004) 53 *International and Comparative Law Quarterly* 171, 178–86.

evident in prompt release cases is the difficulty that ITLOS faces in undertaking an acceptable balancing of coastal and flag state interests.[124] ITLOS has faced similar issues when dealing with provisional measures applications arising from the seizure of ships that fall outside of the scope of the Article 73 and 292 prompt release mechanisms.[125]

C. Jurisdictional Limitations and Exceptions

There are several significant limitations to the jurisdiction of the four Article 287 courts and tribunals which are set out in Section 3 of Part XV, and states retain the option of indicating which of the formal third party mechanisms they prefer by way of a declaration. Article 298 declarations may be made by states with respect to three types of disputes:

1. disputes with respect to the delimitation of maritime boundaries and the application of Articles 15, 74 and 83 of the LOSC, or disputes involving historic bays or titles;
2. disputes concerning military activities; and
3. disputes in respect of which the United Nations Security Council is exercising its functions.

Article 298(3) makes clear that states taking advantage of one or more of these exclusions cannot then submit any dispute in relation to them against another state party without the consent of that party.

A total of 32 states have lodged declarations in reliance upon Article 298(1) of the LOSC (see Table 18.2). The declaration can relate to any one or more of the procedures provided for under Section 2, such that the state can exempt the dispute from only some of the Section 2 procedures or all of the Section 2 procedures. An Article 298 declaration may raise issues as to its interpretation, and whether the state is able to only issue the declaration activating the particular optional exception or whether the terms of the declaration can include some statement of understanding with respect to the effect of the declaration. Given the potential ambiguity that may exist with respect to what constitutes 'historic bays or titles', for example, there may be some merit in a state lodging a more expansive declaration so that it can precisely identify how it interprets those provisions.

Declarations may be withdrawn by the state party, or the party may elect to submit a dispute covered by the declaration to any of the procedures specified in the LOSC.[126] There thus exists a level of flexibility with respect to how a state may seek to modify or withdraw its Article 298 declaration, or to even elect ad hoc to not be bound by the terms of the declaration in any particular instance.[127] Likewise, the lodgement of a declaration does not impact upon proceedings that are pending before a court or tribunal.[128] However, it is

---

[124] See the discussion in Andrew Serdy and Michael Bliss, 'Prompt Release of Fishing Vessels: State Practice in the Light of the Case before the International Tribunal for the Law of the Sea' in Alex G Oude Elferink and Donald R Rothwell (eds), *Oceans Management in the 21st Century: Institutional Frameworks and Responses* (Leiden, Martinus Nijhoff, 2004) 273.
[125] See eg *Arctic Sunrise (Netherlands v Russian Federation)* (provisional measures) (2014) 53 ILM 607.
[126] LOSC, art 298(2).
[127] *Virginia Commentaries*, vol V, 115 [298.12].
[128] LOSC, art 298(5).

Table 18.2: Summary of declarations under Article 298 of the LOSC

STATE PARTY	CATEGORY OF DISPUTE EXCLUDED
Angola	(a) if brought before Annex VII arbitration
Argentina	(a), (b) excepting military activities by government vessels and aircraft engaged in noncommercial service and (c)
Australia	(a)
Belarus	(b) and (c)
Canada	(a), (b) and (c)
Cape Verde	(b)
Chile	(a), (b) and (c)
China	(a), (b) and (c)
Denmark	(a), (b) and (c) if brought before Annex VII arbitration
Ecuador	(a), (b) and (c)
Equatorial Guinea	(a)
France	(a), (b) and (c)
Gabon	(a)
Iceland	(a) in relation to disputes concerning the interpretation of Article 83
Italy	(a)
Mexico	(a) and (b)
Montenegro	(a)
Nicaragua	(a), (b) and (c)
Norway	(a), (b) and (c) if brought before Annex VII arbitration
Palau	(a)
Portugal	(a), (b) and (c)
Republic of Korea	(a), (b) and (c)
Russian Federation	(a), (b) and (c)
Saudi Arabia	(a)
Slovenia	(a), (b) and (c) if brought before Annex VII arbitration
Spain	(a)
Thailand	(a), (b) and (c)
Trinidad and Tobago	(a)
Tunisia	(a), (b) and (c)

(continued)

Table 18.2: *(Continued)*

STATE PARTY	CATEGORY OF DISPUTE EXCLUDED
Ukraine	(a) and (b)
United Kingdom	(b) and (c)
Uruguay	(b)

Key:
(a) Disputes concerning the interpretation or application of LOSC, Articles 15, 74 and 83 relating to sea boundary delimitations, or those involving historic bays or titles.
(b) Disputes concerning military activities, including military activities by government vessels and aircraft engaged in non-commercial service, and disputes concerning law enforcement activities in regard to the exercise of sovereign rights or jurisdiction excluded from the jurisdiction of a court or tribunal under LOSC, Article 297(2) or 297(3).
(c) Disputes in respect of which the Security Council of the United Nations is exercising the functions assigned to it by the Charter of the United Nations, unless the Security Council decides to remove the matter from its agenda or calls upon the parties to settle it by the means provided for in this convention.
Source: www.un.org/Depts/los/settlement_of_disputes/choice_procedure.htm

important to note that this limitation does not apply with respect to a dispute, but rather only with respect to proceedings that are pending. Article 298 declarations can therefore have an impact upon an existing dispute which has yet to reach the stage of proceedings before a Section 2 court of tribunal.[129]

There are also some automatically applicable limitations on the adjudication of disputes set out in Article 297. Importantly, Article 297(1)(a) affirms that disputes with regard to the exercise by a coastal state of its sovereign rights or jurisdiction will be subject to Part XV where it is alleged that a coastal state has interfered with freedoms and rights of navigation, overflight, or laying of submarine cables and pipelines, or in regard to other internationally lawful uses of the sea as set out in Article 58. Article 297(1)(b) provides that Part XV also applies where it is alleged that a state exercising these freedoms has acted in contravention of the LOSC, or the laws of the coastal state adopted in conformity with the LOSC. Article 297(1)(c) states that Part XV extends to disputes where it has been alleged that a coastal state has acted in contravention of international rules and standards relating to marine pollution set by, or adopted under, the LOSC such as where exorbitant jurisdiction is claimed or exercised by a coastal state. Klein has noted that although Article 297 is included in a Section setting out limitations to Part XV, its effect is to reaffirm the comprehensive coverage of Part XV rather than to circumscribe its application to the three matters referred to.[130]

There are then two specific, non-optional, exceptions to jurisdiction. Under Article 297(2), coastal states are not obliged to accept submission of a dispute concerning a decision not to grant consent to undertake marine scientific research in the EEZ or on the continental shelf. However, such disputes are made subject to compulsory conciliation, under Annex V, section 2, provided that the commission does not call into question the coastal state's discretion to designate areas where marine scientific research may not take place because exploitation or exploratory operations are occurring, or will occur within

---

[129] As to the date from which an art 298 declaration takes effect, see the discussion in *Virginia Commentaries*, vol V, 140–41 [298.44].
[130] Klein, *Dispute Settlement* (n 46) 141.

a reasonable time.[131] Nor may the commission question the coastal state's jurisdiction discretion to withhold consent to marine scientific research in the circumstances set out in Article 246(5) where it is, for instance, of direct significance for the exploration and exploitation of natural resources.

Under Article 297(3)(a), a coastal state is not obliged to submit disputes 'relating to its sovereign rights with respect to the living resources in the exclusive economic zone or their exercise, including its discretionary capacity, the allocation of surpluses to other States and the terms and conditions established in its conservation management laws and regulations'. However, where a coastal state has 'manifestly failed' or 'arbitrarily refused' to meet these responsibilities then this may be the subject of compulsory conciliation.[132] Given that 90 per cent of commercial fishing occurs in the EEZ, the exclusion of EEZ fisheries disputes from compulsory judicial settlement is a 'very far-reaching exception'.[133]

D. ITLOS

Although there is no formal hierarchy among Article 287 courts and tribunals, ITLOS as a new permanent institution dedicated to resolving law of the sea disputes is rightly regarded as being at the centre of the Part XV dispute resolution system.[134] The creation of a new international dispute resolution institution such as ITLOS inevitably attracts a great deal of comment and speculation, as has also been the case with other dispute settlement systems, such as the WTO's Dispute Settlement Understanding, and the International Criminal Court.[135] In relation to ITLOS, the commentary has focussed on issues including the extent of its jurisdiction and relationship with the ICJ, its capacity and expertise, and its potential workload.

Despite some pessimistic assessments,[136] ITLOS has performed well, particularly in generating a body of jurisprudence on issues relating to prompt release and provisional measures where it has residual compulsory jurisdiction. It has also sought to ensure that it is accessible to all parties to the LOSC. Mindful of the expense of international litigation, a trust fund was established in 2000 by the United Nations Secretary-General to provide assistance to developing states to gain access to justice.[137] The fund mirrors that established for the ICJ in 1989,[138] and was used to assist Guinea-Bissau in the *Juno Trader* case.[139]

---

[131] See LOSC, art 246(6).

[132] Ibid art 297(3)(b).

[133] Robin Churchill, 'The Jurisprudence of the International Tribunal for the Law of the Sea Relating to Fisheries: Is There Much in the Net?' (2007) 22 *International Journal of Marine and Coastal Law* 383, 389.

[134] Tullio Treves, *Le Controversie Internazionali: Nuovi Tendenze, Nuovi Tribunali* (Milan, Giuffre, 1999) 102. See also Gudmundur Eiriksson, *The International Tribunal for the Law of the Sea* (The Hague, Martinus Nijhoff, 2000).

[135] Donald R Rothwell, 'Building on the Strengths and Addressing the Challenges: The Role of Law of the Sea Institutions' (2004) 35 *Ocean Development and International Law* 131, 138.

[136] See, eg, Jillaine Seymour, 'The International Tribunal for the Law of the Sea: A Great Mistake?' (2006) 13 *Indiana Journal of Global Legal Studies* 1.

[137] UNGA Resolution 55/7 (2000). For discussion see Charles Claypoole, 'Access to International Justice: A Review of the Trust Funds Available for Law of the Sea-Related Disputes' (2008) 23 *International Journal of Marine and Coastal Law* 77, 90–92.

[138] 'Secretary-General's Trust Fund to Assist States in the Settlement of Disputes through the International Court of Justice', UN Doc A/47/444 (1992).

[139] *Juno Trader (St Vincent and the Grenadines v Guinea-Bissau)* (prompt release) (2004) 44 ILM 498.

ITLOS was established by Annex VI of the LOSC, which sets out the structure, composition and basic rules of procedure for the operation of the tribunal. The tribunal is composed of 21 independent judges who have 'recognized competence in the field of the law of the sea'.[140] The composition of ITLOS is to be representative of the principal legal systems of the world, and there is to be an equitable geographical distribution.[141] Judges are elected for a term of nine years, with one third of the court retiring every three years.[142] The elections take place at the meeting of the states parties, at which the judges elected will be those nominees who obtain the largest number of votes and a two-thirds majority of the states parties present and voting.[143] At the fifth SPLOS it was decided that an agreed number of judges would be elected to represent each of the five geopolitical regional groupings within the United Nations.[144]

A standing Sea Bed Disputes Chamber within ITLOS, comprising 11 members, was created by Annex VI, Article 14, and possesses a distinctive jurisdiction, including the capacity to provide advisory opinions. ITLOS is also able to form additional chambers, composed of three or more of its elected members, to deal with particular categories of disputes.[145] It can also form a special chamber of three or more judges to deal with a specific dispute, if the parties request this,[146] as occurred in the *Swordfish Stocks* case.[147] The Chambers that ITLOS has established for particular categories of dispute are: the Chamber for Fisheries Disputes, the Chamber for Marine Environment Disputes, the Chamber for Maritime Delimitation Disputes, and the Chamber of Summary Procedure.

The general subject matter jurisdiction of ITLOS is essentially of two types. The first is with respect to disputes and applications submitted in accordance with the LOSC. The second is with respect to 'all matters specifically provided for in any other agreement which confers jurisdiction upon the Tribunal'.[148] Subject to agreement of the parties, this jurisdiction can also be extended to treaties or conventions that predate the LOSC with respect to disputes 'concerning the interpretation or application of such treaty or convention'.[149] Although ITLOS does not have a general advisory jurisdiction, it was on this basis in 2015 that ITLOS in plenary handed down its first Advisory Opinion following a request made under Article 33 of the 2012 Convention on the Determination of the Minimal Conditions for Access and Exploitation of Marine Resources within the Maritime Areas under Jurisdiction of the Member States of the Sub-Regional Fisheries Commission (MCA Convention).[150]

---

[140] LOSC, annex VI, art 2(1).

[141] Ibid annex VI, art 2(2).

[142] Ibid annex VI, arts 4 and 5.

[143] Ibid annex VI, art 4(4).

[144] Churchill, 'Dispute Settlement under the UN Convention on the Law of the Sea: Survey for 2008' (n 95) 605.

[145] LOSC, annex VI, art 15(1).

[146] Ibid annex VI, art 15(2).

[147] *Conservation and Sustainable Exploitation of Swordfish Stocks in the South-Eastern Pacific Ocean (Chile/European Community)* (removed from docket 17 December 2009) www.itlos.org.

[148] LOSC, annex V, art 21.

[149] Ibid annex VI, art 22.

[150] *Request for an Advisory Opinion submitted by the Sub-Regional Fisheries Commission (SRFC)* (Advisory Opinion) 2 April 2015 www.itlos.org (*SRFC Advisory Opinion*).

Article 138(1) of the ITLOS Rules[151] provides that '[t]he Tribunal may give an advisory opinion if an international agreement related to the purposes of [the LOSC] specifically provides for the submission to the Tribunal of a request for such an opinion'. However, the issue of jurisdiction was contentious because neither the LOSC nor the ITLOS Statute makes express reference to ITLOS possessing advisory jurisdiction.[152] Article 288(1) of the LOSC speaks of jurisdiction extending only to a 'dispute concerning the interpretation or application of [the LOSC]'. On the other hand, Article 21 of the ITLOS Statute is cast in more general terms, providing that the jurisdiction of ITLOS 'comprises all disputes and applications submitted to it in accordance with [the LOSC] and all matters specifically provided for in any other agreement which confers jurisdiction on [ITLOS]'.

In the *SRFC Advisory Opinion*, ITLOS unanimously decided that it had jurisdiction to give the Advisory Opinion sought.[153] ITLOS observed that under Article 318 of the LOSC, annexes to the Convention, including the ITLOS Statute (contained in Annex VI), constitute 'an integral part of [the LOSC]'. Therefore the ITLOS Statute has the same legal status as the LOSC, and Article 21 of the statute 'should not be considered as subordinate to article 288 of the Convention'.[154] Article 21 refers to three elements of the tribunal's jurisdiction— over 'disputes', 'applications', and 'matters' provided for in any other agreement. The tribunal found that 'matters' must mean something more than just 'disputes' and must include advisory opinions.[155] The tribunal observed that Article 21 of the ITLOS Statute does not itself establish its advisory jurisdiction—rather it is an enabling provision allowing other agreements to confer jurisdiction.[156]

In terms of its personal jurisdiction, ITLOS is open only to the states and the European Community.[157] As with the ICJ, natural persons and corporations therefore have no standing before the tribunal. However, in relation to disputes over Part XI and the 1994 Implementing Agreement the standing rules are relaxed, so that not only states and the European Community, but also the ISA, the Enterprise, and natural and juridical persons parties to a contract relating to the Area may appear.[158]

Since it commenced operation in 1996, ITLOS has dealt with 19 distinct cases, delivered three judgments and two advisory opinions, and made many prompt release, provisional measures and associated procedural orders. Two cases were removed from the ITLOS docket without substantive orders or a judgment being issued (see Table 18.3). While ITLOS has not been as extensively utilised as was expected at the time of its establishment, when the tribunal's 11 cases during the 2000s is compared with the nine listed matters between 2010 and 2015 there is evidence that the docket is growing. The relatively small number of cases dealt with by ITLOS is reflective of the fact that in respect of two major areas of controversy in the law of the sea—maritime boundaries and EEZ fisheries—states have been

---

[151] Rules of ITLOS, ITLOS/8, March 17, 2009, available at https://www.itlos.org/fileadmin/itlos/documents/basic_texts/Itlos_8_E_17_03_09.pdf.
[152] *SRFC Advisory Opinion*, [40].
[153] *SRFC Advisory Opinion*, [219].
[154] *SRFC Advisory Opinion*, [52].
[155] *SRFC Advisory Opinion*, [56].
[156] *SRFC Advisory Opinion*, [58].
[157] The European Community is an 'international organisation' within the meaning of LOSC, art 305(f) and annex IX, art 1 as an intergovernmental organisation constituted by states to which its members have transferred competence over matters governed by the LOSC.
[158] LOSC, annex VI, art 20.

Table 18.3: Cases brought before the ITLOS

Case No 1: *M/V Saiga (Saint Vincent and the Grenadines v Guinea)* (Prompt Release) (1997)
Case No 2: *M/V Saiga (No 2) (Saint Vincent and the Grenadines v Guinea)* (Provisional Measures) (1998) (Admissibility and Merits) (1999)
Case Nos 3 and 4: *Southern Bluefin Tuna (New Zealand v Japan; Australia v Japan)* (Provisional Measures) (1999)
Case No 5: *Camouco (Panama v France)* (Prompt Release) (2000)
Case No 6: *Monte Confurco (Seychelles v France)* (Prompt Release) (2000)
Case No 7: *Conservation and Sustainable Exploitation of Swordfish Stocks in the South-Eastern Pacific Ocean (Chile/European Community)* (removed from docket 2009)
Case No 8: *Grand Prince (Belize v France)* (Prompt Release) (2001)
Case No 9: *Chaisiri Reefer 2 (Panama v Yemen)* (Prompt Release) (removed from docket 2001)
Case No 10: *MOX Plant (Ireland v United Kingdom)* (Provisional Measures) (2002)
Case No 11: *Volga (Russian Federation v Australia)* (Prompt Release) (2003)
Case No 12: *Land Reclamation by Singapore in and around the Straits of Johor (Malaysia v Singapore)* (Provisional Measures) (2003)
Case No 13: *Juno Trader (St Vincent and the Grenadines v Guinea-Bissau)* (Prompt Release) (2004)
Case No 14: *Hoshinmaru (Japan v Russian Federation)* (Prompt Release) (2007)
Case No. 15: *Tomimaru (Japan v Russian Federation)* (Prompt Release) (2007)
Case No. 16: *Delimitation of the Maritime Boundary between Bangladesh and Myanmar in the Bay of Bengal* (Merits) (2012)
Case No. 17: *Responsibilities and Obligations of States Sponsoring Persons and Entities with Respect to Activities in the Area* (Advisory Opinion request to the Seabed Disputes Chamber) (2011)
Case No. 18: *M/V Louisa (Saint Vincent and the Grenadines v Kingdom of Spain)* (Provisional Measures) (2010) (Merits) (2013)
Case No. 19: *M/V Virginia G (Panama/Guinea-Bissau)* (Merits) (2014)
Case No. 20: *ARA Libertad (Argentina v Ghana)* (Provisional Measures) (2012)

(continued)

Table 18.3: *(Continued)*

Case No 21: *Request for an Advisory Opinion by the Sub-Regional Fisheries Commission (SRFC)* (Advisory Opinion) (2015)
Case No. 22: *Arctic Sunrise (Kingdom of the Netherlands v Russian Federation)* (Provisional Measures) (2013)
Case No. 23: *Dispute Concerning Delimitation of the Maritime Boundary between Ghana and Côte d'Ivoire in the Atlantic Ocean (Ghana/ Côte d'Ivoire)* (Provisional Measures before an ITLOS Special Chamber) (2015) (Merits before an ITLOS Special Chamber) (ongoing in 2015)
Case No. 24: *Enrica Lexie Incident (Italy v India)* (Provisional Measures) (2015)

highly reluctant to confer jurisdiction on ITLOS. In the case of maritime boundaries this is undoubtedly because the ICJ presents itself as the natural forum for resolving such matters, given the pre-eminence of its judges, the long history of its settlement of such cases, and the extensive jurisprudence that it has established on the topic. ITLOS acquired its first maritime boundary dispute in late 2009 in *Delimitation of the Maritime Boundary Between Bangladesh and Myanmar in the Bay of Bengal.*[159] The dispute had initially been submitted to arbitration under Annex VII of the LOSC by Myanmar, but was subsequently brought to ITLOS with the consent of both parties. Neither Bangladesh nor Myanmar had made declarations pursuant to Article 287(1), and hence by operation of Article 287(3) were deemed to accept Annex VII arbitration. For the purpose of referring the matter by joint consent to ITLOS both parties subsequently made declarations under Article 287(1) accepting the jurisdiction of ITLOS.

In *Arctic Sunrise*, ITLOS dealt with its first instance of default of appearance. The Russian Federation did not participate in the proceedings as it was of the view that its Article 298 declaration with respect to law enforcement activities excluded the dispute that had arisen with the Netherlands regarding the boarding and detention of the *Arctic Sunrise* and its crew within the Russian EEZ. Referring to the extensive jurisprudence of the ICJ on the matter, ITLOS was of the view that 'the absence of a party or failure of a party to defend its case does not constitute a bar to the proceedings and does not preclude the Tribunal from prescribing provisional measures, provided that the parties have been given an opportunity of presenting their observations on the subject'.[160] Default of appearance, which is anticipated in Article 28 of Annex V, has been described by Judges Wolfrum and Kelly in their Joint Separate Opinion in *Arctic Sunrise* as 'contrary to the object and purpose of the dispute settlement system under Part XV of the Convention'.[161]

---

[159] *Delimitation of the Maritime Boundary between Bangladesh and Myanmar (Bangladesh/Myanmar)* (judgment) 14 March 2012 www.itlos.org (dispute submitted 14 December 2009).
[160] *Arctic Sunrise (Netherlands v Russian Federation)* (provisional measures) (2014) 53 ILM 607 [48].
[161] Ibid Joint Separate Opinion of Judge Wolfrum and Judge Kelly [6].

E. Annex V Conciliation

Procedures associated with conciliation under the LOSC are to be found in Annex V. Two types of conciliation are provided for. The first, referred to in Section 1 of Annex V, is voluntary conciliation consistent with Article 284, which is located within the general dispute settlement procedures found in Section 1 of Part XV. The second is found in Section 2 of Annex V, and importantly is titled 'Compulsory Submission to Conciliation Procedure Pursuant to Section 3 of Part XV'. To date, there are no recorded instances of the LOSC conciliation mechanisms having been applied. The procedures outlined in Section 2 deal with the particular dynamics of compulsory conciliation and address the institution of proceedings,[162] the failure to reply or to submit to conciliation[163] and the competence of the conciliation commission.[164] In sum, it is made clear that conciliation is a compulsory procedure that can arise under Article 298(1)(a) and that, once commenced, the other party to the dispute 'shall be obliged to submit to such proceedings'.[165] Failure on the part of one of the parties to submit to the proceedings is not a bar to the proceedings,[166] though it is clear in Article 13 that the competence of the conciliation commission may be challenged. Such a challenge could arise on the grounds that the dispute arose prior to the entry into force of the LOSC, that a reasonable period of time had not been allowed to pass prior to the commencement of proceedings or that the dispute was one that concurrently involved consideration of a land dispute.

Other than these distinctive features of Section 2, Annex V, conciliation commenced under Article 298(1)(a) proceeds under the general conciliation procedures laid down in Articles 2–10 of Annex V.[167] A feature of these procedures is flexibility, including the manner in which the procedure to be adopted by the conciliation commission is agreed upon,[168] which extends to whether oral or written submissions are received, and the capacity of the commission to 'draw the attention of the parties to any measures which might facilitate an amicable settlement of the dispute'.[169] Reaching an amicable settlement is further reinforced in Article 6 of Annex V, which makes clear that the functions of the Commission are to 'hear the parties, examine their claims and objections, and make proposals to the parties with a view to reaching an amicable settlement'. The final matter of procedural significance is that the conciliation commission is to report within 12 months of its constitution.[170] The report is to be deposited with the Secretary-General of the United Nations, who is to transmit the report to the parties.[171]

---

[162] LOSC, Annex V, art 11.
[163] Ibid Annex V, art 12.
[164] Ibid Annex V, art 13.
[165] Ibid Annex V, art 11 (2); the *Virginia Commentaries*, vol 5, 326 [A.V.33] observe that 'Through this unilateral institution of proceedings and this obligation to submit to the procedure, a much more thorough system of conciliation than is found in earlier conventions has been created, especially with regard to the obligatory submission of disputes to the conciliation process'.
[166] LOSC, Annex V, art 12.
[167] Ibid Annex V, art 14.
[168] Ibid Annex V, art 4.
[169] Ibid Annex V, art 5.
[170] Ibid Annex V, art 7(1).
[171] Ibid.

The general procedures with respect to conciliation are varied in an instance of compulsory conciliation arising under Article 298(1)(a) once the commission's report has been presented. Whereas Article 7(2) of Annex V makes clear that the report of the commission is not binding upon the parties, Article 298(1)(a)(ii) provides that upon presentation of the conciliation report, 'the parties shall negotiate an agreement on the basis of that report', thereby suggesting some level of compulsion on the part of the disputing parties to engage with the commission report in good faith.[172] In the absence of such an agreement being reached, the parties are to mutually submit the dispute[173] to one of the procedures provided for under Part XV, Section 2, unless they agree otherwise.[174]

The consequence of these procedures is that the parties are given every incentive to either endorse the report of the conciliation commission or negotiate a settlement of the dispute on the basis of the report. Failure to reach such an agreement will then see the fundamental dispute settlement provisions of Part XV, Section 2 activated, with the consequence that the state that originally lodged an Article 298 declaration so as to exempt a dispute with respect to maritime boundaries, historic bays or titles from Section 2 procedures will eventually be forced to engage in those procedures if it has been unwilling to settle the dispute through Annex V conciliation. This raises for consideration where conciliation has at face value failed to settle the dispute, and once Section 2 procedures have been activated how the 'mutual consent' of the parties could in these circumstances be determined.[175] One view could be that such consent needs to be reached by separate agreement to refer the matter to a Section 2 court or tribunal. In the *Virginia Commentaries* it is observed, with respect to Article 298, that:

> In case no substantive agreement is reached through such negotiations, there is also the further obligation to at least try to reach an agreement to select one of the procedures under Part XV, section 2, or some other procedure for settling the dispute. This agreement must also be negotiated in good faith, but can come into effect only by mutual consent.[176]

A critical procedural issue that arises is how 'mutual consent' is attained, and whether this is consent which is specific to the dispute in question or consent that may previously have been given by the parties. The fact that 'consent' and not 'agreement' is referred to in Article 298(1)(a)(ii) is significant. As such, it should be possible to refer to where the parties have mutually given their consent to resolve the dispute in either a general or specific context. The better view would therefore be that in the absence of the parties mutually agreeing between themselves to utilise one of the Part XV, Section 2 courts and tribunals, the default would become arbitration in accordance with Annex VII, consistent with the default procedures reflected in Article 287. Here 'mutual consent' could properly be identified through

---

[172] Tullio Treves, 'What have the United Nations Convention and the International Tribunal for the Law of the Sea to offer as regards Maritime Delimitation Disputes?' in Rainer Lagoni and Daniel Vignes (eds), *Maritime Delimitation* (Leiden, Martinus Nijhoff, 2006) 63, 76 refers to the 'pressure' upon the states to settle their dispute arising from these procedures. It is observed that 'the pressure on the State that is not ready to follow the recommendations is great'.

[173] LOSC, art 298(1)(a)(ii) uses the term 'question', which in context is taken to have the same meaning as 'dispute'.

[174] A further exception to these procedures applies in the case of a 'sea boundary dispute' settled by an arrangement between the parties, or by a bilateral or multilateral agreement binding upon the parties.

[175] See LOSC, art 298(1)(a)(ii).

[176] *Virginia Commentaries*, vol 5, 134 [298.31].

the consent of a state becoming a LOSC party, by which that state agrees to become subject to the Part XV procedures with respect to dispute settlement, including the compulsory procedures found in Section 2. Under those procedures, while Article 287 provides for a choice of procedure, in the absence of a state having made a choice by way of a declaration, the default procedure is Annex VII arbitration.[177] Likewise, if the two disputing states have not accepted the same procedure, then the default once again becomes Annex VII arbitration.[178]

F. Annex VII Arbitration

Given the history of arbitration as a means of dispute settlement in international law, including law of the sea disputes,[179] it is not surprising that specific reference is made in Part XV, Section 2 to arbitration mechanisms for the compulsory resolution of law of the sea disputes. Article 287 provides for two types of arbitral tribunals: an Annex VII arbitral tribunal, which, subject to the choice of procedure by the parties, has similar subject matter jurisdiction to ITLOS or the ICJ; and an Annex VIII special arbitral tribunalm which has a more limited jurisdictional scope. Annex VII arbitral tribunals have proven to be popular amongst states, with ten arbitrations having been commenced between 2010 and 2015. As can be seen in Table 18.4, some arbitral proceedings were discontinued because the matters were settled, or proceedings originally instituted before an Annex VII arbitral tribunal were discontinued and then referred by special agreement between the parties to an ITLOS Special Chamber.[180] There has also developed a trend whereby states instituting proceedings before an Annex VII arbitral tribunal have sought provisional measures before ITLOS pending constitution of the tribunal under the mechanisms provided for in Article 290. While this approach allows applicant states to urgently seek provisional measures before ITLOS as a standing institution, as was highlighted in *Southern Bluefin Tuna*, there remains the potential for ITLOS and a separately constituted Annex VII arbitral tribunal to come to differing views as to jurisdiction. The by-product of these procedures is that ITLOS and Annex VII arbitral tribunals from time to time judicially interact during different phases of proceedings that have been separately instituted.

The jurisdiction of Annex VII arbitral tribunals is as noted above, and accordingly much of the substance of Annex VII concerns how the tribunal is formed, the appointment of arbitrators, general matters of procedure and the award. As the tribunal is ad hoc, a critical aspect of Annex VII is the constitution of the tribunal, which is provided for in Article 3. An Annex VII arbitral tribunal will generally comprise five members,[181]

---

[177] LOSC, art 287(3).

[178] Ibid art 287(5).

[179] As highlighted in maritime boundary disputes; see generally ch 16.

[180] See eg *Dispute Concerning Delimitation of the Maritime Boundary between Ghana and Côte D'Ivoire in the Atlantic Coast (Ghana/Côte D'Ivoire)* (provisional measures) 25 April 2015 www.itlos.org.

[181] LOSC, Annex VII art 3(a); in 2013, in *Duzgit Integrity (Malta v São Tomé and Principe)*, the parties agreed to a three member Annex VII arbitral tribunal, applying the provisions of art 3 *mutatis mutandis*; the President of ITLOS was involved in appointing two of the arbitrators: 'Press Release: Two Arbitrators Appointed in the Arbitral Proceedings Instituted by the Republic of Malta against the Democratic Republic of Sao Tome and Principe in Respect of a Dispute Concerning the Vessel *Duzgit Integrity*', ITLOS/Press 209 (18 March 2014) www.itlos.org.

Table 18.4: Cases brought before an Annex VII arbitral tribunal

M/V Saiga (No 2) (Saint Vincent and the Grenadines v Guinea) (discontinued and transferred to ITLOS 1998)
Southern Bluefin Tuna (Australia and New Zealand v Japan) (Jurisdiction and Admissibility) (2000)
MOX Plant (Ireland v United Kingdom) (Suspension of Proceedings on Jurisdiction and Merits and Request for Further Provisional Measures) (case withdrawn 2008)
Land Reclamation by Singapore in and Around the Straits of Johor (Malaysia v Singapore) (case settled 2005)
Barbados v Trinidad and Tobago (2006)
Guyana/Suriname Arbitration (2007)
Delimitation of the Maritime Boundary between Bangladesh and Myanmar in the Bay of Bengal (discontinued and transferred to ITLOS 2009)
ARA Libertad (Argentina v Ghana) (case settled 2013)
M/V Virginia G (Panama/Guinea-Bissau) (discontinued 2011)
Bay of Bengal Maritime Boundary (Bangladesh v India) (2014)
Dispute Concerning Delimitation of the Maritime Boundary between the Republic of Ghana and the Republic of Côte D'Ivoire (Ghana/Côte D'Ivoire) (discontinued and transferred to ITLOS 2014)
Atlanto-Scandian Herring (Denmark v European Union) (case settled 2014)
Chagos Marine Protected Area (Mauritius v United Kingdom) (2015)
Arctic Sunrise (Netherlands v Russian Federation) (2015)
South China Sea (Republic of Philippines v People's Republic of China) (proceedings ongoing)
Duzgit Integrity (Malta v São Tomé and Príncipe) (proceedings ongoing)
Enrica Lexie Incident (Italy v India) (proceedings ongoing)

who will preferably be chosen from a list of arbitrators drawn up and maintained by the Secretary-General of the United Nations.[182] Each party is entitled to appoint one member of the tribunal, with the other three members to be appointed by agreement between the parties. A default procedure exists whereby the President of ITLOS can make the necessary appointments.[183]

Once constituted, an Annex VII arbitral tribunal can determine its own procedure unless otherwise agreed by the parties.[184] The parties are to facilitate the work of the tribunal[185] and, unless otherwise decided by the tribunal, the expenses of the tribunal are to be borne equally by the parties.[186] Decisions of the tribunal are to be taken by a majority vote, with the president having a casting vote.[187] The award is final and without appeal, and is to be complied with by the parties.[188] Any subsequent controversy regarding the interpretation or manner of implementation of the award may be submitted to the arbitral tribunal for decision, or to another Article 287 court or tribunal.[189]

One of the most significant Annex VII arbitrations is the 2013 claim by the Philippines against China with respect to a dispute over the South China Sea,[190] which raised a number of jurisdictional and procedural issues. The first related to China's acceptance of the jurisdiction of the tribunal to hear and determine the Philippines claim. In 2006 China made an Article 298 declaration indicating that it did not accept any of the procedures for dispute resolution referred to in Article 298(1), which includes disputes with respect to 'historic bays or titles'.[191] This raised issues as to whether elements of the Philippines dispute with China in the South China Sea fell within this exception, including what precisely are the historic titles that China asserts in the South China Sea.[192] The second issue was that on 19 February 2013 China indicated that it would not participate in the proceedings.[193] This position would appear to be based upon China's view that, consistent with its Article 298 declaration, the Annex VII tribunal lacks jurisdiction. On 1 August 2013 China submitted a *note verbale* to the Permanent Court of Arbitration, which acted as registry for the proceedings, indicating that 'it does not accept the arbitration initiated by the Philippines' and that it will not be participating in the proceedings.[194] However, Annex VII of the

[182] Ibid Annex VII, art 2; each state party to the LOSC is entitled to nominate up to four arbitrators, 'each of whom shall be a person experienced in maritime affairs and enjoying the highest reputation for fairness, competence and integrity'.

[183] This procedure was utilised in the *South China Sea (Republic of Philippines v People's Republic of China)* Annex VII arbitration after China refused to participate in the proceedings; see 'Press Release: Arbitrators Appointed in the Arbitral Proceedings Instituted by the Republic of the Philippines against the People's Republic of China', ITLOS/Press 191 (25 April 2013) www.itlos.org.

[184] LOSC, Annex VII, art 5.
[185] Ibid Annex VII, art 6.
[186] Ibid Annex VII, art 7.
[187] Ibid Annex VII, art 8.
[188] Ibid Annex VII, art 11.
[189] Ibid Annex VII, art 12.
[190] Republic of the Philippines, *Notification and Statement of Claim* (22 January 2013).
[191] China: Declaration made after ratification (25 August 2006) at www.un.org/Depts/los/convention_agreements/convention_declarations.htm.
[192] See discussion in Zhiguo Gao and Bing Bing Jia, 'The Nine-Dash Line in the South China Sea: History, Status, and Implications' (2013) 107 *AJIL* 98, 113–15, 121–22; Florian Dupuy and Pierre-Marie Dupuy, 'A Legal Analysis of China's Historic Rights Claim in the South China Sea' (2013) 107 *AJIL* 124.
[193] Permanent Court of Arbitration, *The Republic of the Philippines v The People's Republic of China* (2013).
[194] Ibid.

LOSC contains procedures whereby if one of the parties chooses to not participate in the proceedings, an arbitral tribunal can nevertheless be constituted and proceed to a hearing of the application.[195] In this instance, the Annex VII arbitral tribunal will need to make a determination that it possesses jurisdiction over the dispute, and also that the claim is 'well founded' in both fact and law.[196] The Philippines filed its memorial in this case on 30 March 2014. On 3 June 2014 the arbitral tribunal issued its Procedural Order No 2, in which it fixed 15 December 2014 as the date by which China was to submit its counter-memorial responding to the Philippines' memorial. On 21 May 2014, China submitted a note to the Permanent Court of Arbitration in which it restated its position that 'it does not accept the arbitration initiated by the Philippines'.[197] In July 2015 the Annex VII arbitral tribunal commenced its hearing of the Philippines' claim in the absence of China.

G. Annex VIII Special Arbitration

Annex VIII provides for a special arbitration tribunal which, consistent with Article 287, has limited jurisdiction to deal with disputes regarding the 'interpretation or application' of LOSC articles with respect to fisheries, protection of the marine environment, marine scientific research and navigation, including pollution from vessels and by dumping.[198] The general procedures of an Annex VIII special arbitration duplicate those of Annex VII arbitration, and this is reflected in Articles 4 to 13 of Annex VII applying *mutatis mutandis* to Annex VIII.[199] There are, however, three significant differences between arbitration under Annex VII and Annex VIII. The first is that a special arbitral tribunal is to comprise five members, of which the parties to the dispute can each choose two members, one of whom can be its national.[200] The parties jointly appoint the tribunal president, unless they are unable to reach an agreement, in which case the appointment is made by the Secretary-General of the United Nations.[201] The second is that the arbitrators are preferably to be appointed from a list of experts, of which four lists have been established reflecting the distinct areas of specialised jurisdiction exercised by the special arbitral tribunal.[202] Each LOSC state party may nominate two experts in each of the four fields, including not only legal experts but also those with competence in 'scientific or technical aspects' of the field.[203] The third distinctive aspect is that the special arbitral tribunal also has competence to undertake fact finding upon the request of the parties.[204] This is the only example in Part XV of the LOSC where an institution is given specific competence to undertake fact finding, the outcome of which will be considered to be conclusive unless otherwise agreed to by the parties.[205] As at 1 July 2015, no disputes had been referred to an Annex VIII special arbitral tribunal.

[195]   LOSC, Annex VII, arts 3, 9.
[196]   Ibid Annex VII, art 9.
[197]   Permanent Court of Arbitration, 'Press Release: Arbitration between the Republic of the Philippines and the People's Republic of China' (3 June 2014).
[198]   LOSC, Annex VIII, art 1.
[199]   Ibid Annex VIII, art 4.
[200]   Ibid Annex VIII, art 3.
[201]   Ibid Annex VIII, art 3(e).
[202]   Ibid Annex VIII, art 2.
[203]   Ibid Annex VIII, art 2(3).
[204]   Ibid Annex VIII, art 5.
[205]   Ibid Annex VIII, art 5(2).

V. Further Reading

AO Adede, *The System for Settlement of Disputes Under the United Nations Convention on the Law of the Sea* (Dordrecht, Martinus Nijhoff, 1987)

Alan E Boyle, 'Dispute Settlement and the Law of the Sea Convention: Problems of Fragmentation and Jurisdiction' (1997) 46 *International and Comparative Law Quarterly* 37

Gudmundur Eiriksson, *The International Tribunal for the Law of the Sea* (The Hague, Martinus Nijhoff, 2000)

Natalie Klein, *Dispute Settlement in the UN Convention on the Law of the Sea* (Cambridge, Cambridge University Press, 2005)

John Merrills, *International Dispute Settlement*, 5th edn (Cambridge, Cambridge University Press, 2011)

Bernard H Oxman, 'Courts and Tribunals: The ICJ, ITLOS, and Arbitral Tribunals' in Donald R Rothwell, Alex G Oude Elferink, Karen N Scott and Tim Stephens (eds), *The Oxford Handbook of the Law of the Sea* (Oxford, Oxford University Press, 2015) 394

19

Oceans Governance

I. Introduction

The Preamble to the LOSC acknowledges that 'the problems of ocean space are closely interrelated and need to be considered as a whole'. This entreaty to manage oceans issues in an integrated and coordinated manner is at the heart of 'oceans governance', an approach to oceans management that has gained increasing currency in the law of the sea in recent decades.[1] This is in recognition of the reality that many contemporary ocean threats, particularly environmental pressures such as overfishing and pollution, are difficult or impossible to resolve via the traditional issue-by-issue and zone-by-zone approach to oceans management.[2] Under that model, the hallmark of the law of the sea throughout most of its history and reflective of the Westphalian conception of state sovereignty,[3] oceans management is demarcated according to jurisdictional authority and the specific subject matter of concern. This chapter examines the important ways in which this approach has been challenged and replaced by 'integrated oceans management' in the LOSC era at national, regional and global scales.

Although the LOSC makes no mention of 'oceans governance', the Convention provided a vitally important legal framework to enable the shift from a sovereign-rights and issue-specific perspective to an integrated approach to oceans management. In large part this is because, as Allott has observed, there are considerable areas of mediation between 'all-power' and 'all-freedom' in the maritime zones recognised or established by the LOSC.[4] In the early law of the sea, ocean space was divided into a multitude of areas under national jurisdiction, where individual states enjoyed exclusive or primary rights, and areas beyond national jurisdiction, where states enjoyed unencumbered freedoms consistent with the Grotian vision of the *mare liberum*. By contrast, the LOSC introduced a new regime in which the 'shared zone has now become the rule rather than the exception'.[5]

---

[1] See, eg, Jon M Van Dyke, Durwood Zaelke and Grant Hewison (eds), *Freedom for the Seas in the 21st Century: Ocean Governance and Environmental Harmony* (Washington DC, Island Press, 1993); Marcus Haward and Joanna Vince, *Oceans Governance in the Twenty-First Century: Managing the Blue Planet* (Cheltenham, Edward Elgar, 2008); Karen N Scott, 'Integrated Oceans Management: A New Frontier in Marine Environmental Protection' in Donald R Rothwell, Alex G Oude Elferink, Karen N Scott and Tim Stephens (eds), *The Oxford Handbook of the Law of the Sea* (Oxford, Oxford University Press, 2015) 463.

[2] Donald R Rothwell and David L VanderZwaag, 'The Sea Change Towards Principled Oceans Governance' in Donald R Rothwell and David L VanderZwaag (eds), *Towards Principled Oceans Governance: Australian and Canadian Approaches and Challenges* (London, Routledge, 2006), 3.

[3] Douglas M Johnston, 'The Challenge of International Ocean Governance: Institutional, Ethical and Conceptual Dilemmas' in Rothwell and VanderZwaag, *Towards Principled Oceans Governance*, ibid 350–51.

[4] Philip Allott, '*Mare Nostrum*: A New International Law of the Sea' (1992) 86 *AJIL* 764, 767.

[5] Ibid.

With the exception of internal waters, the LOSC's regulation of all maritime zones is built upon fundamental duties of cooperation between states in order to balance competing ocean uses, and to achieve common objectives. As a result, Allott argues, the oceans must now be regarded as neither *mare liberum* nor *mare clausum*, but instead as *mare nostrum*.[6] With all sea areas, including the territorial sea and the high seas, conceived as 'an area of power and interest shared by two or more state systems'[7] the law of the sea has become less a matter of apportioning rights between rivalrous sovereign states, and instead 'an inextricably complex systemic interaction of science, technology, economics and human values that cannot be organized simply by occasional text-centred lawmaking'.[8]

II. The Concept of Oceans Governance

A. Oceans Governance Defined

The disaggregated character of authority in the international legal system, and the transboundary nature of most oceans issues, means that oceans 'governance' must be clearly distinguished from oceans 'government'. Government entails the making and enforcement of decisions by a centralised formal authority, something clearly absent from the international system, whereas governance, in the international context, connotes a process in which there is cooperation by states and other actors to achieve desired objectives.[9] Oceans governance may therefore be described as those formal and informal rules, arrangements, institutions and concepts which structure the ways in which sea space is used, how ocean problems are monitored and assessed, what activities are permitted or prohibited, and how sanctions and other responses are applied.[10] It is therefore a broad conception of oceans management, implicating an array of global and regional organisations,[11] directed at 'integrat[ing] the management of activities that impact upon or affect the oceans across sectors, space and time under a unified over-arching vision'.[12]

B. The Ecosystem Approach and Area-Based Management

The starting point for effective oceans governance is the identification of an appropriate scale of management. In this respect, the ecosystem paradigm has become the dominant

---

[6] Ibid 773.

[7] Ibid 785.

[8] Ibid 782.

[9] Johnston, 'The Challenge of International Ocean Governance' (n 3) 349. For a critique of the use of the governance concept see Martti Koskenniemi, 'International Legislation Today: Limits and Possibilities' (2005) 23 *Wisconsin International Law Journal* 61, 74.

[10] Lawrence Juda and Timothy Hennessey, 'Governance Profiles and the Management of the Uses of Large Marine Ecosystems' (2001) 32 *Ocean Development and International Law* 43, 44.

[11] Louise de La Fayette, 'The Role of the United Nations in International Oceans Governance' in David Freestone, Richard Barnes and David M Ong (eds), *The Law of the Sea: Progress and Prospects* (Oxford, Oxford University Press, 2006) 63.

[12] Scott, 'Integrated Oceans Management' (n 1), 465.

frame of reference,[13] and the 'ecosystem approach' has been increasingly incorporated into fisheries and other law of the sea treaties since its pioneering use in the 1980 Convention on the Conservation of Antarctic Marine Living Resources.[14] The ecosystem approach functions only when the relevant biogeographic area selected for management effectively encompasses the living and non-living components that are closely interrelated within a marine area. An example of the growing sophistication of the ecosystem approach is the Large Marine Ecosystem (LME) concept. In the 1980s the LME was proposed by the marine science community as a way of identifying major ocean ecosystems for the purposes of more effective ocean use management.[15] LMEs are large areas, approximately 200,000 square kilometres or larger, that are adjacent to the continents in coastal waters where primary productivity is generally higher than the open ocean. Around 80 per cent of the world's wild fisheries catches are taken from LMEs each year, and many LMEs are facing a range of environmental problems, including coastal ocean pollution, habitat degradation and biodiversity loss.

Two central features define the LME approach to managing marine areas. First, the boundaries of LMEs are based on ecological criteria, rather than being drawn according to legal, political or economic factors. These four ecological criteria are: (i) bathymetry; (ii) hydrography; (iii) productivity; and (iv) trophic (that is nutrient) relationships. On the basis of these, 64 distinct LMEs have been identified on the coastal margins of the Atlantic, Pacific and Indian Oceans (see Figure 19.1, below). The second aspect of the LME concept is that it calls for a five-module approach for monitoring LMEs, and formulating management plans. These are concerned with (i) productivity and oceanography; (ii) fish and fisheries; (iii) pollution and ecosystem health; (iv) socioeconomics; and (v) governance.[16] The LME approach received strong support from the 79 states that adopted the Manado Ocean Declaration,[17] a non-binding commitment to address common oceans challenges that was adopted at the 2009 World Ocean Conference in Indonesia. While it is only one approach among several for dividing the world's oceans according to ecological boundaries,[18] and the concept of the ecosystem is susceptible to upwards of 40 definitions,[19] the LME has been particularly influential, and forms the basis of practical measures to improve marine management such as several projects financed by the Global Environment Facility.[20]

[13] Juda and Hennessey, 'Governance Profiles' (n 10) 43.
[14] See further ch 15.
[15] Lewis M Alexander, 'Large Marine Ecosystems: A New Focus for Marine Resources Management' (1993) 17 *Marine Policy* 186. See further K Sherman and G Hempel (eds), *The UNEP Large Marine Ecosystem Report: A Perspective on Changing Conditions in LMEs of the World's Regional Seas* (Nairobi, UNEP, 2008) and Timothy M Hennessey and Jon G Sutinen (eds), *Sustaining Large Marine Ecosystems: The Human Dimension* (San Diego, Elsevier, 2005).
[16] Juda and Hennessey, 'Governance Profiles' (n 10) 44.
[17] 2009 Manado Ocean Declaration at www.cep.unep.org/news-and-events/manado-ocean-declaration/at_download/file, [16].
[18] See, eg, the 232 marine ecoregions identified by the WWF and the Nature Conservancy.
[19] Bruce G Hatcher and Roger H Bradbury, 'Marine Ecosystem Management: Is the Whole Greater Than the Sum of the Parts?' in Rothwell and VanderZwaag, *Towards Principled Oceans Governance* (n 2) 205, 208.
[20] See, eg, the GEF, UNEP and World Bank supported Strategic Partnership for the Mediterranean Sea Large Marine Ecosystem approved in 2007: www.medsp.org.

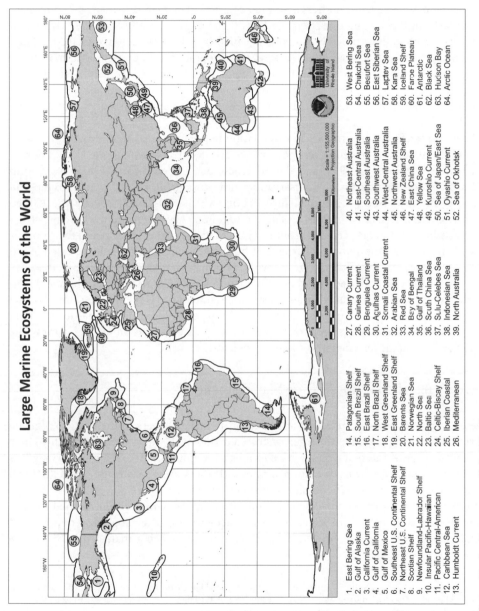

Figure 19.1: Large Marine Ecosystems of the World

Because LMEs are confined to marine areas of continental margins, they have limited relevance for the management of high seas areas. High seas governance has proceeded on its own distinctive and generally more limited basis because of its character as an open access regime. However, it is increasingly well-recognised that more integrated and formalised arrangements are needed to address a number of interlinked high seas management issues, particularly the threat to biodiversity posed by overfishing as operators have been displaced from fishing grounds within EEZs, many of which have become better managed.[21] High seas management is fractured along sectoral and geographical lines, with a large number of treaties and regimes under the IMO and regional fisheries management organisations (RFMOs), which do not cover all high seas areas and are subject to limited coordination, all having a role to play.[22] Additionally, the FSA does not apply to fish stocks found on the high seas alone.

There is therefore a 'governance gap' in relation to the high seas. Significant efforts have been made to develop new high seas governance arrangements through the UNICPOLOS, which was established in 1999, and the Ad Hoc Open-Ended Informal Working Group to Study Issues Relating to the Conservation and Sustainable Use of Marine Biological Diversity in Areas Beyond National Jurisdiction, which was established by the United Nations General Assembly in 2004.[23] These discussions have seen the resurfacing of the long-standing tension between an absolutist Grotian vision of the free seas and the communitarian notion that the common heritage of humankind principle should be extended to address marine living resources in areas beyond national jurisdiction. The discussions have now come to a head, with the United Nations General Assembly resolving, in June 2015, 'to develop an international legally-binding instrument under the [LOSC] on the conservation and sustainable use of marine biological diversity of areas beyond national jurisdiction' and, to this end, to establish a preparatory committee to meet in 2016 and 2017 prior to the holding of an intergovernmental conference thereafter.[24]

C. Area-Based Tools for Marine Management

The ecosystem approach directs the attention of oceans managers to the need to regulate marine uses having regard to the interconnected reality of the marine environment. There are now a range of interrelated area-based management tools that assist in achieving this objective, including marine spatial planning (MSP), marine protected areas (MPAs), MARPOL special areas and PSSAs, and world heritage sites.

MSP is a public process for assessing and allocating activities within defined marine areas, usually at an ecosystem scale, in order to achieve desired ecological, economic and social objectives.[25] Depending on the maritime area that is being managed, MSP can be

---

[21] Rosemary Rayfuse and Robin Warner, 'Securing a Sustainable Future for the Oceans Beyond National Jurisdiction: The Legal Basis for an Integrated Cross-Sectoral Regime for High Seas Governance for the 21st Century' (2008) 23 *International Journal of Marine and Coastal Law* 399.

[22] Ibid 402.

[23] UNGA Resolution 59/24 (2004), [73].

[24] UN Doc A/69/L/65 (2015).

[25] Frank Maes, 'The International Legal Framework for Marine Spatial Planning' (2008) 32 *Marine Policy* 797, 798.

implemented by one or several national authorities, and involves a step-by-step approach to planning by taking into account possible competition between the variety of actual and potential human uses of the marine environment. It involves the gathering of information through the use of geographical information systems and other mechanisms, and a systemic planning process to ensure the long-term health of marine ecosystems.[26]

There are around 120,000 terrestrial protected areas, accounting for over 12 per cent of the Earth's land surface.[27] By contrast, MPAs are much more limited in coverage, extending over only 2.8 per cent of the global ocean.[28] Around 10 per cent of the area of territorial seas, five per cent of 200 nm zones and just 0.12 per cent of the high seas are included within MPAs.[29] MPAs, particularly of biologically rich zones such as coral reefs, are recognised for delivering multiple ecological, social and economic benefits, including building resilience against the negative impacts of climate change.[30] The 2009 Manado Ocean Declaration emphasised the importance of MPAs, with states resolving 'to further establish and effectively manage marine protected areas, including representative resilient networks, in accordance with international law, as reflected in [the LOSC], and on the basis of the best available science, recognizing the importance of their contribution to ecosystem goods and services, and to contribute to the effort to conserve biodiversity, sustainable livelihoods and to adapt to climate change'.[31]

In 2010, the CBD adopted a number of biodiversity targets, including to ensure that, by 2020,

> 10 per cent of coastal and marine areas, especially areas of particular importance for biodiversity and ecosystem services, are conserved through effectively and equitably managed, ecologically representative and well connected systems of protected areas and other effective area-based conservation measures.[32]

Previously, in 2008, the CBD had adopted a decision on marine and coastal biodiversity that set out scientific criteria for identifying areas that require protection.[33] Such networks are being established on a national and regional basis by individual states and groups of states.

National examples include Australia's representative system of MPAs, and the United Kingdom's Marine and Coastal Access Act 2009 which sets out the legal basis for the designation of Marine Conservation Zones in United Kingdom waters. The United Kingdom's declaration of an MPA around the Chagos Archipelago in 2010 was at issue *In the Matter of the Chagos Marine Protected Area*,[34] commenced by Mauritius under Part XV of the

---

[26] See further Charles Ehler and Fanny Douvere, *Marine Spatial Planning: A Step-by-Step Approach Towards Ecosystem-Based Management*, Intergovernmental Oceanographic Manual and Guide No 53 (Paris, UNESCO, 2009).

[27] L Coad et al, *State of the World's Protected Areas 2007: An Annual Review of Global Conservation Progress* (Cambridge, UNEP-WCMC, 2008) 17.

[28] UNEP World Conservation Monitoring Centre, Official MPA Map at www.protectplanetocean.org/official_mpa_map.

[29] Coad et al, *State of the World's Protected Areas 2007* (n 27), 27.

[30] See 2008 Valencia Declaration of the World Congress of Marine Biodiversity; Jorge A Angulo-Valdés and Bruce G Hatcher, 'A New Typology of Benefits Derived from Marine Protected Areas' (2010) 34 *Marine Policy* 635.

[31] 2009 Manado Ocean Declaration, [15].

[32] Decision X/2, UN Doc UNEP/CBD/COP/DEC/X/2 (2010).

[33] Decision IX/20, UN Doc UNEP/CBD/COP/DEC/IX/20 (2008).

[34] *In the Matter of the Chagos Marine Protected Area Arbitration (Mauritius v United Kingdom)* (18 March 2015) www.pca-cpa.org.

LOSC. Mauritius contended that the United Kingdom was not entitled to declare the MPA as it was not the coastal state having sovereignty over the Chagos Archipelago, and was incompatible with fishing and other rights enjoyed by Mauritius under the LOSC. When Mauritius became independent from the United Kingdom in 1965 the Chagos Archipelago was detached from Mauritius and retained under British control in order to accommodate the presence of a large United States defence facility on Diego Garcia, the largest island of the archipelago. The tribunal was careful to avoid ruling on the issue of sovereignty over the Chagos Archipelago, or on the merits of the MPA itself (it advanced 'no view on the substantive quality or nature of the MPA or on the importance of environmental protection').[35] Instead, the decision turned on the effect of undertakings given by the United Kingdom, which the tribunal found were legally binding, to respect the rights of Mauritius in the territorial sea and EEZ of the Chagos Archipelago. The tribunal concluded that in establishing the MPA, the United Kingdom failed to have due regard for Mauritius' rights, as required by Articles 2(3), 56(2) and 194 of the LOSC, because it did not conduct meaningful consultations with Mauritius and had 'failed properly to balance its own rights and interests with Mauritius' rights arising from [the undertakings]'.[36]

In addition to national level MPAs, there are also examples of multilateral MPAs established in several ocean regions, including on the high seas. These include the network of over 300 MPAs established within the area of operation of the OSPAR Convention, including six high seas MPAs.[37] Another regional example is seen in the Southern Ocean, under the auspices of CCAMLR. In 2009 the CCAMLR Commission established a high seas MPA surrounding the South Orkney Islands and covering around 94,000 square kilometres.[38] In 2011 the Commission adopted a 'general framework' for the creation of CCAMLR MPAs, which elaborates criteria for designating MPAs, including the protection of ecosystems, species and habitats.[39] There has been progress in identifying appropriate areas for protection, with New Zealand and the United States proposing an MPA in the Ross Sea, and Australia, France and the European Union proposing seven areas adjoining Eastern Antarctica. However, these proposals have not been accepted and implemented by the Commission to date. Several CCAMLR Commission members, notably China and Russia, have questioned the scientific basis of the proposals, and whether the boundaries of the MPAs accurately reflect the distribution of ecosystems and biotypes,[40] and have even argued that it is beyond the competence of the CCAMLR Commission to establish MPAs.[41]

Under the auspices of the IMO a number of 'special areas' and PSSAs have been designated, having regard to the need for a special or higher level of protection from pollution from shipping. Under MARPOL, Annex I (relating to oil), Annex II (relating to other noxious substances) and Annex V (relating to garbage), certain sea areas may be defined as 'special areas' requiring the adoption of mandatory methods for preventing pollution. Annex I special areas include a number of enclosed or semi-enclosed seas such as the Mediterranean, the Baltic, the Black Sea, the Red Sea, and the Gulfs Area, along with other ecologically

---

[35] Ibid [544].
[36] Ibid [535].
[37] OSPAR Commission, *2012 Status Report on the OSPAR Network of Marine Protected Areas* (2013).
[38] CCAMLR Commission, Conservation Measure 91-03.
[39] CCAMLR Commission, Conservation Measure 91-04.
[40] CCAMLR Commission, *Report of the Thirty Third Meeting of the CCAMLR Commission* (2014), [7.50].
[41] CCAMLR Commission, *Report of the Second Special Meeting of the CCAMLR Commission* (2013), [3.26].

vulnerable areas such as the Antarctic and Southern South African waters. In addition, under Annex VI to MARPOL (which relates to air pollution from ships), the IMO has to date identified several 'emission control areas' in the Baltic, the North Sea, North America and the Carribbean, where the volume of merchant traffic calls for stricter controls on air pollution from ships.

A PSSA is defined in the IMO's Revised Guidelines for the Identification and Designation of Particularly Sensitive Sea Areas[42] as 'an area that needs special protection through action by IMO because of its significance for recognized ecological, socio-economic, or scientific attributes where such attributes may be vulnerable to damage by international shipping activities'.[43] When a PSSA is designated, an 'associated protective measure' must be approved or adopted by the IMO to prevent, reduce, or eliminate the threat or vulnerability identified in relation to the PSSA. These include measures such as routing, piloting requirements and strict application of discharge prohibitions and limits. The criteria for 'special areas' and PSSAs overlap to a significant extent, such that both designations can exist within the same area. The Great Barrier Reef (GBR) in Australia was the first PSSA to be designated (in 1990), and the GBR PSSA was extended in 2005 to include the Torres Strait. This was controversial because of the associated protective measure deployed by Australia which includes a requirement of compulsory pilotage of certain vessels passing through this international strait.[44] Other PSSAs, in order of adoption by the IMO, are the Sabana-Camagüey Archipelago (Cuba), Malpelo Island (Colombia), Florida Keys (United States), Wadden Sea (Denmark, Germany, the Netherlands), Paracas National Reserve (Peru), Western European Waters, Canary Islands (Spain), Galapagos Archipelago (Ecuador), the Baltic Sea area, Papahānaumokuākea Marine National Monument, (United States), the strait of Bonifacio (France and Italy), the Saba Bank (Netherlands) and the Coral Sea (Australia).[45]

D. Transparent and Participatory Decision-Making Processes

In addition to identifying an appropriate biogeographic scale for managing the marine environment, the concept of oceans governance directs attention to effective and legitimate processes for regulating ocean uses.[46] Particular emphasis has been placed on more participatory and transparent decision-making involving all stakeholders, including not only all interested states but also non-state actors such as civil society.[47] This is in line with developments in public international law more generally, and international environmental law in particular. In this regard, the 1998 United Nations Economic Commission for Europe Convention on Access to Information, Public Participation and Decision-Making and Access to Justice in Environmental Matters (the Aarhus Convention) has particular significance. The Aarhus Convention gives effect to Principle 10 of the 1992 Rio Declaration, which

---

[42] IMO Assembly Resolution A.982(24) (2006).

[43] Ibid [1.2].

[44] See the discussion in ch 11.

[45] See further www.pssa.imo.org.

[46] See Juda and Hennessey, 'Governance Profiles' (n 10); Lawrence Juda, 'Considerations in Developing a Functional Approach to the Governance of Large Marine Ecosystems' (1999) 30 *Ocean Development and International Law* 89.

[47] *Oceans and the Law of the Sea, Report of the Secretary-General*, UN Doc A/70/74 (2015), [90]–[98]; Rothwell and VanderZwaag, 'The Sea Change' (n 2) 4–5.

provides that 'environmental issues are best handled with the participation of all concerned citizens, at the relevant level'. It is concerned principally to improve domestic governance in environmental matters, including in the marine environmental context, by requiring that environmental information be disclosed, that the public be permitted to participate in environmental decision-making, and that they be given access to justice in environmental matters. However, it also has potential international application, in that Article 3(7) of the Aarhus Convention requires the parties 'to promote the application' of these principles 'in international environmental decision-making process and within the framework of international organisations in matters relating to the environment'.

The relevance of the Aarhus Convention to oceans governance in Europe was at issue in the *OSPAR Arbitration*,[48] which arose out of requests by Ireland for information from the United Kingdom concerning environmental risks associated with a nuclear reprocessing plant under the OSPAR Convention.[49] Ireland sought access to the full contents of two reports commissioned by the United Kingdom that examined the economic justifications for the plant. A majority of the arbitral tribunal found that the information sought was not environmental information within the meaning of Article 9 of the OSPAR Convention.[50] Specifically the majority concluded that the Aarhus Convention, which was not then in force for the parties or generally, was not relevant for determining the information that the United Kingdom was required to disclose.[51] Now that the Aarhus Convention has entered into force, and is widely ratified,[52] this conclusion may need to be reconsidered in future cases not only under OSPAR but also under Part XV of the LOSC to the extent that the rules set out by the Aarhus Convention can be considered relevant rules of international law applicable in the relations between the parties.[53]

E. Scientific and Other Cross-Disciplinary Influences

The oceans governance concept is also associated with an interdisciplinary perspective that seeks to incorporate a consideration not only of legal issues but also economic, scientific, social, political and ecological matters relevant to the management of ocean space. Over the last century the various branches of marine science—biological, chemical, geological and physical oceanography—have been given an increasingly prominent role in oceans management. This occurred initially from the nineteenth century onwards through the role of fisheries science in the management of living marine resources. More recently, scientific research has been brought to bear in addressing a broader range of marine issues, including marine pollution, bioprospecting and mining. International relations scholars have explained the way in which these developments in scientific knowledge have had important

---

[48] *OSPAR Arbitration (Ireland v United Kingdom)* (final award) (2003) 42 ILM 1118.
[49] *Basic Documents* No 50.
[50] Art 9 of the OSPAR Convention provides that the parties shall ensure that competent authorities of parties shall make available information on the state of the maritime area, on activities or measures adversely affecting or likely to affect it.
[51] *OSPAR Arbitration (Ireland v United Kingdom)* (final award) (2003) 42 ILM 1118, [99], [103]. But see the Dissenting Opinion of Gavan Griffith QC.
[52] There are 47 parties to the Convention.
[53] 1969 Vienna Convention on the Law of Treaties, art 31(3)(c).

effects in catalysing the formation of new structures for oceans governance through the concept of 'epistemic communities', where issues of concern have been identified in the scientific literature and have then led in some cases to new international regimes.[54]

Scientific knowledge is vital to sound decision making in marine planning and management, and the LOSC places special emphasis on increasing the stock of marine scientific knowledge, devoting Part XIII to safeguarding the right of pure scientific research on the high seas and within EEZs, and referring in many other places to the importance of scientific criteria for oceans management.[55] However, although important, science is neither the sole nor the dominant perspective in oceans governance, and is only one among several influences on policy and decision-making. For instance, although scientific studies have revealed problems with maximum sustainable yield as an overarching fisheries objective, and has suggested that a range of stocks may be under significant threat of commercial extinction,[56] fisheries science is frequently ignored in management decisions in favour of economic and political interests.[57] This underscores the flexibility of oceans governance, and the ongoing contest between a number of disciplines and values, all of which have some relevance to the process. To some extent such interaction between competing values is guided by notions such as the precautionary principle, which provides that in situations where there is a threat of serious or irreversible damage, scientific uncertainty should not be used as a justification for postponing measures to protect the environment.[58] However, how this mediation occurs remains controversial, as is evident by the general reluctance of states to accept precaution as a principle, let alone a binding rule of law, and a preference instead for referring to the concept in a more generic sense as an 'approach'.

F. Normative Influences on Oceans Governance

The oceans governance concept also represents an acknowledgment that there is a broader range of normative influences upon the contemporary international law of the sea than only conventional and customary law.[59] In this regard there is growing dependence upon soft-law instruments such as the main documentary products of the 1992 United Nations Conference on Environment and Development: the 1992 Rio Declaration and Agenda 21. Chapter 17[60] of Agenda 21 contains detailed discussion of oceans issues from a global environmental perspective and has been a core text in the emergence of integrated oceans governance. The use of such policy instruments allows standards to be developed in a more

---

[54] See, eg, Peter M Haas, 'Do Regimes Matter? Epistemic Communities and Mediterranean Pollution Control' (1989) 43 *International Organization* 377.

[55] See, eg, in relation to fisheries LOSC, art 61(2), and in relation to marine pollution LOSC, art 201.

[56] See, eg, RA Myers and B Worm, 'Rapid Worldwide Depletion of Predatory Fish Communities' (2003) 423 *Nature* 280.

[57] This is a long-standing criticism of the EU's fisheries policies: Tim Daw and Tim Gray, 'Fisheries Science and Sustainability in International Policy: A Study of Failure in the European Union's Common Fisheries Policy' (2005) 29 *Marine Policy* 189.

[58] Rio Declaration, Principle 15. See generally Jacqueline Peel, *The Precautionary Principle in Practice: Environmental Decision-Making and Scientific Uncertainty* (Leichhardt, Federation Press, 2005).

[59] Allott, 'Mare Nostrum' (n 4) 764.

[60] *Basic Documents* No 48.

dynamic and responsive way than 'hard-law' in respect of which a high degree of international consensus is required, and in which attention is required to be paid to formal law-making processes.[61] However, increasing use of soft-law also means that oceans governance is a moveable 'open-textured' approach that can change rapidly.[62]

III. The Global Legal Framework for Oceans Governance

Three distinct phases may be identified in the development of a global legal framework for the international law of the sea that has been able to facilitate oceans governance. The first of these was the period up until the Geneva regime of 1958 and its four conventions addressing the territorial sea and contiguous zones, the high seas, fishing on the high seas, and the continental shelf. In this period the primary focus was upon the rights of states in maritime space, particularly within the territorial sea which was expanding as a result of unilateral claims. There was only limited attention given to cross-cutting issues such as shared, straddling and highly migratory fisheries, or marine pollution which by its nature can have significant transboundary impacts.

The second phase extends from 1959 until the conclusion of the LOSC in 1982. This epoch was marked by growing appreciation of marine environmental threats that needed to be addressed in a coordinated fashion, an objective that could not be attained through a zonal approach. This was particularly evident in the case of vessel-source pollution and ocean dumping where the jurisdiction of coastal states, which tended to experience the worst effects of these activities, was significantly limited. Principle 7 of the 1972 Stockholm Declaration on the Human Environment called on states to take all possible steps to prevent pollution of the seas, and there were a raft of treaties concluded to give effect to this principle.[63] Fisheries management also acquired fresh attention, particularly on a regional basis. In addition, this period saw the emergence of more holistic regional agreements concluded under the auspices of UNEP's RSP. These seek to regulate in a comprehensive manner the environmental pressures affecting common bodies of water. Hence they deal with interlinked marine environmental issues from marine resource exploitation to marine pollution, and establish a process for monitoring and assessing environmental indicators in regional seas, for establishing plans for managing activities, including by controlling wastes and pollution emergencies, and set out standards for incorporation in national legislation.

The end of this phase, and the beginning of the third, was marked by the conclusion of the LOSC in 1982. The LOSC not only permits, but actively encourages, the development of a holistic approach to managing ocean issues. The LOSC is a 'package deal' convention, developed on the basis that all uses of the oceans are interrelated and therefore need to be addressed comprehensively. Moreover, the LOSC has a constitutional character, and seeks to provide fundamental rules and principles for the ordering of ocean space, while allowing

---

[61] See generally Alan Boyle and Christine Chinkin, *The Making of International Law* (Oxford, Oxford University Press, 2007) 211–29.

[62] Rothwell and VanderZwaag, 'The Sea Change' (n 2) 5.

[63] See the discussion in ch 15.

the implementation of the LOSC's objectives to be given effect through specific agreements under the 'umbrella' of the Convention.[64] In these rules and principles the LOSC represents a sea change from the 1958 Geneva regime, because it shifts the focus of the law of the sea decisively from being concerned solely with sovereignty and jurisdictional rights and freedoms to being concerned also with a shared responsibility to protect and preserve the marine environment in its totality.[65] Freestone has noted that this is most obvious in the context of fishing, where the Geneva regime's essentially unqualified freedom of fishing on the high seas has been replaced in the LOSC with a conditional right of high seas fishing.[66]

In this third phase the constitutional foundations for oceans governance provided by the LOSC have been built upon through global and regional agreements and soft-law instruments consistent with the LOSC. In this respect, Allott has described the LOSC as being in 'a slow-motion metamorphosis',[67] in which its conceptual structures are developed through subsequent practice.[68] There have been two particular areas where this transformation has occurred. The first of these is in the context of fisheries, in relation to which the LOSC imposes an obligation of cooperation upon states to manage shared, straddling and highly migratory fisheries and several other specific species, including cetaceans. This obligation has been discharged through bilateral and regional agreements establishing fisheries commissions and other arrangements. In relation to straddling and highly migratory fisheries the most important development in oceans governance has been the adoption of the FSA, a major implementing agreement under the LOSC.[69] The FSA is highly significant from the perspective of oceans governance because it operationalises the precautionary and ecosystem approaches, and places the objective of optimum utilisation of fisheries within a sustainability context.

The second main area of the LOSC where the Convention establishes a framework for governance which is specifically designed to be expanded upon is found in Part XII, which addresses the protection and preservation of the marine environment, especially from vessel-source, land-based and atmospheric pollution, and from intentional dumping. Part XII functions by setting out general obligations of protection, and then referring the achievement of these to supplementary rules and standards such as those adopted by the IMO, which has been responsible for sponsoring and coordinating the adoption of a multitude of treaties and guidelines on pollution issues.[70]

In addition, there exist many regional and multilateral agreements that complement the LOSC and aid in the achievement of its objectives, including in areas as diverse as improved labour standards for seafarers via treaties adopted by the International Labour Organization, to the protection of marine biodiversity under the CBD.[71] The CBD has been an important

---

[64] See Shirley V Scott, 'The LOS Convention as a Constitutional Regime for the Oceans' in Alex G Oude Elferink and Donald R Rothwell (eds), *Oceans Management in the 21st Century: Institutional Frameworks and Responses* (Leiden, Martinus Nijhoff, 2004) 9.

[65] David Freestone, 'Principles Applicable to Modern Oceans Governance' (2008) 23 *International Journal of Marine and Coastal Law* 385, 387.

[66] Ibid 387.

[67] Allott, '*Mare Nostrum*' (n 4) 765.

[68] Ibid 782.

[69] See the discussion in ch 13.

[70] See the discussion in ch 15.

[71] See further United Nations, *Obligations of States Parties Under the United Nations Convention on the Law of the Sea and Complementary Instruments* (New York, United Nations, 2004).

forum for advancing efforts to protect marine biodiversity, particularly on the high seas. The CBD brought marine and coastal issues into sharp relief in the Jakarta Mandate[72] that was agreed at the second conference of the parties in 1995 and which calls on states to use integrated marine and coastal area management to address human impacts on marine and coastal biological diversity. It was followed by a decision in 1998 on a programme of action for implementing those provisions of the CBD relevant to marine environmental protection.[73] The parties to the CBD have also adopted several further decisions, including a 2008 decision requesting parties to place a moratorium on ocean fertilisation activities for the purposes of water column sequestration of carbon dioxide from the atmosphere in order to mitigate climate change, until there is an adequate scientific basis on which to justify such activities, including assessing associated risks.[74]

Another environmental regime where oceans issues have tended to be more controversial is the 1973 Convention on International Trade in Endangered Species of Wild Fauna and Flora (CITES). CITES seeks to protect threatened species, including a range of aquatic species that are listed in appendices to CITES, by imposing restrictions on their international trade. For instance, most species of great whale are listed in CITES, Appendix I as 'threatened with extinction', and must not be traded internationally. Importantly, Article I addresses not only imports and exports across international borders, but also the 'introduction from the sea'[75] where flora or fauna are taken from 'marine environment not under the jurisdiction of any State'.[76] Hence landings of cetaceans listed in Appendix I that were taken from the high seas would be trade, and permissible only where not detrimental for the survival of the species and where the animals are not to be used for primarily commercial purposes.[77] This has implications for the operation of the International Whaling Commission established by the ICRW, which expressly permits scientific whaling in Article VIII, and whether CITES and ICRW can operate harmoniously or in tension remains an unresolved question.[78] Similar issues arise in the relationship between CITES and some RFMOs. Some parties to CITES have strongly resisted the listing of commercially valuable fish species, notwithstanding that they meet the criteria for inclusion, often as a result of RFMOs being unable to manage effectively a fishery for reasons ranging from deadlock among participants, to the failure to deal with free riders, including IUU fishers.

IV. The Policy Framework for Oceans Governance

The two most fundamental policy documents for integrated oceans governance emerged at the 1992 United Nations Conference on Environment and Development. The Rio Conference adopted the 1992 Rio Declaration, which sets out 27 principles, many of which

---

[72] Decision II/10, UN Doc UNEP/CBD/COP/DEC/II/10 (1995).

[73] Decision IV/5, UN Doc UNEP/CBD/COP/DEC/IV/5 (1998).

[74] Decision IX/20, UN Doc UNEP/CBD/COP/DEC/IX/20 (2008).

[75] CITES, art I(c).

[76] Ibid art I(e).

[77] Ibid art III(5).

[78] See Peter H Sand, 'Japan's "Research Whaling" in the Antarctic Southern Ocean and the North Pacific Ocean in the Face of the Endangered Species Convention (CITES)' (2008) 17 *Review of European Community and International Law* 56, 63.

have direct relevance for oceans management.[79] In addition, the Rio Conference adopted a detailed and prescriptive action plan, Agenda 21, which sets out a policy agenda for addressing global environmental challenges. Chapter 17 of Agenda 21[80] addresses oceans and seas issues, and is regarded as the main international blueprint for sustainable oceans governance.[81] It provides a plan of action to achieve sustainable development of the oceans, coastal areas, and seas through the programme areas of integrated management and sustainable development of coastal areas, including EEZs.

A decade after the 1992 Rio Summit, the 2002 Johannesburg Plan of Implementation, adopted at the 2002 World Summit on Sustainable Development included clear targets for improving oceans management. The Plan of Implementation encouraged states to ratify the LOSC; promote the implementation of Chapter 17 of Agenda 21; establish an effective inter-agency coordination mechanism on ocean and coastal issues within the United Nations to apply by 2010 the ecosystem approach; promote integrated, multidisciplinary, and multisectoral coastal and ocean management at a national level; strengthen regional cooperation and coordination, including through UNEP's RSP; and assist developing countries in the conservation and sustainable management of fisheries.[82] It also called upon states to maintain or restore fish stocks to levels that can produce the maximum sustainable yield with the aim of achieving these goals for depleted stocks on an urgent basis, and not later than 2015.[83] In the 'Future We Want' resolution adopted by the General Assembly at the Rio+20 United Nations Conference on Sustainable Development in 2012, governments recommitted to this goal, and the other targets in the 2002 Johannesburg Plan of Implementation.[84]

Also relevant to the policy framework for oceans governance are the Millennium Development Goals adopted by the United Nations General Assembly in 2000[85] which reiterate the importance of supporting the principles of sustainable development set out in Agenda 21. Several of the Millennium Development Goals and the specific targets for achieving these goals, are germane to oceans governance. These include Goal 1, Target 3, which is to halve by 2015 the proportion of people who suffer from hunger, the achievement of which depends in part on the productivity of coastal fisheries, and Goal 8, Target 4, which is to address the special needs of least developed landlocked countries. Also significant are Goal 7, Targets 1 and 2, which relate, respectively, to the integration of sustainable development principles into country policies and programmes, and the achievement of a significant reduction by 2010 of the rate of biodiversity loss. Regrettably, while there has been progress on many other development goals and targets, the loss of biodiversity, including marine species, continues apace.[86]

---

[79] See Jorge E Viñuales (ed), *The Rio Declaration on Environment and Development* (Oxford, Oxford University Press, 2015).

[80] *Basic Documents* No 48.

[81] De La Fayette, 'The Role of the United Nations' (n 11) 66.

[82] Plan of Implementation of the World Summit on Sustainable Development, UN Doc A/CONF.199/20 (2002), [30].

[83] Ibid [31].

[84] UN Doc A/RES/66/288 (2012), [158]–[177].

[85] UN Doc A/RES/55/2 (2000).

[86] United Nations, *The Millennium Development Goals Report 2015* (New York, United Nations, 2015) 56–57.

V. Norms and Principles of Oceans Governance

One of the features of the period following the conclusion of LOSC has been the articulation of norms and principles for oceans governance that reflect new international priorities for managing ocean spaces. Most of these principles have an overtly environmental dimension, such as 'sustainable development' and the 'precautionary principle/approach'. Others have involved instead the elaboration of principles already hardwired into the LOSC and in general international law, such as the general duty to cooperate, and the duty to prevent transboundary damage, including environmental harm.[87] Fundamental principles of oceans governance have filtered down to the national level, with a growing number of states seeking to implement policies of sustainable use, precaution and integrated oceans management. Examples include the Canadian Oceans Act and Australia's *Ocean Policy*.[88] Both of these are examples of initiatives by very large coastal states in which they have adopted an ecosystem-based and integrated approach in implementing oceans policies, and sought to address jurisdictional and sectoral overlaps and conflicts shared by both federal systems through regional planning processes for marine ecosystems.[89]

Definitively cataloguing the principles underlying oceans governance is difficult, as there are diverging views about which principles are relevant, the meaning of those principles and what weight they are to be accorded. Nonetheless it is possible to identify a core set of concepts that have influenced not only the development of new regimes but, perhaps more importantly, have impacted the ways in which existing law has been given effect. Although these principles cannot modify the LOSC, they may legitimately be considered when interpreting the LOSC and implementing its provisions. Given the lengthy period that has elapsed since the Rio Declaration, it would be desirable for these principles to be consolidated in a single instrument specifically in the oceans context.[90] Declarations such as the Manado Ocean Declaration partially perform such a consolidation function, but not in a dispositive manner akin to the Rio Declaration.

Principles of governance that animate the LOSC include the protection and preservation of the marine environment, the principle of preventing transboundary harm,[91] the principle of cooperation, and the common heritage of humankind principle, in respect of the Area. While it now passes largely without mention, the obligation to protect the marine environment in Article 192 of the LOSC was novel, and represented a reorientation of the law of the sea away from a purely instrumental attitude to ocean space, to one which recognised the need to protect the marine environment for the benefit of humanity as a

---

[87] Freestone, 'Principles' (n 65) 390–91.

[88] Marcus Haward and David VanderZwaag, 'Implementation of UNCED Agenda 21 Chapter 17 in Australia and Canada: A Comparative Analysis' (1995) 29 *Ocean and Coastal Management* 279. See also Donald R Rothwell and Stuart B Kaye, 'A Legal Framework for Integrated Oceans and Coastal Management in Australia' (2001) 18 *Environmental and Planning Law Journal* 278.

[89] For an assessment of these approach see respectively Aldo Chircop and Larry Hildebrand, 'Beyond the Buzzwords: A Perspective on Integrated Coastal and Ocean Management in Canada' in Rothwell and VanderZwaag, *Towards Principled Oceans Governance* (n 2) 19 and Joanna Vince, 'Ten Years of Implementing Australia's Ocean Policy: From an Integrated Approach to an Environmental Policy Focus' (2008) 159 *Maritime Studies* 1.

[90] Freestone, 'Principles' (n 65) 391.

[91] LOSC, art 194(2).

whole both within and beyond the limits of national jurisdiction. The principle that states must prevent transboundary environmental harm is an obligation of customary law, and is restated in the maritime context in Article 194(2) of the LOSC. Despite its fundamental importance, and various instances of transboundary marine environmental damage, the principle has not been directly applied by an international court or tribunal in the maritime context, although it was implicated to some extent in the *Nuclear Tests* cases[92] in the ICJ, and in the *MOX Plant* case[93] and *Straits of Johor* case[94] in ITLOS.[95] In *Responsibilities and Obligations of States Sponsoring Persons and Entities with Respect to Activities in the Area* (*Seabed Mining Advisory Opinion*),[96] the Seabed Disputes Chamber of ITLOS noted that Article 194(2) was an example of an obligation of 'due diligence' or 'of conduct'.[97]

The principle of cooperation is a long-standing one in public international law and in the international law of the sea. It has received particular attention in fisheries disputes where there was early awareness that as fish are no respecters of national jurisdiction, a high level of coordination is required to avoid overfishing. In the *Fisheries Jurisdiction* case[98] the ICJ issued an important statement in this regard, noting that the laissez-faire treatment of marine living resources on the high seas has been replaced by a duty to have regard to the rights of other states and the needs of conservation, and that states have an 'obligation to keep under review the fishery resources [of shared fisheries] and to examine together, in the light of scientific and other available information, the measures required for the conservation and development ... of those resources'.[99] More recently, in several decisions of ITLOS relating to requests for provisional measures, the duty of cooperation in relation not only to fisheries but also the prevention of pollution has been highlighted. In the *MOX Plant* case, ITLOS noted that 'the duty to cooperate is a fundamental principle in the prevention of pollution of the marine environment under Part XII of the [LOSC] and general international law'.[100] In the *Request for an Advisory Opinion Submitted by the Sub-Regional Fisheries Commission (SRFC Advisory Opinion)*, ITLOS expressed the view that cooperation between states on issues relating to the conservation and management of shared fisheries resources, and promoting the optimum utilisation of those resources, 'is a well-established principle in the [LOSC]'.[101]

The common heritage of humankind principle was an important innovation in the LOSC as it was the first time that this principle had been given definitive legal force and was accompanied by an institutional structure to give it effect. However, in the LOSC it

[92] *Nuclear Tests (Australia v France)* (interim measures) [1973] ICJ Rep 99 (merits) [1974] ICJ Rep 253; *(New Zealand v France)* (interim measures) [1973] ICJ Rep 135 (merits) [1974] ICJ Rep 457.

[93] *MOX Plant (Ireland v United Kingdom)* (provisional measures) (2002) 41 ILM 405.

[94] *Land Reclamation by Singapore in and Around the Straits of Johor (Malaysia v Singapore)* (provisional measures) 8 October 2003 www.itlos.org.

[95] See the discussion in ch 15.

[96] *Responsibilities and Obligations of States Sponsoring Persons and Entities with Respect to Activities in the Area* (2011) 50 ILM 458 (*Seabed Mining Advisory Opinion*).

[97] Ibid [113].

[98] *Fisheries Jurisdiction (United Kingdom v Iceland)* (merits) [1974] ICJ Rep 3; *(Germany v Iceland)* (merits) [1974] ICJ Rep 175.

[99] *Fisheries Jurisdiction* ibid [72].

[100] *MOX Plant (Ireland v United Kingdom)* (provisional measures) (2002) 41 ILM 405, [82]. In his Sseparate Opinion, Judge Wolfrum described the obligation to cooperate as 'a *Grundnorm* of part XII of the Convention as of the customary international law for the protection of the environment' (at [16]).

[101] *Request for an Advisory Opinion Submitted by the Sub-Regional Fisheries Commission (SRFC Advisory Opinion)*, Advisory Opinion of 2 April 2015, [213].

has application only to mineral resources found in the Area and is not a general principle for redistributing oceanic open access resources. Although in the course of negotiations on the deep seabed regime, and many times since, there have been arguments that it should be extended further, to apply to the high seas generally and the living resources found within them, this has not attracted any significant support. Hence it remains most appropriate to refer to the common *concern* of humankind as the operative principle in relation to resources in areas beyond national jurisdiction.

Another principle central to the LOSC is the use of best scientific knowledge. The LOSC makes reference in several provisions to the need to take account of 'the best scientific evidence' in relation to fisheries management[102] and pollution;[103] however, more recent instruments dealing with matters beyond fisheries also give science a more central role in marine assessments and decision-making, and emphasise the need to utilise cutting-edge technologies, as seen in the principles of best available techniques, and best environmental practice.[104]

In addition to the core LOSC principles of oceans governance, are further principles relevant to oceans management, including the polluter-pays principle, the ecosystem approach, the precautionary approach/principle, environmental impact assessment and sustainable development. The polluter-pays principle provides that the costs of pollution should be borne by the polluter.[105] It receives no direct reference in the LOSC, but is implicit in many of its provisions addressing marine pollution, particularly Article 235(2), which provides that states must ensure that recourse is available for prompt and adequate compensation for damage from pollution of the marine environment.[106] The provision was considered in *the Seabed Mining Advisory Opinion*,[107] where the Seabed Disputes Chamber of ITLOS observed that it served the purpose of ensuring that sponsored contractors operating in the Area provide reparations for any damage caused by wrongful acts committed in the course of their deep seabed mining activities.[108] The polluter pays principle is also given effect in a number of conventions agreed under the auspices of the IMO to prevent vessel-source pollution,[109] to impose liability for pollution accidents[110] and to enhance preparedness for oil pollution emergencies.[111]

The terms 'ecosystem' and 'ecological' receive few mentions in the LOSC. In the context of preventing marine pollution, states are encouraged to adopt measures 'necessary to protect and preserve rare or fragile ecosystems'.[112] In relation to vessel source pollution,

---

[102]   See, eg, LOSC, art 61(2).

[103]   See, eg, ibid art 201.

[104]   See, eg, OSPAR Convention, *Basic Documents* No 50, which requires parties to apply best available techniques which it defines as 'the latest stage of development (state of the art) processes, of facilities or of methods of operation which indicate the practical suitability of a particular measure for limiting discharges, emissions and waste': OSPAR Convention, app 1, art 2. Best environmental practice is defined as 'the most appropriate combination of environmental control measures and strategies': OSPAR Convention, app 1, art 6.

[105]   Rio Declaration, Principle 16. See Priscilla Schwartz, 'Principle 16: The Polluter Pays Principle' in Viñuales, *The Rio Declaration on Environment and Development* (n 79) 429.

[106]   See especially LOSC, art 235.

[107]   (2011) 50 ILM 458, [139].

[108]   Ibid [140].

[109]   See especially MARPOL.

[110]   See, eg, the 1992 Civil Liability Convention.

[111]   1990 Convention on Oil Pollution Preparedness, Responses and Cooperation.

[112]   LOSC, art 194(5).

Article 211(6)(a) provides coastal states with the capacity to adopt mandatory pollution control measures in clearly defined areas where the 'ecological conditions' require them. In a similar vein, coastal states with ice-covered areas within their EEZ may adopt strict laws for the prevention of marine pollution from vessels to avoid 'irreversible disturbance of the ecological balance'.[113] Also, the ISA is to adopt appropriate rules to prevent 'interference with the ecological balance of the marine environment' from mining activities in the Area.[114] Nonetheless, as has been seen, the ecosystem approach is now regarded as fundamental to oceans governance. This is largely as a result of the strong emphasis placed on the protection of ecosystems in Chapter 17 of Agenda 21, and this has influenced developments in treaty law, including the FSA. In the FSA one of the guiding principles which states must bear in mind in giving effect to the duty to cooperate is to assess the impact of fishing and other human activities on ecosystems, and, where necessary, adopt management measures having regard to ecosystems to which targeted species belong.[115]

The precautionary principle/approach has also become prominent in the marine environmental context, again largely as a consequence of the Rio Declaration and Agenda 21, and treaties such as the FSA, which refers not only to precaution in an abstract sense, but gives it meaning in the specific arena of fisheries management.[116] The precautionary principle/approach has been invoked in a number of disputes under Part XV of the LOSC, although it has only recently been expressly endorsed and applied. In the *Southern Bluefin Tuna* case[117] ITLOS granted provisional measures under Article 290 of the LOSC to restrain Japan from undertaking an experimental fishing programme. In its order ITLOS encouraged the parties to 'act with prudence and caution in order to ensure that effective conservation measures are taken'.[118] Although ITLOS did not expressly refer to, or endorse, the precautionary principle, its decision revealed a classic precautionary approach.[119] ITLOS noted that there was scientific uncertainty surrounding the measures necessary to conserve stocks of southern bluefin tuna, but that the tribunal was not in a position to assess this evidence conclusively, and that the urgency of the situation demanded measures to preserve the rights of the parties and to avoid further deterioration of the tuna stocks.[120] The majority order of ITLOS did not venture a view as to whether the precautionary concept is a legal principle,[121] although several individual judges suggested either that it was better treated as an approach,[122] or that the issue was not strictly relevant as precaution is inherent in the Article 290 provisional measures jurisdiction, given that it may be invoked to prevent serious harm to the marine environment.[123] In later provisional measures orders in the *MOX*

[113] Ibid art 234.
[114] Ibid art 145(a).
[115] FSA, art 5(d), (e).
[116] See further Simon Marr, *The Precautionary Principle in the Law of the Sea: Modern Decision Making in International Law* (The Hague, Martinus Nijhoff, 2003).
[117] *Southern Bluefin Tuna (New Zealand v Japan; Australia v Japan)* (provisional measures) (1999) 117 ILR 148.
[118] Ibid [77].
[119] David Freestone, 'Caution or Precaution: "A Rose By Any Other Name…?"' (1999) 10 *Yearbook of International Environmental Law* 15.
[120] *Southern Bluefin Tuna (New Zealand v Japan; Australia v Japan)* (provisional measures) (1999) 117 ILR 148, [80].
[121] On this issue, see further Jacqueline Peel, 'Precaution: A Matter of Principle, Approach or Process?' (2004) 5 *Melbourne Journal of International Law* 438, 494.
[122] *Southern Bluefin Tuna (New Zealand v Japan; Australia v Japan)* (provisional measures) (1999) 117 ILR 148, Separate Opinion of Judge Laing.
[123] Ibid Separate Opinion of Judge Treves.

Plant case[124] and in the *Straits of Johor* case[125] ITLOS repeated its 'prudence and caution' formulation, and again refrained from any express reference to the precautionary principle/ approach. In more recent decisions ITLOS has taken a stronger position on precaution. In the *Seabed Mining Advisory Opinion*, the ITLOS Seabed Disputes Chamber considered mining regulations adopted by the ISA which made specific reference to the precautionary principle, and observed that these had the effect of 'transform[ing] this non-binding statement of the precautionary approach in the Rio Declaration into a binding obligation'.[126] And the Chamber went further, stating that:

> the precautionary approach has been incorporated into a growing number of international treaties and other instruments, many of which reflect the formulation of Principle 15 of the Rio Declaration. In the view of the Chamber, this has initiated a trend towards making this approach part of customary international law.[127]

Connected with precaution is environmental impact assessment (EIA), which is a procedure for evaluating the likely environmental effects of a proposed activity.[128] The purpose of EIA is to ensure that these environmental effects are understood, and taken into account in making a decision whether or not to approve a proposed activity.[129] There is growing recognition that EIA ought to take place not only at the development stage, but also at an earlier point in the origination of policies, plans and programmes. In this context EIA is described as 'strategic' EIA.[130] The LOSC requires parties to monitor the marine environment and to evaluate and assess the extent to which activities they permit are likely to pollute or otherwise harm the marine environment.[131] Article 236 is most clearly on point, in requiring states, when they have reasonable grounds for believing that planned activities may cause substantial pollution of the marine environment, to assess the potential effects of such activities. In relation to deep seabed mining, section 1(7) of the Annex to the 1994 Implementing Agreement requires applicants to the ISA seeking approval for deep seabed mining to accompany the application with 'an assessment of the potential environmental impacts of the proposed activities'. The EIA requirements for activities in the Area are elaborated in the Mining Code.[132] In the *Seabed Mining Advisory Opinion*, the Chamber advised that 'the obligation to conduct an environmental impact assessment is a direct obligation under the Convention and a general obligation under customary international law'.[133] Among the

---

[124]   *MOX Plant (Ireland v United Kingdom)* (provisional measures) (2002) 41 ILM 405, [84].

[125]   *Land Reclamation by Singapore in and Around the Straits of Johor (Malaysia v Singapore)* (provisional measures) 8 October 2003 www.itlos.org [99].

[126]   *Seabed Mining Advisory Opinion* (2011) 50 ILM 458, [126].

[127]   Ibid [135]. Citing the ICJ's statement in *Pulp Mills on the River Uruguay (Argentina v Uruguay)* [2010] ICJ Rep 14, [164] that 'a precautionary approach may be relevant in the interpretation and application of the provisions of the [bilateral treaty at issue in the proceedings]'.

[128]   For comprehensive discussion of EIA in the law of the sea see Robin Warner, *Environmental Impact Assessment and Spatial Planning in the World's Oceans: Conserving Marine Areas Beyond National Jurisdiction* (Abingdon, Edward Elgar, 2011).

[129]   Neil Craik, *The International Law of Environmental Impact Assessment* (Cambridge, Cambridge University Press, 2008) 4.

[130]   *Oceans and the Law of the Sea: Report of the Secretary General*, Addendum A/64/66/Add.2 (19 October 2009).

[131]   See, eg, LOSC, arts 204–06.

[132]   See ch 6.

[133]   *Seabed Mining Advisory Opinion* (2011) 50 ILM 458, [145]. The Chamber again cited the ICJ in *Pulp Mills* [2010] ICJ Rep 14 and its conclusion, at [204], that 'it may now be considered a requirement under general international law to undertake an environmental impact assessment where there is a risk that the proposed industrial activity may have a significant adverse impact in a transboundary context, in particular, on a shared resource'.

treaties applicable to the marine environment that require EIA are the 1976 Convention for the Protection of the Marine Environment and Coastal Region of the Mediterranean,[134] the 1996 Protocol to the Convention on the Prevention of Marine Pollution by Dumping of Wastes and Other Matter,[135] the FSA[136] and the 1991 Protocol on Environmental Protection to the Antarctic Treaty.[137]

Sustainable development was defined by the World Commission on Environment and Development as 'development that meets the needs of the present without compromising the ability of future generations to meet their own needs'.[138] In seeking to reconcile ecological protection with economic development it is a meta-level principle incorporating many of the other environmental principles already discussed. In many ways the notion of sustainability has 'set a course towards rethinking and redefining human-nature relationships',[139] including humanity's engagement with the marine environment. However, although recited in legal and policy texts in international law and the law of the sea, the underpinnings of sustainable development remain open to ongoing debate. This includes, fundamentally, the ethical content of sustainability and whether it can effect a genuine transformation of the law of the sea from its utilitarian and anthropocentric origins to a truly balanced legal system that recognises that human beings are part of, and not separate from, the natural environment.[140] The United Nations Secretary General's 2015 report on oceans and the law of the sea focused specifically on the role of sustainable development in relation to the oceans, observing that sustainable development has three dimensions—environmental, social and economic—the integration of which 'is at the core' of the LOSC.[141]

VI. Institutions for Oceans Governance

The institutional framework for oceans governance has a complex, multi-level structure, involving global, regional, national and sub-national institutions and organisations. Globally, the most important elements of the institutional framework for oceans governance are the bodies created by the LOSC and the United Nations and its specialised agencies, such as the IMO, and programmes such as UNEP.

One of the distinctive features of the LOSC in contrast to the earlier Geneva regime is the significant additions it makes to the institutional architecture for the law of the sea.[142] Since the LOSC entered into force in 1994, these institutions have begun to operate, and have

---

[134] *Basic Documents* No 23, art 4(3)(c).

[135] *Basic Documents* No 19, art 14.

[136] *Basic Documents* No 56, art 6.

[137] 1991 Protocol on Environmental Protection to the Antarctic Treaty, arts 6–8.

[138] World Commission on Environment and Development, *Our Common Future* (Oxford, Oxford University Press, 1987) 43.

[139] David L VanderZwaag and Donald R Rothwell, 'Principled Oceans Governance Agendas: Lessons Learned and Future Challenges' in Rothwell and VanderZwaag, *Towards Principled Oceans Governance* (n 2) 407.

[140] Ibid 407–408. See also Allott, '*Mare Nostrum*' (n 4) 773; Douglas M Johnston and David L VanderZwaag, 'The Ocean and International Environmental Law: Swimming, Sinking and Treading Water at the Millennium' (2000) 43 *Ocean and Coastal Management* 147.

[141] *Oceans and the Law of the Sea, Report of the Secretary-General*, UN Doc A/70/74 (2015), [5].

[142] Donald R Rothwell, 'Building on the Strengths and Addressing the Challenges: The Role of Law of the Sea Institutions' (2004) 35 *Ocean Development and International Law* 131, 132.

had a major impact on the implementation of the Convention. The permanent institutions established by the LOSC are the CLCS, the ISA and ITLOS.

The CLCS is a specialist, technical body charged with assessing submissions of data by coastal states concerning the establishment of the outer limits of their continental shelves. It has a particularly important role in the delineation of the boundary between the continental shelf and the Area because the limits established by coastal states on the basis of recommendations of the CLCS are final and binding. The CLCS is without question the most active of the LOSC's institutions, so much so that the extent of its workload has been of concern to parties to the LOSC, and there is a significant backlog in its consideration of continental shelf data.

The ISA is the institution at the fulcrum of Part XI of the LOSC, which establishes a system for giving effect to the common heritage of humankind principle in relation to the mineral resources of the Area. Since the ISA began to operate in 1996 as a fully autonomous international organisation there have been two main elements to its work programme. The first of these has been the finalisation of organisational arrangements such as the privileges and immunities it enjoys in Jamaica, where it is headquartered. The second is more substantive and relates to the completion of regulations for mining in the Area (the Mining Code), and contractual arrangements with pioneer investors. In developing the Mining Code, the ISA has been particularly aware of the environmental impact of deep sea mining. Reflecting the role of principles in the work of institutions for oceans governance, the Mining Code requires the ISA and sponsoring states to apply a precautionary approach as reflected in Principle 15 of the Rio Declaration.

The third permanent institution established by the LOSC is ITLOS, which is given a prominent role in the resolution of law of the sea disputes under Part XV of the Convention. A number of criticisms were made of ITLOS at the time of its establishment, with concerns being raised as to how it would relate to existing bodies, especially the ICJ that has a lengthy and distinguished history in law of the sea dispute settlement.[143] ITLOS has had a respectable but at times far from busy docket since its first case in 1997. Almost all of its initial cases concerned matters in which ITLOS had residual jurisdiction—provisional measures and the prompt release of arrested vessels. More recently, however, it has been called upon to resolve a broader range of law of the sea disputes, and to provide advisory opinions. ITLOS is not the only body that can be called upon to resolve law of the sea disputes; Part XV also permits LOSC disputes to be referred to the ICJ, and to ad hoc arbitral tribunals established under Annexes VII and VIII of the LOSC. Annex VII arbitral tribunals have proven to be the most popular bodies for addressing LOSC disputes.

The LOSC does not establish a general organisation akin to the World Trade Organization to supervise the implementation of the Convention. Indeed, proposals to establish a general international commission for the oceans were rejected at UNCLOS III.[144] In lieu of such an organisation or commission, the United Nations Secretary-General and the meeting of parties to the LOSC have performed important governance tasks. Under Article 319

---

[143] Shigeru Oda, 'Dispute Settlement Prospects in the Law of the Sea' (1995) 44 *International and Comparative Law Quarterly* 863.

[144] Alex G Oude Elferink, 'Reviewing the Implementation of the LOS Convention: The Role of the United Nations General Assembly and the Meeting of States Parties' in Alex G Oude Elferink and Donald R Rothwell (eds), *Oceans Management in the 21st Century: Institutional Frameworks and Responses* (Leiden, Martinus Nijhoff, 2004) 295, 302.

of the LOSC, the United Nations Secretary-General not only functions as the depository for the Convention, but is also given a wide-ranging mandate to report to all parties on issues of a general nature that have arisen with respect to the Convention.[145] There is specific reference made to the potential for the Secretary-General to convene a Meeting of States Parties to the United Nations Convention on the Law of the Sea (SPLOS).[146] However, SPLOS does not resemble conferences or meetings of parties under other multilateral agreements that are given governing roles in reviewing progress on implementation and in adopting programmes of work through binding decisions.

SPLOS has a highly circumscribed role in reviewing the LOSC.[147] The only express functions the LOSC empowers SPLOS to perform are administrative and financial in nature, such as the election of members of ITLOS and the CLCS, although it does not rule out SPLOS taking on a more substantive role. The majority of the decisions of SPLOS have been administrative in character, with few exceptions, such as the decision in 2001 extending the time limits for making submissions of data to the CLCS.[148] This had the practical effect of amending the LOSC's requirement that submissions be made within 10 years of the entry into force of the Convention for the state concerned.[149]

As a result of the limited role of SPLOS, the central institution for international oceans governance has been the United Nations, particularly the Secretariat and the General Assembly. In 1993 the General Assembly requested the Secretary-General to report on developments pertaining to the LOSC, and all related activities.[150] Since that time the Secretary-General has prepared and submitted to the General Assembly annual reports dealing with oceans issues, and the scope and detail of these reports have expanded greatly over the years. Significantly, the Secretary-General's reports often address compliance issues, occasionally referring to situations where parties have not conformed with specific provisions of the LOSC. The Secretariat, one of the five principal organs of the United Nations, also contains the Division for Ocean Affairs and the Law of the Sea (DOALOS), which is one of six units of the United Nations Office of Legal Affairs. DOALOS provides to states, and to international organisations, information, advice and assistance relating to the LOSC and the FSA in order to promote their improved understanding, wider acceptance, uniform application and effective implementation.

Since 1984 the law of the sea has been an annual agenda item for the General Assembly, and following the entry into force of the LOSC in 1994 the General Assembly has carried out annual reviews of the implementation of the LOSC and other issues of ocean affairs. In this way the General Assembly performs a function for the LOSC that is similar to that discharged by conferences of parties to other instruments such as the 1992 United Nations Framework Convention on Climate Change. The General Assembly is a principal organ of the United Nations, and one in which the views of all members can be heard. As a result it

---

[145] LOSC, art 319(2)(a).
[146] Ibid art 319(2)(e).
[147] Oude Elferink, 'Reviewing the Implementation of the LOS Convention' (n 144) 295.
[148] UN Doc SPLOS/72 (2001). See also UN Doc SPLOS/183 (2008).
[149] LOSC, Annex II, art 4. See Oude Elferink, 'Reviewing the Implementation of the LOS Convention' (n 144) 309; See also Tullio Treves, 'The General Assembly and the Meeting of States Parties in the Implementation of the LOS Convention' in Oude Elferink and Rothwell, *Oceans Management in the 21st Century* (n 144) 55.
[150] UNGA Resolution 48/28 (1993).

is centrally situated to advance sustainable oceans governance for the international community as a whole. The United Nations Security Council has also considered oceans issues from time to time, but only those such as piracy and maritime terrorism that constitute a threat to international peace and security and therefore come within the Security Council's limited remit to address matters of collective security under Chapter VII of the UN Charter.

The annual review by the General Assembly is informed by the annual reports of the Secretary-General, and culminates in resolutions dealing with a variety of specific oceans issues, which vary from year to year. As with all resolutions of the General Assembly, these are not legally binding; however, they can have a major impact on state practice, generate customary international law, and stimulate negotiation of international agreements, as was the case with the FSA. There are two General Assembly resolutions dealing with oceans affairs each year: an omnibus resolution under the title 'Oceans and the Law of the Sea', and a further resolution on 'Sustainable Fisheries, Including through the 1995 Fish Stocks Agreement and Related Agreements'. These resolutions address a variety of issues, call for the production of comprehensive annual reports, reports on specific subjects (such as flag state implementation, marine biodiversity on the high seas, fisheries and so on). They may also call for the convening of meetings to deal with particular topics.

In 1999 the General Assembly in Resolution 54/33 established a subsidiary body, the ICP. The ICP, for which DOALAS performs secretariat functions, reports to the General Assembly on developments in ocean affairs and the law of the sea, and is an important source for the General Assembly's resolutions. The ICP is open to all members and accredited observers of the United Nations, and to intergovernmental organisations that have competence in oceans affairs. The ICP was originally established for a three-year period, but this has been subsequently renewed. It meets in June each year.[151] In addition to the ICP, the General Assembly has also established other subsidiary bodies on an ad hoc basis, including the Ad Hoc Open-Ended Informal Working Group to Study Issues Relating to the Conservation and Sustainable Use of Marine Biological Diversity Beyond National Jurisdiction[152] and A Regular Process for Global Reporting and Assessment of the State of the Marine Environment Including Socio-Economic Aspects.[153]

A number of specialised United Nations agencies also contribute to oceans governance, including the IMO, which is concerned with shipping, the Food and Agriculture Organization, which has a significant fisheries focus, the Intergovernmental Oceanographic Commission and the World Meteorological Organization. UNEP, the Commission on Sustainable Development, and the United Nations Development Programme also address ocean issues. Beyond the United Nations system there are many governmental and non-governmental organisations which are concerned with oceans issues, including most prominently the IUCN, which is particularly active in the field. The IUCN's Marine Programme has directly engaged with oceans governance issues, and has distilled and elaborated 10 principles for high seas governance: conditional freedom of activity on the high seas, protection and preservation of the marine environment, international cooperation, science-based approach to management, public availability of information, transparent and open decision-making

---

[151] For the report of the 2009 meeting see UN Doc A/64/131 (2009).
[152] UNGA Resolution 59/42 (2004), [73], [74].
[153] UNGA Resolution 60/30 (2005).

processes, the precautionary approach, the ecosystem approach, sustainable and equitable use, and the responsibility of states as stewards of the global marine environment.[154] These principles have been reflected to varying degrees in the ongoing deliberation on a new implementing agreement to LOSC to protect biodiversity in areas beyond national jurisdiction.[155]

VII. Regional, Sub-regional and National Oceans Governance

The LOSC, in multiple provisions, encourages the establishment of regional regimes to implement aspects of the Convention, especially in relation to marine environmental protection and fisheries conservation. Article 311 makes clear that while the LOSC prevails over the four Geneva conventions as between parties, it does not prevent parties from concluding agreements that implement the LOSC so long as these do not undermine the object and purpose of the Convention. In relation to marine environmental protection more generally, Article 237 preserves the entitlement of parties to the LOSC to adopt additional regional agreements where they are consistent with the general principles set out in the LOSC. Regional cooperation can be more effective in achieving governance objectives for the reason that the defined region may relate more appropriately to the area that needs to be managed, and further that on a regional basis it may be possible to achieve greater level of cooperation among states than that which is achievable globally.[156] An exhaustive discussion of all regional oceans governance initiatives is beyond the scope of this chapter, and what follows is an outline of the practice in several important and indicative regional arrangements.

A. UNEP Regional Seas Programme

The agreements adopted under, and associated with, the UNEP's RSP are the most developed structures for regional oceans governance. The RSP was established following the 1972 United Nations Conference on the Human Environment, and seeks to facilitate cooperation among states that neighbour and share marine regions to achieve sustainable management of the marine environment. The RSP has grown to involve 143 states and operate in 18 ocean regions: the Antarctic, Arctic, Baltic, Black Sea, Caspian, Eastern Africa, East Asian Seas, Mediterranean, North-East Atlantic, North-East Pacific, North-West Pacific, Pacific, Persian Gulf, Red Sea and Gulf of Aden, South Asian Seas, South-East Pacific, Western Africa and the Wider Caribbean. The RSP operates through regional action plans, addressing matters such as environmental assessment, environmental management, environmental legislation, institutional arrangements and financial arrangements. In most cases these

---

[154] IUCN, *10 Principles for High Seas Governance* at cmsdata.iucn.org/downloads/10_principles_for_high_seas_governance___final.pdf.

[155] See Alex G Oude Elferink, 'Governance Principles for Areas Beyond National Jurisdiction' (2012) 27 *International Journal of Marine and Coastal Law* 205.

[156] See further Haward and Vince, *Oceans Governance* (n 1) ch 3.

action plans are given a binding legal basis through regional conventions and protocols. UNEP administers five RSPs itself, a further seven are non-UNEP administered, and there are five independent programmes linked to, but not established by, UNEP (the Antarctic, Arctic, Baltic Sea, Caspian Sea and the North-East Atlantic).

B. European Union

The European Union (EU), the economic and political union of 28 states on the European continent, is one of the most important international actors in oceans affairs, not least because of the extensive coastal and maritime areas of EU member states, the size of the EU fishing industry operating in European and distant waters, and the key role that EU states play in the international shipping industry. Special provision was made in the LOSC for the European Community, which is now subsumed within the EU, to become a party to the Convention in its own right.[157] This is because the LOSC permits an international organisation to which member states have transferred competence over matters addressed by the LOSC to join the Convention if the majority of its members have also joined the regime. The EU is presently the only such organisation that meets the conditions for membership.

In terms of regional oceans governance, the EU has characteristics akin to federal states such as the United States, Canada and Australia where power to manage marine and coastal domains is distributed between the central government and peripheral states and provinces. For the purposes of European law, the LOSC is a 'mixed agreement' in that it addresses some matters within the exclusive competence of the EU, and others that it shares with its member states. The EU has exclusive competence in relation to the conservation of marine biological resources through the Common Fisheries Policy (CFP) adopted by EU member states.[158] In the other area of key relevance to regional ocean governance—marine environmental protection—the EU shares competence with member states. How this shared arena of oceans policy operates in practice was at issue in the *MOX Plant* case[159] which raised a range of environmental matters, over which the EU is vested with competence by the Treaty Establishing the European Community. Ireland contended that it could raise marine environmental issues under the LOSC dispute settlement system as it involved issues in which competence had not been transferred to the EU. However, the European Commission took the view that even if this were the case, the dispute with the United Kingdom could only be brought to the European Court of Justice because that court alone has exclusive jurisdiction over matters relating to the interpretation or application of the EC Treaties, which incorporates by reference those provisions of the LOSC dealing with marine environmental protection, that are within the reach of the EU's competence. The European Court of Justice agreed.[160] It is not entirely clear what the implications of the *MOX Plant* case will be

---

[157] LOSC, arts 305–07 and Annex IX.

[158] See Declaration of Community competence attached to the EC's acceptance of UNCLOS at www.un.org/Depts/los/convention_agreements/convention_declarations.htm.

[159] *MOX Plant (Ireland v United Kingdom)* (provisional measures) (2002) 41 ILM 405; *MOX Plant (Ireland v United Kingdom)* (merits) (2003) 42 ILM 1187.

[160] *Commission of the European Communities v Ireland* C-182/89 (2006) 45 ILM 1051. See the discussion in Paul James Cardwell and Duncan French, 'Who Decides? The ECJ's Judgment on Jurisdiction in the *MOX Plant* Dispute' (2007) 19 *Journal of Environmental Law* 121.

for oceans governance within the EU; however, by clarifying the respective powers of the centre and the periphery, it may provide a surer basis and greater imperative for improved intergovernmental cooperation.

In EU oceans governance the priority issues are marine environmental protection and sustainable fisheries. In relation to the marine environment, it is identified as one of the seven policy areas in the Sixth Community Environment Action Programme which was adopted by the European Parliament and Council in 2002. Key initiatives include the 2005 Marine Strategy Framework Directive, which sets out the obligations of members to formulate and implement a marine strategy. To this end, the directive requires members to carry out a comprehensive assessment of their marine areas, ascertain the impacts from human uses and undertake a socio-economic analysis of those uses. EU waters are divided into three regions for the purposes of the directive: the Baltic, the North-East Atlantic and the Mediterranean. To a significant extent the directive is linked to the obligations of EU member states under the regional arrangements for these three areas. It is one component of a broader EU oceans policy framework developed under the banner of the 'Integrated Maritime Policy for the EU' (IMP), which was the title of a major Communication from the Council in 2007.[161] The IMP observes that 'all matters relating to Europe's oceans and seas are interlinked' and that 'sea-related policies must develop in a joined-up way'. Marine spatial planning is specifically identified 'as a fundamental tool for the sustainable development of marine areas and coastal regions, and for the restoration of Europe's seas to environmental health'. Although the IMP has its limitations, for instance MSP has not been mandated for EU member states, it has been important for advancing integrated oceans governance in Europe generally and for the main regional European seas.[162]

There has been very limited progress made in the adoption of sustainable fishing practices within the EU. The EU's CFP was first agreed in 1983, and was considered necessary because of the truly common character of marine living resources given the mobile nature of many important fish stocks. The CFP, which has since been revised on a regular basis, addresses four subjects: the conservation of fisheries; infrastructure such as vessels, port facilities and the like; the organisation of the common market; and external fisheries policy. The latter has become an increasingly important part of the CFP as fishing fleets from EU members leave exhausted fisheries grounds in northern waters and seek more profitable harvests, particularly in the waters of African nations, with which the EU has concluded a network of fisheries agreements. The total allowable catches, limits on gear, and limits on fishing effort and overcapacity set under the CFP have not successfully achieved the EU's fisheries conservation objectives, as seen most obviously in the case of North Sea herring and cod fisheries.[163] If stocks are to recover there will need to be a major reform of the CFP and the EU fishing industry, a process that will require large-scale structural assistance. This

---

[161] European Commission, *An Integrated Maritime Policy for the European Union* (2007). See also European Commission, *Towards a Future Maritime Policy for the Union: A European Vision for the Oceans and Seas* (Green Paper, 2006).

[162] Scott, 'Integrated Oceans Management' (n 1), 474. See further Robin R Churchill, 'The European Union and the Challenges of Marine Governance: From Sectoral Response to Integrated Policy' in D Vidas and PJ Shei (eds), *The World Ocean in Globalisation: Climate Change, Sustainable Fisheries, Biodiversity, Shipping, Regional Issues* (Leiden, Martinus Nijhoff, 2011) 395.

[163] Haward and Vince, *Oceans Governance* (n 1) 69.

is well-recognised by the many EU member governments and by the EU itself;[164] however, implementation of any reform remains politically unpalatable.

C. Asia-Pacific Economic Cooperation

Asia-Pacific Economic Cooperation (APEC) is the main forum for promoting economic development in the 21 nations in the Asia-Pacific region that constitute its member economies. As with the EU, APEC has very significant interests in effective oceans governance to sustain the health of the marine environment of its members and the continued productivity of their fisheries, which supply around 80 per cent of global aquaculture production and around 65 per cent of global capture fisheries.[165] However, by contrast with the EU, APEC possesses a very limited institutional structure to achieve a consistent regional policy for integrated marine and coastal management.

The work of APEC is based around annual Leaders and Ministers Meetings, regular meetings of senior officials, and specialist working groups. Two of these are directly charged with addressing oceans policy: the Marine Resource Conservation Working Group, and the Fisheries Working Group. In 1997 APEC adopted a Strategy for the Sustainability of the Marine Environment, which aims to promote an integrated approach to coastal management, reduce marine pollution, and achieve the sustainable management of marine resources. Subsequently, in 2002, Korea hosted the inaugural APEC Oceans-Related Ministerial Meeting, which adopted the Seoul Declaration that took APEC oceans policy forward significantly by expressly referring to the need for ecosystem-based management at national and regional scales. This was a significant achievement in the context of a regional economic cooperation arrangement that has been predominantly focussed on economic growth objectives. A programme for achieving this was set out in the 2005 Bali Plan of Action Towards Healthy Oceans and Coasts for Sustainable Group and Prosperity adopted at the second APEC Ocean-Related Ministerial Meeting, which is similar in a number of respects to Chapter 17 of Agenda 21, although somewhat vague in many other respects. For instance, no direct mention is made to the threat posed to the marine ecosystems of APEC members by climate change, despite the prevalence of vulnerable systems such as coral reefs within the seas of a number of APEC members. In 2014, following the publication of the extensive *APEC Marine Sustainable Development Report*,[166] the Fourth APEC Oceans Ministerial meeting adopted the Xiamen Declaration.[167] The Xiamen Declaration acknowledges that 'APEC members share one ocean' and that the Pacific is vitally important for fisheries, livelihoods, trade and its ecosystem services, and called for:

> the establishment of more integrated, sustainable, inclusive and mutually beneficial partnership through ocean cooperation among APEC members, that implement previous commitments, and focuses efforts on collaborated and concerted actions in the following four priority areas: (1)

---

[164] See European Commission, *Improvement of the Economic Situation in the Fishing Industry* (2006).
[165] Seegenerallywww.apec.org/Groups/SOM-Steering-Committee-on-Economic-and-Technical-Cooperation/Working-Groups/Ocean-and-Fisheries.aspx.
[166] Available at http://publications.apec.org/publication-detail.php?pub_id=1552.
[167] Available at www.apec.org/Meeting-Papers/Ministerial-Statements/Ocean-related/2014_ocean.aspx.

Coastal and marine ecosystem conservation and disaster resilience; (2) The role of the ocean on food security and food-related trade; (3) Marine science, technology and innovation; and (4) Blue Economy.

Significantly, the Xiamen Declaration goes on to elaborate specific goals in these priority areas, including a commitment to conserve at least 10 per cent of coastal and marine areas within effectively managed MPAs. The strong influence of the concept of integrated oceans management upon the Xiamen Declaration, and the activities of APEC members in implementing its recommendations, demonstrates the ever-growing salience of the principles, rules and institutions of oceans governance discussed in this chapter.

VIII. Further Reading

Philip Allott, 'Mare Nostrum: A New International Law of the Sea' (1992) 86 *American Journal of International Law* 764

Marcus Haward and Joanna Vince, *Oceans Governance in the Twenty-First Century: Managing the Blue Planet* (Cheltenham, Edward Elgar, 2008)

Simon Marr, *The Precautionary Principle in the Law of the Sea: Modern Decision Making in International Law* (The Hague, Martinus Nijhoff, 2003)

Donald R Rothwell and David L VanderZwaag (eds), *Towards Principled Oceans Governance: Australian and Canadian Approaches and Challenges* (Abingdon, Routledge, 2006)

Karen N Scott, 'Integrated Oceans Management: A New Frontier in Marine Environmental Protection' in Donald R Rothwell, Alex G Oude Elferink, Karen N Scott and Tim Stephens (eds), *The Oxford Handbook of the Law of the Sea* (Oxford, Oxford University Press, 2015) 463

Tim Stephens and David L VanderZwaag (eds), *Polar Oceans Governance in an Era of Environmental Change* (Cheltenham, Edward Elgar, 2014)

INDEX